MW01505465

Fighting in Paradise

Fighting in Paradise

*Labor Unions, Racism, and Communists
in the Making of Modern Hawai'i*

GERALD HORNE

University of Hawai'i Press
Honolulu

© 2011 University of Hawai'i Press
All rights reserved
Printed in the United States of America
16 15 14 13 12 11   6 5 4 3 2 1

Library of Congress Cataloging-in-Publication Data

Horne, Gerald.
  Fighting in paradise : labor unions, racism, and communists in the making of
modern Hawai'i / Gerald Horne.
      p. cm.
  Includes bibliographical references and index.
  ISBN 978-0-8248-3502-6 (hardcover : alk. paper) — ISBN 978-0-8248-3549-1
(pbk. : alk. paper)
  1. Labor unions—Hawaii—History. 2. Labor unions and communism—Hawaii—
History. 3. Hawaii—Race relations. I. Title.
  HD6517.H3H67 2011
  331.8809969—dc22

                          2011008965

University of Hawai'i Press books are printed on acid-free
paper and meet the guidelines for permanence and durability
of the Council on Library Resources.

Designed by inari

Printed by Sheridan Books, Inc.

Contents

A Prefatory Note

Traditionally, Japanese names—e.g., "Ichiro Izuka"—are often referred to by reference to what English readers would call the first name, or "Ichiro" in this example (e.g., those not familiar with me referring to me as "Gerald" and not "Horne"). Readers will note that the principals I quote employ both the traditional and nontraditional modes, as do I from time to time, given the context.

The diverse archipelago also presents a challenge in how various racial and ethnic groups are denoted; for example, those called "white" or "Euro-American" on the mainland are often referred to as "haole" in the islands. Readers will note that I employ all of these terms, just as I use interchangeably the terms "black," "Negro," and "African-American." Those with the longest roots in the islands are referred to as "indigenous" or "indigenes" (I shied away from use of the term "native," though I quote those who did use this term). I also refer to "Americans of Japanese Ancestry"—or "AJAs"—which I use interchangeably with "Japanese-Americans."

There are also in these pages a number of indigenous terms—"Hawai'i," "Kaua'i," and the like—and there I use diacritic marks (although those I have quoted do not).

Harry Bridges (*center with lei*) meets with Hilo stevedores in 1949. The Australian-born union leader was accused repeatedly of being a Communist Party member by the US authorities who sought to deport him—or, alternatively, imprison him. Courtesy of Labor Archives and Research Center, San Francisco.

Introduction

The workers kept coming, streaming in rivulets of protest. These men—they were mostly men—were predominantly of indigenous Hawaiian, Filipino, and Japanese origin and were departing angrily from the docks of pleasant Honolulu and balmy Hilo and the plantations of Kaua'i and Lana'i. It was in the early afternoon in mid-June 1953, roughly three years after the United States had embarked on a bloody war on the Korean peninsula and Hawai'i had become a primary point of departure for supplying the battlefield of this anticommunist conflict. Yet these men who numbered in the thousands were protesting, since their union leadership and the Communist Party leadership, which were thought by their adversaries to be equivalent, had been convicted on anticommunist grounds of violating the notorious Smith Act. The docks, usually a beehive of activity in light of the jolt provided by war contracts, were strangely silent, as if the men had been summoned by a modern Pied Piper.[1] Though closer to Osaka than Boston and considered relatively isolated, the ports of Hawai'i were among the most efficient in the world when it came to handling cargo, and with harbor entrances directly facing the Pacific Ocean,[2] their importance increased as military tensions waxed in Korea—then Vietnam—and tensions rose accordingly.

In protest of the conviction of the seven leftist leaders, and, most particularly, their leader—Jack Hall—stevedores voted quickly to virtually double their wage demands in current contract negotiations. Ships were being stranded in port, and sugarcane and pineapple began to decompose in the field.[3] This was not the first time that Hawai'i workers had gone on strike in reaction to a slight against a presumed Communist. The same thing occurred in August 1950 after the jailing of these workers' union leader, the Australian-born Harry Bridges, head of the International Longshoremen's and Warehousemen's Union (ILWU), based in San Francisco. Then about 10,000 workers went on strike; this time the workers decided to up the ante, as 20,000 walked out.[4]

Bridges, who was widely thought to be a Communist—or Red, as Communists were known colloquially—should not have felt bad about the smaller number of strikers in 1950, for in September 1952, when a federal appeals court ruling upheld his perjury conviction, 20,000 workers went on strike in Hawai'i.[5] This response was extraordinary and totally unlike the reaction to any other trial and conviction of leaders of the beleaguered Communist Party USA on the mainland, where if demonstrations erupted in response, they often were in celebration of the jailing of Reds. How and why was Hawai'i different?[6]

In contemporary US parlance, Hawai'i is probably the bluest of the blue states, a dependable vote for Democratic Party presidential candidates. Republicans wishing to survive in this island chain in the Pacific must minimally appear to be "Democrat lite," as the kind of conservatism that is de rigueur on the mainland is a nonstarter in Hawai'i. This state is second only to New York in terms of union members as a percentage of workers—a typically reliable measure of progressivism—weighing in at 25.8 percent, a nose behind the Empire State's 26.1 percent.[7] But it was Hawai'i, not New York, that instituted the first negative income tax for the poor. It was Hawai'i that was the first state to legalize abortion and to ratify the ultimately failed Equal Rights Amendment. It was Hawai'i that led in abolishing the death penalty, and it was Hawai'i that was the first state to mandate prepaid health care for workers. In the most fundamental ways, Hawai'i has the most progressive politics of any state, with a political coloration—and, not unconnected, a demographic makeup—as distant from the mainland as the thousands of miles of ocean that separate it from the nation to which it ostensibly belongs.[8]

This is not a recent trend.[9] In 1966, ILWU leader David Thompson stated proudly that agricultural workers in Hawai'i enjoyed the world's highest farm wages; it was the first state—and then the only one—in which all the workers in large-scale agriculture belonged to a union. It was the only state in which agricultural workers had decent wages, comprehensive medical plans, dental plans, pensions, paid vacations and holidays, sick leave, severance pay, and the like,[10] all the result of labor's struggle.[11] Robert Hasegawa, Hawai'i's director of labor and industrial relations, claimed in 1966 that his state had the "best labor laws in America" in terms of "minimum wage, unemployment compensation, workmen's compensation, temporary disability insurance, and a pioneering Fair Employment Practices Act."[12] Given that the majority of Hawai'i's population is made up of "minorities"—mostly of Asian-Pacific descent—this state may hold lessons for the nation as a whole as it evolves in this direction, particularly since historically Euro-Americans have been the bulwark of conservatism in the United States.[13]

The transformation of Hawai'i was a dramatic turnabout from relatively recent times. In 1947, speaking of Ni'ihau, "'the Forbidden Island,'" a correspondent informed Senator J. Howard McGrath of Rhode Island, a Democratic Party leader and crony of President Harry S. Truman's, that its entire "72 square miles is owned by the Robinson family," that "no one can visit the island," and that "so-called real Hawaiians who elect to work on the island for the Robinson Family cannot leave without special permission." This family was "the dictator"; its word was law.[14] Ten years earlier, things were probably worse on Niʻihau. It was a "feudal isle," said one journalist, and the "owners of this island are holding their workers in practical peonage"; the owners were "deliberately violating the educational law of the territory which states that children must attend school up to the age of 16 years," while "nothing but Republican ballots have been allowed to be distributed" in elections.[15] Visiting Hawaiʻi[16] in March 1937, Edward J. Eagen, regional director of the newly minted National Labor Relations Board, was astonished by what he saw. "'A number of the laborers are more like slaves than free people,'" he thought. "'I have seen them remove their hats when officers of the "Big Five" [corporations] pass. They live from hand to mouth. Surrounded by 2,000 miles of water, they have no chance to change their jobs or to get away from their present environment. They speak in mumble[s] [and] in undertones.'" A congressional visitor concluded three years later that "if there is any truer picture of fascism anywhere in the world than in the Hawaiian islands, then I do not know the definition of it"; there was "close cooperation between the Army and Navy intelligence units and the 'Big Five'" corporations that dominated the local economy.[17]

The island of Lanaʻi[18] was wholly owned by the Hawaiian Pineapple Company for a good deal of its modern history, and its employees were treated harshly.[19] Yet with all this quotidian repression, one analyst was not far wrong when he suggested that the archipelago's "wartime government"— with certain regimes in the Deep South conspicuously excepted—was "the only true fascism which has ever existed on American soil," in that there was martial law, arbitrary detentions, gross restrictions on unions, strictly enforced curfews, and the like.[20]

This cruel repression contributed to pent-up resentment that burst forth at the war's conclusion with the efflorescence of labor organizing, notably by the ILWU, a union that was not hostile to Communist Party (CP) participation. The year of the 1953 walkout, Hawaiʻi had a population of about 500,000, and the ILWU membership was about 24,000, including the stevedores—so important for the unloading of merchandise in the island chain that was 2,400 miles from North America.[21] Because of the varied influences of seafarers who frequently visited these islands and stevedores influenced by the ILWU, Hawaiʻi long had developed a justified reputation for working-class consciousness,[22] which the union was able to parlay into major gains. Indeed, Harry Bridges, who led the group for decades, was friendly toward the Soviet Union, considered himself a Marxist, and acknowledged that he had access to the highest levels of CP decision making. In November 1992, scholars Harvey Klehr and John Haynes claimed that they had located a document in recently released files in Moscow that established that Bridges was also a member of the Central Committee of the US Communist Party as early as 1936—a point vigorously denied by Bridges over the years and, as well, a point flyspecked relentlessly by courts that were seeking to deport him.[23] Still, his first wife—Agnes Brown—testified in 1945 that Bridges was indeed a Red and kept his CP card hidden under the linoleum in their home. (They divorced during that same tumultuous year.)[24]

Despite such explosive charges, which customarily destabilized leaders on the mainland, the ascetic Bridges inspired loyalty among those he led, not only because his union delivered real benefits but also because of the personal example he set. His son recalled later, "He always stayed in cheap hotels, he traveled on weekends to save money. There was nothing extravagant about him"; he "never made a lot of money [and] made a point of making as much"—and no more—"as the highest paid longshoreman," in stark contrast to fellow labor leaders.[25] Despite—or perhaps because of—this asceticism, Bridges was hounded by the US authorities. In 1941 some of Bridges' confederates decided to reverse the usual pattern and spy on the FBI. They were rewarded as they watched through their spyglasses while government agents wearing earphones and wielding recording equipment engaged in close surveillance of Bridges whenever he entered a Manhattan hotel room.[26]

The influence of figures like Bridges caused Senator James Eastland of Mississippi, who took a keen interest in the territory's affairs, to claim in 1956 that "'the power of the Communists in Hawaii is a thousand times stronger than it is in the continental United States.'"[27] This was an exaggeration but not a gross one.[28]

The left in Hawai'i faced off against a major regional economic powerhouse, given that the Bank of Hawaii and Bishop National Bank were among the 100 largest commercial banks under the US flag and, as of 1953, there were 7 Hawai'i firms among the 1,000 largest within the federal government's jurisdiction.[29] Hawai'i's representative in Washington, D.C., observed more than seven decades ago that "in 1936 Hawaii purchased more products from the rest of the United States, than were purchased by any but five foreign countries," just behind Britain, Canada, Japan, France, and Germany and ahead of Cuba, South Africa, Mexico, Australia, and Italy.[30]

What was undeniable was the deep sense of grievance in the islands, particularly among indigenes, who even today are about 20 percent of the population, and among those of Japanese origin, who are now the plurality of Hawai'i and were specifically invited to reside there by the Hawaiian Kingdom precisely as a bulwark against US imperialism, which was to seize power as the twentieth century was dawning.[31] "They had lost the islands to the missionaries and to the haoles [Euro-Americans]," recalled ILWU leader Louis Goldblatt, "and they wanted them back. They saw the union as the first effective fighting organization to come along."[32] Attorney Grover Johnson reported that when he visited Hawai'i in 1934, "all the while . . . I was besieged by natives who claimed to have been defrauded of their land and wanted to bring suit to get it back." It was "much the same situation as the

Indians at Wounded Knee."[33] During the summer of 2005, a visiting journalist in the islands found a "deep sense of dispossession among native Hawaiians, who make up about 20 percent of the population."[34]

Many of the Filipinos had experience in one of the more sophisticated guerrilla operations in this planet's history—the fabled Huk Rebellion[35]—and Tokyo had long been the site of vigorous and thriving socialist and Communist movements that dwarfed their counterparts in the United States. When the Hawai'i Communist leadership was placed on trial in 1952, the prosecution introduced an article penned by the legendary Sen Katayama, who had been a founder of the Communist Party in the United States in addition to being a leader of the party in Japan. In the article, he termed Hawai'i as "the strategic knot of the Pacific" and "the most important strategic point in the Pacific Ocean"; given that fact, he was elated to note, "Among the Japanese workers in Hawaii there was a group which was long under the influence of the Japanese revolutionary movement. The members of this group came chiefly from the Japanese islands of Riu-Kiu [Ryukyus], where, at one time, the Japanese Workers and Peasants Party (which supported the CP [of] Japan and was dissolved by the government in 1928) had a strong influence."[36]

An article retained by Senator Hugh Butler of Nebraska spoke dramatically of a "Japanese Communist Master Plan" in pursuit of the "Japanization of Hawaii." This scheme "progressed so well," said the writer, "that a notable Communist, Hozumi Ozaki, succeeded in penetrating to become an unofficial advisor to the Japanese Cabinet on the eve of Pearl Harbor. He was a trusted intimate of Prince Fumimaro Konoye, the Premier." As he saw things, it was the CP in Tokyo—not Moscow—that "threatens the entire world."[37] Weeks before war erupted on the Korean peninsula, Senator Butler received from Hawaiian attorney James Coke a picture with a caption he found disturbing: "200,000 . . . in the Imperial Plaza in Tokyo to hear Japan's Communist Party leader, Sanzo Nozaka, deliver his May Day Address."[38]

Many of the most militant workers in Hawai'i hailed from the radical region singled out by Katayama. "I'm an Okinawan," said Yasuki Arakaki, one of the more dedicated of ILWU members during its pre-statehood heyday. "As I was growing up, I knew I was not Japanese. I was not treated as Japanese." Like minorities worldwide who felt a deep sense of grievance—including African-Americans on the mainland—this helped to generate within him a fierce progressivism. "So when a person is discriminated [against] . . . , you have a feeling of fighting back, you know." Thus, he continued reflectively in a 1991 interview, "if you see today, many of the business people on the Big Island [Hawai'i], the Kaneshiro family, the Food Fair, and many of the merchants in Honolulu, the Star Market, many of the markets [are owned by] Okinawans. And Okinawans[,] because they are discriminated [against], they stick together and help each other out." Once he had a would-be sweetheart whose mother compelled her to reject him, "'because you're an Okinawan,'" he was informed curtly. He was "deeply hurt[,] naturally," as he felt like a "low-class Japanese." But dialectically, he said, "that gave me some impetus to prove that I'm not a leper. I'm going to prove to her and others that I'm equal or better"[39]—which he did by becoming one of the leading unionists in the archipelago, as did other similarly situated Okinawans.

In sum, many of those who resided in Hawai'i had roots in Japan, not only a nation whose radical movement was more widespread than its counterpart in North America but also a nation less profoundly influenced by anticommunism. Thus, the de facto leader of Hawaiian Communists at the time of the Smith Act trial (designed to eradicate alleged subversion)—and one of the key defendants—was Jack Kimoto, who had been born in Ewa, Hawai'i, in 1908 but had studied in Japan and was bilingual. He worked as a reporter, a translator, and a cab driver and lived in his ancestral home from 1914 to 1916. From 1931 to 1938 he resided in Los Angeles, where he joined the Communist Party. Rather small and with bespectacled brown eyes, he blinked rapidly as he declaimed. "I got interested in the left-wing movement—the one in Japan," he recalled in a 1974 interview, "because their publications would come to Hawaii." In other words, his knowledge of another language meant that he could escape the hegemony of English reporting, in which—because of the conservatism of the United States and Great Britain—radicalism and Marxism were overwhelmingly and disproportionately portrayed as unfavorable.[40]

Another Smith Act defendant was Koji Ariyoshi, a stevedore, journalist, and founder of the archipelago's leading and most widely read left-wing journal, the *Honolulu Record;* its popularity has yet to be equaled since and whose very success was a key reason that led to the 1952 trial.[41] This man of Japanese ancestry, the son of an impoverished Kona coffee farmer, attended the University of Hawai'i for two years and then the University of Georgia before joining the US military. While in the service, he wound up as an adviser to Mao Zedong in the caves of Yenan, before decamping to Manhattan, where he worked as a translator of Chinese. He was also a dedicated Communist, arguing that the ILWU—which had rescued Hawai'i—would not have been organized but for the CP, which was the "basic fibre . . . the starch . . . the brains" behind it.[42]

Still, the man often given principal credit for the strength of the union, which also built the Democratic Party into the hegemonic force it is today, was Jack Hall, who was born about 1915 in Wisconsin and joined the CP in 1936. A ferocious imbiber of alcohol beverages, an aficionado of jazz, a brilliant mathematician and reader of balance sheets, a man who did not know how to drive a car (perhaps a good thing, since he didn't see very well)—Hall was a mass of contradictions.[43] He was well over six feet tall and weighed more than 200 pounds, and his great friend, according to his admiring biographer, was "named Jack Daniel and then he made the acquaintance of Jim Beam." Eventually, his dissolute living was to leave him with diabetes, prostate problems, high blood pressure, arteriosclerosis, gout, and Parkinson's disease. He was an expert poker player, which helped make him an adroit negotiator with management.[44] An excellent cook, he exhibited a good deal of imagination in the kitchen—fungible skills that allowed him to concoct delicious recipes for higher wages and better working conditions for his membership. He steered clear of tobacco and complained that the smoke from this weed bothered his already beleaguered eyes. He was an excellent typist too, and his influence was later magnified when his daughter married into the politically influential family of John and Phillip Burton in San Francisco.[45] Most of all, he was a tireless worker; his colleague David Thompson found him to be "brilliant," saying that he "works like a goddamn mule; gets more work done than any other 6 guys put together—and he's a damn rare thing, he's a great strike leader."[46]

Nevertheless, as Thompson also put it, Louis Goldblatt, the university-educated ILWU leader based in San Francisco, "was the general and Hall the lieutenant in the field."[47] John F. Murphy, an executive at the major island firm Castle and Cooke, recalled that, during negotiations, Hall often "had been running them" and then would be "displaced" by Goldblatt, a "clever" man in Murphy's estimation. Goldblatt was a "better negotiator" than Hall, he thought. Goldblatt realized, said Murphy, that while business was monolithic, a union was not. "The president of a company gives a directive" and minions salute and execute, but a union was different. "It is full of mavericks," Murphy said. "It's a political entity." And Goldblatt, he felt, recognized this more than most.[48]

Goldblatt grew up in the Bronx and received a Berkeley degree in 1931 and did two years of graduate work before becoming an organizer of Hollywood labor and then moving to San Francisco. There he threw in his lot with the newly organized ILWU, which had just spearheaded a weighty General Strike.[49] According to someone who knew him, he was a piano player, a sports fan, and a devotee of sculpture, painting, philosophy, and the history of art. Yet while Goldblatt provided direction to Hall, O. Vincent Esposito, a graduate of Harvard Law School who was Speaker of the House in the Hawai'i legislature in the 1957–1958 term, asserts that Hall during that period was the most powerful man in the territory. "I was the Speaker," Esposito averred, and "he was a much stronger person than I was—by far, when I was the Speaker," adding that Hall was "one of the most important men in the history of Hawaii, in my judgment."[50]

Governor John Burns, a founding father of statehood in Hawai'i, frequently sought to make surreptitious visits to Hall's home, leery of how his tête-à-tête with the isles' resident radical might be viewed by some. "He'd drive in a ramshackle car," perhaps so as to camouflage his presence, "but of course," said Yoshiko Hall, his spouse, "the minute" he stopped at their door, "all the kids in the neighborhood would say, 'Governor Burns is here. Governor Burns is here!'" The two men also often met at the governor's place "at 6 o'clock in the morning before Burns went to mass"—and perhaps before nosy reporters were awake.[51]

Burns acknowledged that Communists gave him his start in politics. "If you ever look at my papers that were filed in 1948," said this former cop who once served as the territory's representative in Washington, D.C., "you'll find all those names [of Reds,] Jack Hall, Jack Kawano, down the line. I wasn't even around when the papers were filed."[52]

Yet if Hall was the lieutenant and Goldblatt the general, then—according to Ariyoshi—Bridges was the political commissar, for "the line came from [him]."[53] Well-born in Melbourne, Bridges was struck by the writings of Jack London, which inspired him to go to sea. Then he wound up in San Francisco, where he led the General Strike and organized a union he headed for decades. A man with a resonant Aussie accent, Bridges was a consummate leader of workers, and the federal government sought to deport or imprison him more than once. He was a thin and dapper man and sharp—sharp of face, sharp of nose, sharp of dress, sharp of manner, sharp of speech, sharp of gesture. Even his mouth was a thin, tight-lipped—and sharp—line. His face was a sharp triangle, with the sharp apex not at the chin but at the long, thin, sharp nose. His high, sloping forehead was topped with wiry hair, rapidly graying. His cheekbones were high and sharp. He was well-barbered, well-manicured, and so adeptly tailored that he resembled a courtroom version of a man of distinction—a man who, it was suggested, could have been played in the movies by the actor George Raft. But of all his embodiment of sharpness, it was his sharp mind that allowed him to remain a radical of alien birth in a nation determined to jail or deport him.[54]

Bridges' sterling qualities notwithstanding, it must be stressed that the very nature of his industry allowed him to flourish. Dockworkers, along with miners and seafarers, lost more workdays to labor disputes than other workers. Stevedores globally knew that their well-being depended on collective action, since otherwise the oversupply of brawny men with strong backs who were desperate for a job that provided decent—and not starvation—wages, seemed to generate a kind of labor solidarity that served to propel a man like Bridges, who knew how to speak to this concern.[55] Dockers knew that the ILWU—unlike their New York–based competitor[56]—sought not to collaborate with management to their detriment but instead to spearhead fierce class struggles. Before the advent of the ILWU in the islands, the notorious "shape-up system" prevailed, whereby in the morning and/or afternoon, stevedores seeking labor went to a pier and stood in a circle and a hiring boss stood in the middle and selected the men he wanted to work that day. There might be 200 or so in the circle—but only a lucky dozen or so were chosen and the remainder were left to drift away. Eventually, these workers learned that if they promised the hiring boss a kickback, their chances for work were greater—which opened the door to racketeering, internal squabbling among workers, and all manner of ills. Strapped workers often felt compelled to steal cargo, not necessarily for themselves but for gangsters, a practice that led inexorably to double crosses—and then, perhaps, murder. But in the San Francisco–based ILWU, workers were hired through a hiring hall, jointly supported and controlled by the employers and the union.[57]

In Hawai'i the union was also sufficiently perspicacious to notice the split between irrigated and nonirrigated plantations. The former were more prosperous—e.g., Waialua and HC&S—whereas the Hamakua plantation was among those that were more dependent on rainfall and didn't make as much money as others. Labor could gauge the weather and then strike—or not strike—accordingly, something that management realized.[58] The non-irrigated plantations were also not as susceptible to early mechanization as the irrigated segment, a difference that also helped shape union strategy.[59]

Months before the commencement of the epochal Smith Act trial, leading labor journalist Victor Riesel took on this troika—Bridges, Goldblatt, and Hall. The latter was a "glowering, thick set, full-faced man in silver-rimmed spectacles" who directed Bridges' "real base of power, the Hawaiian sugar and pineapple workers," and was guided by Goldblatt, a "crew cut, dirty blond, arrogant little fellow." Riesel also described Goldblatt as a "'Sather Gate orator,'" a reference to his halcyon days in Berkeley, and as "an accomplished pianist, a sugary, swaying speaker, a financial genius." Aghast that this radicalism could occur amidst a Red Scare meant to root out remaining Red influence, Riesel noted that "Bridges' men control unions in atomic energy installations, electronic, aircraft, jet motor plants, in the copper mining and smelting fields, in auto, tank, gun and agricultural implement factories, on our most strategic docks, in our vital warehouses, on fishing fleets in waters neighboring Soviet Russia, in metal fabricating shops, meat packing houses, and thousands of commercial units."[60]

Riesel's dream that the ILWU would be stripped of representation over many of its members came true, but he was correct in observing that the "real base of power" was the sugar and pineapple workers in Hawai'i (along with the stevedores there), and they refused resolutely to yield. One reason was that they didn't have much choice, since conditions for agricultural workers were so abysmal. Speaking before Congress in 1949, Bridges pointed out, "The average wage—and I am only talking about 5 years ago—was 28 cents an hour. No such thing as overtime." He continued, "Workers out in the field would get up about 4:30 in the morning. They were in the fields at 5 in the morning. At 5:30 they would have breakfast, a bucket of rice and fish. They would scoop it out; 11 o'clock lunch, a little more of the same."[61] Aiko

Reinecke (who was of Japanese origin), was born in Kahuku, Oʻahu, in 1907. Child labor was not unusual then, and she began to toil in the fields at the age of 11, carrying jugs of water. She arrived at 7 in the morning and departed at 3:30 in the afternoon; she was earning a nickel per day and resided with her parents in a camp that was "just a couple of rows of barracks" in which "each family had a room"; there was no running water, electricity, or oil stoves.[62]

Even after the union gained traction in the islands, the backlog of oppressive conditions proved difficult to extirpate. In the summer of 1956 a journalist found families "living in tents down on the beach," while others were residing in automobiles. "Thousands of others are today living under inhuman substandard conditions," the writer lamented; "relatives and friends who have doubled up are not on speaking terms because they have gotten in each other's way for so long." It was "not uncommon to find 15 to 20 persons living in a two bedroom unit"; and "in the Punchbowl area [of Honolulu] families were found living under houses, without excavated basements," as "rats interrupted their sleep."[63] As late as the 1950s in Ewa, where Communist leader Jack Kimoto was born, plantation workers lived in an area with open sewers and complained that rats bit their backsides in dilapidated outhouses in segregated camps termed "Filipino Camp" or "Japanese Camp" or "Korean Camp," etc.[64]

There was a consistency of horrible working conditions across the islands, though each one had a certain uniqueness. The Big Island—also known as Hawaiʻi, with Hilo as its largest city—was larger in territory than all the other major islands combined; Oʻahu, where Honolulu, the major metropolis, was sited, was the most populous. The largest payroll in the archipelago was that of the military, which provided a counterweight of sorts to the radicalism of labor.[65]

These abominable conditions provided fertile soil for the rise of radical labor and their complement—astute Communists. Yet the question needs to be posed: how did a nation like the United States, where die-hard white supremacists, Jim Crow devotees, and Dixiecrats of various stripes wielded power in the midst of Red Scare hysteria, find itself in the position of simultaneously entertaining the idea of admitting Hawaiʻi—where those of European descent were in a distinct minority and where Reds and radicals were influential—into its hallowed union as a state? In short, statehood for Hawaiʻi was concocted when this territory was basically an apartheid state with the GOP as the leading party. It became difficult to ditch statehood even after Communists became powerful and the Democrats roared back into contention, because by this point statehood was being viewed as a referendum on how Washington viewed Asians—i.e., rejection for statehood of a territory with the largest population of Asian descent under the US flag might be viewed as a racist slight, something to be avoided during the Cold War.

This road to statehood was complicated further when in 1954, in direct reaction to the creeping Red Scare as evidenced by the Smith Act trials (interpreted widely as an assault on the ILWU), the GOP lost its firm grip on Hawai'i for the first time in 50 years—since the US annexation. This altered the calculus for those who were in favor of statehood as long as it seemed that it would produce two Republican senators or at least legislators akin to the moderate white men who routinely represented the islands in Washington.

Part of the answer as to why statehood was granted in 1959 rests also with the white supremacists' being overtaken by events; that is, when they began trumpeting the idea of Hawai'i joining the union, this territory seemed to be firmly within the ambit of unalloyed racism and, thus, a decent fit for the United States. As late as 1948, for example, W. K. Bassett—the top aide to Honolulu's popular mayor—complained that no "bride of Chinese ancestry, Japanese ancestry, Filipino ancestry or Puerto Rican ancestry is permitted to have her picture appear in any one of the first five pages of the 'Honolulu Advertiser's' Sunday social section"; in the metropolis' most widely read periodical, "pictures of whites appear there exclusively."[66] In 1949 passengers departing for the mainland on the American President Lines were segregated: Euro-American Communist Stephen Murin and his spouse discovered this when they were refused the cheaper third-class accommodations, which were reserved only for so-called non-haoles (i.e., those not deemed to be "white").[67] Thus, there was a persistent practice of "wage differentials for haoles and non-haoles in various Big Five [corporations] and their subsidiary establishments," the progressive *Honolulu Record* editorialized in 1951, also noting that "haoles go up fast in promotions and in many offices"—a reality that the mainstream press ignored persistently.[68] Strikingly, in 1952 on the police forces on Maui and the island of Hawai'i (as opposed to the entire island chain), there were "more Caucasians," as one journalist put it, "than any other ethnic group"; of course, the "police commissioners" were "practically all Caucasian," as this was deemed necessary to make sure that white supremacist diktats were enforced ruthlessly.[69] There was also a sizeable number of unwarranted sterilizations of "non-haole" women and vasectomies of "non-haole" men.[70]

One reporter acknowledged in late 1952 that African-Americans, whose numbers in Hawai'i were quite small, were the most discriminated against, with Puerto Ricans—who had been brought to the islands in the wake of the overthrow of the kingdom—a close second; then Filipinos, then indigenes, followed by Chinese and Japanese. Since the latter hailed from a power that was scorned because of the attack on Pearl Harbor, however, and since they appeared to present the stiffest challenge to white supremacy and, besides, were more numerous than the other groupings, they were a special recipient of bigotry.[71]

Contemporary Euro-American writer Susanna Moore, who grew up in pre-statehood Hawai'i, has asserted that in Hawai'i "there was a fairly unconscious racism all around us" and also quite a bit of this bile that was "institutionalized" in the form of "restrictions and bylaws that kept non-haoles not only from private clubs, but from certain neighborhoods." In that era this praxis was largely "unquestioned"—at least by the white minority.[72]

Just as in today's United States, when those who seek to raise the issue of bias against minorities are accused of "playing the race card," there was something similar at play in pre-statehood Hawai'i. During the Smith Act trial when the defense lawyers sought to point out the racist conditions that had given rise to both unionism and leftism—and to jury pools, e.g., in the case at hand, in which whites were overrepresented—the prosecution reacted sharply asserting, "They are trying to stir up racial hatred here."[73]

Inevitably, white supremacy unleashed a strong counterreaction. Smith Act defendant John Reinecke, whose persecution by the authorities in 1948 was the opening shot in an anticommunist purge, remarked in that pivotal year that when he arrived in Honolulu in the 1930s "haoles . . . comprised less than 10 percent of the population" but "haole hating," a "quite accepted local term," was highly "prevalent." In fact, he said "it is still one of the problems here" and was a "problem in the labor unions," an ironic situation. Although these bodies with their stress on class struggle and the class ethos were a major antidote to racial antipathy, they had an uphill climb.[74]

Senator Butler of Nebraska discovered this when he began his post–World War II assessment of whether Hawai'i should become a state. Lucile Paterson, a resident of Honolulu informed him that the "much bruited racial integration and mutual respect" was "largely a myth"; she perceived an "undercurrent of hostility against the haoles or whites by the mixed Oriental population." As she saw it, the "numerous 'hoodlum attacks'" then capturing headlines were symptomatic of "Orientals vs. haoles" since the latter were targeted in her eyes. "My son is an excellent barometer," she said with regret. "He came here totally unaware of 'race' as such [but] he has already acquired a wary manner in his dealing with Orientals of his own age and has finally accepted the fact that he is a 'damn haole.'"[75]

When Senator Butler held confidential hearings in 1948 in Honolulu on the prospects for statehood, he was greeted with an outpouring of nervous sentiment from whites who, despite their privileged position, complained repeatedly about racial harassment. Like many of the witnesses, Francis D. Houston opposed statehood—if Hawai'i, why not Fiji? he asked querulously—and asserted that white sailors and soldiers were special victims of physical attacks, as if, to non-haoles, they were symbols of the colonial status that Hawai'i endured. "Non-haoles [would] catch a haole sailor alone and beat him up. That exists today," he cried, "and it exists to a pronounced degree."[76] In so many words, this sentiment was echoed again and again.[77]

Though historians have cast serious doubt on the alleged disloyalty of Japanese-Americans during the Pacific War, many whites disagreed vehemently.

Martin E. Alan, who told Senator Butler of his wonderment as to why so many white Communist men—including Smith Act defendants Jack Hall and John Reinecke and, ultimately, Bridges himself—were married to women of Japanese origin also claimed that farmers of Japanese origin in Hawai'i had stopped growing vegetables after 7 December 1941 in order to sabotage the war effort. Alan also declared that "from 1920 to 1940 an average of $1,200,000.00 annually was sent to Japan by the nationals here, in the form of gold and silver coin." As he recalled things, "Planes and submarines made regular and periodic visits here [from Japan] until the very end of the war in 1945. It's all hogwash about the loyalty of the Niseis [Japanese-Americans] and the aliens," as there "were acts of sabotage, plenty of them." But now, he asserted, those of Japanese origin had shifted from allegiance to Tokyo to allegiance to Moscow, for "Communism is working through the Orientals," as certain matrimonial tendencies supposedly suggested.[78]

This fear that "non-haoles" generally might be disloyal to a state that, after all, treated them like rubbish may shed light on why, when the "Major Disaster Council" of Maui met in emergency session at "10:40 A.M. following receipt of word via radio and telephone from Honolulu that O'ahu had been attacked" on 7 December 1941, only one of the 22 people present had an Asian surname.[79] Then an investigator from the US Navy opined that those of Japanese ancestry in Hawai'i might assist Japanese invaders.[80] Of course, such sentiments could have been motivated, as much as anything else, by guilty fear as to what white supremacy might have induced.

Unsurprisingly, after receiving an earful from whites, Senator Butler was in no mood to push for statehood in a territory where reputed Communists might be able to elect two US senators and where his racial compatriots were complaining about a veritable state of siege. This sentiment was held most dearly by Dixiecrats. Senator Olin Johnston of South Carolina, who was opposed adamantly to statehood, stressed that the *"non-haole peoples are taking Hawaii just as surely as a lava flow over-runs a volcanic region,"* for *"non-haole births were 9 times as [many] as haoles and the Japanese alone nearly 4 times as great."*[81] His comrade in arms and the epitome of white supremacy, Senator J. Strom Thurmond of South Carolina, proclaimed proudly, "I do not believe there is anyone in the Senate who is more opposed to the admission of Hawaii to statehood than I"—though many of his fellow Dixiecrats disputatiously disagreed.[82] Daniel Inouye, a chief beneficiary of the historic Democratic Party landslide that swept the GOP aside in Hawai'i in response to the Red Scare and the Smith Act convictions, recalled after statehood that one senator during the time of these passionate debates had asked wonderingly, "'How would you like to be sitting next to a fellow named Yamamoto?'"[83]

US elites had to decide whether it would be easier to contain the Left as a colony or a state—and the latter option was chosen. As then Vice President

Richard M. Nixon put it in early 1959, "Hawaii will be less susceptible to any control by Communists as a State than it is as a Territory."[84] The wily Nixon may have been listening to the likes of the powerful Henry A. White, president of the Dole Hawaiian Pineapple Company, who as early as 1946 recognized that statehood provided more leverage to otherwise grossly outnumbered white elites and was yet another lever to circumvent domination by the overwhelming majority.[85]

As it turned out, these sensitive senators had to sit next to counterparts named Inouye and Fong and Akaka after the granting of statehood in 1959 and did not appear to be any the worse for it. Hawai'i was transformed in the process from a feudal outpost in the Pacific to a state that plays the fortunate role of injecting a jolt of progressivism into an otherwise conservative United States, and for this the ILWU and the CP are largely responsible. Ray Jerome Baker, a left-leaning photographer—and a white—who arrived in Honolulu on a visit in 1908 and began residing there in 1910,[86] mused in 1952 as the Smith Act trial was launched, "I have seen the feudal conditions" abolished in Hawai'i, as "wages increased from about $20 per month to $10 per day."[87] This spectacular rise in wages was largely due to the energetic activism of an ILWU that was led by radicals.

Still, it would be a mistake to leave it at that, for there are still lessons to be learned about this experience that it would be ill-advised to ignore. These concerns reside in two profound areas—the matter of racism and the very question of statehood. On the former matter, Bridges—who often clashed with the eminent union leader Hall—recalled subsequently that he had wanted "some local people who were non-haole" in leadership of the union. "I promised those guys years ago that we were at the end of importing mainlanders. It was like an imperialist domain down there," he said, speaking of the strongest branch of the union he headed. It was "colonial," said Bridges; it was "paternalism, this patronizing [attitude that] because the poor people are uneducated [and] they're non-white, [they] need smart people to lead them around by the hand and to take care of them like this." Bridges' close ally in union leadership, J. R. Robertson—who also crossed swords with Hall—said that Hall had failed because "he failed to develop leadership," while relying heavily on whites from the mainland.[88]

Hall's reliance on white mainlanders was even more remarkable in that figures like Ariyoshi—who had advised Mao, started a pioneering newspaper, and more—were quite available. Yet as statehood approached, Hall and the union, instead of supporting the collapsing *Honolulu Record*, started a lighter—less ideologically sharp—version of this journal, and it folded quickly. To the extent that Hawai'i may provide an inkling to the future of a United States where those of European descent are not in the majority, it is troubling that some ILWU leaders seemed to have difficulty in working in equality alongside "non-haoles." To give a balanced picture, however, it must be noted that the notoriously insecure Hall also seemed to be wary of any potential challengers. When the Euro-American Communist Stephen Murin arrived in Hawai'i in 1947, Hall nervously said to him, "'I hear you're a Communist.'" Murin replied, "'I am,'" to which Hall—who may still have been a CP member at that juncture—retorted, "'We don't need Communists from Boston.'" Murin went on to become a stalwart of radicalism within labor and on the Left.[89]

At the same time, the ILWU leaders pushed for a kind of affirmative action, repeatedly requesting that leaders of Japanese origin in the union step aside so that Filipinos could be promoted[90]—yet it seemed beyond their comprehension (Bridges and Robertson aside[91]) to view the overrepresentation of white men in the leadership as problematic and to consider asking some of them to step aside. This grievous flaw may have stemmed from the fact that the Communist Party—which had long been a trailblazer in the fight against white supremacy—was in retreat even as the stunning 1953 demonstrations that greeted the Smith Act convictions were unfolding, and this helped to nudge Hawai'i in a more conservative direction than it might have gone otherwise. Moreover, both the party and the union were born and bathed in the amniotic fluid of the old racist order and could not easily escape this troubled heritage. As thousands of protesters poured into the streets of Honolulu and Hilo in 1953, Communists were virtually underground. Robert McBurney Kempa, a former Red who testified against Communists in 1953, noted that after war commenced in Korea, party cell meetings took place in moving automobiles—which obviously limited participation: "No telephones were to be used, homes were not to be used for meetings, no written records." The only writing was done on a "magic slate," i.e., a "black piece of waxed cardboard covered by a piece of wax paper covered by a piece of cellophane" that "could be immediately erased."[92] The party was the venue where these issues of racism in labor leadership could have been engaged and hashed out more effectively, but this was not easy to do while meeting in cars in busy Honolulu traffic. The union itself found such discussions hard to accomplish, as it too battled for survival and as Hall could easily interpret such discussions as attacks on his otherwise meritorious leadership.

More puzzling is why the party and the union chose to crusade for statehood, though they were more aware than most of the blatant imperialism that led to the deposing of the kingdom and the imposition of rule by Washington, D.C. At the 1948 hearing in which he was castigated for being a reputed Communist, Smith Act defendant John Reinecke spoke eloquently of how "in 1893 the business centers by *coup d'etat* overthrew the established government" and "set up what was openly an oligarchy of small sections of the Caucasian population," while "Oriental Hawaiians were not allowed to vote at all." Then, he said, "in 1895 a number of native Hawaiians, abetted by some of the whites rose in rebellion." Although he described the rebellion as "futile and anachronistic," he declared, "But I certainly could not blame them. If I had been living here in Hawaii at that time and had been of an age to join them, I think I would have joined them." Shockingly for the time, he added, "Looking at it from the vantage point of history now, I should say that they would have done better to have waited for annexation." He disagreed with the notion that "Hawaii should have its independence," though he recognized that it was a "colony."[93]

In a lengthy undated document probably written at the time of the Smith Act trial, the CP too acknowledged the obvious: Hawai'i was a colony. In a nuanced manner, it noted that the idea of independence—raised by the party early on—had not been bruited of late because it was "too far in advance of the present level of consciousness of the national movement in the country," although it was "urgently necessary to caution against ruling out for all time this particular slogan." Statehood "cannot solve the national problem," and the CP "cannot favor statehood as a solution," it was said. "Nor should the party make its main point of departure that opposition."[94]

The ILWU, which contrary to its detractors was independent of the CP, did not adhere to this line, but belatedly in September 1959, after statehood was a reality, union leaders began to grapple with what it actually meant to be a state in an otherwise retrograde United States. Noted was the impending "rapid change in the social and political outlook of our electorate with the influx of tens of thousands of adult conservative Caucasians from the mainland who will tend more and more to 'Miami-ize' our islands and bury its real traditions." Rather tardily, it warned, "We may lose our identity, traditions and liberalism altogether within the next decade."[95]

It is entirely possible that as the CP was being chased into underground status and Hall failed to renew his membership as a direct result of requirements of the draconian Taft-Hartley legislation, he saw measures to diversify the top ranks of the ILWU and to rethink the union's support for statehood and the *Honolulu Record* as all part of letting go of an unrealistic Left turn illbefitting a mature union that was about to determine the selection of US senators. These flaws notwithstanding, the Communists in the earthly paradise that was Hawai'i may have had more influence and impact than Reds anywhere else under the US flag. They spearheaded the building of a union, the ILWU, which still thrives and which brought democracy to a virtual despotism as it rescued thousands from the brutal clutches of white supremacy.

CHAPTER I

Confronting Colonial Hawai'i

It was in the mid-1930s when the Communist Party in San Francisco summoned Bill Bailey—the gruff and plain-talking seaman—to its Haight Street office for the prospect of an enticing assignment. Very tall and rugged, with lively blue eyes and hair that would soon gray, he had an accent that betrayed his East Coast origins. He had gone to sea at the age of 14 and early on became friendly with Jack Hall.[1] Only recently had the ILWU been organized in this city of steep hills, gray skies, and cool weather. Now a CP leader handed Bailey 50 blank membership application cards, which he tucked away, and instructed him simply to travel westward, to the Hawaiian Islands, and organize. Five days after he left California, the beautiful sight of Diamond Head in Hawai'i loomed invitingly on the horizon.[2] His suitcase stuffed with more CP propaganda than clothes, he had adopted beachcomber style, deigning only to bring a pair of dungarees, a blue denim shirt, two pairs of socks and underwear, and a handkerchief—along with his union book and seamen's papers—but no hat or coat. He had been dispatched by the party, and not his union, for, as he recalled things, "at one time Harry [Bridges] didn't want to even entertain the idea that the islands should be organized."[3]

Bailey seemed to be a glutton for unrest, arriving in an archipelago teeming with turmoil, just as he had left a city similarly seething:[4] strikebound San Francisco.[5] Hawaiians, particularly indigenes, in San Francisco were involved in the city's General Strike in large numbers and bonded tightly as a result. They were deemed to be the toughest men on the waterfront—particularly in relentlessly pursuing scabs and strikebreakers—and that was saying something, since the docks were notorious for attracting the most abrasive of roughnecks.[6] Bailey's journey reflected their presence in California.

The Hawai'i that greeted Bailey was likewise embroiled in conflict, for Honolulu was still buzzing about the notorious Massie case. It was a Pacific reenactment of the Scottsboro Nine case, then brewing on the mainland, as African-American youth were being charged with the rape of two white women.[7] In Hawai'i the alleged interracial molestation in the Massie case involved a white woman versus two indigenous Hawaiians, two young men of Japanese ancestry, and one of Chinese-Hawaiian origin,[8] a flaming example of injustice that had captured the attention of the Communist press.[9] Near the same time, famed sociologist Robert Park was stunned to find in Hawai'i "two cases where Orientals were victims of murder by white men" and "these white murderers were given merely imprisonment," as opposed to the punishment that might have been imposed if the roles had been reversed on the mainland: the death penalty. "They now realize that here in Hawaii exist two laws—one for the white man and one for the Oriental," Park ascertained.[10]

Racist miscarriages of injustice were nothing new to Hawai'i; such emerged almost effortlessly from a land where the distinctly minority ideology of white supremacy was being implanted forcibly. It was in 1880, just before the arrival of a large wave of Japanese, that leading Euro-American William Armstrong confessed bluntly, "The Chinese question troubles me." Speaking of perceived danger to his fellow whites, he warned, "Here there are over 10,000 of them. They can rise and kill us all."[11] Armstrong, who was close to Hawai'i's royal family, may have felt that bringing in more Japanese to the archipelago could serve as a counterweight to the Chinese he so feared, because a few months later he was in Tokyo on a historic mission with the monarch, as the politics of race and ethnicity played out.[12]

Yet Armstrong's exultation was short-lived, as the effluvia of bigotry spread almost seamlessly to these most recent arrivals, the Japanese. In 1898 a man of Japanese origin, Hiroshi Goto, was lynched in direct response to his refusal to provide false testimony in a controversial court case.[13] Already sensitive to the perceived danger of relying too heavily on labor from a rising and increasingly militant Japan, the barons of Hawai'i turned to labor thought to be more reliable or at least without roots in a rising power: African-Americans. By 1901, Negro laborers had begun to trickle into Maui. There were 20 from Tennessee in the cane fields working among a mixture of Chinese, Japanese, Puerto Ricans, South Sea Islanders, Portuguese, Italians, and Galicians[14]—but the rebellious tendency of these darkest of workers wrecked this experiment.

Hawai'i was straining from the brunt of rapid change, in any case. According to Ichiro Izuka, a onetime Communist, the first labor organization in Hawai'i was forged in 1908. In an illustration of how labor and racism were joined at the hip, there was a felt desire to push for equal pay for equal work since the white skilled workers were then paid $4.38 per day, the Hawaiians $1.68, the Portuguese $1.61, the Chinese $1.06, and the Japanese $0.97. As if the white elite was consciously courting a potential confrontation, laborers with roots in a rising Japan were paid the least; in response, over 9,000 O'ahu Japanese workers went on strike.[15]

Maui was hardly an improvement. It was not easy to reach this amiable island named after a legendary hero and demigod of Polynesia. At 728 square miles, it was the second largest in the chain—dwarfed only by the Big Island. Maui was 2,100 miles west of San Francisco and 90 miles from the capital and main population center, Honolulu, and on the eve of the new world brought by the Pacific War, it had a population slightly over 50,000.[16]

Thus, the sugar and pineapple plantations that dominated in O'ahu and Maui particularly had to rely on those akin to the Massie case defendants in order to meet their perpetual problem of securing labor, a problem that was growing as rapidly as the crops they harvested. For example, in 1856 the entire crop of sugar in the islands was 547 tons, but by 1925 the crop amounted to over 776,000 tons as the sweet tooth of the planet—particularly due eastward in North America—demanded constant satisfaction. By this latter date a number of the plantations employed more than 2,000 men each, and some more than 3,000 men; by 1926 there were 51 of these sprawling plantations, although there had only been 5 in 1857.[17]

The plight of the young men of the Massie case, ensnared by criminal charges, was emblematic of the new type of Jim Crow system these agricultural workers faced, whereby Euro-Americans were positioned at the top of the socio-economic order, while others—e.g., the defendants—were the horse to their rider. Arriving shortly after World War I, the peripatetic writer W. Somerset Maugham confided, "Nothing had prepared me for Honolulu"; "I could hardly believe my eyes," he confessed, as he espied shacks "cheek by jowl with stone mansions" and "dilapidated frame houses stand[ing] next door to smart stores with plate glass windows," while "every third house is a bank and every fifth the agency of a steamship company." Euro-Americans also generally tried to distinguish themselves by their dress. "Ignoring the climate, [they] wear black coats and high, starched collars, straw hats, soft hats, and bowlers," Maugham observed, while the "Kanakas"—"pale brown" indigenes "with crisp hair," looked and dressed differently.[18]

Many of these indigenes were not happy with the annexation of their homeland by the United States at the end of the nineteenth century, and certainly the former royal family—many of whose members were still around when Bailey arrived on these congenial shores—were decidedly in that category. The same could be said of many within the burgeoning population of Japanese origin, whose presence was the result of a calculation by the monarchy. Vainly seeking an alliance with Tokyo in order to forestall the larger threat from Washington, the monarchy opened its doors to immigration from Japan—a process that Armstrong helped engineer. That few beyond Euro-Americans were allowed to vote in what had become an apartheid state was not pleasing to Tokyo in particular, and it had the means to object, as the events of December 1941 were to demonstrate.[19]

This migration from Asia nonetheless helped create one of the more diverse populations under the US flag, and one partial result was a thriving laboratory involving what Edwin R. Embree of the Rockefeller Foundation termed "research in race biology."[20] A "station for racial research"[21] was proposed in 1926 for the recently established University of Hawai'i, which would involve—inter alia—"a program concerned primarily with the biological aspects of racial amalgamations" and the "complex genetic problems which have risen from race mixture."[22] This kind of thinking underpinned a racially stratified labor force whereby workers were grouped and given posts according to what the Hilo Sugar Company termed "racial ancestry," with "Anglo-Saxon males" at the top, followed in order by "Japanese males," "Filipino males," "Chinese males," "Puerto Rican males," "Portuguese males," and at the bottom the original inhabitants, "Hawaiian males."[23]

Such conditions had provided fertile soil for the implantation of radical ideas. The Japanese-American Communist stevedore and intellectual Karl Yoneda has argued that quite a few of those who came in the first wave from Japan in the early 1880s were socialists. Those who arrived in Lihu'e, Kaua'i, began publishing the biweekly *Yoen jiho* (Plantation times), whose printing of numerous articles on Marxism and socialism did not bar it from having wide circulation throughout the islands. By 1929, systematic study of Marxism had been launched in the community of Japanese, marked by the publication of a magazine, *Kenkyu* (Studies), as well as a newspaper, *Jiryu* (Current tides), and by 1932 there was the monthly *Hagurma* (Wheels). All of these were short-lived, but from such acorns the mighty oak of the Communist Party in Hawai'i grew, and it included numerous members of Japanese ancestry. By 1925 the Communist League of Hawaii had been organized by George Wright, former head of the American Federation of Labor in Honolulu.[24]

But Japanese-Americans were not alone in their radicalism. In 1921 a small Korean weekly in Honolulu was charged with advocating direct action to gain Korea's freedom.[25]

By 1921 there were about a dozen comrades of Japanese origin in the US Communist Party, but aggressive recruiting was to produce a different result, so that by April 1933 the veteran Communist organizer Sen Katayama reported on growth in radicalism in Maui as represented by the Yuaikai, the "'Hawaiian Proletarian League,'" the "'Social Science Study Group in the University of Hawaii,'" and "'a literary group centered around the "Haguruma" (The Gear).'" This development was facilitated by a trans-Pacific, two-way communication between Japanese immigrant organizers on the West Coast of the United States and Japanese seamen traveling between Japan and the United States—all of whose influence was often left in Hawai'i.[26] Thus, in the US Communist Party, the Chinese group was much smaller than the Japanese, whose numbers soared above 200. There was a CP paper in the Japanese language that printed 2,000 copies.[27]

Japanese migrants played a central role in organizing the CP in Hawai'i and California. One analyst argued that the CP in Japan "threatens the entire world" due to its heft and that "from 1926" to the postwar era "the favorite meeting place" of these particular Reds was "the Owl Restaurant in Little Tokyo of Los Angeles, which was owned by Yotoku Miyagi, Japanese artist and spy."[28]

A few years earlier, in 1922, Communist organizer George Wright had been seeking valiantly to unite labor in Hawai'i, with little palpable success.[29] Jan Valtin, who billed himself as a courier from the Moscow-based Communist International, arrived in Hawai'i to distribute propaganda in 1925 and, likewise, was distressed by the weakness of labor and the Left.[30]

The ships plying the waters between Japan and Hawai'i were often bringing fleeing radicals eastward to the archipelago. In 1933 in Japan, 1,304 Communists and their sympathizers were arrested, including the majority of the Central Committee and the editor of the party's principal organ; a number of comrades were murdered, and 200 Reds were placed on trial in Tokyo. At this point there were Communist nuclei in shipyards and factories alike, and rooting out this radicalism was perceived in Tokyo as a precondition to global conquest,[31] but repression spurred migration and, ultimately, helped give rise to radicalism in Hawai'i.

It was in February 1925 that Paul Crouch (later a primary and hostile witness against the CP in the Smith Act trial) and Walter Trumbull, then in the US Army, were court-martialed at Schofield Barracks, O'ahu, for behavior that amounted to sedition. Arrested with them were 10 other soldiers of the 21st Infantry stationed at Schofield. Crouch and Trumbull were tried, found guilty, and sentenced, respectively, to 40 and 26 years at hard labor, reputedly the heaviest sentences ever accorded in peacetime for military activism.[32] Crouch was born in Jim Crow North Carolina in 1903, and his father was a Baptist minister. Perhaps in revolt against his staid upbringing, he joined the Young People's Socialist League at the age of 14. He arrived in Hawai'i by 1924, where he became part of the Communist League and then the CP, reportedly remaining a member until 1942 (though it is unclear when he became a government agent).[33] Contrary to Yoneda's assertions, Crouch claimed, "We openly formed the Hawaiian Communist League . . . and had letterheads printed at the Army's printing shop at Schofield."[34] He was punished, Crouch said at the time, "because we defended the Soviet Union"[35] and because he was responsible for the "first organized revolutionary movement in the American army"; the Communist League had only "15 members," he said, but had a "mass following of about 75."[36] Later, Crouch said, he traveled to Moscow, where he was reputedly told that Hawai'i "should be a concentration point, second only to Panama in importance, followed by the Philippines and military posts around the port cities of New York and San Francisco."[37]

In words deemed sufficiently important to be retained by the Dixiecrat Senator James Eastland of Mississippi, Crouch declared that the rise of the CP in Hawai'i developed "according to scheduled plans worked out by the Kremlin many years ago" and that at its apex of influence the local party "received the personal supervision of the highest officials of the Soviet Government and the Red Army General Staff." It was in December 1927, Crouch claimed, that he traveled to a frosty Soviet Union, remaining there until April 1928. During that time he averred that he was involved in "high level policy meetings" in which there was "exclusive discussion of the role of Hawaii as a strategic point and the necessity of building the Communist movement there." In Moscow, he allegedly conferred with Communist stalwarts such as Sen Katayama, James Allen, and "two Filipino Communist leaders, Cristano Evangelista and Jacinto Manahan." He reported that "the Moscow plans included infiltration of Hawaii through the Filipinos [via] relatives of the Communists in the Philippines Islands." Moscow, he stated, "recognized the necessity of capturing Hawaii as the necessary step in obtaining control of the United States." To that end, he said, by 1933 there were "2,500 members" of a "Hawaiian Proletarian Soviet" with "branches on the five major islands of the group." Crouch asserted that until about 1936 the CP argued for Hawaiian self-determination, but presumably as part of the Popular Front against fascism and the need to woo a broader front in the United States, this demand was ditched and "it was decided to make Hawaii a part of District 13 of the Communist Party, the California District,"[38] which is why Bill Bailey of San Francisco found himself in Diamond Head in the mid-1930s with 50 membership blanks in his suitcase.

Surely, many of Crouch's recollections are far-fetched, but it remains true that the oppressive and racially coded conditions of Hawai'i were made to order for the rise of radicalism. Felipe Lariosa was born in Cebu in the Philippines in 1916 and arrived in Hawai'i when he was three years old, residing in Ewa. As a laborer when he was older, he received a dollar a day for 10 hours of work. Food was served outside, and baths were also taken in the wide-open air upon returning home to a shack owned by the plantation. He felt further isolated since he was Visayan, of which there were "very few" while "plenty" of his compatriots in the islands were "Ilocanos."[39] ILWU leader A. Q. McElrath—the Chinese-American spouse of fellow labor leader Robert McElrath—recalled that by 1927 there were 27 sugar plantations and 30,000 workers, whose families resided in "quite old" plantation housing, "some with outdoor plumbing, some without." Working conditions were, put simply, "lousy." The boss looked at workers as if they were "cattle" or "jute bags."[40] One journalist reported that in Kaua'i in the 1930s there were shacks where "4, 6 and even [more] men are crowded" in a "room 8 by 12," the "kind of room you rent in Hawaii's slums for eight dollars a month"; workers "even have to supply their own beds," the reporter maintained.[41]

Pablo Manlapit, a leader of island labor of Filipino descent, observed in 1934 that the basic wage for sugar plantation laborers was a meager dollar per day for 10 to 12 hours of work, and this wage encompassed 32,000 of the 50,000 workers he found toiling on plantations—which included child laborers. As was its wont, the Hawaiian Sugar Planters' Association, representing approximately 41 sugar corporations, was recruiting even more laborers from the Philippines in excess of the needs of the industry, in order to depress wages further. Since most of them were noncitizens, these workers were subjected to a further heightened exploitation. Besides manipulating immigration laws, Manlapit said, the planters' association was "spending large sums of money to frame-up charges against the leaders of sugar plantation laborers" and was "using the Public Prosecutor's office and the Police Department to carry on its object in destroying and disbanding the labor organizations," which were "making a militant fight." Manlapit was aghast that whenever workers held a meeting, plantation officials and police officers were present, intimidating the laborers and jotting down their employee numbers.[42] Filipinos, whose numbers in Hawai'i began to grow when the Philippines and Hawai'i became linked as the twin colonial Pacific possessions of Washington, were enduring a notably rough time under the US flag.[43]

In 1934, California attorney Grover Johnson—affiliated with the re-nowned International Labor Defense, which was known to be close to the CP—arrived to defend these Filipino workers. "I flew from Oakland to Hono-lulu," he recalled later, and "the fare was $365," a hefty amount sufficiently for-bidding to explain why the islands remained so isolated. "I landed in Honolulu," he continued, "and then took a two-engine Sikorsky seaplane to Maui. When we landed[,] there was a crowd of three or four thousand. A big band was play-ing."[44] Johnson left with an idea that had occurred to many in the US Left—Hawai'i, though despotic, was ripe for radicalism. The treatment Johnson received may have reflected that although he was a radical, he was also white.

There was more that Johnson in his narrative could have added about the sorry plight of agricultural workers in 1930s Hawai'i. Routinely, plantation bosses ordered their employees to vote a certain way, and the press generally was a toothless watchdog.[45] In those bad old days, recalled Hideo Okada, who worked in the sugar fields of O'ahu for more than 40 years, "the company put all the employees on the truck, during working hours, and they [would] drag them to the voting precinct."[46] The man known as Doc Hill recalled condi-tions in those difficult days: "The manager was the king. No king ever ruled his domain with a firmer hand." There was "complete control—fire a man, raise his pay, kick him out of the house," traditionally owned by the planta-tion, "or do anything that they want." He added, "And they [workers] were getting a dollar a day."[47] Not surprisingly, the pivotal election of 1934 re-sulted in a complete disintegration and rout of the Democratic Party ticket in

Hawai'i, though the committeewoman of the Democratic National Committee in the islands claimed that the island chain had "participated abundantly in the benefits accruing from the New Deal."[48]

Bill Bailey, the colorful and irreverent seaman, found himself residing in a "whorehouse" as he vainly sought to rally support from existing trade unions that "existed all right, but most of them were for the elite—plumbers, electricians, bartenders," while the major corporations, the infamous "Big Five," sought to control "everything but the weather."[49] Bailey's perception that existing unions tied to the American Federation of Labor amounted to a "haole job trust" was not far wrong.[50] But a careful observer, as Bailey proved to be, might have noticed that something was percolating in Hawai'i. It was in the early days of the FDR regime that the longshore local in Hawai'i was organized, with Hilo leading the way.[51] Bailey arrived at a propitious moment, for an imminent shipping strike in October 1936 affected the entire Pacific Coast, and a number of stevedores in Hawai'i joined the job action. About a thousand seamen were "beached" in the islands for almost four months, and their presence and active propagandizing added fuel to the flames of labor radicalism.[52]

In early 1936 a headline in the *Daily Worker*, the CP organ, announced: "Hawaii docks strike spread to small ports."[53] William Crozier, then chairman of the Central Committee of the Non-Partisan Party of Hawaii, along with his co-leader, Charles M. Kekoa, blamed a pillar of the Big Five, the Matson Company, and its "dictatorial, domineering" policies; also accused were the local GOP and the Democrats too since this latter party was said to be "speechless."[54] What had happened was that, spearheaded by Harry Kamoku, stevedores were organized in Hawai'i in 1935, as a direct aftermath of the unrest in San Francisco. Born in 1905, Kamoku was the leader of the first real and fighting union to be recognized in the isles as a bargaining representative.[55]

His task was not easy,[56] something Kamoku knew better than most.[57] Yet there was also something radically right about it, for symptomatic of the heightened organizing of the stevedores was that the first issue of their "rank and file trade union paper" was published in late November 1935.[58]

A year later the International Longshoremen's Association leadership in New York was informed that stevedores in both Hilo and Honolulu had built a growing union across racial and ethnic lines. The "potential membership of the port of Hilo is 250, of which 175 members are paid up to date," and in Honolulu the "potential membership is 1,000, of which 140 are paid up to date and about 300 in arrears,"[59] it was said.

Reflecting the attempt to break from the "race-based" unions of the past was this union's provision of interpretations in Japanese and Filipino languages during meetings.[60] This wise policy proved useful when workers struck in 1936, a job action that revealed how sensitive these isolated islands were to the ministrations of organized labor. Governor J. B. Poindexter had to intervene to aid stranded California travelers.[61] An engineer aboard the SS *Lurline* developed a "highly nervous condition through worry over his wife and two children in San Francisco," said a Castle and Cooke executive, who noted that the "prolonged separation from [his] family, brought about by the present maritime strike," could "easily develop into a complete nervous breakdown and permanently impair his mental facilities."[62] A group of white businesswomen lamented, "We are absolutely isolated without transportation by water," while "oranges and lemons have been imported by parcel post, and were obtainable only at a dollar a dozen up!" Meanwhile, warehouses were "full of products that could not be shipped," and it was observed that the "unemployment situation, bad enough at any time, has been tragic during the strike."[63] The Japanese Poultrymen of Honolulu told the governor that "owing to the present maritime strike," they too were in "dire distress."[64]

It was not only the chickens that might have been on the verge of starvation. According to the territory's governor, the "situation regarding certain food staples" was "becoming serious," since the "visible supply [of] potatoes and similar vegetables except taro and sweet potatoes" was "exhausted," while "rice [was] nearly gone[,] ditto poultry feed and flour." Ernest Gruening of the Interior Department in Washington, D.C., which had oversight of this colony, was informed that if the "supply [of] milk [was] not received within [a] few days infant mortality will increase." The "situation will soon become desperate," the governor cried, since there was "little hope for relief from foreign sources."[65]

The governor's frantic appeal was in response to appeals he in turn had received from local businesspersons. The Chamber of Commerce in Kaua'i, an island that was to become a bastion of labor radicalism, complained that the "stock of fruit and vegetables are practically exhausted," the "local rice crop has been practically exhausted," and the "situation in regard to essentials will become acute by the end of the year."[66] That they might not have been crying wolf was suggested when the Hilo Chamber of Commerce complained that "potatoes, onions, oranges, apples and lemons are non-existent."[67]

This complaint about a dearth of citrus brought a fierce response from physician Lyle G. Phillips. He also happened to lead the gathering anticommunist bloc, as the strike fomented both radicalism and antiradicalism alike.[68]

Pulses were quickening, temperatures were rising, and stomachs were tightening and growling as labor flexed its muscles, and those who theretofore had seemed to rule unchallenged were displeased. Walter F. Dillingham, the informal leader of the white elite, took to the radio airwaves in January 1937 and carped bitterly. Though tensions with this Asian nation were increasing, it was left to Japan, most notably, to furnish limited amounts of food supplies during this emergency.[69]

This food relief from Japan could have been deemed to be strikebreaking rather than a humanitarian intervention, however. What doubt there was tended to evaporate when, rather boldly, strikebreakers went to work in Hilo unloading the Japanese steamer *Rakuyo Maru*.[70]

Dillingham had reason to be concerned, nonetheless. In mid-December 1936, Kamoku was informed, "It has been 6 weeks and two days since the strike has started. And solidarity is getting better and better." A bit of "financial difficulty" had arisen, however. There had been "very good attendance," said stevedore Richard Bodie, at a "mass meeting to which the public was invited," at Honolulu's McKinley High School Auditorium. "I want to sleep for about two weeks to catch up with all of the sleep that I have lost to date," said Bodie. "I am busy with a typewriter about twelve hours per day."[71]

Internal conflict within the ranks, however, seemed to be raging twenty-four hours per day, with militants charging that their opponents had "tried to sell out this union," leaving the Port Allen Waterfront Workers Association in particular "in a very bad position." By August 1937 they were on strike nonetheless. Acknowledging that it would "be a very tough fight because most of the workers have family and are at present living in company houses," the strike committee noted: "The minute they go on strike[,] the company [has] the right to throw them out of their houses."[72]

The authorities were not accustomed to the kind of militancy to which the otherwise blissful islands had been subjected. The organizing of the stevedores—propelled by a global economic depression whose chilly winds had reached the South Seas—introduced a new dynamic in Hawai'i. Close students of labor should not have been surprised by this turn of events. Earlier, Governor Poindexter had refused to accept the credible assertion that in Maui a "machine gun" was "mounted on an army truck had been driven through a crowd of strikers . . . for the purpose of intimidation," and "guns had been mounted in a look-out at the sugar mill."[73] This armed response to restive labor reflected the hysteria of the white elite in the face of a challenge. Yet the repression in Maui did not intimidate labor into submission; it was part of a wave of unrest that was to accelerate further in coming years.

Bill Bailey, still on the scene on behalf of the CP, had noticed that the activism among stevedores had reached agricultural areas. "At present the plantations look like a camp headquarters of the National Guard," he said, "as there are so many special deputy sheriffs around, parading around with their rifles on their shoulders."[74] But Bailey continued to believe that organizing the docks was the key to organizing labor as a whole, an intuition that proved to be accurate. Thus, in Maui, he told "Dear Comrade Harry" Bridges that in Honolulu there was a "possibility that the majority of workers will vote against the union thru past fear," so "naturally they will look to Hilo to see what the workers there will do first." And Hilo did not disappoint.[75]

As August 1938 approached, a strike had been called targeting the Inter-Island Steamship Company. One of its boats was slated to dock at the Big Island—and labor objected. As with the most recent labor unrest, the stevedores were showing that they were the real power in a string of islands utterly dependent upon imports. With a sense of déjà vu, the Hawaii Island Poultry Association complained to the governor about the impact of the "present strike," which was "simply murderous," with staples like eggs and vegetables being notably affected.[76] Labor had its own problem in trying to coordinate simultaneous activity on isles separated by miles of water.[77]

Nevertheless, few should have been overly surprised on the first of August, when Hilo was the scene of a sizeable demonstration. Marching eight abreast and in orderly fashion, with patrolmen keeping order and with many demonstrators gripping picket signs, organized labor in a procession of about 500 marched to Pier 2 down a public highway and through police lines, tear gas brigades, and firefighters forebodingly wielding their hoses. They reached their destination but then were halted by men with fixed bayonets, riot guns, sidearms, rifles, menacing machine guns, Thompson submachine guns (the notorious "tommy guns"), and more. Perhaps intimidated by labor amassed, law enforcement gave the signal to fire. By that point, the procession had halted and the demonstrators were sitting on the ground, laughing, joking, singing, and playing cards in a semicircle from one end of the pier to another—they were sprayed with bullets nonetheless.

All hell broke loose as what came to called the Bloody Hilo Massacre commenced, ignited by the Hilo County police. Protesters were fleeing in all directions, and even the wounded carrying the wounded were not spared; instead, they were fired on again and again. Others were chased, clubbed, gassed, and bayoneted, with a blazing ferocity. It seemed as if ages had passed before the firing stopped and the surroundings were left strewn with the bodies of defenseless men and women, many bleeding profusely. Bert Nakano, who became one of the archipelago's leading unionists, was among the wounded. Labor was not cowed, however, and in what came to be a pattern when they were attacked, they struck back vigorously. They started by calling a 24-hour work stoppage, then upped the ante by birthing the Hilo Industrial Union Council on 9 September 1938.[78] It was that council that lamented what it described as the authorities "armed with riot guns and fixed bayonets" who "fired flush into a crowd of unarmed and helpless workers," leaving dozens wounded "so seriously that the hospitals of Hilo were filled."[79]

The authorities were also compelled to investigate this bloodshed. Hawai'i attorney general J. V. Hodgson interviewed 242 persons on the Big Island, which then had a population of 81, 952 (Hilo had about 14,459 residents). Hodgson was struck that "those of Hawaiian ancestry seem to predominate" in the newly formed unions and that "some aliens are members."

It was "due to the higher wages paid for this class of labor" that "stevedoring work had attracted or was attracting many local high school boys."[80] Hodgson's conclusion was that only 250 people were in the procession, which was "very peaceful." They came within 25 yards of the police, then stopped. As he reconstructed the scene, "there were much more of the curious around them than actual demonstrators," including almost 40 women. Confusion erupted, however, when the county sheriff asked the protesters to halt, for "many unionists saw the upraised hands but heard no order to stop," and "those in back of the [assembled] ranks said that they heard nothing," because of the noise. In addition, "those who could hear denied that he said anything beyond commanding them to stop." Perhaps the timbre of his voice had been overridden by the raised cries of those in the front of the column singing enthusiastically, "'the more we get together the better we will be,' while the women in the rear sang 'hail, hail, the gang's all here.'" Evidently, the sheriff, not seeing his commands obeyed, gave an "order to the tear gas detail to throw grenades." Stunned protesters picked up the grenades and threw "them either back at the police or away from the demonstration." The choking fumes of tear gas were wafting promiscuously, causing a stampede and heightening disorder, as the assembled scattered in several directions. But another group refused to budge and simply sat down; the police "begged the union men to go back or keep back or to advance no further." Apparently some "testified" that "Lieut. C. J. Warren was singled out from the other police officers and that a number of threatening statements were made to him," including "'You black S- of a b'" and other less choice epithets.

According to Hodgson, "Sheriff [Henry K.] Martin stated that a few minutes before he ordered the police to fire on the crowd" in response to this perceived affront, "he gave an order directing all police officers to change the ammunition in their riot guns from buckshot to birdshot." Protesters asserted that prior to the firing they "were given no warning that the police were going to fire towards them." One officer said that he saw the aggrieved Lieutenant Warren "hit D. Kupukaa in the face with the butt of his gun," while "Sheriff Martin, some police officers and other witnesses stated that from the beginning the firing was general and that they did not know who fired the first shot," though the fusillade lasted for almost two minutes. Why fire in the first place? Sheriff Martin claimed that he "ordered the firing, first because he had heard the rumor that the crew of the ship" that was at the pier and in solidarity with the protesters "was armed," which did not bode well, and "second[,] that the crowd was rushing the police officers." All told, 50 were wounded and 25 hospitalized, though "no physician saw any wound which was caused by a rifle or pistol bullet." Hodgson's report noted that all "pellets which were removed were buckshot or birdshot," suggesting that firing from the ship did not occur.[81]

Speaking years later, Bert Nakano, who emerged as the most visible victim of the unrest, recalled—his memory perhaps inflated—that "we had about 3,000" marching "with the flag leading us." The police "stopped us," Nakano said. Then a "Hawaiian boy" (referring to a police officer) "whacked" the startled Nakano "right across the chin." Nakano said that "as soon as the rifle came down," the officer shot him "right on [the] ankle." It was then, he said, that chaos erupted, as he got hit by "four buckshot." As Nakano recalled, "They [spun] me around and knocked the hell out of me. I got two that hit my side and one hit my artery," and "they caused . . . great damage," as "they thought I was going to die." Gangrene set in: "I lost three toes," he said, and he gained a noticeable limp. He spent "17 months in the hospital" and "had to walk with a cane."[82] Subsequently Lieutenant Warren was pointed to as a trigger for unrest, since he was said to have "struck [Kai] Uratani three or four times on the face with a butt of a sawed-off gun," yet the grand jury "refused to indict anyone."[83]

Nevertheless, sparks from Hilo helped energize labor. A few days after the guns had cooled, the attorney general informed the governor that the "situation has quieted down considerably," but he added that he could "still feel a tenseness over the trouble of last Monday," now memorialized as "Bloody Monday." With resignation, he reported that "labor union people" were "indignant and probably inflamed" by the events, and "fears" had congealed that "rioting, fighting and even bloodshed will occur"; there was a "grave possibility of danger," he warned morosely.[84] The "police force at my command is entirely inadequate to maintain order," responded Sheriff Martin, as he made an urgent "request that the National Guard be immediately called out."[85]

Besides Kamoku, Maxie Weisbarth should be accorded credit for this labor upsurge that had shaken the foundations of the islands. He was a "real, hard-punching Hawaiian of the old school," said Edward Berman, a seaman who arrived in the islands from the mainland in 1931. Like so many who flourished in labor circles in Hawai'i, he too was a "Wobbly," or a member of the once-vibrant Industrial Workers of the World, which had wielded significant influence in mainland mines, most notably a few decades earlier. He was a "good labor man," said Berman.[86] Of mixed Hawaiian and German descent, he was 33 in 1935 when labor unrest was brewing, but had already been working for two decades, having begun as a laborer at the age of 11. Despite his high-pitched, thin voice and his limited height of five feet eight inches, the sailor was not above using his fists, having once thrashed Jack Hall. "[I] knocked him down the stairway, kicked him in the ass," he claimed in 1975, two years before his death.[87]

Kamoku, the other man often accorded credit for labor's 1930s upsurge, at the time congratulated Weisbarth for being "the one Hawaiian who had the guts [to] start organization of the Hawaiian Islands"; as a result, he rhapsodized, "you are enshrined in the hearts of all Hawaiians who toil for their daily bread."[88] Paul Kalina, a union sympathizer in Honolulu, concurred, telling Kamoku that "due credit should be given to Maxie Weisbarth for the good work that he has done."[89] At this juncture, Weisbarth, who had been a member of the Sailors' Union of the Pacific, was serving as chairman of the board of directors of the recently organized Longshore Association of the islands.[90]

In addition to Weisbarth and Kamoku, there was Jack Kawano. Born on the Big Island in 1911, he was an early spark plug for labor. He in turn hailed Weisbarth, underlining that he was "part Hawaiian, part white," and thus "he could talk at the whites and he could talk also at the Hawaiians." It was the husky Weisbarth who was willing to put his body on the line for his fellow workers. Yet Kawano said that in 1936, when he tried to join the longshore union, "I was rejected because I'm American of Japanese [descent]. . . . [T]hey couldn't reach first base. So they changed their policy [by 1937]." Thus, Kawano was told pointedly, "It was *you* really, that organized the Honolulu waterfront." Kawano replied simply, "I'm the man who done it. Many folks tried it. . . . Berman tried it. . . . Jack Hall tried. . . . Harry Kealoha, he tried. Maxie Weisbarth. They tried. They all tried."[91] But Kawano succeeded.

He—and Weisbarth and others—succeeded in the face of a stiff rebuff. In response to the violence unleashed on Bloody Monday, the Communist Party branch in Santa Barbara assailed the "unwarranted and brutal attack of the armed police upon the CIO pickets at Hilo,"[92] while Honolulu photographer Ray Jerome Baker termed what occurred as "one of the most brutal and cowardly events of recent Hawaiian history."[93] The CIO Council of the Industrial Council of Los Angeles—"representing 40,000 organized workers," as it informed the Civil Liberties Committee of the US Senate—voted unanimously to back the members of its counterpart in Hilo.[94]

Meanwhile, labor had to regroup. "We are making every effort to secure the help of the International Labor Defense," said William Kaluhikau of Hilo labor, referring to the CP-influenced legal defense organization, in order to "assist in the prosecution of those responsible for the shooting down"[95] of peaceful protesters.[96]

Bill Bailey, who had arrived in the islands to stir the pot of radicalism, had found that even with his formidable organizing skills, there was enough cloth at hand already to construct a formidable tapestry of labor solidarity. He was the first Red that Jack Kawano—who was to become a Red himself—met. Bailey, said Kawano, "asked us to volunteer in the Spanish [Republican] Army, but no one volunteered,"[97] but this gruff seaman from Hoboken had more success otherwise. Within a week of his arrival, he had collected $60—enough to facilitate the printing of 3,000 copies of a newspaper, the *Voice of Labor,* which was to become an interisland staple. Soon after arriving, he met a budding Red and indigene named Jack, who asked him, "'Does this mean . . . that if the

Communists took control of the islands, the land the missionaries stole from us would be taken back?'" Replied a confident Bailey, "'That would be Number One on the list.'" Well, said Jack, "'that's good enough for us.'" And with such tactics Bailey found that within three months of his arrival, "I would accept 22 applications for the Party."

With such vim and vitality, Bailey helped organize a May Day demonstration in Maui and discovered that "every half mile the Hawaiian Planters' Association had their stooges out, tabulating the number of marches and taking pictures." But, he added, "word had gotten to the people in Kahului that we were coming. They lined the streets to welcome us as we entered town. We marched into the ballpark and held our meeting. History had been made." Picking up a newspaper soon thereafter, he could not help but notice a story suggesting that he faced a decade in prison for having supposedly violated the Criminal Syndicalism Act. Forewarned, Bailey departed—but not without satisfaction. "The nucleus I had left behind," he said, "would one day make the Hawaiian Islands one of the strongest bastions of unionized labor."[98]

CHAPTER 2

An Apartheid Archipelago?

Soichi Masuda was upset. Fortunately, he was among friends—his co-workers in the Hilo Longshoremen's union—but what he had to tell them did not reflect fraternity. Recently, when he had reported for work at the powerful firm that was Matson, he had been assaulted by the foreman. Berating him as a "Yellow Belly," a term Masuda saw as having racial connotations, the foreman told him bluntly that his union would soon oust him, adding, "Then you will have to go to work for the plantations." Speaking partly in English and partly in Japanese, Masuda spoke movingly of this unfortunate incident, concluding to thunderous applause, "I did not realize until this morning how strong the Longshoremen's Union in [the] port of Hilo really is, and then I too realized that I was glad to [be] a part of it." As his fellow union members, contrary to the foreman, embraced him, he continued, "That it is a rank and file organization [was] today proved to me and many others."[1]

Shortly thereafter, an unidentified indigenous Hawaiian sailor made his way to the Jim Crow citadel that was Galveston, Texas. He boarded a streetcar and sat down in the first seat he saw. It happened to be the section reserved for the so-called ruling race, of which he was not a part, and since the conductor was unsure where Hawai'i rested on the totem pole of racialism, he concluded, "'Well, no matter where you come from, no colored folks are allowed in these seats.'"[2]

Such incidents were only partially random, as they reflected an infrastructure of bias. Bill Bailey discovered that, as a result, the Hawaiian Islands were a happy hunting ground for those seeking to recruit Reds. One reason was the nagging persistence of white supremacy in a string of islands where those of European descent were a distinct minority; an apartheid colony had been built with a white elite at the top at a time when the very existence of a rising Japan was signaling the abject peril of such a gross misadventure. Yet those of Japanese descent were the plurality in these sparkling island beads in the Pacific, and white supremacy was sufficiently irrational that mere realities could not alone force a retreat.

Soichi Masuda's story was not unique. Jack Kawano was compelled to leave school after the seventh grade. By 1934 he was toiling on the waterfront, where there was no union. Then in 1935 the Sailors' Union of the Pacific and the West Coast Firemen's Union "opened a hiring hall" as an organizing drive was launched. "However, I did not join the union at that time," Kawano said, "because they did not permit workers [of] Oriental descent to become members of that organization. I joined the Longshoremen's Association of Honolulu in November 1935 when the organizers changed their policy." Two years later he was an organizer working without pay, which was very difficult. The union gained speed by the spring of 1941, when it won its first agreement, but before that a strike of sugar workers on the Puunene plantation in 1937, which lasted for two to three months, had provided momentum to Kawano's union.[3]

The Congress of Industrial Organizations—the CIO—and the Communist Party, which Kawano eventually joined, rose in tandem in Hawai'i. An official body in the territory adjudged that as of 1936 "there were slightly more than 60 Communist Party members among the waterfront and maritime workers in Hawaii." Harry Kamoku was said to have "organized what may have been the first 'cell' of the Communist Party ever to exist in Hawaii," and it was "composed entirely of Hilo waterfront workers."[4] As unions were organized, the more advanced workers began to consider gaining political power—which is where the Communist Party entered the picture.[5] Journalist Sanford Zalburg, who was no radical, captured the consensus of the party's impact when he concluded, "If it had not been for the Communist Party here, I have a feeling there would not have been any real labor movement here." The American Federation of Labor in the islands, he said, "wouldn't even admit Orientals," as "they [AFL leaders] were racists."[6]

The rise of Franklin D. Roosevelt had buoyed the Left,[7] though criticism remained of his party's local leading figures, such as Takaichi Miyamoto.[8] Nolle Smith, a local legislator, confessed during this tumultuous era, "It is true that I was one of the very good Republicans who went down to defeat in the Democratic landslide of last November," referring to the New Deal, whose hurricane force had reached the Pacific.[9] At this juncture, Communists in Hawai'i, who were generally supportive of the New Deal, were thought to be too close to Moscow, while non-Communist progressives, the bulk of them not white, were often thought to be too close to Tokyo, as in the case of the derided Miyamoto. This dilemma—being trapped between Moscow and Tokyo—was to haunt the archipelago for years to come.

Thus, it was not long before seven radical unionists were on trial for reputedly seeking to use dynamite to injure property, i.e., an interisland ship.[10] Because FDR was seen as being pro-union,[11] this activism inevitably had a negative impact on the Democratic Party in the islands.[12] Simultaneously, in these pre-Internet days, it was difficult for these isolated islands to get news from elsewhere, while left-of-center forces were hammered by the related fact that the mainstream Honolulu newspapers, whose views of the Left were less than positive, reached Asian ports a week ahead of mainland papers of the same date, thus shaping views in Asia of most regions under the US flag.[13]

Still, the decided advantages held by the white elite—control over the commanding heights of the economy, along with state power—did not bar the slow but steady rise of a local Left led by the Communist Party. California attorney Grover Johnson and seaman Bill Bailey both had remarked that when they arrived in Hawai'i, indigenes had expressed to them directly their land hunger and their avid desire to reverse the results of US annexation. At this point, the CP spoke directly to these concerns, with its articulation of the unavoidable reality that Hawai'i was little more than a colony that—conceivably—was entitled to self-determination up to and including secession, then independence. This slogan—"independence for Hawai'i"—was raised at the eighth convention of the party in Cleveland in 1934. In Hawai'i there was a common territory, there was a common economy, a common culture, a common language, a common history—all requisites of a developing nation. Besides, it was thought, the nation of Hawai'i could exist independently of the United States and, possibly, flourish insofar as it could negotiate advantageous deals with potential partners in Tokyo, Canberra, Wellington, Suva, and elsewhere.

The party came to recognize, as leader Celeste Strack subsequently put it, that the "basic *class* division in the Islands actually parallels the division between whites ["haoles"] on the one hand and the various nonwhite national groups on the other." There was a "deep seated chauvinism and white supremacist ideology at work," which was "expressed, among other things, in the forced 'Americanization' of cultural life," including the compelled hegemony of the English language and the forced decline of the Hawaiian counterpart. In the 1930s the CP did not support statehood and instead called for independence of Hawai'i, along with the same for Puerto Rico and the Philippines.[14]

In 1937 the Communist-influenced *Voice of Labor*, too, derided the notion of statehood. This radical journal argued that "there is no advantage in statehood to Hawai'i except to the Sugar Barons," as it would "only serve to strengthen that much more [their] grip on the life of the land."[15]

Still, the long-term success of the CP was not derailed by the fact that its campaign for Hawaiian independence was ultimately aborted. Rather, its success lay in its antiracist and pro-union crusade, which, despite certain oversights, marked a turning point in the archipelago's trajectory. For example, during the tumultuous agricultural strike of 1920, management was able to drive a wedge between two unions, one representing workers of Japanese origin and the other representing Filipinos, to the detriment of both.[16]

This tendency continued until the CP and the ILWU intervened forcefully.[17] What radical labor did was to overcome this barrier.[18]

Yet the path was strewn with obstacles beyond those that separated Filipinos and Japanese. John Burns, a founding father of modern Hawai'i, a governor who served from 1962 to 1974, and a good friend of Jack Hall's, has gone further, agreeing "with Harry Bridges that 'every Oriental has an inborn resentment against the haole.'" Burns also felt that "the Hawaiian does too." As a journalist reported, "He said that when he gets into a Hawaiian meeting, a closed meeting, he makes the following point: 'no hate the Japanese, the Japanese on your side. The haole the one who hold you down, he taken everything away from you. Get together with the Japanese, fight back for yourself.'" This was not exactly the message conveyed by Communists, but it is indicative of the racial politics they had to confront; in fact, the existence of white radicals like Bridges aided in overcoming this bias against "haoles" as a whole, helping to convince those of Asian-Pacific origin who might have had doubts that not all people of European descent were consumed with the preservation of racial privilege.[19]

This racism was not a "thing in itself" but was part of the underpinning of a profitable system of exploitation. Before World War II, economist James Shoemaker declared, "'There is a well-known comment on wages in Hawaii.'" He was referring to the "'three levels of wages'" in the archipelago: "'what the "haole" pays the "haole," what the "haole" pays the "Oriental," and what the Oriental pays the Oriental.'" Shoemaker found that wages in hotel work reflected a bias, with the average rate "per half month" for "Caucasians" being $51.45; that for those of Japanese origin, $28.15; and that for Filipinos, $25.05.[20]

Before the war, the Left charged that indigenes were "jim-crowed on Navy Defense jobs." At US sites at Midway (soon to be an important battleground in the war with Japan), Palmyra, and Samoa, there were "separate barracks, messhalls and canteens" for "'haoles' and Hawaiians." As war approached, where solid unity would be a necessary requisite for victory, it was reported that indigenes were "being eased out of . . . island jobs and being replaced by mainland 'haoles.'"[21] When the US military started to bring in a "Negro Labor Battalion" of about 600 men to handle cargoes as relations with Tokyo took a nosedive, Hawai'i's representative in Washington objected on racist grounds.[22]

But it was not only Negroes who were feeling the hot winds of bigotry as war approached. George Cass, an executive at the Dairymen's Association, acknowledged that "in a recent advertisement in the 'Help Wanted' column of a local newspaper, we asked for truck helpers and specified Hawaiian, Portuguese or Haole"—yet he simultaneously denied that discrimination was an issue.[23]

Plantation life was no prize either. "What I saw [there] helped make me a Marxist sympathizer," said the Communist John Reinecke, underscoring once more how the crude extremities of Hawai'i dialectically helped forge a Communist Party. "Under W. P. Naquin, a Creole from Louisiana, Honokaa was probably the most backwardly run plantation in Hawaii," Reinecke observed, as "class lines were sharply drawn," with Filipinos excluded so vigorously that they "were a foreign people to us." Plantation bosses targeted for defeat Democratic Party candidates for electoral office who sought to oppose this system. These plantations were "physically" a "disgrace," Reinecke said. "I once asked our maid how her camp could be improved," he recalled. "'Burn it down'" was her terse reply.[24]

Still, part of the paradox of Hawai'i was that it was *not* the Deep South, despite its apartheid-like bias against those not defined as white. If the island chain had been Mississippi, then it would have been hard to explain Nolle Smith, a Negro; actually he was the son of a Scotch-Irish father and a Negro mother. Born in Wyoming in 1888, he had attended the University of Nebraska. Dark-skinned, with the tightly coiled hair that marked those perceived as indigenously African, he eventually migrated to Hawai'i. There he worked for the quintessential Big Five company, Matson, started a construction business, and then was elected to the territorial legislature in 1928 as a Republican. His rise suggested how flexible white supremacy under the US flag could be, in that the dearth of Negroes in the islands meant they were hardly the issue there—not the way Issei and Nisei and indigenes were—and thus could be absorbed into elite circles. Yet when Smith visited Washington on government business, he was subjected to Jim Crow and had to be accommodated by the then Howard University professor and future United Nations diplomat Ralph Bunche. Smith, on the other hand, accommodated himself to Hawai'i, learning the language of the indigenes, just as his children learned Japanese.[25]

Frank Marshall Davis, who proudly considered himself to be an African-American and later befriended Barack Obama (who wound up moving to Davis' old Chicago neighborhood), was among those who objected to Smith's distancing himself from identification with the beleaguered Negro.[26] Bill Eubanks was a Dartmouth graduate who had studied in Scotland and fought in Spain before arriving in Hawai'i. This highly cultured Negro found Smith to be a "slick, high class Uncle Tom." With asperity, he added, "I understand that he has told his children they are to bring home no Negro in-laws." Thus, his daughter "married a haole," a son was courting a Chinese woman, and another daughter "passes for Hawaiian on the mainland."[27] Smith did not consider himself to be a Negro, in any case, and since there were only 255 of this group in Hawai'i in 1940 out of an overall population of 423,000, this was an identity easy to discard.[28] Smith also accommodated himself to the political status quo, testifying at the Smith Act trial of the Communists in 1953, where he affirmed that the reputation of defendant John Reinecke for loyalty was "bad."[29]

The presence in Hawai'i of a man like Smith was indicative of a pattern of race relations that distinguished the islands from the mainland: prior to the war the Negro hardly existed in the direct experience of most people in the region. The very few Negroes who lived in Hawai'i were commonly thought of as part-Hawaiians—a situation that often led to resentment from actual Hawaiians who thought this suggested their own nationality was being liquidated and they were being shoehorned into an identity (that of the Negro) perceived widely as being inferior. As the march toward war accelerated, more Negroes began to trickle into Hawai'i, courtesy of the US government. This contributed to tensions when white servicemen openly expressed their resentment when local women were attentive to these dark-skinned visitors. According to one study, "many young women of Oriental and of Hawaiian ancestry developed aversions toward the Negroes solely through the associations with white servicemen." As Japan seized Manchuria and butchered Nanking, many whites were similarly seized with the idea that locals of Japanese origin might exercise a subversive influence upon the newly arriving Negroes, and it did seem that some Nisei manifested considerable interest in African-Americans and identified with them.[30]

Frank Marshall Davis, a leading African-American poet and journalist, migrated to Honolulu in 1948, but what he detected early on preceded his arrival, as he pointed to wide antiwhite hostility in the islands among the Asian-Pacific majority. He felt an instinctive bond with Okinawans; "several told me privately," he noted, "[that] they felt a strong bond of kinship with me as a Negro because of the fight they faced to get equality, not only with white America but with other Japanese." Like Negroes on the mainland, Okinawans were often in the vanguard, he thought, as they "lead other Japanese proportionately in the trade unions and progressive activities in general, just as on the mainland Negroes lead other groups proportionately in the fights for civil rights and full democracy."[31] Likewise, he was struck that the stereotype used to describe indigenous Hawaiians—"'lazy, carefree, loud, happy, superstitious and childlike'"—was "painfully close to the old stereotypes of Afro-Americans," an insight that raised searching questions about the real reason for these views.

Once Davis addressed an Okinawan club, the Hui Makaala, and he recalled that in the question period "I could have closed my eyes and imagined I was back at a meeting in the Parkway Community Center in Chicago, so similar were questions and Okinawan reactions to prejudice shown by Japanese and whites." Portuguese had begun streaming into the islands in the late nineteenth century in search of work but were not accepted wholly as true whites. They were a "kind of in-between group," thought Davis, who observed that "generally they resent being called 'haole'" and "many accept without embarrassment African ancestors," though they themselves ranged from "blonde to black." According to Davis, "At the same time a considerable number resent Japanese and Filipinos while accepting Chinese, Hawaiians and Afro-Americans." Davis himself, with dark skin and bushy hair, was "mistaken frequently for Hawaiian, Tongan and Samoan"—he was stunned when he noticed that indigenes "frequently call each other 'nigger.'" Davis had to squint when he saw "kinky haired Chinese and Japanese," which sheds light on why he noticed, that "as time passed . . . not only Hawaiians but members of other groups like me because I was not white." He added wonderingly, "At the same time, I developed strong friendships with many haoles because I am not Oriental"—a circumstance that also helps explain the rise of Nolle Smith.[32]

Davis also came to realize a basis for why he may have been seen as someone he was not. "There is a strong kinship," he said, "between the rhythms of Samoa, Tahiti, Old Hawaii and Africa."[33] "I have seen," said an agog Davis, "Hawaiians, Samoans, Filipinos and even a few Chinese, Japanese and Koreans who could easily be first cousins of Negroes I know all over the mainland. . . . I have also met and talked with a few Orientals here in Honolulu who lived with Negro families and attended Negro colleges on the mainland. For all practical purposes they were a part of the Negro community where they lived."[34]

The racial combinations and accords in Hawai'i were so different from those obtaining on the mainland that it led to the premature idea that the islands were a racial paradise. This mythologizing hardly explained what one researcher noted in 1925: "under the laws of the United States and of Hawaii the immigrants from Portugal, Spain and Porto Rico have been eligible for naturalization so far as race is concerned, while those from China, Japan and Korea have been ineligible."[35] It was Davis—the reputed Black Communist—who was the keenest observer of the racial dynamics of the islands.[36] Hawai'i was the "most complex community under the American flag," he opined.[37] Later Davis noticed that his small business on O'ahu often received support from Asian-Pacific businessmen because he was seen as one who defied the "'Big Haole.'"[38] Wilbur Wood, a Negro who migrated to the islands in the mid-1920s, agreed with Davis.[39]

There were not that many Negroes in any case, so they were hardly the sole target of bigotry, which was a relief from the situation on the mainland—and added to the complexity on the islands. Richard Masuda, who grew up in Maui before the war, recalled, "There were only two Negroes on the island. One was a lawyer and the other a musician. They were accepted by the community as individuals."[40]

Smith Act defendant Koji Ariyoshi, like Davis, saw parallels between the white supremacy of the Deep South and that which was manifested in Hawai'i. He was born in Hawai'i in 1914 and attended the University of Georgia in Athens, graduating in 1941.[41] Traveling on the mainland before the war, he "tried to recall where . . . I had seen the first 'For Whites Only' signs. Why did I go into the lavatories marked 'For White Only'?" he asked himself. "Why was I riding up forward in the bus with white passengers? I was not white but colored." He was "deeply tanned from stevedoring under the Hawaiian sun," he remembered, "but no one questioned my sitting up front. Nevertheless," he confessed, "I began to feel uncomfortable." He was as difficult to pigeonhole in the mainland as Davis was in Hawai'i. Ariyoshi knew he was different from the haoles; when he was growing up in Hawai'i, his mother had "explained" that "Jesus Christ is a white man's God" and that "our God was Amaterasu-Omikami, the Sun Goddess who descended on Japan and started the Imperial dynasty and the Japanese people." Hence, he was not predisposed to accept an ersatz "honorary haole" status on the mainland. "[The US South] made me think of Kahala," he said, "and the restricted upper Nuuanu residential districts in Honolulu, where the white people kept non-whites from buying property. But, as in the southern restaurants that did not serve Negroes but employed them for services, the white residents of Honolulu's 'For White Only' districts employed Oriental yard boys and maids and cooks. In both instances," he concluded with bitterness, "white supremacy showed itself in its ugly form."

What might be called Ariyoshi's racial consciousness was strengthened further by what his father used to say: "He told us that Negroes and Jews will be oppressed as long as they do not have a strong nation to look after them. He said as long as Japan is strong, we would be treated decently in America. This was a feeling shared by many of the older generation years before the last war." Visiting Pahoa in the islands, Ariyoshi noticed that the white boss' home was a "carry-over from the old days when the plantation bosses felt like kings among slaves." He also observed the practices on the docks of Honolulu: "The haole firms did not seem to approve of white laborers working with us. Haoles became clerks or watchmen, holding down what appeared to be cleaner jobs. Only a rare haole became a longshoreman or was hired as such."[42] Strikingly, the perception expressed by Ariyoshi's father—that a "strong" Japan would influence how those of Japanese origin were treated in the islands—was suggested when the Rockefeller Foundation insisted in 1926 on the "importance of having a Japanese scientist associated in a responsible capacity with the research project in race biology," so as to give this initiative credibility it otherwise lacked.[43]

Aiko Reinecke, yet another progressive intellectual of Japanese origin, had experiences that paralleled those of Ariyoshi. She visited Washington, D.C., in the 1930s. "I was very shocked to learn," she later recalled, that "schools were segregated" and that "as we went further south it was sharper and uglier." The Negro students in the seminars in which she participated "were not allowed to stay in the same hotels as we did." In Atlanta, she remembered, "I boarded a streetcar and found that it was separated into two," a vivid racist divide.[44] Such encounters with raw Jim Crow helped radicalize figures like Ariyoshi and Reinecke.

There were other forms of garish exploitation. As an outpost in the Pacific, visited often by footloose sailors and tourists seeking excitement that they dare not pursue at home, in the midst of brown-skinned beauties whose undulating and swaying hips helped make hula a craze on the mainland, Hawai'i had developed a ramified network of bordellos. "Prostitution is a problem on the island," progressive writer Carey McWilliams was informed in 1937. But even in this arena Jim Crow was not absent, as there were "'houses' which have two or more entrances, one for the whites and one for the Orientals," and "some 'houses' cater[ed] only to whites, some only to Orientals."[45] The state was complicit, in that the Left charged repeatedly that Honolulu's police force controlled prostitution.[46]

Sadly, for many workers prostitution was one of the few alternatives to unemployment,[47] which was fostered by the dearth and weaknesses of unions.[48] Yet this antiunion stranglehold was loosened progressively as the 1930s unfolded, a development fueled by unity across ethnic and racial lines, due to the efforts of figures like Davis, Ariyoshi, and Reinecke.

This unity was needed because labor was facing a formidable foe. Maui was the birthplace of Alexander and Baldwin, a firm that was tied to the Hawaiian Commercial and Sugar Company, the largest sugar producer in the archipelago. Sugar was at the heart of Alexander and Baldwin's fortunes, but this commodity not only was dependent on an increasingly militant labor force but also was affected by such problems as earthquakes, tidal waves, floods, bubonic plague, fire—and worse. Ironically resembling the keiretsu (networks of interlocking corporations) of the presumed antagonist Japan, this leading member of Hawai'i's notorious Big Five was also tied to Matson Navigation Company, one of the nation's largest steamship lines as the Pacific War approached. Matson also had been involved in oil exploration, hotels and tourism, military service, even the airline business.[49]

"Hawaii was dependent almost entirely, at least 85 percent to 90 percent[,] on West Coast shipping," said ILWU leader Louis Goldblatt, adding, "Matson had about the nearest thing to a complete monopoly on all trade to Hawaii." This apparent strength could also become a gigantic weakness if ILWU could organize the docks—which it proceeded to do. "I read everything I could put my hands on [in] terms of the economy of Hawaii," said Goldblatt, a labor intellectual who had worked with the ILWU from its inception in 1935. As he quickly ascertained, "Power did not lie in the shipping industry, or in one particular type of business; the power lay in the hands of the Big Five. Those were Alexander [and] Baldwin, C. Brewer, American Factors, Castle and Cooke, and Theo Davies." The latter was "primarily held by British capital and British royalty," a relic of a time when London was jousting with the United States for influence in the Pacific.[50] "If you tied up longshore effectively," Goldblatt said, "you could eventually squeeze the entire islands. On the other hand, if you confined your organization to longshore, then the employers could bring the full weight to bear of everything else that they controlled[,] from sugar to pineapple to finance." And, he noted, "they could bring that full weight to bear against the one small group of guys"—i.e., stevedores. As Goldblatt saw it, "Unless you can shut down every single plantation, on every island, from top to bottom, field to mill, you couldn't win. . . . [S]ooner or later the split would take place either industrially, island by island, or race by race."[51] Goldblatt's insight was confirmed inferentially by FDR's secretary of the interior, Harold Ickes.[52]

Sugar, as Goldblatt well knew, was the foundation of great fortunes in the islands, and the growing of this crop there was different from growing it in competitor regions. For example, sugar production was more completely integrated into the economy of the islands than in other regions; in Louisiana, Puerto Rico, the Philippines, and even the sugar-beet areas, a farming system existed prior to the growth of the industry. Hawai'i's industry began on land that was relatively undeveloped and was organized along industrial rather than farming lines. As a result, the Hawaiian Sugar Planters' Association—the chief antagonist of the ILWU—was a tightly knit grouping.[53] Moreover, there had been a historically powerful connection between leading forces in San Francisco and those in Honolulu. That relationship gave added ballast to the elites of Honolulu but simultaneously provided impetus to the ILWU, which was based in the very same California city and therefore found it easier to pressure those who were holding the puppet strings there. Thus Claus Spreckels of San Francisco came to Hawai'i to enhance his fortune by investing in sugar, after approval of an 1876 treaty between the United States and the archipelago. Similarly, Hawaiian interests, especially in the sugar industry, became deeply involved in antiunion activities in San Francisco, in turn giving further incentive for the ILWU to strike back in the islands.[54] With this thought firmly in mind, the ILWU launched its organizing drives, which did not take flight until the war commenced.[55] Yet, despite their intelligence and skill, the ILWU leaders did not have an easy time in their confrontation with the Big Five.[56]

Against a backdrop of racist persecution, labor exploitation, and promising union organization, Jack Hall arrived in the islands. Born in 1915 in Wisconsin, he was an ordinary seaman at the age of 17. He was to marry Yoshiko Ogawa, whose parents had been born in Japan. In 1944 he became an ILWU official. Despite his reputed Communist Party membership he served on the police commission of Honolulu from September 1945 to November 1946.[57] He said that instantly on arrival he saw the abasement of indigenes by "'white masters'" in the Pacific, and this marked him indelibly. He also found that antiwhite bias was strong among workers in Hawai'i, which meant suspicion of him for the longest time before he was accepted.[58]

As a way station between the United States and Asia, Hawai'i was often visited by a diverse array of sailors, who were known to reflect all manner of ideologies—on the Left.[59] Hall fit in well in this regard. "I'm supposed to have been a Marxist," he acknowledged much later; yet, he conceded, "I always felt emotionally closer to the Wobblies"—referring to the once-popular anarcho-syndicalists—"except for their denial of the importance of political action."[60]

Hawai'i at the time was a stew of competing ideologies, with maritime workers like Hall deeply influenced by anarchist, socialist, Trotskyite, and Communist currents. Hall—according to Edward Berman, who arrived in the islands in 1931—was a "lean, lanky, half-starved kid who had been an ordinary seaman"; he had been "kicked out of [the Sailors' Union of the Pacific] for so-called Communist activities and kicked out for 99 years," a punishment that drastically reduced his potential for earning a livelihood and predisposed him to remain where he was, as a labor activist. As Berman recalled him, "he was a very, very fervent—I don't want to use the word Marxist—fervent believer in destroying the government." Berman, who spoke of Hall at a time when their relationship had deteriorated, said, "He confided in me in the early days." Berman noted that his onetime comrade had had a difficult childhood, which "probably pushed him into the left-wing movement," like "lots of guys who were frustrated and had bad beginnings, you know, are looking for some kind of revenge[, so] they take it out on society that doesn't quite meet up with their expectations." This troubled upbringing also might account for what many, besides Berman, saw as a defining trait of Hall's: "he was as close to an alcoholic as I've ever seen and could function," Berman said. Hall drank whiskey—"Not beer: whiskey. Strong stuff"—yet somehow he found the energy to "read every goddamned leaflet that came out of San Francisco," referring to the radical variety. "All I know is that Hall was a confirmed Communist in his mind until the day he died," confided Berman. "All he was reading was Communist literature." Berman didn't think Hall read *Das Kapital*, but "he never read anything else" beyond radical literature. This was particularly noticeable during the labor unrest of 1936–1937. "That was the strike that united [labor]," said Berman, "the first time that all of the seafaring and longshore of the country were united in one strike," as "there was no movement between [Hawai'i] and the mainland for 98 days."[61]

Berman's view of Hall has been confirmed in large part by others. His biographer agreed that Hall—arguably the most powerful man in the islands in the run-up to statehood and thereafter—officially joined the CP early in 1936, though there "was not yet an official Communist Party organization in Hawaii" at that point, and a "'seaman's faction' ran the 1936–1937 maritime

strike." This faction included perhaps the leading Communist in the islands—who happened to be of Japanese origin—George Goto.[62]

Born Noborum Furuya in 1910 in Hawai'i, Goto was short and thin,
with deep sunken eyes, and he smoked constantly. Educated in Japan, he had
returned to the islands in 1929. As he saw it, Hall "didn't know a damned
thing about Marx and Lenin" and, besides, was a "very hard man to get along
with" because "he was too hot-headed." As for Berman, he "was never a member of the Party," despite what he alleged, a discrepancy that casts doubt on
his recollections, including those of Hall.[63]

Apparently, Hall's arrival in the islands was not a matter of serendipity
but the result of a party mission, for he was dispatched by the well-known
African-American Communist maritime leader Revels Cayton.[64] Cayton arranged for various sailors to chip in so that Hall had about $20 to live on
when he arrived in Hawai'i.[65]

A man who was to become one of Hall's closest comrades also arrived at
this point. Robert McElrath, of Dutch-Irish descent, was a seaman born in
Spokane in 1916. He attended the training school for budding Communists in
San Francisco in 1939 and was part of the core of radical leadership that administered the ILWU in Hawai'i. As he recalled later, Hall "felt that the American
employers, the American capitalists, were unreconstructed, [and that] the only
way people could live and enjoy life was through a socialist order of society." He
also verified Hall's tastes in literature: "I think Jack probably read an awful lot
of what's called 'the Little Lenin Library' and pamphlets," but Hall, akin to
"the ordinary guy," didn't "have the time or the facility to read Marx." On that
subject McElrath boasted, "I probably read more than most people here,"
though he conceded that "[Red leader Jack] Kimoto read a hell of a lot" also.[66]

John F. Murphy, a vice president of Castle and Cooke who sat across the
table from Hall in negotiations, corroborated the ILWU leader's taste for alcohol, saying, "Sometimes [Hall] went into a quasi-coma at 10 o'clock at night.
From drinking, I guess."[67] Rachel Saiki, a Japanese-American woman short and
squat in stature, was involved in strikes in the islands beginning in 1938—"I've
been in many picket lines," she confessed. Thus, she worked closely with Hall,
a circumstance she did not find too thrilling, since "at times [he] would make
passes" at her "while drunk."[68]

Yoshiko Hall also mentioned her husband's drinking habits, but she
painted a more complex picture of this leader than others did, noting his poor
eyesight—if he took his glasses off, anything farther than four inches away
started to blur—his love for jazz, his skill as a cook (a frequent trait among sailors), his inability when it came to driving cars, and his disregard for fine
clothes. "He didn't have a decent suit to his name, really," she said. She also
pointed out that his feet were small (size 9) and "very dainty."[69] Nevertheless,
those small feet managed to traipse about the islands repeatedly.[70]

A. Q. McElrath worked with Hall on the progressive journal *Voice of Labor* while she was still in college. She had attended Honolulu's McKinley High School, referred to as "Tokyo High School," as she recollected, "because there were so many Japanese." By 1938, she recalled, Hall had organized the Kauai Progressive League, which was associated with the United Cannery, Agricultural, Packing and Allied Workers. Consonant with the CP's thrust, he persuaded a store owner by the name of J. B. Fernandes to run for the territorial senate—and he won. It was Senator Fernandes who introduced the so-called Little Wagner Act, the Magna Carta for unions, in 1939. The bill did not pass then, but when it did in 1945, it turbocharged the organizing efforts of the ILWU.[71] Fernandes, born and raised in Kapaʻa, Kauaʻi, was among the island's leading political figures, serving in the territorial senate and house of representatives and the Board of Supervisors of Kauaʻi County. A former president of the Kapaa Ice and Soda Works and also a former president of the electric company in Kapaʻa, he met Hall in 1937 and testified positively in his favor during the Smith Act trial.[72]

Later Hall and another union sympathizer, Koichi Imori, rented an old house behind the Royal Brewery on Queen Street in Honolulu, which the future ILWU leader called "the Kremlin" because it quickly became a beehive of Red activity in Oʻahu. This was in contrast to Kauaʻi, whose CP branch was "no powerhouse," Hall thought, as it "met irregularly and 'functioned weakly.'"[73] In 1938, Hall met William Crozier, who had won election to the colony's house of representatives in 1932, the first Democrat to do so in "twenty years," as Crozier later recalled. In September of the year they met, "we had hung up a sign that we were going to have a meeting at Makaweli Plantation." Although it was election season and the GOP was allowed to campaign within the plantation, Crozier noted that "the social worker [there] told us that we could not go into the Makaweli Plantation to make a political speech or to talk labor organization or unions." Undaunted, Crozier and Hall "stopped in front of the plantation store, which [was] also the Post Office, which [was] Federal property," and they "took the loudspeaker out and put it on the veranda of the Post Office." Crozier remembered that "the loudspeakers were turned up so high that the voices of the speakers [reached] directly into the camp"—but "the only audience" was "five police officers," as "the people were afraid to come to the rally because the non-partisans and even the Democrats were considered bad people." Back then, he said, "it was a sin not to be a Republican in Hawaii."[74] Yet as the strength of radicalism grew steadily, these discriminatory barriers began to crumble.

Hall and McElrath were instrumental in building the union in the face of such adverse conditions. Yet those of Japanese origin also proved to be critical to radicalism's fortunes.[75] Robert McBurney Kempa, a graduate of Roosevelt High School in Honolulu and then a seaman who joined the CP, also spoke of having transported Red literature across the Pacific, in his case from the Soviet Union to Japan. "I had to smuggle the books out one by one," he said. "[I] had been in contact with the local Communist Party in Yokosuka [Japan] who had assisted me in this matter." Kempa had been part of a CP branch in the Mānoa section of Honolulu, which included—he said—his spouse and A. Q. McElrath.[76]

Ichiro Izuka, born in 1911, worked with Hall during the famed strike in Port Allen, Kauaʻi, in 1937. Izuka became a Red in 1938 and resigned in 1946; during that time he participated in a six-week-long CP training school in the islands that took place at the home of John and Aiko Reinecke in Honolulu. As CP treasurer, anticipating the scrutiny that was to come, he kept membership lists in a coded language of Russian, Japanese, and English.[77]

Jack Kawano met both Jack Hall and Bill Bailey in 1937, in the latter's room on Lusitana Street near Beretania, in a Honolulu boardinghouse. The room, he recalled, "had a big red flag pasted on the wall with a big hammer and sickle insignia against it." It was then that he too joined the CP. There were weekly meetings that featured Hall, Berman, and A. Q. McElrath and quickly became so well attended that "it was impossible to have meetings in small rooms." For a while Kawano was a leader of the CP, and in 1938 he worked his way across the Pacific so he could attend party training school at 121 Haight Street in San Francisco. The course lasted for five weeks, and he stayed with Karl Yoneda, the leading Japanese-American Red. Party school was rigorous, with classes lasting from 9 a.m. to 5 p.m. at the CP headquarters, which faced sideways on a sloping street in a building that used to serve the Young Men's Hebrew Association. The main room was large and formerly a basketball court.[78]

More non-Japanese were being attracted to the radical banner too. Emil Muller, born in 1913, joined the party in 1938, paying his "ten cents dues" and an initiation fee of a mere "25 cents,"[79] at a time when most members were stevedores.

Events were changing rapidly in Hawaiʻi, and not only because of the approaching war in Europe, as progressives of various stripes—Wobblies, New Deal liberals, and Communists alike—joined hands. But the war would also have an impact in this isolated Pacific outpost, for it was then that refugees from China, displaced by rampaging Japanese troops, began flocking to Hawaiʻi.[80] Their very presence was a reminder—if one was needed—that the white elite was discriminating against a group of Japanese origin whose powerful patron in Tokyo was smarting over the perception that people from their homeland were not treated fairly, a reality that Koji Ariyoshi's father had foreshadowed. Governor J. B. Poindexter chose to retain an article from a Deep South periodical that argued that the colony's "appeal for statehood has become so complicated by the dangerous swirl of Far Eastern events as to evoke a hot controversy in the 48 states"; concern was expressed "lest some 90,000 Japanese in Hawaii, now barred from immigration to the United States proper should seize upon statehood to migrate to the mainland."[81]

This was to become a salient fear as war crept ever closer. Despite this fear, however, the white elite proceeded as if the racial bias and labor exploitation they had perpetuated was immutable, for they were secure in the belief that the radicals—like Hall—who had sought to reverse this situation would remain ineffectual. They were to be proven wrong.

CHAPTER 3

The Race of War

Conservative whites were furiously suspicious in the aftermath of 7 December 1941. The community was buzzing with the rumor that, on the fateful day in which the Japanese military bombarded Pearl Harbor in Hawai'i, the saloons, taverns, and bars run by those of Japanese origin "knew in advance of the sneak attack" and joined in, since "alcohol was their weapon," as one disgruntled man put it. "Jap bartenders graciously and generously distributed free drinks (compliments of Hirohito!) the night before the attack," he said, a strategy said to be essential to the success of this military mission, since reputedly "fifty-four percent of the legal liquor joints in Hawaii were operated by Japanese."[1]

Some whites firmly believed, as an authoritative study put it, that "Japanese plantation workers had defected and fired on American soldiers." There was an enduringly persistent "story about a milk truck that had opened machine gun fire on Hickam Field," and there was another "rumor that there was a renegade radio station operating" in aid of Tokyo's forces, as well as a number of "reports that fires were deliberately being set in cane fields."[2]

The veracity—or mendacity—of these assertions aside, the point here is that they reflected a guilty fear that the apartheid that had been visited upon those of Japanese origin in particular had backfired catastrophically. The Pacific War, which ensnared an archipelago with a plurality of residents of Japanese origin, unleashed in response a bitter fusillade of invective against this very same population, which also happened to be heavily represented in the radical and trade union movements then growing.

Though the ILWU generally stood tall against attempts to exact special penalties at the expense of the besieged population of Japanese origin, it is nevertheless likely that the rise in the union leadership of figures like Jack Hall and Robert McElrath was facilitated by their being of non-Japanese origin, amounting to a perverse form of affirmative action. In other words, since Americans of Japanese ancestry were being besieged, it became easier for whites to surge to the leadership of the labor movement.

Similarly, the war also exacted a heavy penalty on the overall business class. For example, in April 1941 the *Kauai Herald* editorialized that "the Japanese merchants of Kauai have taken a more progressive stand on the wage and hour bill than did the Japanese merchants of the other islands," yet rather than their progressive influence being extended, it too was squashed by the war.[3] ILWU leader Robert McElrath recalled later that as early as 1939 the employers on Kaua'i, where a sizeable employer class of Japanese origin resided, had generally begun to seek conciliation with the union.[4]

At the same time, the draconian regulations that fell upon Hawai'i in the wake of the war—combined with a restive working class that had been on the verge of an organizing surge when this conflict erupted—eventually, as the war was winding down, led to an explosive growth in the ranks of union membership that was to transform the islands dramatically and decisively.

In a perverted way, the war came at a propitious moment for those then routinely referred to as the "boss haole elite," for the outburst of bloodletting provided yet another convenient rationale for political repression, a phenomenon that handcuffed progressive unionists in the first place. The well-known investigative reporter Drew Pearson was horrified by wartime Hawai'i: "the press is not free," he said, "labor has lost its traditional rights," and there was even a "dog curfew at 8 o'clock."[5] Wartime censors read incoming and outgoing mail, listened to interisland and trans-Pacific telephone calls, censored newspapers, and controlled other means of communication ranging from cables to carrier pigeons.[6] Decades after the Pearl Harbor debacle, a leading Honolulu newspaper conceded that "no American territory, including the rebellious states during the Civil War had been subject to such a loss of civil rights," a fiasco that was not terminated until October 1944.[7]

The fateful year—1941—had been unfolding as a successful one for the ILWU. Actually, the picture was mixed for unions. A scant year before the attack on Pearl Harbor, the ILWU was enduring a crisis. While Bridges' men were organizing the docks, a fellow union was organizing laborers in the sugar and pineapple industries—a potential cache of 70,000 new members[8]—but a push led by Jack Kawano caused a turnaround for the ILWU among the latter groups.[9] By June 1941, stevedores in Honolulu had won their first union contract, which served as a launching pad for further organizing in the fields.[10] By September 1941, Kawano could take heart from events in San Francisco, where, on Labor Day, Koji Ariyoshi arrived just in time to view the thousands upon thousands of workers march through Market Street. The parade was "immense," he exultingly reported, "continuing for four hours until the 75,000 people [passed] the city's reviewing stand,"[11] a demonstration that augured well.[12]

The union, in sum, had completed the organization of stevedores, with the exception of those working on Maui, and since six of the seven stevedoring firms were controlled by sugar interests, this augured well for organizing the plantations. On two islands, Kauaʻi and Hawaiʻi, the union movement had become particularly significant—with the former claiming an estimated 10 percent of the population as union members. Yet within a few weeks after the war's outbreak Hawaiian unions were reeling, on the verge of extinction. Labor under martial law received extraordinarily intemperate maltreatment as the islands were placed in the vise of a virtual dictatorship. US regulations meant that ILWU stevedores were devastated, as those of Japanese origin were excluded from military areas, which constituted a good deal of the archipelago and its port facilities. At the latter sites management blithely paid little attention to the unions, returned to antiquated methods of hiring, and exerted bias against union members. On Kauaʻi in April 1942 the Communist union leader Ichiro Izuka was arrested and detained for 123 days at the behest of an adjudicating committee that included three plantation managers and one representative of the military.[13]

This union leader was understandably irate, complaining that "without questioning" he had been "detained and taken to Waialua jail." While "locked in," he was unable to see his family, and his assets were frozen. It was "impossible" for the adjudicators to "prove my pro-Japanese attitude," he said, so "instead [they] did some red-baiting. They asked about Harry Bridges."[14]

The use of fascist tactics to fight an antifascist war was one way to describe what befell the Communist stevedore Koji Ariyoshi. "I remember being marched off the docks at bayonet point," he recalled later. "Uniformed state guards also marched in front and beside me with drawn pistols"; the "hysteria created against those of us [of] Japanese ancestry was almost beyond description," he added.[15] Ariyoshi was Japanese-American, but ultimately close to 2,000 Japanese aliens were "evacuated" from Hawaiʻi during the war.[16]

John Reinecke, a leading Red intellectual, was so stunned by what he saw as the white elite attempted to use the exigencies of war to undermine labor—by manipulating racism—that it convinced him that this class could easily opt for full-blown fascism in the future.[17] On the other hand, Jack Hall, who was to become the embodiment of labor radicalism, was quoted as having "endorsed the Speak English campaign," which was sponsored by the Kauai Morale Committee. Hall expanded on this initiative, widely seen as targeting the population of Japanese origin: "'This Territory is going to remain American for all time,'" he announced ambitiously, "'and people who live here cannot learn to speak and think as Americans too soon.'" Then he asserted, "'The campaign may be difficult but it is a necessary one. . . . [The] influx of war workers and service personnel in the past few years has been tremendous. For many of these people, a foreign tongue—particularly Japanese—breeds an unhealthy suspicion and distrust.'"[18] Hall went further, arguing in early 1942, "I have never kidded myself into believing that a great number of first generation Japanese—and a surprisingly large number of citizens—do not have strong emotional ties with the Shinto Empire. This was all too well demonstrated to me many times back in 1937," when certain progressives were "frankly afraid to include Hawaii in the nationwide trade union 'boycott of goods made in Japan.'" Why was the boycott not carried out in Hawai'i? "Applying such a program here [it was said] would be like expecting it to be effective on the Ginza in Tokyo." Hall thought that "strong emotional bonds" united those of Japanese descent in the western and central Pacific. As he saw it, "those of Japanese ancestry in the Territory are in a peculiar category" and "will have to demonstrate in even more concrete ways than the non-Japanese that their loyalty lies undivided with America."[19] The Kaua'i periodical in which Hall penned these disturbing words argued that "evacuation of Japanese from vital war areas under the present circumstances should be looked upon as essentially for their own protection."[20] That Hall, who was a legitimate symbol of progressivism, was swept up by the hysteria of the moment, was indicative of how poisonous the environment had become.

Anti-Nippon bias was one lever used against unions that had a high level of Issei and Nisei membership. Congressman John Rankin of Mississippi, who had become notorious because of his bigotry targeting African-Americans, leapt quickly into the maw of anti-Nippon bias. The internment policy directed at Japanese-Americans was much too mild, he said; "American people are sick and tired of this policy of pampering the Japs in these concentration camps," he added, while more ferocity was needed to confront the "brutal apes in the Pacific."[21] When the War Department proposed sending Japanese-American soldiers from the isles to Mississippi, Rankin objected violently,[22] a response not unique in his state.[23] Honolulu resident Ray Jerome Baker was fair-minded and was surrounded by "Japanese or Chinese" daily, yet he, too, casually and insultingly referred to "Japs,"[24] suggesting how unpleasant the archipelago had become.

It was this atmosphere that may have influenced an unnamed interlocutor of the epitome of the "boss haole elite"—Walter F. Dillingham—to unburden himself of grave apprehensions about the Nisei and Issei in his midst. "By 1941 there were 174 Japanese language schools operating in Hawaii," it was said, that "developed racial solidarity"; at this juncture Nisei and Issei "assistance to Japan had become so important that a delegation of Japanese from Hawai'i, including US born Nisei, visited Japan and were honored by Emperor Hirohito," and the "Hawaii Japanese became the first Japanese community outside Japan to donate a plane to the Fatherland." According to this source, "the presentation ceremony was broadcast from Japan to listeners in Hawaii" and "the plane donation was followed by gifts of military trucks, each truck bearing the name of the district in Hawaii responsible for it." Dillingham was informed that "a local Japanese newspaper on January 3, 1939[,] said that there were a total of

1,050 Japanese organizations at work in Hawaii, from sewing circles to Chambers of Commerce and industrial associations." In this memorandum to Dillingham, the capital city itself—Honolulu—was derisively termed "'Little Tokyo,'" as a "large segment of Hawaii's Nisei conclusively proved before Pearl Harbor that they wanted to develop their 'superior traits' under the flag of Japan." It was stated that the "Japanese in Hawaii are regarded by Japan as the most important Japanese overseas" and that the "Japanese alone of all immigrants brought their culture intact to Hawaii and have retained it intact"—which was not deemed reassuring.[25]

The Black Dragon Society of Japan—the most chauvinistic and bellicose force in the emperor's kingdom—was thought to have infiltrated US territory in advance of the war. "It is from the Black Dragon Society," complained one propagandist, that "Japanese patriots have come, disguised as immigrants, students, fishermen, farmers, scientists, businessmen to settle [and] establish themselves as long-term residents." It was alleged that a "retired Japanese naval captain, Otojiro Endo[,] and a retired Japanese Army major, Masichi Sughihara, visited the West Coast states and held secret meetings with Japanese societies" before the war. Reputedly, a book circulated by them asserted that "there are one hundred and fifty thousand Japanese [in Hawai'i], one half of whom are Nisei," and that "once the news of Japanese naval victories reach[es] Hawaii, the Japanese there will quickly organize a volunteer army." Thus, concluded this propagandist, "no Japanese language newspapers should be permitted to operate in the United States or in any of our territories or possessions" and "every Japanese school and temple must be closed."[26]

Actually, this kind of hyperbolic hyperventilating had been occurring for some time. As Tokyo's meteoric rise accelerated in the 1930s, the Ku Klux Klan, which had had a growth spurt of its own, became concerned about the influx of Japanese into territory controlled by the United States.[27] Its "100% American Platform" had only six points, two of which were directly relevant to Hawai'i: "drive out Communism" and "preserve white supremacy."[28]

After the war a number of whites in the archipelago, perhaps reading through the lens of bitter retrospection, happened to recall numerous incidents in which the loyalties of their neighbors of Japanese ancestry seemed questionable during the war. Emma Richey, a Honolulu landlord, asserted in 1948 that "they knew"—meaning those of Japanese ancestry—about the coming attack. As proof, she offered a story about "a friend" of hers: "Mr. Lee took care of a pumping station overlooking Pearl Harbor. Their maid on December 6 asked for her pay. She said she was not coming back any more. He saw quite a few Japs going up the hills early the next morning before the planes came." This, Richey concluded triumphantly, "shows what lies underneath."[29]

In a confidential interview with visiting US senator Hugh Butler of Nebraska, Joseph Whitfield, who had arrived in the islands in 1914 and was personnel director for the Royal Hawaiian Hotel from 1934 to 1938, recalled an incident at the hotel, where "the majority of those employees were Orientals." One night he wandered into a "tea party" and "heard the remark made by a Japanese, in [the] Japanese language, 'here come another bunch of damn haoles,'" he reported. "I understand a lot of the Japanese language," he acknowledged, "and they thought we were a bunch of tourists." Once, in wartime, he was sitting on a bus—buses became mobile sites of conflict during the war, as they brought together in a confined space various ethnicities—"driven by a Japanese[,] and someone at Bishop and King started to board the bus and he slammed the door and caught his foot on the door; and something was said." The driver then opened the door and let in the frustrated haole passenger, who retorted, "'What are you trying to do, kill me?'" Whitfield, still bitter years later, said, "The Japanese never said anything until he walked away and there happened to be another bus driver, Japanese, sitting behind him talking to him and he said, 'if I had, it would have been good riddance.'"[30]

Senator Butler accumulated a good deal of material during his journey to Honolulu that helped convince him that the behavior of many individuals of Japanese origin during the war disqualified the archipelago from attaining statehood. During the war a white man complained that when he was playing tennis at the University of Hawai'i and the national anthem played, all stood to attention—except unnamed members of the population of Japanese origin. Attached to this communication to Senator Butler was a story of US national Masao Akiyama, who at age 27 renounced his citizenship during the war. He had been born in Hawai'i and had lived in Japan from the time he was 6 until he was 17. "'Although the United States has given its reasons for this war,'" he declared, "'I do not consider those reasons to be just.'"[31] There was also 22-year-old Mamoru Sadanaga, born in Hawai'i, who was among those who professed loyalty to Tokyo and failed to appear for induction,[32] a list that apparently included others.[33]

William H. Tilley, who arrived in the islands in 1916, had been assigned during World War I to train and equip the "first Japanese[-American] soldiers" in the US Army, and he was not impressed. "The Oriental here has never struck against an Oriental employer, never has and never will," he told Senator Butler bluntly. Tilley believed this was not bound to change[34]—a feeling growing among others that led to calls for mass deportation.[35] This combustible mixture of patriotism and prejudice meant that management saw the unionizing of a workforce heavily composed of those of Japanese ancestry as a serious long-term problem that—as one journal put it—"might jeopardize the strong controls which local white residents have long exercised."[36]

The *Christian Science Monitor* followed up with a report on elite concern about the "enthusiasm with which Hawaiian workers of Japanese descent are responding to the organizers' appeal." It was also true that AJAs—Americans of Japanese Ancestry—in particular were horrified at what was happening to them and, in response, sought to organize their ranks, which meant a boost in union membership. This led to criticism of what some termed ungenerously their "'cockiness' and 'independence,'" terms that reportedly had been heard with increasing frequency following the transportation slowdown involving 500 Honolulu bus drivers, "65 percent of whom were of Japanese ancestry," as one reporter pointedly noted. This was the first serious work stoppage since the start of the war and outraged those unable to make critical distinctions between the foe in Tokyo and individuals in Hawai'i who physically resembled them. Supposedly one employer with a brother interned in Manila paid off his drivers and prepared to sell his trucks rather than negotiate with a trucking union headed by a person of Japanese ancestry. Yet the observant journalist could not help but notice that the war was "tending gradually to eliminate or at least modify the dual standards under which Oriental labor in Hawaii has received less pay than Caucasian labor."[37] During the summer of 1943 certain Honolulu businessmen sought to exert pressure on Japanese-Americans to keep them from joining unions. The wartime regime's stance was apparently that civilian workmen were in the same position as soldiers and sailors in labor units.[38]

Hence, not long after the bombs stopped falling on Pearl Harbor, the authorities pounced. Union membership, a mere 500 in 1935, had grown to almost 10,000 shortly before the bombing of Pearl Harbor, and the war provided an opportunity to curb this trend, as the retreat of civil liberties was a roadblock in the path of this kind of growth. Unlike on the US West Coast, where the bulk of Japanese-Americans residing there had been interned, any attempt at large-scale internment in Hawai'i would have brought the economy of this important Pacific port to a screeching halt, because of the sheer numbers of Japanese-American workers there. About 1,450 people of Japanese origin were taken into custody during the war in the isles nonetheless, and about a third of these had been born in Hawai'i and were US citizens. Virtually the entire corps of Buddhist and Shinto priests, who were thought to have a special relationship to Tokyo, were swept up, along with Japanese consular agents, language school officials, many commercial fishermen—and labor leaders and politicians. Three of the most influential institutions among the community of Japanese origin—Buddhist temples, Shinto temples, and the language schools—became inactive, which was a demoralizing and disorienting blow; 8 out of 10 children in this community attended these language schools for an hour or so after the regular school day, and the clampdown was quite harmful to the Nisei and Issei. Even Chinese language schools were discontinued, which easily leads to the perception that what was at play was as much anti-Asian racism as anti-Nippon bias. The dragnet encompassed some against whom there was no more evidence than that they were leaders in the "alien" Japanese community. About

800 of these were shipped to Arkansas, while the property of many of them was expropriated, including the Japanese Social Club at Ewa; school buildings at Kaimukī, Kalihi, and Wahiawā were transferred to the YMCA; the Japanese language school at Mōʻiliʻili was given to the Moiliili Community Association, and the McCully School was turned over to the City and County of Honolulu. Arms were twisted to force many of Japanese origin to withdraw altogether from politics, their participation being perceived by the white elite as aggravating racial tensions.

This was part of the panic that seized the elite who thought there might be a national security concern embedded in the dense populating of the archipelago with those of Japanese descent. Coincidentally, the number of unskilled male laborers on sugar plantations dropped from 37,000 in 1939 to 30,000 in 1941 and 20,000 in 1945. The number of pineapple workers likewise declined. This trend increased anxiety among workers at a time when this feeling was already prevalent, given the restriction on civil liberties. Yet it did not take long for a labor famine to set in. The Hilo Chamber of Commerce passed a resolution condemning "labor pirating," and retail stores had fewer employees as a result of this drought. By 1944 there were almost 15,000 unfilled posts in Oʻahu, and the same held true in services, such as stevedoring, trucking, transportation, construction, repair shops, laundries, restaurants, and hospitals, all of which were desperately seeking workers. Acute shortages of women in the workforce in general were intensified in the kinds of positions they held traditionally, including jobs as domestic and laundry workers, waitresses, clerical workers, teachers, and nurses. In Hawaiʻi during the war a larger percentage of the total population was at work than in virtually every other land under the US flag; many individuals held one or more part-time jobs, along with a full-time job. The unique situation in Hawaiʻi facilitated regulations that allowed prosecution and the imposition of jail sentences for absenteeism—miss work, go to jail. The repressive measures inflicted on labor dialectically led to the passage in 1945 of the Little Wagner Act, making Hawaiʻi the only land under the US flag—beyond Wisconsin—to extend collective bargaining to agricultural labor, which in turn spurred the explosive growth of the ILWU.[39]

Part of the wartime crackdown on the working class of Hawaiʻi had to do with rising inflation. "Prices are up in spite of the establishment of price ceilings," said left-leaning photographer Ray Jerome Baker during the midst of the war. "Toilet paper costs double what it did a year ago," he observed, while "labor which has been frozen to its jobs, is restless and dissatisfied and reports come in that some deliberately commit acts to get themselves fired."[40] Prostitution had "become a big racket, a big business"; sex workers could earn a staggering "twenty thousand or more a year."[41] Later Baker noted, "[The] population of Honolulu has about doubled during the war; if one had dog kennels to rent, no doubt people would want to rent them to live in."[42]

In a way, the tidal wave of repression that crashed on the shores of Hawai'i veritably preordained a counterreaction—a growth of unionism—and, ironically, it caused some to feel that if the archipelago were to become a state instead of remaining a colony, that would prevent a recrudescence of such harsh measures in the future. Of course, the push toward statehood was not an inevitable result of this repression; progressives could just as well have pushed for independence. However, by 1945 the population of Japanese origin was on the defensive, blamed implicitly—at times explicitly—for the Pacific War, and the Euro-American Left was not sufficiently farsighted to see beyond the immediate horizon. This population of Japanese origin had been sorely hurt by the penalizing of Buddhist clergy, since the latter had supported workers and allowed their language schools to serve as shelters and centers to organize.[43]

Reflective of, perhaps, the weaknesses of the white Left, even John Reinecke, the soft-spoken Communist, acknowledged in 1948, "I felt and I still feel that the Buddhist churches [sic] here did maintain Japanese chauvinism to a certain extent"; however, he did oppose the attempt to curb "Shinto temples."[44] For his part, labor leader Art Rutledge contended, "The corporate interests [were] largely responsible for permitting the continuance of Shinto practices in Hawaii during peace times. They gave every assistance to language schools, etc. because they wanted to maintain a docile, unassimilated group of workers."[45]

Unfortunately, extreme skepticism toward the good intentions of those of Japanese ancestry was not limited to whites. Kilsoo Haan of the Korean National Front Federation, along with the Washington-based Sino-Korean People's League, claimed that US nationals of Japanese origin were "members of the Japanese Occupation Army which Japan plans to use after she invades the American mainland."[46] Haan also told Washington in "confidential" terms that that he desired detention of not only Japanese-Americans but also those friendly to them.[47]

Haan's skepticism reflected the reality that the measures imposed on wartime Hawai'i were so breathtaking in their reach and sweep that it was understandable, to a degree, why progressive forces were left flat-footed. Thus, in Maui, regulations mandated that "firearms, ammunition, explosives and weapons in the possession of persons of Japanese ancestry, naturalized American citizens who were citizens of Germany or Italy, and American citizens whose parents were German or Italian citizens, will be turned in to the nearest police station immediately."[48] One study declares that, in internment camps where they were all housed, "Japanese always ate after the German and Italian internees."[49] These crude distinctions between and among those with roots in the Axis nations suggested how those who constituted the plurality of the islands' population faced a special discrimination that bled ineluctably into the workforce.[50]

Thus, just after the attack on Pearl Harbor several government officehold-
ers from this community did not seek reelection, but others did run. Within
days some island newspapers printed an editorial from the mainland averring
that the "'sour part of the news is that five out of seven Japanese candidates who
ran for various nominations won out over assorted white, Chinese and Hawaiian opponents'"; thus, the editorial concluded, "'it seems inescapable that we
have [got] to exercise some old style imperialism in Hawaii for the duration of
the war to be on the safe side . . . and if the Japanese in Hawaii do not like that
attitude they had better go back where they or their ancestors came from.'"[51]
Speaking to Senator Butler after the war, Martin E. Alan was among the whites
in Hawai'i who took issue with this community's voting patterns.[52]

Such statements were representative of the extreme rhetoric—often accompanied by extreme action—that characterized the war years. Japan, said
one white writer, was "'our major menace and our principal enemy'" because
that nation—unlike Germany—desired "'the crushing of white civilization.'" The Japanese and Japanese-Americans were the "yellow hordes storm-
ing the gates of European civilization," a "Yellow Octopus." It was said that
even the biblical passages "Revelation 16:12–16 and 9:13–21 refer plainly and
unmistakably to Japan" in uncomplimentary terms. Tokyo, it was reported,
wanted "unification of the yellow peoples of the world, a sort of United States
of Asia," and though Moscow was now a wartime ally of the United States, it
was deemed "very significant that today Russia and Japan enjoy the most
friendly relations as 'neutrals.'" That relationship was said to cast doubt that
"Japan really desires a German victory"; rather, it was thought, Japan "would
prefer a war of exhaustion in Europe" as a way to bring about Nipponese supremacy, a mortal danger to haole rule in Hawai'i. After all, it was asserted,
"Orientalism took control of Russia through the advance of Bolshevism,"
which suggested that even if Washington managed to prevail during this
conflict, there would still have to be a bruising confrontation with a resident
Communist Party that seemed to be draped in the finery of "Orientalism."[53]

John Reinecke acknowledged that "from as far back as 1937" he had detected a heightened hostility toward those of Japanese origin. "By 1940 it was
a considerable factor," he said. "I remember that the Democratic Party in
January 1940 had rather a heated argument over whether or not it should
condemn the foreign language broadcasts over the radio here [in Honolulu]."
In 1948 he recalled earlier discussions that contended that "'one or more
Caucasian American[s]'" must be present whenever those of Japanese ancestry assembled and that "'no language other than English'" could be spoken at
such assemblages.[54] Given the redolent anti-Nippon atmosphere, it is surprising that only one-fourteenth of the Nisei population, or about 6,000
people, renounced their citizenship when the mainland government provided an opportunity to do so. (In contrast, at the Tule Lake internment

camp in California, about 70 percent of citizens over the age of 18 renounced their citizenship.)[55] Interestingly, during the war apparently some individuals of Japanese ancestry changed their names to signify another Asian identity,[56] so brutal was the persecution they faced.

Those of Japanese ancestry were not the only ones to endure a blistering racial experience. In the spring of 1941, as the hoofbeats of war began to pound ever more insistently, Secretary of War Henry Stimson proposed to dispatch a labor battalion of some 600 Negro men to the islands. A protest ensued.[57] Similarly, the NAACP was upset—and told FDR so a year later—that in "recruiting laborers for work in Hawaii," the "War Department has made a ruling that no Negroes may be recruited," a policy that "dangerously impedes essential war work."[58]

Ultimately, approximately 1,800 men from the so-called Harlem Hell-fighters arrived on the islands, with the core having roots in a ten-block radius within this overwhelmingly African-American neighborhood in northern Manhattan. These men, routinely subjected to white supremacy yet compelled to fight in a war with an antagonist—Japan—that had made a specialty of appealing to them (and not altogether unsuccessfully) on the basis of joint opposition to white supremacy, were in no mood to accept supinely the bigotry that was to be accorded them in Hawai'i. Their presence led to a spate of black-white fistfights in the streets of Honolulu, an abject lesson—if any were needed—to indigenes and others that white men too could have a glass jaw and be felled by a powerful punch. There were dozens of these racial fracases and at least four mini-riots. Panicked, US Naval Intelligence raided the library of the University of Hawai'i in a sleepy Honolulu neighborhood and hastily removed all copies of the NAACP's principal journal. An NAACP chapter was formed, buoyed by the growth in the population of Negroes in the islands from a few hundred in 1940 to 10 times that many soon after. The *Pittsburgh Courier,* the weekly bible of black militancy, as a matter of course sold every issue that was shipped in, at times a hefty 1,000, as Negro troops helped deliver a new spirit of aggressiveness to the islands.[59]

Many of the Hellfighters wound up on Maui, where they ingratiated themselves by learning to dance the hula. Their main task was to take care of night defense in 13 locations on the island, where they guarded troops and installations against attack. Returning to Maui four decades after his departure, the now elderly and graying Hellfighter Robert King confessed, "'We loved Maui,'" though love was hardly in the air when the Hellfighters first arrived and confronted white racism.[60] But since Maui was the only island in the chain that had been shelled four times by foreign ships, stretching back to 1825, the presence of these Harlemites had to be somehow tolerated,[61] a perception fed by the generally warm reception they received from the population of Asian-Pacific origin.[62]

Even before the Harlem Hellfighters brought their own swaggering menace to the ramparts of white supremacy, Negroes had begun to see the need of banding together,[63] a feeling fueled by the NAACP.[64] Earlier the NAACP had sought to intervene in the notorious Massie case[65]—Hawai'i's version of the Scottsboro Nine case—involving spurious charges of molestation of a white woman.[66] That effort had struck a chord, though at that time Honolulu's Negro population could be counted in the scores.[67]

Still, the NAACP was reluctant in 1941—before the war—to commit resources to the organizing of the islands.[68] Even the battle-hardened William Pickens, an NAACP leader who had seen the worst the United States had to offer, observed in 1941 that "up until the time I visited Hawaii about five years ago, it was undoubtedly the freest place and freer from color prejudice of any part of the United States territory."[69] Yet even during this pre–Pearl Harbor period, viewed by many as a sunny era of good feelings, it was not African-Americans who took the lead in seeking to form an NAACP chapter in the islands. It was Jacob Prager, a native of Boston who spearheaded the campaign, a man who, as he put it, "for years . . . held an active interest in the Negro cause, perhaps because of my Jewish origin."[70] "The enthusiasm is here," he said, for he "noticed that on the defense projects, Negros still get the small pick and shovel jobs, not because they cannot fill other jobs, but, because of their prejudice."[71]

Thus it was Prager who rounded up 53 of the interested men and women who wanted to form an NAACP chapter,[72] as they overcame the concern expressed by the association's premier leader, Walter White.[73] This trepidation was overcome, and soon the NAACP leadership was informed that a member wanted to scrutinize the "alleged ruling by a downtown café prohibiting service to Negroes"; that a Honolulu nightclub was "reported to have refused service to a legislator of Chinese ancestry"; and that the "increase in national defense activity in Hawaii" meant an "influx of many mainlanders who have strong racial prejudices."[74]

As it turned out, the NAACP and its sympathizers had their hands full during the war. The USO, which sought to provide recreation for the numerous sailors and soldiers passing through Hawai'i, was allegedly seeking to establish segregated sites exclusively for Negroes; already there were separate USO sites for men of Chinese origin.[75] This concern was magnified because Negro troops—like those of Japanese ancestry—also were suspected of being disloyal and were being watched carefully by military intelligence, to the extent that if they were seen consorting with people of Asian ancestry, they were all looked on with suspicion. As one report put it, "some suspect that there may be a collaboration of the dark races against the white races."[76] The authorities began telling various men and women of Asian descent in the islands that it would not behoove them to be too friendly to Negroes; it was thought that seditious ideas would spread from the latter to the former.[77]

This combustible brew meant that if a Negro entered certain restaurants, the white soldiers present instigated arguments and fights.

The arrival of Negroes, the group most predisposed to confront white supremacy, provided an object lesson for the Asian-Pacific masses of Hawai'i and was a spark that helped ignite a labor revolt. Many indigenes and people of Asian origin were horrified by the way Negroes were being treated in Hawai'i. An unidentified group of Chinese-Hawaiians were cited as saying that "after the war we are going to have lots of Negroes in Hawaii" and that unlike on the mainland "they don't have to ride on special buses, or eat in separate restaurants"—"they go everywhere here in Hawaii." The Chinese-Hawaiians had noticed something that was happening on buses: "Sometimes there's a seat occupied by just one Negro soldier. The other seats are all occupied. A haole soldier or a group of them board the bus. No one will take the seat beside the Negro. They'll stand instead."[78]

Even Riley Allen, the influential editor of the *Honolulu Star-Bulletin*—viewed widely as the islands' most liberal newspaper—was accused of surrendering to racism with his journal's repetitive habit of distinguishing between "'soldiers'" and "'Negro soldiers,'" which was leaving the impression that the latter—who could be easily distinguished on the streets—were largely responsible for the disruption brought by the arrival of so many military men in the islands. Allen was unrepentant. "'The colored troops should never have been brought over here in the first place,'" he thundered. "'We don't want them in the community,'" since "'all they cause is trouble.'" Yet the Asian-Pacific majority in Hawai'i, having begun to connect their own plight to that of African-Americans, were concerned about the maltreatment of Negroes: "Because of the darkness of their color," said an unidentified observer, they were "given treatment generally accorded to Negroes in the U.S." and "they objected to and were hurt by this treatment."[79]

NAACP leader Walter White was beyond anger in confronting Riley Allen. It was "heartsickening," White cried, "to see the things that are happening over here," such as "the establishment of Jim Crow USOs." Angrily perplexed, White asked rhetorically, "Just what are we fighting for[?]"[80]

One islander reported being informed "by several basketball fans" of practices involving teams of servicemen: "When the 'white' teams play the 'colored' teams, the civilians boost the 'colored' teams. If the civilians do not, the colored fellows have no supporters outside of the small number of colored men in the audience. When the 'white' teams play the 'civilian' teams, the colored fellows boost the civilians. When the 'colored' teams play the 'civilian' teams, the civilians boost their own teams, but are generous in their applause for colored players who make 'good plays.'" Inadvertently, the "white teams" were bolstering Tokyo's propaganda, isolating themselves and preparing the ground for future sociopolitical earthquakes.[81]

When Negroes began arriving in Hawai'i in significant numbers, their presence added a new element to the mix in the struggle against racism. The antiracist rhetoric of the antifascist war could not be kept from the South Seas, and it caused many there to question the foundation of white supremacy—i.e., Negrophobia—thereby undermining the white elite. On the mainland—in Seattle, for example—Negroes and Japanese-Americans often sat together in the balconies of theaters,[82] a reflection of their dual dearth of European ancestry and the bonds that shared trait helped to forge.[83] Aiko Reinecke, persecuted by the authorities after the war because of her presumed political affiliations, recalled later, still aghast, that "during the war, we took some of the Negro soldiers to eat in the Honolulu restaurants and in one instance particularly, were denied—we were denied food."[84]

On the other hand, since Hawai'i was an encampment for soldiers, Negro men in particular passed through the archipelago in profusion, often leaving in their wake progressive ideas. The list of such progressives included Ewart Guinier, a future Harvard faculty member who visited Ray Jerome Baker.[85] Also visiting Baker was Vernon Jarrett, who became a prominent Chicago journalist and was quite well known among African-Americans.[86] The upsurge of labor militancy, in short, was entangled with a similar upsurge in antiracism, as exemplified by the stirrings of the NAACP, in reaction to the elite—an elite that under the cover of an antifascist war had expropriated Americans of Japanese ancestry and smashed unions. An indicator of militancy can be gleaned from the stunning number of fistfights[87] that seemed to erupt between white servicemen and indigenous Hawaiians.[88] Fortunately, present within the archipelago was a union—the ILWU—that specialized in forging class unity across racial and ethnic lines.

There were also union leaders tied to the competing American Federation of Labor, principally its idiosyncratically crusty Arthur Rutledge. "I was bootlegging in Seattle," he admitted, before deciding to decamp to the islands. He had ties to the Teamsters Union, which wound up competing with the ILWU along the West Coast, and those ties influenced his often star-crossed relationship with the union of Hall and Bridges. Rutledge was born in Poland early in the twentieth century under the name "Avrom Rotleider," and he had once been arrested for "vice."[89] Yet he hired John Reinecke at a time when others would not touch this Communist, suggesting that in Hawai'i even the federation was more farsighted than its counterpart on the mainland.[90]

Hawai'i would need every ounce of this positive attribute in order to confront a complex wartime situation in the islands. At a time when some were cheering as Americans of Japanese Ancestry were being marched at gunpoint from the docks, it was Rutledge who objected.[91] A material interest was involved in Rutledge's objection, for removing those of Japanese ancestry from the workforce would have crippled the islands. As he observed in 1943, "among local unions, the following have large percentages of Japanese-American members: carpenters, 80 percent; dairy workers, 75 percent; longshoremen, 17 percent; teamsters, 75 percent; street railway workers, 70 percent; drydock workers, 30 percent; brewery workers, 70 percent."[92] This heavy representation of AJAs in particular presented a major challenge for Rutledge and for labor in general,[93] a challenge that was met with the wise aid of John Reinecke.[94]

A leading member of the elite, J. A. Balch—who had resided in Hawai'i since 1907—was among those worried about this heavy representation of AJAs in the workforce. Thus, he declared, "our government cannot afford to leave the Japanese here as the dominant racial group." Like other elites he was particularly concerned about "the matter of increasing numbers of Japanese driving buses for the Honolulu Rapid Transit and other transportation utilities"—this trend "should be investigated and corrected," he proclaimed, but he did not describe how this was to be done when labor markets throughout Hawai'i were under stress. Undeterred, Balch suggested that "as soon as conditions warrant, at least 100,000 Japanese should be moved to mainland farming states." Speaking during the midst of war-related turmoil in 1942, he reported, "I gave an order over ten years ago, when President of Mutual Telephone Company, that no further men or women of Japanese extraction should be employed by that company if avoidable"—he was seemingly unconcerned with the profound discriminatory implications of that policy. He proposed that more Filipinos and Puerto Ricans be brought to Hawai'i in response.[95]

Likewise, Secretary of the Navy Frank Knox informed his superior, President Roosevelt, that he wanted all those of Japanese ancestry on O'ahu removed.[96] The White House chose to retain a provocative article that inquired tantalizingly, "If you were one of four white people on a raft in the middle of the ocean, and two Nisei were also seated there—scared and glad to be alive—would you push them off?" What if "you knew that they could supply ninety-one percent of the food, eight percent of the milk and butter and sixty percent of the drugs"? Pointing to Knox' plan, the article noted that it was "much discussed" at the highest levels in Washington and "favored by some,"[97] though ultimately was infeasible.[98]

In response to this furor, Governor Ingram Stainback informed Rutledge that "Americans of Japanese descent should [be able to] participate in union activities" and should "have the same right as every other American citizen in this matter." The governor, whose roots were in the former slave South, then observed that "thus far we in Hawaii have been remarkably free from racial prejudice," unlike that demonstrated by the "Zoot Suit Riots" in Los Angeles, for example, and by other "un-American incidents" that had gripped Detroit and Harlem.[99]

As the war plodded on mercilessly, John Reinecke, soon to be a Smith Act defendant, complained that the "chief organ of Jap-baiting" was the powerful

Honolulu Advertiser. "It has got worse," he thought, "maybe because its circulation among the armed forces has increased." The unions "had been pretty much put out of commission during the early months of the war," he noted, "and only toward the end of 1942 was the Central Labor Council (AF of L) re-established." Until 10 March 1943, "all labor was under the direction of the Military Governor," he observed, and when Art Rutledge "went to the office of the MG to protest that employers were using military rule as an excuse for breaking their contracts, he was told by one of the aides that if he made any trouble he would get a bayonet up his arse."[100]

CHAPTER 4

The Labor of War

Frank Thompson had been dispatched to the islands in mid-1944 by the ILWU to survey the possibilities for the union's advance there. He arrived on a Saturday morning in July and immediately felt at home,[1] but it did not take long for him to become displeased. "The Port Allen local has been non-existent since Dec. 7th, 1941," he grumbled in a letter. Kaua'i was languishing under martial law, and "all meetings of any kind were banned." Since "the heat naturally fell on the Japanese," Thompson noted, many of them were "scared stiff."[2]

This latter point was no less true. Weeks after Thompson's arrival, the US Office of Naval Intelligence was accused of "doing a first class job of running to hell off the waterfront the best manpower available for longshore work, not only the aliens but also the American born Japanese," with special reference made to Yoshito Watanabe.[3] This behavior was "uncalled for," Thompson charged.[4]

Thompson was shocked to find how brutally the population of Japanese origin was treated in Hilo.[5] These "Hitlerite tactics" had ignited other "fascist minded groups," he said. Given this "miserable situation," Thompson instructed Goldblatt, "You should raise some holy hell both with the Navy and the Manpower Commission." These "smug employer bastards," he argued, were "making an attempt to play off one national group against another" and were simply "breeding race hatred."[6]

The question of employment of Japanese-Americans in the handling of ammunition was also at issue, said Thompson.[7] In response, Goldblatt reminded his comrade that "we have gone to bat . . . on the whole business of employment of Americans of Japanese ancestry in Hilo and other ports," and, he insisted, "if necessary, we will reopen the entire question, perhaps on the floor of Congress."[8]

Yet few recognized at the time that the dawn of labor's rise was nigh at precisely its darkest moment. Meeting Harry Bridges in 1938 in San Francisco, Jack Kawano noted that his longshore unit was affiliated to the ILWU and the CIO, and the thankful Bridges provided him with funding so he could purchase a public address system upon his return home, which proved quite useful in an explosion of successful labor organizing. The Big Island was effectively organized into the ILWU camp; i.e., even before the passage of the Little Wagner Act was drafted, the ILWU had organized from fields to mills. The chronology was reversed, Kawano said, in that the "pressure of the organizing was so powerful that legislators had to pass a special law." Thus the bill was enacted as the war was winding down.[9]

In short, in early 1944 the ILWU had a few hundred members in the islands, but beginning later that year the union rapidly won 132 elections, covering 10,984 workers in the sugar, pineapple, stevedoring, and other industries, and emerged as one of the most powerful organized forces in an island chain approaching a population of 500,000.[10] The union leaders accomplished this in the face of stiff resistance.[11]

Kawano, the forgotten man in Hawai'i's turbulent labor history, had long been a union stalwart. In early 1941 he recalled, "Nearly five and one-half years ago our union was born in a dank meeting hall at the foot of Maunakea Street which had just been opened by the Marine Firemen and Sailors' Union" at a time when "working conditions were rotten, wages low [and] discrimination terrible."[12] In 1938 the aptly named *Voice of Labor* had editorialized that "in Jack Kawano[,] their leader," stevedores "have produced as careful an organizer and as keen a negotiator as can be found anywhere."[13]

It was because of his yeoman service that in 1943 Kawano was given a raise by the union.[14] Hence, a few months later Kawano reported to Bridges that "we have been able to make some progress on the Big Island" since "at least sixteen Sugar Mills there alone" were leaning strongly toward unionization; "these plantations," Kawano said, "are spread out in a territory of about more or less than 200 miles in diameter." The Australian-accented Bridges probably took keen notice when Kawano added that the "real power" of the San Francisco–based union's adversary, Matson, "lies in the Hawaiian sugar plantations"; these plantations, stressed Kawano, "are the backbone of the political reaction in the Territory." Things were progressing nicely, thought Kawano, in that "[the] docks are organized by the ILWU [and] the railroad gang who transport sugar from all of the Big Island plantation mills to the docks are members of the ILWU"; in addition, plantation workers were moving in a similar direction. Kawano noted, however, that a "reactionary AFL leader has the blessing of some of the plantation managers" to broker sweetheart deals. This brokerage was blunted, but there was no guarantee the concord would last. Therefore, Kawano insisted, "we must act and act now," and there was ample reason to do so, since the wages were "terrible" and, he said, "the number of men engaged in this type of work is not less than fifty thousand." "[The] sugar industry is a stabilized industry," he observed, "and so they don't move the mills from one place to another," unlike, say, a textile factory. Kawano advised Bridges, "Drop everything, pick the right guy and send him over here right now."[15]

The moment was propitious, Kawano thought, since the "reactionary" Jack Owens of the AFL had split with his fellow federation leader, Art Rutledge. Kawano deemed Rutledge to be "progressive," since he "asked me whether there was any possibility of the CIO getting the Rutledge faction into the CIO,"[16] as the two men had collaborated[17] fruitfully[18] on a number of fronts.[19]

Thus, contrary to popular belief, it was not Jack Hall who organized island labor in the first place—if any one person deserves credit, it is Kawano. "Kawano is the one that organized the sugar workers in Hawaii, not Jack Hall," contends ILWU stalwart Yasuki Arakaki. Perhaps Kawano was overlooked because he was "not very verbal in his spoken English," Arakaki said, noting that "he was born and raised in 'Opihikao in Puna, really in the boondocks," which ill prepared him for becoming known prominently.[20] Hall's sympathetic biographer notes that "Hall didn't organize the union" and admits that many islanders "resent a haole from the mainland getting all the credit," concluding, "And they are surely right. Hall didn't [do it]."[21] Hall himself basically concurred,[22] a gracious concession on his part.[23] Of course, Kawano's choosing to become an anticommunist stool pigeon, seeking to tear apart the union he had helped build, not only is a human drama of Shakespearean dimensions but also has colored indelibly how he has been viewed subsequently.

Nevertheless, in the period leading up to Thompson's arrival, pressure was building on the ILWU to fall in line behind the anti-Nippon campaign—despite the importance of figures like Kawano—and it came even from quarters not usually found in conservative ranks. Such sources of pressure decidedly included the exceedingly competent labor lawyer Carol King of New York City, who was a friend and comrade of Goldblatt's. In May 1942 she instructed "Dear Lou" that he was "screwy on the Japanese [issue]"; "my hunch," she continued, "is that the Japanese cause is a lost cause."[24]

Goldblatt did not flinch. Hysteria was skyrocketing in early 1942—not least due to the blow to white supremacy just administered in Singapore—when the pudgy labor leader trooped before a congressional committee that had come to San Francisco to take testimony. The distressed Goldblatt was unsparing, decrying the "old flames of racial suspicion" that had been "fanned to full blaze" and the "ill-considered and vigilante-inciting epithets against the Japanese born in this country" that had the "wolf pack" in "full cry." Meanwhile, Goldblatt said, "most of our State and local officials, rather than standing as bastions of justice and equal protection under law, have joined the hue and cry against the Japanese native-born." Angrily, he charged, "This entire episode of hysteria and mob chant against the native-born

Japanese will form a dark page of American history. It may well appear as one of the great victories won by the Axis Powers." His assessment was that, horribly, "all of us who failed to speak in time contributed to this victory of the isolationist fifth column in America." Hence he asked, "Shall we follow in the footsteps of [press baron William Randolph] Hearst and turn our war effort into an illusory battle against the 'yellow menace'?" Goldblatt was concerned that in the fight against fascism the United States was being drawn magnetically toward the more egregious methods deployed by its foes. "If our treatment of the Japanese becomes the index of the future," Goldblatt told these complicit solons, "we can readily foresee the course of America. Hitler and Mussolini will not hesitate to sacrifice the Italians and Germans in this country if it suits their policy of total war. New incidents will occur, in which Americans of Italian and German descent are involved. Then the fifth column in America will demand the evacuation of all Germans and Italians. And this is not the end. What of the other European nations that are now cooperating with the Axis Powers, some of which have declared war against us?" What of "Austria, Rumania, Hungary, Finland, Bulgaria, Denmark—right down the list"? His intensity rising, Goldblatt insisted, "If we do not call a halt—and call it now—America will be a nation divided against itself. It will be an armed camp with half the population guarding the other half." As he saw it, bigotry was now metastasizing, in that "much damage has already been done to this unity [of the nation] by such practices as discrimination against Negroes." He continued, "Time may well show that among those who yell most loudly for the evacuation and hounding of the Japanese are fifth-column elements who are quietly going about their work under the smoke screen of protective hysteria." Seemingly distraught, Goldblatt advised, in words that have yet to be fully comprehended, that "discrimination against races and nationalities will ultimately end in race riots, national antagonisms, bitterness, and hatred." Thus, he counseled, "no concentration camps or forced labor should be imposed upon Japanese or other aliens" and "the same principles governing evacuation" should be applied to "other aliens of enemy nationality," e.g., those of Italian origin, who were well represented in the ILWU's ranks in San Francisco.[25] Goldblatt, befitting his intellectual candlepower, was more prescient on this matter than other ILWU leaders.[26]

Confirming Goldblatt's dismay, by mid-1942 Bert Nakano was informing Jack Kawano with regret that "as far as the local [union] is concerned, we have 107 book members left on the waterfront after the Japanese elements were frozen out."[27] This distressing pattern had begun to appear even before the war.[28]

Thus, formidable barriers were strewn in the path of labor. One of the Japanese-Americans who had been ousted was Koji Ariyoshi. By the time of the war he was working on the docks of San Francisco and was extremely unhappy with the bigotry to which he had been subjected. "I deeply felt the effect of the white supremacy and racist propaganda every time the sentries stopped me on the Embarcadero," he recalled bitterly. "Germans and Italian aliens were not stopped, and they did not have to take their sandwiches out to show that eggs or luncheon meat were between the slices of bread, and not dangerous weapons."[29]

The Japanese-American Communist Karl Yoneda recalled what happened when he was departing for Camp Shelby in Mississippi: "[A] group of MPs came aboard as our train left Chicago on the way south. They told us Nisei to move to the forward 'Whites Only' section. One of us said, 'we're not white. Why do we have to move?' The MP captain replied, 'this section is for 'Colored Only.' Now move, that's an order.'" He added that "a similar incident took place at Camp Shelby where we used the 'Coloured Only' latrine," as white supremacy was again reinforced.[30] Ariyoshi, one of the more distinguished sons emerging from this community, was interned during the war at the appropriately named Camp Savage on the mainland, and it was there that he "saw the difference between Nisei brought up in different environments": "For example, the Hawaiian-Nisei would not stand 'Jap' baiting. . . . On the other hand, the West Coast Nisei were generally less aggressive and outspoken and would not throw their fists when the white men called them 'dirty Japs.'" The West Coast Nisei were less confident than their island counterparts, not least because they were not the plurality of the population. As Yoneda saw things, "the Hawaiian-Nisei were more like Negroes in the Northern states" with their feistiness, while the Nisei from the West Coast were more like southern Negroes.[31] Yet white supremacy was so potent under the US flag generally that even the isles were not exempt from its reach: speaking from Kahuku, O'ahu, Soichi Yonemori confided in January 1945 that the reason he—and perhaps others—avoided participating in unions may have been to deflect the concern that those of his ancestry were seeking undue influence.[32]

The war had stopped labor organizing in its tracks, which was part of the point of Goldblatt's impassioned denunciation of the opprobrium attached to those who disproportionately comprised the archipelago's workforce. In any case, the prewar spurt in union growth, a development that portended so much, was not of long standing.[33]

Just before Thompson set foot on Hawai'i's shores, Roy Gutsch, a member of ILWU Local 6 on the mainland who was stationed on Kaua'i, provided his own survey of the landscape. He went to Honolulu for a visit and found to his dismay "hundreds of unorganized longshoremen." Describing the situation, he reported, "The absenteeism is great. Men don't show up for work weeks at a time. The employers just advertise in the local papers for new men. The results are more union finks on the docks, [which] obstructs the union's bargaining power." Gutsch worried that "if that keeps up in these islands," it "leaves the door open for [the] AF of L"—the AFL was the bitter rival of the ILWU, which was tied to the competing CIO. Gutsch felt that the adverse conditions faced by labor in wartime Hawai'i meant that the "loads on Oahu" that were carried by stevedores were "like mountains," which "slows up the work and adds many injuries." The picture was mixed for labor, he thought: "On Hawaii the situation is good," while "Maui and Kauai are unorganized." He appealed to Bridges' self-interest, adding cogently that "by organiz[ing] out here, we protect the West Coast," removing the possibility that deteriorating conditions in the archipelago could spread like an oil slick to San Francisco.[34]

Part of the explanation—repression aside—that illuminated how labor could fall from the euphoric promise of the late 1930s to the knuckle-scraping lows of wartime was that the Communist Party, which had helped engineer the former state of exhilaration, had gone into remission. At the Smith Act trial, Jack Kawano, testifying on behalf of the prosecution, recalled that Robert Fitzgerald of the CP in San Francisco had arrived in Hawai'i after the onset of war and recommended that the party disband. Why? Kawano related the reason he was given: "Because the composition of the Communist Party members in Hawaii was not the same with that of the mainland. In other words, there have been too many Orientals." And that raised too many problems. Moreover, since Washington and Moscow were allies, it was imperative "not to do anything that might irritate the Army and Navy, particularly because there were some Orientals in the membership." Hall, Jack Kimoto, and Robert McElrath all objected—to no avail. They appealed—and lost. Then Kimoto announced that "although we disagreed with that decision, we were going to abide by it." Thus, the mimeograph machine was stored in the ceiling of "Mr. [John] Reinecke's Pahoa Avenue home." It was in early 1943 that Ichiro Izuka, Kimoto, and Alice Hyun, another stalwart comrade, were "caught digging up some Communist literature at the Koko Head farm of Peter Hyun," where it had been buried—which infuriated Hall.[35] According to Izuka, however, he, Kimoto, and Hyun had proceeded surreptitiously to the Koko Head farm, where they were "about to burn books which had been plowed up by a farmer," when the FBI caught them in the act.[36]

Jack Kawano embellished this story subsequently, recalling at another point that after the Pearl Harbor bombing, Red seafarer Walter Stack sailed into Honolulu, bringing the message that party units must disband; hence "there were no official activities of the Communist Party in Hawaii during the war." He confirmed that Jack Kimoto and Jack Hall "argued very strenuously" against this thinking. "I burned my material," Kawano asserted.[37]

The withdrawal of the Communist Party from Hawai'i was a devastating blow, and not just to the fortunes of the radicals but, as well, to the ability of those of Japanese origin to thwart the forces who were bedeviling them. Given the role of the CP in the abortive labor upsurge, its retreat was also not helpful to all those who toiled for a living. The ILWU, which was affiliated to the upstart CIO—both of which were perceived as carrying a Red taint—was handcuffed by the exigencies of war in a way that the competing AFL was not. Kawano had agreed with Art Rutledge to establish a "joint AFL-CIO organizing committee," but "when it came time to put up the money[,] Rutledge reneged," so the ILWU organizers were "forced to carry the burden by ourselves." By mid-1944, Kawano and his organizers had "60 to 70 percent of the sugar plantations completely organized." Then, just before the day that Tokyo surrendered, a message was received from the CP in San Francisco, requesting that they "reorganize and reactivate" party units in Hawai'i.[38] Even after he had defected from the ranks of the Communists, understandably, Kawano seemed to take pride in his vanguard role in labor organizing even when he testified for the prosecution at the Smith Act trial.[39]

In short, though Hall was given credit for launching this formidable task of organizing, it was actually men like Kawano who were responsible. For it was not until mid-June 1944—when labor organization on the islands was well under way—that Hall reported that he had just then signed on with the ILWU, resigning from what he termed his "comfortable position in charge of the Wage and Hour Division in the Territorial Department of Labor."[40]

The happy confluence of the lifting of martial law in October 1944, which in turn boosted labor organizing and encouraged the Communist Party to re-emerge, was all good news for a beleaguered workforce. There were other factors too, which the local press had not ignored. "Post-war Hawaii will face the problem of too many people for too few jobs," said the *Honolulu Advertiser* in the summer of 1943. The islands "are in for labor unrest after the war," since "the almost certain great scarcity of jobs in postwar Hawaii will force workers into unions as a means of safeguarding their security," the newspaper warned. "Plantation workers on Kauai are deeply conscious of this." But that was not the only gloomy news—from the viewpoint of the elite—since the *Advertiser* also advised that "there will be less tendency than in the past [to] permit discrimination by employers," the kind of divide-and-conquer tactics that had worked to a fare-thee-well in pre-ILWU Hawai'i.[41] Subsequently, Thompson recalled reflectively that he basically agreed with this analysis.[42]

Thompson may have overestimated the influence of sailors like Bill Bailey and Jack Hall on the explosion of organizing in 1944—but he was not wrong in sensing the imminent growth of unions. A. Q. McElrath recalled that the ILWU won union recognition elections "by as much a hundred percent [or] ninety percent" for the most part. "None of the plantations which we had organized in 1944," she insisted, "fell below ninety percent," but as she perceived things, it was the wartime conditions—more than any other factor—that drove this success. Martial law and the arrival of mainlanders with retrograde racial attitudes combined with the preexisting terrible conditions on the plantations to drive events.[43] Steve Sawyer, who arrived in the islands in 1939 with future ILWU attorney Harriet Bouslog, agreed,[44] as did

Anna Duvall, a Hawaiian resident, who recalled a time when workers were "often whipped"; plus, workers had to wear "bango tags" that identified them by a number, "so they weren't even called by their names." And "if Filipinos would strike," Duvall added, "they'd hire Chinese and pay them more."[45]

Even after the war had concluded, restrictions remained for a while against Japanese-Americans—as opposed to Japanese nationals—working on the waterfront. By October 1945 the military chose to lift the restraints imposed on Japanese-Americans, but they continued to be excluded from working on ammunition and at Pearl Harbor, though Tokyo had been defeated.[46]

As it turned out, it was men not of Japanese origin—men like Jack Hall—who were able to take advantage of the unjustifiable suspicions that haunted the bulk of the archipelago's laborers. There were also some unintended benefits to the ILWU. In February 1945, Thompson told Goldblatt that some of the workers at the Olaa plantation had been part of an association that built a Japanese language school. The school was forced out of business when the war began, and the former headquarters—worth a considerable $12,000—had been vacant for three years. After martial law was lifted, the former members of the Japanese school association called a meeting. Undoubtedly nervous about resuming language instruction, which would have been misinterpreted intentionally by the elite, they decided to donate the building, free of charge except for taxes, to the ILWU.[47]

Yet despite the magnanimity of workers of Japanese origin, it would prove to be difficult to remove from them the unfair stain they were said to carry as a result of the Pacific War. Thompson charged that the US government, even as late as February 1945, was seeking to intimidate these men on the waterfront despite—or perhaps because—they were the most hardworking and conscientious "of any racial group on the island,"[48] no small matter.[49]

But indicative of the foul pervasiveness of the environment was Thompson's instructing Goldblatt, "For your information, Lou, there are some of these Orientals that can be awfully stubborn and dumb-acting" and "There is only one way to handle them and that is to really lay it on the line to them."[50]

Goldblatt gently sought to push Thompson in a positive direction toward the requisite sensitivity toward those who were, after all, the archipelago's backbone—Asian-Pacific workers. Goldblatt reminded him that the "use of pidgin English" in communication with them was discouraged, since this was "like one of us going into the South and imitating that southern speech": "Generally it is taken as though we are poking fun at their form of speech. The experience of most Hawaiian people with the haoles has not been good." The workers, he continued, "are still pretty suspicious of them [haoles] and are bound to watch them carefully." So, he counseled, "work with them on a very businesslike although personal basis, until they gain enough confidence to understand our own habits."[51]

Thompson and Goldblatt were an odd pair, their differing sensitivities aside. Thompson was a "funny guy," thought Kawano. About six feet tall, Thompson loomed over most of the workers he purported to represent, and he used "bad language," i.e., profuse profanity. "I got along with him," said Kawano; then again, he recalled, "I got along with almost everybody, because I'm the kind of guy that makes allowances for some weaknesses"—of which Thompson had more than one.[52]

Upon arrival in Honolulu, Thompson had stayed with John and Aiko Reinecke. "He lived with me for a while," said John Reinecke, and he was "arrogant in a heavy-handed sort of way." Reinecke recalled that when an election was held at the Olaa plantation and the workers "elected a slate of all Japanese and perhaps one or two Portuguese, no Filipinos," the feisty Thompson said, "'You can't run a union this way, you've got to have mixed leadership,'" Reinecke continued: "And he was right but the way he went about telling it . . . to [Yasuki] Arakaki, who was one of the proudest men I know, was that it burned up Arakaki. He couldn't stand that. The detestation was mutual."[53] But it was an example of the unusual affirmative action pushed by the union leadership, whereby those of Japanese origin were at times asked to step aside for others—but rarely was this requested of haole men.

Yoshiko Hall, Jack Hall's spouse, remembered that Thompson had poor hygiene habits; she made him shed his clothes so she could wash them. Thus, in the early stages this union, composed overwhelmingly of people of Asian and Pacific descent, had Thompson as de facto second-in-command behind Jack Hall—though the union did see fit to assign Yoshiko Hall to organize the outer islands.[54]

Saburo Fujisaki emerged at Olaa as a leader of the ILWU, and it was he who, on behalf of a large group of workers, chose to go "on record to protest and argue the dictatorial and fascistic practices presently carried out by Brother Thompson."[55] As Fujisaki saw things, Thompson was "causing a split between the Japanese and Filipinos,"[56] effectively doing the dirty work of the elite. According to Fujisaki, Thompson had charged that he—Fujisaki—along with a number of other workers of Japanese origin, had called a meeting for the purpose of "ousting the haoles from the top ranks of the ILWU."[57] Angrily perplexed, Fujisaki remonstrated.[58] At times it seemed that Thompson played too heavily on the differences between and among the workers rather than stressing their commonalities.[59]

"What you have got to understand," Thompson insisted, "is that the different racial groups particularly on this Big Island do not trust one another [and that] this has to be told to these people by an outsider like myself, because these people mistrust one another in trying to get together by themselves."[60] To some, Thompson seemed like an undercover arsonist embedded in a fire department, throwing gasoline on the flames instead of extinguishing them.

"You might not believe this," he informed Goldblatt "but there is no doubt that Bert Nakano," viewed heroically because of his trailblazing role in organizing the Hilo waterfront, "is anti-haole in no uncertain terms." He was happy to report, however, that he had "broken the back" of his "cockeyed scheme."[61]

In addition to being insensitive and having poor hygiene, Thompson also was "big-mouthed and pretty forceful," concluded the Communist Jack Kimoto. In speaking with Kimoto about Thompson, journalist Sanford Zalburg mused in passing that "the trouble with those guys from the mainland" was that "they sometimes retained a little of that racism in them." Kimoto did not disagree, recalling, "I heard that . . . one of the meetings"—attended by labor pioneer Harry Kamoku—"was going on for a long time, quite late," and Kamoku "was lying on the floor sleeping." When "the time came to disband," Hall "kicked Kamoku's leg" while yelling, "'Hey Harry, come, let's go.'" Fred Kamahoahoa "got mad" and "went against Hall." Kimoto continued, "That's what I heard. He thought Hall was—he took it as a white man kicking a Hawaiian." Hall probably meant nothing offensive by this gesture, but it reflected his lack of the kind of sensitivity that was needed in a racially split colony like Hawai'i. Kimoto also did not think highly of another member of the ILWU's haole leadership. "In the early days, among longshoremen, especially Hawaiians used to call him 'make rat' [or] 'dead rat,'" he said, speaking of Robert McElrath. "They didn't like him."[62]

Thompson, viewed widely as similarly tactless, was a grandson of a German socialist and, like many in the ILWU, had a Wobbly background, having started working in lumber camps at the age of 14. He was an "irascible guy in many ways," said Goldblatt, and "a difficult guy." The steady Goldblatt, by way of contrast, had contemplated a doctorate in economics and in the process had studied the Wobblies; he had spoken at length with mine, mill, and smelter workers, the hard rock miners, and the profusion of "Wobblies [who] went to sea." Many of this last group were "loners," yet "they played a certain role in the history of this country, a role that is terribly underestimated," he concluded sagely—as he indirectly bolstered the case for Thompson.

Goldblatt resembled an old Samurai warrior in that he was balding, with a high forehead, a soft, curved nose, high arched eyebrows, and slits that revealed baby blue eyes. He had a wonderful and warm smile that lit up his face—but frowns often creased his visage when he considered his union's leadership in the archipelago.[63] In addition to having to defend Thompson, the chain-smoking Goldblatt also had to contend with the grave reservations about Jack Hall. There was much he admired about Hall—"there was something of the Wobbly in him," he said, "no question about that," but he did not admire his fondness for alcoholic beverages. Goldblatt seemed to sympathize with Hall's weakness when he referred to Hall's rationalizing his often excessive drinking by averring that "Hawaii didn't possess sufficient 'mental stimulus.'"[64]

Whatever the case, Hall—like Thompson—did have some initial teeth-ing problems in relating to the union leadership. Thompson informed Gold-blatt that he had "had a long talk with [Jack Kawano]" and that "in his own way" Kawano had been candid with him. "It is his opinion," Thompson said, "that Jack Hall is not a guy he can sit down with and have any mutual confi-dence in business, because of Hall's attitude, and he very frankly informed me that other people in our local organization feel likewise."[65]

But things were changing swiftly, driven by the rapidly rising currents of war. Reaching Honolulu from San Francisco, where he was based temporarily just before the war, Koji Ariyoshi found work on the waterfront to be "much different," not as oppressive, perhaps because of the different racial and ethnic composition there.[66] Such experiences made it difficult for island stevedores to accept the apartheid-like conditions to which many had grown accustomed—despite the manifest strength of the opposition they confronted.

It was not just the powerful Matson that the ILWU—and Ariyoshi—had to press; there was also C. Brewer, the biggest of the Big Five, according to the union, and the "key corporation in island industry, the one of the Big Five most closely tied to the sugar industry." Since 1909, it was said, "the smallest dividend it has paid has been over 20% on actual capital."[67]

But these employers were contending with a formidable array of orga-nizers, Kawano in the first place—and others too. This list included Yasuki Arakaki, born in Hawai'i in 1918 and a reputed Communist. A small, well-knit, tough-fibered man with strong shoulders and a very strong face featur-ing flat eyes and a curved chin, he had a tremendous talent for organizing and running strikes and laying the strategy for same. Born and raised on a plantation, he went to high school in Hilo, where he graduated in 1935, then promptly began work at Olaa as a carpenter's helper. Ambitious, he desired to attend Waseda University in Tokyo but was unable. For a while he dated Florence Yates, daughter of a prominent politician, territorial senator Julian Yates, but there was bitter opposition to this romance by him. It was in 1944 that Kawano arrived at Olaa and explained that the ILWU—unlike the AFL—did not discriminate, particularly against noncraft workers. At this moment, Filipinos were mostly in the field, and their Japanese counterparts were in the mill—300 of the latter and 700 of the former. Arnold Wills, a federal government bureaucrat with roots in New Zealand—and a labor portfolio—"spent many nights with me at my house," recalled Arakaki. "He laid down the [organizing] strategy during the whole year of 1944. It all started at my house [and] Arnold Wills was the brain. It wasn't Goldblatt and it wasn't Bridges and it wasn't Jack Hall." Rather, a "government man did the organizing for us."[68]

"We organized Olaa first," said Arakaki. "We went to Hilo Sugar [next]. We went to Pepeekeo [next]. We cleaned up the thirteen on this island first.

Then with this success, the rest of the organizing team cleaned up Maui, Oahu and Kauai. So the organizing started on the Big Island."[69]

Tall, with a perpetual quizzical expression and not much of a Kiwi accent, Wills—along with Kawano and Nakano and Arakaki—is also credited with labor's 1944 upsurge.[70] Kawano concurred that it was Wills, a social democrat, who aided them when other officials insisted that labor organizing could not occur as long as martial law persisted.[71] This was ironic since Wills was considered to be a highly bitter anticommunist aiding a union reputed to be led by Reds.[72]

Bert Nakano, on the other hand, who carried throughout his life bullet wounds from the Hilo Massacre was sidelined.[73] Nevertheless he too—along with Jack Kawano—deserves some credit for the organizing of island labor. In December 1943 he called both Kawano and the AFL's Art Rutledge, requesting that they assist in organizing the plantations, but the latter was hesitant. Nakano and his allies started with Onomea Sugar and were largely successful. Born approximately in 1910, Nakano had become a stevedore in 1930 and also cut sugarcane; he joined the Communist Party in 1947, a time when others were beginning to flee this beset organization.[74]

Despite the evident talent and skill of those like Nakano, Kawano, Ariyoshi, Arakaki, et al., there were repetitive complaints that the ILWU had difficulty in developing leadership with roots in the archipelago. As early as 1945 Goldblatt warned Jack Hall, "The most disturbing feature in the island picture still remains the dearth of well-developed local leaders. We will never be able to administer a union which may in the foreseeable future have a membership of thirty thousand or more over many scattered units unless we undertake, as a major part of our work, the training of local leadership."[75] Until the dawn of statehood in 1959, this remained nonetheless one of the ILWU's prime weaknesses.

Still, this justifiable concern of Goldblatt's took an unusual—though repetitive—turn. It was also in 1945 that Kawano, Hall, Goldblatt, and others met at ILWU headquarters in San Francisco, where worry was expressed about too many union leaders in the islands of Japanese origin—though the disproportionate number of white men at the highest level of leadership did not cause as much concern. "The imperative of racial unity in the islands," it was concluded, "makes it imperative that steps be taken to put Filipinos, Hawaiians, Portuguese and others into prominent positions, even though in some cases they might not be as qualified or capable as Japanese. It may well mean that Japanese of considerable ability will have to step back."[76] No concern was expressed, however, about white leaders having to take a "step back."

Again, to his credit, Goldblatt cautioned separately, "We have to beware of a mechanical approach to a broadening out [of] leadership along the racial lines represented in Hawaii. If this followed purely on the basis of having everyone represented regardless of numbers, it might well lead to a situation where we completely frustrate Japanese leadership and then turn them into a hostile force." Arguably, that is what occurred with Kawano and Izuka, among others.[77]

Evidently Jack Hall did not always hew to this approach. Shortly after the union sank roots in the archipelago, Hall told Shigeo Takemoto, president of Local 144 in Maui, "There seems to be a good deal of resentment developing against the leadership of Japanese ancestry on your island. This springs primarily from [Joseph] Kaholokula's fear that Tom Tagawa or some other member of Japanese ancestry is going to run against him for presidency of the local. I find that he has been stirring up the Filipinos . . . to support him for presidency on the basis of preventing the Japanese from taking over control of the local." Hall, who was not prone to request white leaders of the union to stand down, stressed, "Such opposition to Kaholokula at this time would result in a split within the union and the development of sharp racial feelings. If it is the desire of yourself or anyone else in the local to defeat Kaholokula, obviously, the best method would be to have a non-Japanese run against him."[78]

Likewise, Thompson, in the name of diversified slates, placed a "great deal of emphasis on the importance of having Filipino leadership,"[79] which was fair enough and could have been better accepted if he had shown a similar awareness to the sight of having so many white men in the top ranks of the ILWU. Hideo Okada, born in Hawai'i about 1910, worked on sugar plantations for about four decades, yet this staunch ILWU member recalled that at the height of the organizing drives "the Portuguese people were the hardest to sign because they had the best jobs,"[80] further narrowing an already contracted base for leadership, if those of Japanese origin were to be asked to take a step back.[81]

But even before Goldblatt constructed his insightful formulation, a fateful step had been taken that was to reverberate in the archipelago for decades to come. Harry Bridges had become interested in the islands as early as 1934 when he recognized the outsized role of Hawai'i's Matson in the Pan-Pacific shipping industry. Stretched resources, he said, had prevented the ILWU from intervening in Hawai'i as quickly as he had wanted, but, as is apparent, when the union did step in, it made a huge splash. Still, he was blunt when asked in 1975 why he and the union leadership had acquiesced to the recommendation that Jack Hall be picked over Jack Kawano—who was, arguably, more qualified—for the plum post of regional director of the ILWU. Well, said Bridges, Kawano was a Nisei, and "the feeling of the people themselves, especially of Japanese ancestry, was against having one of their own people in the jobs"; at that sensitive moment when the elite was still seeking to disrupt labor by scapegoating workers of Nipponese origin as the complicit culprits in the Pacific War, "the idea of any Oriental holding any kind of important position" was viewed skeptically. "There was plenty of non-haole material," said Bridges, "educated, well-educated and so forth," so, ironically and per-versely, "race" played a signal role in Hall's selection.[82]

Kawano was highly skilled in organizing plantations, thought Matt Mee-han, a union official who was responsible for recommending Hall. "All whom I have come in contact with, have confidence in Kawano," he declared. "He is the spearhead of the labor movement in the islands as far as the CIO is concerned and I find him very capable." But, he concluded, "he is under a great handicap at the present time [because] he is of Japanese ancestry";[83] hence, Meehan said, "it will be necessary to have a haole—white to you—to front for him."[84] The well-connected journalist Sanford Zalburg recalled that even Thompson had told him that Meehan "made a number of enemies" in the islands. "I don't mean just Kawano," said this Hall biographer. "He may have had a little of that brusque-ness that mainlanders sometimes have when they come over here."[85] John Reinecke described Meehan as a "man of average height" who was of Irish de-scent and "strongly built." His spouse, Aiko Reinecke, felt that Meehan "was a wino," for "he always had a bottle of wine" in his hand. She had reason to know, since the Reinecke house had two bedrooms and the couple housed Meehan in one of them when he arrived on the islands in 1944.[86]

J. R. "Bob" Robertson, a Texan of Cherokee, Scotch-English, and Dutch origin who was born in 1903 and had not completed elementary school, was a painter before becoming a leader of the ILWU in San Francisco. He recalled that Meehan recommended Hall because the latter "was there on the scene, and he was a haole," and "that had a great deal to do with Meehan's recom-mendation." As Robertson saw it, this was not wise, since Hall's "greatest weakness was his lack of confidence in others and it reflects an inferiority complex." Like his union adversary, Goldblatt, Robertson felt that Hall too "was afraid to trust people."[87]

Kawano in turn characterized Meehan as a "white supremacy type of guy" who looked down on peoples of the Asia-Pacific basin. Thus, on the questionable Meehan's recommendation, it was Hall—not Kawano—who became the local head of the ILWU in June 1944 at the not inconsiderable sum of $75 per week.[88]

Yet Meehan had objective barriers to consider. Even as the war was wind-ing down in 1945, restrictions remained on workers of Nipponese origin.[89] Army regulations meant that Jack Kawano, quite specifically, was denied ac-cess to the Honolulu port area.[90]

In June 1945, Isami Uwaine felt compelled to resign from his "present job as carpenter" because, he said, "in 1942, May 17, I was denied the right to work on the waterfront by the US Coast Guard because of my Japanese ancestry."[91] After the war, Jack Hall informed Takumi Akama, secretary of the ILWU local in Kaua'i, that "because of the difficulty in clearing any AJA in time to get to the convention [on the mainland,] it is unfortunately necessary that [the]

Indonesian workers are accorded solidarity from the ILWU at their San Francisco head-quarters in the early postwar era. Unlike many of its US counterparts, the ILWU believed fervently in working-class solidarity across borders—not least as a counterweight against the strength of management. Courtesy of Labor Archives and Research Center, San Francisco.

delegates selected be either a citizen of non-Japanese ancestry or a Philippine national."[92] The union's law firm acknowledged in the spring of 1946, "We have had numerous complaints from our brothers on the islands on the immigration regulations pertaining to Orientals coming to the mainland from the islands. Japanese and Filipinos particularly are subject to discrimination on the part of the Immigration Department. They are required to furnish proof of citizenship and identification photographs before they can board a ship or a plane for the mainland. Other citizens are not required to furnish any such proof."[93] Just after the war, when someone from the ILWU staff called the Pickwick Hotel in San Francisco to arrange reservations for two members arriving from Hawai'i, the staffer was told that quarters were available—but then the clerk requested their names, then their nationality. When given this information, the staffer was informed that "[the] hotel would not reserve a room for these people since [we] do not cater to Orientals." The union promptly protested this "flagrant example of discrimination,"[94] but such restrictions hamstrung attempts at effective organizing, serving to render whites more effective and providing a rationale for Hall's appointment.

The other barrier the ILWU confronted—not always successfully—was the widespread notion among some white men that there was something illegitimate about a union's leadership mirroring demographically the composition of the rank and file. That seemed to be the sentiment of Ray Bascom and his spouse, Evelyn; it was she who complained that she was "summarily discharged without previous warning or consultation with the union" by Hall, and then her husband "was rejected by the ILWU Regional Office upon his application for the position of Regional Educational Director solely upon policy grounds of non-Oriental origin."[95] "I was rejected for policy reasons—I am not an Oriental," said Ray Bascom.[96] Actually Ray Bascom was seen as being all too close to the Teamsters, who even then were seeking to raid the ILWU for members, but the wider point was that some seemed to feel there was something questionable about an overwhelmingly Asian-Pacific workforce having Asian-Pacific leadership.

This was not the only problem that leaders like Hall, Thompson, Meehan, and McElrath had with leaders of Asian-Pacific origin. Wilfred Oka was a Communist but in 1950 was serving as both a leader of the Democratic Party and as a county commissioner.[97] Born in Honolulu in 1912 with a fisherman as his father, Oka received a degree from Springfield College in Massachusetts, then worked for the YMCA. His Japanese language skills were poor—"You know what they tell us," he said subsequently. "It was un-American to learn Japanese." But his English language skills were formidable, and he once served as secretary to future governor John Burns. Yet he was not good enough to work for the ILWU, since Hall and McElrath opposed his being hired; the excuse in his case was that he was deemed to be an intellectual, which the skeptical critic could translate to mean that he could more readily challenge them. He was good enough for the CP and the Democrats and local government—but not the ILWU. Ultimately he married a millionaire and enjoyed a comfortable life.[98]

Maxie Weisbarth, of Hawaiian descent, also had his problems with Hall, though he appreciated that Hall was a "strong Party man[, v]ery, very strong." Kaua'i was the "hardest island to organize[,] even today," he conceded in 1975, and Hall took on this formidable task nonetheless at a time when others shrank in retreat. Yet when Hall was sent to Maui to organize, he "couldn't do any good because of the language barrier." Weisbarth confessed that he didn't like the man he had once defeated in a fistfight, because Hall "didn't want anybody that was smart" around him, and if someone was that smart, he'd be "purged" posthaste.[99]

Myer Symonds, the ILWU's Australian-born and Hawaiian-based attorney, disliked Hall intensely, accusing him of being a "name dropper" and of avoiding "the local Communists" despite his own political orientation. Symonds also felt that Hall was something of a "snob" who, as he grew in stature, "liked to pal around with people like the Dillinghams," leaders of the hegemonic Big Five. Hall "strongly disliked intellectuals" and also despised "liberals," according to Symonds; he "would rather have a good, honest moss-back conservative 'that he could trust.'"[100] Even Hall's comrade, Robert McElrath, observed that "Meehan actually recommended that the union hire John Reinecke for educational director" and the insecure Hall replied dismissively, "'We need organizers and not school teachers,'" suggesting that Hall's insecurity could be manifested in a transracial fashion.[101]

Not only that, but it was Kawano, the man given credit for organizing the ILWU, who was also given the lion's share of credit for organizing the Democratic Party, with both entities pushing the theretofore hegemonic GOP out of the winner's circle. Tokuichi "Dynamite" Takushi was an early member of the Democratic Party, asserting that he had joined when "only Hawaiians would join." At that time, he recalled, "Orientals were afraid to" and "all jobs in the state, city and county went to Republicans." Takushi was the "first Oriental," he said, "to join the party," whose foundations were constructed through the Herculean labor of Kawano. "He did [it]," said Takushi speaking of Kawano. "That's true." In the Communist Party, of which Kawano was a member, "discussions of what to do in the political field" had led to two possibilities: "one was to start a labor party, a separate party, and the other was to build up the Democratic Party," a process that proceeded on a parallel track with the organizing of the ILWU. It was "such a weak party and there were so many unorganized precincts," Takushi said. "If we got into the Democratic Party and built the precinct clubs, we would have a great influence, see?" So it was Kawano who "helped to make up their minds," speaking of comrades and allies, "to get into the Democratic Party and build" at a time when "their candidates were not even allowed to have rallies in the plantations, election rallies" and the like. Kawano was concerned that a labor party would "split [the] working class and poor vote." Takushi said decades after the fact, "I still think it was correct tactically."[102] It was true that months after the consolidation of the ILWU in the aftermath of the war, Kawano, Jack Burns, Ernest Murai, and Chuck Mau, a future power broker, helped forge the Democratic Party, at a time when Mau declared that "'there were few haoles even interested'" in this organization.[103]

Yet McElrath did not recall Kawano fondly, albeit after he had deserted the ranks of the progressive forces. "You'd say something to Kawano," he noted, "[and] there'd be no facial expression. No physical reaction at all. You don't know if he understands, [and] you felt that what he was doing was translating what you said into Japanese, thinking in Japanese and translating it back into English." McElrath said that "many of the old Japanese" did this, and, in their cases also, their often impassive reactions contributed to further questionable stereotypes about their alleged stolidity.[104]

The Communist John Reinecke had fonder memories of Kawano. "He was a tower of strength to the union for several years," he said. "I give him great credit. He had a wretched little wooden shack at the head of Pauoa Valley where he lived. He was married, had a family and he lived in the country shack." Back then, "Hall used to sleep there frequently on the floor"; after the war, Reinecke recalled, "when the Communist Party had been abolished for several years in Hawaii," Kawano "wanted it back so it would give discipline to the union members who might join it"—i.e., an antidote to conservative influences. "Don't forget," Reinecke reminded, "the influence of the Catholic Church on a large part of the ILWU membership," particularly Filipinos, Portuguese, and Puerto Ricans.[105] Kawano had seen such influence as problematic. A well-oiled Democratic Party too could serve as a counterweight to conservatism, thought Kawano.

Another Japanese-American, Jack Kimoto, was the de facto leader of the Communist Party, which presided over the tremendous growth in both the ILWU and Democratic Party. He was in frequent touch with seafarers, who often acted as couriers for the CP in San Francisco, bringing materials and instructions to the islands. "From 1938 until the trial," i.e., the Smith Act prosecution in 1952, Kimoto—by his own admission—was the "key man" in the CP. "In the beginning," Hall consulted with him frequently, "but later on he sort of grew away"; "that's right," said Kimoto, "later on he probably developed a resentment against me." As time passed and hysteria rose accordingly with Red strength, Hall had an incentive to put distance between himself and Kimoto, forcing the band of Communists to meet sometimes in Kimoto's house and "sometimes in a car." The bilingual Kimoto, who worked during the war "translating and sometimes announcing on the radio in Japanese" for the US authorities, had good reason to be confounded by the persecution—on racial and political grounds—of men like himself, which marginalized a generation of Japanese-American labor leaders.[106]

Yet despite the fierce internal squabbling and the vile racism directed at those of Japanese ancestry, the ILWU managed to prevail—providing an abject lesson in that its success suggests that even the most formidable internal and external obstacles can be overcome by organized workers. Thus, as 1945 was coming to a close, an elated Jack Hall was able to report that "the pineapple industry was almost completely organized" and stevedoring was "finally completely organized," all of which meant "nearly ten million dollars in the pay envelopes of [the] workers represented"[107] over the length of the contract. In early 1944 the ILWU had 900 members in Hawai'i, but by the time of Hall's striking remarks about 33,000 were enrolled. And in the field of social legislation, only Wisconsin compared with the archipelago.[108] These advances were largely due to the ILWU, which, in addition to battling in legislatures, was fighting aggressively for wage increases and improved working conditions, while pursuing numerous grievances of ordinary workers, providing them with an enormous sense of empowerment and collective self-esteem. This union was also well organized, holding classes for stewards and other union officials, and highly democratic, with biennial conventions, regular meetings of the rank and file, and the publishing of numerous pamphlets, while unafraid to subscribe to and allow for the dissemination of Communist Party publications.

CHAPTER 5

Sugar Strike

Howard Babbitt knew the score. This executive of C. Brewer was living large in postwar Hawai'i, but he knew the same did not hold true for those he employed. He realized in particular that conditions were harsh for the wartime working class in the archipelago. "[They] worked long hours," he recalled years later, "10 and 12 hours a day, and under blackout conditions that were pretty disagreeable. The mills were all blacked out[,] so that it was stifling hot." That was one of the many reasons why he thought that unionization spread like a prairie fire throughout the islands, transforming the politics of Hawai'i in the process. These onerous working conditions were "one of the reasons that the men were so easy to organize, unionize after the war," he observed. "[T]hey just have been working so long and so hard that they wanted a vacation. A strike, in a large part, was a vacation to them[;] most of them had pretty large savings because they couldn't spend money during the war." As he recollected, still in disbelief, "No new automobiles came in! There were no new appliances. The plantation employees just sort of had forced savings so they weren't hurt financially [when the first strike occurred in 1946]."[1]

This first strike—from which the union emerged triumphant and the archipelago was transformed definitively—was the beginning of what one study termed a "three year 'showdown' which has been compared to the American Civil War," this time a fight between the radical left and conservatives,[2] a struggle (particularly with the Left triumphing) that was far distant from anything that occurred on the mainland. It was a confrontation in which the union entered united. Balloting on 33 sugar plantations resulted in 99 percent of workers voting for a strike, as they demanded a minimum cash wage of 65 cents per hour, overtime pay after 40 hours per week, and a union shop. The Sugar Strike, which began on 1 September 1946, lasted 79 days, with the union emerging victorious—a gigantic step in transforming Hawai'i from an apartheid outpost to the closest thing to social democracy that existed under the US flag. This was the culmination of a process whereby roughly 30,000 workers

The ILWU organized sugar workers like these—en masse—as World War II was winding down. Courtesy of Anne Rand Library, ILWU–San Francisco.

predominantly from the sugar, pineapple, and waterfront industries had joined the ILWU in the relatively brief period from 1944 to 1946.[3]

Months before this eruption of labor unrest, Philip E. Spalding, president of the Hawaii Sugar Planters' Association had told Governor Ingram Stainback that because of a "sharp continuing decline in the labor supply" and stiff global competition, he wanted more labor imported from the Philippines.[4] The plantation bosses were in an advantageous position to execute their dreams of manipulating labor. In Maui the only newspaper was owned "lock, stock and barrel," as Frank Thompson put it, by the Baldwins, a leading family, and was in a position to massage public opinion. The island's territorial senator, Harold Rice, was a former Republican; he had married a Baldwin, who afterward died. The senator had a "big ranch up on the slopes of Haleakala," said Thompson, and was flush with cash—not the typical profile of an ILWU supporter.[5] The fact remained, Thompson emphasized, that it was "the Baldwin interests that practically own the whole island of Maui,"[6] where sugar was king.

Nonetheless, the Sugar Strike demonstrated that the Big Five were facing a union that was not without weapons. In early 1945 a union official referred contemptuously to this "tightly held feudalistic, monopolistic system" that "sprawls like a many threaded spider web over every possible consumer and wholesale interest." "[The] monopolistic control exercised by these five companies over every facet of life in the islands," the official stated, "has obliterated in the past many attempts at organization of labor." But times were changing.[7]

The workers were hardly prone to accept a status quo that allowed Rice and the Baldwins to live like royalty, while they were ciphers by comparison. As the time for the strike approached, Jack Hall reported, "Our membership [is] plenty hot at this writing. There is more strike talk, slow-down threats, feigned illness, etc., than we have seen for many a day. Conditions are damn intolerable and we are going to be hard pressed to keep the lid on." Workers were "completely fed up," he said, and were straining on the leash. Filipino workers were so discontented that one leader, Pablo Manlapit, had inquired if the ILWU would authorize him "to organize [the] CIO in the Philippines."[8]

However, unlike the Sugar Planters' Association, Hall did not believe that Hawai'i suffered from a dearth of labor, at least not to the same extent as the association did. He concluded, "[The] sugar [industry] with a payroll covering 54,000 workers in 1932 produced slightly in excess of one million tons of sugar. During 1945 with little more than 20,000 adult workers it is producing nearly 900,000 tons."[9]

Kawano, on the other hand, stressed in August 1945 that acceleration of unionization was as much a defensive measure as it was an offensive one. For it was he who recognized that "there may be thousands of defense workers and servicemen who may be stranded or who may wish to remain in Hawaii" and that "these men will compete with the local workers for jobs," particularly on the waterfront. Bulking up with plantation workers was a formidable hedge against such an employer maneuver.[10]

Jack Hall was essential to labor's upsurge[11]—but so was Kawano, who reported in mid-1945 that the union had "grown by leaps and bounds during the last few months."[12] By the spring of 1946 Frank Thompson was enthusiastically speaking in similar terms.[13] A few months later, ILWU leader Henry Schmidt echoed this observation.[14] Thompson, the ILWU representative in the archipelago, had yet to dispense with some of his less attractive habits, but even his typically narrow approach to those he purported to represent could not obscure the real progress that was being made. "Beginning in November [1945], less than 3,000 out of 9,000 sugar workers on the island of Hawaii were dues paying members. The figures will show," he rejoiced, "that at the end of April, practically 6,500 sugar workers are now dues paying workers and more are being organized every day in all three of the existing sugar locals on the islands of Hawaii."[15]

The ILWU was rampaging through the sugar industry, busily organizing sugar workers with pent-up demands. Even before the war concluded, they had won the right to bargain for one-third of the entire industry in the archipelago.[16] During that same prewar period, the union won the right to represent workers at the largest sugar mill in the islands, the HC&S plantation; owned by the Baldwins, it was also billed as the second-largest sugar mill in the world. Stretching across the full width of the isthmus of Maui, it was about 10 miles long and 4 miles wide.[17]

Union organizers were almost giddy about the prospects of organizing these behemoths. In response to management's cry of a labor shortage, the legislature had mandated that children in the seventh grade or above could work. With their children thrust into Hobbesian competition with them, working parents were outraged by this policy and prepared the ground for a walkout.[18]

These were powerful winds impelling islanders toward militant action. Days after Japan's surrender, Bert Nakano was complaining about the controversy rising in Hilo as an outgrowth of the employment of schoolchildren in the plantations. This meant, he complained, that "these schoolchildren must sacrifice one day of their school study per week." Perversely, though management was reportedly short of workers, it was seeking children to labor— though it was loathe to employ their fathers with overtime work that would have obviated the need for child labor.[19]

In September 1946, Bob McElrath in one of his earliest broadcasts for the union, informed listeners huddled around their radios that "one of the reasons why 25,000 sugar workers in Hawaii are on strike today is that the industry has rejected their demand on housing." At the time, management provided workers with pitiful quarters, for which they paid excessively. The

Postwar Hawai'i was rocked repeatedly by strikes—akin to this one in 1946—spearheaded by a union that critics charged was dominated by Communists. Courtesy of Anne Rand Library, ILWU–San Francisco.

ILWU, said McElrath, wanted management to "account for the money it deducted from the employees' pay envelopes in the past six years for housing additions, replacements and maintenance." Harry Shigemitsu, leader of the union at the Kahuku plantation, bemoaned the existence of "'open ditches running through the whole length of the camp, with everything under the sun flowing down.'" He added, "'Often-times the ditches are chocked with dead animals and other refuse, and worms all over them.'" Then there were the putrid outhouses. During the night if children needed to relieve themselves, they often simply used the ditch rather than tempting fate by visiting what was euphemistically considered a toilet. More than two-thirds of all plantation houses had no indoor plumbing, and the size of most of these shacks averaged less than 500 square feet for a family of five, with as many as eight persons living in a room of about 100 square feet.[20] Living on a plantation, claimed Frank Thompson, was the equivalent of an "island reform school."[21]

   The sugar negotiations were tense, as both sides knew that a victory for the union would be transformative. As pulses raced and tempers rose in intensity,

Jack Hall reported to Louis Goldblatt, "Strike votes are rolling in. Waianae Company voted 116 to 1 in favor of the strike. In the five departments at Olaa where balloting was completed the vote was 164 to 0." Hall noted that "the prime concern of our members," which came up repeatedly, was the "question of whether or not they can remain in plantation housing during the strike,"[22] for as pitiful as it was, company housing was better than sleeping in the great outdoors.

This strike was the climax of a remarkable labor advance. In a brief 18-month period, from January 1944 to July 1945, the sugar industry in Hawai'i had been almost completely organized. Organization of the pineapple workers followed shortly thereafter, and by the middle of 1946 workers in every basic industry, with few lagging exceptions, had been organized. Before the war the ILWU had completed the organization of stevedores, except on Maui, and since six of the seven stevedoring firms were controlled by the sugar barons, this accomplishment set the stage for the postwar surge. Hawai'i's sugar industry represented the first agricultural industry under the US flag to be completely unionized. But it was the 1946 strike that intimidated the theretofore seemingly invulnerable elite, who complained that the vaunted Big Five had been shrunk to the "Big One"—with that being the ILWU.[23]

"Whenever I think of democracy," union lawyer Harriet Bouslog told an island crowd on Labor Day in the early 1950s, "I think of a meeting I attended at Lahaina, Maui[,] in November 1946 at the end of the 79 day sugar strike." There were "600 to 700 people at that meeting," she recalled with stirring pride. Having been through an enervating strike, "they were people whose children needed shoes and clothes and food," she noted. "Everything said at the meeting was translated into three languages"—English, Japanese, and Ilocano—and "no less than 40 or 50 people spoke." Yet the message, the language difficulties notwithstanding, was clear: the ability of these workers to hold out against the elite meant that Hawai'i would never be the same again.[24]

This strike, which left mills idle and irrigation ditches dry, was one of the most significant in the islands' history. As a result, for example, the workers at Ewa doubled their annual wages and then the emboldened ILWU moved aggressively into politics, and not only in November 1946. The next year, union members helped elect fifteen Democrats to the state's lower house, where, as one critic put it, they "took seats behind the [legislators] to see that they voted right."[25] Thus, after transforming the economy, they had then transformed politics. One study concluded that the strike "frightened the employers" and "created a general awe of the union power on the part of workers, employers and the general public." In addition, "for the first time in Hawaiian history the employers had been soundly and deeply thwarted," the study observed.[26] This turnabout appeared to be linked to trends then occurring in Australia and New Zealand, whose influence in the archipelago cannot be discounted.[27]

Union members and supporters march in 1946. Courtesy of Anne Rand Library, ILWU–San Francisco.

But respect would not come easily. There was good reason for management to be angry about the strike, for sugar plantations had been gushing fabulous amounts of cash for decades, and from its viewpoint the enhanced strength of the union compromised the reliable source of profit. Management also had good reason to believe that a loss in the sugar fields would translate easily into losses at the ballot box. Waialua Agricultural Company (WAC) was one of 34 sugar plantations doing business in Hawai'i at the time of the strike. In 1945 these had produced 821,216 tons of raw sugar, and of this amount WAC alone produced 56,193 tons, or slightly less than 7 percent, and thus it ranked as the third-largest producer of this commodity in the territory during this pivotal year. At the time of the strike, these sugar plantations employed 29,517 workers, approximately 28 percent of the total number of persons privately employed in the islands. During the war, Hawai'i produced about 13 percent of all sugar, both beet and cane, that was distributed for consumption in the United States, and given the pervasive sweet tooth in this nation, the archipelago was an essential part of the appetite that obtained under the Stars and Stripes.

This, along with the high perishability of sugarcane, gave the union quite an advantage. For this commodity starts to deteriorate immediately after harvesting and must be processed into sugar, syrup, or molasses within a few hours after it has been burned or severed from the ground. Cane-growing land in Hawai'i was crisscrossed with a network of plantation field roads and a narrow-gauged plantation-owned railroad, making these plantations resemble industrial factories. Employees worked in the fields and moved from one area to another, depending upon the program of plowing, planting, irrigating, fertilizing, applying herbicides and insecticides, weeding, and harvesting. At WAC there were ten worker classifications and hourly wage rates, ranging from a minimum of 80 cents to a maximum of $1.38. Herbicide gangs, in mortal danger due to the noxiousness to which they were subjected, were composed of 13 to 19 men. Fertilizer gangs had 12 men. After the construction of firebreaks was completed, a crew of 6 men proceeded to set fires among the firebreaks. Tractors, cane-loading machines, portable air compressors, and diesel and gas locomotives were serviced daily by 6 men; there were 15 employees in an electric shop, and about 25 carpenters, 5 painters, and 6 plumbers. There was a stable with 35 horses and mules, and a number of workers attended to them. For efficient operation, sugar mills had to be closed down annually for general repair, given the complexities involved. WAC owned 820 houses for workers, all of which were located on the plantation and gave the appearance of a feudal arrangement.[28]

Before the strike began, Hall was informed that the quality of medical service provided to plantation workers as perquisites, like the housing provided, was "poor, if not dangerously bad," since "doctors are incompetent" and "hospital facilities are often inadequate." A widely circulated story held that plantation doctors engaged in extensive sterilization of workers, reportedly without their consent. Thus, the "sterilization rate in the territorial hospitals," it was reported with concern, "is far higher and unjustifiably higher than the national average." This heinous practice was presumably done by the doctors when they felt that families of workers were getting too large. "Closely related to the feudal colonialism of the plantations," this was "a matter we should expose," Hall was informed. It was also "closely related to the tightly held monopoly of Honolulu medicine, which has no 'reciprocity' (i.e.[,] refuses to let doctors practice here unless they have interned here[,] and won't let mainland doctors come in here)." Furthermore, "no governmental agency or medical association exercises any real supervision over standards of plantation doctors," as "all plantation doctors are haoles[,]with real discrimination against good, non-haole physicians."[29]

The working conditions were not ideal either. Thomas Yagi, a Wailuku Sugar laborer who began working for the union in 1944, noted subsequently, "Some of the longshore organizers were deported from Maui. That's how strict it was." Organizers would "go in the night, meeting with various workers" surreptitiously, he recalled. "We didn't have an automatic dues check-off," Yagi said, and "as a result, we went over to various individuals [to] pick up the dues money." This necessity, however, had the advantage of bonding more adhesively the shop stewards to the members with whom they were mandated to have frequent contact. The union quite handily won the election to become a bargaining agent for the workers in March 1945, and the following year it was on strike.[30] Because of such victories, as of 1946 the ILWU was representing, according to Hall, "35,000 workers regularly employed in Hawaii's basic industries," which meant that it was the most powerful organized force in the archipelago.[31]

Eddie Lapa, who toiled at Waialua, recalled that in the heavy equipment shop, there was a "lot of favoritism"; for example, "if you happen to be a relative of a supervisor," he said, there was a "better chance in getting promoted." Those not in this charmed category would "have to work two times harder." As a result, support for the strike was strong at Waialua, just as support for organizing the union months earlier was similarly formidable. Lapa, a key organizer in the latter effort, recalled how he lobbied his fellow workers: "I would call them to the restroom, saying 'I want to talk to you.' [The worker] would come to me in the restroom and we would be sitting—he would be sitting in his bowl. I would sit in my bowl and I would pass the card underneath." Lapa would ask the worker to sign the card. Lapa continued: "[The worker] said, 'I'll think about it.' I tell him, no, do it now." Lapa noted that "many were afraid," though there were ethnic cleavages in this regard. "The Japanese and the Filipinos were much more cohesive," he said. "But [with] the other . . . groups that were born here, uh, to me," he added hesitantly, "[there] was a—a little stumbling block." Similar trends obtained during the 1946 strike, though these apprehensions were to erode, not least because of growing confidence in the union. Hence, when the strike was called, "we had at least ninety-eight to ninety-nine percent [in] favor of the strike," Lapa declared. This solidarity was also evidenced during the strike at meetings that occurred "maybe every other day at the union hall"; of the hundreds of workers at Waialua, the overwhelming preponderance attended these meetings. The workers developed a "victory garden," where vegetables were grown and shared among workers and their families, while fishermen and hunters acted similarly. This was part of the secret of Hawai'i's record of successful strikes: it was not easy to starve in this earthly paradise. Free movies were screened, virtually every night; there were games and sports activities too that kept workers engaged and bonded.[32]

The crude racial difference that separated the masses of workers from the "boss haole elite" also provided fuel for struggle—there was only one scab among the hundreds of workers. When ILWU leaders showed up, they brought with them another shock, simply because of the way they looked. "We don't see too many white people," said Lapa, and when they did, it was mostly as putative or actual management bosses. So when J. R. "Bob" Robertson, from the San Francisco headquarters, came to Waialua and told the assembled that the boss was the "worst enemy" of the workers, they were stunned. "We never heard things like that in our life," Lapa noted. "This guy was so aggressive." Apparently Robertson inspired the workers, since Waialua went on to have "more strikes than all the other units compared." Lapa added, "We went on strike in '46, we went on strike in '50, we went on strike in '56, and we went on strike in '58."[33]

But it was not just Robertson who impressed the workers. They were also taken by A. Q. and Bob McElrath. It was "these two," said Lapa, who were the "most influential people, husband and wife, that organized this union"; they "were the nucleus," clearly "instrumental" in so many ways. For example, A. Q. McElrath was the one who helped Lapa learn "how to read and understand union contracts."[34]

Joe "Blur" Kealalio, an indigene who was also a union stalwart, had a similar evaluation of the leadership negotiating on his behalf, terming both Hall and Goldblatt "terrific guy[s]," though the former was a "hard drinker." Kealalio also described Hall as a "hard worker," and of Goldblatt he said, "When he speaks, you know, he do [*sic*] a lot of illustrating, you know, lotta movement in his hands [and] in his body, his eyes." Robert McElrath, another key participant, was a "loner" but "amazing," a "real knowledgeable person" who was "not a big guy" but "small" and "rough"—"You don't push [him] around." His spouse, A. Q. McElrath, "was always around . . . doing this, doing that," Kealalio said. "Always." Union attorney Harriet Bouslog he found to be "just a tiger" and a "go-getter" who "was involved even with, uh, some of the decision making we had to make in the union" and was "tremendous." He also had high praise for Yasuki Arakaki: "everything is go see Yasu," during the strike. The workers came to "find out he had the place [the critically strategic Olaa plantation] "sort of, hey, real organized." Arakaki and his Nisei and Issei counterparts were "the backbone," Kealalio emphasized. "The backbone. The Japanese. On the waterfront [too] they were the backbone."[35]

Yet with all her personal help to Lapa, the energy poured by union staffers like A. Q. McElrath into making sure that strikers remained cohesive proved to be essential in the strike's success. To keep the members involved and bonded, union member George Kruse remembered a volleyball tournament, singing, dancing, telling jokes, and softball.[36] Likewise, Martha Kruse recalled that she "had just had a baby the year before" and was understandably concerned about the future, but her worries were diverted by the union's activities, which included "staging amateur programs" and sponsoring "women's athletics." Such recreational outlets were even more critical because the times were "very stressful," Kruse said, with even her six-year-old getting caught up in the emotions and calling "a blond, blue-eyed classmate, a scab." Kruse boasted, "I thrive on stress," which was useful, since the strike brought so much of it.[37]

Tony Bise agreed with the idea that A. Q. McElrath, a frail though dynamic woman of Chinese descent, was critical to the union's ultimate success, which flowered in 1946. "I learned a lot from her," said union member Bise, who worked at Ewa. "In fact," he added, years after the furor the strike had brought had diminished, "all what I know today about membership and everything, was through her. She teach me a lot. And I admire her, you know. Because she's the type of woman that really works for the workers." So moved was Bise by her energy that he "asked her one day, how come you working for the union? You know, when you can get a good paying job with some top companies[?]" Bise continued: "She said no, she grew up as a poor woman and she think she want to help the people. And she did a lot of work for . . . especially those people that going back to the Philippines." This was at a time when "even the church was a little segregated," he recalled with exasperation.[38]

In short, it was hard to disentangle the success of the union—and the strike—from the person of the slender, almond-colored A. Q. McElrath: she was instrumental in developing the sophisticated level of organization that proved so important in bringing management to retreat from its initial intransigence. During the strike, she recalled later, "each unit had, first of all, a negotiating committee, a political action committee [and] a housing committee"; then there was a "unit strike strategy committee," and under that was a "unit bumming committee," tasked with requisitioning "money or foodstuff." There was also a "morale committee" and a "unit credit committee." She concluded, "If you multiply twenty-eight thousand workers who went out on strike by three, or at that time probably by four [i.e., the number in a family] you had practically a quarter of the population of the Territory of Hawaii who was on strike. The active workers plus their family members." Targeting them all were "union papers, unit bulletins, division bulletins [and] territorial bulletins," all in three languages.[39]

The "Territorial Sugar Strike Machinery" was illustrated in a sophisticated flowchart that had a "Strike Strategy Committee" at the top, linked to, e.g., finance and purchasing, negotiations, publicity, and "liaison & communication." Beneath that was an "Island Strike Strategy Committee," whose subcommittees covered finance, publicity, transportation, and "liaison & communications." Next on the chart was a "Unit Strike Strategy Committee," which stood above subcommittees on morale, women's corps, picket organizing, police, publicity, relief, finance, and transportation. Then on the flowchart came subcommittee responsibilities designated as store, water, planters, kitchen, garden, miscellaneous food, medical, purchasing, bookkeeping, and fundraising, followed by subcommittees for kitchen, hunting, fishing, garden, merchants, and farmers.[40] Still, despite her formidable skills, McElrath had plenty of assistance. Yasuki Arakaki claims—and not inaccurately—that it was he who "drafted the strategy for the sugar workers in Hawaii," noting that "the manual is still there."[41]

Avelino "Abba" Ramos, born on the Big Island in 1934 and a witness to the 1946 tumult, was also a pivotal player. He recalled that the Big Five had "horizontal and vertical control," as signified by their being able to take the cane out of the ground, process it, and ship it to shore, where it was placed on one of their ships to be sent eastward to the mainland. There were 14 plantations all along the Hamakua coast, stretching from the port of Hilo all the way up to Hamakua. And each plantation had camps for hundreds of workers, Ramos recalled. The "camps were separated by ethnic groups," he said, which facilitated lack of cohesion among laborers. Perhaps more debilitating were the herbicides and insecticides often promiscuously sprayed on the crops—they "stunted the growth of the weeds and it became like a mutation," he said. "We used a lot of arsenic," he added, and other specialties from Dow Chemical, whose skill in producing elements that destroyed weeds and workers alike was notorious.[42]

With such toxins poisoning labor and the atmosphere alike, it would seem inevitable that workers would rise in rebellion. A central problem was the forced separation compelled by management, which segregated workers by nationality in various camps and, not accidentally, hampered united action. The union faced a dilemma in how to confront this matter, since workers spoke different languages, which militated against addressing them all in one tongue and, naturally, did not facilitate the desired cohesiveness. The union chose not to hold separate meetings of different language groups, feeling that this would only feed divisiveness, but it had a bevy of interpreters. The union also chose to print summaries of general membership meeting discussions in Ilocano and Japanese, as well as English.[43]

Besides toxins and tongues of various sorts, there were other formidable barriers to labor's progress, among which were the simple logistics of coordinating a strike on far-flung islands.[44] When Frank Thompson headed to Hana just before an important meeting was to commence in the run-up to the strike authorization vote, the union, as it often did, had hired a pilot to take him there in a small plane, but to Thompson's dismay, there was no airport and the "pilot had to put the plane down in a cow pasture." The frantic pilot "had to land his two-motored outfit with a crosswind blowing across the pasture," and the frazzled duo "almost ran out of the field into the brush on the opposite side." This was "big fun," he noted archly, "if you have no nerves."[45]

Yet a potential plane crash, as unnerving as it was, was minor to what Thompson had encountered earlier. For in the period preceding the strike, a massive tsunami had struck the islands. "Our membership was hit and hit hard by the wave," said Jack Hall. "Had it come an hour earlier or later the loss of life would have been ten times as great. As it is, we have 115 identified dead and 57 still missing, probably dead." On one island the local union's office and records—"everything"—were gone; a shaken Hall admitted that the "fury of a little water is more than a little frightful."[46] A "huge tidal wave . . . hit these islands," said Thompson, and "all of the exclusive beach homes and property of the Baldwins, and the military officers' clubs . . . situated along a nine mile stretch of beach from Kahului to Paia have been totally destroyed." Joseph Kaholokula, an indigene who served as leader of the union's Local 144, "was able to escape with his wife and three kids and nothing else," Thompson recalled. "His car, his home, furniture and everything else went out with the tide." The "destruction on all the islands is considerable," Thompson concluded. "Hilo on the Big Island is pretty well wrecked," along with "everything from Bert Nakano's office." It was a "good thing that these island people get up about 5 o'clock in the morning," he said wearily. "Otherwise the loss of life would have been terrific. [A]s it was the wave hit about 7 AM when most people are already up and about." There was also "considerable wreckage in Honolulu along Waikiki," he added." Senator Rice, who had a "$100,000.00 beach home here in Maui on the beach[, could] not even find the foundation where the home was."[47]

Such tumult was distressing, though for workers it was comparable to the disruption of the dislocation already induced by the strike. Sadao Kobayashi, for example, could testify to the stress induced by this militant walkout. "I worked for [a] dollar thirty-three cents a day," he said, involving "nine hours of work" as a carpenter. Perhaps because of the discipline induced by the need to improve paltry wages or the rigor brought by the union—and for various other reasons—the union "didn't have no strikebreakers during those days." What they did have, he recalled haltingly, was "something like [a] court, kangaroo court," to try alleged transgressors. "We used to bring the person" to an informal hearing, he said, to obtain a "court finding" in cases where, for example, "some of the boys got lazy" and "didn't want to turn out to picket duty." So, he observed, "we have the police going around, our union police," and "we bring that person in and we ask them a question." The general question posed was "What's the matter with you[?]" and a suitable answer was demanded. There were communication problems, since many of the workers didn't speak English, "so we all talk Pidgin," he said, e.g. "half Filipino," though "sometimes we talk English." Yet despite these formidable hurdles the union was able to prevail. "We got a two dollar raise [per] day" and a "medical plan," plus significant housing improvements, Kobayashi recalled. Such emoluments meant that this father of seven was able to put "five of them [through] universities."[48] Workers like Kobayashi realized that there might be a pot of gold at the end of the rainbow, and this helped him—and them—to persevere.[49]

Just in case of recalcitrance, workers at Waipahu were—according to the Honolulu Police Department—"threatening a number of small merchants[,] declaring that stores would be picketed unless the merchants gave support to the strike."[50] To hammer the point home, 6,000 marchers took to the streets of Hilo, presenting a picture of labor to which the islands were hardly accustomed.[51]

Yet with all this, perhaps the ultimate insult was management's rejection of a contract clause targeting racial discrimination. As one ILWU official put it, "The industry claims there is no discrimination; hence, there is no necessity for such a clause." Yet it took no particular insight to notice that daily newspapers carried advertisements for employees or lodgers, specifying "race" or national descent. "Differentials are maintained in wages and housing accommodations . . . because of race or national descent," the union objected.[52]

It seemed that this campaign against racism was noticeably deemed irksome by the elite. An editorial in a Honolulu newspaper declared that the very act of raising this matter was needlessly divisive, an assertion to which the ILWU took immediate umbrage, observing that many whites "feel that bringing the subject up is ungracious, impolite and should be taboo."[53] Still, the question of racism continued to fester, with those of Japanese origin continuing to raise this matter sharply.[54]

The union's own internal problems with racial wrangling did not aid the union in fighting the external battle in this important sphere. Besides, there was a not-so-subtle reason that management did not desire an alteration of the status quo on the sensitive matter of racial discrimination. It thought that this status quo was a trump card, particularly playing upon real and imagined differences between those with roots in the Philippines and those of Japanese ancestry. After the war started, management began to import more laborers from the Philippines, which had just undergone a brutal occupation by Tokyo. In addition to persistent reports of tensions, as one analyst put it, "between Filipinos and Japanese," there was dissension between single and married men, the former wanting to strike, and the latter not wanting to. When the strike did erupt, rumors circulated of pickets being armed. As one man carrying a placard put it, "'I came here from the Philippines to work. I killed Japs before and I can do it again if necessary.'"[55]

"We had guys among the new Filipinos," recalled Goldblatt, "who had belonged to the Huks," the fierce anti-Tokyo guerrilla fighters. Then, he said, "you had the Japanese here who felt that they were really maltreated during the war[;] they had been kicked around from hell to breakfast. There wasn't a single Japanese family here that wasn't hurt. Either an older man who had been barred from whatever his employment was; like you take the Issei who were working on the waterfront, and there were a tremendous number of them. They were barred from the waterfront." Goldblatt also mentioned a particular source of tension between two groups: "[The] Filipinos had the worst camps; your Portuguese and particularly Portuguese lunas had the best ones." The "perquisite system had to go," he maintained, referring to the peculiar system of lodging for workers that had distinct feudal overtones; it was a "real holdover from colonial days" and contrasted sharply with the commodious housing enjoyed by the elite. Then there was the "vicious anti-Semitism" that Goldblatt maintained was aimed at him specifically. Cartoonists had a field day, he said, with depictions of the "kolea bird," which had a "special significance" in that this ornithological favorite was "the same thing as a plover[,] . . . a bird that steals from other birds' nests."[56]

Thus, just before the strike was launched, management chose to import 6,000 fresh new laborers from the Philippines, on the premise that they would be effective strikebreakers. Yet the executives no doubt were quite surprised when these workers came strolling down the gangplank with ILWU buttons pinned to their shirts, thanks to organizing on the trans-Pacific journey by union allies in the similarly progressive National Union of Marine Cooks and Stewards. "When those employers saw those buttons, man, their faces dropped a foot-and-a-half," Frank Thompson said exultingly.[57]

Plantation executives, said Thompson, "were up bright and early rubbing their hands and smiling all over" before the truth hit them. The workers arrived "packed like sardines" in the hulk of a ship—it was "in pretty bad shape and worse than a cattle pen," he thought. "I have never seen a more dirtier and more rotten mess in all my life for human beings to live in," Thompson confessed, adding that the "smell in this hold would almost knock you down." But, instead, felled were the dreams of management.[58]

It was an error, thought Hall, to bow to the importation of these 6,000 laborers. He chose instead to "violently protest shipping . . . Philippine labor to Hawaii plantations while veterans are still overseas awaiting transportation"; this "will aggravate anticipated unemployment here in six months," he announced in late 1945.[59] "In principle we have no objection to the temporary importation of labor," he said; "residents of the Philippines have suffered much under the heel of Japanese militarism and unless they are thoroughly indoctrinated with the plain fact that local residents of Japanese ancestry are just as bitterly against such imperialism as they themselves, an ugly racial situation might result." That potential problem was part of management's idea, it was believed. The proposed migrants were to come from Ilocos Norte, Ilocos Sur, Abra, and Pangasinan, "from whence came most of those Philippine nationals presently residing in [Hawai'i]."[60] Management "did not need" these workers, according to Hall. "It was a criminal mistake," he emphasized, "to bring them here. But since they are here, we must see to it that they are kept here and not pressured to leave. Therefore we must make the severance pay attractive enough to make them want to leave with enough money to make a new start in their home country."[61]

As Yasuki Arakaki recalled, Hall was afraid that these recent migrants had been "mistreated" by Tokyo's military in their homeland and would not "assimilate" with "local Japanese" and might become "scabs." But the new arrivals proved to be "very hearty" and took to their union "membership cards" like fish to water. Some of them even sang "Japanese military songs" learned during the occupation.[62]

As the tempestuousness of the strike merged seamlessly with the excitement generated by the 1946 elections—the first since the war's conclusion—passions rose accordingly, along with allegations of racism. Marshall McEuen, leader of the islands' CIO Political Action Committee—and thus at the confluence of these two trends—reported during the height of the strike that some ugly stories were circulating in Honolulu about a local radio personality who was "told that he might have double the salary formerly paid if he would take the following attitude as a commentator: 1. play up white supremacy. 2. play down labor. 3. play up management." Such a fetid atmosphere could not be helpful to a striking union whose members overwhelmingly had "skins [that] were not quite light enough."[63] Similarly, Major General Wilton B. Persons reported credible allegations that "racial discrimination is being practiced by the Hawaiian Air Depot"; as the strike was reaching a crescendo, simultaneously there was a "protest against the policy of housing colored and white employees together" that had been "presented orally to the Commanding General of the Hawaiian Air Materiel Group by a group of Caucasian girls."[64]

Thus, it was not surprising that in such an environment, when the 21 members of management sat at the negotiating table across from the 34 members of the ILWU, this ticklish matter of racial discrimination loomed large. "We could document these cases by the thousands," said Goldblatt, speaking of cases of racism. Union leader Harry Shigemitsu pointed out that "haole houses are always repaired[,] for one thing," while "Orientals always have to pay for repairs." Another union leader, Amos Ignacio, declared, "A manager on Hawaii told me: 'as far as I am concerned any plantation manager I ever have will always be a haole.'" Jack Hall made a general denunciation of "race discrimination in hiring, housing, promotion, etc.," but the other side continued to insist that "the presence of the [non-discrimination] clause itself [tends] to promote discord on racial lines."[65]

Henry Walker, a cog in the management machine who crossed swords with the union during this time, recalled that "once the contract was negotiated, Jack Hall ran the strike, but not the negotiations. Lou Goldblatt did that." Goldblatt "used to discipline Jack Hall publicly in the negotiations," Walker recalled. "We can't say that," he admitted, "but it's true. He used to yell at him." Goldblatt, he said, was a "wild man" in negotiations and was not above seeking

The union often had to confront violence when it initiated strikes, compelling heightened forms of organization, such as "union guards." Courtesy of Anne Rand Library, ILWU–San Francisco.

to intimidate. This was part of Goldblatt's attempting to "handle the theatrical portion of the negotiation," Walker observed, whereas Hall was "very able" and "would do the nitty-gritty work." It was a "remarkable crew," with Goldblatt being "fiery, imaginative, well educated [and] bright," and an "actor" besides; Hall, "a man of value, of character," who was "thinking only of the worker [being] poorly paid"; and Bridges, "who was probably a Marxist," with the resultant class rigor. Yet generally at the negotiating table it was Goldblatt who was in charge, and he "enjoyed the pleasures of alcohol" and the "pleasure of ladies"; Goldblatt "was quite a ladies' man," Walker noted, and a "good looking guy." Hall was "quite different"; he had an "inner . . . torment" and felt deeply that "there has to be an uplifting of the downtrodden masses," Walker conceded, adding that he "really felt that way," that it "was a serious thing with him." But the "moment of truth" came when Bridges "would arrive at the negotiations with a quart of milk," Walker recounted. "And he'd smack that down on the table and he said, 'I've got to go get out of here, let's wind this thing up.' And in two days, the thing would be wound up. His signal for that was a quart of milk." But what allowed Bridges, Hall, and Goldblatt to perform so credibly was a united membership behind them. Union members, driven by war-imposed burdens, were straining to revolt. "I think," said Walker, "there were times when the union felt it needed to strike because it needed to reestablish its control of its members, [and] '46 was probably one such occasion."[66]

This awe-inspiring strike led directly to the local Red Scare as the union's opponents, rather than connecting labor unrest and subsequent victories to deteriorating working conditions and paltry wages, instead began to think dark thoughts about an alleged conspiracy of Communists. It is true that the party did revive in the wake of the war's end. An official inquiry found that as of 1936 there were about 60 Reds in Hawai'i among the waterfront and maritime workers, with Harry Kamoku given credit for having organized the first CP unit ever to exist in the archipelago; it was composed wholly of stevedores in Hilo. But concomitant with the rise of the ILWU in 1944, there rose similarly a Communist Party, whose premise was that class struggle was the motive force of society, that workers generated value that was appropriated by their bosses, that these same employers controlled the political process to their benefit—and that workers needed a revolutionary party like the Communists to overturn this rigged game. Thus, from 1945 to 1947 there existed, it was reported, at least 15 basic units of the CP, 11 of which were located on O'ahu. Membership had increased dramatically, with the stevedores of O'ahu split into two cells. Arakaki of the ILWU was seen as one of the top Red leaders, and total membership had virtually tripled since 1936, with most of this growth being among the population of Japanese origin and with those of Chinese ancestry hardly represented in this growth.[67]

Jack Kawano, who was in the vortex of these swirling events, recalled subsequently that his party comrade Dwight Freeman "said that our policy on recruits" should be "very stringent as far as the uptown people or the white collar people were concerned," presumably because informants and other disruptive elements traditionally emerged from this stratum. But "in the event of people working in basic industries," Kawano was informed, "such as the waterfront, pineapple or sugar industries," then "it was not necessary for him or her to understand the theory of Marxism"—a policy that at once stressed militant activism and increased membership rolls. This differentiation also reflected the Communists' theory about the strategic importance of workers in these basic industries who produced wealth, confronted management more critically as a result, and thus were essentially positioned to push for radical change.[68]

At the Smith Act trial, Kawano spoke of the time when the CP decided to reactivate, telling the jurors that there had been "quite a bit of change" in the ranks: "[Jack Hall] stated when we de-activated there were anywhere between 60 to 70 members. But since then, during the war, a lot of members have left the islands." According to Kawano, Hall "also stated that since we had organized so many people into the ILWU that we do some concentration work within the membership of the ILWU," i.e., political education and recruiting. That was followed by a party gathering on the grass lawn on the Waikīkī end of Ala Moana Park, with about 40 members present, but in the next year or two, buoyed by the 1946 strike victory and other triumphs, membership increased to almost 200. These growing numbers led to a CP convention in 1946 as the dust kicked up by the strike had yet to settle; it was held, said Kawano, "in the YMCA camp in Kokokahi, Kailua or Kaneohe," with approximately 50 delegates present and Reinecke chairing the event.[69]

The CP cooperated with the similarly inclined California Labor School in San Francisco in imbuing workers and union leaders alike with the kind of intellectual understanding that would be required in order to confront the Big Five effectively. There was an incentive for workers to participate, for as David Jenkins, the Labor School's leader, informed Bridges, "veterans who are coming to the school not only receive $65 a month if they are single and $90 if they are married, but all school costs, tuition and textbooks are paid for by the Veterans' Administration." As Hawai'i workers were arriving in this ocean-bound metropolis, Jenkins was reporting that "some 35 Negro veterans from Alabama, Tennessee and Georgia are taking advantage of this opportunity who ordinarily could not go to school in their native South."[70]

Thus, early in 1946, months before the strike, special seminars were established that featured such island stalwarts as Thomas Yagi, a leader in Maui; Yasuki Arakaki, president of the Olaa local; Harry Kamoku, leader of the longshore local in Hilo; and others—10 in all. Topics included "History of the Labor Movement," "why workers should understand economics," "History of the ILWU," "understanding the contract," and so on. An overarching theme was the notion that "all workers are brothers regardless of race, color or creed." These classes went further by underlining that "to try to 'Americanize' everybody in the islands by destroying their whole cultural inheritance would be saying that their cultures are inferior." Though it was said that "of course, all groups should learn to read and speak English," this was coupled with the admonition that racism should be made "illegal."[71]

Thomas Yagi, born in Maui in 1922 and of Okinawan origin, was among those who found the Labor School extremely valuable.[72] A critical part of their curriculum was classes in the "theory and practice of trade unionism" and in "political economy." The lineup in 1946—the year of the pivotal strike—included classes in "stewards' and officers' duties," "recent strike struggles," "union building," "labor law and legislation," "world labor: past, present and future," "collective bargaining and research," and much more.[73] Arakaki, who was deeply influenced by both Mao Zedong and Ho Chi Minh, was so impressed with his experience in San Francisco that upon his return to the islands he wrote a pamphlet on how to conduct strikes.[74]

The key man in San Francisco was neither Mao nor Ho but Harry—Harry Bridges. He had defeated the best that San Francisco had to offer in 1934 and had the kind of experience in devising strike strategy that was largely absent among his opponents. Later, Bridges related that as he saw it, a strike was a pitiless struggle for power, not unlike a war or a dress rehearsal for revolution. "Temporarily, we take over their property, seize their property, expropriate their property, and say: 'we own it. Temporarily. You'll only get it back when you pay us.' That's the one weapon workers have nobody else has got," he stated sagely. "And if you know how to use it, you're on top of the world."[75]

Buoyed by their classes at the Labor School and motivated by a felt desire to transform an archipelago where sterilization, child labor, poor housing, dangerous toxins, pestilent racism, and poor wages obtained, workers embodied Bridges' words by shutting down the sugariness of the Big Five's profits until they capitulated. Six weeks into the strike, Hall was able to report that the "membership is solid and the employers' sweetness and light technique continues," as harsher tactics had failed miserably. The "general public is on our side by and large," an outcome not particularly surprising given the racial makeup of the business elite and the demography of the archipelago. Besides, a rift was developing within the elite; Hall thought the "real reason for the friendly situation of the man in the street is the favorable treatment we are receiving in the '[Honolulu] Star-Bulletin.'" Although "[Walter] Dillingham's '[Honolulu] Advertiser' is rabidly against us," at that juncture the latter did not "have the circulation and the influence of the 'Bulletin,'" Hall reported, and "Joe Farrington, the 'Bulletin's' publisher has been more than fair to us." This was no accident, as Bridges had recommended that the union locals in Hawai'i back Farrington's attempt to get reelected as the islands' congressional delegate in Washington. "Your insistence that we make a deal to support Farrington's campaign for reelection is paying off," Hall told his immediate superior. "As long as the 'Bulletin' continues its kokua [aid], our chances of complete victory are excellent." The union's candidate "came through very well in the primary election," and "many members of the Republican Party are raising hell with him and demanding he disavow us," Hall continued. "He has refused to go along with them and as a result he is being red-baited in some circles of the GOP," a tendency that was to reach titanic proportions rather shortly.[76]

Motoring along, the ILWU had had all of its "union machinery in work in the campaign," Hall said. "Kawano, McElrath and Oka are spending almost all of their time on this work as are many of our local and unit leaders. We feel that a strike victory depends to a large extent upon the election of Farrington. If he doesn't win," Hall warned, "we'll have one heck of a time keeping his paper from following the lead of the 'Advertiser.'" Cagily, Hall advised Bridges that "it might be a good thing to play up Farrington with Marc and our other friends back in Washington," referring to the left-wing congressman from

East Harlem, Vito Marcantonio. "Farrington loves attention," Hall pointed out, "and he'll need the feeling that he's accepted in pro-labor circles even though he is a Republican."[77]

Ray Jerome Baker, the Honolulu photographer who was quite close to the union, disagreed. By his own admission he had "voted for all the candidates recommended" by the union, but one. "The only exception was that I voted for [William] Borthwick instead of for Farrington for delegate to Congress," since the former, he thought, "represents the interests of labor better than Farrington."[78] The union's enthusiasm was not shared, as well, by the then Communist Ichiro Izuka, who was rapidly becoming disenchanted with the CP. Kawano testified that his fellow Japanese-American was "opposed to the idea of having to support Mr. Joseph Farrington, a Republican," and that this led to a "complete showdown" that angered him further.[79]

Thus, as strikers marched and chanted, they were simultaneously striking back at the ballot box. This provided the union with a tremendous wind at its back that considerably increased labor's ability to prevail. This was a harbinger of things to come in 1947, when the union and the radical Left were to face their most severe challenges to date, as internecine conflict was bolstered by a rising Red Scare that ultimately was to topple the archipelago's counterparts on the mainland. By way of contrast, fortified by the successful Sugar Strike, the ILWU and the radical Left on the islands were able to sail boldly into the headwinds they faced. For Hawai'i was different from the mainland, as one island organ sensed after the November 1946 elections: "Comparing the local election against the national results, it would appear as if Kauai is about four years behind the normal national trend. Kauai goes Democratic and to the Left in a big way, [and] the nation goes Republican and to the Right just as decisively."[80]

CHAPTER 6

Red Scare Rising

In the aftermath of their smashing victory in the Sugar Strike, the ILWU and the Left seemed to be sailing along smoothly, managing to avoid the choppy seas that were not infrequent in the Hawaiian Islands. But 1947 brought leaping waves of discontent, symbolized by the failure of the union's strike of the pineapple industry. As if that were not enough, there were other clouds that blurred their apparent rainbow of success. The gentle radical John Reinecke summed it up in his year-end letter that he sent to friends and colleagues in lieu of holiday greetings. The tone for this tumultuous year had been set in November 1946, when during the elections in which labor and the Left effectively flexed their growing muscle, "one Republican candidate went about Jew-baiting," a developing trend no doubt influenced by the instrumental role in the sugar negotiations of Louis Goldblatt. One local Honolulu newspaper—it was "semi-fascist," said Reinecke—"carried cartoons of three repulsive, hook-nosed carpetbaggers raking in union dues." The CIO's endorsement of Joseph Farrington was another sore point with some, but not for Reinecke, since Farrington was publisher of the largest daily, the *Honolulu Star-Bulletin*, and for the islands was "something of a liberal." Reinecke also pointed out that "he is a persistent and effective fighter for statehood, which is the ILWU's great goal also," a point made without necessary elaboration. But as Reinecke saw it, the opposition to this goal was sufficient explication, since "today some of the important men are against it, mingling 'Jap' and 'Red' in their arguments," which was becoming de rigueur in the archipelago. So the CIO, with one eye on statehood and the other on the neutrality of the *Star-Bulletin* during the strike, endorsed Farrington over William Borthwick, Democrat, the candidate of Governor Ingram Stainback. As a partial consequence, by the end of the strike, which coincided with the close of the elections, Stainback and the ILWU were bitter political enemies, a factor that was to weigh heavily in the islands in the near term. Moreover, within the union too there was some dissension over the endorsement of Farrington, since some within labor and the Left were already busily pursuing their goal of transforming the Democratic Party from the carcass it had become into a vehicle for progressive aspirations. Farrington was elected, said Reinecke, even though the silk-stocking precincts ditched the Republican ticket for the first time in history and voted for Borthwick, suggesting the flux that had entered Hawai'i, a region that was a typical indicator of incipient change. In short, "'Moscow's kiss of death,'" which is how unkind critics had characterized the CIO's embrace of Farrington, did not frighten the voters, who were rapidly developing an immunity to the ideological viruses generated by an elite that had become—unbeknownst to itself—isolated from the overwhelming Asian-Pacific majority of the islands.[1]

So foiled, this elite doubled down with its Red-baiting tactic, when Ichiro Izuka—a former progressive pillar who became a tormenter of those he had formerly epitomized—published in March 1947 a popular pamphlet charging that Jack Hall, Robert McElrath, and John Reinecke were all Reds, explosive charges that seemed to detonate more forcefully on the mainland than in Hawai'i. Izuka was aided by Edward Berman, a tall, strongly built, sallow man who seemed always to have a dissatisfied sneer on his face. He led the 1938 Inter-Island strike and then went to San Francisco to work as a longshoreman and study law. But the union leadership in Honolulu cold-shouldered him because his reputation from San Francisco was so unfavorable. Izuka and a number of other AJAs were distressed by what they saw as their being sidelined from top leadership posts in favor of whites like Hall and McElrath, and Izuka's predilection then merged with Berman's unhappiness to produce a blockbuster publication. Berman became friendly with Borthwick and the governor and, along with Izuka, campaigned strongly against Farrington and began denouncing the leadership of the ILWU. They were then joined by Art Rutledge, the wily AFL leader who had assisted Reinecke himself more than once. "The 'Izuka' pamphlet has had great effect within the ILWU," concluded Reinecke without enthusiasm.[2]

In June 1947 came the pineapple strike—which the ILWU termed a lockout and which lasted only five days. Then the union went back to work, practically on the employers' terms. In this case the union had been flummoxed by strikebreakers. High school students wanted jobs during their vacation, and public sentiment was against the strike. The pineapple units went out almost "criminally unprepared," said Reinecke with disgust. "The president of the pineapple local, a drunken and incompetent and dishonest fellow, had been thrown out a few weeks before and was going about Red-baiting" while the brutal "treatment [workers] got from the police might have been specially ordered straight out of the opening pages of [V. I. Lenin's] *State and Revolution*." ILWU leaders "had spent too much time at their desks" and not enough in the fields with workers; "the leadership has not succeeded either in integrating the social life of the plantations into union activities," he observed, "so meetings are poorly attended," while "some of the Catholic clergy are helping" bosses. Then at the end of 1947 Amos Ignacio of the ILWU bolted and formed a new Union of Hawaiian Workers, claiming 4,000 members. These tumultuous events forced Reinecke to conclude that "every splitting device—race, religion, the 'mainland carpetbagger' argument, and of course the menace of Communism—will be used to the full in the next few months."[3]

Reinecke had reason to believe this. He had appeared as an expert witness in a suit brought by Chinese schools to challenge the constitutionality of the wartime act that virtually closed foreign language schools. An array of experts and prominent persons appeared on behalf of the Territory of Hawaii. Reinecke was the sole expert testifying for the schools, a fact that conservatives found displeasing and for which they were to retaliate: strike one. Then there was the case of the Maui County grand jury, which had indicted some pineapple strikers for throwing two foremen into a harbor. Grand juries for years had been drawn preponderantly from the white minority, and Reinecke again appeared as an expert: strike two. This led directly to a public hearing in 1948 whereby Reinecke and his similarly progressive spouse were both ousted from their positions as schoolteachers: strike three.[4]

The earthly paradise that Hawai'i was thought to be was undergoing a typical bout of strain in the postwar environment. "Here in Honolulu there is a miniature building boom on," Ray Jerome Baker wrote in 1946. There was a serious shortage of lumber, and, as well, a serious shortage of labor—"they are even talking of recruiting 2,000 laborers for work [from] Japan," he added with wonder, which did not necessarily augur well for an ILWU planning to strike.[5]

This economic stress saw no surcease in 1947 in Baker's eyes. "Rising prices and food shortages have been particular topics of conversation," he confided to his diary. A shipping strike that lasted two months had meant that no fresh vegetables arrived from California and the local supply was very short. As a result, prices soared, reminding those who might have forgotten about the perils of residing on isolated islands in the middle of the planet's massively definitive feature—the Pacific Ocean. Moreover, with demobilization reducing army personnel, the dependence was more and more, he thought, on the prisoners of war to keep the services going. They did work in the laundries, on farms, in nurseries, in warehouses, and on construction jobs. Some were plumbers, some electricians, cabinetmakers, mechanics, and stevedores, to the notable consternation of the ILWU. They worked in commissaries, hospitals, and radio stations. They polished the brass doorknobs at the post headquarters, mowed the lawns, and weeded the flower beds. Some "would have liked to remain," he said, especially Japanese but also some Italians and Germans as well. Moreover, "hundreds of service men and women want [to] remain in Hawaii," and, in addition, "thousands of mainland workers began to inquire about permanent employment." There were other alien invaders that were having a noticeable impact on the economy too. Coming in as stowaways on the hundreds of planes passing through Hawai'i during the war, nearly a score of new insects had arrived "as immigrants."[6]

The new potential workers were drawn magnetically to the archipelago by visions of perpetual sunshine, cascading ocean waves, gently warm breezes, and swaying palm trees. With Hawai'i functioning as a way station during the war, thousands of soldiers and sailors had touched down in the islands and had communicated to thousands more these seductive images. Other factors were drawing migrants to Hawai'i as well—migrants who might compromise the bargaining leverage the ILWU had won only recently and who could once again allow the business elite to manipulate the labor supply to the union's detriment. "It seems uncanny," said Baker with delight, "that we can now come from Honolulu to San Francisco overnight when we used to spend six days making the same trip."[7] With so many wishing to reside in the Shangri-la that Hawai'i was thought to be, inexorable pressure was placed on the existing labor force, as management now had a ready-made reserve army of labor.

What was also new was the growth in transoceanic air transportation—what had captured the delight of Ray Jerome Baker—and the fact that it was a building block for a burgeoning tourism industry that was developing beyond the grasp of the Big Five, thereby creating another power center in the mid-Pacific and potentially weakening the theretofore firm grip on the islands held by Matson and its allies.[8]

Thus, labor and the Left did not have an easy path before them, faced as they were by a rapidly changing postwar landscape that featured prisoner-of-war labor, increased migration from the mainland, expensive housing, and a relatively high cost of living. Such considerations did not discourage labor and the Left: they had confidence that they could effectively confront the Big Five even in their formidable redoubt that was the pineapple industry. By 1947 this industry employed a maximum of 23,500 workers, of whom almost 12,000 were regular year-round workers and the rest were seasonal.[9]

Whatever the case, in the run-up to this ill-fated pineapple strike, Jack Hall exuded optimism. In February 1947 he reported to Goldblatt, "The situation on Kauai, Molokai and rural Oahu is excellent. There are some dangers in the Lanai situation, however." Although the latter island happened to be a major seat of pineapple production, Hall noted that "only about 400 workers turned out for the Lanai meeting out of a membership of more than eleven hundred."[10]

"We can sum up the pineapple situation," said Hall in May 1947, "by saying that the membership is restless"; put simply, "there is no inclination to accept the industry's proposal." Even in sugar, scene of a recent triumph, the situation was "quite bad, except in a few cases," said Hall; "whirlwind tours are not the answer," he suggested, though he was "interested in the purchase of a plane," which would facilitate such.[11]

The immensity of the sugar victory, coupled with Hawaiʻi's bucking of the national trend of turning politically to the right, may have given the ILWU a false sense of invincibility that backfired during the pineapple strike. McElrath was breathing fire, advising that the "Big Five has not tossed in the sponge since the beating we gave them in the sugar strike but on the contrary bandaged their wounds and apparently are out to take us on in another round."[12] That they were.[13]

Visiting Pauwela on the lovely isle of Maui in July 1947 during the pineapple strike, Rhoda V. Lewis, the territory's acting attorney general, noticed that the large number of pickets served to dissuade management. Trucks were kept idle, and field workers were not picked up by company trucks and conveyed to harvesting areas. In Maui 600 strikers prevented management from moving vehicles from their own garages. "Strikers are alleged to have blocked a highway," she said nervously, "by stretching out on the ground." There was intimidation too, she said: "Five strikers visited the home of one Sonny Fernandes to warn him against operating a loading crane. Fernandes disregarded the warning and reported to work as usual at the loading dock. He was assaulted by them and finally had to jump into the ocean to escape from the mob." Still angered, pursuing strikers continued to hurl loose pineapples at him from bins that had been smashed open, and the beleaguered man was forced to dive and swim under the water to escape injuries. Another nonstriker was assaulted, she said—he received a considerable beating—while two other company workers were forced to cease loading. From her perspective, Lanaʻi residents were the most apprehensive of what might happen—though their Kauaʻi neighbors might disagree, notably when 600 angry strikers gathered at the Hawaiian Cannery. Police were escorting nonstrikers through picket lines, to the consternation of the ILWU, and three trucks of pineapples belonging to the cannery were being diverted to Hawaiian Fruit Packers for canning. But police were unable to clear away the picketers, and after the drivers finally abandoned the trucks, the pineapples were left spoiling on the highway. Then a truck loaded with pineapples was confronted by strikers who broke the windshield and deposited boxes of pineapple onto the thoroughfare. The union's Juan Reyes Tamo was arrested and charged with carrying a deadly weapon after he was found with a concealed knife with an eight-inch blade. Lewis, increasingly nervous, warned of a breakdown of law enforcement on Kauaʻi, with its police force, "numbering 62 in all," denoted as "inadequate."[14]

Though this strike was largely determined to be a failure as far as the union was concerned, that outcome was not due to a dearth of militancy. Management warned frantically of chaotic conditions that were lurching "beyond remedial action"; bosses claimed that they possessed a wealth of detail to document the approach of anarchy in these islands, where a kind of lawlessness was already rampant: "Men have been beaten. Real and property damage ha[s occurred]. Trespass upon private property, prominently marked[,] has been constant. Missiles have been thrown into windows of private homes. Wives and children have been threatened. Foul language and threats have been hurled at workers and the families of workers. Masses of illegal pickets have blocked public highways and private roads and plants, " it was said. Seemingly suffering a nervous breakdown, this management representative denounced the union and reeled in the face of the "rape of law and order before our very eyes." The authorities were advised that the necessity for taking swift and sure curative measures was mandatory while "the patient may still be cured," a prospect that seemed to be melting with every passing summer day. "Save the situation and perhaps save Hawaii from ruin and shame," the governor was told with escalating rage.[15]

Even before these anguished words were uttered, local authorities worried that "there will be local tacks on the highway when they start hauling pineapple," placed by union saboteurs to cause flat tires, and it was requested that the county purchase a machine magnetized to draw all nails or metal articles from the highway.[16] Unsurprisingly, there was sweeping surveillance of the union in 1947.[17] Frustration was rising within the union correspondingly.[18]

To hear union members tell it, it was they who needed to be rescued, along with Hawai'i, from the ruin and shame brought by the authorities. There was a "campaign of terror and police intimidation," the ILWU charged. "Scabs are being herded and run into struck plants with police protection. Court injunctions against picketing are being issued. Peaceful union assemblies are being broken up and our members are being arrested on [a] wholesale scale."[19] Jack Hall once said that "island working people in plantation areas or with plantation backgrounds will fight far longer and far harder, much harder than American workers any place in the nation, except perhaps in some of these coal-mining towns," and the events of 1947 did little to shake his supposition.[20]

Yet with all that, the ILWU was left to lick its wounds after roundly being perceived as vanquished. Jack Hall was left to bluster, informing Honolulu police chief William Hoopai quite curtly that "police brutality during the recent pineapple strike" was unacceptable and that his union would not "participate in any star chamber investigation" of their reaction.[21] With the union staggered by the inflicted blows, in early August 1947 the strike in the archipelago's multimillion-dollar industry was settled with contracts covering 11 plantations and 9 canneries and about 8,000 pineapple workers.[22] Management found it hard not to gloat[23] and preen after its triumph,[24] not least because it had seemingly won a sidebar contest—being able to drink more alcohol during negotiations[25] than its labor counterparts, no small feat given Hall's reputation.[26]

While Howard Babbitt's management negotiating teams, having never negotiated before, were "complete greenhorns," the union representatives were quite astute, but this did not save them during the pineapple strike. This development validated Harry Bridges' notion that mobilized members—rather than smart leaders—were the ILWU's trump card. There would be negotiations "where the union might bring 30 to 50 representatives," Babbitt later recalled, and "industry would bring in 30 to 40"; "then there'd be smaller meetings," followed by "off-the-record meetings between [management] and Bridges and Goldblatt and Hall.[27]

Yet Reinecke had a point in acknowledging that the union mishandled the pineapple strike.[28] Sanford Zalburg, Jack Hall's admiring biographer, conceded that the union gained little from this 1947 job action in pineapple. Hall lost one. Industry stood its ground. The strike was settled for the most part on employers' terms. Nevertheless, the ILWU claimed a victory. Fortunately, this stumbling block made Hall aware of the neglect of the rudiments of organization within the union and the commonsense notion that ill-planned economic maneuvers could spell disaster. Given that this thrashing was accompanied by the significant defections by Izuka and Ignacio, it caused the union to become more closely knit, wary, and thorough and yet—as Zalburg saw it—"more militant and autocratic."[29]

For his part Harry Bridges, in a sense, felt vindicated. "We disagreed with Hall," he said, who he thought "favored this high-fallutin' type of unionism," whereby "the workers are taught that what produces a good contract is fancy negotiations, especially by haole people with college degrees," and not the "basic rank and file strength of the workers, which is what counts." That the pineapple strike was effective only on Lana'i was quite indicative, he thought. The "way to handle a strike" was outlined by this man who well knew how: "You start off and you hold some reserve forces so you can call them up. Not pull everybody off." But this was not done in 1947.[30] Bridges' comrade in the ILWU leadership in San Francisco, J. R. Robertson, agreed. He later asserted that Hall and the local leadership wanted a pineapple strike while Goldblatt, Bridges, and himself disagreed.[31] Thus the growing rift between Hall and the San Francisco–based leadership of the union deepened.

The union's foes were ecstatic.[32] As a premonition of what was to occur during future ILWU strikes, well-drilled elite white women sought to organize what was euphemistically termed "volunteer labor" in order to undermine ILWU labor.[33]

"The '47 pineapple strike was a fiasco. We lost islands-wide bargaining and didn't get it back for four years," said ILWU staffer Dave Thompson. "We walked into a trap." The union was bargaining for a settlement "and thought we were very close to an agreement, but the employers stalled while the strike deadline passed," he recalled. "By then our guys were setting up picket-lines." The problem was there were lots of seasonal pineapple workers who had no solidarity with the union. They were encouraged by the employers to cross picket lines, and they did. As union weakness was exposed, the ILWU called in the entire territorial leadership from all the industries and raised the perspective of saving the pineapple strike by fighting on all fronts. But the sugar leaders said they couldn't do this because their members would not understand why they should support a strike in another industry—a profound frailty in the Left's ability to generate class consciousness and worker solidarity. "The lesson of this was that we had to get closer to our rank and file," Thompson said. The Sugar Strike had demonstrated that labor and the Left were a force to be reckoned with in Hawai'i; the November 1946 elections had provided evidence to buttress this notion, just as these results suggested that the ILWU's counterparts on the mainland were simply not as strong[34] as they were in the islands.[35]

What went wrong? Curtis Cosmos Aller Jr., who had served on the Territorial War Labor Board in Hawai'i, felt that the pineapple worker clearly did not have the same intense feeling of hatred for the employer as did the sugar worker. The former was paid better, was more carefully selected, and was given somewhat better treatment on the job; plus, Aller thought, there was a "strong sense of identification with the crop which generally pervades the work-force[,] with the result that the workers view any avoidable destruction of the fruit as criminal." This may have been an exaggeration; what was accurate, however, was that Hawai'i had a stronger foothold in the global pineapple market than it did in sugar, which might have given workers in the latter industry more determination, given the more difficult odds they faced.[36] Seeking to take advantage of this leverage, the union was said to have deliberately stalled negotiations for several months in order to call a strike at the peak of the pineapple harvest,[37] but this proved to be unavailing.

This delaying tactic had collided with another imperative, for it was in late May 1947 that nervous leaders in the fields of education and social work began to express concern that a prolonged strike in the pineapple fields and canneries would eliminate employment opportunities for thousands of Hawai'i students. Traditionally, as many as 10,000 students worked in this industry each summer,[38] a consideration they brought to Governor Stainback.[39] It turned out that even some teachers—thought to be sympathetic to labor—chose to scab,[40] suggestive of the union's setback.[41]

From the high of the victory in sugar, the union was now gasping for air, for just as strikers sought to shut down the pineapple industry, their old foes in the American Federation of Labor and the Teamsters began an initiative to oust the ILWU from its role as bargaining agent for these workers.[42] "The AFL has declared war on the ILWU,"[43] claimed Bridges' colleague Henry Schmidt, no small matter since the Teamsters were notorious for discriminating against Asian-Pacific workers on the Pacific Coast.[44] McElrath was quick to spread the accurate report that, just before seeking to raid the ILWU, the journal of the Teamsters had an editorial asserting that "quote[,] a Jap is always a Jap[,] unquote."[45]

Bridges typically was even more explicit—and angry. The Teamsters, he said, "assessed the membership . . . one cent per member per month for a fighting fund to move into Hawaii, ostensibly in an organizing drive"; this would "preclude any of our energy going towards any high falutin political schemes," he said, and would mandate avoidance of "super-militant or leftist drives and tendencies." Like Jack Kawano, Bridges stressed the importance of emphasizing the Teamsters' anti-Asian bias—"if necessary," he recommended, "paid ads" should be used to disseminate this news.[46] Though militant episodically,[47] AFL unions were ill-equipped to organize workers of Asian-Pacific origin.[48]

Yet with all their sophistication and militancy, labor and the Left found that they were overwhelmed, as rightist currents drifting from the mainland landed with a wallop in the islands. Walter Dillingham, who was not only president of the powerful Oahu Railway and Land Company but, as well, unofficial titan of the Big Five, had traveled to the mainland just as strikers were lifting their placards; he found, he said ominously, "the widest interest ever shown in Hawaii" since he had been traveling to California, New York, Boston, and Washington, D.C., "over a 50 year period." His ire rising, he denounced the "'un-American attempt to establish a dictatorship by labor in these islands'"; it was "'so disturbing that the whole country is taking a new view of our strategic and economic situation from the standpoint of statehood,'" he warned. Thus he left it for all to ponder the obvious implication as to whether the United States, which was moving steadily on a path of anticommunism, would seek to incorporate Hawai'i as a state, when it seemed to be moving in an opposing direction,[49] a prospect that did not escape leading union members.[50]

As Dillingham was issuing his weighty edicts, on a typically warm Friday afternoon in Honolulu in the early summer of 1947 some 1,400 grim and silent—mostly white—businessmen listened in mounting anger about what was to befall their beloved Hawai'i. At this emergency meeting of the chamber of commerce, they listened stonily as they were informed of the amount of strike dynamite that was about to be detonated. There were more than 100 union contracts that could be opened for wage discussions within coming months, at a time when the AFL was seemingly in a competitive contest with the CIO to determine which of the two would wear the mantle of labor's chief defender. It was a potential disaster, they were told, dwarfing the past damage of earthquakes, tidal waves, and war—combined. That CIO unions were reputedly controlled by Communists only increased their hysteria at a time when headlines blared globally about a Red offensive.[51]

Local elites seemed confounded by the fact that the mainland seemed to be heading in a conservative direction as the archipelago headed in a different direction. One noted business journal observed in the spring of 1947 that the general shellacking administered at the polls the previous November to the CIO Political Action Committee on the mainland served to obscure "one important PAC triumph.".: In apt wonder, it was announced: "Hawai'i's CIO political wing, in its first big political sortie there, backed 15 winners in the election for the 30 member lower house of the territory's legislature. The gains have enabled the PAC to block the passage of any legislation it opposes." With evident irritation, the journal stated, "Today the Democratic Party is only a front. The rear echelons of the party take their inspiration, direction and dynamism from the Political Action Committee."[52] And in turn the PAC was thought to be controlled by Communists. *Newsweek* pointed out that of the "fourteen Democrats the CIO-PAC had endorsed on election day, four of them [were ILWU] officials"; the magazine added that the "ILWU's attempt to capture the House had failed [but] its men [control] half the committee chairmanships."[53] Similarly worrisome to some was a report in the Communist press that boasted that "five ILWU members now sit in the [territorial] legislature."[54]

The unique events in Hawai'i, which was heading left as the mainland was veering rightward, were snaring the attention of a growing number regionally and nationally. The *Honolulu Advertiser* noted that one popular magazine averred that "'labor is in the saddle'" in the archipelago; it was labor "'that is largely Asiatic in blood with a grievance going deeper than wages, hours and working conditions'" that was of pressing concern. Philip E. Spalding of C. Brewer and Company responded by declaring that the Big Five had now become the "Big Six—the Big Five and Harry Bridges." To his credit, he thought the war and martial law—rather than Moscow—had driven this dilemma: "this four year diet of dictatorship during which islanders were jailed or ordered to donate blood for such insignificant infractions as traffic violations, leaving a light burning or being out after curfew" had helped create a new—and radicalized—Hawai'i.[55] But management, which sensed the tide turning toward anticommunism,[56] was not exactly retreating.[57]

Unfortunately for labor and the Left, it was not simply the pineapple setback that had them reeling. Goldblatt had warned that the ILWU should be careful when declaring that those of Japanese ancestry might have to take a backseat in the interest of, e.g., promoting Filipino leadership. The avuncular Goldblatt may have had a perverse sense of vindication when Ichiro Izuka defected spectacularly from the ranks of the ILWU and the broader Left in 1947. He had been a valiant and sturdy leader in the 1930s, at a time when the islands bordered on feudalism; he had been a vice president of the ILWU in Kaua'i from 1939 to 1941 and president from 1941 to 1942. But in the hinge year of 1947 he penned a startlingly received booklet, *The Truth about Communism in Hawaii*. Setting the tone for the attacks the ILWU and the Communist Party were to absorb in the run-up to statehood, it put forward a lurid story of Red manipulation and domination of the union in particular.

Born in Hanapēpē, Kaua'i, on 5 June 1911, Izuka was the sixth child in a large and sprawling family. His parents had migrated from Fukuoka, Japan, in 1900, and like others so situated, he had endured suffering: "there was continual debt bondage to the plantation store," he recalled, and "we workers had no incentive to go for our money on payday, for most often the envelope was empty." In 1938 he joined the Communist Party, and it was he who kept the books for the organization—given his unparalleled intimacy with the CP's innards—using both Russian and Japanese for camouflage. But he resigned in November 1946, driven in part by disgust at the decision by labor and the Left to back Farrington over Borthwick as the archipelago's representative in Washington—at least, that is what he said.[58]

As Jack Kimoto recalled it, Hall had heard that Borthwick had made anti-Semitic remarks, and this, along with temptation to seek to co-opt Farrington's influential *Honolulu Star-Bulletin*, pushed him toward the Republican even though Izuka and Kimoto felt they "should support a Democratic candidate." That spawned a rift: "The ILWU leaders of the outside islands—like Maui and Kaua'i—they were not satisfied [either]," Kimoto asserted, and they began to show signs they would back Borthwick. McElrath, who was present, "got excited," said Kimoto, "and I guess he tried to talk them into changing their minds and support Farrington." When he didn't succeed, McElrath requested that Kimoto "be sent over" to talk them out of it "because [he] was the only one that [could] really make them [back Farrington]." So Kimoto "took the plane" and had the meeting in which he stressed that the main thing was unity. The workers were convinced—but Ichiro Izuka was not.[59] It was even more startling that the union's decision to back Farrington was taken so much to heart by Izuka, since Chuck Mau, a leader of the Democratic Party, acknowledged that Borthwick was "aloof" and "didn't mingle with the Oriental groups," characteristics not unusual among "mainland haoles."[60]

Weeks before this pivotal 1946 election, Jack Kawano met with Stainback and found that the governor "did not talk about the relief ships or food situation but talked about politics." The territory's chief executive was bent on compelling the ILWU to support Borthwick instead of Farrington—though the ILWU leader maintained that "Farrington is a better man."[61]

Yet the support for Farrington was not the only electoral decision that caused flutters of concern within the union. In the spring of 1946 Jack Hall went to bat for Governor Stainback—soon to become the Left's deadly foe—informing the secretary of the interior that this increasingly conservative executive should be reappointed and remarking that "opposition stems from persons with selfish motives."[62] Subsequently, this maneuver caused some members to question Hall's judgment, eroding his popularity.

In any case, Izuka's booklet was a highly explosive depth charge in the archipelago, coming as it did at a time of growing apprehension in Hawai'i about a force that was being demonized on the mainland—the Communist Party. The publication was treated as if it were "a book of the Bible," according to one study. It was wielded against John and Aiko Reinecke when the time came to oust them from their jobs as schoolteachers, and it was devastating for the ILWU and the party itself, even though, says scholar John J. Swissler Jr., "its veracity is highly dubious." It came out at the same time that another bombshell book—*The Plot to Sovietize Hawaii*—was published. It featured a cover with a photograph of Soviet foreign minister Vyacheslav Molotov and Harry Bridges toasting each other over the caption "Cronies"; the photograph had been taken during the wartime entente with Moscow.[63]

Izuka and the pineapple defeat notwithstanding, by 1947 it appeared that the CP was on the rise, propelled by its influence in the ILWU—which helps explain why the union was attacked so viciously and dramatically. Seaman Robert McBurney Kempa, who was a Communist himself at this point, recalled that when he joined the Mānoa branch in March 1947, Dwight Freeman told him "there was a secret group or closed group," as well as other groups that were more open. "There were two trade union groups," "a pineapple group," and "a group on each of the following islands: Hawaii, Lanai, Maui and Kauai." A telling indicator of the CP's resurgence was that there were 125 subscriptions in the archipelago to the party's theoretical journal, *Political Affairs,* at that juncture, which was a rough approximation of how many Reds were enrolled. An indicator of the CP's activism was that Kempa attended 25 party meetings from March to November 1947.[64]

To say that the IWLU and its comrades were displeased with this onslaught would be gross understatement. McElrath accused Art Rutledge of the AFL of being the culprit behind Izuka's metamorphosis. "The Filipino edition [of Izuka's booklet] was paid for with money that Rutledge put up," he asserted, while Arnold Wills—the Socialist of New Zealand origins who was unfriendly toward the Communists—was also seen as culpable.[65]

Yet the ILWU approached the matter in a way that probably enhanced the union's appeal to its members. Ichiro Izuka was invited to a major ILWU confab where Hall, Goldblatt, and local leaders presided. There he stood, facing a constant barrage of questions, accusations, catcalls, laughs, and mockery from those who felt he meant them ill. But it was not only this apostate who was subjected to withering criticism. The *Honolulu Advertiser,* the American Legion, organizations known as Spearhead for Americanism and We the Women, and others of that ilk were denounced in harsh terms. Izuka began speaking at 2:41 p.m. and remained on the platform—battered and slightly bowed—until 5:27 p.m., in the face of shouted inquiries demanding to know on whose payroll he was serving. Goldblatt concluded the gathering with a flourish, speaking for 45 minutes and insisting that the ILWU was democratic, as evidenced by the leaders' having invited Izuka to share his "findings" with those most directly affected by them.[66] Goldblatt deemed this to be an excellent example of democracy, though those labeled as Red did not seem to be as welcoming to Izuka.

Thomas Yagi, an ILWU stalwart who was accused of being a Communist, called his accuser a liar—Yagi said he was a member of the Democratic Party. Nonplussed, Izuka was asked if he espied any Reds in the room and he replied coolly, "Yes," identifying "Lou [Goldblatt], Johnny Elias, [Ernest] Arena, Harry Kamoku, [Bert] Nakano and [Yasuki] Arakaki."[67]

Others were not buying this line. Izuka had raised a "point that every American citizen of Japanese ancestry may well consider," a Maui writer said. "Izuka names names," the writer continued, adding that "most of these names are of Japanese origin and nearly all are active in labor leadership." His concern was explicit: "Is the average American citizen of Japanese ancestry who thought he proved his loyalty to America beyond any doubt in the war, going to be forced to prove it all over again, as far as Communism is concerned?"[68] What many found striking about Izuka's exposé of the Communist Party of Hawaii, in short, was the ethnic makeup of the membership. Senator Hugh Butler of Nebraska, who had taken a keen interest in the territory, was informed by John Stokes of Honolulu that "the members of the local CP mentioned in Mr. Izuka's pamphlet total 53" and that of these there were "29 Japanese, 10 mainland whites, 6 Hawaiian and part-Hawaiian, 3 Chinese, 3 Korean and 2 miscellaneous." Therefore, Stokes calculated, "35 out of 53 are of Oriental extraction," and he also noted that "at least four of the mainland whites (who are the leaders) are married to Oriental women (described as highly intellectual)"—including Hall, McElrath, and Reinecke. "As stated in Hawaii by a Japanese priest to a friend of mine: 'the lowest Japanese is higher than the highest haole,'" said Stokes. "Japanese have been taught for centuries that they are a very superior people." Izuka's bombshell, which was the more powerful coming from one of his ethnicity, sent anticommunism into stratospheric heights, fueled by lingering hysteria about Japan and Asia. This hysteria was to materialize once more during the war with Korea.[69]

Another point that illuminates the Izuka controversy was the ongoing conflict between some of the haole and non-haole leaders of the union and the CP—and Jack Hall was often at the center of this dispute. Hall was on the Central Committee of the Hawaii CP at this juncture, along with Kimoto, John Reinecke, and Charles Fujimoto, the intellectual Japanese-American who was to lead the organization—but not McElrath or Koji Ariyoshi. Kimoto did not have a high opinion of Hall's emerging as one of the most powerful men in Hawai'i, however. Kimoto felt that—among other things—Hall was not very well versed in Marxist literature. When asked whether he ever read the classics of Marxism and Leninism, Kimoto replied simply, "Probably not." Hall, he thought, could be "regarded generally as a labor leader but not a Communist leader," for "he's not the type that grasps theory." It was unfortunate, Kimoto added, "that [Hall] and Izuka[,] who were chosen by the Party to attend the party school on the West Coast[,] didn't have the chance to get that training because the war started" and so "they came right back"—though "Kawano attended." When they did make it to San Francisco, "Izuka's resentment for Hall started around that time," Kimoto said, because Izuka "didn't think he was being treated properly by Hall" while there. Izuka "expected Hall to take him around," but "Hall was drinking," a frequent preoccupation of his, and "from then on [Izuka] had no feeling for Hall."[70]

By way of contrast, Yasuki Arakaki was a voracious reader, consuming volumes on US labor history and the works of Yugoslav Communists, such as Tito. He learned about strike strategy by reading the work of Mao Zedong— also a favorite of Koji Ariyoshi's. He studied strike strategy at the California Labor School—and he too was no friend of Jack Hall's.[71] Koji Ariyoshi did not like Hall either. "There are people who came up from the ranks, matured and developed and then began to lose their links with the rank and file," Ariyoshi said, "and that's what happened to Hall." It was Hall, he thought, who had blocked him from working on the waterfront. "Kimoto was the ideological leader" on the islands, "but he was not a forceful man but very patient," Ariyoshi stated, whereas Hall "had a left-wing bent—but fuzzy." What Ariyoshi said about the similarly defecting Jack Kawano could just as well be applied to Izuka: "When a person does so much to build a movement and when he begins to feel that his recognition is being taken away or is eroding, then the change takes place in a person and I think that's what took place in Kawano. . . . [I]t's the immaturity of the trade unionism in Hawaii, not being able to [accept] people[,] and it still persists."[72]

Thus, it was in late 1952 that Izuka testified in the Smith Act trial against Hall, recalling that the then young seaman gave him Communist literature in 1937 in Kaua'i,[73] thereby boosting the case for conviction. Izuka's defection was hardly minor, for at this same trial Jack Kawano testified that "he remembered Izuka carrying a black diary [whenever and] wherever he went [and] wrote down into the diary the places where they met and the date they met, who was there, what subject they discussed." This was why he was "able to get so much information and put such information into the book"; Kawano found it "amazing how accurate that book was."[74]

Interviewed almost thirty years after he defected publicly from the union and the CP, Izuka was unrepentant. A short and compact man with strong arms and a smooth face set off by spectacles, he continued to speak in a brogue, betraying his Japanese origins. He recalled the conflicts within his party branch in Waikīkī, where he was the leader and where Hall, McElrath, Frank Thompson, Koichi Imori, yet another Japanese-American leader, and others flocked. Fees were minimal; the initiation fee was 50 cents, those making over $100 per month had to pay $2 in monthly dues, and those making less than that princely amount had to pay $1 monthly. But McElrath, he said, didn't want to pay, which set conflict in motion. The disgruntled Izuka eventually met with Wills and Edward Berman at Wills' home in Kailua, the latter two brimming with anti-Red sentiment and excited to snare a defecting Red. "Berman changed one or two sentences" in his celebrated book, he recalled, "but the main writing was done by Wills," though the latter hardly trusted the former.[75] Wills, who resembled Abraham Lincoln, tall and lanky—albeit without a beard[76]—was instrumental in dividing the house of Hawai'i labor against itself. But he could not have done this without Izuka, and Izuka was driven by antipathy toward Jack Hall. Kawano testified under oath that "Izuka took the position that Mr. Hall was not a good Communist and that he would not belong to the same Communist Party so long as we allowed Mr. Hall to remain a member."[77]

Unfortunately for the ILWU, the context for Izuka's thunderbolt was a preexisting pattern of unsettled race relations within the union.[78] Arakaki—who spearheaded organizing at Olaa, whose workers, he said, were "the first local to organize [a] Hawaii sugar plantation back in '44"— also complained about what he perceived as white leaders demanding that leaders of Japanese origin, like himself, take a backseat.[79]

A strike requires a leap of faith, an abiding belief that the rich and powerful can be confronted and defeated. When that does not occur, it feeds resentment, anger, and doubt. Particularly when the union does not prevail, the strike's failure saps confidence in leadership and forces to the surface tensions that might otherwise have been submerged. It appears that Izuka fell victim to this cycle. Seemingly the same could be said for Amos Ignacio, an ILWU leader of Portuguese descent who also infamously defected, driven from the union by the force of Izuka's demarche.[80] Ignacio left with Izuka and joined his self-styled Union of Hawaiian Workers, which had 4,000 in its ranks at its inception and was active on the biggest sugar plantation in the archipelago.[81] The formation of the Union of Hawaiian Workers was "the most significant news in the history of Hawaii," crowed one journal extravagantly.[82] It was "no tempest in the teapot," according to John Reinecke. "It damned near cracked the teapot," for Ignacio and Izuka were able to "neutralize the local's and the international's direction on about half a dozen plantations on the Big Island" and "it took an awful lot of work to reduce his strength."[83] For his part Ignacio, like Izuka and others, claimed years later, "Actually I was the spearhead of organizing the union and Jack Hall moved in and took all the glory."[84] But at the time, Ignacio's revolt was in tune with Izuka's: the union charged that Ignacio reproduced 20,000 copies of the inflammatory anti-ILWU booklet *The Plot to Sovietize Hawaii* to propel this anti-ILWU initiative.[85]

Yet, said Arakaki, after Ignacio was dislodged, the ILWU members were informed by San Francisco that his replacement could not be Filipino or of Japanese origin but must be of Portuguese descent—which was fair enough except that the general homogeneity in the headquarters leadership still was hardly challenged. To Arakaki, this was quite troubling, since the "element leading the workers toward organization was the Japanese," who were "the most educated" because of the presence of "Japanese schools." These institutions served to "build morally and ethically"—and "culturally"—a "good citizen of the community." Arakaki's ethnicity was the "most cohesive" on the islands.[86]

The backstory to Arakaki's annoyance was that the much-complained-about Frank Thompson was accused of favoring Ignacio over all others, giving him undue prominence. Thompson relied on Ignacio for information, once informing Goldblatt, "Amos tells me that Arakaki is not liked at Olaa by the races other than Japanese and these people think he is too domineering. This may be so, [particularly because] there are some of these orientals that can [be] awfully stubborn and dumb acting." His plan? "I am going to get hold of Bert Nakano and tell him to talk to this guy as one Jap to another."Arakaki with his "bull-in-the-china closet tactics [is] responsible for the trouble here in Olaa," Thompson asserted. "This control has given this ambitious little character some big ideas, not only for Olaa but also for the rest of the sugar plantations on the Big Island." Arakaki, said Thompson with contempt, "walked up to me like Julius Caesar approaching a plebian and ordered me away." The aggrieved haole said, "[I] almost lost my temper to the extent of breaking every bone in the little bastard's body; however, I controlled myself and backed him up against the wall and really told the little bastard off. I asked him who the hell he thought he was anyway [and] I then pushed him to one side. [He] ran in behind me and around in front of me like a terrier and shouted." To Thompson, that was "really funny." He continued: "All these little men sitting around the table with a sheepish and chastened look on their face[s] didn't bat an eye. I pushed Arakaki to one side and walked over to the front of the table and informed them that I had something to say and that I intended to say it." He then stormed off with Amos Ignacio in tow: "When we got into the car and drove off, Amos told me that he had wanted to kill Arakaki, he was so mad. I told Amos to forget about it, as Arakaki had lost enough face for one evening." Thompson said that, finally, "Kawano told us that Arakaki hated Ignacio's guts" and "Arakaki told Kawano that he hated my guts." This heated episode revealed, inter alia, not only that the union's designated leader—Thompson—was insensitive to the plurality of the archipelago but, perhaps worse, that his ham-handed tactics were alienating a stalwart like Arakaki as he catered to a renegade like Ignacio.[87]

Even McElrath questioned Ignacio, a "very fair Portuguese" of whom McElrath said, "If his name wasn't Ignacio and [he] lived in the mainland, you would have assumed he was North European." Worse, "he was anti-Oriental," McElrath said. "He was anti-Filipino. He used to refer to Filipinos as 'these monkeys.'" Yet this man whom McElrath called "an opportunist" was being supported—at least for a while—by Thompson,[88] even though that support had paved the way for the potentially catastrophic defection of Ignacio.[89]

It would be an error to overstate or dwell unduly on Izuka or Ignacio, as both eventually faded into obscurity after flashing meteorically across the skies of Hawai'i. In 1972 Ignacio retired as a boiling-house superintendent after 24 years of service.[90] More representative of the union's mettle was a figure like Arakaki, who harbored similar complaints but, instead, fought internally and externally for justice. Scarcely a year after Ignacio's revolt, his Union of Hawaiian Workers lost spectacularly in a representation election sponsored by the National Labor Relations Board, which was simultaneously a major setback for those seeking to derail the ILWU and foil the union's radical allies.[91] Yet Izuka and Ignacio were only the leading edge of ever stiffer challenges that the CP and the ILWU were to face as the Red Scare was rising.

CHAPTER 7

Purge

A leftist juggernaut seemed to be rolling along in the isles. Neither interne-cine conflict, anticommunist bombshells, nor failed strikes appeared to halt what seemed like an unstoppable ILWU and Communist Party in Hawai'i. For in 1947, a year that had been thought to represent a setback for labor and the Left, Jack T. Osakoda of the ILWU was reporting gleefully that his union had organized soft drink plants, the meatpacking and newspaper industries, magazine distributing plants, the Sears, Roebuck department store, and the ice cream and refrigeration industries. All of the warehouses organized were in some way or another connected with longshore operations, with the exception of the newspaper industry, he added proudly. This was no trivial matter, given the vanguard role that the Honolulu press in particular played in opposing the ILWU's rise. Now that industry's inner sanctum had been breached by its staunchest foe, for the union had organized the Circulation Department of the newspaper industry, which consisted of street sales delivery and home edition delivery personnel, mailing room employees, and maintenance employees.[1]

The Communist Party was perceived as accepting instructions from Moscow and seen as controlling the union besides. More to the point, it had not been so long ago that the Big Five and their acolytes had sway in the ar-chipelago, and now it seemed they were being supplanted by the Big One—the ILWU. This was a kind of whiplash-inducing dramatic change that was bound to generate anxiety. Still, it was just before the pineapple strike that Jack Hall waspishly began to analyze the import of the Taft-Hartley law, re-cently passed in Washington, which had ominous implications for the union.[2]

This law, whose enactment was followed by the Smith Act trial, basically forced Hall and others to distance themselves from the Communist Party. When the CP was fundamentally illegalized, this disrupted severely the rise of labor and the Left, not least since the party was a forum whereby devilishly dif-ficult issues of race and ethnicity and democracy could be disentangled.

The words of Ichiro Izuka had kicked off this new phase in Hawaiian his-tory, but as the dust settled, it was evident that neither he nor his denunciation had been received with equanimity.[3] Following the explosive Izuka offering —which was disseminated widely in the archipelago[4]—the authorities fired a shot over the bow at the leading Communist, John Reinecke, and his spouse, Aiko Reinecke. Both schoolteachers, they were targeted for ouster from public education.[5]

This targeting of the Reineckes was part of a larger crackdown. John Reinecke alleged that the refuse collectors made special examination of his garbage, along with that of Jack Hall and others on the Left.[6] This was the run-up to a public hearing exploring how it was that two presumed Communists could become schoolteachers and thereby be in a position to mold young minds. They were charged with being members of the Communist Party in Hawai'i under a provision of a law originally enacted in 1884 that declared secret societies illegal. They were ousted summarily, though after the political climate had changed, in 1976 the Board of Education voted to restore his teaching credential, apologize to them both, and recommend the restoration of their pensions.[7]

But such an outcome was hardly envisioned when the inquisition commenced.[8] Broadcast across the archipelago, it was intended as a public flogging, akin to beating two slaves to keep the entire plantation in line.[9] Photographer Ray Jerome Baker knew the Reineckes better than most, having shared more than one dinner engagement with them over the years.[10] He realized the charges were unfair, but his was a voice hardly heeded then.[11]

The Reineckes, however, did not necessarily project the popular image of whiskered conspirators with darting eyes. He was a tall, rather gaunt man whose professorial mien seemed straight from central casting, replete with a dollop of dry humor. She was tiny, with a similarly shy and gentle manner.[12] Koji Ariyoshi recalled being in a Communist Party meeting with John Reinecke when a moth was flying around a light bulb. The gentle leader caught the insect but did not crush it; instead, he took it outside and let it fly away.[13] Born in Kansas in 1904, John Reinecke was by his own admission an "academic dilettante" and a linguist of no small talent. His spouse was one of seven children of a father who was both a preacher and a foreman in the agricultural industry.[14]

Yet the couple's apparently nonthreatening image dovetailed with the ascending idea that alleged Communist "infiltration" had penetrated so deeply that the prototypical next-door neighbor should be suspected, facilitating an all-encompassing witch hunt. But, alas, intentions can be waylaid, and a heavily Asian-Pacific majority in Hawai'i was hardly in the mood to attack those in the ILWU and the CP perceived widely as having rescued them from an ill-fated destiny, or to follow an elite that was seen correctly as spearheading this new crusade.

Thus, a leader of the Communist Party of California, Celeste Strack, was called to testify early in the hearing that led to Reineckes' dismissal. She was of the opinion that the "Reineckes are known and loved throughout the islands—and because this represents the Party's first public appearance in any capacity in Hawaii," the "response of the workers to our Party is terrific,"[15] a conclusion she gleaned after speaking at packed meetings and on various radio stations.[16]

Strack was on the witness stand for four hours at the Reineckes' hearing—with testimony beamed island-wide—and was examined by the exceedingly competent ILWU lawyer Richard Gladstein, who had flown over from San Francisco for the occasion. About 100 spectators were present, quite a few of them workers from the plantations and the waterfront,[17] there to witness her impressive presentation.[18]

The services of the feisty and flamboyant Gladstein did not come cheaply,[19] which led to a hectic round of fund-raising. Since the fund-raising campaign was centered in the fields, mills, and docks, it had the added advantage of solidifying union support for the Reineckes.[20] Many of these same workers were to be found in the line of march in the massive Labor Day demonstration led by the ILWU that coincided with the hearing. Strack noticed that "in the workers' ranks there was only a sprinkling of white workers." Commenting admiringly that "row after row of workers passed by," she added knowingly, "Class and national lines almost coincide [in the islands]. The Big Five, many smaller business people, a great many professionals and a number of the skilled workers are 'haoles.'" That was all the more striking she said, since "over half a million people" resided "on the islands, about 200,000 being sugar and pineapple workers and their families." Though she was a leading representative of an organization that was presently being reviled on the mainland—the Communist Party—she was overwhelmed by her positive reception in Hawaiʻi. She visited Kauaʻi, the maverick island, where her first meeting was at Hanapēpē ("which means 'make a baby!'" she said with wonder). It would have been more appropriate if the slogan that day had been "Make an uproar," as several hundred pamphlets from her soon-to-be-virtually-outlawed party "vanished in ten minutes, mainly the pamphlets on socialism by . . . Nemmy Sparks"; she "could have sold more" if available. Strack was not moved by the idea that the archipelago was a "paradise." With evident disgust, she said that the "housing, rented to the workers at exorbitant rates," was "disgraceful," describing it as "tumbledown shacks, like those in southern plantations on the mainland, which the workers try their best to keep clean and neat—an almost impossible job." She added with amazement, "Sanitation facilities are almost completely absent."[21]

Her experience in Hanapēpē informed her testimony in Honolulu. Oscar Iden, a member of the staff of US senator Hugh Butler, felt that attorneys opposing the Reineckes were "no match for Miss Strack." During these electrifying hearings, scores of observers were usually present, most expressing "considerable sympathy for the Reineckes," to Iden's consternation. Somehow,

Iden became quite well acquainted with Dr. John Reinecke and the couple's attorneys, though he found the doctorate holder to be a "low thinker" and "vindictive, crafty and resourceful" besides, not to mention "potentially dangerous." Ms. Reinecke was found to be merely "innocuous," but the couple's lawyers—Myer Symonds and Harriet Bouslog—were deemed to be "extremely radical." On the other hand, the chief witness—Izuka—"under cross-examination by Gladstein was pathetic," as he "became confused."[22]

But those adjudicating the case of the Reineckes seemed unmoved, not least by Strack. In her time on the stand, probably longer than that of any other witness, she testified at length about the nature of imperialism—of questionable relevance, according to some, in a hearing about the fitness to teach. She was asked about her two marriages, her roots in Chicago and San Diego, her attendance at UCLA and Berkeley and the University of Southern California, her joining the Young Communist League in 1933, and her presence at the 1943 gathering in Manhattan that led to the creation of that organization's successor, American Youth for Democracy. The August 1948 hearing was a rehearsal for the Smith Act trial. Hoary quotations from ancient texts of Marx and Lenin were read, with their conclusions then imputed to the Reineckes, particularly notions of dislodging the government by force and violence—which was ironic since it was force and violence that had been deployed so adroitly to bring US rule to Hawai'i in the first place. Of course, extended queries about racism were ruled to be immaterial and irrelevant. The government's chief witness was Louis Budenz, a former Red himself and then a professional stool pigeon who earned a tidy living testifying at anticommunist trials. He received a sympathetic hearing from the adjudicators—who were overwhelmingly white and whom the Reineckes' attorneys had unsuccessfully challenged for bias.

A more successful witness from the adjudicators' viewpoint was Izuka, whose booklet had unsettled the archipelago only recently. "During my official capacity at Local 135 at Port Allen," he testified gravely, "the party members got together before the executive board of the ILWU gets together and these party members . . . had all the agenda fixed." Since these alleged agenda fixers were in turn supposedly manipulated by Moscow, this meant that Hawai'i faced a threat no less formidable than that on 7 December 1941.[23]

Izuka proved to be a persuasive witness, at least to those who favored him.[24] Yet whatever his verbal circumlocutions, Izuka hammered home the point he had emphasized in his now infamous booklet: a veritable conspiracy of Communists to control the islands was afoot. As he later put it, there was an "axis" consisting of Jack Hall, George Goto, Jack Kawano, and John Reinecke—and it was the latter who was the first to fall victim to his ire.[25]

Yet despite the attempt to yoke the ILWU leadership to the Reineckes, leading Communist journalist and former stevedore Koji Ariyoshi later said that Hall was actually against the union's taking a strong stand on behalf of the two besieged schoolteachers. Ariyoshi was probably also correct in asserting that had the union failed to back the Reineckes, the ILWU itself would not have been as well prepared to back the Smith Act defendants in 1952.[26]

By a chain of twisted logic, this supposed immense conspiracy extended to the two mild-mannered schoolteachers who were effectively on trial—though the witnesses who appeared did not tend to bolster these bold imaginings. Azores-born John Luiz, a 35-year-old father of three, was principal at the Benjamin Parker School when Aiko Reinecke taught second grade there in the late 1920s; "her teaching was very good," he testified. Luiz had met her spouse in 1938 when she was teaching third grade at Waialae School, where he was principal. Ann McClellan Pfaender, a librarian at Leahi Hospital, had two children and had known Aiko Reinecke since 1925; when testifying, Pfaender was wily but no less supportive. Beatrice Krauss, born in Hawai'i and a worker in plant physiology at the University of Hawai'i, had known John Reinecke for decades and had nothing bad to say about him. Edith Keen, a counselor at Farrington High School since 1943, was well acquainted with him. "I know of class-cutting of his classes" was perhaps the most damaging thing she had to say about him. Sarah Kamakau, married with two children, spoke softly though firmly about her ties to the Reineckes. She had met Aiko Reinecke in 1921 and, beginning in 1938, taught in the same school as she for nine years; Kamakau also had nothing bad to say about her. Samuel Kapikula Stevens of Hilo—a true son of the islands, being "part Hawaiian, quarter Chinese and quarter Irish"—sought to rebut Izuka's testimony.

For his part, Reinecke, a skilled linguist, displayed his easy familiarity with various languages from the Philippines. Reinecke spoke over the heads of those who were judging him and directly to a wider audience. "At that time there were virtually no non-haoles appointed to the senior high schools," he recalled of the days preceding the rise of the ILWU, "and it was something of a sore point . . . among the teachers." But he neatly dodged the central question of the hearing: whether he was a dues-paying member of the Communist Party.

At the time of the hearing, the Reineckes were living at 1555 Pi'ikoi Street in Honolulu, a home they shared with over a thousand books resting unsteadily in the parlor and hallway on "about 33 shelves," Reinecke said. "Possibly two out of those 33 shelves may be called Marxist," he was quick to add.[27] But the authorities were not buying this rendition of a quiet and gentle John Reinecke—though it happened to be accurate. Their view of him was glimpsed in an incident a few months before the hearing; he had been punched in the mouth while distributing circulars for a protest,[28] an assault that was seen as a just desert by some. Yet the bulk of the population did not accept this antagonistic approach to the Reineckes,[29] nor the anticommunist surge that underpinned it.[30]

Unlike on the mainland, the majority of the working class in the islands rejected anticommunism[31]—which made all the more necessary the persecution of the Reineckes as a kind of demonstration project illustrating what might befall those so bold as to challenge the status quo. This was the backdrop to the testimony of Aiko Reinecke on 16 September 1948, as she was examined by her attorney Harriet Bouslog. Speaking softly, the witness told of her birth in Kahuku, Oʻahu, in 1907: "My father and my mother both came from Japan. My father came to Portland[,] Oregon[, when] he was 26 and lived on the West Coast for eight years[, where] he converted to Christianity," though he had been "born into a Buddhist family." He then "prepared for the ministry" and in 1899 "was sent to Honolulu to become assistant pastor of the Japanese Methodist Episcopal Church," she said. "During the 1900 Chinatown fire his church was destroyed so that he was sent on to Lahaina, Maui." Her mother "came from Japan to Lahaina to be married to my father."

Times had been tough for her family when Aiko Reinecke was a child. "In those days," she said, "[there were] outdoor toilets and all the cooking for the children was done in our kitchen." In 1913 her father "went to work for himself," she recalled. "Libby, McNeill and Libby Company was opening up pineapple fields above Kahuku and my father went as an independent grower. That is, he contracted to grow certain acres of pineapple and he was to sell the fruit to the company and borrowed money to do so but at the end of two years he gave that up." Thus, she said, "from 1914 until several years later [we] worked for the pineapple company." When she was 13, in 1920, "that was the year that the Japanese workers on the Oahu plantations went on strike," and "all my friends, all my playmates in the camp were being evicted," she remembered. "The company—the camp police drove them out of their homes and these people bundled up what little they had in 'furoshiki' [cloth bundles]," she lamented. "Suddenly all my friends were gone and I was left alone."

These tumultuous events left an indelible impression upon her. Speaking so softly that she was barely audible, the affecting witness spoke of becoming treasurer of the Honokaa Union Church in 1932. Then, "as a result, I suppose of the Depression," she said, "I developed a condition which is called hyperthyroidism," which was quite disabling.

She had met her future husband during the summer of 1928, and they rapidly became a pair. In 1937 she was able to get a job teaching at Kawananakoa School; by that time she was married to John Reinecke, who was unemployed. This was during a time when he had written a controversial pamphlet that bruited the idea of sovereignty for the islands and was greeted rudely by the authorities. Like her spouse, Aiko Reinecke demurred during the hearing when asked if she were a Communist. Yet she did admit that while visiting Manhattan, she had made her way to Madison Square Garden to hear a debate between Communist leader Earl Browder and Norman Thomas of the Socialist Party.

Pineapple workers vote in midst of 1947 strife. Though their critics considered the Communist-influenced ILWU to be antidemocratic, actually the opposite was the case. Courtesy of Anne Rand Library, ILWU–San Francisco.

Despite—or perhaps because of—the Reineckes' evident radicalism, hundreds signed a petition demanding that the two be reinstated to their teaching
posts. Part of the file assembled on John Reinecke included his 1947 testimony
in a contentious case in the islands. He had detailed that Maui was essentially
an agricultural county with 10 plantation units, some four or five subsidiary
firms, and about four or five large ranches. There the Baldwin family was estimated to control something like $15,000,000 out of the $24,000,000 in sugar
assets of this island, with pineapple interests trailing behind, followed by
ranching as a poor third. In Lana'i there was the all-powerful Hawaiian Pineapple Company, and on Moloka'i there were two pineapple plantations, along
with a major cattle ranch. But what probably drew attention to Reinecke's recounting of these unremarkable facts was his delineation of the "racial origin"
of ownership—"it is almost entirely Caucasian" or "haole"—and his outlining
of the peculiar racial dynamics of the archipelago: there were "552 names listed
of men who held positions from water luna [foreman] up to manager, and 91%
of these, roughly 501 to be exact[, had] haole names." Ironically, in 1948, the

year apartheid was proclaimed officially in South Africa, a form of that system already prevailed in the islands. This was an inconvenient truth that the authorities did not want in the spotlight, and John Reinecke's having called attention to it in his 1947 testimony, along with the Reineckes' ties to the organized Left, led to their losing their jobs[32]—despite the outcry throughout the islands.[33]

At a September 1948 membership meeting at Pier 11 in Honolulu, John Reinecke came to thank the Oahu Division of ILWU for its "splendid support" of his and his wife's struggle. He revealed that one union member had already been fired for attending the hearing. Suggesting the union's unwillingness to back down, Celeste Strack was then introduced, after the members were first asked if they objected to her addressing them and, with unanimity, no objection arose. In fact she was given a tremendous ovation, particularly after she outlined her participation in the 1934 General Strike in San Francisco that led to the founding of their union: she had walked the picket lines and was beaten by the police. The questions from the floor were not hostile but inquisitive— e.g., "What is Communism?" and "Can another political party be formed in the Soviet Union?" (Her response to the latter query was "1 single union. Single political party.")[34] It is unclear how many of those assembled were swayed by her responses,[35] though it was clear that some were.[36]

Yet the ILWU,[37] as John Reinecke saw it, had been somewhat reluctant in backing him and his spouse, as there was wariness about the union's seeming to align with intellectuals deemed to be Communist—though such wariness was decidedly not present among the rank and file of 'Ōla'a and Hilo. So, after being bounced out of the public schools, Reinecke faced the prospect of economic woe. Art Rutledge, a cagey operator who had helped to inspire Izuka's bombshell booklet that led directly to the Reineckes' losing their jobs, then hired the former schoolteacher as a staffer. They had met in 1939 and had had a star-crossed relationship since—Dave Beck of the Teamsters, also an AFL leader, once "ordered" Rutledge to fire him as a staffer. Reinecke wound up working for Rutledge for more than a decade and survived financially because of this employment and other work given him by union lawyers Harriet Bouslog and Myer Symonds.[38]

The islands were starkly different from the mainland in responding to the rising Red Scare.[39] The difference was that the overwhelmingly Asian-Pacific working class was reluctant to accept the elite-led anticommunist crusade as legitimate. These workers' perception was validated when Ronald Jamieson, a prominent Honolulu attorney and a member of the American Civil Liberties Union, agreed that the case against the Reineckes was bogus. "I am not now and never have been connected with the Hawaii Civil Liberties Committee," he said of the ACLU's local rival that stood to his left, thereby establishing his credentials. He agreed that "a teacher should not be removed for disloyalty or for lacking the ideals of democracy if he has neither said nor done anything which shows disloyalty,"[40] but his counsel was ignored.[41]

This pummeling of the Reineckes had occurred in the midst of what it was designed to forestall: a burst of strikes and union militancy, though this time Art Rutledge's AFL was deemed to be the culprit, as competition with the ILWU was driving this federation to new heights. A strike by bus drivers in Maui[42] was followed by yet another by their counterparts in Honolulu,[43] as well as other signs of unrest.[44]

Labor was straining to regain ground lost during the war and to confront the rising costs of everyday living. Simultaneously a telephone workers' strike took place on the islands, hitting rural areas notably hard; saboteurs were said to have slashed cable, disrupting telephone service, including service to the military.[45] The dock strike on the West Coast erupted as the Reinecke case was being mulled, and soon automobile batteries and tires joined the list of hard-to-get items in O'ahu. This list quickly came to include various food items, particularly those that were perishable such as fresh produce; supplies of citrus, lettuce, celery, and other vegetables began to dwindle, not improving the mood of some islanders.[46]

Militancy and repression seemed to be yoked together in perverse harness, for as strikes mounted, Communist leader Dwight Freeman was reported to have advised that comrades should not use the telephone unless it was absolutely necessary and that it was "not a good policy for all the members of the Executive Board" of the CP to "take notes of the meetings," for fear of what might happen to these scribblings.[47] Baker himself was summoned to the Lions Club, of which he was a longtime member, and was informed that he "had been specifically charged with disrupting the meeting by bringing John Reinecke." Baker reported, "Then I was questioned [and] asked if I was a member of the Communist Party. I stated that I was not and never had been." Then he was asked if he was "a member of any foreign Communist Party." Nolle Smith, the club's leading Negro member, "stated that the reputation of the club was involved," so Baker was "expelled."[48] (Though not a member of the Communist Party, Baker actually was one of the two remaining members of the old Socialist Party of Hawaii, having joined in 1910.[49])

Earlier Baker had bumped into Smith, who acknowledged that the kind of financial distress he was facing made him malleable to a purge. He "confided to me," said Baker, "that he intends to give up the liquor business" since the war's end meant there was less of a need for a site where "Negro soldiers could go unmolested and drink." Smith was thinking of selling his home in Honolulu and moving to Maui, where his son was a rancher.[50] No matter. At a secret meeting "at which I was practically commanded to appear," Baker said ruefully, "it was intimated that in introducing Dr. John Reinecke to Lion members . . . I had embarrassed and insulted" all assembled.[51]

The bulldog attorney of the Left, Myer Symonds, took Baker's case, threatening to sue the club and go to the press. The Lions got a severe case of the jitters and agreed to reinstate him. But Baker was not mollified, and resigned instead, since "we [himself and Symonds] were both convinced that Red-baiting has received a major setback."[52]

Though not a Red himself, Baker was familiar with this organization generally and its frequent companion—Red-baiting—recalling that when the Communist International, which was based in Moscow and comprised all the parties of this stripe globally, was dissolved in 1943, he had been informed that "it will knock the props out from under [the] ever-lasting Red-baiting,"[53] since "it means that capitalist reaction in the United States [or] anywhere else cannot justly hold the Communist Party of the Soviet Union [responsible] for anything said or done by Communist parties outside the Soviet Union."[54] He was sorely misinformed, however.

Still, the sacking of the Reineckes was not the only burden that radicals in Hawai'i had to bear as the Red Scare rose and the Cold War crept stealthily toward the island. During the same month that the Reineckes lost their jobs, it was reported that nine bars in Honolulu were routinely refusing service to non-haoles, principally African-Americans,[55] and those who backed Jim Crow also tended to back anticommunism.[56] This shift toward Jim Crowism was a function of two trends spreading from the mainland to the islands: a postwar influx of African-Americans whose arrival helped ignite mainland white sentiment that bristled in their presence; and the ongoing rise toward power of the Asian-Pacific population, whose growing influence coexisted uneasily with that very same white population and heightened its nervousness about the arrival of yet another community of color.

This problem was proliferating and exacerbating already parlous class relations in the archipelago—indeed, since the Negroes and the Asian-Pacific population were generally absent from the elite, the class and "race" struggles seemed to merge seamlessly, inflaming both. Many whites appeared to grow more insecure as their relative economic hegemony was challenged ever more fiercely and such challenges then seemed to generate within some amongst this group an attempt to assert more forcefully their racial privilege in compensation. One man who tirelessly sought to analyze these two interlocking struggles was Frank Marshall Davis, an African-American born in Arkansas City, Kansas in 1905, who had made his mark as a journalist and poet in Chicago before decamping to Honolulu at the suggestion of his good friend Paul Robeson.[57] The well-positioned Davis was also a good friend of the legendary writer Richard Wright.[58]

Arkansas City had prepared Davis for Honolulu in a sense, in that this town of 10,000 had a Negro population of 400. Perhaps because of these disparities, Davis confessed, "I spent so much time at the library that the librarian

used to call me her bodyguard." By the time he was 8 years old, he had con-
quered Victor Hugo, whose works, he said, "developed in me a taste for good
literature that continues to exist." Subsequently, he became known as the
"poet who looks like a prize fighter," since at maturity he was well over six
feet tall and weighed 200 pounds—"and people just didn't like to fool with
me," he added proudly, not least "since I look so much like Joe Louis." Thus,
he "met and became a personal friend of Jack Johnson," the heavyweight box-
ing champion; "we had a very good relationship," Davis noted. By 1934 he
was executive editor of the highly influential Associated Negro Press and
every day, as a result, read 35 daily newspapers, including some from Britain,
Africa, and the Caribbean, which gave him a breadth of knowledge of contemporary affairs that was hardly equaled when he arrived in Honolulu. Because of his widespread knowledge, he recalled that he "often had the FBI
contacting me" as they "wanted to find out whether . . . a person who had
applied for a job in Washington was a good [security] risk." Puckishly and
subversively, Davis "determined [that] if this brother who had applied for this
job in Washington was an Uncle Tom[,] then I would tell the FBI that this
person was . . . no good[, and] if a person was sufficiently militant, [I] would
praise him to the highest." His journalistic duties led to his meeting Harry
Bridges in Chicago. "I was involved with the Abraham Lincoln School," said
Davis, which was closely tied to the Communist Party. Davis' Euro-American
wife inherited a trust fund serendipitously in 1948, which allowed him to
contemplate moving to Hawai'i.[59]

"I am 42 years old and married," Davis told Jack Hall in mid-1948.
"Around the first of December, my wife and I plan to leave Chicago to live in
Hawaii, although neither of us has ever been there."[60] Davis had established
himself well in the Windy City and was hardly in need of a job. "Late in 1945
and early in '46," he told his good friend Langston Hughes, "I had a disc
jockey show plus news and comment over a local station and the 15 minute
daily period kept me hopping." But he was tiring of the travails of mass communication in Chicago and longed for a change of scenery. So he considered
heading west, seeking to reside "preferably on a small farm on one of the islands other than Oahu which would give me time for creative writing that's
just impossible as an active newspaperman."[61]

But it was not only the magnetic pull of warm ocean breezes that was
bringing Davis to the mid-Pacific. "If you hear of my being brought before the
Rankin Un-Americans," he said of a potent congressional committee in 1947,
"don't be too surprised."[62] Escaping to the Pacific might mean an escape from
the House Un-American Activities Committee, he thought wrongly. He was
able to wangle $20 monthly from the Associated Negro Press, with whom he
had served as an editor for 13 years by the time of his departure, and with that
(and his spouse and her inheritance) he headed to Honolulu.[63]

"Japan's attack on Pearl Harbor," Davis pointed out, "took place 7 December 1941. We launched our invasion of Hawaii by leaving Chicago on 7 December 1948. Some cynics say that in certain ways, the second was worse than the first"—and he was only exaggerating slightly.[64] Like any new visitor, after the beauty of palm trees and perpetual sunshine had worn off, Davis began to grumble, immediately complaining that "food and rents are very high," with "eggs at $1.10 per dozen" and milk at "20 cents a quart"; tiny "'studio' apartments cost from about $80 up per month." Davis was a bit perplexed by local customs, e.g. "taking off your shoes at the door."[65] But he was a quick learner and an early adapter, which served him well in the island. Later realized that when it rains, "some people take off their shoes, on the theory it's easier to wash your feet than clean your shoes," for "some of the streets here are dirt and some paved streets don't have sidewalks."[66]

The uncomplicated pleasures of Honolulu made it easier to forget the hardships of the mainland.[67] The dark-skinned Davis admitted that he—along with his spouse, who was white—seemed to "like Honolulu" right away,[68] though being isolated in the mid-Pacific had its drawbacks.[69] Davis' editor preferred that he remain in Chicago, and, evidently, so did many others[70]—the list included the influential Roy Wilkins, the moderate leader of the NAACP, who at this juncture spoke warmly of the burly radical.[71]

Yet there was a larger reason why Davis came to appreciate Honolulu. "For the first time I felt I had some dignity," he said of his new hometown after living there for decades. Though often described as a card-carrying Communist, he had served during the war on the staff of the Republican Party and "had no objection," he recalled, to backing Wendell Willkie, the party's past presidential hopeful.[72] Thus, his hard-boiled attitude toward mainland racial practices was driven by experience more than ideology. He feasted on Waikīkī, with its "overwhelmingly light brown to black look which my eyes hungrily devoured." Finally, Davis cried, "I felt that somehow I had been suddenly freed from the chains of white oppression." Hawai'i, he stated, became the "only area in the United States which has successfully shown the possibility of integration with integrity"; the "determination to maintain group identity and respect undoubtedly is largely responsible for the deepening of equality existing in Hawaii," he concluded."[73]

Davis wasted little time plunging into the complex maelstrom that was Hawai'i. He encountered an archipelago that was undergoing a wrenching transition, driven only partially by the growing impact of progressive labor. Robert Greene—chairman of the newly organized Hawaii Civil Liberties Committee (HCLC), which eventually was to affiliate with the Communist-led and Manhattan-based Civil Rights Congress[74]—was distraught about the proliferation of Jim Crow practices, including the refusal to serve Negroes in bars and dance halls. Although blacks were the primary victims seemingly, he added that "cases of such discrimination have been reported against other non-Caucasians" as well. "This is logical," he stressed, since "if one race can be insulted with impunity, so can others."[75]

As so often occurred under the US flag, African-Americans had been herded into a small neighborhood in Honolulu. "When folks talk about Smith Street as a section where there are Negroes," said one writer, "they mean only one block—the block between Pauahi and Beretania."[76] Others were more concerned about how the HCLC was supposedly digging its tentacles into the NAACP. This came clear when a letter from the NAACP was read at the HCLC meeting in October 1948; it announced a mass meeting and requested the Left's cooperation in an effort to eliminate discrimination. That the HCLC had a considerable $2,943.89 in its treasury suggested why its cooperation was sought.[77] But the NAACP was courting danger by deigning to cooperate with the HCLC, given the obtaining political climate. Congressional staffer Oscar Iden noted that he "had the good fortune to gain the confidence" of the HCLC and thus was invited to its meetings. He found it curious that though "persons of Japanese ancestry" predominated, "some time ago Negroes in considerable numbers began to attend the meetings."[78]

Bias was a principal concern at these gatherings. Thus a "Negro woman, a graduate of a California university, told me," said Davis, that "she was asked in sincere curiosity by an Oriental girl in her office to show her long, monkey-like tail!" There was a "whispering campaign to keep Japanese, Koreans, Chinese and Filipinos divided" that augmented neatly this anti-Negro campaign, he declared, underscoring his repetitive theme that antiblack racism was instrumental in propelling bias against others.[79]

At the University of Hawai'i at Mānoa, Davis was stunned to find that virtually all the professors and instructors except the "teachers of Oriental languages" were "haole." He noted that there were "capable, even brilliant" non-haoles "either teaching or otherwise employed" on the mainland, "but efforts to get the administration to hire them are fruitless," he said with incredulity. "They will employ clerks and assistants and general personnel but the top jobs are reserved for whites. That, incidentally, is a pattern that exists throughout the islands."[80]

Davis egged on his fellow victims of discrimination to unite instead, an effort to forge class and race solidarity and strengthen both simultaneously. "Is there any sound reason why the Japanese, Filipino, Korean, Chinese, Hawaiian, Puerto Rican and Portuguese people here should throw aside their historic cultures and become mere rubber stamp proponents of the ideas and customs of Western Europe as revised by the mainland?" he asked. Within days of his arrival, Davis expressed amazement that the "struggle goes on relentlessly to remake the brown and yellow peoples of Hawaii into brown and yellow imitations of a haole from New York or Memphis." Seeming, with irony, to make a valedictory just after he arrived, he advised that "these beautiful islands can still chart their own future"[81]—though like most people of the Left, his questioning of the cultural genocide unfolding in the isles did not extend to questioning statehood, which was a factor driving this unfortunate process.

Yet even with such a cultural strangulation, the isles could still manage to chart a useful future. The problem in no small part was the navigators, and here the archipelago was lacking, insofar as the NAACP was concerned. Or so thought Davis, who said of his new home, "I doubt if, anywhere else in the world, there is an NAACP branch similar to the one in Honolulu." Pointing out shortly after his arrival that on its books the organization claimed, "roughly, over two hundred members," including "a sizeable number of Caucasians," he noted that "it is among some of them [the Caucasians] that the difficulties have originated," for there were two bitter factions embroiled in a miniature civil war. Leading the right-wingers was a white woman, secretary of the Republican club, who blandly told Davis that there was no prejudice against Negroes "'as a group'" and who insisted that Negroes "must 'prove their worth.'" This strange civil rights leader did not favor enactment of a civil rights law for the territory. This was the official Republican position, for the party swore that there was no Jim Crow in the isles—this at a time when more and more cafés and taverns barred Negro patronage. Working with her were several Catholic leaders and quite a few Negroes, he said with astonishment. The other faction was led by members of the resurgent Democratic Party, which had been revived only recently by the ILWU—and the Communists.[82]

The NAACP branch had gotten off to an auspicious start during the war. Interestingly, it was a similar left-wing Chicago mate of Davis'—Oscar Brown Jr., the performer and raconteur who simultaneously led the NAACP branch in the Second City—who instructed the association leadership in early 1944 that he was forwarding "petitions bearing 102 names of citizens of Honolulu" and the Philippines who desired "immediate establishment of a branch" in Hawai'i.[83] From its inception this branch reflected the diversity of the archipelago, as evidenced in the leading role played by Esther Park, who was of Korean ancestry though born in Hawai'i.[84] Also from its inception, the branch found it necessary to rebut the myth that Hawai'i was a racial paradise, somehow transcending the messiness that defined the mainland.[85] This illogical supposition was further repudiated when one NAACP leader was informed reliably that the manufacturers and industrialists in the islands had gotten together among themselves and agreed not to hire any more Negroes and to discontinue any immigration.[86]

The formation of the NAACP branch was a manifestation of the settling in the islands of a number of African-Americans as an outgrowth of their wartime service and others, like Davis, drawn by Hawai'i's charms—along with some whites originating from the mainland who were loath to leave behind the

peculiar folkways of Jim Crow. Thus, even before the Pacific War had concluded, branch leader Katherine Lackey had concluded bitterly that "the pro-
verbial racial equality here is more fiction than fact," as "ownership of land,
monopoly of shipping, control of press, education, utilities, transportation,
etc.," were "*all* by one small group of people." Noting that "this group is white,"
she contended, "There is not a colored group here which has not felt discrimination in some form or other." Nevertheless, she was heartened that the phe-
nomenal rise of labor would be a countervailing force to this hegemony[87]—a
trend tellingly backed by some Negroes who had accommodated themselves to
the status quo.[88] Discrimination in employment, salary schedules, housing, and
social activities all demanded attention, she insisted.[89]

The inappropriately named Lackey was quick to denounce newspaper advertisements blaring boldly, "HAOLE SECRETARY WANTED" for the affluent
Bishop Trust or "'mechanic wanted, haole'" or "'rooms available, only haoles
need apply.'" Besides there was an unwritten law, she maintained, that restricted certain areas for haoles only; such vile practices had led, she reminded,
to the "Damon Tract Riot which lasted nearly a week."[90]

Even the most shamelessly obsequious Negro could not accept easily
that the Central YMCA was largely for whites and the Nuuanu YMCA was
for others. Filipinos were denied life insurance by some island companies.
One particular firm did not issue insurance to Chinese, Japanese, Negroes,
or Filipinos. Chinese, Japanese, and Negroes were turned away routinely at
various times from various clubs and restaurants, while schools followed the
same general lines. "There is no law, no regulation by the Department of
Public Instruction"—so hawkish in its pursuit of the Reineckes—"which
stipulates that students of certain racial groups [attend] certain schools,"
Lackey lamented. Nevertheless, the haoles attended Punahou, the Hawaiians
attended Kamehameha, and those of Asian descent attended the public high
schools, the Chinese favoring Roosevelt and the Japanese favoring McKinley.
In addition, she added with rising fury, "that strange phenomenon in American education known as the English and non-English standard school, allegedly established on the basis of ability to use the English language[,] also
tends to segregate students according to racial groups."[91]

Moreover, few white students attended the local public university, as the
islands' elite did not look there for leadership; its alumni rarely reached the
top flight in the employment scale in the local economic setup, which had a
long-established policy of a double wage scale, one for whites and one for
others. Lackey remarked that at a recent conference "the Japanese reported
the most oppressive discrimination in employment" and "the Hawaiians reported less prejudice socially."[92]

Little wonder that Lackey informed NAACP organizer Ella Baker som-
berly that "there are difficulties facing the chapter."[93] Though by 1948 the

reported 3,000 Negroes residing in Hawai'i (2,000 of whom were said to be in the military) constituted a tiny minority in a population of a half million, they seemed to be a chief locus of bigotry. But their numbers had leaped from 255 out of 423,000 eight years earlier, so their proportion of the overall population had increased dramatically, perhaps unsettling some.[94]

Visiting Communist leader Celeste Strack had a chance to see racially segregated "restricted areas"—for instance, in the neighborhood of heiress Doris Duke's huge mansion.[95] General Wayne Carleton Smith at the Schofield military base was hailed when he ordered every GI, every officer, every civilian worker, to sign a pledge promising not to discriminate on the grounds of "race." The effort was admirable, but the fact that this urging had to occur in December 1947 itself was a troubling indicator.[96]

Though Lackey was elected president of the Honolulu NAACP branch unanimously, she conceded openly that the bulk of the drudgery was to fall upon Kenneth Sano, a Japanese-American leader.[97] Sano proved critical in this organization—an indication, as Lackey stressed, that the "NAACP can make a special contribution to *all colored groups*."[98] Sano's leadership was all the more remarkable since the composition of the branch as of mid-1946 was 75 percent Negro, 10 percent white, and 15 percent Japanese, Chinese, Portuguese, Filipino, and Hawaiian.[99] Unsurprisingly, by 1947 the group's stationery billed the chapter as "the voice of minority groups."[100] Yet resting 2,000-plus miles from the mainland and having a palette of issues that was not always congruent with headquarters' was a liability.[101]

Nonetheless, as the Red Scare gained momentum on the mainland, inexorably its fierce gales reached the archipelago. Frank Marshall Davis, like Paul Robeson, the man who had brought him to Hawai'i, was known to be close to the Communists; thus, Claude Barnett, who employed Davis as a writer, decided against sending out a letter urging resistance to the gathering anticommunist wave.[102] Davis was not so inclined, and soon the Federal Bureau of Investigation was monitoring him.[103]

Simultaneously, Gloster Current of the Manhattan–based NAACP leadership raised the specter of purging radicals from the local branch,[104] and if the NAACP's sacking of its founder W. E. B. Du Bois was any indication,[105] the result Current wanted to see was the ousting of supposed Reds and the blocking of all other supposed subversives from the membership rolls.

Morris Freedman of the Honolulu NAACP supported such a purge.[106] Current agreed that there were far too many radicals in the branch's ranks.[107] Branch leader Catherine Christopher concurred, declaring that "our branch has been infiltrated by the Hawaii Civil Liberties Committee," an organization frequently charged with being a "Communist Front."[108]

But her opponents charged that it was Christopher herself who was at fault. She was a practitioner of a "queer sort of parliamentarism [*sic*]," according to

Charles Bouslog. She felt that "to take any public action concerning any problem would be to 'create racial tension by admitting it existed,'" though the
"Negro workers in Hawaii [are] singled out specially by the Honolulu police for
sudden arrest without charges, for beatings without cause or arrest, [and] for
practical unwritten restriction for eating and entertainment to one small area
of the downtown district." There was "staggering evidence" for all this that
"was collected [by] committees of the NAACP here." For example, "photographs were taken showing Negroes being refused entrance to dance halls" and
restaurants. There were a dozen or so cases in the courts of false arrest and
police brutality against Negroes. In the Navy housing area, many civilian police had launched a war of nerves against Negroes and generally made things so
unpleasant for them that they would feel compelled to begin to move back to
the West Coast in disgust. The NAACP was also seeking to "attract a large
number of fine members of Filipino stock, as the single Filipino frequently gets
the same public treatment here as the single Negro." Hawai'i may have seemed
far, far away from the mainland and its more crudely complex racial problems,
but since the "plane fare from San Francisco or Los Angeles to Honolulu can
now be obtained for as little as $250 a round trip," these problems were arriving
in the Pacific with increasing rapidity.[109]

Bouslog, unlike Christopher, was not engaging in puffery about deadly
harassment of Negroes. Riveting Honolulu in 1948 was the bloody case of
Frederick Penman, who had died in police custody,[110] amidst credible allegations of his being subjected to racial epithets.[111]

Some of this anti-Negro sentiment was laid at the doorstep of Governor
Stainback, who hailed from Jim Crow Tennessee. Or so thought Newton R.
Holcomb, in his mid-thirties at the time and territorial director of the US Employment Service. He was not sure that Stainback had gotten rid of all his ill
feelings about the Negro, he said, since he had "instructed Nils Tavares, the
Attorney General, to create the policy whereby mainland Negro servicemen
could not remain in Hawaii." Holcomb had a suspicion that the chief executive
had also been active in preventing Negro stevedores from coming to Hawai'i
before the war.[112] This reputed anti-Negro bias was of consequence to the
ILWU, for by late 1946 about 22 percent of the longshore and warehouse membership on both sides of the Pacific was African-American. This amounted to
about 11,000 Negroes out of a membership of 50,000; on the West Coast of the
United States, the proportion in the sealers' locals was estimated as being as
high as 60 percent in San Francisco and 50 percent in Los Angeles. In the large
San Francisco local, the proportion was about 25 percent, while 50 percent of
the scalers and 10 percent of the warehousemen in Los Angeles were Mexican.
Of course, of the 30,000 ILWU members in Hawai'i, only a tiny percentage
were Negroes, but their high proportion on the mainland still meant that racism toward them could hardly be ignored.[113] Yet the branch leadership that was

not close to the union was more interested in purging real and imagined Communists,[114] and its influence was not diminishing.[115]

Alfred Stacy, then the leader of the Left in the branch, felt that he won the election just concluded in early 1949 and should have been declared president but was blocked, as his opponents complained that fighting bias was indicative of Red influence.[116] Frank Marshall Davis was among those who found this idea bizarre.[117] Publicly, Davis was more forthright. Having argued in one of his many newspaper columns that he doubted if "anywhere else in the world, there is an NAACP branch similar to the one in Honolulu," he added, "And for the sake of Negro advancement, I hope not," for the archipelago was enduring a sapping Red Scare.[118]

Edward Berman, who had mirrored Izuka's retreat from left to right, was not buying Davis' argument. The journalist-poet had "suddenly appeared on the scene" from Chicago, he proclaimed, and then proceeded to "propagandize the membership about our 'racial problem' in Hawaii." In Berman's opinion, "He had just sneaked in here on a boat and presto! [He] was an expert," though actually, Berman asserted, Davis was a "front for the Stalinist line." Davis was foremost among those who sought to "create a mythical racial problem here," though "we have no Harlems, little or big in Hawaii" and "there is no segregation." Aghast, Berman informed Wilkins that "the Communist Party was deliberately trying to stir up racism in an area where [there is] racial unity and harmony." These Reds were "more concerned about the speedy assassination of Tito [of Yugoslavia] than they are about the advancement of the colored people of these United States." Thus, he argued, "it is better to have no organization than to have these tactics continue."[119]

Worn out by the wrangling, Davis agreed with the idea of suspending activity.[120] Charles Bouslog, also of the Left, was in accordance, demanding that the "charter of the branch must now be revoked."[121] Wilkins agreed, rescinding the branch's charter in mid-1949,[122] just as the archipelago was undergoing a whirlwind of unrest generated by an ILWU strike on the docks. All things considered, this decision was quite harmful to the Left, which needed as much organized support as it could get, given the heft of the Big Five. More than this, removing from the scene a skilled fighter against racism did little to buttress a disproportionately Asian-Pacific workforce with problems in this realm all its own. Later Berman boasted to the House Un-American Activities Committee that he had helped break up the local NAACP branch.[123] The Reineckes were purged from the teaching profession, and then the entire branch of the NAACP was subjected to what amounted to a purge—ill omens for the ILWU.

CHAPTER 8

Surge?

"To All Workers" was the headline on an important and widely disseminated ILWU leaflet in the fall of 1948, just as the Reineckes were being purged and Frank Marshall Davis was packing up in Chicago and preparing to head west. "Election day will be Saturday, October 2, 1948," it was said, "and you who are able to vote will be asked to vote and help the Democratic candidates get nominated. Those who are unable to vote will be asked to work at the voting booths," with the aim of putting forward "the poor man's candidates, the Democratic candidates." Lurking as an issue was that the GOP was "saying that the 'RED' [strength] prevented Hawaii from becoming a state."[1]

This revival of the once moribund Democratic Party was to culminate in the stunning defeat of the GOP in pivotal 1954 elections, which were to set the political tone for Hawai'i for decades to come. Yet the foundation for the ouster from power of the instrument of the elite—the Republican Party—had been laid by the ILWU and its allies in the Communist Party, and this trend had begun to appear as early as the elections of 1944.[2] This did not bode well for the Big Five.[3]

When the union was just attaining liftoff in mid-1944, Jack Hall observed that it would be extremely easy to change control of the legislature from plantation control to plantation worker control, because of the unique districting and allocation of representatives in Hawai'i. Like most states, the territory of Hawai'i was gerrymandered to the advantage of nonmetropolitan areas. Thus the so-called "outside" islands such as Kaua'i and Lana'i—almost entirely plantation communities—sent 18 of the 30 representatives to the legislature, leaving metropolitan Honolulu but 12. Hall therefore found "an almost even chance of getting a fairly liberal legislature for 1945" to be a top priority.[4]

In 1946, Ray Jerome Baker observed that "reaction won to a large extent throughout the mainland" but "here in Hawaii about 35 of the fifty-odd candidates [backed] by the CIO won office."[5] Jack Kawano, a diminutive Communist of medium build with black hair, brown eyes, a light tan complexion, and a distinguishing burn scar on his upper right arm,[6] was reputedly told by Hall that actually 18 of 30 of the candidates backed by labor in 1946 had won seats in the territorial legislature.[7] At the Smith Act trial, Kawano testified about a late 1947 meeting of 65 individuals who crammed into Hall's small house for an intense discussion about work within the Democratic Party.[8]

A scant year later, a local newspaper warned that "under present conditions the union can take over the [Democratic] Party, if that is its objective."[9] The ILWU was certain to be prominent as a factor and an issue in the territorial and county campaigns of 1948, said one journalist nervously.[10] Within the Democratic Party there was an inrush of ILWU members, encouraged by their leaders to join. The influx was pumping new blood into what used to be a very anemic body. O'ahu for the first time in 16 years had a Democratic organization in every precinct, and the resultant fight between progressivism and reaction was expected to cause just as great a tumult within the Republican ranks as within the Democratic.[11] More than 20 Hawai'i labor leaders had been elected to the party councils in the recent precinct elections, an indication of things to come.[12] Thus, even before the results of the important 1948 election had been registered, the leading progressive Ray Jerome Baker observed that "all our people have been joining the Democratic precinct clubs and working for the Democratic Party." There was "considerable talk to the effect that the Communists have taken over the Democratic Party," he said, but as he saw it, the point was that "when the masses really participate in the elections and exercise clear judgment in the selection of candidates, then the Fat Boys will start violence."[13]

It was true that the ILWU encouraged its members to participate in this party's structures.[14] In September 1948, Marshall McEuen, a top political operative with the CIO, stopped by the Honolulu home of Ray Jerome Baker and confirmed this.[15] Joseph Farrington, the powerful publisher that the union had backed—the maneuver that had outraged Izuka so—was paying dividends to the union, assailing in increasingly bitter terms their mutual foe: Governor Stainback.[16] Most of these new Democratic Party leaders were ILWU leaders, and by June 1948, according to the *Honolulu Star-Bulletin*, the ILWU had seized the majority of Maui Democratic Party posts.[17]

"It has often been charged," said McEuen, "that the legislature of Hawaii has been under the dictatorship of Hawaii's businessmen"[18]—but times were changing and shortly that would not be so. Jack Hall's chronicler was no doubt correct in asserting that "to a large degree, the ILWU helped create the modern Democratic Party of Hawai'i."[19] For after challenging the Big Five economically, the ILWU then chose to challenge them politically.[20]

Jack Kawano was well positioned to declaim about the Democrats, for as with the ILWU, he played a central role in its revival. Mitsuyuki Kido, a graduate of the University of Hawai'i in 1928, asserted that it was Kawano—along with himself and Jack Burns—who was responsible for the revival of the Democratic Party in the islands. The diminutive Kido—five foot three inches tall and weighing 150 pounds—acknowledged that "all of us knew that Kawano was a member of the Communist Party," but they also knew that he could deliver labor, which was essential. "At that time the AFL was more the aristocrats of labor," Kido explained, "and they wouldn't join us, see. They would be more on the Republican side, you see." Thus, he said proudly, "I got elected on the strength of the ILWU." It was Kawano who "just took me from one stop-work meeting to another" during the monumental Sugar Strike of 1946, "and that's how I got elected," he recalled. "It was the first time I ever ran for office," he said, and he succeeded in joining the territorial legislature.[21]

But Kawano was not singular. Koichi Imori, a short, bandy-legged man with immense shoulders,[22] was typical of the strength the Left brought to politics.[23] By his own admission, his strength as an organizer was his acute memory for faces and names. "'I called 48 guys by name'" at one union election, he said. He claimed to be the father of the Teamsters in Hawai'i and had served as leader of the Central Labor Council, tied to the AFL—though he was a reputed Red.[24] He was a dynamic recruiter for the CP too,[25] having reportedly brought to their ranks a number of members.[26] The larger point was the wide influence exercised within the Democratic Party by the union, as exemplified by figures like Imori.[27] The union had "taken over the party," it was said.[28] The ever more furious Governor Stainback was not reclining in the face of this counterattack, however.[29]

"The Communist organization has been very active in the recent primary elections," said the nervous governor, "although it has kept hidden in the background. It supported the bi-partisan combination of Mayor John Wilson, a Democrat, for re-election as Mayor [of Honolulu,] and Joseph Farrington, the Republican Delegate." Thus, Stainback pointed out, "at many of the polling places there were workers with Mayor Wilson ribbons on one side of the coat and with Farrington ribbons on the other." The mayor was 76 years old, and his executive assistant, W. K. Bassett, was for all practical purposes the acting mayor, thought Stainback, and was seen as all too close to the Reds. The CP, Stainback argued, had concentrated on getting control of both the city and the county of Honolulu, through the mayoralty and the county Board of Supervisors, rather than attempting to get control of the territorial legislature.[30]

The authorities also thought they had good reason to be suspicious of another leading Democrat—Bassett—since the professional anticommunist Paul Crouch referred to him as the "notorious Communist founder." Bassett "boasted," according to Crouch, "that he had been a friend of Harry Bridges for thirty years and used his official credentials to go through the gates of the Honolulu Airport to meet Bridges as he stepped off the plane,"[31] sentiments that echoed Stainback's.[32] Stainback's opinion was not his alone. Movie mogul Cecil B. DeMille warned Congress of the purported Red threat to Hawai'i as he blasted away at the Communist Party: "'Faint hearts, gentlemen,'" he advised, "'do not win either fair ladies or elections.'"[33]

Prominent mainland organs were echoing this mordant concern about what was going on in the islands, as Hawai'i's politics were becoming a national issue. In the popular *Saturday Evening Post*, concern was expressed over the "actual switch of wealth into the hands of Asiatics," which had ignited a "surge of confidence bordering on cockiness [within] the Asiatic element of Hawaii's population." With apprehension, it was said, "Today Hawaii is a white man's paradise, with a question mark after 'paradise.'"[34]

As some saw it, this issue of "race" was not inconsequential in explicating the rise of the Reds. Certainly this was the viewpoint of Victoria K. Holt. A Democratic Party leader, she had been a party member for three decades before she had a "confidential interview" with the staff of Senator Hugh Butler, who had arrived in Honolulu in 1948 to conduct hearings about the prospects for statehood. She observed that at a recent party convention Jack Hall and his comrades were so well trained in parliamentary procedure that when any motion was introduced, they were able to carry it to the floor without any opposition; this taught her that the "power of the Communist Party does not show in the number of people that are registered," not least since the "Japanese people" over whom they held sway "pay allegiance to their leaders." They had "lived under a feudal system for thousands of years" and were "very obedient to their parents" besides, and this deferential attitude was transferred easily to the Communists, said this mother of nine.[35] Martin E. Alan, also white, concurred, but from a different perspective, pointing to the alleged monolithic "race hatred by the Japs," which was "deepseated." He told the senator's staff, "I went to Jap language school for two years—I know."[36] Stainback found time to visit the convention of the Young Buddhist Association in Hilo, where he discussed with sorrow his perception that "more than half the known Communists in Hawaii are of Japanese blood."[37]

Since much of his maneuvering was behind the scenes, many did not realize the utter danger of Governor Stainback's crusading effort to link AJAs, the ILWU, the CP, and the Democrats in a conspiratorial quadrangle. Thus in 1948 Hall and his colleagues were strategizing to replace the appointed governor—Stainback—with someone more congenial to their tastes. They had their eyes on Robert Shivers as the designated replacement, but US attorney general Tom Clark, who was vetting the process, was informed by Honolulu lawyer J. Harold Hughes about the "anomalous" relationship that existed between Shivers and the Communist Party. Hughes alleged that during the war, while Shivers was a special agent in charge of the FBI office of Honolulu, it was said that he publicly supported the "local Japanese element" and "now considers he has their vote in his pocket," which was indicative of his "close connection with the Communist Party."[38] Hughes found this terribly suspicious—Shivers had blocked internment of Nisei and Issei, and now they wanted him as governor, in league with the Democratic Party, which was reportedly controlled by Reds. "He has betrayed his Government," Hughes said of this FBI agent; furthermore, Hughes felt that his view was "shared by the majority of leading citizens" among Hawai'i's all-important "Caucasian Element."[39] Again, Governor Stainback attempted to substantiate this supposed connection between Nippon and Communists in Hawai'i, informing the Department of the Interior—which administered the colony—in "personal and confidential" terms that the "list of enrolled Communists in the Territory [reads] like a directory of the officials of the ILWU, with most of the members being of Japanese descent"; he attached the list to support his point.[40]

Governor Stainback had ignited a crusade—not to save his job from being given to Shivers, as he saw it, but to save the colony from the AJAs, the ILWU, the Reds, and their alleged Democratic Party front. "The most dangerous factor," he told Washington, "is the inroads of Communism upon the Japanese of the community, particularly those connected with labor organizations." This group was "considerably embittered, many of them connecting the white race and its government with tyranny and oppression," Stainback stated. "Moreover," he asserted, "the Communists are using as propaganda the appeal to race prejudice," for as one Red had supposedly said, "Hawaii is the 'most fertile field for Communism in the whole nation.'"[41] Furthermore, "the citizens of Hawaii have a larger voting percentage than any state in the nation," the governor said, adding, "I believe about 89% of those eligible to vote take part in the elections."[42] According to Stainback, this degree of voter participation suggested that, if they so desired, the alleged Nipponese-Communist-ILWU-Democratic tie-up could simply take power via the ballot box.

The governor was not singular in this campaign. One who communicated with Senator Butler came full circle in linking the nervousness about Japanese-Americans and Communists to the resuscitation of the Democrats. He sent Senator Butler a clipping from a Honolulu newspaper featuring "Daizo Sumida, President of the Businessmen's Association" and wrote alongside: "He is the one who was reported to have been taken in by the military on December 7th 1941 after the Pearl Harbor attack. He was interned for the duration by the authorities—and *now* is very active." "How soon we forget," he moaned. It was also generally rumored in intelligence circles, he indicated, that Sumida had been the governor designate of the Japanese military who would have been installed should the Japanese have taken over after Pearl Harbor.[43] Could it now be that the alleged anti-haole sentiments of the Nisei and Issei had been transferred from Tokyo to Moscow via the Democratic Party?

Yet it would be an error to see the Democratic Party's moving to the Left as solely a product of the feverish imaginations—or organizing—of Communists. The much-reviled Mayor Wilson certainly did not think it was. By the time of the Smith Act trial in 1953 he was in his second term, having been first elected to office in 1924. The problem that Stainback and those of his ilk encountered was that there was a popular basis for Wilson's Red and labor-friendly approach. Wilson, an engineer, had been appointed mayor in 1919 to fill an unexpired term. He served intermittently as the metropolis' leader from then until the 1950s, in addition to being appointed as postmaster by President Roosevelt from 1934 to 1939 and serving as a national committeeman for the Democratic Party for forty-two years. He was also a former organizer of stevedores and thus testified at the trial on behalf of Jack Hall.[44]

Testifying at the very same trial, Stainback angrily disagreed with Wilson's assessments—and political outlook. By then he had lived in the islands for over four decades, arriving in 1912 directly from law school and, suggestive of the policy of affirmative action for haoles, had become attorney general by 1914. He went on from there to become US attorney in 1934, a federal judge in 1940, then governor and a member of the territorial supreme court. At the trial he recalled the fight within the Democratic Party in 1948 that had cost him a prominent role at the group's convention, which he found upsetting.[45] At the Philadelphia convention he was generally ignored by his fellow delegates—despite his elevated status. Still, he was elated when "President Truman [himself] had inquired about Communistic activities in the Territory of Hawaii, as had powerful Hugh Butler," the senator from Nebraska who had congressional oversight of the colony.[46]

In light of the disadvantages he faced, what should have been preoccupying Stainback was the tactical acuity of his comrades within the Republican-oriented local elite,[47] which, not least because of its lack of real contact with the members of the isles' Asian-Pacific majority, often alienated them. Because of such blunders, the Democrats continued to soar in the archipelago—though, understandably, labor and the Left had one foot planted firmly in the camp of Henry Wallace, the defrocked former FDR vice president who challenged Truman from the Left in 1948 on the Progressive Party ticket. Though assessing this ticket's campaign generally positively, Louis Goldblatt was critical of what he saw as some of its sectarian traits,[48] a critique shared by Baker.[49]

After conferring with Bridges, Goldblatt contended that the ILWU had made its own blunder in the islands, beyond the avid friendliness toward the Wallace crusade. It was as if the union had scored a catastrophic victory, for its political success had so inflamed the bloodlust of Stainback and the local elite—who, like others, had come to see the Democrats as the ILWU's political arm—that it magnified and concentrated their hostility.[50]

Hall, on the other hand, was elated in the aftermath of the important November 1948 election, since although the GOP controlled the territorial senate 9–6 and the house 20–10, the union felt sufficiently confident that it could neutralize the Republican advantage. The bounce back on Kaua'i and Maui was telling, solidifying these islands' gathering role as Democratic strongholds.[51]

The concern about Wallace was not misplaced,[52] but the union in Hawai'i was operating at a stratospheric level that its counterparts on the mainland could hardly comprehend. While the ILWU in San Francisco was flailing about in its attempt to dislodge GOP governor Earl Warren, the ILWU in Honolulu was seeking to place its man in the territory's chief executive's chair. The union in the islands faced a different set of challenges, as its opposition was much more dependent upon Washington to balance the scales against the Left. That was a major reason why radicals became so pro-statehood, on the premise that locals should elect the powerful force that was the governor, as opposed to having him appointed from officials 5,000 miles away.[53] Their desire for influence in Washington was also propelled by the passage of anti-labor laws there, such as Taft-Hartley.[54]

Driven by the Taft-Hartley law, Ricardo Labez, formerly of the ILWU and a prominent Filipino leader, called on Reds in the union to identify themselves.[55] Bolstered by Taft-Hartley, the anticommunist surge from Washington was beginning to have impact in the isles.[56] The union was compelled to enter the electoral arena not least since its opponents were seeking to compensate for losses at the bargaining table by making gains in the political realm[57]—a trend that had become painfully evident.[58]

The critique of Wallace's Progressive Party was reflective of a larger split developing within the Communist Party and "fellow travelers" concerning to what extent these forces should be more aggressive politically, particularly with regard to Marxists coming out of the closet and revealing their true political identities, and the wisdom of doing so as a Red Scare was surging. The impact of Taft-Hartley, followed by the perceived leftism of the Wallace campaign and the Democratic Party victories locally, caused some to wonder if radicals might be moving too fast too soon and were, as a result, inviting a sharp counterattack by their opponents. Jack Kawano recalled the time in 1948 when Archie Brown, the tough California Communist, arrived in Hawai'i. He was a "white man, [a] Jewish fellow," said Kawano, who was about five foot ten and weighed about 175 pounds.[59] Born in Sioux City, Iowa, the stocky and muscular Communist had arrived in San Francisco in 1926 and had been a stevedore since the mid-1930s—he journeyed to Honolulu for a week in 1948. Subsequently, Brown recalled speaking to Hall about the sensitive matter of some Communists revealing their true political identities. "Jesus Christ," Hall responded, "the union has enough trouble"—but Brown was unconvinced.[60]

Disputing this recollection, Jack Kimoto said that Brown had come to Hawai'i "not to make us [Reds] come out in the open." "Well," said Kimoto, "we always wanted to come out in the open," but "it was Hall and those guys who were afraid to come out." It was a fraught time, as he recalled J. R. Robertson of the ILWU leadership saying, "'You know, these two weeks will be remembered as the two weeks that shook Hawaii.'" Kimoto concurred: "We had terrific discussion and argument about whether to come out in the open," with one side arguing vociferously that "it was time the party should come out and state the facts" about its CP membership. This side argued that doing so would make things easier for the union, as the CP would become "like a lightning rod," deflecting heat away from the ILWU. "Guys like [Robert] McElrath, Dave Thompson, [and] Ernie Arena" were all against this initiative, Kimoto said, and so there was a compromise: "We did come out in the open [but] not the entire party." Only the titular leader, Charles Fujimoto, revealed his CP membership, thereby becoming the public face of radicalism. Opponents were against even that, but those who prevailed wanted to go further and "have at least one union man come in along with Fujimoto."[61]

Robert McBurney Kempa, a seaman who had graduated from Roosevelt High School, was then a Communist and attended this important gathering at Ewa Beach. There were heated discussions, he said and he opposed the Hall-McElrath faction, which was against more openness but was defeated by Kimoto, Dwight Freeman, et al. Kempa was among those who did not want Fujimoto as the CP spokesman, but the retort was "they wanted a kamaaina [island-born person], and they wanted [him] to be someone who wasn't a haole." At this tense moment, "the Executive Board was considering having several trade unionists announce their [CP] membership to the unions"; the sugar and pineapple unions were considered, but longshore "was the only one that was strong enough to protect any such individual if they came out and said, 'I am a Communist, too.'"[62]

When asked about this tumultuous meeting years later, the tactful McElrath recalled that it was the "uncontradicted testimony" of Kawano that "there was a meeting and that I took Archie on and as a result of that, I think he said I was kicked out of the party." Still seemingly miffed about it all, McElrath observed that "the Communists in those days were philosophers" and that Archie Brown, most notably, fit this bill, demanding, "'Let's take the machine guns off the shelf and go!'"[63] But standing against McElrath at this meeting at the home of the Fujimotos were, among others, the respected union attorney Harriet Bouslog, the Reineckes, and Charles Fujimoto himself.[64]

Hall and McElrath were apprehensive about a Communist offensive in the face of Taft-Hartley legislation, which forced them to file affidavits attesting to their being non-Communists. It was suggested that they simply resign from the CP, sign the affidavit, and then rejoin, but this may have been too cute by half. Jack Kawano chose this moment to leave the CP, suggesting that Brown's demarche was not timely. Though he was to testify against his former comrades subsequently, Kawano pointed out decades later that "even today I still believe what the Communists say about capitalism"—i.e., that it "breeds war" and is "based on greed." Thus, Kawano, who could speak but not write Japanese, continued to reflect the leftist trends of his ancestral homeland; yet he suggested that whatever its merits, the California Communist initiative may have placed undue pressure on comrades who were unable to absorb it.[65]

Jack Hall was equally dismissive of Brown. John Reinecke felt that Hall, the regional director of the ILWU, had many substantial differences with the Communist leadership on the West Coast, believing that they meddled too much with union affairs. Yet Reinecke's cautious assessment also inferentially revealed why this leadership might have had a problem with Hall's approach, which was increasingly reflecting his insecurity, perhaps exacerbated by heavy drinking. Thus Hall despised Claude White, a Negro from Washington, D.C., as Reinecke recalled him and a student at the university under the GI Bill who was raising funds for progressive causes. Hall also was suspicious of Steve Murin, though this hardworking radical spent his whole career as a union man. The fundamental feeling that Hall conveyed in both cases was distrust of "outside intellectuals," said Reinecke, who added, "I think that is characteristic of the ILWU," though Hall, McElrath, and much of the top leadership could easily be characterized as "outside intellectuals" themselves. In fact, said the soft-spoken Reinecke, although Hall didn't consider himself an intellectual, he "probably did more thinking on basic intellectual issues than most people who are commonly called intellectuals," speaking of his ability to engage in tactical maneuvers during strikes. Reinecke, who knew Hall well, thought the former seaman to be a "very self-sufficient man" who "knew his own ability very well," which "gave him a certain arrogance" that did not go over well with figures like Archie Brown. It was not as if Reinecke disliked Hall, though Reinecke did have a lingering resentment since the ILWU chose not to employ him. Despite this, he recalled fondly a time from the early 1940s, before Hall's marriage, when the future ILWU leader stayed at his home and showed himself to be "one of the most considerate and gentlemanly persons" Reinecke knew. "One thing that was typical," Reinecke said, "was he came home late one night, found both doors locked, which was unusual, so he got in the back seat of our Ford and curled up [and] slept there," rather than rouse his hosts.

But Hall had other liabilities that clouded his thinking, making it difficult for him to get along with Communist—or any other—leaders. "I remember we had one bottle of whiskey," said Reinecke, "and we hid it away in the closet to keep him from laying his hands on it"; in addition, "when he was around our place, I didn't see him read books to a great extent, of any kind."

This combination of drinking and intellectual failings did not inspire confidence among Communist leaders, who might have reacted to his staunch opposition to their proposals by automatically thinking that Hall was reflecting his incipient alcoholism and failure to study.[66]

Communist leaders also might not have appreciated that Hall did not get along very well with Harry Bridges, whose tenacity and leadership was so well respected among radicals. Ernest Arena, who once had been a Communist himself and was a longtime ILWU leader, recalled a time when the split between Hall and Bridges was so intense that the regional director would make calls outside of his office for fear that the top ILWU leader was spying on him somehow and monitoring his telephone.[67]

Koji Ariyoshi, also a Communist, would argue that this was all part of Hall's insecurity. He felt that Hall lacked confidence in the rank and file, an insecurity that colored his every move. "He got off into trade unionism and became an administrator and technician,"[68] Ariyoshi noted, an assessment not intended to be complimentary. These perceived weaknesses of Hall's in turn did not inspire Communist leaders to have confidence in him.

Nor did his alcoholic binges inspire confidence. The leader of the pineapple and cannery workers local of the ILWU, which had just undergone a bruising confrontation with management, felt compelled to inform Bridges in late 1948 that during important negotiations "Jack Hall has gone on a drunken spree for as long as a week and has failed to attend a number of important committee meetings when we most needed his advice and guidance." Once, the local's leader had called on Hall at 5:30 p.m. and found him "sleeping[,] as he had been drunk"; further, he had "been guilty of the same offense during previous pineapple negotiations." This was not just one man's opinion but the consensus of the negotiating team. "I have no personal grudge. . . . I have the highest respect and admiration for him," another team member said, noting that Hall had apologized, but "something must be done," since "the whole organization in the Territory is too loose."[69] Philip Maxwell, who represented management in negotiating with the union, recalled a time when Hall was so drunk that he spread guacamole all over his face and had to be helped to his car in order to make it home.[70]

Moreover, despite the admirable—if not astonishing—growth of the union, radicals had good cause to look skeptically at the union with which Hall was so closely identified. Early on Roy Gutsch, an ILWU member then stationed in Hawai'i, told Bridges that he had little confidence in Hall and much more in Kawano,[71] an opinion shared by others. As early as December 1945 Hall and Kawano met with Bridges, Goldblatt, and Robertson, and the minutes reflected the conclusion reached: there had been no "true collective leadership in the ILWU in the territory."[72] Weeks later Kawano complained that "there existed an unfortunate situation in Hawaii where personality difficulties among the ILWU leaders of the Big Island are impeding the work of the ILWU there."[73] J. R. Robertson, a prominent member of the San Francisco–based leadership of the ILWU and a man known to be close to Bridges, was informed of complaints from workers that "they were never told of what had been happening in the union" and that "in some instances, no meetings had been called by the officers since the last encounter with the employers." Consequently, it was reported in late 1947 there was a "diminishing interest in the affairs of the union."[74]

Though they were heartened by the evident successes in Hawai'i, there had long been concern in San Francisco among both the ILWU and the CP about a number of occurrences within the union—grumbling from the Nisei and Issei members, for example. Much of this discord centered around what had been thought to be a union success—its weekly radio broadcasts. "In addition to our regular Sunday radio programs at 6:15 PM," said Hall in the summer of 1946, "we have obtained further time [and] broadcasting will be by remote control from our offices." He added, "This costs us only $20 per program.[75] "I sold more radios in this town for the business community because of those broadcasts," boasted McElrath. These programs were wildly popular, he claimed, saying, "We cost these employers hundreds of millions of dollars."[76]

Yet others were not so happy with these programs and thought they revealed a fundamental flaw that reflected poorly upon both Hall and McElrath, an opinion that Communist leaders could hardly ignore. The debate about whether Reds should come out of the closet was, in a sense, a surrogate for a wider discussion about the perceived failings of Communist leaders of the ILWU. Even McElrath's astute spouse was critical, informing Hall that there was "very little response" to the English language programs: "very few families listen," she averred, and "a couple of individuals said frankly that they were bored by the program and did not wish to listen to it." The Japanese language program received "the least response," though she conceded that of them all it was the Filipino program that seemed to have "the most response." Suggesting the complexities of building a union in Hawai'i, however, she said that "a number of Visayan families have said that they do not understand Ilocano and would appreciate something in either Visayan or Tagalog."[77]

Validating her criticism was an influential leader of the pineapple and cannery workers local who complained about the "Regional Officers and its staff," principally Hall and McElrath, whose maneuverings were "unhealthy." McElrath's pride and joy were his regular radio broadcasts, but this local leader felt that the program was a good illustration of broader problems. "The script of the first radio program was prepared by the Regional Officers themselves and not a single local officer was consulted," he observed, and thus "none of the rank-and-filers understood their language." Furthermore, after the Izuka pamphlet and the Ignacio revolt, the "top leadership of the

Regional Officers was so confused and bewildered that their reactions reflected a great deal upon the secondary leaders." On the other hand, J. R. Robertson—who often clashed with Hall and McElrath—was praised.[78]

"One of the biggest criticisms that I have," said this leader who identified himself as "T. Oshiro," "is that the Regional Officers are unwilling to accept any kind of suggestions offered by the local officers in regard to radio programs." He charged that they were reluctant to take criticisms or accept suggestions from anybody besides themselves. In addition, McElrath, who was assigned to work with the sugar local, was reportedly never to be found in his office or anywhere near the union hall. "The first and best chance of locating him would be to inquire at this pet bar in town," Oshiro said with disgust.[79] Since Hall and McElrath were so adamantly opposed to a more public role for the CP, their other alleged failings served to undermine their overall position.

Moreover, the California Reds were understandably concerned with the anticommunist surge, which was proliferating, though no actual and identifiable Communists were stepping forward in rebuttal. Thus, the Hawaii Civil Liberties Committee was organized in response to the persecution of the Reineckes and played a key role in inviting Celeste Strack to speak on their behalf. The committee was immediately punched with a forceful body blow of anticommunism in the form of a charge that it was no more than the lengthened shadow of the Communist Party. Roger Baldwin of the American Civil Liberties Union hastened to distance his national group from the local committee,[80] though ACLU members in Hawai'i were not as charitable.[81]

It was in this charged and volatile context that Charles Fujimoto unveiled himself as the spokesman for the Communist Party in Hawai'i in October 1948, just before the November elections. Speaking on radio station KHON, Fujimoto portentously intoned, "This is the first time a member of the Communist Party of Hawaii is addressing you, the people of Hawaii," as he proceeded to lay out his party's unique perspective on things.[82] Ray Jerome Baker was among those who were unimpressed. Fujimoto "had good material," Baker thought, "but his voice was not too good for radio and his manner of speaking was not very forceful"; those who opposed him "had a much better delivery."[83] Fujimoto also simultaneously held a press conference at 1526 Kaihe'e Street in Honolulu that was attended by the inquisitive journalist Adam Smyser, then toiling for the *Honolulu Star-Bulletin*. Smyser recounted this episode as a witness against Fujimoto at the Smith Act trial. "He said that the Party had been formed here about 1938," said the witness, "and that he had become a member of the Party about 1941." Getting along on $318 per month as a scientific worker at the University of Hawai'i, the altruistic Fujimoto "said he was taking about a one-third pay cut to work for the Party here." He also said "that he had been born on the island of Kauai and he had been born into a very poor family," Smyser recounted.[84]

These internecine conflicts should not suggest that relations had broken down between the CP and the ILWU. Actually, a year before the 1948 showdown with Archie Brown, the flow of union members across the Pacific to study at the California Labor School—which maintained close relations with the Communists—seemed to be accelerating. David Jenkins, the school's director, spoke of a group of approximately 20 Hawaiian members of various locals who had indicated a desire to attend sessions in San Francisco.[85]

Those choosing to make the trek to California were some of the union's rising stars, and there they also had the opportunity to see in action an even larger Communist Party than was in place in their homeland.[86] The professors at this school who were teaching the basics of class struggle included Bridges, Goldblatt, Robertson, and others. Among the topics covered were the union's history, racism, and how to mobilize members.[87]

Thus, when Fujimoto stepped before the microphone in the wake of the Sugar Strike, the revival of the Democratic Party, and the rise of the ILWU, he seemed to confirm in febrile imaginations that a veritable Bolshevik takeover was nigh—and that he was simply foreshadowing a more formal announcement. J. B. Matthews, a flaming anticommunist who was billed as an expert on radicalism, helpfully provided an "outline of [the] Communist Party leadership strategy for [a] coup resulting in control of the Democratic Party of Hawaii." This, he warned forebodingly in his "confidential" report, "portends the CP objectives of eventual economic dictatorship" and formation of a "socialist state, as well as the important immediate objective of control of shipping and all harbor facilities."[88]

According to an official body in Hawai'i, when the Democratic Party convention was held at the auditorium of McKinley High School in Honolulu on 2 May 1948, a relatively large number of Communists had been chosen as delegates and 41 Communist Party members held credentials, while several Reds secured appointment to the standing committees of the Democratic convention. Yet when a resolution was introduced in this party in June 1949 that required all prospective Democratic Party members to swear that they were not and had never been members of the Communist Party, it was debated extensively rather than accepted meekly. Then, after a bitterly contested three-hour session "highlighted by an exchange of invectives between the 'right' and 'left-wing' committee members, the resolution was rejected by a vote of 8–7," it was reported with incredulity—though, admittedly, 15 members of this leading body were absent.[89]

J. R. Robertson, by way of contrast, was pleased with the results. Tweaking their opponents, the ILWU leaders chose to meet in the citadel of power, the Board of Supervisors' headquarters in Honolulu, where Robertson exulted. It was just a "Big Lie that the Communist Party was moving in and trying to take over," he complained. "I recall reading it in the 'Advertiser' and hearing it over the radio," but, fortunately, he continued, the union was able to beat back the counterattack.[90]

The presence of Communists in Hawaiʻi was a direct threat to national security—or so thought investigators from the US House Committee on Un-American Activities. In their hands was a report that stated that, late in 1948, Masao Kauwai, then a civilian employee of the US Far East Command, was intercepted in Honolulu while in possession of classified military documents; he was tabbed as liaison agent between Okinawan and Japanese Communists, and Aiko Reinecke was allegedly in contact with this reputed agent upon her return to Hawaiʻi in 1948. Ominously, "Russian vessels have also stopped over in Honolulu," the report added.[91]

Since Hawaiʻi seemed to bring together the two leading fears of Washington—fear of Japan and fear of Russia (in the form of Japanese-American Communists)—it seemed to raise hysteria accordingly. After the Izuka bombshell, morale in the CP plummeted, and attendance at meetings declined; there was a corresponding perception that surveillance was rising— telephone wiretapping, rifling through garbage pails, and the like—with a concomitant fleeing of members in a kind of death spiral. Rather than slink deeper into the closet, the CP leadership felt that a bolder and more open approach was mandatory.[92] There seemed to be a connection between the CP's discovery in mid-1948 that Fujimoto's telephone was tapped and the decision for him to emerge as a Communist spokesman.[93]

Those who were hounding the CP were pleased with their handiwork. One congressional investigator reported elatedly that in 1948 Jack Hall had listed in his own handwriting a set of security regulations to be used by the Communist Party, which included "not to discuss Communist Party business over the telephone, throw Communist Party material in the wastepaper basket, etc." Yet, it was said, this document was "written by Jack Hall in the rough draft form and thrown by him in the wastebasket," where it was gleefully retrieved.[94]

These precautions were an ironic reflection of the growth and militancy of the ILWU and the fact that it was an open secret that the CP had ignited this effort; given this background, the party had reason to believe that this was no time to run and hide. Did not simple honesty—and premature glasnost—mandate that Reds unveil themselves? When Dwight Freeman attended a meeting of 60 in Maui in mid-1947, Jack Kawano recalled that Freeman "was happy to see [that] practically half of those people assembled at that meeting joined up, signed up into the Communist Party."[95] By the time of Celeste Strack's 1948 arrival in the islands, the CP had about 200 members in Hawaiʻi,[96] though, like many on the mainland, the anticommunist John F. G. Stokes of Honolulu was more concerned with the heavily Asian composition of the CP.[97]

Thus, Henry S. Toyama was recruited into the CP by Doris Ozaki in 1947, when he was 21 years old. He felt compelled to assume a nom de guerre,

"Al Young," on his membership card; at the time the stated goal of the CP was to become a mass organization, doubling its membership. Most of the meetings he attended lasted about an hour and a half, but, inevitably, nervous members were apprehensively noticing whether anyone seemed to be taking detailed notes or engaging in other behaviors that might suggest duplicity—none of which was conducive to the success of the CP's membership goal.[98]

This added pressure might also have contributed to what appeared to be a crackdown on seemingly laggard members, even erstwhile champions. It was in late 1948, as the Red Scare deepened, that a perceptibly irked visitor strolled into an office on Pier 11 at the Honolulu docks. It was Kawano's fellow Communist Jack Kimoto. He "came into my office," Kawano recalled, "and told me that he was sent to have a heart-to-heart talk with me by the Executive Board of the Communist Party," since there were "quite a bit of complaints about myself"—e.g., his skipping meetings—as well as "rumors that I had been more interested in playing golf than my Communist activities" and "complaints from longshoremen on the waterfront that I was not spending enough time on the waterfront." Kawano was informed curtly, "The only thing you have in your mind is the union," which presumably was not a good thing. Kimoto told him brusquely that he "must learn how to study more seriously" and that he did not "understand the Communist theory." Then, Kawano said, "he asked me if I had a copy of [the book] 'History of the Communist Party.'" Kawano replied simply that he did. So Kimoto reportedly switched tack, telling him, "You should take that book during your spare time and go through that book, not once but many times." Supposedly, the demanding Kimoto said, "Unless you do that we cannot consider you a good Communist. And for that you might even be dropped." Party members were concerned about him because "some of my friends had paid my dues for me," and he was a "very poor example." This "heavy criticism" was from Kimoto "in particular" but echoed by "Mrs. Fujimoto," spouse of the new CP spokesman, and by Freeman also. Kawano confessed that these criticisms were not misplaced. Beginning in 1947 the union had to write him more than once to spur him to attend meetings. "I shot pool once in a while," speaking of how he was spending his time. "I played golf once in a while" and "played poker, just like Jack Hall," he said, launching a glancing blow at the man who had nudged him out of union leadership and whose weaknesses too were similarly glaring. Yes, he "deeply hated" Hall, he admitted, but answered no when asked bluntly, "You might kill Jack Hall, didn't you say that?" On the other hand, he acknowledged that he was "pretty friendly" with Charles Fujimoto and his wife—"As a Marxist I had great respect for him at that time," Kawano said, but "maybe not as much [as] my respect for Mr. Kimoto," he added. Yet soon he was to become alienated from them all, though he regarded Kimoto especially as a "sincere man."[99]

Kawano was becoming progressively disgusted with this party he had helped build. Before this confrontation with Kimoto he had traveled to an ILWU board meeting at the union headquarters at 150 Golden Gate Avenue in San Francisco. On the sidelines of this gathering he found time to meet with Strack, Brown, and Robertson and starkly informed them that there was a terrific amount of dissension and ill feelings among the Communists in Hawai'i on the question of coming out into the open. The case of the National Maritime Union, where unveiling Reds made it easier to slaughter them, was cited as a negative example. After Kawano's testy encounter with the Reds, it was Hall's turn. "He told me he was going to make a trip to San Francisco," said Kawano. "He stated that he was getting disgusted with his work because the Communist Party had been riding herd on him" and that "the orders he received from the International [ILWU–San Francisco] sometimes were contrary to the orders of the Communist Party" in Hawai'i. But "he was a paid employee of the International," and "as a result of that he found himself in Dutch with all of the Communists." Thus "he was getting disgusted and he was going to San Francisco to have a showdown"; and "if the showdown was not satisfactory to him, he was already determined to come back and quit the Communist Party and the union and everything."[100]

According to Kawano, Hall was in a very happy mood upon his return and stated that everything was all ironed out. A method had been worked out so that he did not have to follow the orders of the Communist Party of Hawaii, and if there was a conflict, he could ignore the CP. The CP would have to contact its counterpart in San Francisco, which would then huddle with the ILWU in that city to work things out—and if they could not smooth over problems, the matter would be forwarded to CP headquarters in Manhattan, which would presumably have a say.[101]

It is unclear how many raging disputes the beleaguered CP leaders in Gotham had to sort out, but it is evident that the simultaneous surge of labor and the Left generated a corresponding pushback by the authorities, which contributed to a maelstrom of conflict[102]—including a spate[103] of lawsuits[104]—that demanded time,[105] cogitation,[106] money, and even fistfights.[107] Finally, in the fall of 1951, Edward Berman—a onetime union ally turned mortal foe—cracked under the pressure. He found himself in the hospital after slashing his wrists and imbibing turpentine in an apparent suicide attempt. After he was revived, his physician acknowledged what was evident—his patient was in a deep "'state of depression'" and that "'the whole thing has got him down.'"[108] Berman's precipitous decline was symbolic of what was simultaneously about to befall the CP, at a moment when it felt sufficiently confident to propose a policy of openness,[109] igniting a debate that sent radicals generally into a tailspin.[110]

Yet the strength of the Left was such that it could absorb such setbacks. Certainly the mood of the Big Five did not improve when renowned performer and activist Paul Robeson, known to be quite close to the top levels of the CP leadership, chose 1948 as the time for his arrival in the archipelago. He had come to perform for the benefit of the ILWU, and, in any case, he was a favorite of the union's leadership. Already Robeson had become a regular on the union's periodic radio broadcasts, with his rendition of "The Canoe Song" being a staple[111] on the airwaves.[112]

Robeson "had this amazing quick ear," Goldblatt marveled, and "within a couple of days he had picked up Filipino songs, a Hawaiian song and, of course, he already had Chinese songs"; his was "a very effective tour."[113] A. Q. McElrath was happy to report that "we have lined up a Japanese tenor and a Hawaiian soprano who would be willing and eager to coach him in Japanese and Hawaiian, respectively."[114] The response to his visit, she said, "has been terrific, despite conscious baiting, last minute sabotaging, etc. and there has been a wild clamor for more of Robeson."[115] Robeson's celebrity candlepower was such that even the mainstream press in Honolulu could not afford to ignore his performance at Roosevelt High School that was sponsored by the ILWU.[116] The "Maui concerts, particularly the one at Baldwin High, went very well," said Jack Hall; "Baldwin High was nearly packed."[117] Ray Jerome Baker also found the concert "packed"—"every seat has been sold," he noted.[118] "The high school where he sang was filled to capacity both nights," Baker said, adding, "He is certainly giving the unions a good boost."[119] Robeson did not disappoint, as he sharply criticized the economic arrangements in the archipelago as "'medieval and feudal'"—before singing songs in Japanese, Chinese, Filipino, Russian, Hebrew, and Polish, as well as English. During his 11 days in the Pacific, he performed in 14 public concerts and as many private performances.[120]

But the annus horribilis that was 1948—for the Big Five—was not capped by Robeson's arrival. After all, he came—and went. But the founding of the *Honolulu Record* by Communist stevedore and intellectual Koji Ariyoshi was an even clearer sign that radicals had sunk deep roots in the archipelago. The *Record* was a unique weekly that engaged in far-reaching investigative journalism uncovering the manifest inequities of the islands, published stinging editorials, and provided space for eloquent voices, such as that of Frank Marshall Davis. The founding of this journal was accompanied by the arrival of the similarly inclined *Hawaii Star*, which targeted the Japanese community and was printed in part in their language. Nicheibei Minshu Kyokai of the Japanese American Association for Democracy, organized in August 1946, helped spawn this journal.[121]

It was in early 1947, said Kawano, that he, Kimoto, Bert Nakano, and a number of affluent Japanese "aliens" met to discuss forming this latter enterprise,[122] though the CP owned 20 percent of the shares of this paper.[123] The *Record* appeared on newsstands in August 1948 from its offices at 811 Sheridan Avenue in Honolulu after the *Star* discontinued its English language version[124]—upon receiving intense scrutiny.[125]

Controversies aside, the left-leaning political line of these periodicals found a willing audience in Hawai'i.[126] Thus the *Record* quickly attracted attention, albeit some that was unwanted. A congressional investigator pointed out subsequently that it was "sent abroad in quantities to Communist countries, notably Red China,"[127] a reflection of Ariyoshi's wartime camaraderie with Mao Zedong.

Mao? A growing CP that was holding press conferences? A surging Communist-led union that was thought to dominate the Democratic Party? Now a weekly left-wing newspaper? What next? What was next was the decision by Washington authorities to shine their investigative spotlight on Hawai'i, now beginning to be viewed as Uncle Sam's troubled nephew.

CHAPTER 9

State of Anxiety?

"My visit to Hawaii, supported by many interviews on the islands, leaves me with the deep conviction that international revolutionary Communism at present has a firm grasp on the economic, political and social life of the Territory of Hawaii." So spoke Senator Hugh Butler of Nebraska in 1948 after a series of exhaustive hearings in the archipelago that exposed dangerous fault lines in the quest for statehood. More than that, it raised difficult questions for Washington as to what to do about what had become something of a problem colony at a time when labor and the Left had become fierce proponents of statehood and the Big Five was having second and third thoughts.

Some of the senator's confreres had gone further, suggesting that statehood for Hawai'i would mean the Kremlin would get to choose two new members of the US Senate. The Nebraska senator had arrived in Honolulu in May 1948, and his staff had been there from mid-August to late October of that same year; they conducted 77 confidential interviews. "I personally talked with more than 100 citizens whose remarks were not made a matter of record," he said, and their comments were explosive. He found that there were 11 branches of the CP in O'ahu and one each in Hawai'i and Kaua'i. Worse, he argued, was that the CP controlled the Democratic Party, and now "statehood for Hawaii is a primary objective of Communist policy in the territory."[1]

State senator Edwin A. Rogers of Colorado, a confidante of the investigators, had resided 16 years in Honolulu and was quite close to leading members of the Republican Party in Hawai'i, and he agreed that it was "inadvisable to give Hawaii statehood at the present time." This was the gathering consensus among conservatives, generated by the rise of trade unionism in the isles. The ILWU, fundamentally, had taken over the colony, he thought, for in the territorial senate there were "eight Republicans and seven members of the CIO," and in the territorial house, "fifteen Republicans and fifteen members of the CIO."[2]

Senator Butler believed that the rise of the CP in Hawai'i was part of a larger challenge to Washington's interests in the Pacific basin. He linked its ascension to a similar rise of the Communist Party in the Philippines and was concerned about migration to Hawai'i from Central Luzon, where the latter organization had a base of support.[3] He had gone as far as visiting General Douglas MacArthur in his home in Tokyo, where the US military man was acting as a kind of viceroy in a prostrate Japan, so concerned was he about the purported ties between Communists in the Philippines, Hawai'i—and Japan.[4]

But equivalent to or perhaps even surpassing this alleged threat from the Left were the gnawing racial anxieties that permeated the atmosphere with a miasmic haze. Indeed, there was an overlap between the two, since the "threat" from the Left was widely seen as being borne by Japanese-Americans and was part and parcel of the anomalous minority status of Euro-Americans. "Contrary to common belief," Senator Guy Cordon of Oregon was briskly informed, "there is racial friction" in Hawai'i, tourist brochures about "paradise" notwithstanding.[5] Writing to the senator from Hilo, Edward Silva lamented that "certain sections of Hawaii are becoming more and more Japan-like each day." He was perplexed: "Why don't they celebrate American holidays?" he wondered. "Why do they Japanize Hawaii?" Their ceremonies and rituals "turned my stomach," he carped. Why, he fumed, "they would have been perfectly contented if Japan had won the war."[6] Joseph Whitfield of Honolulu told Senator Cordon that his city was similar to Hilo. He felt a "fear of retaliation" if he told the truth, which was that those of Chinese and Japanese ancestry were "very clannish people and marry their own kind as a rule," though the Nipponese were particularly problematic because they "will not buy from any other nationality" and "will not employ anyone of another nationality." His rage rising, he asked, "Why is it that in almost every paper we pick up, there is something about a bunch of hoodlums, of Japanese ancestry, making unprovoked attacks upon United States soldiers, sailors and marines on the streets of Honolulu?"[7] Calvin C. McGregor spoke in like terms to the solons, though he added that the same was also "true in the Jewish race," but this was little comfort on islands with an Asia-Pacific majority more than 2,000 miles from North America.[8]

Samuel Pailthorpe King, a Republican lawyer and a Yale graduate who had been born in China, told Senator Butler that these concerns were not peculiar. "My grandfather," King said, "was Secretary of the Interior of the Republic," which dislodged the kingdom in the 1890s, and prior to that he had had the same position in the provisional Government that followed the overthrow of Queen Lili'uokalani. Furthermore, his great-grandfather "was a Justice of the Supreme Court," and his great-great-grandfather was the first governor of O'ahu under King Kamehameha. Thus, King was not provincial and, in fact, had studied the Japanese language in the navy—yet this apparent cosmopolitan acknowledged that "of course, there is a racial problem" in Hawai'i.[9]

Robert Parker Lewis also harked back to the halcyon days of the dislodging of the monarchy. He was born in Hawai'i in 1878 and thus had experienced this tumult. "First I joined the white people," he said. "We overthrew the monarchy." Then he departed and returned in June 1948, disgusted with what had transpired in the interregnum. "Oriental influence and customs and everything else is predominating in Hawaii," he groused. The remedy was clear: "What I want now," he insisted, "is to do away with that and restore the custom and atmosphere and the sphere of influence of the Caucasian race, make it the supreme race, and if that would be successful, then have it become a part of the mainland."[10] Harry I. Kurisaki, one of the few persons of Japanese ancestry to provide a confidential interview to the congressional delegation, was a dentist and a graduate of the University of Southern California who, like many, wondered why "so many of the boys of Japanese extraction" were "members of the so-called Communists." He was one of the few so bold as to offer an explanation, pointing to the bias to which his community was subjected. Fujimoto's emergence was seen as noticeably worrying, and Kurisaki also pointed to the Japanese language schools as a vector of possible subversion.[11] These critical institutions had been barred since the war erupted, but their reemergence seemed to unsettle some.[12]

Yet when Lucile Paterson arrived in Hawai'i in 1947, her eleven-year-old son in tow, she too was concerned about language instruction—but of a different sort. She was not prepared for the fact that "we should have to place our son in a private school so that he might continue to speak the English language."[13]

John F. G. Stokes, who had worked for 30 years at the Bishop Museum in Honolulu, was concerned about a challenge from the Left. "Bridges, who I am sorry to say is a fellow countryman of mine"—Stokes, too, hailed from Australia—"should be lynched but that should not go into the record." Stokes, who kept close tabs on such matters, told Senator Butler that "ten or twelve years ago labor [had] opposed statehood for Hawaii," and now he thought it quite suspicious that labor had reversed field.[14] James Coke, former territorial senator and, perhaps, the leading attorney in the islands, spoke similarly.[15]

Ruby Thelman was worried about violence too—but the kind that had gripped the borderlands decades earlier. "I grew up in Southern Texas," she told Senator Butler, "and we had a little trouble there in 1916," referring to an alleged plot to liquidate the Euro-American male population. "I remember that very well," she said as she evoked the specter of such an occurrence in the islands.[16]

Alfred Yap, yet another anomalous Asian-American who addressed the legislators, was so concerned about his sedulous assessments becoming known to a wider audience that he often used a pseudonym, "Jonathan Lee." He too was concerned about the alleged dearth of patriotism that animated the Nisei and Issei. For him the choice was clear: "Between the two evils, Big

Five control [or] Jap control of these beautiful islands, we of the minority groups believe in the continuance of the present status quo."[17]

It seemed that some in the islands thought that they might be in jeopardy if their unalloyed opinions were to be wider known. "This is my second letter and written in confidence with the request that my name be withheld," said one correspondent to Senator Butler. "I am alarmed," it was said, "at the growing tendency to 'plunk'"—i.e., "[a] ballot marked for a single candidate in a given category of offices, although there are several vacancies to be filled, thus building up his total and blanketing all the others in the same category." The correspondent warned, "This evil is growing" and was so widespread that he and others would "not go before him and tell him these facts," for fear of retaliation. "Race has been set against race" in the islands, he moaned— and simultaneously "Hawaii has become a breeding ground for Communism and pro-Soviet sympathy." He concluded, "The Serpent has entered Eden, and on his venomous head he bears a symbol—the Hammer and Sickle."[18]

The confidential interviews that Senator Butler conducted with—disproportionately—haoles were even more revealing of the intertwined "race" and class tensions that had enveloped Hawai'i. A flood of emotions burst forth that at times was overwhelming. Many interviewees had been backing statehood publicly but privately were scornful of the very idea, and the tension of living this lie had fomented internal disruption and cognitive dissonance, for which Senator Butler provided an outlet. Why were they reluctant, in any case, to reveal their true feelings, aside from a left-influenced political discourse that valorized statehood? Senator Butler was informed that their reluctance dated back to the Roberts Commission, which had investigated the Pearl Harbor attack. That committee pledged secrecy to those who testified, but the promise of secrecy was not kept, it was said, and exposure had resulted in ruin. A second reason appeared to be fear of one of the local newspapers, presumably the *Star-Bulletin*. So confidential interviews were the proposed solution, and, it appears, the vow of confidentiality was kept—until now.[19]

William H. Tilley, who had arrived in the islands in 1916, was hotly opposed to any kind of bilingual or multilingual initiatives in Hawai'i, since "we are afraid of the Malayan and Asiatic ideology," and if not careful, "we will have a Japanese feudal state here." As a consequence, he was "unequivocally and absolutely" against statehood.[20]

Lucille Martin of the Ladies Auxiliary to the Veterans of Foreign Wars, who was born and raised in the islands, concurred. During the war, she recalled, some of her neighbors of Japanese ancestry had said, "'Some day Japan come, all islands take.'"[21] Ralph E. Woolley, who was the leader of the influential local branch of the Church of Jesus Christ of Latter-day Saints—the Mormons—was anti-statehood, since he believed that "until these Japanese have become Christians . . . they are easy prey to Communism."[22] Richard

Kellett, the resident manager of the brokerage house Dean Witter and Company, argued that statehood had "few supporters at this time among the business leaders of Hawaii," and, he advised Butler, "if you succeed in obtaining their [businessmen's] off-the-record viewpoint" on statehood, this could be ascertained easily, the reason being that "the ILWU can control the Japanese vote whenever it deems necessary."[23] Car dealer A. M. Wilson, though born in South Dakota, had lived in Hawai'i for 32 years, and he too was opposed to statehood.[24]

Bill Ritchie, an attorney from Omaha, told his senator—"Dear Hugh"—that while visiting Honolulu as Stainback's guest, he had met "numerous businessmen and other persons [who] told me that they did not favor immediate statehood, giving as their chief reason that the Japanese had such a large vote" and could not be trusted. "While I was there," he added, "a meeting of some 4,000 Japanese was held for the purposes of explaining to the people of the islands that Japan really won the war and MacArthur was being held as a prisoner in Japan and the stories that America had won the war were mere white propaganda."[25]

Andrew Kalinchak of Honolulu, a resident of the islands for two decades, similarly opposed statehood because of the preponderance of AJAs. He felt as if he were living in Tokyo. "When you wake up on Sunday morning three of the five radio stations are on the air with about 2 or 3 hours of Japanese programs *only*." Moreover, "during the week the Japanese programs are so frequent that a stranger might think that he landed in Japan accidentally," he grumbled, "instead of Hawaii, a United States possession." Instead of statehood, "I say annex this territory to Japan, [and] call it Honolulu-ken, Oahu Jima," and be done with it. Besides, he said, "I would not want to see a Congressman Sakehara, Yamamoto or some other Japanese name."[26] In the same vein, Roman V. Ceglowski of the Detroit Civic League wailed that "for the preservation of the integrity of the White Race," statehood should be opposed.[27]

Yet with all the fire-breathing rhetoric emanating from these tinderbox hearings, few exceeded in intensity the hotly charged remarks of a wounded veteran who had joined the Honolulu police force, Bill Du Bois. His hostility to statehood knew no bounds—ditto for his antipathy toward communities of color. "You probably are familiar with this word 'pelau,'" he began. "That is a Hawaiian word but the Orientals use [it], and it means no good, and anything that is white in Honolulu is pelau, no good. The white man is the underdog here," he complained angrily, "and he is discriminated against. You can find cases every day where they gang [up] on the service men here, their dependents and wives and kids [too] and they beat them up." Plus, the prospect of statehood had political implications, since "about 90 percent of the Communists in the islands would be Japanese followers." Indeed, "a number of Japanese and Chinese have stated to me alike," he said, "that if their daughters ever married a haole, they would kill them[;] and they have spit on the American flag, and anything that is American, they are against it." He denounced the heralded 442nd Regimental Combat Team, composed of Japanese-American soldiers, because he had fought in Italy and Sicily, where they were sited, but, he said, "I never heard of the 442 until I returned to the islands." They "did not even fight in Africa," he spat out. Anyway, he wondered, "why didn't they send the Japs against the Japs in the Pacific instead of sending them against a white man in Italy?" Why were "they . . . always cramming the 442nd record down the people's throat?" he asked pointedly. His sour comments regarding statehood were not his alone either, he said: "99 per cent of the white people, the haoles of the islands, and the Hawaiians would sign a petition against statehood." It was the "Jap, the Chinaman and the Filipino that wants statehood and not the Hawaiians," he insisted. "I know the Hawaiians well." Though he claimed that indigenes were not pro-statehood, he also asserted, "The Hawaiians hate us so badly, and believe me, they hate us"; he thought that the haole was "the most hated man in the South Pacific." He went on to assert, "Our local police are controlled by a Chinaman and the Chinese businessmen, [who] monopolize all of the businesses," adding, "They hate [the] white race of people [too]." The "god of the Chinese is usually money," he said. "That is all they talk about, the pelau haoles."[28]

But what of the "conflict between the Chinese and the Japanese?" he was asked. "There is no conflict among them at all," he retorted. "They work hand in hand." As he saw things, "Chinese are the worst citizens that the United States has, in my opinion." He was persistent in arguing against Hawai'i entering the Union: "If you make this place a state," he proclaimed, "you might as well make Japan a state." It all came back to the Nisei and Issei, he thought, since they were "for Communism" because they thought it was "against the white man, against the United States," and "they hate the United States, because we beat the devil out of their relatives." He had firsthand knowledge: "I work with them every day," he said. "I have never heard a Jap or a Chinaman say anything against [a] Communist government."[29]

Dr. Guy Milnor agreed that those of Nipponese ancestry "are haole haters down in the bottom of their hearts," for "they don't like the white people very well."[30] There was "deep racial hatred" in Hawai'i, said Dr. Virgil Harl, who had arrived in the islands in 1921. "It is impossible for there not to be racial problems," he asserted. "Before[,] the Hawaiians used to have a saying in every campaign, 'look to the color of the skin before you vote.'" And, like Du Bois, Harl had "never yet seen [an indigene] that was in favor of statehood."[31]

To be sure, so many of those who conveyed their opinions to Senator Butler and his staff spoke so passionately about the linked issues of "race" and "Reds" precisely because so many of the questions they were asked related to these sensitive matters. Yet the issue at hand was statehood, and solons were concerned about—as they put it—inadvertently depositing two Communist senators in Washington or, as others might have it, sending two non-haoles there (or worst of all: both). Thus, William Stryer of Princeton, New Jersey, grasped the nettle when he instructed Senator Butler that "any clear thinking American will realize that the threat of Communism in Hawai'i, if it actually exists at all, could [more] successfully be combated were the territory a part of the United States." He put it bluntly: "Hawaii as a territory is indeed in danger from Communist influence; Hawaii as a state definitely would not be."[32] As it turned out, it was his viewpoint that prevailed in 1959.

Yet others were prone to argue contrarily that the ILWU and the CP had to be repressed before statehood could become real—this was also part of the dialectic that drove the archipelago until 1959. The other critical aspect was stated succinctly by Democratic Party leader Chuck Mau when he addressed his party's convention in 1948. "The peoples of China, India, Japan and all of the Pacific isles are watching with keen interest the kind of treatment that is accorded to the territory of Hawaii by our nation," he asserted. "They know that we aspire to statehood."[33]

The question of "race" also drove the statehood debate, as even Senator Butler admitted—in his own way. "The other night you asked me," said Ernest Gruening, founding father of Alaskan statehood, to the Nebraskan, "'if you were certain that Hawaii would elect a couple of Japanese Senators within a few years, would you vote for statehood for Hawaii.'"[34] Speaking to a constituent, Senator Butler confided, "My own suggestion to the people who come to me that ask [about] immediate statehood is why wouldn't it be better to make the Hawaiian islands, one or two counties of California. California then would be about the same width east and west as it is north and south at the present time. We would still have two Senators, but the real Americans would still be in the majority. A lot of other people have asked if I want to see two Japs in the United States Senate." His locution made his answer evident: "No, I don't," he insisted. "This may warm up into a real fight next session," he warned, adding ominously, "We will get a lot of help from the Southern Democrats."[35]

Senator Butler's correspondent, Esther Van Orsdel, had similar concerns. She had been poring through the newspapers of the archipelago, "looking for pictures of people that are pure white," and was distressed to report: "I don't find them." She was dismayed to observe that "the pure whites, haoles are definitely in the minority & will be practically driven out of Hawaii in order to preserve their pure strain of ancestry," for "that strain if kept pure will be forced to leave Hawaii if given statehood—it cannot possibly survive in a political state in which it is a pitiful minority." Rest assured, she continued, "when Japanese are in control & they will be, [are] you sure they will be 100% U.S. in 'thinking'? They are 100% smart actors already." It was not as if there were not precedents. "You know we have a pretty fair example right here in the U.S.A.

How about Miami Beach? People you and I know used to love to go there. Do they go any more? No! Why? Does anyone enjoy Atlantic City anymore? When places are taken over by 'types'—we will use that instead of 'racial,'" she said demurely, "you see what happens to them." Obviously frustrated, she concluded, "I had to get it out of my system!"[36] while Senator Butler told her soothingly, "You made some good statements in your letter."[37]

Senator Zales Ecton of Montana, a Republican, opposed statehood precisely because of fear that it would create a "'backdoor'" for Asians to enter the United States. "'Think about what happen[s] 25 to 30 years from now,'" he posed. "'They could come into Hawaii from Asia and get themselves elected to the United States Senate.'" Emphasizing his point, he said with imprecision, "'Think about it[; if] they go to Hawaii they would be only 1,400 [sic] miles from the United States.'"[38]

When Knight Woolley, a member in good standing of the US ruling elite, visited Hawai'i, he was stunned at the prospect of statehood—as he rapidly informed his business partner, the then undersecretary of state Robert Lovett. "The fear seems to hinge around the possibility that the mixed Asiatic population under certain circumstances might develop a strong Communistic trend," i.e., "a Communistic dominated legislature and even a Communist Governor."[39]

Frank Marshall Davis was among the unimpressed,[40] and he was not alone.[41] The British embassy in Washington was of the opinion that the "local feeling in favour of statehood is far from being solid or even vocal"; in fact, "as a subject of general interest and a topic of conversation, however, it runs a bad third to the more pressing questions of high prices and the local labour situation." Detected was apathy on the subject of statehood, though "local opposition to statehood is even more amorphous and elusive than support of the measure," propelled in part by the explosive "charge of block voting" by those of Asian-Pacific ancestry, "rich Orientals" not least. The "feeling towards the Americans of Chinese ancestry who profited by the near panic following Pearl Harbor to buy up real estate at sell-out prices, is not, of course, very cordial." As the embassy put it, "Basically, the statehood issue turns on the racial question," a point that was "summed up by a Negro serviceman's remark: 'back in the states they called me a dirty nigger: right here I'm a Royal Hawaiian'."[42]

In the face of this cascading concern, some in the broader Left sought to reassure skeptics that statehood would not be so bad after all. Autopilot politics seemed to be at play, with conservatives opposing statehood because the Left seemed to back it—and the Left backing it because conservatives seemed to oppose it. Strikingly, the Left rarely addressed consistently the point that statehood could hamstring the Left itself. Mayor John Wilson, who was to provide character testimony on behalf of indicted Communist leaders in the Smith Act trial, dismissed the idea that statehood would entrench Big Five domination. Granted statehood, he argued, Hawai'i would have reapportionment in the territorial legislature, and that would mean breaking the power of the Big Five. Consider, he said, that "[O'ahu] has only one representative in the House for every 5,400 votes while Hawaii County has one for every 2,200, Maui County, one of every 2,100 and Kauai County, one for every 1,900." He pointed to Honolulu as an example of what would occur with reapportionment in that, since 1909, there had been "18 municipal elections" and the Democratic Party, "always opposing the big interests, has won 11 times and the Republican Party, 7." He also noted, "For 25½ of the 39 years the city has been in existence a Democratic Mayor has been in office. Republican Mayors have only served 11½ years."[43]

There was much to be said about the acuity of Mayor Wilson's comments, but as so often happened with pro-statehood arguments by those of the Left, much was left unsaid. Thus he could have mentioned that even without reapportionment, the growing strength of the ILWU and the Left in the "outside" islands spelled ill for the further flourishing of the whims of the Big Five in this key region. Moreover, attaining statehood in order to curb the Big Five seemed as straightforward as a Rube Goldberg contraption or akin to burning down the house in order to roast the pig. Still, when the union was drafting its first issue of its newspaper, it chose to follow Bridges' idea that it regularly include material on the ILWU program: "Making statehood for Hawaii the first point, is an excellent idea," said Robert McElrath, giving a telling indication of priorities.[44]

During his journey to the archipelago, Robeson gave his seal of approval to statehood. Describing himself as "'an advanced New Dealer,'" the famed activist performer remarked that "'it would be a tremendous impact on the United States if Hawaii is admitted as a state,'" not least since "'Americans wouldn't believe the racial harmony that exists here.'" He speculated that statehood "'could speed democracy in the United States,'"[45] another widespread view that saw the enlightened archipelago as enlightening the retrograde mainland.

"Statehood makes strange bedfellows," A. Q. McElrath admitted, adding that "we can't be sure that the Big Five sincerely desires statehood."[46] Maybe so. The larger point is that union leaders did not seem to think carefully about the ramifications of statehood and the imprimatur of legitimacy it placed on the questionable seizure of the islands a few decades earlier.

Jack Hall also agreed largely with the mayor. The union demanded "Statehood Now!" Hall exhorted in early 1946. He felt that opposition emerged from both progressive and reactionary sources in Congress, in that the former feared that economic control of the Big Five extended to political control, and the latter were of a similar stance because a considerable part of the population was of Japanese ancestry and it was claimed they would vote en bloc. Hall hastily reassured Governor Stainback, "Workers of Japanese ancestry make up a good fifty percent of our present membership. Yet the roster of our leadership is completely representative of all our various races and nationalities. . . . [O]nly on Oahu is a worker of Japanese ancestry the elected head man. He is Jack Kawano," the soon-to-be-alienated leader.[47] The idea that those of Japanese ancestry would vote as a bloc was a "fabrication," Hall said, since proportionally they always had less than their "racial share" in the legislature; "a person of Japanese ancestry has never been elected to the Board of Supervisors of the city and county of Honolulu," he said in 1946, "even though many have tried with the full support of the highly organized Republican Party."[48] Providing testimony to Congress in 1946, Hall acknowledged that much congressional opposition to statehood for Hawai'i appeared to be an apprehension that citizens of Japanese ancestry did and would vote in racial blocs and by reasons of their numbers would control the political life of the islands if statehood were granted. But instead of confronting this racial bias frontally, Hall continued to assert that the underrepresentation of those of Japanese ancestry should be reassuring.[49]

Hall could have reassured statehood opponents further if he had added that whites were overrepresented in the leadership of his union. More to the point, progressivism would have been better served if Hall had informed the governor that—to cite one example among many—in Maui, haoles were 3.6 percent of the population but 42 percent of the jury pool, while (as Harriet Bouslog detailed) the "percentage of Koreans, Hawaiians, Puerto Ricans and Filipinos [in the pool] was zero."[50] Stressing underrepresentation of Nisei and Issei as a justification for statehood was wildly misplaced reasoning.

Still, to be fair, the union was not unaware of the racist aspects of the labor setup in the island or of the statehood battle.[51] Subsequently, the union was adroit in pointing to an account from Washington that showed a photograph of the Board of Supervisors in Honolulu captioned in bold print, "Not a White Man Among Them." It was "common knowledge for some time that the foes of statehood for Hawaii—both locally and nationally—have been using racism," said an ILWU spokesman. "Many a prominent local resident has come back [from] the mainland and talked about the so-called Japanese problem, and said that the only way the white man could control Hawaii was by remaining a territory. Not one of these gentlemen," it was said with disdain, "[has] the courage to say the same thing here in Hawaii."[52]

On the other hand, the radicals in the archipelago had to consider how the rising Red Scare had placed them in the bull's-eye, since they were—by far— the most influential Left under the US flag; they thought that the election of a governor, rather than a White House selection, made more sense (interestingly, these radicals had removed the option of independence for this colony). Thus Harold D. Dillingham, of the prominent Big Five family, was a friend of "Dear Franklin" Roosevelt and the family of the powerful Robert Morgenthau— "delightful people," said this scion of a major island fortune—and he was "happy

An archipelago in the middle of the Pacific, Hawaiʻi was heavily dependent on imports and exports for its survival—and, therefore, dependent on the union-organized stevedores who handled both. Courtesy of Anne Rand Library, ILWU–San Francisco.

to contribute something to their fun while here."[53] President Roosevelt was effusive about "Dear Walter" Dillingham, telling him at one point that he and "Harold . . . must both come to see me in Washington soon," this after his "wonderful three days in Honolulu."[54]

Thus, in the spring of 1946, progressives in the isles found themselves in a familiar position: wringing their hands as the Big Five were maneuvering to have their man appointed as governor.[55] With such Big Five leverage in Washington, radicals thought it prudent that statehood and elections of the chief executive were the way to go.

Moreover, the mayor and others similarly situated seemed curiously blind to the pro-statehood commentary emerging from circles that were not friendly to them. "There will not be less Communism in Hawaii if it is left in territorial status," said one mainland newspaper; "statehood, with its more definite political obligations and greater governmental authority" might make curbing the Left easier.[56] The "current paralysis in the islands," said the *Tampa Tribune*, speaking of the epochal 1949 ILWU strike of stevedores, "would not be tolerated if a state were involved."[57] Yet another journalist opined that statehood "might change some of the conditions which have enabled Communists to get whatever hold they have."[58]

In any case, the ongoing status of Hawai'i as a colony meant that Washington had to file reports regularly to the United Nations on its status, raising the more than niggling matter during the Cold War that Moscow and its allies could plumb this ticklish matter more assertively.[59] That Honolulu was considered at one point to become the headquarters of the United Nations itself—an offer backed by Governor Stainback and transmitted by Alger Hiss of the State Department—was suggestive of how the islands were not off the radar of the international community.[60]

Of course, beyond the Left there were others who had reason to think statehood for Hawai'i was a bright idea. Curtis D. Stringer, a real estate broker in Lebanon, Oregon, certainly thought so, informing Governor Stainback that statehood "would give to the West a larger voice in the Congress and in our government"; "wresting a part of the political power now held by a small group of thickly settled and financially powerful states up in our Northeast corner" was his goal.[61] Perhaps that is why certain prominent residents of the Eastern Seaboard vigorously opposed statehood, a list that included the highly influential Nicholas Murray Butler, best known as a president of Columbia University.[62] Senator Henry Cabot Lodge, a similarly influential man, noted that "there is already a movement on foot to submit an application on the part of the British Crown Colony of Newfoundland" for statehood—"some of us have already been approached." He noted that "in the Italian election," just concluded, there were "several thousand people who voted in favor of having Italy join the United States as a state." What next, he mused? "The matter of the size of the

Union members picket Hawai'i's governor when he arrives in San Francisco in 1949. The union had a substantial African-American membership on the mainland, which was less susceptible to the then prevailing anticommunism. Courtesy of Anne Rand Library, ILWU–San Francisco.

United States Senate is something to be seriously considered," he said, since "every time we add more Senators to the Senate, we decrease the relative importance of every existing Senatorship." Thus, why shouldn't Hawai'i simply "become part of California" and be done with it?[63] His Bay State compatriot Lieutenant Governor Arthur W. Coolidge concurred.[64]

Speaking to his comrade Governor Stainback, Coolidge said, "You are not alone out there in the Pacific," for "we saw what happened to Czechoslovakia yesterday," referencing the Communist surge to power in that nation. "We want no duplication in Hawaii," he advised. In a speech, the text of which he forwarded to Honolulu, he said with gravity, "I have in my possession a Photostat copy of orders, issued by the Communist Party, outlining a program to gain control of labor unions and education, to weaken the National Guard, to attack religion and to make Hawaii the most completely Communist area under the Stars and Stripes. This document was sent to me by the Governor of Hawaii, Ingram M. Stainback."[65]

Contemporaneously, J. Howard McGrath, who was to become US attorney general, was informed that the islands were "certainly nothing like Rhode Island," his homeland, and were "not ready for statehood and probably never will be"; the sensitivity of "race" was specified as a central reason, since "if it weren't for the Armed Forces, the number of whites would be negligible." Yes, "those missionaries who came to pray" stayed and "preyed"—but this was hardly justification for statehood, the eminent senator from Rhode Island was told.[66]

Inadvertently, by pushing for statehood, labor and the Left had placed themselves squarely in the spotlight, which was not necessarily to their advantage. For when the union began to push aggressively for better wages and working conditions in the midst of hysteria generated by the fantasy-driven notion that the Kremlin would soon select two new senators from Hawai'i to be seated in Washington, they were quickly engulfed by a tidal wave of anticommunism. The ILWU saw things differently, of course. Early in 1949, just before the game-changing stevedore strike that was to erupt in full force in the spring, McElrath took to the airwaves to inform those huddled around their radios that the military had reigned supreme over labor, both organized and unorganized, during the war; thus wages were frozen, and workers were frozen to their jobs. Employees failing to report to their jobs were arrested and hailed before the provost marshal. Many were sentenced to contribute blood to the blood plasma bank. Others were sentenced to serve nights in jail, while working in the daytime. Still others were forced to invest in bonds that could not be cashed in for the duration of the war. Union organizers—even organizers working full-time at their regular phase of employment—were intimidated. Japanese workers on the plantations were told it was unpatriotic to join a union while the country was at war.[67] Well, McElrath, said, labor was still laboring under the remnants of these extraordinary conditions, and the time had long since arrived for the ILWU to claw back what workers had surrendered only recently. Presumably, statehood would help them to do so.

Yet 1949 was shaping up as the "rubber match," the tiebreaker between labor and management after the 1946 success of the strike in sugar and the 1947 setback in pineapple. The stevedores' struggle would give an indication of the correlation and balance of political forces between labor and capital and therefore would serve to determine the trajectory of statehood. Frightened by the revival of a left-leaning Democratic Party and chastened by the ILWU's rise, management sent a signal that it was not willing to back down as the struggle along the waterfront began to intensify. Senator Butler's hearings were the opening gambit in this regard, designed to place radicals on the defensive.[68]

Serendipitously, at this pivotal moment, the union leadership in Hawai'i was able to have an in-depth conversation with Kurt Auler, who was working with the famed Clark Kerr, a preeminent scholar of labor-management relations. When Auler had visited Hawai'i, Dave Thompson took him to dinner—and received an earful. Auler had been talking to management and said that it was clear that there was a split in their ranks. The so-called moderates (Castle and Cooke) had prevailed, and the industry was reconciled to the idea that the

Mexican and Cuban sugar workers meet with their Hawaiian counterparts in San Francisco in 1947. On the far right is J. R. Robertson. The ILWU remained close to Cuban sugar workers after Fidel Castro came to power in 1959—the year of statehood—which caused considerable consternation in Washington. Courtesy of Anne Rand Library, ILWU–San Francisco.

union was here to stay; now it would oppose the ILWU only on issues, not merely because it was a union. Auler felt that management would like to see leadership of the union changed but would try to live with the union; failing that, it would seek to "soften up" its adversary. Management had ascertained that "'Communist' doesn't seem to excite people too much," so a renewed approach was called for—though Auler had allowed earlier in the conversation that the employers could always keep the union on the defensive by Red-baiting at opportune times. As Thompson put it, summarizing Auler's words, management "used to be scared as hell of us," but "after watching us fluff off on contract administration," management was changing its collective mind and now was beginning to "feel cocky," since the bosses "feel we can never achieve real democracy in our union." Auler prefigured the union's future by telling Thompson that the ILWU was "missing [a] bet in not solving our problem by political mean[s]," via a legislative push for minimum wages, socialized medicine, progressive taxation, and so on. Thompson replied that it "must be fun to be an intellectual," but it was apparent that Auler was on to something, for as he was sharing his ideas over dinner, management was already in the midst of implementing the plans it had shared with him.[69]

J. R. Robertson sensed this shift when he observed in early 1948, "Things are too quiet and it is just the lull before the storm."[70] He was prescient. "At midnight today," said Jack Hall on 9 October 1948, "1,300 workers on the island of Hawaii will be locked out of their jobs by the Olaa Sugar Company"; this was occurring even though "the union, bear in mind, has no wage demand," he complained. "We asked [for] the continuation of the present wage, and even offered to accept a cut of 5 cents an hour in order to expedite a settlement."[71] Days later, Hall remained upbeat, despite pointing to a persistent weakness: "a few of the Portuguese might be eventually sucked [back] to work but the number will be small." All in all, Hall foresaw "surprisingly good results."[72] The larger point, however, was that a coordinated offensive against the ILWU, driven by Senator Butler and management's dual concerns, was apparently being launched.

By the third week of this lockout,[73] nonetheless, Robertson was informed that the union's fight back was going strong, and the morale among the workers was high. One of the bright spots, it was reported, was the high spirits being shown by the women pickets,[74] though by December 1948, stalemate reigned.[75]

Actually, it was complicated too, particularly after management demanded police protection for nine laborers who desired to work but were afraid to do so because of the picket lines. "Somebody turned on the ignition keys of 13 trucks," Hall said passively and blandly, "and ran the batteries down; also brake lines were cut. I rather suspect it was performed by some scab," since "we have warned the guys strongly against any violence."[76] Hall was being coyly tactful, perhaps mindful of the surveillance of his mail, for the public record revealed that at one point nearly 300 ILWU members amassed at the home of a worker who had sided with management in this broiling dispute; they proceeded to hurl insults at him for more than 30 minutes.[77]

The difficulties at Olaa suggested that despite its manifest victories since 1944, the ILWU continued to face formidable barriers. Ricardo Labez, then a prominent member of the ILWU staff, pointed out that "employers will not stop trying to split our union along racial lines." As he announced in March 1947, "They are now active in this connection. They have purchased more radio time and more newspaper space for employer propaganda in Filipino."[78] Even at this late date, long after the celebration of the defeat of Imperial

Japan, Jack Hall had to make special arrangements for AJAs who desired to travel to an ILWU convention on the mainland.[79]

These racial tensions had impact. "Never have I seen so many people so downhearted," said writer Jared Smith, speaking of the Olaa lockout at the time. Neighboring Hilo had been "hit pretty hard," and "war shortages, the tidal wave, the abandonment of the railroad," and more had decimated the Big Island. "Olaa plantation is unique among all of Hawaii's sugar production units," he said, "in that half of its cane area is owned by 435 independent farmers who produce about half of the processed crop." Because the "majority finance their own operations," that put "their group in the same class with prosperous mainland farmers"[80]—and complicated enormously the ability of the ILWU to organize.

As if this were not enough, the islands were hit powerfully by a strike of stevedores on the West Coast. This militant action set the stage for a similar outbreak of unrest in the archipelago itself, but more directly, it heightened fears about the power and reach of radical labor, as it inflicted heavy blows on the economy of Hawai'i and, thus attracted the prying eyes of Senator Butler. In the midst of the tumult centered at Olaa, a battered Honolulu seemed pleased when it received a two-week supply of potatoes from New Orleans, even though the price had zoomed 40 percent and these valued items arrived spoiled after the hot, humid 17-day trip via the Panama Canal.[81] The strike was costing the isles an estimated $400,000 daily, according to Lorrin P. Thurston, president of the Chamber of Commerce. Among his riveted listeners was one Senator Hugh Butler.[82]

"This strike has caused the layoff of a lot of the waterfront workers here in Honolulu," said Ray Jerome Baker; "builders are running out of materials and supplies." Then there was an unrelated strike of bus drivers that was warping nerves[83] throughout the isles.[84] Ultimately, this 95-day stevedores' strike cost the Matson Navigation Company alone an estimated $1,789,252.[85] Matson had to endure a complete suspension of operations for three months; taken separately, the company's operations in 1948, exclusive of capital gains, would have shown a modest profit if there had been no shipping strike.[86]

The ILWU was flexing its finely toned muscles at a time when the elite felt beleaguered[87]—though, predictably, management was not alone in its angst. "It is almost impossible to locate a house," Frank Marshall Davis was informed just before his departure from Chicago, and "rents are terrifically high in the islands."[88]

The housing crisis was eroding the marrow of the economy. Straining to move away from the spheres already dominated by the ILWU, the economic royalists made an attempt to develop tourism. But this initiative, which was to bear rich fruit ultimately, immediately collided with the housing crisis, in that the construction industry was torn between building hotels or homes. "We do not have many tourists," said Ray Jerome Baker in 1948, "largely because there are no hotel accommodations for them." There were beach hotels, but these were "very expensive." Housing, he said, "is still very short here," though "much building [is] going on." Just recently, Baker said, a couple had moved out of one of his "small rental places," and "immediately . . . half a dozen callers [bid] for it."[89] The royalists felt that the housing shortage, as exemplified by this incident, harmed economic growth.[90] With high housing costs draining income, less money was available for other matters,[91] including food and transport,[92] which also harmed the union.[93] Mechanization—a response to union strength—was also beginning to bite.[94]

In sum, as hysteria was escalating due to the rise of radicals, simultaneously the economy was taking a downturn and workers were on the march. All of this, along with the arrival of Senator Butler's road show, was bound to increase tension.[95] The situation was being worsened by the growing complexity of negotiations, particularly with the sugar barons, as the union seemed to be empowering lawyers and experts at the expense of the rank and file.[96] But if the union was to prevail, a mobilized membership was the primary guarantee.[97]

Thus, as the conflict in Olaa spread, the ILWU leaders perceived that, despite their best efforts, they were losing ground. The so-called Ignacio Revolt, the Izuka booklet, and the gathering Red Scare had taken a toll. The arrival of Senator Butler only contributed to the burden faced by a union leadership already under siege.[98] A self-described "rank-in-filer," reflecting the pressure the ILWU was under, informed Hall that "our union here in Maui is completely destroyed. . . . [A]ll the Filipino brothers are quitting the union too."[99] Hall felt it necessary to scurry to Maui, where he found that the racial tensions also had exacted a price, with complaints being made about alleged misdeeds by those of Japanese origin.[100] Fortunately, the "membership is holding solid at Olaa," Hall added hopefully.[101] Despite all of the complex problems of the union, the ILWU had hidden strengths. It was in mid-1948 that A. Q. McElrath conducted a survey gauging the attitude to the union of women on the sugar plantations, which proved to be positive[102] and thus made for a bright outlook for the union.[103] Senator Butler's interest in Hawai'i was an indication of the growing concern that inevitably accompanied the union's optimism. The leading solon saw fit to insert in the *Congressional Record* a lengthy and far-reaching missive to him from the archipelago that rang alarms about CP and union strength.[104] Something had to be done, it was said.

Something was done—which even the Foreign Office in London anticipated.[105] The administrators of the California Labor School in San Francisco, the presumed locus of purported "radical indoctrination," were hauled before a congressional committee. It was a contentious confrontation, with the school's leader, David Jenkins, complaining, "First you say that I can have an attorney and then you throw him out of court. What goes on?" The attorney in question, Norman Leonard, declared, "I want the record to show that I am being forcibly escorted from the room." Jenkins was able to point out to the doubters that his school was no nest of subversion but instead "112 subjects" were taught, including "ceramics, finger painting, sign painting," and "poetry appreciation." Congress was not buying it. Jenkins, a member of the ILWU's labor comrade, the Marine Cooks and Stewards, was subjected to parching examination. "Is it possible to get a drink of water, or do I have to go through special anxiety on the stand? I am very thirsty," he insisted. But his desiccating examination continued unabated. Soon, his school had passed into history.[106]

The ILWU, with a membership of 80,000, had a stranglehold on imports and exports to the then booming West Coast, where California was destined to become the richest, most populous, and most powerful state in the Union. Yet of those impressive numbers, there were 30,000 members in Hawai'i who were exercising outsized influence in an archipelago with a population of a half million.[107] They not only had a grip on imports and exports but also had come to dominate the sugar and pineapple industries and were moving into other spheres. This was a union in which Communists played a leading role on both sides of the Pacific, and the question that some in Washington were pondering was whether statehood for Hawai'i would mean—as it was then phrased—the Kremlin having a role in the selection of two US senators. It was such union strength that showed that pessimism about Olaa and the alleged decline of union units in Kaua'i and Maui was premature, as the ILWU was able to emerge from these scrapes largely intact and, indeed, with propulsive momentum that would be needed for upcoming battles. Thus, as the ILWU in Hawai'i was about to emulate its counterparts on the West Coast and engage in a strike of stevedores, the *Washington Post* reported apprehensively that a "hot backstage row over statehood for Alaska and Hawaii has the House Rules Committee in a tizzy."[108]

CHAPTER 10

Stevedores Strike

The stevedores' strike in Hawai'i lasted from 1 May to 24 October 1949.[1] It was "one of the longest strikes in the history of the United States that was won," said Louis Goldblatt of the 2,000 men who tied up the ports and heightened anxiety at a time when the Red Scare was rising. "It is a rare thing," he added, "to win a strike that goes that long."[2]

How true. It was the longest strike to that point in the maritime industry and, arguably, the most important strike in Hawai'i's history—surpassing the Sugar Strike of 1946.[3] It was "Hell in Honolulu" one newspaper screamed,[4] while another said simply the strike was "destined to make labor history."[5] Months before the strike ended, Joseph Farrington had concluded that the strike had "created a crisis without parallel in the history of Hawaii."[6]

Harry Bridges felt that the strike "established the union and forced the employers to give up their notion that they'd drive us into the ocean" since "that was their program."[7] Looking back years after the fact, a Honolulu newspaper asserted that this was "an event never to be forgotten," ranking "behind only the Pearl Harbor attack and statehood among the significant happenings of the 20th century" in the isles, for it brought Hawai'i "to the very brink of violent civil war," as the "ILWU ended all lingering hopes that it might be destroyed." The crux was that the union wanted a wage increase of 32 cents per hour, but management reluctantly offered 8 cents, then 12. Graciously the ILWU offered arbitration of the dispute but was turned down flatly.[8]

Decades after it ended, Dave Thompson of the ILWU argued that the 1949 strike "did two things": "It set the stage for tremendous gains by the union[,] since we won. At the same time it isolated the union from a part of the community," due to the economic distress the strike caused and the effectiveness of the Red-baiting—buoyed by trans-Pacific currents—to which the union was so deftly subjected. The strike jerked Hawai'i forcefully into the mainland's consciousness, in a way unseen since 7 December 1941. During this time of turbulence, President Harry S. Truman sent a personal plea to the Hilo stevedores, requesting that they back down. "I remember that very vividly," Thompson said, since at that moment he was on the docks with a "godforsaken looking little bunch of guys" who were "barefooted. They had ragged pants. The morale committee was playing ukuleles and guitars and it was real country stuff"[9]—but these mournful strings did not entice these workers to heed the plea from the White House.[10]

Stevedores had to deal with dwindling bank accounts, deteriorating shoe leather from constant picketing, angry neighbors upset with the disappearance of basic necessities from grocery shelves, and an outraged Washington fearful that Communists had established a foothold in an archipelago that was viewed as the open backdoor compromising the security of the mainland. All this ensued because stevedores in Hawai'i simply wanted parity in wages with their counterparts on the mainland.[11]

The stevedores were resolute, particularly in the early stages of the strike.[12] They were more than ready to raise their lagging wages and transform their onerous working conditions. Frederick Tam Low, born in 1913 and a graduate of high school in Hilo, was a short and fattish man, appropriate for the burdensome labor at the docks. By 1940 he was vice president of the Hilo local of stevedores and by 1949 was chairman of the Strike Strategy Committee. These men were mostly indigenes and of Japanese ancestry and were tasked with the job of hauling sugar sacks weighing 110 pounds, fertilizer sacks that could weigh 215 pounds, and other heavy loads. Low was only five inches taller than a mere five feet and carried 160 pounds on his frame, yet even his size and build—not atypical for men on the waterfront—often buckled under the loads he was compelled to endure,[13] though he made less than his counterparts elsewhere[14]—even in the Deep South.[15]

This strike occurred as the postwar economy of Hawai'i, or at least the fortunes of those who dominated it, appeared to be surging. Corporations engaged in pursuits other than agriculture had grown—by 1946 their number stood at 689, with one of every three corporations engaged in wholesale and retail trading. By 1948 the total assets of the 831 corporations in the archipelago amounted to $902,974,170—considerable, yes, but less than the total assets for Socony-Vacuum Oil Company and less than one-quarter the size of American Telephone and Telegraph.[16]

Yet this postwar growth on islands that may have been as far from neighbors as any other site on this small planet was heavily dependent on the good wishes of a group of Communist-led stevedores. Sensing the potential danger, as early as 1946 Walter Dillingham told a fellow member of the ruling elite, Joseph Farrington, of his fears of a strike of stevedores. Inflamed just thinking about this worst-case scenario, Dillingham pondered "who the heck is running our government," and others were to answer that it was Harry Bridges who actually was in charge.[17] But bluster aside, management did not hold a hand full of winning trump cards during this high-stakes battle. Philip Maxwell, who negotiated on management's behalf, acknowledged later that there was "extreme dissension" within his ranks; C. Brewer, for example, was "desperate for cash," although others were not as pressed.[18]

Yet since a chain is only as strong as its weakest link, the string of islands that constituted the colony of Hawai'i and was in turn chained to the United States was bound to have an impact on the mainland when those who handled imports and exports abandoned their posts. By mid-June, *Life* magazine, the flagship of the Manhattan-based publishing empire of Henry Luce, was reporting vigorously on the "showdown in Honolulu," stating that the "languid land of the lei was as restless as a hula dancer's hips." The ILWU, which had a "heavy list to port" had created a circumstance whereby poultry was being killed off, dairy herds were drying up for want of feed, and affluent housewives—"irate" and "broom-wielding"—were picketing longshore picketers. There was murmuring, it was said, about "tarring and feathering Harry Bridges."[19]

Surely Albert Bean of the Tnemec Company in Kansas City, Missouri—which was involved with preservative and decorative coatings—was devastated by this strike thousands of miles away and demanded action.[20] The drawing of a parallel between events in blockaded Berlin and Honolulu had emerged initially in the archipelago itself.[21] Picking up the charge, one journalist chided those who seemed to be spending more time hyperventilating about Reds abroad rather than those at home.[22]

J. C. Duran of General Insurance in St. Petersburg, Florida, concurred, asking his US senator for help.[23] Mrs. C. A. Weil of Ferguson, Missouri, had been "listening to letters received and read by [broadcast entertainer] Arthur Godfrey on the air," and she too demanded action.[24] "As a mainland supplier to the territory," said H. E. Turpin, president of Neevel Manufacturing Company in Kansas City, "we are suffering a loss in business and a reduction in personnel (10 jobs) just at a time when full production is so vital to the nation's economy,"[25] simply due to the strike. "It makes my blood boil to see something like this go on and on," said D. J. Biller, president of Day-Brite Lighting in St. Louis. "When are we going to deport foreign-born Commies, like Bridges, whose main purpose is to cause trouble?" he asked.[26]

Hawai'i, said the vice president of Davol Rubber Company in Providence, Rhode Island, "can be considered part of our foreign market," since for "many, many years we have supplied the majority of the pineapple companies with special gloves used in the canning industry, which kept one of our departments in production, giving employment to several persons"; but now, he complained, "production has either been reduced considerably or has completely stopped."[27] The same held true in North Carolina, where industrial baron A. P. Steele of Statesville was equally distraught,[28] and in Florida, where Roger F. Dykes of the chamber of commerce in Cocoa, objected vociferously to the strike.[29]

Dykes' counterparts in Hilo were not consoling.[30] Shipping served as a pipeline from Hawai'i's mills to the refineries in the vicinity of San Francisco; when that pipeline closed, raw sugar began to pile up.[31] William H. Soper of the Honolulu Paper Company informed Secretary of the Interior J. A. Krug that "we may shortly face a situation which will be dangerously analogous to Pearl Harbor," for "the citizenry is developing a mass hysteria" and a "cold deliberate rage is building up here."[32] Fred Barnett, another Honolulu businessman, seemed to be in the grip of the hysteria that Soper had detected.[33]

In short, this strike in the Pacific had vast repercussions on the mainland. But that was not all. The idea that these 2,000 men had placed their hands firmly on the windpipe of the isles' economy was not far-fetched. The local press found that it had trouble obtaining the stock needed to publish newspapers,[34] reducing its product's size.[35] A little more than two weeks after the strike erupted, there had been a run on such items as rice and tinned milk, new cars were hard to get, and plantations were compelled to halt grinding operations when their warehouses became filled with bagged raw sugar.[36] Like dominoes falling in line, one after another of the local firms began cutting salaries and workweeks due to the strike. The tobacco habit as a means of alleviating nervousness was losing its effectiveness when the cigarette supply began to diminish. As a result, this valuable item, along with cigars and pipe tobacco were shipped parcel post at the rate of $4.73 a case, whereas ordinary freight was a mere 83 cents. Drowning one's sorrows in alcohol was also becoming less of a possibility as supplies began to dry up. De facto prohibition seemed to be descending in an archipelago where bacchanalian revelry was an evident trademark.[37] Bakers began to close their doors because of a shortage of eggs.[38] Relief rolls were mounting, and months before the strike was to conclude, the well-informed journalist Ray Coll ascertained that "if the strike continues another month the real estate dollar won't be worth 50 cents."[39]

The day after Coll weighed in, another journalist noted that on the surface Hawai'i did not seem to be hit hard by the stevedores' action: "Hotels have plenty of food, rooms, excellent service. Public entertainment is well-patronized [and] many stores continue to do a fair business." But Hawai'i resembled the duck gliding along on a pond, seemingly tranquil—while beneath the surface there was frantic and energetic paddling. For many small businesses had suspended operation, and thousands of high school students on vacation were unable to earn their accustomed money for the coming school year; in fact, just before the school semester ended, teachers were reporting that their many children were coming to school hungry.[40] Canned tuna, one of the colony's major export items, faced a shutdown.[41] Islanders may have thought this was a good thing, since by late July Maui was faced with an acute food shortage.[42] As bakeries were shuttering, dairy farmers were thinking along similar lines, and so were poultry producers.[43] Humans had it better than fowl, for by early June 13,000 chicks and eggs had been destroyed on O'ahu because of a shortage of feed.[44]

During this labor unrest, sugar valued at more than $35 million was strike-bound, along with more than 50,000 tons of molasses, while lack of fertilizer was proving to be increasingly serious.[45] The union had chosen a propitious moment to walk out, for it was in April that the sugar barons had reported, "California sugar refineries will process the greatest tonnage of Hawaiian sugar in history during the year 1949."[46] In addition, the idea that tourism was unaffected by the strike may have been a mistaken one, since shortly after the stevedores walked out, there was a sharp reduction in tourist air travel from the mainland to Hawai'i,[47] and by mid-July, hotel occupancy was down 37 percent from that of the previous year.[48] By early September, tourist business losses were estimated at $4 million,[49] a sizeable chunk extracted from a $35 million industry.[50] "Tourist trade is off 35 percent," screamed headlines, while "18,800 men and women" were "out of work."[51]

Despite the hysteria on the mainland about the strike in Hawai'i, its worst effects were concentrated in the mid-Pacific, which gave the ILWU a dubious advantage.[52] Small business was suffering,[53] infuriating a potential union ally. Hundreds of small businesses had collapsed, complained one pundit, and "total loans granted by the two major banks are estimated at around $70 million." Big firms also borrowed from mainland institutions, which jeopardized their future viability. "To say that Hawaiian business is in hock to the extent of $150,000,000 would be conservative," argued Ray Coll. "Hawaii today is very close to being broke," he carped.[54] Even the pineapple industry was singing the blues.[55]

"No other labor dispute here or on the mainland," declared Governor Stainback, "can take place in which the actions of so few are disastrous to so many. Except for food, medicine and other highly critical supplies, no ocean-borne commerce has entered [Hawai'i] during this period."[56] Of course, Stainback had reason to emphasize the disruption of the strike, since it was led by his eternal opponents, the ILWU; he was noticeably irked when, during a visit to San Francisco as the strike was unfolding, union pickets hounded his every move, carrying signs with evocative slogans like "'Stainback, Strike Breaker'" and "'Go Back to Honolulu.'"[57]

Yet he was not alone in his denunciation of the stevedore walkout. The strike "has played havoc with the economy of he islands," concluded soon-to-be-governor Oren Long. By early October the combined total of estimated losses had soared beyond $100 million.[58] Senator Hugh Butler's already huge concern about the isles escalated further.[59]

Weeks before the strike concluded, the president of the University of Hawai'i was strolling in his lovely neighborhood in Honolulu, but what he saw was not so pretty. "I saw 'for sale' signs on five houses. These houses did not bear such signs a month ago. The economic machine is breaking down," he warned the US secretary of the interior, who had oversight of the colony, "and with it the feeling of security which is essential to every happy community. People of all classes are emotionally, as well as financially disturbed," he cried, "and that sort of thing leads to social disintegration. I hear every day of people losing their jobs, selling out and going to the mainland." The well-respected academic don Gregg M. Sinclair was to the point of whimpering as he observed that "tragedies are piling up." In his view, "The debacle here up to now has been worsening by arithmetic progression; from now on it will worsen by geometric progression."[60]

Needless to say, given the avid attention paid to Senator Butler's hearings and their implication that Hawai'i was coming under the domination of a Communist foe that was being confronted in Europe, Asia, and elsewhere, a strike led by a union thought to be led by Reds was viewed with something akin to hysteria. "Where Tojo failed, Bridges succeeds," was the cry in the halls of Congress, referring to the Japanese general who some believed had been responsible for the Pearl Harbor attack.[61] This retrospective analogy lacked the potency of the present-minded appeal of the veteran anticommunist bomb-thrower J. B. Matthews, who turned up in Honolulu in early July. As he saw things, the stevedores had coordinated their job action with a strike of miners in Australia and with the impending seizure of power by the Chinese Communist Party, which was to occur as the strike was winding down. Ominously, the vitriolic and rabid Matthews was introduced to an adoring audience by O. P. Soares, leader of the GOP in Hawai'i.[62]

That Matthews, an unremitting segregationist, was now spouting remarks that were being adopted by the union's mainstream opponents was worrying. The strike, said the parroting local press, was "America's Pearl Harbor," as the Communists were "trying a new formula of conquest in Hawaii"; the isles were a "test tube for 'the perfect experiment,'" for "if the new technique works, it may be tried in the Philippines next—and eventually the United States."[63]

The *Honolulu Advertiser* led the charge, featuring for virtually the entire length of the strike a provocative series of front-page "Dear Joe" editorials—i.e., presumed letters to Stalin from his comrades in Honolulu that provided a running account of their activities. "What are we going to do about these Wahines, Joe? They may get dangerous"—this was one typical broadside, with the Hawaiian term for "women" used to address the leading ladies of the haoles who had taken it upon themselves to picket the ILWU picketers.[64] "With government help we're building a New Russia, Joe," said another.[65] Continuing this propaganda barrage day after day, the *Advertiser* played an instrumental role in this battle royal, once displaying an illustration of a hammer and sickle piercing Hawai'i, with the slogan affixed, "Communist control of territorial economy." Mimicking Matthews, others now termed the strike the "Second

Pearl Harbor," this time involving an "invasion of the Communists." Bridges was no more than a "Communist and tool of the Kremlin," they said; quite simply he had "invaded and occupied" the isles, led by "Red Forces" who were "directed from the Kremlin."[66]

Lorrin Thurston, an economic titan who resided in the Hawaiian home once occupied by King Kamehameha, was a millionaire many times over at the time of the strike. He wrote all of the "Dear Joe" editorials, and years after the fact his ire had yet to be squelched. "I hated the guts of unions," he confessed, while his Big Five comrade Walter Dillingham "hated the Japanese basically[,] though he had Japanese in the house as servants"; nonetheless, Dillingham "hated their guts" and thus opposed statehood.[67] That men of Japanese ancestry were in the forefront of the strikers was not lost on either man.

Such hyperbolic maunderings were reflected among some ordinary citizens as well. According to Wilfred Oka, a key operative in both CP and Democratic Party circles, the tremendous growth of the white population in the years preceding the strike had been accompanied by "quite a number" of problems as the newcomers "brought their hometown prejudices" with them. The alarmed Oka noticed that "at many of our athletic events there has been displayed a growing unsportsmanlike conduct on the part of a number of people who use epithets like popolo, paele, eight-ball, Alabam, etc.," and other hurtful language. This was the "assumed superiority complex of maladjusted and misinformed persons," he contended stoutly[68]—and it complicated attempts by mostly Asian-Pacific workers to obtain concessions from a white elite.[69] With the populace pumped up by propagandistic bilge, it was not long before aggressive actions to thwart the ILWU were afoot. By late July there were disturbing reports of violence directed at union members and their families. The home of Calixto Damaso, ILWU vice president in Oʻahu, was bombarded repeatedly with rocks and stones, then set afire. The union brandished a recording of a telephone conversation between the besieged union leader and a man with the voice of a Hollywood film gangster who threatened that if the strike was not halted forthwith, Damaso and his colleagues would be leaving Hawaiʻi in "wooden boxes."[70] Because of such violence, Jack Hall in particular was under threat. Dr. Theodora Charmian Kreps, the daughter of an anthropologist, worked as a researcher with the ILWU in Honolulu from 1948 to 1953; as an anthropologist herself, this chain-smoker may not have had the necessary fieldwork to comprehend her disbelief when she found a guard of five longshoremen posted around Hall's house during the strike.[71] Henry Schmidt of the union, who was staying at Hall's abode, found the guard to be needed "just in case somebody might have screwy plans to do something."[72]

"Nearly all of the union's leaders," complained Schmidt, "including those of Hawaiian birth, are daily getting threatening phone calls. [An ILWU leader], a Filipino, has been the victim of several attempts to burn down his house during the night. They throw bottles containing inflammable fluid at the side of the house, but so far no fire," he said with relief. Noting that during the third week in July, "the windows of this house were broken by bricks," he added with sobriety, "We have taken appropriate steps to defend our headquarters just in case of attack[,] by hurriedly organizing a baseball team,"[73] brandishing dual-use Louisville Sluggers. Preparation for potential attacks by antiunion factions was needed more than was realized, for in June 1949 an attempt was made to destroy the union headquarters by arson.[74]

ILWU members did not necessarily conduct themselves as if they were passive pacifists either. Violence flared at Port Allen in Kaua'i when 150 strikers overturned two cars carrying five scabs to work.[75] It seems that weeks later 300 strikers and their sympathizers, armed with clubs, rocks, knives, and other weapons, attacked a group of adversaries; 19 persons were hospitalized as a result, including a few strikers and one police officer who suffered a broken arm.[76] This union raid on the offices of a nonunion stevedoring concern was reportedly conducted by combatants.[77] Then, as the strike was winding down, a fight broke out in Oregon at the Northern Pacific terminal yards when two loads of Hawaiian pineapples were unloaded—strikebreaking, was how the union described it. Thus, two drivers were knocked down and pummeled.[78] This was "war," cried an editorialist, saying it could "not be called less than war."[79]

Contributing to the escalating tension was the organizing of a group of mostly white women who began harassing the picketers in the guise of representing grassroots opposition to the strike. As early as May 1949 they had become picturesque fixtures on the docks, at times numbering a reported 300 carrying signs attached to brooms. "We the Women" as they were called, created quite a stir.[80] "I'd say a good 95 per cent or more," were haole, said Robert McElrath.[81]

"They used to have these cars with loudspeakers which went around town denouncing the union," recalled Yoshiko Hall, spouse of the ILWU leader.[82] The slogans on placards carried by these women were revealing. "'We are not paid stooges'" was one; "'Communism is like cancer'" was another; "'Married Men, are your wives and children eating?'" one asked. And, perhaps most telling of all, was the sign that said, "'Communists took over Shanghai, don't let them take Hawaii.'"[83]

These otherwise prim and proper women were not above taking matters into their own hands, as when a brigade of them stormed and all but broke up a meeting of parents and teachers because Harry Schmidt of the ILWU happened to be addressing the assembled. Bitter recriminations flowed freely as the enraged women accused the PTA of not adopting what they perceived as the correct approach to real and imagined Communists.[84] Yet, their aggressiveness aside, Ruth Yap, an alert local, was among those who noted what might have been their most distinguishing characteristic. "Why is it," she asked wonderingly, "we see few of our Oriental women in the 'Broom Brigade'?" This was "not just a 'haole' fight," she insisted—though others were not as certain.[85] Beseeching "calls for more Chinese marchers" to join the women were becoming common, but such imploring could not obfuscate the fact that, disproportionately,[86] opposition to the strikers came from haoles.[87]

Like others, these women linked the actions of Reds at home and abroad,[88] and bolstering this gnawing concern was the arrival in Honolulu of the notorious anticommunists Benjamin Gitlow and Elizabeth Bentley and other emblems of reaction's heavy artillery, whose presence demonstrated how seriously this island struggle was taken.[89] Thus, by late July, Henry Schmidt of the union reported contemptuously, "[The] Broom Brigade is still with us but no one pays attention to them any more. Our men don't even bother to heckle them any more now." The distress expressed by the Broom Brigade had diminished since "there never has been any shortages around here of any commodity except rice, and that has been taken care of by the relief ship."[90]

If one looked carefully, one could almost see the veins bulging in temples and faces reddening as the strain of the strike began to take its toll. Bud McConnell, one of these angry objectors, warned threateningly that "there will be no peace on the waterfronts of the Pacific Coast or the Hawaiian islands until the people rise up en masse and rid the communities of those who are undermining their very existence." What was needed, he said worryingly, was the equivalent of the "Vigilantes of 1852 in San Francisco."[91] A self-described "Hilo Housewife" writing on behalf of "We the Women" exuded this growing fascination with violence when she warned that "Hall and the rest of them might learn first hand what is meant by 'the female of the species is deadlier than the male.'"[92]

Ray Coll, the columnist with excellent sources among the local elite, by early September was reflecting their anxiety. He had been engaged in intense conversations with "some of the men of Merchant Street," Honolulu's version of Wall Street, and they were highly displeased. More than this, they were weary, "as weary as a general whose lines have been unable to advance for many weeks," he said, and "they have no solutions to offer." This "once Paradise of the Pacific," he complained, "feels that it is without a friend in court. A stepchild cast adrift and at the mercy of that Communistic fog."[93]

With Hawai'i in turmoil, seemingly descending into barbarism if not a death spiral of anarchy, and with international tensions rising as Communists began ascending to power in China and elsewhere, it did not take long for the conclusion at which Senator Butler had arrived—second and third thoughts on the possibility for statehood—to receive a wider audience and a more sympathetic hearing. Fanning the flames was Governor Stainback, who reaped a rich harvest in Washington.[94] "I believe many . . . thought that I simply had a Communist complex, so to speak," he said, but now they knew better. Evoking his favorite metaphor, he again compared the Reds to the kolea bird, which arrived in the isles "emaciated" but left "fat."[95]

One congressional insider thought he knew who had become "fat" as a result of events in the archipelago—and it was not who the governor had in mind. "With the war came a significant transfer of wealth from the whites to the Asiatics," according to William R. Tansill of the Legislative Reference Service of the Library of Congress, "[for] the Chinese, third and fourth generation, acquired much of their wealth through the simple process of buying property during the war from faint-hearted whites. There are Chinese huis [groupings] in real estate, frozen foods, music, bottling, bowling, meats, groceries, hotels and ranches." He said with wonder, "With a population approximately one-sixth as large as that of the Japanese, the Chinese own more property than the latter." Of course, "the whites still own three-fourths of Hawaiian property, either directly or as stockholders," he observed, but that was apparently insufficient for this minority of 15 percent of the population. Tansill's report, prepared to inform congressional decision making as the statehood debate revived, noted that "attitudes among the Japanese have altered markedly," as "the men who fought so gallantly in Italy lost all sense of inferiority, despite the fact that many of the whites continued to keep them at a distance."[96]

Hawai'i, it was said, continually contributed more to the United States Treasury than had been expended by the federal government in the territory's behalf (excluding military appropriations). But taxation and expenditure policies disfavoring an archipelago with an Asian-Pacific majority was not Tansill's primary concern: he was more riveted by what he thought was outsized Chinese wealth.

On 5 November 1940 the colony had its first plebiscite on the issue of statehood. Of the 68,552 who voted, 46,124 registered approval and the rest voted against it, and about 20 percent of the 84,000 registered voters did not cast ballots—all in all, not exactly a ringing endorsement for statehood. Even Jack Hall conceded that the working class made up most of the opposition to the proposal, though his spin was that their vote was more an expression against the control of Hawai'i by the Big Five, not a vote against statehood itself. But indicative of the skewed perspectives on the isles was that in 1940 the Republican National Committee labored under the strange belief that the Hawaiian islands constituted a part of the Philippines. One of Henry Luce's magazines posited that Hawai'i was a "separate nation," and it found "strong secret anti-statehood sentiment" there. Other mainland elites looked on those of Japanese origin in Hawai'i in the same way they viewed Negroes in their own vicinities.[97]

But now, with spiraling labor unrest and serious allegations of Communist penetration, the debate on statehood had been transformed. As Senator Butler put it, "'when our mainland territories became states there was no world-wide condition as faces us today and no threat of Communism.'" Tansill hastened to bring to Congress' attention the recently concluded and protracted battle for control of the Hawai'i Legislature between left and right—Democrats and GOP—and the leading role of Jack Hall, who, it was said, presumed to dictate to the Democratic representatives their every move in the struggle for the Speakership. "For eighteen days neither side would yield, and the unorganized House could do no business," Tansill reminded. The "impasse was finally broken when a freshman Democrat reluctantly sided with the Republicans," he said, and "a Republican was thereupon elected Speaker." ILWU "protégés won half of the committee chairmanships," though—and this was the territory now being bruited as a state? Tansill requested that instead Congress should remember that "the basic objective of the Hawaiian Left . . . was succinctly revealed in 1946 when it circularized the ancient Hawaiian proverb, 'it is prophesied that the rulers will come down, the commoners go up.'"[98]

Inexorably, the tumult in the isles—the specter of a union, thought to be dominated by Communists, effectively shutting down the Pacific Gibraltar of Washington as Reds surged to power in China and rattled their sabers in Korea and elsewhere—led to grave concern on the mainland. Senator Butler chose to retain an illustrative cartoon from the *Los Angeles Times* that was published at the height of the stevedores' strike; it portrayed Stalin in a hula dress on the beach at Waikiki emblazoned with a hammer and sickle and the words "Communist inspired strikes."[99]

Taking this image to heart, a correspondent who identified herself simply as a "school teacher" informed Senator Butler that he did not "have the facts" that were "obscured by hula dancers, leis and cocktail parties"—which too often seduced visiting dignitaries.[100] President Truman, emerging triumphant from a bruising 1948 electoral battle, did not flinch in continuing to back statehood,[101] but other well-connected politicians were to reconsider.

Like the nervous citizens interviewed by Senator Butler's staff or the apprehension reflected in William Tansill's words, the racial and ethnic composition of the isles was increasingly influencing the debate on statehood and the strike, both of which were front-page news in 1949. Even the *Honolulu Advertiser*, obtuse in the best of times, noticed this issue. "On the surface," it reported, "harmony still exists among the racial minorities," but "for the first time authorities are aware of a tension seething beneath the surface." This startling perception arose when Jack Kawano stood before his fellow union members and shouted: "'Why don't they give us the same wages they pay on the coast?'" The theatrical Kawano then paused dramatically and answered his searching inquiry by pointing to his arm and posing another query in roaring reply: "'Because the color of our skin is brown?'"[102] Another observer insisted that "it is high time that we stop kidding ourselves about the Communist smokescreen, very conveniently used by opponents of statehood[,] and face the real issue obstructing Hawaii's statehood." What was that? "This is the racial issue," was the response. "Opponents of statehood are afraid that if Hawaii were ever granted statehood, a Japanese or a Chinese might some day be elected to the governorship."[103]

The dilemma for many isle residents and their patrons in Washington was that as they confronted the knotty issues of strike and statehood, they were faced with dueling poles of race and radicalism—either the fear of Asian-Pacific hegemony or the fear of Communists. The latter was symbolized by the increasing prominence of Harry Bridges, now widely portrayed as the éminence grise of the islands, the evil genius of labor unrest, the Communist mastermind who would have veto power over who was to occupy two US Senate seats and what might become two more seats in the House of Representatives.[104]

William Glazier of the ILWU staff in Washington, D.C., captured their message thusly: "'If we are successful in our prosecution of Bridges it may be that we can break the Hawaii situation without any intervention.'" Among those who feared unions and Communists, the idea was growing that if Bridges could be done away with, problems would disappear magically.[105] Earlier, Glazier noted that a New York newspaper had carried a letter urging the journal to "play up the Hawaii strike in order to facilitate the deportation of Bridges."[106]

Thus, during the midst of the strike, Bridges, Robertson, and Harry Schmidt of the San Francisco–based ILWU leadership were all indicted at the behest of Attorney General Tom Clark on three counts of criminal fraud and conspiracy based on their alleged lies about Communist Party membership. The union prevailed in this standoff, but not minus immense strain. Bridges and his colleagues were tried and convicted in 1950; then their bail was revoked after Bridges called for a cease-fire in the newly launched war in Korea—and he was jailed, then freed after three weeks behind bars. By May 1953 his conviction was overturned, but then Jack Hall was about to be convicted for violating the Smith Act, and the union's travails continued.[107] It was not long before Myer Symonds, the attorney representing both Hall and the ILWU, found that the House Committee on Un-American Activities was following up aggressively on Governor Stainback's desire that the committee thoroughly investigate this effective advocate about his supposed CP membership, which—it was thought—he was dissembling about.[108]

Still years from the age of retirement at the time of his indictment, Bridges was born into a family that held extensive real estate interests, and his uncle was a member of Parliament. He was reared and educated as a Catholic. The union had become his life, and his only possessions were a mortgaged automobile and a vacant lot in Australia, as he was probably the lowest-paid leader of any importance in the United States. His union elected officers annually by secret ballot, and any act of the International Executive Board, which he led, could be subjected to referendum by the entire union at the request of 15 percent of the membership. No union contract could be ratified without secret majority vote, and neither he nor any other ILWU official received a penny in salary when strikes ensued. Oscar-winning screenwriter Dalton Trumbo, a friend of Bridges', said that Bridges' union was "the finest example of democratic trade unionism in America,"[109] and he was not exaggerating. Early in life, Bridges had demonstrated his precocity. "I joined the Australian Seamen's Union," he said, during the "first World War in 1916"[110]—he was a teenager then.

Controversy rages as to whether Bridges was a Communist Party member, his vigorous denials notwithstanding. Certainly he was an unrepentant Marxist, not unfriendly to Moscow, and that in itself has raised suspicions in some. Such eminent intellectuals as Arthur Schlesinger Jr., Nathan Glazer, Daniel Bell, and Irving Howe were among those who rejected his denials, though a defender of Bridges has argued just as assertively that "excessive focus on the issue of his relationship with the Communist Party" was misleading, for "if parallels existed between Bridges' political views and the party line of the American Communists, historians miss the point" that even some of their own pet causes—civil rights and equality for minorities, for example—could easily get them labeled as Reds.[111] One journalist writing for an anticommunist audience at the time of Bridges' vicissitudes maintained, "The relationship between Harry Bridges and the Communist Party was not one in which the party gave orders and Bridges mechanically obeyed. Rather, the party generally found it necessary to 'handle' Bridges, sometimes wheedling, sometimes cajoling, always feeding his ego."[112]

In a sense, the 1949 strike was not the only reason the government had sought to get rid of Bridges. Consider that in early 1945 one writer argued that "Bridges is closer to deportation now than he has been at any time since the government started investigating him almost nine years ago."[113] Before that, a champion of Bridges moaned that "for the first time in its history the House of Representatives of the United States on June 13, 1940, passed a bill to deport one individual—Harry Bridges."[114]

What was often missed was that, his San Francisco associations aside, Bridges—and the ILWU—relied heavily on Hawai'i as a base of support, and thus events in the isles were a factor in prompting his latest persecution. When he was raising funds in 1943 to avert yet another attempt to oust him, Honolulu's Local 137 of the ILWU provided more support than either the San Francisco CIO or the Alameda CIO, across the bay and centered in Oakland.[115] As Dave Thompson recognized, the ILWU in Hawai'i "was the big cog in the union wheel," controlling "more political power commensurately than the mainland ILWU" could possibly have, due to the size of the islands and the proportion of the ILWU to the size of the place.[116]

By the time of the epochal 1949 strike, the support for Bridges had not wavered. This he found when he appeared before striking stevedores during the first week of August. He was in Hilo, which was probably not accidental. According to Jack Hall, the stevedores there were "always the most militant," and he had "always considered them as the guys that really got started in the modern day labor movement here in Hawaii"; on the other hand, Hall noted, Honolulu "was extremely backward in the trade union sense, even though you would think that because it's an urban community it would have been easier." It was in Hilo, he said, "primarily because of a close affinity to the seamen and so many of them being ex-seamen," where there was a "militancy that was uncharacteristic of the rest of the Hawaiians."[117] Thus, perhaps because of the nature of his audience, Bridges—candid in the worst of times—was unusually frank. Though the strike was to plod on for two more months, he did not hesitate to tell the assembled that, in his judgment, "the strike is won," though "we haven't got the strike over yet." This strike, he detailed, was "in reality a strike against the Big Five," and "not a strike against the shipping companies," as it appeared. "Among these seven companies," he argued, "the big company, the powerful company, of course, is Castle and Cooke, the biggest of the Big Five," and the "main employer in this strike is the Matson Navigation Company." But as he saw it, "this strike is really a strike against[Matson]," which was "owned by all of the Big Five." Thus, he insisted, "the key to this strike is to stop Matson from running its ships taking sugar to the refineries in San Francisco, taking pineapple over to the canneries in California and [operating] the Durline, running tourists from the mainland down here to live in the hotels Moana and Royal Hawaiian"; for, continued Bridges, "as long as Matson can't operate, your strike is over 80% effective," and "as long as Matson ships are not operating, you have a more effective strike here than any longshore strike we have ever had on the Pacific Coast."[118]

How so? "Well," said Bridges, "in every strike we have had on the Pacific Coast, more than 20% of the cargo would move by other means than ships"—trucks, rail, etc.—"and yet we won these strikes, despite that." Bridges did not know "how long it will take before the Big Five and Matson wake up to the fact that they are beaten," as he made it clear, "I am not here giving you a pep talk. I am not kidding you." Stormy applause erupted at this juncture from the stevedores. "A couple of years ago, I had to come around the islands at the time of the pineapple strike," Bridges said. "At that time, my purpose was to say—we have lost the strike [because] we made a mistake." But times had changed, for "we have already been told by one union, the Marine Cooks and Stewards," which had similar progressive leadership, "that they won't man the ships," Bridges observed, and "there are just not enough scabs to work these ships." Therefore, he was supremely confident of the union's ability to prevail but added a cautionary note: "If we lose this strike, believe me, [and] you people trust me to know what I am talking about, that is the end of unions in these islands for some time to come."[119] As it turned out, Bridges' confidence was not misplaced.

This grim reality had dawned slowly on his opponents, and they were not gleeful at the prospect. While still in Hawai'i, Bridges was being interviewed—"grilled and harassed" is probably a more accurate description—by a panel of journalists on the popular radio station KIPA, and he was giving as good as he got. "I don't [think] that anybody could accuse me of going to church," said this leader who resided in a nation proud of its religiosity. Unbothered, Bridges added, "I believe in God as a private person and individual." The moderator of the discussion replied, "We have enough questions that have been phoned in. I think we are going to be busy here all night if we keep them coming in." Callers were no doubt moved by Bridges' salty assertions, including his riposte that "you can't turn sideways in these islands without running up against the Big Five."[120] KIPA had become the station to tune into for information about the union, with Hall once boasting that the ILWU-sponsored "daily radio program" was getting a "large response"[121]—and the kind of unvarnished comments provided by Bridges at the height of a straining strike was a central reason why (even though the station's general manager complained, "Your broadcast is bringing us numerous phone calls, none of them complimentary").[122]

A few days later, after a series of tough and bitter negotiating sessions, Bridges was at the airport in Honolulu. Amidst the sunshine and swaying palm trees he was greeted by a delegation of 200 persons who did not necessarily wish him well. In fact, they greeted his arrival with a volley of spirited boos and other imprecations. Nattily dressed as ever, in a gray pin-striped suit, a white shirt with a red tie, and brown wing-tipped shoes, Bridges stopped short at the sounds, turned, and smiled, and the sight of his big white teeth bared for all to see served to accelerate the velocity of the epithets. Draped with three leis and toting a box of paradise flowers and a box of candy, Bridges was the picture of the radical in paradise, exerting power and influence at a level far beyond those of his counterparts—and even himself—on the mainland. [123]

Bridges was crisscrossing the nation, attempting to at once lead and bolster his beleaguered troops. A few days earlier he had been in Washington, and Senator Butler, who had seen him, was hardly impressed. "Bridges was in town the other day," he muttered. "I stepped into the committee hearing long enough to get a look at him, [and] one look was enough." His temper flaring, the senator proclaimed angrily, "He should be [de]ported and his unions should be broken up just like we break up large corporations. There is a movement on here now to prepare such a bill," he assured. As an aside that cast light on his true feelings, Butler added, "I think the [fascist] Spanish government should be recognized and should receive . . . assistance in fighting Communism" since General Franco "believes in Christianity,"[124] unlike Reds.

Butler may have seen Bridges at a hearing convened by the crustily idiosyncratic Senator Wayne Morse of Oregon, in which the solon, in the union leader's recollection, "stood up and declared that he had never seen a worse bunch of employers" than those in Hawai'i. Bridges stoked this idea by noting that he had never seen such hysteria whipped up against a union since 1934 and the San Francisco General Strike. On one occasion, he said, in support of his contention, he was having lunch with Henry Schmidt and some shipowners at a public eatery, and some "screwball" recognized him and started screaming "'Lynch Harry Bridges.'"[125] The screamer—and those like him—were not pleased when Morse chose to back the union's demand for arbitration and was joined by other congressional heavyweights, e.g., Senators Warren Magnuson, Claude Pepper, and Elbert Thomas.[126] When Riley Allen of the *Honolulu Star-Bulletin* dared to report in a manner deemed not to be critical of Morse's demarche, he "lost $50,000" in advertising, said Ray Jerome Baker, and "it was a lesson that Mr. Allen never forgot."[127]

Then the isles' congressional delegate, Joseph Farrington, met with President Truman to ask his intervention to get the strike settled.[128] This dramatic gesture by Farrington was insufficient for the union.[129] The union pressure was evidently working, for when Glazier spoke with Oscar Chapman of the Interior Department "at some length," he "agreed with my comments on the Governor's actions," said the union man, "and the motives behind them."[130]

Bridges and the ILWU, along with their CP colleagues, had Washington in a bind, prompting the conniptions of some. The United States was coming to see how white supremacy—which had been essential to its fortunes and the seizure of Hawai'i in the first place—had been challenged forcibly during the Pacific War and was now compromising the nation's ability to credibly charge Moscow with human rights violations in the then raging battle of ideas. Retreating from the more egregious aspects of white supremacy was in order or, minimally, placing decorative window dressing upon it. Instead, these elites were confronted with the spectacle of the worst of all worlds—a race-tinged labor battle in the strategically critical archipelago.[131]

Yet despite the ILWU's manifest power, it was not preordained that the union would emerge triumphant at the end of this arduous struggle. But they had assets beyond the purview of mainland counterparts. John Burns, a leading member of the Democratic Party and a founding father of modern Hawai'i, was prevailed upon by the union to travel to Washington, D.C., to lobby on the union's behalf. It was "the first time I had ever been," he said, suggestive of the union's reach and impact. Burns took the opportunity to confer with representatives of the potent House Committee on Un-American Activities who "gave me the agreement that they wouldn't come out [to Honolulu] while the strike was in progress." That was a concession, albeit minor, since the committee arrived shortly after an agreement had been reached between labor and management. During the course of this journey, he found himself on the same plane as that of Secretary of Labor Maurice Tobin, and Burns also cajoled him on behalf of the union. Burns' kneading and arm-twisting compelled Tobin to admit that he backed the union's view that arbitration was the way out of this crisis. Subsequently, Hall declared that this "was the straw that broke the camel's back" and forced management into a more realistic posture.[132]

Arbitration had become the critical question. Goldblatt observed that the "weaker side" usually favored arbitration, but that was not "really the issue" since, he said, "as far as the employers were concerned, as long as we were in favor of it, they were opposed to it."[133] When the managers were compelled to retreat from their dug-in position, it signaled their impending defeat. They also thereby laid the groundwork for future setbacks, for just as Burns, a future power broker, found himself in league with the ILWU in 1949, it was during that same year that the man who was to become Hawai'i's long-standing US senator, Daniel Inouye, visited the offices of management in search of information about what was going on—and was rebuffed. Then he visited Hall, Bridges, and Goldblatt, and as he recalled it, "they greeted me like a long-lost brother." During those tense times, Inouye spoke to at least 100 workers and asked them their feelings about allegations about Red leadership of the ILWU, notably Hall, and "the usual response was, 'I don't know what a Communist is. All I know [is] he's okay. He's taking care of us. He don't break no laws.'"[134] Thus, as McElrath recollected, when an attempt was made during the course of the strike to form a "strike breaking committee" composed of Japanese-American military veterans, this effort proved unavailing. Moreover, prominent members of the emerging Chinese elite—e.g., future US senator Hiram Fong—aided the strike by preventing foreclosures, extending time for payments of overdue bills of workers bereft of income,[135] and other thoughtful gestures.[136]

Thus the union remained strong. "Only a handful of weak sisters," said Mamoru Yamasaki, a strike leader, "have deserted the ranks in spite of all the pressure and propaganda." He added, "Stainback and his stooges predicted that from 150 to 200 of our Honolulu members would go to work scabbing for the Territory. Yet, this prediction has fizzled down to just eight finky guys."[137] The union had dispatched its top generals to the scene to help ensure that defections did not spread, including not only the usual troika of Bridges, Goldblatt, and Robertson but Henry Schmidt as well. Of Dutch-German descent—his father was German—Schmidt had enchanting blue eyes and pink skin encasing a dumpy figure featuring spectacles perched on his nose, just below a balding pate. He arrived in Honolulu originally at an auspicious moment—"the day after the tidal wave," as he recalled it—in April 1946 when he was approaching the age of 48.[138]

A veteran stevedore, he was well versed in the outs and ins of labor struggles. Thus it was Schmidt who in early July 1949 instructed isle stevedores on the mechanics of organizing a soup kitchen for strikers and their families. It was designed, he said, not only for feeding the hungry. "It will be a morale builder," he added, "since it will be necessary for all of the strikers to get to-gether in the kitchen several times each day and also because several of your members will find it necessary to work there constantly," thereby becoming vectors for transmission of information—and solidarity. "You should also go to the [Public Welfare Department]," he instructed, "accompanied by a large committee of strikers [and] insist that Department also render you assis-tance," for "need is the basis on which they should agree to render aid."[139] That proved to be timely advice.[140]

Schmidt also was coordinating a kind of intelligence operation. "You fel-lows are renting an airplane and several speed boats to check if any additional barges are on the way," he informed a union leader in Seattle. "Territorial scabs are loading pineapple on some of the big East Coast vessels, and these vessels will proceed to the East Coast via the Panama Canal." The idea was to mobilize friends and supporters to harass and boycott these ships and cargoes.[141]

It was not foreordained that the union would mobilize—as it did so adroitly.[142] As it turned out, steadfastness paid dividends, for after the strike concluded, union pillar Joe Blur told Hall, "As a result of the strike, Port Allen is a changed port. It's leadership, and in fact the whole unit are really militant." Things had progressed to the point where "they even had the finks (deserters and strike breakers) supporting them in the job actions they have been pulling."[143]

Paul Fagan could not have been very happy about how things were going. It was August 1949, and the millionaire shipping magnate was ensconced at his lush and well-appointed estate in Maui, entertaining Harry Bridges. The two men lounged on the beach, seemingly relaxed, in swimming trunks and sport shirts. "'I talked to him casually about the San Francisco Seals,'" said Fagan with what must have been a suppressed frown, in a reference to the much-beloved baseball team of which he was the majority stockholder. To believe Fagan, the issue of the strike and how it was affecting Matson, of which he was a key director, did not emerge in his discussion with Bridges.[144]

Yet it is reasonably certain that Bridges' encounter with Fagan was among a number of essential meetings that led to a settlement of a strike that was not only draining revenue from Matson but also reducing the amount of taxes that the government in Honolulu needed to collect. The dwindling tax revenue was not good news in an archipelago that was already reeling from the burden of inadequate housing stock and rising prices for the most mun-dane of goods—the latter being influenced directly by the strike. Such con-cerns led to the arrangement of another high-level meeting, a few weeks after Bridges was lolling on the beach in Maui. "Brother Kawano and I called upon the Governor at the latter's request," Schmidt reported. "We arrived at his offices at 3 PM, where we were allowed to cool our heels in the anteroom for 30 minutes. When they finally met Stainback face-to-face, the session proved disappointing, as it was apparently difficult for the governor—a man who viewed the union as an existential danger to Hawai'i's well-being—to recognize that the ILWU was about to attain a victory that would not only cement its reputation for delivering victories to its members but also prove that it had become a permanent fixture among the powerful of the islands. Thus, before departing the governor's office, the ILWU delegation, said Schmidt, "agreed that we would say nothing to the press," which was surprising, since "the only affirmative statement that was made was regarding his [the governor's] question regarding long-term contracts."[145]

Stainback was not alone. Jack Hall felt that Manila—the home of a number of union members—was also perturbed by the ILWU's solidarity, as the consulate was pressuring Filipino workers: "McCabe segregated the Filipinos on buses from Pearl Harbor and attempted to drive the buses to the Consulate for a 'meeting.' The workers objected and piled off before the buses reached their destination," but the attempts to sway their opinion continued.[146] The consul general, Aurelio Quitoriano, did not cease his efforts. His (probably inflated) opinion was that about 75 percent of stevedores in Honolulu were Filipinos and that the alleged 14 percent wage increase recommended by the governor was just and fair.[147] The consul did not share his view of Stainback's effort, as the ILUW put it, "to smash [the union] by seizing the docks and putting the strikebreakers to work"; nor did Manila's man express his opinion of the union's "warning [that] ships would not be worked on the mainland if they are loaded by scabs and strikebreakers."[148]

Bridges backed up these threats when he settled into the witness chair in a federal courtroom in Honolulu. Looking hungry but smiling frequently, he thundered occasionally as he lashed out at the colony's longshore strike legislation. He alternately waved or wore his horn-rimmed glasses and grimaced often.[149] An evidently impressed Judge Delbert Metzger ultimately decided that the dock seizure law was unconstitutional.[150] This was just another indication that the strike was not evolving in a direction favorable to management. Ray Coll, who often reflected management's views, acknowledged in early September, "Folks back there [on the mainland] still can't understand why we won't arbitrate. I tried to make the point by saying you can't arbitrate with the Communists."[151] But this notion, which seemed like common sense on the mainland, struck many islanders as little more than stubborn arrogance.

Ultimately, the strike was won. This came clear in August in San Francisco when the ILWU leadership was joined by other maritime unions. The purpose of the meeting, said Bridges, "was to inform the maritime unions that should the ship-owners try to load ships from San Francisco to Hawaii, the ILWU will pull the coast, contracts to the contrary notwithstanding," leading to a Pacific strike. "One part of the ILWU is not going to be used to scab on another part," he warned. "We may be back where we were in 1934"—alarming news to those familiar with these previous apocalyptic events. "Even if we told the rank and file to load the ships, they would tell us to go to hell," he advised the doubters. Eddie Tangen of the National Maritime Union echoed these threats, proclaiming, "Unless we put our finger in the buzz-saw now, we are going to put our whole god-damn arm in. If they get away with what they are trying to do in Hawaii with refusal to arbitrate and with threats of violence and calling for violence [we] will have to take the same thing here."[152]

On 6 October 1949, Schmidt reported, "Honolulu is an uproar at the moment. Bridges has just left by plane and he has issued a statement indicating under what terms the union would be willing to settle the strike. We have concrete information that the employers' camp is split wide open." His thoughts were interrupted before he returned to his message and further informed F. T. Moore, vice president of the ILWU local in Wilmington, California, "P.S. The beef is over! And we win; there is no mistake about that, taking into consideration that it was the employers' program to wipe us out completely."[153] Shortly thereafter, Bridges announced a settlement to a circle of reporters and union men just as the first call was sounded for passengers to board his plane from Honolulu to San Francisco, this at a moment when negotiations seemed to have broken down. First management denied this was so, but then was compelled to agree,[154] thus vindicating Bridges' confident assertion that, unlike coal or movies or steel, "you can't store transportation," which gave the stevedores an advantage unavailable to other workers.[155]

CHAPTER 11

Racism—and Reaction

"We do not just have a cyclical depression in Hawaii that will one day crawl up the graphs of the professional economists to the peaks of prosperity." Such were the ominous words of Jack Hall, just after the monumental strike of stevedores had concluded. No, he insisted, "Hawaii has reached the stage of chronic unemployment—chronic unemployment of an alarming degree." The island paradise was "already worse off than any state in the union," with the "prospect of one worker in four being without a job." The vaunted sugar industry was slated to produce in 1949 nearly one million tons of sugar with a workforce of less than 20,000 hourly paid workers; to produce the same tonnage in 1932 had required a workforce of 54,992. Yet, astonishingly, during those same years the permanent population of Hawai'i increased by 150,000.[1]

There were contrary trends. Ray Coll felt that the stevedores' strike would help island farmers, given that it blocked competition from the mainland because fewer ships were making the journey due to inability to unload upon arrival. In Waimea, for example, early on he noticed that farmers who had been plowing under lettuce because the Honolulu market was glutted were—with the strike—able to both increase output and sell it.[2]

Yet this did not obliterate the realities perceived by Hall. Drawn by the advertisements of Hawai'i as an earthly paradise, the impressions rendered by visiting soldiers and sailors, and a long-standing tradition of seeing the archipelago as worthy of residence, migrants from the mainland had been traveling westward particularly since the end of the war. Their taking up permanent residence in Hawai'i had placed pressure on employment rolls. More than this, the changing population and economic climate placed added strain on the exceedingly intricate racial makeup of Hawai'i, which—in turn—created the opportunity for management to pit one group against another. This increased racial diversity was taking root as the United States itself was moving to the right, driven by war in Korea and the purging of Reds from public life.

As these migrants who made up this enhanced reserve army of labor increased in number, ready to be deployed against unions—as management

saw it—unions responded accordingly. By early August 1950 a local periodical complained that there had been 18 work stoppages already—with more
planned. Worse, said this writer, in each instance the ILWU was the bargaining agent of the employees involved. "No other union has engaged in a
strike so far this year," it was announced prematurely.[3] By December the
same journal was complaining of an AFL bus strike in Honolulu in terms
that echoed what had been heard when the stevedores walked out.[4]

The bus strike led to an astronomical intensification of traffic congestion,
with vehicles ensnarled bumper to bumper and with prospects for further
chaos.[5] One frustrated journal posed what had been thought unimaginable:
"Should government control the buses?"[6] Worse—or so it was thought—was
that this problem could not be blamed on the ILWU, as it was Art Rutledge's
AFL-affiliated union that was responsible.[7] Rutledge's AFL had a membership
of about 10,000 in Hawai'i, although only half of this number were organized
in private industry. The remainder were union members employed at the Navy
Yard at Pearl Harbor.[8] These numbers were far from negligible but paled in
comparison to the ILWU's figures, thus highlighting the latter's potency.

But there were other changes in the makeup of Hawai'i that had attracted
the attention of Hall's antagonists. Oscar Iden told his employer, Senator
Butler, that he should "compare the 'curves' of Negro and white births and
deaths in some of the southern states where the present Negro population is
close to a majority." He noted nervously, "When the Negro electorate does
reach a majority in a few short years, may we not expect a few, and possibly
radical BLACK Senators[?] Isn't is probable that under such circumstances,
there would be a 'block' of the Hawaiian and Negro Senators[?]"[9] As it turns
out, Iden's worries were wildly overblown, but this nervousness was driven to
no small degree by the specter of white supremacy's retreat in the face of the
Pacific War and the concomitant surge toward equality by all those not defined as "white"—a reality that, in a sense, reached its zenith in Hawai'i.[10]

A leading Honolulu politico at the time, Bill Borthwick, lamented, "The
census of 1950 has developed some facts that to say the least are astounding. 90
thousands haoles have left since 1947 and there are thousands more going.
Many young Portuguese are leaving. Because when they apply for positions in
answer to ads they are told Japs are preferred."[11] Senator James Eastland of Mississippi, who also had taken an interest in Hawai'i, chose to retain an inflammatory analysis detailing the alleged "decline of Caucasian Population in Hawaii,"
which had purportedly gone from 82,385 in July 1950 to 78,539 months later
and to 70,176—or 15.3 percent of the overall population—shortly after that.
The information in Eastland's hands noted apprehensively that "these alien
Filipinos constitute the core of the Harry Bridges Communist machine."[12]
Senator Eastland, a Jim Crow advocate, also found worth keeping a report on
"dangerous factors in proposed Hawaiian statehood," which included the theme

that "racial birth-rates are of the essence." The "atom bomb terrifies us," it was said, "but perhaps it is not more deadly than the explosion of peoples," which was a reference to "Japan's new weapon[, a] flood of babies." The question was simple, according to the report: "Will the haoles disappear" since the "fast-growing groups are driving out the haoles[?]" The report concluded that "whether or not the fear of the Japanese [is] justified, it is undoubtedly very real and wide-spread."[13] This whispering behind closed doors emerged into public view when a local newspaper blared the headline, "Caucasian Group in Big Population Drop."[14]

As the twentieth century entered its second half, the themes foreshadowed by Hall and his antagonists—the ILWU seeking to consolidate its gains, and the racist reaction to it—were to duel dancingly. A kind of hysteria had enveloped many in Hawai'i and on the mainland, as it seemed their prewar fears about the planet's Asian majority merged almost effortlessly with their postwar fears about Moscow: the ILWU, a mostly Asian-Pacific union led by people thought to be Communists, became the focus of this nervous apprehension—particularly after war was launched in Korea in June 1950.

What was concerning to the ILWU, however, was that the monumental strikes they had launched in the fields and on the docks had attracted the concerted attention of an ever-growing number of powerful solons, reflective of the idea that Hawai'i was becoming a problem for Washington. Rulers there were unsure as to what to do about a place where Communists seemed to be ascending—in contrast to their retreat on the mainland—and where those not defined as "white" were rising in number, with the two factors seeming to be related. Amid the leafy and bucolic setting of the headquarters of the Rockefeller Foundation, which long had taken an interest in Hawai'i, executives were poring over a report they had funded, and they were not overly pleased with what they read. There was an "alleged Japanese menace," while "'Communism is strong among the Japanese,'" reported the foundation's correspondent, Bernhard L. Hormann of the University of Hawai'i: "In contrast to the Caucasians and Hawaiians, the Chinese and the Japanese in particular expressed very strong support of statehood. Among the Japanese there was less than one out of twelve who opposed statehood." On the other hand, "Hawaiians and part-Hawaiians expressed the least enthusiasm for statehood." Thus, there was a proliferating "fear that the favorable state of race relations [might] be jeopardized by statehood" and a concomitant "fear that Communist infiltration in the islands has already gone so far as to make statehood unwise." Simultaneously there was "uneasiness over the possible domination of island politics and industry by Orientals," all of which amounted to a "'Yellow Peril' Scare" that eerily corresponded to the mainland's Red Scare.[15]

One reason why Hawai'i was a site where the Red Scare seemed to morph easily into the "Yellow Peril Scare" was the triumph of the Communist Party in

China—in the same month, October 1949, that the ILWU had its most significant victory in Hawai'i—followed swiftly by the onset of war on the Korean
peninsula; in each instance Communists were the primary antagonists. The
Korean conflict was to have gargantuan consequence for Hawai'i, as the islands
became a major staging ground for the United States' deployment of troops and
tons of materiel to Asia (a process that was to accelerate in coming years when
Vietnam became the target of war, again with Communists being in the cross-
hairs). The economic consequence for Hawai'i was enormous,[16] but that was not
all. The political consciousness of Chinese-Americans grew in Hawai'i when
the idea was floated of interning them there as tensions with Peking grew.[17]

It was in November of that pivotal year, 1950, that Joseph Farrington
contacted the future US president, Senator Lyndon Baines Johnson, who like
most well-informed politicians on the mainland kept a close eye on the Pacific. "Casualties among Hawaii's sons in [the] Korean war" had reached 425,
a rate "almost five times that for [the] country as a whole," Farrington pointed
out. In fact, he remarked, "if losses for [the] entire country were at same rate
as those [of] Hawaii they would now be close to 150,000 instead [of] 29,996."[18]
Tellingly, shortly after Farrington's pained remarks, the left-wing *Honolulu
Record* blared in a front-page headline, "Few Haoles among 480 Draftees."[19]

The local elite and their counterparts in Washington had to ponder the
logic of fighting Communists to the death in Asia while they seemed to be
gaining ground in Hawai'i. These power holders had to consider further the
import of an increasingly confident Asian-Pacific majority in the isles who
not only were loathe to take an electoral backseat to the elite but were hungry
for a taste of power themselves.

This had crossed the mind of left-wingers, and foremost among these was
African-American writer and activist Frank Marshall Davis. He had become a
small businessman, purchasing an 11,000-square-foot lot on Mount Tantalus
in O'ahu. From there he could peer down upon the city of Honolulu and the
surrounding ocean. He spent his days rubbing shoulders with individuals from
small settlements of Hawaiians and Samoans who lived mainly by fishing and
growing their own taro, from which came the famed local dish poi.[20]

Davis was rapidly integrating himself into the life of the islands in a way
that was making him a fixture on the Left, as he strolled around in shorts or
swim trunks—bereft of shoes.[21] When his new daughter was born in the
midst of the stevedores' strike, he signaled his deepening attachment to the
islands by naming her "Lynn Makaleka Davis, giving her a Hawaiian middle
name in honor of the place of her birth."[22]

As his new daughter's name suggested, Davis found that "the more I get
acquainted with [indigenous] Hawaiians, the closer the emotional and cultural resemblance to Negroes" he observed. "At times I think I'm back in
Chicago," he mused, as he noticed that some indigenes "have picked up jive

talk" and many liked "jazz and blues,"[23] similarities that also suggested why they were treated like Negroes.[24] At his flourishing small business, where he sold various kinds of paper goods, most of his customers were of Japanese ancestry and quite friendly.[25] He felt he had landed on another planet when he was able to conclude, "It's gotten so now that you don't pay attention to the ethnic background of the people you know."[26] His solidarity with the islands deepened further when in late 1950 he fathered another child, a son, Mark Kaleokualoha Davis, with his middle name too being Hawaiian.[27]

Yet as the complexities of racism and radicalism—and anticommunism—continued to unfold in the islands, their effects were manifested acutely, hardly leaving time for the idyllic existence Davis had created for himself. The value of Davis' presence in Hawai'i came clear when a discourse on these interlocked matters erupted at his initiative, a conversation that had been sorely lacking until his arrival. In short, Davis found himself in the midst of a controversy with his fellow progressive John Reinecke, after Reinecke had suggested that "mainland haoles in Hawaii have been a liberalizing force as compared with island-bred haoles." Davis disagreed, and Reinecke took sharp exception, equating Davis' words with "anti-Filipinoism," which was "just as nasty, and I have seen it," he said, "in Orientals who never had an iota of mainland influence."[28] Davis was aghast, almost sputtering in response, "May I ask who is responsible for double standard pay, racial ceilings on promotions, residential segregation and the whole plantation system[?]" Well, Davis continued huffily, "if the mainland haoles as a group have been a liberalizing force, isn't it odd that the rise in anti-Semitism and prejudices against Negroes occurred at a time when mainland haoles came here in such tremendous numbers during World War II?"[29]

Davis' island reverie was interrupted by his festering ongoing dispute with Reinecke, which continued to erupt publicly. The otherwise mild-mannered Reinecke fired a shot over the bow in February 1950, when he criticized the celebrated scholar and activist W. E. B. Du Bois. At that time, Du Bois was about to be tried in federal court for being the agent of an unnamed foreign power—thought to be the Soviet Union—as a result of his crusade against nuclear weapons.[30] Davis found Reinecke's timing inopportune, but the recently defrocked schoolteacher continued to insist that Du Bois was among "some American Negroes [who] have gone to the other extreme," adding, "They have built up themselves a 'history' in which the Negro's role is exaggerated." Reinecke's opinion was that "most of the people of North Africa are still Caucasian in race"[31]—a mind-boggling public statement that at once exposed the ideological frailties of some Communists. An outraged Davis accused his interlocutor of providing aid and comfort to racism, which could not have happened at a worse time. It was a "sad surprise," Davis felt, to see that Reinecke "joins forces with the white supremacists." How could Reinecke form his brain to think—and then write—"'Nobodies like Crispus Attucks are made heroes.'" How could a man of Reinecke's "scholastic achievement" say this, he pondered? "If he is as great a liberal as his reputation indicates," Davis averred, "why is it he does not join in the fight against the publicists for white supremacy[?]"[32] Reinecke's statement, he maintained, "merely proves how deep are the roots of white supremacy even in some of those who have the greatest reputation as liberals."[33] Fortunately, Reinecke did not represent the entire warp and woof of progressive white opinion, in that Stephen Murin charged that Reinecke was "guilty" of being "petty" and scorned the "cynical smart-aleck tone" he displayed.[34]

But it was not Reinecke alone who was thinking such thoughts. Not long thereafter, yet another leader—this time, Bob McElrath—remonstrated the Civil Rights Congress for the seemingly trivial offense of referring to the Hawai'i ILWU as being "'composed mainly of Chinese, Japanese, Negro, Malayan and Filipino workers.'" "The latter is not a fact," McElrath responded tartly. "This union does not have ten Negroes among its membership in the territory of Hawaii," he said, adding that there was "almost a complete absence of Negroes in the work under the jurisdiction of the ILWU." Thus, he concluded triumphantly, "if racism is involved in this attack on the liberties of the people of Hawaii, it is only to a minor degree"—as if "racism" was a term that could be applied only when African-Americans were at issue. That perspective may shed light on why some union leaders were at times so lethargic in responding to racist offenses against the bulk of their members.[35]

But what even the ordinarily perspicacious Davis seemed not to recognize was that Hawai'i was undergoing racial strains in part because of larger political and economic forces. That is, as unemployment rose and Communists grew in influence at a time when fears were escalating about the alleged diminishing number of haoles in Hawai'i, extraordinary strains were placed on the politics of the archipelago—strains to which it was not altogether accustomed. This was manifested in the special attention to a relatively small African-American population—a focus perhaps generated by the speculation to which Senators Butler and Eastland were subjected, which underscored the furor generated by Reinecke's remarks. Davis termed it "Dixie in Honolulu" as he wondered why police officers found it necessary when patrolling to "to use their fists and boots on any Negro whose appearance they don't like." On Smith Street, a main artery in the downtown area, "this has been happening with increasing frequency," Davis said; he had "heard that certain powerful elements in [Hawai'i] want to discourage Negroes from settling in Hawaii and would like to drive out most of those already here."[36] It was more than coincidence, he thought, that just as cutbacks by the military caused many Negroes to return—reluctantly—to the mainland, and the 1,000 or so Negro civilians [dwindled] to about 800, pressure accelerated for the rest to depart forthwith.[37]

Thus, Davis said with a mixture of sorrow and amazement, "the Pleasanton Hotel, reputedly on the advice of the police department, now bans Negro guests," while a recent editorial in the local press in Honolulu said that if they didn't like this treatment, they could get out of Honolulu. Smith Street, between Pauahi and Beretania was now being viewed as the headquarters for "'pimping, dope peddling, prostitution and bootlegging,'" all of which were associated with the Negro presence and seemed to justify the targeted repression of Negroes. But Davis thought he knew why all of a sudden Negroes seemed to be in the bull's-eye, indicating that he was not totally oblivious to what Senators Butler and Eastland were reading. Negroes, Davis related, were deemed to be undesirable because they had "maintained a persistent militancy" and "if enough lived in Hawaii they would be almost certain to identify themselves with non-haoles"—as Davis so clearly had—"and thus strengthen the fight against the various forms of island discrimination"; and this was already occurring even though Negroes numbered "only a few hundred in Hawaii."[38]

The Hawaii Civil Liberties Committee objected strenuously to the rampaging police brutality and to the fact that "such treatment appears to be directed especially at the Negro people, who are the most recent newcomers to Honolulu."[39] Illegal drugs had been prevalent in the isles since the late nineteenth century, and it was only since 1947 that narcotic addiction had become a real community problem[40]—one that was now being used to scapegoat Negroes.[41]

The racist trend was spreading. During the San Francisco trial of "Tokyo Rose," the woman accused of assisting Japan during the war, the witnesses were segregated into two rooms—one for those of Japanese ancestry and one for white,[42] which Davis noticed.[43] Insistently, Davis maintained, "I cannot emphasize too strongly the similarities between the status of the Negro people and the AJAs and other ethnic minorities"[44] as apprehension about one fed nervousness about the other.[45]

As Davis saw it, though Negroes were only a tiny fraction of the island population, this group was a barometer, since the "nation's largest minority sets the pattern for the treatment of all other colored peoples," including "the Oriental, Polynesian and Latin peoples" who "cannot themselves get full, first-class citizenship until Jim Crow is dead and buried." In Hawai'i the list of bias' victims "has been increased and made more complex," Davis said, "because of the physical fact that haoles are an actual minority of the population and therefore they must be more subtle than in Boston or Omaha."[46]

A bittersweet moment for Davis occurred shortly thereafter when—quite mysteriously—his business burned to the ground. Amid the rubble, a shard of good news emerged when a fellow merchant offered to print and provide Davis "with enough letterheads and envelopes to tide me over," as he put it. "Two have offered me temporary storage space for any new stock," he said, still stunned by both the disaster and the hearty response to it.[47] Davis remained upbeat about Hawai'i despite his problems.[48]

Davis may have been justified in being upbeat about the isles—but as his charged exchange with Reinecke suggested, all was not rosy on the racial front in Hawai'i, a situation that complicated the ability of the Left to be effective. This sensitivity to racism had not eluded California Communist Celeste Strack when she arrived in the archipelago to testify on Reinecke's behalf. Perhaps her encounters with him drove her to the perception that there was a "conscious policy of chauvinist condescension." She found it curious that "almost the whole police force is [indigenous] Hawaiian," and she believed that this was a "very conscious measure," perhaps since indigenes were most likely to revolt against a massive dispossession that was in living memory of many of them; this policy was part of a "White Chauvinism," a virulent tendency that Strack had noticed, not least among the Left. Strack said that in the ILWU, as far as she knew, "all international officers and representatives in the islands were white," a problem that had not engaged these leaders to that point. She also had noticed "attitudes of national superiority on the part of some Japanese"; this was being confronted, but, strikingly, "the basic problem of white chauvinism" was "not tackled in [the] same aggressive way." Perhaps Strack had in mind a form of affirmative action the union pursued, whereby a Japanese at times had to step back and allow a Filipino to step forward as a leader, but somehow haoles were not requested to act similarly. She also found it noteworthy that as far as she new, there was not "any organization . . . or movement which raises the question of independence of Hawaii." Thus she found in the archipelago's Communist Party "very grave deficiencies" that emerged "from an underestimation of the importance of this question" of racism and thus reflected "elements of both national and white chauvinism." She found it to be a "rather startling fact that on an issue which has become quite sharp in US politics itself[—]the matter of Hawaiian statehood—our party actually has taken no position at all [and] has virtually ignored the matter."[49]

Strack suggested that the local party back statehood "in a special way": "First we should relate it to the principle of self-determination. This means that we should support statehood not as a final determination of the future of Hawaii, but as a method whereby the Hawaiian people can achieve more equal rights today as a means of enlarging their political rights." Thus, she said, "we should make the point that if, in the future, the people of Hawaii should desire to make further changes in their relations to the U.S., they must have that right." But Strack's all too brief visit to Hawai'i may not have allowed her to perceive the peculiarities of racism in Hawai'i at that moment, as a dwindling number of Negroes were being harassed, the members of a growing Asian-Pacific majority were being viewed nervously by a white elite apprehensive about their ties to radicalism, and all this was occurring as the isles were becoming an object of attention in Washington.[50]

In her lengthy and detailed statement on the intertwined issues of statehood and the Communist Party—perhaps the most sustained scrutiny ever of this matter—Strack mentioned in passing Bridges' avid backing in the isles.[51] This observation was a reflection of the left-leaning climate that was Hawai'i's, in which a man like Harry Bridges could gain support that allowed him to survive when other labor leaders who were similarly inclined had to trim their ideological sails. Put bluntly, the Asian-Pacific majority in Hawai'i was not prone to enlist in an anticommunist crusade spearheaded by its white bosses—this too was a reflection of the uniqueness of the isle's racism and racial makeup. And given Bridges' elevated profile nationally, this also meant that Hawai'i's radicalism was not just an isolated matter for the South Seas alone. In addition, the touting of statehood for Hawai'i meant that the island chain could hardly be viewed in isolation.

Thus Bridges—propelled in no small part by Hawai'i—not only managed to survive but thrived in a way that was unusual for a leader who professed friendliness toward Moscow and no antipathy to Marxism itself. Yes, he was prosecuted and jailed briefly, but the onslaught of support he received globally helped stay the hand of the authorities and also meant that his leadership would be available as Hawai'i labor embarked on a path of heightened confrontation with the local elite. Hence, as Bridges was enduring his travails, the US ambassador in Helsinki heard directly from what he termed the "Communist dominated Finnish Transportation Workers' Union," which hailed the "work of Mr. Bridges [as] praiseworthy" and expressed "deep indignation" at what had befallen him.[52] Washington's man in Yugoslavia received a similar protest from maritime workers there[53]—ditto for Wellington, New Zealand.[54] Naturally, Bridges received support in the islands too, as thousands of workers left their jobs in August 1950[55]—when the mainland was gripped in a fervent hysteria about a Communist upsurge globally—in protest against Bridges' imprisonment.[56]

There was a rising hysteria in the Pacific basin driven by the Communist triumph in China in 1949 and the war in Korea, which followed quickly in 1950—all seemingly buttressed by the undeniable strength of Communists in Hawai'i. The FBI seemed to be considering conflating the armed struggle in Asia with what was emerging in Hawai'i when it concluded that "no evidence has been received of the establishment of Communist Party rifle or pistol clubs." On the other hand, it was reported worriedly that Communist leader Dwight Freeman "owned a Japanese rifle." Yet somehow, more than an arsenal, the Communists had other weapons, including Richard Masato Kageyama. A member of the Board of Supervisors in Honolulu, he was the "only reported [CP] member who is presently the holder of an elective office," it was said with concern—though W. K. Bassett, a top aide of the mayor of this metropolis, had been reputedly a Red in Carmel, California. It was noted that a CP cell met regularly at the home of Benjamin Kahaawinui of the ILWU. Then there was the alleged attempted infiltration by radicals into the local affiliate of the American Civil Liberties Union.[57] In short, though the Left seemed to be in a painful process of retrenchment on the mainland, battered from pillar to post by the anticommunist upsurge, just the opposite seemed to be occurring in the racially different Hawai'i.

It would be an error to assume that conservative pressure was without effect in Hawai'i, however.[58] Fewer and fewer were choosing to attend meetings of the Hawaii Civil Liberties Committee (HCLC). At one small gathering just before the strike of stevedores, journalist Ray Jerome Baker showed up, as did ILWU attorney Harriet Bouslog. In the background were several police officers, who had been there all evening, along with a "stooge"—all of whom were becoming fixtures at HCLC meetings and were surely a visible disincentive for those wishing to attend.[59]

Yet it was at that moment that the HCLC chose to solidify its affiliation with the Manhattan–based Civil Rights Congress (CRC), commonly derided as a "Communist Front."[60] For just as island radicals were bolstering Bridges at his moment of need, they were performing a similar task on behalf of the CRC, which too was under siege.[61] The HCLC then chose to change its name to "Hawaii Civil Rights Congress" as an indication of this new relationship,[62] leaving anticommunists to wonder what it was in the islands that caused some to rush to the embrace of the CRC, while others were fleeing. Actually, the HCLC—or HCRC—was having problems too. During the midst of the 1949 strike, its leadership moaned about "decreasing attendance at meetings."[63] The balance in its bank account was a none too hefty $355.46.[64]

The point was that the strength of radicalism in Hawai'i, which came clear as the territory appeared on the verge of statehood, with the ability to influence the course of the US Senate, generated a massive crackdown that pushed the isles away from radicalism and toward liberalism. Still, that too was different from the present climate on the mostly conservative mainland.

It was as if a figurative noose was tightening around the neck of the CP and those close to it. Robert McBurney Kempa was then chairman of the "Pālolo group" of the CP, as he termed it. The group met every other week and included many members who worked for city and county government in Honolulu, such as Henry and Sylvia Epstein. Suggestive of the claustrophobic atmosphere was Kempa's recollection about the meetings: "The members of the group would gather at one point or in one general area and we would be picked up with the car belonging to one of the group members. The meetings were conducted in the cars." This new approach was implemented during the summer of 1950. Seeking to avoid surveillance, the Reds on wheels would trundle over to the parking lot at Sears, Roebuck, then confer and wait for others, who, if they didn't arrive in five minutes to be picked up, would be left behind. Fortunately for the group, they had access to a sizeable Willys station wagon owned by Bob Wenkam. The meetings were held on the road, as the car weaved in and out of traffic, though a time or two the car was parked while the attendees conferred. Sometimes it was necessary to park, for example, when a document had to be scrutinized by all, as when one such document arrived from Australian Communists.

Not long thereafter, Kempa met with Dwight Freeman. The CP organizer, Freeman was the bearer of bad news, as Kempa recalled: "[He] told me that my group [was] being disbanded along with all other organized groups. That the [CP] in the territory was reorganizing generally, was going underground. That I was being re-assigned to a new group, a group of three, that the party generally was being organized into such groups of three." Kempa's assignment—if he chose to accept it—"would be to contact four other cells." As Kempa recollected, "[Freeman] numbered these cells. The cell that I was placed in was number six. The cells that I was to be [in] contact with were seven, eight, nine and ten." He was given "the name of one person in each of these cells," i.e., "Wilfred Oka, Esther Bristow, Stephen Murin and Frank Marshall Davis." Kempa was placed in a cell that included Pearl Freeman and A. Q. McElrath. "Roughly speaking," he continued, "every two weeks they would be contacted," referring to Oka et al. Thus he reached Davis at his office, which was near the airport in Honolulu, but under such oppressive conditions, members began to drift away, including A. Q. McElrath, who "dropped from the group and the party." The diligent Kempa kept a coded record of dues collections—before he too left the CP and then turned up in court as a key witness against his former comrades.

Kempa's departure was a major loss—and indicative of which way the winds were blowing. He had worked for both the *Honolulu Record* and the HCLC, though his most lucrative employment was with the Board of Water Supply of the capital. He had joined the CP in the spring of 1946 and to that point had spent a good deal of time at the Maritime Bookstore in San Francisco, a "very small place," a "hole in the wall" that was quite "narrow," with a "display window and door, a desk running down one side [and] a counter running down one side of the bookshop." It was a book, in fact, that persuaded him to join the CP—one by "the Dean of Canterbury" that was titled *The Secret of Soviet Strength.* There at the shop, in a city suffused with ILWU influence, he whiled away many an hour before embarking for Honolulu, which was then a potent outpost for radicalism. But then things began to shift. When he began working for the city and county of Honolulu in 1948, he had to sign an oath implying that he was no Red. Then in 1949, when a new law was passed that called for explicit acknowledgment of what had been implicit, he quit his job rather than take such an anticommunist oath. The pressure was too much for him, and soon he left the CP, along with many others.[65]

Leaving with him was Jack Kawano, a man largely responsible for whatever strength the radical Left retained before it began the slow slide to desuetude. He was a member of the CP leadership until mid-1949 and broke with both the party and the ILWU as a result of tensions generated by the strike of stevedores.[66] He was infuriated when, during this critically strategic 1949 strike, he was assigned to patrol the legislature even though he was supposedly head of the longshore unit. He wound up toiling as a janitor at a movie house, which no doubt contributed to his growing dislike for Charles Fujimoto and Jack Kimoto, the leading Reds. He was not very happy with Jack Hall either, who by this point was "not very active" in CP meetings and, said Kawano, "resented being told by certain Communists what to do regarding his job as the Regional Director" of the ILWU. In response to Hall's behavior, Newton Miyagi, an ILWU leader who was "closer to the Communist people," was developing a strong resentment of Hall too.[67]

But such tensions were endemic in an organization that was under siege and where it was hard to tell who was sincere and who was a government agent seeking to stoke ferment. The ferocity directed toward radicals was a compliment to their reach and influence—but it exacted no less of a price, particularly in terms of deteriorating personal relations. Thus Kimoto also did not like Hall, because the latter "didn't want competition," but Kimoto also was no fan of Wilfred Oka's, once ejecting Oka from a CP meeting after he had screened a pornographic movie there. But it was Hall who was his special target of anger, since the regional director was accused—as he was repeatedly—of not cultivating secondary leadership within the ILWU,[68] a point others echoed like a mantra.[69]

Though the opponents of the CP painted it as a steamrolling monolith, the truth was that the organization was torn by discord—a phenomenon generated in no small part by the pressure mounted by these opponents. There were those who dissented from this emerging consensus of opponents, but they were far from being dominant in elite circles. Even before the epochal 1949 strike, J. Edgar Hoover, the bulldog-like federal pursuer of Communists, was informed in a "personal and confidential" message that "the issue of Communism in Hawaii is a 'phony' raised for the purpose of discrediting a 'certain labor leader,'" meaning Jack Hall. At the time, however, James Davis of the Interior Department, which had oversight of this colony, was transmitting to Hoover the insights of a leading academic, Gerald Barrett. What Hall and his cohort were trying to do, it was said, was force a reorganization in the structure of the Big Five by eliminating their holding company gravy, extracted from their many operating companies; yet, Barrett continued, these powerful forces had all come to agree that statehood would be a bad thing in the light of the problems presented by Hall. During the war, largely because of the prodding of Joseph Farrington, they had come around to a passive support of statehood upon the ground that they needed two senators in Washington to assure their sugar quota, but Jack Hall's rise made this seem relatively unimportant and they were now opposed to statehood, although most of them were reluctant to say so publicly. They would much rather lean on the federal government directly, said this analyst, rather than take their chances on an independently elected governor and state legislature. Furthermore, it was said, in the event of an "'emergency'" arising out of a labor dispute, they currently had access to and possible help from the US Army and US Navy, which they might not have if Hawai'i became a state.[70]

What Hoover was being told—and, after all, he was tasked with the huge job of obliterating radicalism from the landscape—was not altogether inaccurate. In such a hothouse atmosphere, with racial tensions rising, Bridges' being jailed, and conflict raging in Korea, further discord erupted within the ranks of the broader trade union movement. For it was at this moment that the CIO, of which the ILWU had been a leading pillar, chose not only to oust this union from its ranks but, as well, to establish an alternative union and raid the ILWU, poaching its members.[71] These actions enraged Hall.[72] Though born in the 1930s with no small aid from Communists, the CIO was now making a separate peace with anticommunists—at the expense of the ILWU.

The CIO sought to place the ILWU on trial, on charges that it was dominated by Communists whose ultimate allegiance was to Moscow. Such a trial would be "illegal," replied the union, not least since it had "never received a bill of particulars." The idea had been instigated by enemies of the ILWU, notably Joseph Curran of the National Maritime Union, who was busily and brutally conducting his own internal purge of the Left so as to solidify his corrupt rule. Moreover, while the ILWU was organizing and growing, CIO membership had dropped sharply. The CIO's claimed membership was six million, but actually half that figure was closer to the truth.[73] Previously, the ILWU had denounced Curran formally for strikebreaking and crossing picket lines after its earthshaking 1949 longshore strike.[74] Now, it was thought, he was seeking revenge.[75]

The much-beleaguered Harry Bridges found time to fly to the islands in early June 1950 to address a territory-wide conference of the four ILWU locals, where he railed bitterly against this turn of events.[76] Though he dismissed the CIO challenge peremptorily, Bridges' heated words seemed to betray concern. The United Auto Workers, the United Steelworkers, and his other erstwhile confederates in the CIO felt that the war machine would keep their members working—but they were mistaken, Bridges argued accusingly.[77]

Another union man who spoke at the conference, Ernest Arena, did seem concerned. Handsome though a bit pudgy, and with curly black hair reflective of his Mexican mother and Italian father,[78] Arena had been born in 1915 and had intimate knowledge of the ILWU and the islands. There were

33,000 dues-paying members in the union in 1945, he said, but at the time of his speaking—in June 1950—this number had dwindled to 25,000 by his count, mostly due to mechanization and union missteps. This trend hampered the ability of the union to move forward aggressively, since there were at least 15,000 workers that awaited organization in manufacturing, trucking, warehousing, bakeries, laundries, wholesale trade, and auto repair shops.[79] Arena's reservations notwithstanding, the ILWU remained the most powerful union in Hawai'i. According to another estimate in 1950, Local 136 of the stevedores had 2,000 members; Local 142 in sugar had 20,000; Local 152 in pineapple had 5,000; and Local 150 (or miscellaneous members) had 1,000—down from a total of 35,000 for the ILWU in 1947. Yet this estimate—calculated by the presumably better-informed Theodora Kreps, the union's chief researcher—acknowledged that through mechanization and rationalization in the pineapple and sugar industries, the bargaining units were shrinking steadily.[80] The point was that the CIO offensive against the ILWU—occurring while Bridges was under siege, the United States was at war, and racial tensions were broiling—had arrived at an inopportune moment.

As Bridges and Arena were putting forward their varying presentations, ILWU officers from the West Coast were holding a special meeting at Pier 11 in Honolulu and authorized the union leaders in San Francisco to sell the ILWU building there for $25,000, since, it was announced prosaically, "the international needs cash."[81] There were other problems too. After the stevedores' strike, J. R. Robertson fretted that those who had scabbed would benefit from the sacrifice of their fellow members; he felt that their very presence was a rebuke to those who had given so much. Previously, the union had dealt very harshly with all scabs, he told the inquiring Koichi Imori, but in most instances the union was unable to get them off the job and they became a continual source of trouble.[82] Management and government had hired 1,900 scabs—amply supplied by the reserve army of labor that had descended in Hawai'i—to handle cargo after the seizure of the docks, and the ILWU's attempt to bar them proved unavailing.[83]

Moreover, the threat from the CIO and other hostile forces meant that the ILWU had to divert precious resources away from organizing and "servicing" members in order to fund more complicated tasks—e.g., establishing an intelligence operation to keep track of foes arriving in Honolulu. Thus, when CIO operative Tim Flynn arrived in Hawai'i, a private investigator acting on behalf of the ILWU shadowed his every move—which included meetings with Art Rutledge of the AFL[84]—but with a healthier budget they could have done more to keep track of them and their confederates.[85]

McElrath realized more than most that, particularly with the onset of war in Korea, the political climate had shifted stridently toward a more fervent anticommunism and that, for a union and a movement thought to be dominated by Communists, this was not good news. Weeks after hostilities erupted on the Korean peninsula, the executive officers of Hawai'i's four ILWU local unions voted to support Washington's initiative there and to cooperate fully.[86] Though the ILWU had thereby thrown peace overboard, its leaders were pursued no less relentlessly by their antagonists; perhaps they were pursued with more vigor, as the anticommunists may have sensed that backing the war was a capitulation and a sign of weakness. Thus the union still felt compelled to announce that it was not "taking orders from Moscow in relation to the Korean War"—though its opponents on the Left charged precisely that the ILWU had "capitulated" to warmongers.[87] The union's early support for the war also did not restrain the hand of the mainstream newspapers, which chose this moment to press the Aloha Network, which broadcast union commentaries on its four stations, to cease doing so. "The censorship it recommends is exactly in the pattern of Joe Stalin," the union retorted. "[The] Aloha Network has sold time to many employer groups in controversial matters dealing with labor problems."[88]

Even when the union endorsed the war, there was lingering concern that its position would generate the reaction it did: give a boost to its opponents. Shortly after its endorsement, a union walkout at Kekaha, Kaua'i, occurred after management sought to increase the workload of the sugar workers there, prompting a local newspaper to editorialize that the strike had been organized by the ILWU leadership to aid Communists in Korea. Touching a sensitive nerve, the union in turn harked back to the bad old days of the Pacific War, when "we suffered under the heel of martial law" and were "frozen to ill-paid jobs under miserable conditions while tens of thousands of other workers were imported for the relatively well-paid jobs in military employment." Was history about to repeat itself, driven by the cruel master that was war?[89]

But it would take more than speaking softly about Korea to compel officialdom to ease the pressure on the Left in Hawai'i, for besides radicals' organizing of the docks and the fields, their rejection of anticommunism, and their antiracism, there was grave concern about what they were doing with what had once been a moribund Democratic Party.[90] Ray Jerome Baker did not seem pleased when Richard Kimball, a party leader, demanded that all those present at a party meeting take non-Communist oaths—though each time he went down in defeat. Presiding, W. K. Bassett ruled Kimball out of order, but he refused to leave the floor, insisting upon talking, shouting, and name-calling. For more than a half hour, Kimball prattled on about communism, Americanism, and the like. In response, Harriet Bouslog in a quiet manner and even voice charged that he was out of order. She remarked that members of the Democratic Party had already signed cards that said, "I have no present affiliation with any other party," and therefore there was no point to the Kimball proposal. Finally Bouslog moved that the endorsement given by the club to Kimball the previous month be withdrawn, and it was—to conservatives' consternation.[91]

Bassett, his opponents charged, had more than theoretical knowledge of radicalism. Hired by a local newspaper in 1919, he was elected to the Board of Supervisors in Honolulu in 1923, with a comfortable margin of victory. He left for a while, then returned in 1946, when he was hired as an aide to Mayor Wilson.[92] He denied repeatedly that he was a Communist, most pointedly after nationally syndicated columnist—and Stainback confidant—Victor Riesel had claimed he was, but Bassett's detractors disbelieved him,[93] to the consternation of Frank Marshall Davis.[94]

In response, conservatives continued to expound, propound, and simply pound the idea that the ILWU and the CP were tools of an alien power bent on destruction of Washington. "For 20 years Moscow has regarded Hawaii as a place of the greatest importance,"[95] said Paul Crouch, who was to bedevil the union during the Smith Act trial. As he saw things, "one factor of great value to the Communists in their work in Hawaii is the continued delay of Congress in granting statehood," since "admission as a state of the union would do much to destroy this Communist argument." Crouch felt he possessed added credibility, since "twenty-five years ago I was Hawaii's first Communist."[96]

Forces more respectable than Crouch were singing from the same hymn-book nonetheless. Senator J. Howard McGrath of Rhode Island, known to be close to the White House, was one of the many.[97] Actually, it was reported, these alleged nefarious plans extended beyond Washington. Supposedly, Moscow was creating a "new 'Pearl Harbor'"—and these plans were said to include "fomenting racial unrest."[98]

The radical Left begged to differ, for as far as the ILWU was concerned, the perpetual burr under its saddle was Governor Ingram Stainback. Even before the stevedores' strike, an assortment of his fiercest opponents had gathered in room 520 of the Alexander Young Hotel in Honolulu. Meeting for more than two hours, the attendees of this top-secret session decided that the governor must be ousted. McElrath accused him of falsely labeling the leadership of the regular Democratic Party as a bunch of Communists and fellow travelers and including Hall within this alleged cabal as the actual leader of these forces.[99]

Stainback was in trouble with his party, even setting aside the staunch opposition he faced from ILWU leaders, and the Red Scare became a convenient way for him to change the subject.[100] "The Democratic Party is on the move," one union leader gloated, "but it doesn't have a chance so long as Stainback remains the nominal head of the party. He is thoroughly discredited locally; he couldn't be elected dogcatcher on the Democratic ticket." That forecast was not altogether inaccurate.[101]

Would the purportedly Moscow-directed Democratic Party convert Hawai'i into a citadel of Marxism at a time when Washington was providing blood and treasure to prevent the same in Asia? And would it do so by ousting its anticommunist chief executive? Such more-than-mundane concerns animated the hundreds of delegates who assembled in 1950 for the Democratic Party convention in Hawai'i, held at Kalakaua School in Honolulu. One reporter was outraged by what he witnessed, pointing to a "howling, screaming mass of humanity" that forced 91 protesting non-leftist Democrats to bolt and depart for the headquarters of the Veterans of Foreign Wars. Outvoted at every turn, the dissidents said the convention was no place for a Democrat, and they surrendered to Lau Ah Chew, John Burns, and the left wing, who won every test by a large majority.[102] Present was O. Vincent Esposito, born in 1916 and a graduate of Harvard Law School who had fought against Japan during the Pacific War. The stated agenda—at least by some—was to throw off the alleged Red domination of the Democrats. But, recalled Esposito years later, "the [Democrats'] Central Committee divided itself into two pieces, just about equal" (an exaggeration most likely of anticommunist strength in retrospect), and thus the mass expulsion of radicals that the Big Five desired did not occur, since the anticommunists could not prevail. Despite credentials that could lead the unsuspecting to think otherwise, Esposito did not hesitate to assert, "I was the leader of the left-wingers," and he was far from being alone in this cohort. Lau Ah Chew, for example, who used to run a pet shop on Honolulu's King Street and was a "real sweet, soft, gentle" man, was in Esposito's group, he observed, along with John Wilson, Honolulu's mayor. That such a powerful figure stood with the Left was indicative of the lineup of opposing forces, and, thus, predictably, scores of the anticommunists—about 10 to 15 percent of the assembled—stormed out. Esposito, who keynoted the convention, sought to explain in his speech that "we Democrats should not be afraid because we [are] going to be called 'Communists,'" but his detractors were not convinced. The result? The party was badly divided and shaken up—but the Left remained in control, which was appropriate, since the ILWU, as Esposito phrased it, "put the whole thing together," meaning the Democratic Party.[103] After this convention, Esposito's antagonists claimed that the archipelago had two Democratic parties: "one opposed to Communism, the other containing a number of persons who refuse to answer whether they are or have been Communists."[104]

Bridges' opinion was that John Burns—a founding father of modern Hawai'i—was a "good man" with "courage and foresight," and Burns felt similarly about those denounced on the mainland as scruffy radicals.[105] Burns and Esposito accepted the reality that the ILWU—and its colleagues in the CP—had built the Democratic Party to the point where it was on the verge of seizing and holding power for generations to come. They saw no reason to destroy this prospect simply because the mainland was moving in an opposing direction.[106]

Helen Kanahele of Honolulu was typical of the new blood that helped revive the Democrats. This laundry worker had been active in the Democratic Party since the age of 12 and in 1950 was also serving as leader of the ILWU Women's Auxiliary. But she was also a leading member of Sodality, a group tied to the Roman Catholic Church, and of the Hawaiian Homesteaders' Improvement Club too. As she noted firmly, one had to be "part Hawaiian or a hundred percent" to belong to this latter group. These were the "old Hawaiians"; "most of them don't understand English," she conceded. Thus she was not a Communist, though she added at a time when it was not popular to say so, "I think they have a right to be Communists if they want to be. It is their privilege." She was friendly to Jack Kimoto, made donations to the Civil Rights Congress, and despite the hype against them, she ascertained that "the things that they did for the community and the territory of Hawaii were very good." She was a regular reader of the *Honolulu Record*, not because of its radical editorials but because it regularly published stories on "safety of the children going to school on . . . Auwaiolimu," the "safety walk, lights and also improvement of roads." Thus, unsurprisingly, as a convention delegate and a member of the all-important Resolutions Committee, she stood with the Left, or "the majority," as she put it. Actually, "it would have to be three quarters" of all those present, she said, revising her estimate of the proportion of leftists at the convention, an indication of the dearth of anticommunism in Hawai'i when it was spreading like wildfire on the mainland.[107]

Mayor John Wilson, perhaps the second most powerful political figure in the islands, also had targeted Stainback. Although Stainback was the leader of the minority faction in the Democratic Party, he was probably the most powerful politico in Hawai'i. "By 1948 he became so unpopular," said Honolulu's popular executive, "we just managed to prevent a resolution being adopted censuring him and asking his immediate removal. This 1950 convention was so bitterly against him that a resolution was this time adopted requesting his removal"; Stainback's response was to raise the Red flag. Wilson saw his rival's decline as part of a transcending historical trend. "Until 1946," he said, "75 to 80 percent of labor voted Republican. It was not until 1948 that most of labor, probably 90 percent started voting Democratic." He added that "it was not until then that Governor Stainback started to talk Communism" in reaction, though there were only "about 130 Communists" in Hawai'i at the time.[108]

Thus the Left emerged triumphant from this sharp clash within the Democratic Party. Conservatives were singed in the process.[109] Yet they got sweet revenge, notably when the House Un-American Activities Committee (HUAC) contemplated bringing its traveling road show to Honolulu, ostensibly to investigate the specter of communism in the islands. The union's decision to endorse the war in Korea did not restrain the House committee. Not long after the stevedores' strike had concluded, Ralph Vossbrink, president of the Oahu CIO, remarked sarcastically that "'February is a very cold month in Washington'" and thus "'it looks like Hawaii's sunshine is beckoning forth [yet] another congressional junket,'" this time to investigate purported sedition by real and imagined Communists. Barely restraining himself, Vossbrink continued his display of sarcasm by asserting, "'As for overthrowing government by force and violence, I believe there are still several families in Hawaii who partook in such activity a few decades back.'"[110] The response[111] from Washington was not pleasant.[112] Though the HUAC faced more resistance in Honolulu than on the mainland, Jack Hall and the other purported top Communists would not have been elated to find that Peter H. Fukunaga, president of the Honolulu Japanese Chamber of Commerce, had told the legislative visitors that he supported their investigation,[113] as others within this beset plurality tried to reassure that—contrary to growing opinion—they were not all radicals.

The HUAC concluded that Dwight Freeman and his spouse were the CP leaders to watch, with his "wife appearing to be the brains" behind the party, along with Kimoto and Frank Marshall Davis, the only figure identified racially in the HUAC's records. Worthy of note, it was thought, was that Charles Fujimoto communicated "on the letterhead of the Democratic Party of Hawaii, Oahu County Committee," suggestive of how the Democrats' organization seemed to be a cat's-paw of the Reds.[114] The HUAC realized that it was entering a strange and exotic venue when it found that Burns' secretary in his role as Democratic Party leader was Wilfred Oka, widely thought to be a Communist leader.[115]

The HUAC's focus on Oka was indicative of the gathering concern about the role of Americans of Japanese Ancestry within the ranks of the organized Left. One response was signaled by a friend of Ray Jerome Baker's who had difficulty in securing a US passport. Walter Tominanga, who spoke freely about communism, was reconsidering his options. "He now says that he will eventually slip away to Japan," Baker reported, "where he can take on Japanese citizenship, take a Japanese passport and travel anywhere he wishes." As Baker noted, "in so doing he would have to forfeit American citizenship,"[116] news that no doubt heartened those who wished to purge the islands of radicals.[117]

The problem faced by Baker and others of his ilk was that they were ensconced in the midst of shifting currents not easy to navigate. As the nation was moving slowly and hesitantly to the unavoidable conclusion that Jim Crow had to go, racism against Negroes was rising locally, though some were more concerned about the fate of the white minority in Hawai'i. This dilemma was framed by the Cold War, which necessitated that Washington get its human rights house in order so that it would be more qualified to point an accusing finger at Moscow. This same Cold War had now turned hot in Korea, and many under the US flag were wondering why Communists should be fought in Asia—and tolerated in Hawai'i. The ILWU, the CP, and their allies had many more rivers to cross, which became clear when the HUAC arrived in Honolulu.

CHAPTER 12

Strife and Strikes

When the House Un-American Activities Committee arrived in Honolulu in April 1950, this investigative body was not greeted with unanimous applause. The tumultuous hearings they held concerned explicitly "Communist Activities in the Territory of Hawaii," which meant an intense focus on the ILWU, which only recently had exhibited its strength. The hearings unfolded at the fabled 'Iolani Palace, once the seat of power of the now deposed monarchy, overthrown not so long ago by subversion and conspiracy—which was now the charge leveled at the radical Left.

John Reinecke's recollection decades later is difficult to dispute. More than a quarter of a century after the HUAC had departed, the soft-spoken intellectual remarked that the CP had "'pretty well disappeared'" by 1950 and was gone altogether by the time the Smith Act trial ended in 1953. "'It was killed,'" he said, "'by two main things: the anticommunist hearings conducted in Hawai'i [by HUAC] in 1950 and the Taft-Hartley Act'" of 1947, which bludgeoned Communists in union leadership posts.[1] When Jack Hall signed a "non-Communist affidavit" in 1950, it was not a pro forma exercise but a signal of the retreat of working-class militancy.[2] Similarly, these highly publicized hearings were virtual theatrical proceedings that sought to shame actual and imagined Reds as they sought to inflame the wider community—and in this sense this project was a victory for anticommunism.

Congressman Francis Walter, the HUAC's leader, was an attorney and a military veteran who had served in both World War I and World War II and, thus, thought he had an idea of what might befall the archipelago if the ILWU and the CP were not halted in their tracks. Of course, it may also have crossed his mind—as it did others—that a junket that involved experiencing Honolulu's delightful sunshine and ocean breezes would be a bracing tonic even if legislation (an ostensible basis for the visit) did not ensue. But as the committee was gaveled to order, Walter uttered a racial note rarely heard in the HUAC hearings on the mainland—and doing so reflected the uphill climb he and his committee faced in these lovely islands. Now it was to be expected, he said, anticipating a line of attack, that "the Communists will shriek from the very housetops that the present inquiry is directed against persons of Asiatic descent[,]that we are interested in promoting racial discrimination."[3]

As the committee quickly got down to business, Ichiro Izuka, whose defection from the ranks of the Left had helped ignite the HUAC's visit, was sworn in as a witness. He recounted the facts already laid out in his infamous booklet and emphasized related points, such as the couriers from ILWU allies like the National Maritime Union: "they are the ones," he said, "who bring the instructions in their heads to local party leaders." Another key witness was Edward Berman, the mercurial attorney who was often in disputes with the ILWU leadership. His time before the HUAC was devoted in no small part to a denunciation of Frank Marshall Davis and his charge of racism in Hawai'i.[4]

Jack Kawano, now in full flight from his previous radical commitments, may have been the most effective witness heard by the HUAC. As the audience buzzed and inquisitive congressmen looked on, he told the assembled that he had attended his last CP meeting as recently as June 1949 and thus had fresh news to deliver. Ralph Vossbrink, whom he identified as a Red, had recently organized the taxi drivers—"there are about 300 or 350," he said—and since these workers "do a lot of talking and see a lot of people," another ILWU tentacle had arisen.[5]

Yet setting aside the explosiveness of such allegations, the most damning testimony provided by this damning witness was his claim that when the US national anthem was played, the Communist comrades would prefer to be "'sitting down,'" but when the Internationale, or Communist anthem, was played, they all "stood with the command[ing]" lyrics "'Arise, you prisoners [of starvation].'"[6]

This drama aside, it was Kawano who probably supplied the most spellbinding testimony since he knew so much about the inner workings of radicalism. The future US senator Daniel Inouye spoke to him just before he testified. "It was an electric day," said Inouye. "When he started to answer[,] people were cursing and screaming and yelling. And when he got all through, he stood up; and people were spitting on him. And he came to," recalled Inouye balefully. "Everyone was watching. And he hugged me. It was an emotional thing. Two of us embracing and everyone is watching and we walked out together." Subsequently, Inouye was propelled by the momentum of this drama to challenge and defeat Wilfred Oka as secretary of the Democratic Party and moved on from there to the US Senate.[7]

A discredited Kawano[8] had a hard livelihood afterwards, so Mitsuyuki Kido and Chuck Mau teamed up to provide him capital, with which he opened a liquor store.[9] It was the increasingly powerful Mau who arranged for Kawano's HUAC testimony and then persuaded the authorities to launch a Smith Act prosecution of Jack Hall.[10]

More lurid testimony[11] was provided by Lloyd M. Stebbings.[12] His words were surpassed, however, by those of others who hammered home the point that the Democratic Party was dominated by the ILWU,[13] which was dominated by the CP, which in turn was dominated by Moscow.[14]

Congressman Walter thought he had found a way to rout the Reds. "'It was very interesting to us,'" he concluded, "'to hear one witness after another testify that he had gotten out of the Communist Party because his wife had found out what communism was.'"[15] Donald Uesugi, a clerk with Mutual Telephone Company, helped reinforce this belief when he confessed that his former wife had recruited him to the CP—before their divorce.[16] Alternatively, speaking of Kaua'i-based ILWU business agent Frank Silva specifically and the issue more broadly, journalist Sanford Zalburg averred that "wives in this thing are always more bitter [about political persecution] than the guys."[17] Still, there was reason to dispute this reasoning. For example, witness Federico Lorenzo placed A. Q. McElrath at a CP meeting in Maui in 1947, though she actually had not been there since 1938.[18]

Senator Pat McCarran of Nevada, whose name had become synonymous with the anticommunist crusade, had taken time out of his busy schedule to fly over to Hawai'i, and he was displeased with what he discovered. After a "careful study," he emerged convinced that "the territory was heavily impregnated with Communist cells and active Communist workers." In fact, said the enraged legislator, "about the most complete Communist organization that I have yet encountered I found to exist in the Hawaiian islands." His concern was bound with his attempt to ensure that Stainback stayed in office, on the premise that dislodging him would be a boon for the Reds.[19] "The Red Flag will be raised over Hawaii," he cried, unless Stainback was reappointed.[20] The legislator's outraged concern contributed to a further draconian crackdown on the Left,[21] including the reading of their mail and the wiretapping of their phones.[22] Hysteria[23] was spreading[24] as a result.

Joseph Farrington's *Honolulu Star-Bulletin* was seen in the union as being less hostile than other mainstream organs—but then it too came under assault. After the 1949 strike, the big advertisers quickly pulled some big accounts, recalled Ray Jerome Baker, and the paper lost $50,000. The paper had been "taught a lesson, and now," he asserted, "it not only red-baits like the morning sheet but it has to red-bait harder, in order to convince its masters that it knows and understands its master[s'] voice."[25] A chastened Farrington sought to blunt the concern that statehood would mean the Kremlin's picking two US senators for Hawai'i, by declaring that accession to the Union was required so that the archipelago could "grapple most effectively with its Communist problem."[26]

It was evident that a central purpose of the HUAC was not only to oust the CP from influence—and weaken the ILWU in the process—but, as well, to weaken the hold of both on the Democratic Party. Intimidation was essential to this process. But the HUAC and its supporters thought they had grasped an ineffable nettle when it was revealed that 6 of the 15 so-called left-wing delegates to the Democratic Party convention had yet to comply with a directive requiring the filing of affidavits attesting to their lack of CP membership—and 5 of the 6 had Asian-Pacific surnames.[27]

Hence, it was after meeting with Congressman Walter that anticommunist Democrats stormed out of the party's convention—an idea "suggested" by the visiting solon, according to one journalist, after "two secret meetings."[28] Party chairman Lau Ah Chew rebuked Walter—and was rebuked in turn by the congressman.[29] Walter's worst fears were realized when the pudgy, bow-tied Richard Kageyama, a powerful county supervisor in Honolulu, confessed that as late as 1947 he had been a CP member.[30] He was also an elected delegate to the colony's constitutional convention, and this revelation, along with the selection to this body of Frank Silva,[31] raised the issue of apparent Communist influence on those tasked with devising the colony's foundational text.[32]

As Reinecke suggested, the HUAC's arrival indicated that a turning point had been reached in the ascendancy of the ILWU and the CP: powerful forces had determined that both organizations wielded entirely too much influence and therefore should be whittled down to a more manageable size. British emissaries, who had maintained a pointed interest in Hawai'i since at least the mid-nineteenth century, sought to put this hinge moment in broader perspective. In the critical year of 1950, London was informed, sugar and pineapple remained key to the overall health of the archipelago, and the viability of those commodities was shaped by events in Cuba, Louisiana, and elsewhere. Events in Asia also determined Hawai'i's destiny, as exemplified by the onset of conflict in Korea and the associated sharp rise in the number of civilian employees in all branches of the armed services. Thus, military expenditures came to be Hawai'i's largest source of income, roughly $50 million greater than even the income from the territory's largest industry, sugar. The war in Korea also meant more planes passing through Hawai'i, leading to increased consumer spending; in addition, all civilian aircraft, whether charter or not, were liable for a territorial tax of four cents per gallon on aviation gasoline taken into planes while in the territory. The territory's income from this source, it was said with no mock amazement, "is exceeding even the wildest dreams of the legislators." In short, the Korean conflict had ignited a boom, and by 31 December 1950 the territory was able to look back on a year that had produced a record tourist influx; the highest production of sugar in a decade, all of which was marketed at ascending prices; a larger pineapple crop than that of the previous year; and increased defense works. In sum, Hawai'i—already a strategic Gibraltar, the backdoor through which attacks on US national security could be launched—was now rising in financial importance as well. The increased government spending meant, on the one hand, that the importance of the workers represented by the ILWU was reduced to an extent; on the other hand, the enhanced national security role for the isles in the context of growing anti-communism meant more intense scrutiny on radicals. London's man was perspicacious in observing the stormy unrest that occurred when the authorities pounced on Harry Bridges, while adding sagely, "It was interesting to note that similar strikes did not take place in the mainland, during the course of the trial and imprisonment."[33]

Well aware that it was targeted, the ILWU braced for the onslaught from the HUAC. The Left was in a particular bind because its purported allegiance to Moscow suggested to some that leftists' presumed opposition to the war in Korea was driven not by prudential concerns but, more so, foreign attachments.[34]

Seeking to go on the offensive as the congressional hearings were about to begin, the adroit ILWU researcher Theodora Kreps investigated the voting records of the HUAC members on the issue of the Japanese evacuation during the war, as the union sought to "expose the anti-Oriental attitudes of the Un-American committee." She also requested a copy of the HUAC bill proposing that all foreign-language newspapers carry English translations; such a measure, "if it had passed, would knock out of business overnight the foreign language press here in Hawaii," which was no minor constituency.[35] Soon the ILWU had taken out a full-page ad in the *Honolulu Advertiser*, referring to such inestimable HUAC members as the recalcitrant racist Congressman John Rankin of Mississippi, who had allegedly referred to "'fat waisted Japs [that] are being released (from relocation centers),'" and the equally objectionable Congressman John Wood of Georgia, who said that the Ku Klux Klan represented "'an old American custom—just like illegal whiskey making.'"[36] The HUAC came to find that the residents of Hawai'i were not a mainland audience that endorsed or winked at racism but instead were infuriated by it.

The HUAC was not pleased with such attacks and launched harpoons of its own. The "Reluctant 39" could attest to this; these were the witnesses summoned by the HUAC who chose not to testify—and were suspected of Red ties as a result.[37] Actually, 28 of the 39 were members of the ILWU, the bulk of whom were of Japanese origin, and they all were charged with contempt for refusing to testify. They were acquitted, however, by Judge Delbert Metzger, whose rulings on behalf of left-wing defendants were to incur the wrath of anticommunists throughout the 1950s.[38]

Metzger's ruling was fortunate for the ILWU, since only the left-leaning congressman from East Harlem, Vito Marcantonio, voted in the House of Representatives against the contempt citations that formed the basis for the prosecution.[39] The fearless Metzger also exonerated Charles Fujimoto, CP chairman, after he refused to produce his party's membership records and correspondence files when directed to do so,[40] a startling victory suggesting how the archipelago was diverging from the mainland.[41]

But there was also convergence: Frank G. Silva, born in 1918[42] and an ILWU member from Kaua'i, was expelled from the islands' constitutional convention on the ground that he was a Communist. Unlike at the Democratic Party convention, at this confab the Left did not hold sway, and the vote was a lopsided 53–7 in favor of his ouster. It was reported that his "contumacious conduct before and toward the Un-American Activities Committee" tipped conventioneers against him.[43]

With the tumult in the Democratic Party, the turmoil brought by the HUAC, and the unrest associated with the constitutional convention, both the ILWU and the CP were on the defensive.[44] The increasingly intense pressure against the Left also included "infiltration" (to use the officially sanctioned term) of its ranks by hostile agents who reported to Senator Hugh Butler of Nebraska, who continued to take a decided interest in the affairs of the islands.[45] "I am right inside the Party," an agent chortled, "and have excellent opportunities to get unusual facts"; besides, he added, "I have my whole heart and soul in this task,"[46] which was understatement.[47]

The infiltrator, John Williams, was happy to report, "Every Sunday I meet either Jack Hall or Robert McElrath privately and shoot the bull. I have access to and the use of the ILWU's so-called research department which[,] in effect, is their blackmail department. It is run by a very smart woman," he said, referring to Theodora Kreps. "Rest assured," he informed Senator Butler, "that the CP has the islands secretly networked, mainly thru Jap employees in every firm, with an underground information system. These undercover agents steal documents, shadow personages, etc. and report into the ILWU research department." Thus he noted worriedly, "If you have any friends coming to the islands, remind them about keeping their private affairs under lock & key [since] the ILWU servants in the hotels are particularly active." Yet amid the exaggerations and falsehoods in Williams' report, there was one truth that was unassailable. "I feel that the CP network in Hawaii," he argued, "is perhaps the best organized & operated under the U.S. flag."[48]

But it was also true that, almost single-handedly, Senator Butler had "infiltrated" this network so thoroughly that one of his agents wound up monitoring another. This occurred when Alfred Yap, who chose to sign his letters as "Jonathan Appleseed Lee," had an appointment with Michael Carey and, to Yap's—or Lee's—surprise, found him to be none other but his "old friend" John Williams.[49]

As Yap saw it, "the Japanese problem and their control of these islands are far more serious and dangerous than the blacks on the mainland." He emphasized that "by favoring statehood for Hawaii, the Senate is showing partiality in recognizing the Japs over the blacks," who, after all, still did not have the right to vote in the region where in numerous precincts they were the majority: the former slave South.[50]

Like Yap, Michael Carey—or John Williams—also found it noteworthy that the majority of the vigorous Communist forces in Hawai'i were "dominated" by leaders of Asiatic descent, particularly Japanese, who were "numerically one-third of the ILWU's rank and file" and were "active and agile unionists" besides. "They are smarter and better educated than their Filipino comrades," he thought, and were close to the powerful Joseph Farrington, whom he called "Moscow Joe."[51]

Bill Borthwick, who had been defeated by Farrington in the pivotal 1946 election in the race to represent the colony in Washington, D.C., was a collaborator with Butler on this spying project, telling Senator Butler at one point that it was "too bad you could not have Carey in your office for a few days," for "he has an amazing file on the local situation going back for 20 years" and had a "streak of genius" in addition. The well-connected Carey was right-hand man to Justice Owen Roberts at the Pearl Harbor hearings that investigated the 1941 attack. Roberts thought so highly of Carey's skills that he conceded, "If I could afford it—I would send him back" to Washington, where his talent in combating Reds might be better appreciated.[52]

What gave the febrile reports of Yap and Carey added heft in the minds of those like Senator Butler was that their words were echoed in the maunderings of others, which were assuming an increasing racial hue, emphasizing insecurity about what it meant to be white in an archipelago where whites were the minority.[53] With the stevedores' strike, the assumed Red seizure of the Democratic Party, and the HUAC hearings, which highlighted both, sober minds were beginning to reconsider statehood. This was the word Senator Butler was receiving.[54]

As time wore on, Hawai'i, with its peculiar ethnic and racial mixture combined with its radical politics, seemed to represent a danger to those who revered the status quo. Certainly, it seemed to disqualify this colony from admission into the hallowed Union. Thomas Paine of New York City did not seem to have the common sense of his most eminent doppelganger in mind when he asked plaintively if Hawai'i would become "our first Mongolian state"; he added, "Shall we Mongolianize? Do you want a Chinese and a Japanese as PERMANENT Senators?" he asked Senator Butler. "Will you cut your own power from one and 1/96th percent down to one percent of your power to Mongolians, who will always be needling you to open your doors to Asiatic immigration and 'FEPC' [Fair Employment Practices Committee; i.e., civil rights]? Hawaii's small percentage of whites," he insisted, "prefer to be ruled by the white mainland rather than local Asiatics!"[55] This theme was repetitive.[56]

With such invective pouring into his ear, perhaps unsurprisingly, Butler stiffened his opposition to statehood, maintaining that it was the "common people, the poor people of Hawaiian descent, who are against [it]," while the Big Five were "desperately for it." Indigenes were anti-statehood, he contended, since it would mean they "would lose all control over that portion of the islands that was reserved for them by an Act of Congress following our acquisition of the territory."[57]

Thus, few were stunned when it was reported that in the battle between O. Vincent Esposito and Mitsuyuki Kido for the lofty post of chair of the Central Committee of the Democratic Party, Kido lost support on the basis that his Asian ancestry would harm prospects for statehood.[58] Belatedly, the left-wing *Honolulu Record* was sensing the dilemma[59] of demanding closer union in a nation drifting dangerously rightward.[60]

Walter F. Dillingham, who epitomized the local elite, had also soured on the idea of statehood, just as the ILWU was rising. Born in 1875, at this juncture he had a magnificent home in Honolulu and a weekend ranch where he raised thoroughbred polo ponies and where he had also built a replica of the New England type of home in which he was born.[61] Amidst the plush pomp of his surroundings, he too had become disconcerted with the demographic makeup of the islands. He retained a lengthy analysis that accused the "statehooders" of using padded figures to increase artificially the size of the haole population. It read in part: "Asiatics[,] who discriminate widely by employing and trading with their own kith and kin, dominate too many economic activities. It is not surprising, therefore, that the Caucasian population has rapidly declined to approximately half what it was on December 7, 1941. As the local saying sums it up: 'Hawaii isn't white man's country any more.'" It was in Honolulu "where the historic clash between the two waves of immigration—the Caucasian and the Japanese—is working out its ultimate destiny"—and it seemed as if the latter were prevailing. "Today there are seven radio stations serving Honolulu, all making Japanese broadcasts which add up to a grand total of 116 hours weekly," it was reported. "Naturally, as the Japanese programs increased, those in the American language decreased—another retreat for the Caucasians!" In the past, the memo stated, "whenever the Caucasian overlordship was threatened, the public veneer of racial moderation was swept aside and the two Caucasian dailies with venomous editorials and cartoons attacked the alien Japanese." This was reflected in the newspaper coverage of the 1909 and 1920 strikes by Japanese workers in the sugar industry, but at the present time, with Joseph Farrington's control of one important local daily, this was hard to do. Thus, the "irrepressible conflict" between "Caucasian Americans and the Japanese" was blocked unnaturally, accompanied by a "suppression of views in public" on this matter and the "driving underground of personal opinions."[62]

Despite these harsh views of his fellow inhabitants of the islands, Dillingham continued to believe that "with this Territory infiltrated if not controlled by Communists, the hazard of sabotage would be greater than what was experienced in the war with Japan."[63] As statehood was being debated in 1950—animated by such beliefs—Dillingham informed Butler that he now opposed the archipelago's joining the Union.[64] Ray Jerome Baker was no friend of Dillingham's.[65] Nevertheless, he had arrived at an opinion akin to Dillingham's, concluding in late 1950, "We are not going to get statehood. The Dixiecrats are too afraid that we will send a 'niggah' (Hawaiian) Senator to Congress [and] they intend to filibuster." After all, he added, "their own Senators go to Congress on about 10% of the vote of the citizens of their states."[66]

Yet with the global climate turning slowly but steadily against overt appeals to racism, it was not easy for opponents of statehood to be racially explicit, at least not publicly. They had to speak sotto voce—if at all—and, more typically, had to encode their inflammatory words in confidential letters not intended for the light of day—not the ideal way in which to conduct a high-stakes political campaign. This may have caused more of an emphasis on the real and imagined influence of Communists in the isles, which was more in tune with the national zeitgeist. Racism had become—officially—radioactive in the Pacific for a reason espied by a liberal journalist: "What happens here [in Hawai'i] is closely watched by all of Asia, as the Voice of America recognized when it sent out a team last spring to make recordings on the most heart-warming aspect of Hawaiian life, the high level of racial tolerance."[67]

Strategically, Hawai'i had been viewed as the backdoor entrance that could allow compromising of the mainland's security—as suggested by the events of 7 December 1941 and the subsequent threat to the West Coast throughout the war. The conclusion of the Pacific War had not ended this perception; instead it was augmented by the idea that now Hawai'i had become a symbol of whether Washington was willing to walk away from the white supremacy to which it had been inured since the nation's birth. And overheated racial appeals were not helpful in that regard—notably as the war in Korea commenced and Asian opponents of Washington began to point to Jim Crow as a clear sign of actual US sentiments. This new outlook was symbolized when President Truman was asked about Hawaiian power broker Chuck Mau. Businessman Samuel Josephson—who, tellingly, was from Senator Butler's state—wanted to know what the occupant of the White House would "think of the possibilities of some kind of Mission to Nationalist China for Chuck Mau, preferably as a personal representative of the President." Enthused, Josephson thought that the "psychological and propaganda value would be tremendous," since Mau's "presence in Asia would reveal an American, a son of an immigrant Chinese laborer," who is now successful. "This certainly stirs my imagination," he declared in the hope that Truman would be moved similarly.[68]

Mau was pleased that the idea had originated from "another friend," Edward Bernays, who happened to be one of the foremost public relations men in the country, thereby signaling the mission's importance and weight.[69] Bernays, who was as influential as advertised, simultaneously instructed Senator Frank Porter Graham of North Carolina that "giving Hawaii statehood would prove to be a very powerful overt act which would be a counter-attack to Communist propaganda accusations that the United States is imperialistic and racist."[70] Agreeing with him was future territorial governor Samuel Wilder King,[71] as did E. R. Burke, the legal adviser to the Hawaii Statehood Commission.[72]

Why Mau was being importuned to travel to Asia and how Hawai'i had become a Cold War racial symbol were inferentially indicated by C. A. Franklin, editor of the *Kansas City Call*, which targeted an African-American readership. "We are in a world crisis with a Third World War possible unless we find a solution for the friction between groups," he informed Senator Thomas Hennings of Missouri. "White supremacy as a springboard in local affairs is expected," he said with an apparent absence of cynicism, "but is intolerable at the present because it adds fuel to the flames internationally." Having seen at the airport the previous night "a trans-oceanic plane being loaded with the flower of American youth on their way to the Asiatic battlefields," Franklin said mournfully, "White supremacy is not worth that price," and therefore he was pro-statehood.[73] Rebuffing statehood was coming to be seen as rebuffing those victimized by white supremacy.

Franklin was not the only person gravely concerned with the racial implications of the Korean conflict. Ray Jerome Baker asserted, "[In Hawai'i] they continue to draft the young Oriental and part-Hawaiian boys to go to Korea to fight. They choose the dark skinned boys so they can convince the Oriental people that this is not a war of the whites against them"—yet this policy was having the opposite impact. Daily there were more casualties involving these young men, and the mortality rates were "twice as many so far in proportion to population as mainland areas." There were wider regional implications that were driving this unfortunate toll, in that Canberra did "not want the Japanese re-armed and the Japanese themselves do not want to carry the burden of armaments, when their living standards are already very low"—thus the need for more infantrymen from Hawai'i.[74] "Over 90 island boys have been killed in the war," Baker announced mournfully in December 1950, "and some three hundred or more wounded. The islands have supplied twice as many men in proportion to population as the mainland. People are sullen and silent about the war. They don't like it." That was not the same mood that was prevalent[75] on the mainland.[76]

Strikingly, the growing distaste in the islands for the war did not submerge the proposal for statehood. Indeed, polling data at the time revealed that one result of the war in Korea was a sharp increase in pro-statehood sentiment on the mainland, since both Hawai'i and Alaska were sites for important military bases.[77]

The ILWU leadership found this encouraging. Jack Hall reported with enthusiasm that the union was engaged in daily promotion of statehood, had participated in congressional hearings on the subject, was represented on Governor Stainback's statehood commission—and more. At the Eighth Biennial Convention of the ILWU in April 1949 in San Francisco, which was attended by 200 delegates from Hawai'i, the union's activism was validated when a resolution urging immediate statehood for the colony was passed with unanimity.[78]

In this campaign the union had strange bedfellows. George H. Lehleitner of New Orleans, a friend of Dixiecrats, suggested that the resultant Hawaiian congressional delegation could conceivably "add strength to our Southern efforts to block such dangerous legislation as FEPC."[79] Lehleitner sought to calm the statehood fears of fellow segregationist and Mississippian Senator John Stennis by reminding him that the colony's legislature "twice (1945 and 1947) killed proposed FEPC bills in committee!"[80] Why worry, he suggested, since the Negro population—the Dixiecrats' primary obsession—was so tiny in the isles, a "negligible three-tenths of one percent!"[81] Anyway, as he informed the similarly segregationist Senator John Sparkman of Alabama, if Hawai'i's citizenry of Japanese ancestry did not send any of their number to Congress in the years when it represented almost half of the populace, what logic could possibly prompt the conviction that this would happen now?[82] Similarly, Stainback and Farrington buried their differences long enough to sign a joint statement to segregationist Senator Spessard Holland of Florida, telling him that "we citizens of Hawaii seek statehood on the same grounds that Southerners stress 'states' rights'"[83]—the doctrine that bolstered Jim Crow.

Statehood supporters of the Left—perhaps because they were spending so much time defending themselves from the HUAC and prosecutors—did not pay close attention to those of the Right with whom they shared a trench. If they had paid attention, they might have been concerned about Lehleitner's contention that viewed Hawaiian statehood as the beginning of an imperial project designed to incorporate far-flung territories into the Union. "Contiguity," he argued, was not "essential to expansion." Just as some had lampooned the idea of the isles' statehood by asking if Fiji or Italy could be next, now this was being raised seriously.[84]

That is precisely what concerned some statehood opponents. William Michels of the Texas Democratic Party, for example, was experiencing pangs of anxiety about the impending, statehood-induced loss of congressional seats for the South. That prospect had energized the "anti-South propaganda brigade screaming statehood for: coral atolls, islands, zones, territories and possessions," all of which risked "radical infiltration in some of these spots."[85]

Hence, those who were paying close attention were not overly surprised when in August 1950, in the midst of the ruckus brought by war, strikes, tumultuous hearings, party discord, and the like, Hawai'i moved closer to statehood. "For the first time in the history of Hawaii," said Statehood Commission leader George McClane, "a committee of the United States Senate has reported favorably on a bill to admit Hawaii to statehood. By a vote of 9 to 1, the Senate Interior and Insular Affairs Committee has recommended that Hawaii be admitted to the union."[86] The sole dissenting voice was that of Senator Butler.[87]

In 1951, Butler was joined by his fellow senators George Malone and George Smathers in yet another minority objection to statehood for Hawai'i on anticommunist grounds. The CP was so respectable in Hawai'i that the reputed leading Communist of them all, Jack Hall, was invited to serve on the board of sponsors of such a widely respected charitable organization as the Society for Crippled Children. Under fire on the mainland, Harry Bridges, had selected Honolulu as the site of his union's first biennial conference since its expulsion from the CIO, because he "knew his strongest supporters were in the Hawaiian locals." Bridges was reelected there "by a tremendous majority, and not one of the delegates from the Hawaiian locals voted against him." It was said with wonder that "in fact, not one of the Hawaiian delegates opposed the Bridges' policies on anything." With a final flourish, Butler and his colleagues concluded that "Hawaii should not be granted statehood until we are sure we are not adding a red star to the 48 white ones on the American flag."[88]

This overheated anticommunist atmosphere did not leave the ILWU unaffected. It may have influenced the union's pro-statehood posture, perhaps on the mistaken assumption that such a position would inoculate its members against a charge frequently leveled at those reputed to be Communists—that they lacked patriotism—an allegation that a call for independence would have enhanced. The union also found that this atmosphere influenced negotiations with management, as the latter was emboldened. Days after the onset of war in Korea, Jack Hall had a meeting with management's Dwight Steele and found that the man sitting across from him "began complaining like hell on the so-called 'commie line of the union'" and that a decision had been made to attack this line within the union. Assuming that the 1949 strike had sobered his adversaries, Hall was horrified to hear that, to the contrary, they had decided that "they couldn't live with us on our present program." Hall was instructed that Steele demanded "'a complete switch, not just a surface change,'" particularly in the ILWU's "allegedly promoting class warfare." Hall was informed that if the union chose to resist, it would lose 3,000 to 10,000 members at a minimum—a number that would mean the destruction of the ILWU. Hall was stunned to find that the man spouting these threats was very cocksure and determined, though Hall also felt that he had overestimated the situation considerably, for already "things were getting hot on the plantations." As he confided this to Louis Goldblatt, Hall was preparing for a trip to Maui, where 3,000 workers had just struck a sugar plantation. Thus, rather than staging a retreat, Hall's inclination was to carry the fight to management. But Hall also knew that the outcome of this standoff would not be solely determined by the relative strength of either side, in that "any deterioration in the international situation could quickly result in a reversal of positions." Thus he was seeking conciliation.[89]

In short, instead of jerking management toward a more realistic position of acceptance of the union, the 1949 strike—when combined with the overriding anticommunist atmosphere—had led the union's enemies to conclude that peaceful coexistence with the ILWU was impossible. This wrenching strike had emitted a clear signal that management was willing to deploy virtually any tactic in order to prevail. In a meeting of the union's executive board on the docks of Honolulu just after this battle had ended, Hall denounced the attempt to legislate the elimination of the very right to strike, which he claimed was unprecedented.[90]

Slowly but surely management was coming to realize that it had a real problem on its hands in the form of militant maritime unions, which controlled the lifeblood of the archipelago—imports and exports. Like a metronome, this realization ensured a forthright response by management. Management's political problem stemmed from the alliances built between and among the ILWU, the National Maritime Union, and the National Union of Marine Cooks and Stewards.[91]

This climate of concern was heightened when, after the advent of war in Korea, the US Navy met with the ILWU and representatives from McCabe—a major firm—and from Castle and Cooke to inform them that all employees of both companies were to be "screened" for subversive influences and that those not passing this test would be barred from army and navy installations.[92] Jack Hall hastened to reassure Rear Admiral C. H. McMorris that the union was uninterested in seeking to impede the movement of military cargoes in the event of a strike. This allegation was "both false and malicious," he thundered. "We'll move this cargo," he insisted. Union opponents were not necessarily convinced.[93]

But it was not just the war that was shaping the battlefield faced by the union. Hall found it obvious that the union's foes were making a concerted "drive to utilize the crap that came out in the hearings against us." Even the Catholic Church was intensifying its effort to harm the ILWU, which meant that now "some of our Portuguese membership is shaky."[94]

The constant drumbeat of anticommunism was taking its toll.[95] Sensing the changing climate, one employer chose to fire a worker for suspicion of being a Communist—and courts ruled this was not illegal. The worker had signed the Stockholm Peace Appeal, seeking to bar nuclear weapons, and placed his union affiliation after his signature. His fellow union members threatened him with violence and also threatened to stop working with him; thus the union—which held a union shop contract with the employer—expelled the worker and demanded that the company discharge him. Now, of course, this was not an ILWU shop, but Myer Symonds, who was the stevedores' attorney, shared this case with Jack Hall with some alarm as to what might occur in the islands,[96] which was not[97] unimaginable,[98] it was thought.[99]

Visiting an ILWU shop in Makawao, Maui, Dave Thompson of the ILWU found more than a hint of ethnic differences that the increasingly conservative political environment was doing little to allay. The Portuguese were "jealous of the positions of the Japanese because they hog the good jobs," while Filipinos, who were a tiny part of the membership at Pauwela and half the membership at Makawao, were also "sore with the Japanese because they refuse to take an active part in the union." Then there was the speedup—the employer had demanded that the workers increase production, without increased pay. "Guys work so hard that they can't talk at the end of the day," he complained. Unionists were quarreling over who was to blame for the state of the union, which quickly descended into dreaded "racial angles"—i.e., a "typical scapegoat reaction when the union is in poor shape," which was the case.[100] The unsanitary outhouses that stained the Kahuku plantation were a living testament to how far the union had to travel.[101]

Yasuki Arakaki was one of the union militants of Japanese origin who could be relied upon to joust with management. It was during the tenseness of the 1949 strike that he had a bitter confrontation with management at a sugar plantation in Naalehu. He had been told that he could not use a loudspeaker there and that if he tried, the police would be called. Arakaki demanded that intimidation of the workers must cease. Dave Thompson, who was there, witnessed the resultant fierce argument as union antagonist Jack Beatty retorted sharply, "'I'm glad to have met you[,] Arakaki. You are a first class Communist.'" An enraged Arakaki promptly grabbed Beatty by the collar and "socked him three or four times in the eye"—then demanded that the bruised Beatty apologize, which he did quite promptly. A satisfied Arakaki extended his hand to Beatty for an affirming shake, but the haole refused to comply, at which point Arakaki called him "chicken shit." All of this unfolded before a large crowd of workers and, according to Thompson, had a "wholesome effect." But Beatty, still not appropriately disciplined and perhaps heartened by the political climate that continued to favor him, tried to elbow his way into a union meeting, suggestive of how the overall political climate could embolden[102] those who appeared to be outnumbered.[103]

Given this brutish climate, spawned in no small part by the massive bloodletting in Korea—which in turn was driven by a hysterical anticommunism—this was not the most fortuitous moment for a purported Communist-led ILWU to go on strike. Yet that is precisely what happened. It was on

27 February 1951 that pineapple workers on the island of Lana'i, on land wholly owned by the Hawaiian Pineapple Company, walked out. By late August, pineapples continued to rot in the fields, emitting a distinct aroma, and the company had suffered losses estimated as high as $40 million. The 750 strikers had received no wages since launching their militant action but remained feisty. Governor Oren Long, who had replaced the beset Stainback, reported disconsolately to his superiors in Washington that "a large number of single Filipino workers [constitute] a militant group [and would] prevent a back-to-work movement by other workers, using violence if necessary." This militancy from the ranks made the typical attempt to blame union leaders for the strike problematic. Long noted that "the rank and file of the Lanai union, rather than the top territorial leaders of the ILWU[,] was responsible for calling the strike."[104]

The casual visitor to this island paradise may have noticed only the facade of a peaceful land festooned with pineapples. But by the end of February 1951 Lana'i had been throttled, swept up in a class confrontation that belied the growing belief that the new decade was to be somnolent. "Even if the company wished to," concluded a visiting journalist, "there are no laborers available on the island to hire in place of the strikers."[105]

Months before the strike, workers at the Maui Pineapple Company and the Hawaiian Pineapple Company had expressed concern that the contracts they had just signed were "far from satisfactory." The union local noted, "Their conditions were, in fact, shoved down our throats and we are presently powerless to resist. Some day it may be different—we hope so, [since] none of the major demands of the union involving the security and welfare of the membership was accepted by the companies."[106]

Visiting Lana'i in 1946, Frank Thompson of the ILWU had found that the only private businesses on the island were owned by small Japanese and Filipino merchants who peddled groceries and dry goods and also operated three eating houses and an ice cream store. Everything else, including the laundry, the bakery, and the theater, was operated by the Hawaiian Pineapple Company. The only hotel on the island was the company's clubhouse, where meals and lunch cost five dollars per day. There was no direct telephone service outside of the island, and the only way someone could get a message in or out of the island was by radiogram or letter—via a building controlled by the company.[107]

Federal investigators also were taken by Lana'i, terming it a "breeding ground for radicalism," suffused with "racial antipathy," and observing that "even hatred exists against all haoles." In fact, it was said, there was "half racial antipathy" and "half commie plot" involved in Lana'i's politics. That ILWU membership there was reportedly 75 percent Filipino was not deemed irrelevant in this context.[108] This militancy was leveraged by the nature of the crop produced, since unlike sugar—which in an emergency could be left standing in the fields for some time without total loss—pineapples had to be harvested at the proper moment and either shipped or processed immediately.[109]

Befitting a small island, Lanaʻi was a microcosm of class and race exploitation. All the lunas and supervisors resided atop a hill with paved roads leading to their comfortable abodes, while the workers endured alongside unpaved roads. Thus, as Goldblatt recalled with a lingering bitterness, "a woman would do her washing first thing in the morning and within half an hour the whole thing was covered with red dust," as a result of the "pineapple trucks going back and forth," kicking up dirt. "Things like that were burning these guys up badly," he said, speaking of his members. "There were nothing but haoles for superintendents," which exacerbated an underlying racial tension. During the sugar strike, management "screamed their heads off" at the union demand for antidiscrimination provisions. "Yet to our guys that was symbolic," Goldblatt said. "So it was a life pattern that had to be changed," and it led directly to the strike. Goldblatt recognized that the "whole thing had to be upset": "You couldn't really have a union that was worth its salt and one that could make any changes [without] at the same time fighting the whole background that I described, and that ran all the way from racial discrimination, racial hostility, refusal to allow these guys a chance to move up."[110] With such pent-up resentment to propel them, the ILWU unsurprisingly prevailed in 1951. Honolulu writer Sanford Zalburg concluded correctly that it was then that the union "cracked the haole superstructure on Lanai for all time," with consequences that touched all of the archipelago.[111]

Ronald Jamieson, the attorney appointed as mediator—or "conciliator"—was not exactly neutral, reminding Long that "the fact that the ILWU is run by the Communists" and "the possibility of a war between the democratic countries and Soviet Russia and Communist China" were connected. "I have felt," he continued, "that there is a possibility that the Lanai strike has been running as the pilot light to widespread labor trouble in Hawaii in the summer," timed to coincide with an Asian offensive.[112] After meeting with Goldblatt, an alarmed Jamieson reported with trepidation that the ILWU leader had told him that "one-half of the strike committee had learned guerilla warfare with the Huks," the fierce and famed fighters from the Philippines. That panic was setting in was reflected when Jamieson reported that he had been told that the "mistake was not shooting five employees to keep the employees in line, the way they do in Malaya,"[113] an area then laboring under a protracted war driven by British colonialism. Yet despite Jamieson's inflamed and improper ex parte communications with the governor, Robert McElrath said publicly that the union had "always considered Mr. Jamieson to be a fair and square fellow."[114]

Perhaps McElrath was making nice in recognition of the difficult straits in which the union found itself. Anticommunist prosecutors were zeroing in on the union leadership, and, besides, the agricultural businesses for which a good deal of their membership toiled were flush with cash and more able to absorb a strike. Pineapple companies particularly were doing well, while, according to a local journal, their cousins in sugar were benefiting since the price of this commodity had climbed steadily since mid-1950 to $127 per ton. With "few exceptions," it was reported happily, "Hawaiian sugar companies have had a good year; many more have had an excellent year."[115]

These businesses were not interested in sharing their bounty with the workers involved in producing these commodities. In fact, one reason the companies were so profitable was precisely that they were busily eliminating jobs. In late February 1951, Ray Jerome Baker found that the same amount of sugar was being produced with half the number of laborers previously used.[116] Something similar[117] was happening in the pineapple industry,[118] which Hall recognized.[119]

As the number of laborers was being reduced, feudal conditions remained. Workers on this pineapple island could not own their own homes or even hope to, while permission was required from the company even for a visitor to arrive there. Union organizers had to journey there in small boats under cover of darkness, and union literature had to be smuggled in.[120]

Harry Bridges was not unaware of these trends, realizing that this industry had to be confronted on all sides. Earlier he had acknowledged in the halls of Congress that the ILWU had to "spread out into the Hawaii pineapple and sugar industry" since "the employers of the longshoremen were in reality the people who owned and operated the basic industries on the island" and they deftly manipulated one body of workers against the other. Matson "kind of operates ships like Henry Ford operates a coal mine," and so this self-professed "left wing trade union leader" who was directing a "left wing trade union"[121] realized that it would be folly to organize workers merely in one sector when their employers were not so limited.[122]

Yet this was not a propitious moment for the union. Yes, the union was a powerful force in Hawai'i at the time. As the strike plodded on, Theodora Kreps reported in April 1951 that the ILWU included 20,000 sugar workers, 5,000 pineapple workers, 3,000 stevedores, and 1,000 other workers in miscellaneous industries.[123] Having such a large membership—that happened to be overwhelmingly of Asian-Pacific origin[124]—helped insulate the ILWU, to a degree, from the conservative consensus that prevailed on the mainland. Though the extent to which Huk influence reached into the ranks may also have been exaggerated, it was unavoidable that the bulk of ILWU membership did not necessarily accept the anticommunist ethos that was so prevalent due east. Hence, as if flexing its muscles, the ILWU chose this moment to hold its convention in Hawai'i.[125] Though Bridges was under siege on the mainland, in Hawai'i he was not only a celebrity but a powerful man who had a good deal of his remarks broadcast on the radio.[126]

Two months into the strike, Yukio Abe of the union reported that although he had hoped for more "activity on the picket lines," the morale of the strikers was "rather high" despite their having "too much free time," which they may have been using in tending gardens and fishing. Nonetheless, the union maintained a soup kitchen kept busy feeding three square meals per day to strikers and their families. There was coffee and bread in the morning and rice and *okazu* (side dish) for lunch, with a repeat of the latter for supper. An official fishing committee supplemented this monotonous fare four or five times per week, depending on the weather. Each meal cost the union about 16 cents, but multiplied times 3 and then times 2,000 to 3,000, the total costs quickly added up: almost 10 bags of rice were used daily to feed the strikers, which included preparing school lunches for 219 children. Hence, the cost of operating the soup kitchen for one week was estimated conservatively to be almost $2,000. Yet despite the grinding hardships, the strike was effective, with weeds covering once-plush fields and thousands of acres of sweet pineapple going to waste. "The plantation is completely shut down," Abe reported, "except for power and water."[127]

The effectiveness of the strike was due in no small part to the solidarity expressed by fellow workers. Thus, in June 1951, stevedores were recruited to grab their turtle nets and hunt for turtles, which many islanders were fond of consuming.[128]

On a tiny island like Lana'i, strong ripples inexorably emanated from this shutdown. Strikers and their families comprised two-thirds of island residents, so when they were fed via the union, this meant they bought less food, which in turn meant that local stores were devastated. The local cinema was affected too, now showing only one movie nightly instead of two, as it had previously. Fortunately for the workers, management did not move to evict strikers from housing, but this battle was no less costly.[129] As losses continued to mount, by early August an estimated 150 individuals had fled Lana'i (though one estimate was about 300)[130]—not a negligible number given the small population.[131]

Hall blasted the employer on Lana'i as "exceedingly arrogant and filthy with money." Despite the company's wealth, however, management did not seem eager to surrender to the workers, even though "they appear to give every indication of being willing to sacrifice their summer crop"; this was "not good business," he advised, though it was "the way they do things in Hawaii."[132] Despite its best efforts, management found itself locked into tough negotiations with the union in an equivalent of trench warfare. Mediation—or "conciliation"—efforts were taking place on the fourth floor of Honolulu's Alexander Young Hotel: company representatives were ensconced in one room, the union in another, and the parties used a third room when the scurrying Jamieson brought them together.[133]

Typically, union negotiations were choreographed, and certainly they were by this point, with the two parties by now quite familiar with each other. For some meetings the union, led by Hall or Goldblatt, would bring a group of workers, and management would bring a like number of its representatives; then there would be smaller meetings, followed by off-the-record gatherings where alcohol flowed freely, heightening one of Hall's persistent problems. Howard Babbitt, who dickered with the union more than once, felt that "Hall was a friend of mine, as I was of his," though it bothered him when Hall and other leaders would "work their members up to such a pitch that when we reached what was thought to be a fair agreement the membership was so worked up they wouldn't accept the recommendation of the leaders."[134] Such apparent disarray was echoed in the press.[135]

Actually, it was the company and the authorities that seemed to suffer most. The crop was lost, and the four police officers on the small island were so overworked that they gained overtime wages.[136] Weeks before the strike ended, Henry White, the company's president, informed his stockholders that already this was the "longest strike in the pineapple industry in Hawaii"; his company had bought Lanaʻi in 1922, and this strike proved to be a landmark.[137] Jamieson sought to reassure Governor Long that things were not as bad as they looked, since tax laws meant that the company's loss would not be as great as it appeared; "I have heard mentioned the figure of $50 [million] as the economic loss from the strike," he noted.[138]

Finally, the authorities had had enough—bowing reluctantly to the union's strength in a coerced settlement that soured further their opinion of the ILWU and its presumed sedition. Early on the morning of 30 August 1951, as the pineapple strike was grinding to a halt with a clear victory for the ILWU, Koji Ariyoshi, the Communist editor of the *Honolulu Record*, was resting in bed in his less than commodious residence at Halawa Housing after a typically lengthy day of toil. He was awakened when a couple of men yelled at the top of their voices and pounded on his front door as if they were about to batter it down. "'This is the FBI!'" they screamed. "'This is the FBI! Open the door! You're under arrest!'" Ariyoshi's spouse, Takeo, put on a robe and ambled to the front door. As she proceeded to unlock the door and turn the doorknob, two agents pushed the door against her and one rushed directly into the privacy of their bedroom. One of these invaders flashed his badge in a frenzy of excitement. Ariyoshi was in pajamas as his arm was grabbed. Then the other agent, who had not had the temerity to invade their inner sanctum, opened the kitchen door that led to the back of the apartment and let in a third agent. The men knew the complete layout of the home. Ariyoshi informed the man who held his arm that he wanted to go to the bathroom. He was allowed to do so, but the agent followed him into this tiny space. "I told him I was going to sit on the stool," Ariyoshi recalled later. "He said for me to go ahead and stood in front of me and watched my every move and expression." Having "moved my bowels," Ariyoshi then "washed my face," then "lathered" it and "was about to pick up my razor when the alert FBI agent reached from behind me and took the razor away." Ariyoshi watched in sadness as his son emerged from his bedroom, "bewildered, half thinking of coming to me but afraid of doing so because of the strangers from the night who had stormed into our house." The boy "stood there, the little fellow in his white sleeping clothes," and then "suddenly he turned and rushed into our bedroom where an FBI agent was watching Takeo and crawled into her arms," Ariyoshi said. "My daughter quickly followed and went to her mother." Unfortunately, he observed with regret, "the minds of both of them were scarred by the behavior of the FBI agents."[139]

A similar scar was left on the ILWU, the CP, and the broader Left as a result of the Smith Act prosecution, the occasion for the FBI's dramatic entry into Ariyoshi's humble home. A similar scene unfolded at the residences of his codefendants, including Jack Hall. This lengthy prosecution was to tie up resources that the Left could have used to organize more workers and attain higher wages and better working conditions—which perhaps sheds light on why these leaders were compelled to endure an ordeal that almost sent them all to prison for lengthy terms.

CHAPTER 13

Radicalism on Trial

Philip Maxwell did not think highly of Jack Hall. Born in 1901, the well-compensated Maxwell, in his role as chief negotiator for the Big Five, often butted heads with Hall. During the same morning that Koji Ariyoshi was detained, Maxwell was looking forward to wrapping up sensitive negotiations with Hall—but then the top ILWU leader was taken into custody too. "We'd been up negotiating all night the morning he got arrested," said Maxwell. "The FBI was waiting down in the lobby of the [Alexander] Young Hotel," waiting to pounce. Not soused, Hall strolled downstairs, confident in the knowledge that a settlement was about to be reached in the Lanaʻi strike and that possibly a sugar strike could be averted. As Maxwell eyed him, "he walked downstairs and they pinched him," he said. "They arrested him." That did not exactly please Maxwell, at least in the short term. "We didn't want him arrested," he insisted. "We didn't want him out of circulation." But his concerns were overridden.[1]

Hall's young daughter had similar feelings. Robert McElrath resided near Hall's home, and after word spread that he had been detained, she came running over to her neighbor's house, shouting, "'They've just arrested Daddy.'" A startled McElrath immediately sprung into action.[2] Almost instantaneously ILWU Local 136 in Maui voted to stop work in protest—a trend that was to become pronounced as the judicial proceedings commenced. Its response was confirmation of what a local journalist noticed—that the simultaneous arrests of seven radicals was "the topic of conversation on every street corner and in practically every business house."[3]

The timing of the arrests—in the midst of negotiations about sugar and as the pineapple strike was winding down—may not have been coincidental. Certainly, the ILWU had to spend time defending itself, rather than devoting energy to obtaining better contracts.[4]

Seven leaders of the Hawaiʻi Left had been arrested, including Hall and Ariyoshi, and they were to endure an extraordinarily lengthy trial—more than half a year—that was to leave the Communist Party in ruins, a process already

The union attracted considerable support from the Asian-Pacific community—the over-whelming majority in the archipelago—even during times of stress and anxiety, such as the 1952–1953 anticommunist prosecution. This union supporter considered the offensive against progressive forces to be *pilau* (rotten or stinky). Courtesy of Anne Rand Library, ILWU–San Francisco.

in motion as a direct result of the Taft-Hartley Act of 1947 and the House Un-American Activities Committee hearings of 1950. They—Dwight Freeman, John Reinecke, Jack Kimoto, Charles Fujimoto, Eileen Fujimoto, along with Hall and Ariyoshi—were tried in federal court, charged with violation of the notorious Smith Act, which had been used and was to be used further against actual and reputed Communist Party members operating under the US flag, all accused of advocating and teaching the desirability of overthrowing the US government. Again, Hawai'i proved its uniqueness during this ordeal. The

defendants were convicted, but unlike on the mainland, this outcome led to repeated strikes and demonstrations involving tens of thousands of protesters.
Because of this protest and the changing political climate, the convicted did not
have to serve the five-year prison terms that had been meted out (the sole woman
received a three-year term; she too did not serve), because a higher federal court
overturned the convictions in 1958, based on a 1957 US Supreme Court opinion. Yet the trial served a purpose in that these leaders were akin to a fire department that no longer could extinguish fires in its neighborhood or dispense
firefighting tips but, instead, had to put out fires at the fire station itself. This
trial was the beginning of the end for a vibrant radicalism that had swept Hawai'i
since ILWU had sunk its tentacles into the archipelago in the mid-1930s.[5]

The trial cost the defendants tens of thousands of dollars, which was borne
mostly by the ILWU, and this left Hall bitter as he thought of the buildings,
union education, and organizational programs this money could have financed.[6] Four other Smith Act trials preceded that in Honolulu—two in Manhattan and one each in Baltimore and Los Angeles—-and two more were in
progress (Detroit and St. Louis) as appeals were launched in what came to be
known as the Hawaii Seven case. Yet the trial in Honolulu, lasting seven and a
half months, was the second-longest of them all, exceeded only by the first trial,
that of the highest CP leadership in New York City; this was an indication of
the importance of the island radicals, just as the fact that theirs was the only
trial in which none of the accused acted as his or her own attorney suggested
the resources these union members could bring to bear that others may have
lacked.[7] A chief prosecution witness in Honolulu—Paul Crouch—summed up
neatly why this trial occurred; speaking before the US Senate, he claimed that
"if the Communist Party on the mainland had the same influence they have in
Hawaii, we would have a revolution in 12 months."[8]

During the course of this lengthy ordeal, one juror got married, four babies
were born—two to jurors' wives, two to attorneys' wives—while over 3.25 million words were transcribed by the man taking down every word; every night
after the court recessed, he would transcribe testimony that at times ran to 175
pages.[9] Ultimately, over 200 pounds of Smith Act case records were shipped to
the archives, including 18,500 pages of transcribed testimony.[10]

Jack Hall probably realized a turning point had been reached on that
fateful morning of his arrest. Certainly he was not a model of repose as he
emerged from the FBI office after his detention. Beads of perspiration trickled
down the furrowed brow of the mountainous man as he walked away. His lips
twitched, and his countenance was grim. He had only gotten a chance to
sleep at 3 a.m., then was rousted less than fours later by the authorities. Continually he asked for water, though hydration may have been the least of his
problems at this juncture. In contrast Eileen Fujimoto wore a perpetual grin,
perhaps recognizing that the evidence against her was the slightest of all; one

observer thought she seemed to relish the popping of flashbulbs. Jack Kimoto mirrored Hall in that he seemed to be extremely nervous, as his eyes blinked constantly and his fingers twisted a rolled newspaper in his hands. He looked pale and ill at ease, while the other defendants rested uneasily between the poles of Fujimoto and Hall-Kimoto.[11]

Fortunately for the defendants, they appeared before Judge Delbert Metzger, and he quickly reduced their bail from $75,000 to $5,000, which outraged countless members of Congress and led to President Truman's reputedly deciding not to reappoint him when his term expired.[12] About 76 years old at the time of this controversial decision, Judge Metzger became the target of national attention and criticism as a result, yet befitting the relaxed atmosphere of the islands—and the relative dearth of anticommunism there—shortly after inflaming public opinion on the mainland, he was observed through his office window leaning back in his chair and casually blowing tobacco smoke in the air.[13] As promised, subsequently Metzger failed to win reappointment to the bench.[14]

But from the defendants' viewpoint, the most important constituency of all—ILWU members, whose dues mostly paid for the defense and whose activism shaped the climate that allowed them to escape incarceration—were relatively unruffled. "The arrest of Jack created not a ripple on the rank and file here in Hawaii," reported Theodora Kreps, a few days after the arrests; further she observed, seemingly surprised, "it is possible that it even resulted in strengthening the determination of the sugar workers to push for a decent agreement."[15]

Hall presented the other side of the ledger when he informed the San Francisco–based leadership of the serious financial problems faced by the Hawai'i locals because of the seven-month Lana'i strike, which was a financial drain, followed swiftly by the Smith Act arrests and a passel of deportation cases targeting a membership composed heavily of non-US nationals, as well as a host of other assaults designed to destabilize the ILWU.[16] Yet even Hall, who had good reason to make a most sober analysis of what was occurring, felt that the union was in excellent shape and found the membership more united than ever, hefty problems notwithstanding. "It looks as if the administration has a bear by the tail in its Hawaii arrests under the Smith Act," he said confidently.[17]

Apparently the union's opponents were disappointed that the arrests did not seem to send the ILWU into a tizzy, with one authoritative voice evidently scandalized that Hall continued to play a leading role in sugar negotiations. "We have already moved from guilt by association to guilty by association," argued the ILWU representative in Washington, William Glazier.[18] But what this authoritative voice seemingly did not realize was that those in Hawai'i may not have overdosed on the gushing anticommunist

news, something that was hardly possible on the mainland,[19] another difference with the federal union.[20]

In fact, not only did fellow unions refuse to aid the ILWU, but they also
chose this difficult moment to raid its ranks. That was the import of the
CIO's sending an agent to the islands before the arrests, and this trend continued, aided immeasurably by the Teamsters and other hostile maritime
unions, including the now conservative-dominated National Maritime
Union and Sailors' Union of the Pacific. This treatment of the ILWU outraged the *San Francisco Sun-Reporter*, which appealed to the city's burgeoning African-American community. "Minority people have fared better in
the ILWU under [Harry] Bridges" than "they have in any other labor union
in the United States," it was reported—"Walter Reuther's United Automobile Workers included." Yet Dave Beck's Teamsters were a "Jim Crow trade
union," and Negroes were "denied gainful employment" by the Sailors'
Union because it had "refused to allow Negroes to membership." The International Longshoremen's Association—the ILWU's competitor—had determined that "no Negroes belong" in ports too numerous to note or else
placed them in "Jim Crow auxiliaries." The National Maritime Union had
systematically purged Negro leadership, including Ferdinand Smith, an ally
of Bridges.[21]

The public face of the Big Five, Walter Dillingham,[22] was unperturbed by
the arrests of the Hawai'i labor activists.[23] Tellingly, his spouse—a bespectacled, matronly, and conservatively clothed woman—became one of the more
ardent fans of the trial, attending daily and wearing a different hat each time.[24]

The local press, which the Dillinghams so admired, had prepared the
battlefield with a withering barrage of anticommunism. "The 'Commies'
want to bust up all business, kick out the churches, tell everybody what to
do—or shoot 'em if they don't," exhorted one inflamed report,[25] as the specter of Stalin was raised repeatedly.[26]

Though closer to Tokyo than Washington, Honolulu—because of the
strength of radicalism there and the resultant fierce and far-reaching reaction against it—had become a central battleground in the US effort to squash
the CP and the unions thought to be close to this group. An internal report
prepared by Saburo Fujisaki for the Hawai'i locals of the ILWU observed
that the "ILWU in the islands has [received] national attention via stories
appearing recently in leading magazines such as the *Saturday Evening Post*
and *Time*." This was not the only way that the often-neglected archipelago
assumed center stage. Elsewhere under the US flag, the mainland locals were
surprised to know that money to defend the accused had been pledged by the
union membership. Thus, there was the distinct impression, Fujisaki noted,
that the "more pressure the government puts on the union (through arrests,
suits, etc.) the tougher and more solid our ranks get."[27]

Since the advent of the ILWU, wages for stevedores had risen from 60 cents an hour before 1940 to $1.76 by the time of the Hawaii Seven trial; sugar base rates had gone up from as low as 19 cents an hour before 1944 to 91 cents per hour by 1951; meanwhile pineapple base wages had accelerated from as low as 55 cents per hour before 1945 to $1.16 by 1951. These wage increases were accompanied by other gains such as paid vacations, paid holidays, and sick leave.[28] During the height of the trial, Hall announced that local stevedores had made the greatest number of gains in the history of any group of workers in the territory in the previous year, and he looked forward to even more, including guaranteed medical care for workers and their families in the immediate future.[29] It was difficult to convince the Hawai'i working class that the Smith Act trial was about subversion of the colony, as opposed to subverting a radical movement that had uplifted the dispossessed.

Fujisaki was not alone in perceiving something unique about the islands. "Our members assumed that the goal of the trial was to destroy the union's leadership and the union," Dave Thompson asserted. Thus, thousands of people came into contact with the defendants through defense activities, which made for an intense rank-and-file participation in the life of the union. Hence, during the Hawaii Seven years, said Thompson in a 2006 interview, "I used to sell a hell of a lot more books to the ILWU members on subjects like unionism, labor history and civil liberties than I do today. There were a lot of intense bull sessions and discussions then." It was "one form of fire that hardened the steel in our case," he said[30]—an opinion shared by others.[31] John Burns was also among these defenders, offering to testify on Hall's behalf.[32] Like a number of other leaders of Hawai'i's modern Democratic Party, Burns had an intimate political relationship with Reds, including Koji Ariyoshi.[33]

On the other hand, suggestive of the ILWU's power was that Samuel Wilder King, who once served as territorial governor, was reluctant to testify against the defendants. The wily King recognized that bearing witness against the popular Hall could be a career killer in the islands.[34] There was a feeling in King's inner circle that "if the present Smith Act case was lost [then] Hall would become a messiah"—and King did not want to be implicated either way.[35] An interlocutor of his was amazed that—at a time when anticommunism was taking on the form of a civil religion, driven by a bloody war in Korea—the isles' top Republican would not testify in a Smith Act trial.[36]

The influential Japanese-American politico Wilfred Tsukiyama was also reluctant to testify on behalf of the prosecution, even when told that he could thereby "dissipate the anti-loyalty criticisms directed against Japanese people" and that "even politically he would emerge a stronger figure."[37] Hiram Fong, who went on to represent Hawai'i in the US Senate, discussed the question of testifying with his business partners—who indicated that he should not testify against Jack Hall.[38]

Jon Wiig may have wished that he had never heard of the Hawaii Seven. This tall—six feet four inches—stately judge was born in North Dakota but graduated from the University of North Carolina and moved to Hawai'i in 1933. He wound up presiding in this controversial case and perhaps would have been well advised to trod the neutral path of Samuel King; subsequently Senator Fong blocked Wiig's appointment to a higher federal court, with his presumed role in the conviction of the defendants being an alleged factor. Elsewhere, men were winning judgeships precisely because of their role in convicting supposed Communists.[39]

Yet Hawai'i remained under Washington's jurisdiction and thus could not be immune from trends there. As the Smith Act arrests were unfolding, the ILWU—meeting in Hawai'i—demanded a cease-fire in Korea and the withdrawal of all foreign troops; shortly thereafter Harry Bridges was imprisoned,[40] as an attempt was made to suppress dissent.[41] Ray Jerome Baker could not help but notice that the islands were "over-run with FBI agents."[42] Despite the best efforts of the anticommunists, however, they failed in their primary objective: jailing Jack Hall.[43]

As leader of the ILWU, Hall wielded—by far—more power than his codefendants, and it was organized labor that, in pushing for wages, better working conditions, and then political power, had given the hegemonic Big Five headaches. As it turned out, this disproportion was mirrored in the legal funding for the trial, with the ILWU picking up the tab for the entire Smith Act defense. Topflight San Francisco attorney Richard Gladstein, fresh from the defense of Communist Party leaders in a 1949 Manhattan trial, leased a nice home on Black Point and parked himself in the islands for the duration of the Hawaii Seven trial. He found this interlude displeasing, although that did not seem to deter the ferocity of his courtroom performance. He had been traveling intermittently to Hawai'i since the ILWU had been organized and invariably felt "awfully depressed" and "lonesome" as a result—or so Frank Thompson thought. Gladstein told him that "he would probably commit suicide if he had to stay [a] couple of years out here."[44]

Gladstein's general unhappiness in the islands was a reflection of the mood of the defendants toward each other and their lawyers, which veered from dismay to fury. The defendants and their attorneys were mired in a snake pit of anger, resentment, and substantive political disagreements—which made their ultimate triumph all the more remarkable. If nothing else, the case of Hawai'i radicals suggests that boon friendship and fond feelings are not unwavering preconditions for political advance. Their case also suggests that the enormous pressure of an indictment and possible imprisonment served a useful purpose in fomenting divisiveness—from the prosecution's viewpoint—even though the defendants were spared lengthy jail sentences.

Thus Hall opposed having any of the defendants testify—and they did not—while Kimoto disagreed, arguing that the seven should be seeking to show for posterity, if nothing else, what the aims and methods of the Communists were; failure to do so, he thought, would lead some to "think we had something shameful, something to hide, so why should they defend us after we get convicted[?]"[45] He had a point: since Kawano was on the witness stand a staggering 13 days, even the most strenuous and dedicated efforts of defense counsel had a difficult time overcoming the points he scored on behalf of the prosecution.[46]

But the major flash point internally was not between Hall and Kimoto but more so between Hall and Ariyoshi, with even Sanford Zalburg agreeing that "the union didn't support [Ariyoshi's] *Record*" properly.[47] Born in Kona in 1914, Ariyoshi, though diminutive—five feet eight inches tall and weighing 143 pounds—was well muscled, befitting his years as a stevedore and a soldier,[48] and intellectually capable, befitting his years at the *Honolulu Record*, perhaps the most erudite and popular local left-wing journal in the history of the United States and its colonies. He was also a war hero. During the war, he had been in charge of a team of nine Japanese-American enlisted men that was deemed by officialdom as "the most effective single fields unit operating tactically against the Japanese forces in any American theater of operations"; Ariyoshi was termed "one of the most completely patriotic, democratic Americans" of all, besides being an "intelligent, balanced adult individual with an excellent . . . sense of humor."[49]

"I was a muscle man," the modest Ariyoshi noted later, toiling regularly on the docks at one point from 7 a.m. to 11 p.m. "I was a tough cookie [in] those days," he said, though he attended the University of Hawai'i from 1938 to 1940, before heading to the University of Georgia, then enlisting in the US military and allying with Mao Zedong.

Ariyoshi's vast array of experiences did not prevent him from engaging in clashes with fellow radicals, however. He thought, correctly, that "Hall and McElrath did not back me" when he led the *Record*, though the busy Ariyoshi was largely responsible for the journal's popularity, editing most of the articles and writing half. McElrath thought he was a spy, said Ariyoshi, and Hall never subscribed, terming it a "shitty sheet," and "tried to line up opposition to the [journal] at every ILWU convention." Why? Said Ariyoshi, "We were for the rank and file and we worked with the rank and file." The ILWU leaders were not alone in their distaste for his handiwork, however. In a typical move, one time in Hilo a "gang of manager's wives," he recalled, "went store to store and threatened shop owners with [a] boycott if they continued to advertise" in his pages. Yet despite such obstacles, the paper managed a weekly circulation of 7,000. This impressive figure helped make him a Smith Act defendant but did not improve his ties with Hall, since—like

Kimoto—Ariyoshi too felt that the defendants should have taken the stand. During the trial, Hall "played it cool toward me," Ariyoshi recalled. "He didn't want to talk to me at first. He was afraid. He had already split from the party," as the "party was split here"—a circumstance fomented in part by the decision of CP leader Charles Fujimoto to emerge from the shadows. Hall, said Ariyoshi, even resisted the campaign in behalf of the defendants; headed by Fujisaki, the campaign did a commendable job in the outer islands and was the ultimate force that saved them all from languishing in dank prison cells. Hall was "afraid of the anti-haole feeling"—which was understandably prevalent—and by the time of the trial he "wasn't much of a Communist" either. Ariyoshi, who published a free newspaper for the benefit of Filipinos—*Ti Mang Una* (The pioneer)—belied the frequently held assertion put forward by some haole leaders of the union that militants of Japanese ancestry were hostile or indifferent to Filipino interests. Ariyoshi felt that Hall had undermined the "most effective guys" in the union's ranks, including Yasuki Arakaki, Sleepy Omori, Castner Ogawa, Justo de la Cruz, and others. Hall, said Ariyoshi, was the "Vishnu or destroyer of the labor movement," and, ironically, it was the trial that "tied him closer to the rank and file," since it converted him into a martyr for their just cause.

Thus, while the defendants sat at their table in the courtroom, there was a bare civility between and among them. As Ariyoshi saw it, Hall also was cavalier in his approach to Gladstein—"he used to curse" him, though the skilled barrister was "like a football quarterback" who saved their hides. Gladstein would lay out precisely what would occur during the upcoming week during the trial, instructing the other defense attorneys as to who should make objections and what points they should raise. Ariyoshi also liked Myer Symonds, one of the attorneys who served on the defense team.[50]

In turn, Hall's comrade Robert McElrath was not too fond of Ariyoshi, feeling that his radicalism was out of touch with reality. "He never got out of the caves in Yenan," where he had liaised with Mao Zedong. "He's still in there," McElrath maintained in 1975, when the controversies of the 1950s had long since passed. Yet even McElrath conceded that elite "Punahou [School] kids used to come down and throw rocks" at the *Honolulu Record*'s office, suggesting that Ariyoshi was not viewed as a cipher.[51]

The beleaguered Ariyoshi borrowed heavily to keep the periodical alive, but the loans had been secured from his relatives and not from commercial loan agencies. Revenues were just enough to allow for bare survival, which makes all the more remarkable that the newsweekly managed to survive the trial.[52]

It was a testament to the relative dearth of anticommunism in Hawai'i that the defendants were able to prevail, despite spending so much time during the trial—counterproductively—at each other's throats. The bad blood between Gladstein and Hall stretched back to squabbles over fees billed to the union in 1945. Ruminating philosophically years later, Gladstein concluded that "Jack's behavior at that point in his life reflected a seething inner conflict between himself and others, between himself and his past, with a frustration that he felt," as well as "rage with former close friends who had betrayed him"—some of whom testified against him. Gladstein came into the trial knowing that "Jack was opposed to my participation in it," and he also knew that "Jack had broken with the other defendants, for whom he had developed an ill-concealed disdain" and that "they, in turn, regarded him with open distrust." The attorney noted that, "indeed, Jack wanted in the worst way to have his trial severed" from that of his codefendants, preferring to be tried alone. Plus, there was a major disagreement between Hall and the other defendants, since the ILWU leader wanted a "narrow trade-union defense for himself, abjuring politics"—which was the subject at the heart of a blatantly political prosecution. "Poor man!" was Gladstein's condescending opinion of him[53] (though Hall's spouse argued later that Hall "had a tremendous respect for Richie," referring to Gladstein).[54]

Yet even John Reinecke realized that though there was a Hawaii Seven, as far as the authorities were concerned, they wanted to bag a "Hawaii One"— Jack Hall. That meant that an inordinate amount of pressure had been placed on Hall in comparison with the others, which may shed light on his ill temper.[55]

The other defendants did not have the weighty responsibilities of Hall, and thus it was easier for them to follow their radical instincts. Sanford Zalburg was present the day that Hall was sentenced after conviction. "I remember Jack betting a buck—I can't remember with whom," said the Hall biographer, "that he would get the maximum prison sentence. And, of course, he did." The trial, said Zalburg, "was aimed at splitting or breaking the union [by] cutting off its head"—meaning Hall.[56]

Hall also clashed with Harriet Bouslog, a woman of Welsh and French descent. As an attorney, she was often surrounded by powerful men, which was nothing new to her. As she was growing up in Bloomington, Indiana, and North Dakota, her father was a professor, and she was often the only child in an adult world. The middle of three girls, reared in what she termed a Christian ethical tradition, she arrived in Hawai'i initially in September 1939 after having graduated law school at Indiana University, passed the bar examination a few days after the attack on Pearl Harbor, and gone to work in Washington for the ILWU. Gladstein and Bridges had brokered the forging of the law partnership she founded with Myer Symonds in Honolulu. Her first marriage dissolved—"he kicked me out of the only house that we owned," she says—and she remarried. Her Hawai'i schedule was hectic, in any case, as the ILWU kept her quite busy—on one occasion in 1946 she was in court on three separate islands in one day, quite a feat even today. She recalled those hectic times: "I never went to bed. I didn't drink. I scarcely ate. I was scared to death." At the time of the trial, she was no fan of Hall's, perhaps because "Harry," as she called Bridges, "likes me,"[57] and Hall was no fan of Bridges. In turn Goldblatt resented her, accusing her of profiting from insider trading based on confidential conversations he had with management that he shared with her.[58] John Reinecke did not like his lawyer either. A. L. Wirin had traveled to Hawai'i from California to defend him and had a wide range of experience with a vast array of civil liberties issues, but Reinecke was unimpressed.[59]

Bouslog was no admirer of her law partner either. Myer Symonds was born in Sydney, Australia, in 1909, though his father—who had roots in Poland—was born in New York. His mother, however, was Australian. A graduate of the University of California, Berkeley, and of Hastings Law School in San Francisco, Symonds began working with Gladstein in 1946 before decamping to Honolulu. Gladstein found it onerous to make a 12-hour trip to the islands for ILWU matters and recruited him to move there. "I had no children and I didn't have a home," Symonds thought, so he decided to move west immediately, particularly since Gladstein offered to finance the firm because other local lawyers shunned the union. Once Symonds asked one of these men, "'If Hall were accused of raping a young girl there would be no hesitation on your part to defend him if he paid you a substantial fee?'" The answer was yes—but labor and political cases were another matter altogether. Symonds arrived in the islands the day before the fifth anniversary of the bombing of Pearl Harbor and found himself in the middle of a labor war, having to defend hundreds of ILWU members then under arrest as a result of a strike. Though he and Gladstein were peers—they had been classmates at Berkeley, and the San Francisco lawyer was only a year older than Symonds—he—like many others—was in awe: "Gladstein is one of the smartest guys I ever met in my life," he said. During the Smith Act trial, he recalled, "we would express our views," but "Richie ultimately was the one who made the final decision."[60]

Despite his selfless toil on behalf of the ILWU, Symonds was not an ideal man: "He'd sit there and he'd tell us the latest accumulation of dirty jokes," said Bouslog with lingering disgust. "Then he'd start talking sports. And I said, 'Sy, I'm not interested in dirty jokes and I'm not interested in sports'"—but he was undeterred. He was not alone, she said, noting when she was interviewed in 1976: "To this day, I don't know more than one or two judges on the bench who aren't the worst male chauvinists I ever saw. Including my partner"—i.e., Symonds—"who is the worst male chauvinist [of all]." She didn't think highly of Hall either, though she noticed that his notorious consumption of alcohol had one positive effect; it "heightened his hearing," making his two loves (including music) strangely compatible.[61]

Hall and Bouslog were not compatible. Actually, he had contempt for both her and Symonds as attorneys, according to Zalburg. Hall wanted to recruit Harvard Law School graduate O. Vincent Esposito of Honolulu for the trial and was angered when he was unable to do so, yet another factor that caused the well-respected Esposito to term Hall "very vindictive."[62] As Hall's wife recalled, Bouslog "professed, or gave lip service to what was supposed to be the good cause, but actually she lived in a style that was far in excess," indeed luxurious. Yoshiko Hall detected a basic unfairness in grand living propelled by a union of workers. Bouslog's "law firm would not be here, except for the ILWU," she said, adding, "They wouldn't have made it."[63] Despite these admonitions, even Jack Kawano, then a sworn foe of the Left, admired Bouslog and Symonds,[64] for, like their legal colleagues, they worked tirelessly.[65] Nerves were wracked during this trial by ordeal: at one juncture, a witness requested a break in order to puff on a cigarette, and Wirin chimed in, "I join in the request although I am not a smoker."[66] Such anxiety contributed to the accumulation of bruised feelings that seemed to propel sour evaluations of Hall and Bouslog particularly.

Hall may have thought he was uniquely positioned to evaluate the lawyers he hired, for Zalburg has observed that the ILWU leader "had a legal brain" and would have "made a great lawyer." According to Zalburg, Hall had "wanted to be a physicist," and thus may not have been terribly impressed with the wizardry of his legal team (particularly since Zalburg mentions that it was Reinecke who "did all the research for those great lawyers").[67] Yoshiko Hall also was employed by the Bouslog-Symonds firm and, she said, "I worked my ass off" while "all the lawyers did was shake hands with the clients." Overriding the tensions that afflicted the defendants was the longstanding conflict at the top. Yoshiko Hall recalls confrontations so intense between Goldblatt and Bridges that once they "almost had a fistfight" in a bar; Bridges and Hall also "teed off on each other" more than once.[68] Zalburg was accurate in suggesting that "the union was clever about not washing its dirty linen in public," notably the notion that Bridges was "not keenly fond of Goldblatt," nor of Hall for that matter. Unfortunately, these antagonisms were not as hidden as those involved might have thought; certainly their clashes were known to the men they negotiated with, including Howard Babbitt of the Big Five, which meant they were probably known to the prosecutors as well. The lineup at the top, with Bridges and Robertson squaring off against Hall and Goldblatt, was hard to hide.[69]

Zalburg contended that "they may [all] be bitter enemies really" but "they don't tell tales about each other." As he put it, they "don't talk stink about each other to strangers" and were well aware of "the great harm that can come out of talking out of school." This approach was a talent that came naturally to Hall, who was a "great poker player" and thus not easy to provoke.[70] However, once Esposito went out drinking with Hall, Bridges, and Goldblatt; one thing led to another, and they wound up denouncing each other, while intoxicated.[71] If J. R. Robertson had been present, he probably would have joined in, so hostile was he to Hall and Goldblatt—as he had difficulty in deciding which of his two co-leaders was "the most insecure person I've ever known in my life."[72]

Still, too much can be made of this bitter infighting, particularly since it did not prevent the parties involved from uniting on a common platform. Moreover, Judge Wiig was favorably impressed with the defense, while the "government attorneys caused me considerable concern." The chief prosecutor "wasn't in Gladstein's class" and, quite improperly, "would do anything to get a conviction."[73]

Since he had lived in the islands for a while, Wiig may have been aware of the obvious factor that distinguished Hawai'i from the mainland—its demographic makeup—which often made residents, notably in Honolulu, not as prone to be stampeded by conservatism. Four of the seven accused were of Japanese extraction, and the community of Japanese descent, the plurality in the isles, was heavily represented in the ranks of progressivism generally. The grand jury that brought the indictment, on the other hand, had a disproportionate number of whites[74]—that this minority generally constituted upwards of 70 percent of grand juries was a source of irritation island-wide.[75]

After various pretrial motions, the actual trial did not begin until more than a year after the arrests. Once it did start, Paul Crouch was the first witness. A tall man, nattily dressed in a tailored suit, he belied his smooth image by testifying in a shrill voice. He spent 27 hours on the witness stand for the prosecution, recalling his time in the islands during the 1920s, when he claimed to have led the initial movement of Marxists there. He was a lonely figure when not testifying, with even the staff of prosecutors seeming to shun this stool pigeon with a confessed "vivid imagination."[76] Yet Crouch's labored testimony was emblematic of the trial: he had little knowledge of radicalism in Hawai'i since the 1920s, and while he was on the stand, the prosecutors spent much of their time introducing "evidence" of Marxist and Leninist writings on insurrection and revolution that were then imputed to the defendants. The trial involved an ironclad syllogism, to wit: witnesses like Crouch were "Communists" who studied Marx and Lenin, and these long-deceased Europeans advocated revolution; the defendants were "Communists" who studied Marx and Lenin too; ergo, the defendants were guilty of violating the Smith Act. As A. L. Wirin put it, the Smith Act was akin to laws promulgated by the licentious Roman Emperor" Caligula, laws "which . . . nobody understood and under which anybody might find himself on trial."[77]

The trial was persnickety slogging as a result, targeting ever tinier points and with virtually every question eliciting an objection from one side or the other. There may have been method to the prosecution's madness, however, for the trial was almost inherently demobilizing, with many in the courtroom fighting to stay awake.[78] Workers asleep in the courtroom and not raising hell at the workplace was just the image that the union's enemies wanted to see.

It was a hard case to defend, given the very nature of the charges, which—fundamentally—placed ideas on trial, as opposed to overt acts. It did not take long before grumbling began to grow louder about the defense, grousing that was helped along by preexisting animus toward some of the lawyers. Jack Hall received a lengthy complaint—possibly from Bridges—that was blunt, expressing concern about the jury being caught in the weeds of dissecting Marxist terms; what was demanded instead was a stipulation admitting these tomes into evidence, without attorneys reading them into the record.[79]

That approach was easier said than done, particularly when part of the demonstration effect the prosecution intended was precisely quoting at length from tattered volumes of long-dead revolutionaries about the presumed immediate feasibility of an uprising. These lengthy readings had a deadening impact. One journalist confessed to having been "lulled by the labored reading of documentary evidence to the point where he wrote [that] three government prosecutors were sound asleep when he meant three spectators."[80] The courtroom itself, about 2,100 square feet in size, was divided roughly in half by swinging doors; there was no armed guard, and if there had been, his job might have been to quiet snoring spectators.[81]

Tout le Hawai'i was present at this sleepy human drama—students, merchants, housewives, office workers. They were dressed in business attire and Hawai'i style—colorful aloha shirts and muumuus. There were servicemen in khakis and well-dressed women wearing hats with veils. But since the ILWU mandated that each unit or gang in longshore would have a day assigned to attend court, union members often filled the 125 seats.[82] The boredom of the proceedings, however, quickly caused a sharp drop in attendance.[83]

Despite the somnolence, heads may have snapped to attention at some of Crouch's testimony, which beggared belief. At one point Gladstein confronted him on cross-examination: "I think you had told us that [there were] some 500 persons whom you had personally brought into the Communist Party, obtained signed applications for membership"—all this in the 1930s, when even during its heyday in the 1940s, there were no more than 300 Reds at any time in the islands. Unfazed, Crouch droned on.[84] Gladstein's remonstrative shaking of his forefinger at the witness led Crouch to lean over the railing of the witness stand and shake his finger right back at the lawyer—then the addled witness responded in a shouting voice.[85]

Shortly after Crouch's testimony, the sound of a falling body was heard, and spectators jerked their heads in time to see the prosecutor, feet in the air, clutching at a chair that had slid out from under him. Evidently he was not fainting in amazement at what he had heard, but because of a reason related to his health:[86] the prosecutor had to undergo an emergency abdominal operation and was replaced.[87]

Like a ghost of Christmas past, Ichiro Izuka came to the stand to reprise his story of Communist perfidy. Symonds trapped him in one inconsistency after another, and the rattled witness began to speak ever more rapidly in response, at times making little sense and even contradicting what he had told the House Un-American Activities Committee. He did acknowledge the many meals he had eaten at the home of the Halls and how he had slept there when he had nowhere else to go. The circuslike atmosphere was enhanced by the presence in the courtroom of a pro-prosecution cheering section of We the Women, the Broom Brigade, and other white housewives who apparently did not have jobs to occupy their time during the days that the lengthy trial unfolded.[88]

Another former ILWU member who testified for the prosecution was Henry Johnson Jr., born in Hilo in 1921. He had joined the CP in 1945, and high drama ensued when he pointed to Jack Hall, attired in a brown coat and light blue shirt, and implicated him as a member of the organization. Johnson had served on the Big Island in 1946 as business agent for Local 142 of the ILWU. By 1947, however, he was singing like a bird to the FBI; the defense contended that his disaffection stemmed from the charge of having mishandled and personally appropriated some of the union funds.[89]

One prosecution witness, Emil Muller, might have been excused, had he fainted with chagrin when he was asked if it was true that he had been expelled from the CP after he was found to be "going out with the wife of another Communist Party member while [said] member was away at sea."[90] Resplendent in white coat and dark slacks, the witness reacted to such undermining questions by going on the defensive, seemingly frightened. He grew angry, and the attempt to rehabilitate him by the prosecutor, John Walsh of New York, was unavailing, as the witness cracked his knuckles and looked glum. The depressed witness was accused by the defense of having been drunk at some of the alleged CP meetings he was said to have attended.[91] As this low comedy was unfolding, the defendants sat mostly expressionless at the witness table.

The prosecution's fortunes appeared to improve after Daisy Caden Van Dorn was sworn in as a witness. She was 68 and had 11 grandchildren and a grandmotherly mien. She had been a Red herself but had joined the FBI payroll, receiving the then queenly sum of $125 per month for services rendered and an additional $150 from other sources. She had worked in San Francisco, where the CP had offices on the seventh floor of a prominent building—"they had the whole floor with the exception of three rooms," she said. It had been in September 1946 that she spoke with Dwight Freeman there, who was on his way to the islands to serve as a party organizer, and the following year she met Charles Fujimoto. But her ability to identify these men as Communists was not her primary value to the authorities, for she regularly emptied the wastebaskets at the party offices and placed what she found in a safe destined for FBI perusal. She had joined the CP herself during the war at the FBI's behest and was well trusted by the party; California Communist leader Bill Schneiderman "said I was the only one he could trust his brief case with [since] he knows it was never tampered with or touched or opened," she said, in a tacit testament to Red folly.[92] "Bloody Daisy," as she was known colloquially, operated the elevator in the building as well and had many opportunities to eavesdrop on conversations as she headed to the seventh floor.[93] The "sweet little old grandma," as she was also called, testified that she had been told that "blood will run in the streets" during the Communist Revolution. According to an observer, however, she was "later tossed to the wolves" by the prosecutors, who "stipulated that Mrs. Van Dorn had lied to Judge Wiig when she claimed to have corrected lies told earlier in the Los Angeles Smith Act trial." Defense demands for a mistrial were promptly rejected.[94]

John Lautner, also a former CP functionary, testified for weeks. Born in 1902 in Hungary, he joined the CP in 1929, while toiling as a bricklayer. Unlike Van Dorn's, his testimony focused on arcane and potentially inflammatory points of Communist doctrine, which were then imputed to the defendants.[95] Verbal hand grenades were detonated when he sought to shout down defense counsel, who noted that though he was a chief witness, he had never met the defendants. As he spoke, the chatter of an air drill being used nearby began drowning out his voice—but not its effect.[96] He did not seem as reluctant to testify as his fellow apostate Robert McBurney Kempa, who spoke softly out of the right side of his mouth, causing Gladstein to complain that "I hear about every other word."[97] A tall, nervous man with a mess of thinning hair, the 29-year-old worker sat with his hands clasped in his lap, his dark eyes rarely straying. Born in Harbin, Manchuria, he had once been chairman of the CP branch in Pālolo.[98] At one point a recess had to be called when the Royal Hawaiian Band began performing its regular Friday concert at the bandstand of the ʻIolani Palace, drowning out the voices of those who were seeking to be heard.[99] This occurred more than once[100]—which the nervous Kempa may have appreciated. Things were not helped by the nature of the courtroom, for the noise from every truck, car, or motorcycle passing by outside made it difficult to hear witnesses' testimony.

Like a number of other witnesses, Kempa too was financially overstretched, providing an incentive to join the government payroll. He had borrowed heavily from his comrades—then paid them back by turning against them in court. His closest friend was Dwight Freeman. When Kempa's car was demolished, it was Freeman who rushed to his aid, he said, just as the Reineckes had provided him with the shoes on his feet. But, supposedly, his wife's family had been pressuring him to abandon the CP when, fortuitously, the FBI paid him a visit with the aim, he said, of enlisting him in a campaign to oust Hall from his ILWU post. His father worked for the US Navy in San Pedro, California, and apparently also had been pressuring his son,[101] a man who appeared haunted during his testimony[102]—a not uncommon occurrence among some witnesses.[103]

Given Kempa's reluctance as a witness, Jack Kawano's testimony was more helpful to the prosecution. He spoke of CP meetings with the likes of Hall, Edward Berman, A. Q. McElrath, et al. Kawano also placed J. R. Robertson at meetings of Hawai'i Communists. Yet despite speaking to prosecutors 20 times over a three-month period leading up to his testimony about what he would discuss at trial—"sometimes an hour and one half; sometimes an hour; sometimes even two hours," he said—and being on the witness stand as long as Crouch and Lautner, suggesting his importance to the case, he hardly painted a portrait of the defendants as bent on overturning the government, let alone advocating same. Instead, by speaking of Ariyoshi's time in China as a liaison between Chinese and Japanese Communists and Kimoto's service during the same time on behalf of US Naval Intelligence (and his radio broadcasts to Japan), he may have inadvertently undermined the prosecution's case. Likewise, it was not clear whose interests he was serving when he spoke glowingly of his experience in San Francisco at a CP school, defended the ILWU aid to the Reineckes when they were under fire, and criticized the booklet by Ichiro Izuka because of "misstatements and mistakes."[104] His heavy jowls quivered when he testified that CP membership had soared from 40 in early 1946 to 280 two years later;[105] his often riveting testimony, redolent with the isles' radical history,[106] may have explained why bailiffs turned away dozens of spectators from the courtroom as he spoke.[107]

An unbiased observer might well have wondered about the prosecution's case, particularly after University of Hawai'i librarian Carl Gerhart Stroven testified that the supposed books of subversion that underpinned the claim of advocacy of government overthrow (and served as the basis for the indictment) were to be found at the campus library.[108] Mabel Mildred Jackson of the territorial library said the same thing. If these texts were so dangerous, perhaps they should have been purged from these libraries—a thought that occurred to even the most diehard anticommunists.[109] Similarly, though the content of Ariyoshi's newspaper was at issue—"The indictment charges the 'Honolulu Record' was a part of the conspiracy," said Gladstein—the prosecution chose not to place reports from it before the jury.[110]

Likewise, the prosecution sought to block Charles Kauhane from testifying. A member of the territorial legislature, he had been with the Honolulu Police Department since 1924, where he investigated subversion. According to Gladstein, during that period Kauhane had found, "after a thorough investigation," not the "slightest evidence that any of these defendants ever advocated" what the indictment claimed.[111]

This wonderment may have increased when territorial senator John Duarte testified warmly on Hall's behalf,[112] followed by Mayor John Wilson of Honolulu.[113] The elderly Wilson laid his brown felt hat on the railing of the witness box, leaned forward, and peered through his familiar pince-nez before launching into a defense of Hall.[114] Senator Duarte of Maui, then 57 years old, was a hotel owner and a printer by trade[115] and spoke similarly.

Strikingly, a good portion of the archipelago's elite trooped to the witness stand to sing the praises of Hall in particular, a facet of this Smith Act trial that set it apart from its mainland counterparts. This lengthy list included Charles Hite, born in Arkansas, educated in Tennessee, and with roots on the mainland stretching back to 1607. A lawyer since 1917, a former deputy attorney general of the territory, and a former prosecutor, he was part of management at the American Stevedoring Company, where he negotiated with Hall's ILWU. In fact, the union was "against me," he conceded, when he served as chairman of the Central Committee of the Democratic Party.[116] This was all the more remarkable since a part of the trial record was a letter from Hite to then Governor Stainback expressing his "grave concern if not actual alarm" at the "sinister and insidious infiltration into our ranks of Communistic influence."[117]

Anthony Baptiste, a businessman who was the equivalent of Kaua'i's mayor, gave similar testimony, in that he did not seem overly disturbed about the existence of Communists.[118] Kimoto, portrayed as the most dangerous defendant of all, was nevertheless endorsed by prosecution witness Keisuke Ikeuchi, who was born in Japan but had lived in the islands for 29 years. Now on the staff of the Hawaiian Pineapple Company, he had previously been a scriptwriter and translator for a local radio station and the Office of War Information. Speaking haltingly, with some questions translated into Japanese for his benefit, he termed Kimoto a "very fine man and reliable man" who had "a very good reputation."[119] William Crozier of Maui was a leading Democrat there, and he spoke fondly of Ariyoshi at the trial.[120]

Harry William Lloyd, born in the islands, was a concrete mason and a hog farmer who also spoke highly of Ariyoshi, having discussed with him "taxes, water, leases, evictions and land monopoly." But what really impressed Lloyd was the time he arrived on Ariyoshi's doorstep with a complaint about the Waikiki School for the Blind, where his daughter, who was totally blind, was a student. There were "about 20 or 25 containers that [were] catching water that was leaking through the roof [there]," he recounted. "I thought that was awfully dangerous," he said, and so did Ariyoshi, who wrote about it in the *Record*, to Lloyd's everlasting satisfaction.[121]

The defense brought to the stand a succession of witnesses who testified to the defendants' probity. Edgar Allen Brenner of Kaneohe, a businessman who had arrived in Hawai'i in 1921 and served alongside Crozier at the highest level of the Democratic Party, called Ariyoshi a "very close friend of mine." Masashi

Arinaga—a carpenter for the Lihue plantation, a former scoutmaster, and a present Democratic Party leader—counted "about twenty to twenty-two thousand" people who made "voluntary contribution[s]" to this organization; he hailed Fujimoto as a "personal friend," plus his "sister was very pretty."[122] Another carpenter, Mac Masato Yamauchi of Maui, spoke enthusiastically of Reinecke, who "should have been a minister or a priest instead of a schoolteacher."[123]

Gladstein sought vainly to elicit admissions that this trial was all about destroying the ILWU. Samuel Wilder King, the territorial governor and real estate baron, was persuaded to testify finally. His prior two decades of service in the US Navy and eight years as the territory's representative in Washington were thought to provide him with credibility. Yet Gladstein reminded him of how he and Hall had "engaged in a very sharp argument concerning the prices at which you intended and tried to sell . . . pieces of property to the workers of the Oahu Sugar Company." And what about the company he formed during the 1949 strike that sought to unload cargo in an attempt to make scabbing profitable? Didn't he serve as vice president of this outfit? Heated words flew back and forth between witness and counsel, with Gladstein admonishing Governor King that since the reporter "can't take your words and mine at the same time, would you please wait until the question is finished?"[124]

King's predecessor, Ingram Stainback, was denounced in similar terms. During his testimony, Gladstein reminded Stainback of his "bitter denunciation of Jack Hall for . . . standing in the way of the desire of the plans of yourself and others to liquidate the Olaa Company" in an attempt to "make a stock killing amounting to many thousands of dollars." And what about the *Honolulu Record*, which "for years has been in favor of extending land ownership in this territory and has expressed criticism of you"?[125] A similar tack was taken with Frank Fasi, businessman and Democratic Party leader. Gladstein asked him about "having bought and paid for the votes of delegates from the outside islands" when he ran for party office.[126]

Nancy Corbett, the spouse of Judge Gerald Corbett, testified that Hall had a "bad" reputation for loyalty to Washington; then she conceded that her father-in-law had hotly opposed the 1949 strike and that she was an anticommunist activist.[127] Farrant Lewis Turner, residing in Hawai'i since the pivotal year of 1895 and thus quite familiar with armed revolt against legitimate authority, confessed that he was a leading member of "IMUA," the anticommunist spearhead, and that his firm had been deeply affected by the 1949 strike. Yet he too claimed that Hall was not loyal to the United States,[128] and Jan Cipar, president of Inter-Island Contracting Company, spoke similarly of Freeman.[129] Harold Chapson, president of his eponymous firm, which dealt in machinery, was a proud Republican—and also proudly denounced Reinecke, though he did not know him.[130] Once in a particularly aggressive cross-examination, Gladstein spluttered, "I notice that whenever I ask a question that uses the word 'Dillingham' there is a great deal of objection."[131]

As the trial proceeded, increasingly every seat was taken, with the judge refusing to permit any more standees.[132] Those present were treated to moments of rank absurdity, such as the time when the prosecutor was droning on and on, reading into the record material about the inevitability of violent revolution—which was then imputed to the defendants (ironically, in a colony that had been seized precisely by force and violence)—when he was interrupted suddenly by a mynah bird that alighted just as he was beginning to speak of the state's withering away. Unmoved by it all, the bird flew in through a window and circled the courtroom several times before coming to rest on a chandelier above the prosecution table, where it perched and listened with apparent disinterest as the proceedings went on.[133]

Absurd touches such as this belied the real stakes at play. As the trial began, there was a waterfront work stoppage that threatened Honolulu and the entire archipelago with shortages of flour and animal feed.[134] A shipping strike on the West Coast of the mainland predictably contributed to dislocation in Hawai'i and hoarding of retailers' and wholesalers' stocks of rice, canned milk, and other basics,[135] including potatoes.[136] At the same time, blood continued to be shed in Korea in a war widely perceived as a righteous battle against Communist encroachment. These were all-too-familiar reminders of the sedition that the defendants were said to represent. After an eloquent appeal for acquittal that lasted 15 hours and 9 minutes over a period of five days and kept the packed courtroom hushed through the final hot afternoon, Gladstein slumped into his chair, shirt collar wilted and awry.[137] Gladstein had made a show of it, leaning on the lectern, chatting amiably, shouting, whispering, winking conspiratorially, squinting for effect. He rapped his knuckles on the lectern, dragged it across the floor, wrote on a blackboard, sneered at prosecutors, fingered his moustache, bounced, and paced the floor—and, of course, lectured on the law. By the end, he seemed to be out of breath.[138]

Finally, in late June 1953, as a truce was being brokered in Korea, the Hawaii Seven stood before Judge Wiig in Honolulu to receive their punishment after being adjudged guilty as charged. Hall and five of the defendants were given five-year terms and fined $5,000 each, while Eileen Fujimoto received a three-year term and was fined $3,000. Indicted on 29 August 1951 and brought to trial on 5 November 1952, they had endured the longest trial in the history of the colony.[139] Hall was visibly shaken as the verdict was read, the fabric of his shirt seemed to tremble as he breathed and pressed his lips together. Kimoto blinked rapidly and moistened his lips with his tongue, while the others seemed similarly distressed.[140]

Labor was bound to be dissatisfied with these verdicts. In late January of that same year, Hall had addressed 300 cheering, stomping union delegates for 45 minutes. Though his trial was ongoing, wisely he focused on the fate of the workers and their attempt to garner medical benefits from employers.[141] In March, 1,500 people had attended a rally in tiny Kaua'i to hear accounts of the trial in one of the largest assemblages in the island's history.[142] Days later, 5,000 heard Hall and Gladstein speak at a rally in Maui. Workers sat under swaying palm trees and stood in an open pavilion out in the hot sun; others stood in long lines that led to barbecue pits, cold drinks, and assorted foods—then feasted on the angry words of protest they were fed.[143]

Hence, the response of labor to these verdicts was sharp and immediate. Shortly after the verdict was returned on Friday at 12:45 p.m., ILWU members began leaving their jobs in protest. Hall announced an indefinite suspension of contract talks with the longshore industry as work on the docks came to a standstill in Hilo and Honolulu. Sugar workers began shutting down plantations on the Big Island in a protest that quickly spread to neighboring islands. By Monday about 20,000 workers in the longshore, pineapple, sugar, and miscellaneous industries were on strike. Longshoremen at McCabe, Hamilton and Renny Company closed civilian stevedoring operations at Pearl Harbor for three days, the longest shutdown ever at the naval base. Throughout the territory on six islands, the protest demonstration was historic, surpassing the demonstrations after the detention of Harry Bridges. The jury in the Smith Act case deliberated for 19½ hours, but its verdict was to resonate for years to come.[144]

Ariyoshi was among the defendants who spent a brief spell in jail, the "eyesore of Iwilei Road," is how he later described his temporary abode in Honolulu. He was placed in a small cell—10 by 6 by 7 feet high—with another inmate. The cells were so small that the two occupants could not stand and stretch at the same time without bumping into each other. One had to sleep or sit on the double bunk bed while the other moved and exercised in the narrow space beside it. Three walls were concrete, and the front, facing the passageway between the rows of cages, was a crisscross of steel bars. Each cell had a padlock, and the entire cell block was padlocked at both ends of the passageway. Lighting was poor; no electric bulb was in any cell. There was one toilet—for about 40 prisoners. Each cell had a bucket, and nightly, just before bedtime, a guard opened one cell at a time and allowed the inmates out to use the toilet and fill the bottom of the bucket with water. A disinfectant was added to the water. Ariyoshi had read of the experiences of the leaders of the 1909 sugar strike, led by the Japanese, who too were imprisoned at Iwilei Road, and he was struck that decades later conditions had hardly changed.[145]

But what had changed was the climate for labor organizing and radicalism, and thus Ariyoshi's time in prison was quite brief. In a sense—and in stark contrast to what was happening on the mainland—he and the movement he represented did not emerge from jail to espy a carcass of a radical movement. Hawai'i was to remain a bastion of progressive strength, but the tocsin had been sounded on its previous destiny as a bellwether of radicalism.

CHAPTER 14

The Trials of Racism and Radicalism

Neither time—nor racism—stood still as the Smith Act trial hurtled toward conclusion. Or so thought Frank Marshall Davis. As Richard Gladstein and his colleagues were busily filing pretrial motions in the summer of 1952, the stocky journalist—now well settled in Honolulu—continued to complain about island racism. Though he counted only 1,000 African-Americans in the isles, there were persistent "efforts by certain influential elements to keep Negroes out of Hawaii."[1]

More than this, Davis felt that the rich ethnic stew that was Hawai'i had led to a bewildering array of tensions that soared far beyond the black-white dyad that defined the mainland.[2] Davis knew that the kind of bigotry routinely visited upon Negroes set the stage for a broader expansion of bias. Thus a number of taverns in downtown Honolulu were accused of barring Negro military men returning from Korea and, as well, indigenes, Filipinos, and Japanese.[3]

Robert McElrath concurred.[4] He sought to connect this ongoing pestilence of prejudice with the obtaining political climate. Quoting at length from a legal brief in another Smith Act case filed by the prominent African-American attorney Earl Dickerson, he argued that this draconian law had suffocating consequences for minorities—who often sought radical solutions to their plight.[5] The McCarran Act had an especially baneful impact in the archipelago, said McElrath, since this law was seen as being particularly harmful to the interests of aliens, of which Hawai'i had a profusion: 8,000 aliens there had failed to comply with its strictures by the end of 1951.[6]

This was the atmosphere in which the Smith Act trial unwound in Hawai'i, and it was inevitable that those involved in the events in the courtroom would not escape unscathed.[7] One witness, business executive Richard Kimball, was accused by the defense of being a racist. He had served three times as a member of the territorial legislature—the first two times as a Republican, and the third time as a Democrat. But Gladstein chose to impeach his credibility by arguing that during the war Kimball had suggested that those of Japanese ancestry in the archipelago were disloyal to the United

255

States and that his present claim that certain defendants could not be loyal was simply a reprise of his wartime charges. The fiery barrister asserted accusingly, "You asked that they remain in the territory because they were needed to work the plantations but they should be interned on Sand Island at night." Kimball denied this claim, saying that he advocated only that they be interned—but not at Sand Island. It was in early January 1942 that Kimball declared, "'[The] vast majority of the Japanese would be loyal to us just so long as we were on top. But they would turn just as soon as the tide began to turn.'" Kimball argued at the trial that since some of his best friends now were of Japanese ancestry, he should now be trusted by this community.[8]

The glowering witness spat many of his responses at Gladstein, who now smelled blood in the water. The crafty San Francisco lawyer responded with extreme politeness, thereby highlighting for the jury—which included a complement of Japanese-Americans—the kind of aggression that Kimball had displayed in January 1942. At times Gladstein strolled silently away from the witness box, leaving the witness to bathe in his own shouting rant, his face flushed, his lips quivering, and his eyes glaring.[9] Sensing that this approach might be insufficient, the prosecution went on the offensive, charging that the defense was "injecting Jim Crowism" into the trial, a reference to the increasingly discredited system that soon was to be junked officially by the elite itself.[10]

Politics in the islands were different from what obtained on the mainland, not least because of the islands' preponderance of men and women of Asian-Pacific origin who, for varying reasons, had reason to believe that the white elite was more concerned about preserving its privileges than anything else. And in any case, how could this elite, which had overthrown the monarchy by force of arms in the living memory of many islanders, blithely accuse others—with skimpy evidence, no less—of attempting the same?

Though the question of racism seemed to have no impact on the verdict rendered, it prepared the local battlefield for a larger conquest of hearts and minds. Thus, when Irwin L. Otterson, an employee of the University of Hawai'i testified, this 32-year-old former resident of Texas was peppered with inquiries about his past assertion that he preferred the Lone Star State "because my kind of people live [there]." The prosecution objected stoutly, but incrementally the defense was building the case that what was at play was an illegitimate, racially driven assault by the government.[11]

This approach did not win over the jurors, but as the walkout of workers suggested after the verdict, it probably influenced the larger jury of public opinion. Gladstein and his colleagues, for example, had tried to fold subtly into their antiracist defense of Charles Fujimoto a civil liberties defense, making them seamless. Otterson's racial imprecations about Hawai'i were equated with an anticommunist prosecution. That the opposing team of lawyers may have sensed this subtly effective turn became apparent when Gladstein had to remind

During the 1952–1953 anticommunist prosecution, the union launched a major public relations offensive, and—unlike in the mainland—was able ultimately to prevail. Courtesy of Anne Rand Library, ILWU–San Francisco.

them as their voices rose dramatically in protest, "I can't out-shout you. I have tried it and I have to admit to failure."[12] At the same time, the ILWU itself was claiming that the prosecution "has as little regard for persons of Oriental ancestry as his assistants who displayed obvious contempt for Japanese, Hawaiian and Filipino defense witnesses."[13] Whites were overrepresented (and those of Japanese ancestry underrepresented) in both the jury pool and the jury itself—which was nothing new.[14]

Thus, Gladstein questioned closely district court clerk William Thompson in the prelude to the trial,[15] bringing out the racism that was embedded in the entire process[16] and could infect the results of the trial.[17] The defense sought valiantly to combat this trend, striking from the pool William J. Paris, who had served in the US military in eastern Europe and been involved in "border incidents with the Russians and the Communistic Czechs" that had soured him on the Left (he felt that Reds were "not worthy of citizenship in the United States of America" and "should have a one-way trip given to them to Russia"). This foreman of the W. J. Paris Ranch declared nonetheless that "I would be able to give them a fair and impartial trial." His being excused from serving as a juror did not eliminate the reality that the archipelago's jury pool was composed disproportionately of white men who had served in the military—not an ideal situation for the defendants.[18]

Delbert Metzger, a jurist under fire for his supposed pro-radical bent, was unsympathetic to the prosecution's claims. By the time of the trial, he had lived in the islands for more than a half century and had served with the military and as an elected official in the territorial senate. President Roosevelt, whom he knew personally, had appointed him to the bench, and at the trial Metzger praised Jack Hall's "fearless honesty."[19] Earlier, he said it was irrefutable that there was an undue proportion of jurors who were haoles; furthermore, it was also irrefutable, he said, that the district and the section of Hawai'i where most of the working class resided were not proportionately given a share of the jury pool.[20]

Dapperly dressed as ever in a dark three-piece suit in defiance of the warmth of the day, and with a small red orchid in his lapel, Metzger clashed acutely with Judge J. Frank McLaughlin over this fundamental issue of racism, declaring it basically unfair that haoles were so grossly overrepresented in both juries and jury pools. Flames of discord were leaping during a tetchy hearing on this fraught matter: this "sudden war" between two respected jurists, as it was described by one observer,[21] featured a sharp, biting tone by McLaughlin,[22] though another commentator called it judicial slapstick and a "sad day indeed when two highly placed federal judges wash their dirty linen in the full view of the public."[23] More to the point, the confrontation between the two was an indication that there was no unified haole bloc in favor of jailing the defendants—or in favor of maintaining the unjust privileges of haoles, for that matter.[24] Nevertheless, right after the verdict, one juror—David Fuller—claimed that he was afraid of retaliation against his family if he voted not guilty.[25] One juror—it was unclear if it was Fuller or not—said that he joined in the verdict for fear of economic retaliation if he did not.[26]

There was a nagging fear that the FBI had exerted undue influence on the jury,[27] not to mention the overriding political atmosphere. Just before the arrests of the Hawaii Seven, five University of Hawai'i deans and more than 200 faculty members publicly protested what the press termed an "anti-Red bill" that targeted the campus, mandating—among other things—loyalty oaths.[28]

There was objection to this measure.[29] Yet even Fujimoto, whose academic background brought with it a certain sympathy, was derided by the local press as "the [ventriloquist] Edgar Bergen whose none-too-well disguised voice he conveys sits not in Honolulu but in the far-away Kremlin"[30]—and this was a difficult charge for sympathizers to confront.

Nevertheless, even Fujimoto—who was certainly harder to defend than, say, Hall, since he did not have thousands of constituents primed to march on his behalf—was a difficult target for the prosecution, given his previous academic post and his ethnicity. Dr. G. Donald Sherman, a soil expert summoned by the prosecution to testify against him, seemed apprehensive about the besmirching he was tasked to perform. The pudgy and bespectacled 48-year-old often mumbled, which made it difficult to understand him, given the problematic acoustics of the courtroom, and he did not help things by even more frequently clapping his hand to his mouth. He appeared troubled; once or twice it seemed he was about to burst into tears, and the next moment, as if he was about to bow his head in prayer. Though he did manage to assail Fujimoto, he also undercut his own testimony by calling Fujimoto a "first class scientist"[31]—as he bit nervously the knuckles of his clasped hands.[32]

Dr. Sherman's evident unease was not unique to him and was quite understandable, for enormous anticommunist pressure had been placed on his employer. Even Linus Pauling, a celebrated scientist, had his invitation to dedicate the new chemistry building at the campus withdrawn after an outcry about some of his more outspoken political stances.[33] Some campus authorities ignited a spirited debate on campus when they sought to bar union members from distributing leaflets protesting the regnant political climate. More than 400 students packed a raucous meeting in the wake of the burning of ILWU materials and the threatening of those who were passing them out.[34] In turn 170 professors signed a petition opposing curbs on their civil liberties.[35]

There were crushing pressures of varying sorts on all the parties involved. The defendants faced prison, which helped impel them to engage in sharp contestation with their lawyers. Five months into the trial there had been eight cases of reported illnesses of the major players, including a switch of both the judge and the chief prosecutor in midtrial. There were taut nerves and strained emotions, with Judge Jon Wiig himself leading the way, falling ill twice.[36] "Scores more of our members," said Hall, "particularly aliens, have been pressured and threatened many times both by agents of the FBI and the Immigration Department," which was not easing nerves rubbed raw.[37] "We are presently confronted with the problem of Coast Guard screening down here," complained one ILWU staffer, referring to an ongoing purge.[38] Angst and maladies were to be expected, for this trial sat astride an unbridgeable chasm between

Hawai'i, where anticommunism was not the hegemonic civil religion, and the mainland, where, in law and practice, anticommunism was precisely that. And it was the mainland's law and practice that ruled in Hawai'i, trapping all parties in a nether land between reality and ideology.

These fraying tensions were reflected not only in Dr. Sherman's tortured courtroom performance. They could also be espied in the courtroom appearance of John Guard, the gruff stevedoring boss who was also, he said, a 33rd Degree Mason.[39] An executive at McCabe, which, along with Castle and Cook, dominated the docks, he initially appeared on Jack Hall's behalf.[40] But weeks later he again ambled casually to the witness stand, wearing a khaki windbreaker over his white shirt and tie—though his explosive words belied his apparent informality. For in one of the trial's most dramatic moments he retracted his earlier testimony in which he had spoken positively about Hall. The prosecution was jubilant, the defense downcast, as could be seen in their eyes and smiles—or frowns. Surprise, anger, and worry were etched on the faces of the defendants—who would renege next? Guard explained himself by simply asserting that a number of his colleagues at McCabe had criticized his earlier appearance.[41]

Attitudes were hardening, particularly among whites, as a result of the trial. The conservative winds blowing from the mainland influenced them disproportionately. For example, Frank Fasi, a rising power in island politics, testified against the defendants during the trial, but, according to Hall, he had good reason to do so—beyond the obvious. He was known by some left-wingers as "Frank Fascist," though the best Hall could muster was that he was "really not that bad," just the "usual young, ambitious and somewhat ruthless guy that's trying to make a name for himself and acquire worldly goods." Fasi, of course, was anti-ILWU, befitting a man who had come to the islands as an ex-GI, got into the surplus racket with his veteran's preference, and apparently made "a pretty good hunk of loot," possibly the "biggest of the post-war crop."[42] Even if Fasi was not as bad as Hall drew him, this up-and-comer with dreams of filthy lucre dancing in his head had to wonder if it made sense to avoid denouncing a purported Red-led union at a time of an intense Red Scare.

The local and national press was also exerting wrenching pressure aimed at those who might bow to the left-leaning culture of Honolulu. The widely read *Saturday Evening Post* blared during the trial's height (in an article widely circulated locally) that "we almost lost Hawaii to the Reds"; according to the *Post*, the indictment had intervened not a moment too soon. With subliminal references to the "pink tinge in the sunset" and blunt references to an "Iron Curtain" descending in the lovely isles, the report no doubt was intended to be chilling. Thought worthy of note were the marriages of McElrath and Hall to "Orientals"—their "wives were to prove valuable as showpieces," said writer Richard English.[43] When Governor Oren Long took issue with the portrait presented and tepidly responded that Hawai'i was not "held captive" by Reds, it was understandable why few believed him.[44]

The local press long since had echoed many of these allegations.[45] Even the *Honolulu Star-Bulletin*, once deemed more realistic in assessing the ILWU, had retreated in the face of a possible boycott and was now featuring the writings of noted anticommunist Fletcher Knebel, who graced its pages with a multipart series titled "Stalin's Plot against America."[46]

Thus, the all-male, disproportionately haole jury—who came to court invariably dressed in a uniform of white shirt and sober tie (though some altered the pattern by daringly sporting two-toned shoes)—judged the defendants to be guilty.[47] "The jury was afraid to look you in the eye," said Koji Ariyoshi. "I tried to catch the Nisei's eye on the jury but he was afraid to look me in the eye."[48] Only one ballot had been taken, though there were heated arguments between and among the jurors. The most discussion focused on Hall, Ariyoshi, and Eileen Fujimoto. In between debate about the defendants' guilt or innocence, they played checkers and other board games. They were not sequestered during the trial but claimed they were shielded from external influences since articles about the trial were deleted from their newspapers, and when they would attend parties, "as soon as we walked into the room, there'd be a dead silence," said one juror.[49]

So there was unanimity on the defendants' guilt, and now the seven faced an uncertain future that seemed to point toward prison. Despite his toil and sacrifices, Hall admitted that he had "somewhat less than a hundred dollars the last time I checked on it in a joint checking account at the Bank of Hawaii with my wife." He added, "I have furniture and books worth perhaps three to four hundred dollars" and "I have two life insurance policies, each for a thousand dollars." The message was that he did not have the means to raise the $15,000 bail, nor the $5,000 fine—and he was still dickering with Gladstein and Bouslog about their ample fees.[50] Ariyoshi could not make bail and spent a week in jail before the money was raised—in contrast to Smith Act defendants elsewhere who mostly spent years behind bars after conviction. "I had only twenty dollars," he said.[51]

John Reinecke had to undergo a hernia operation and thus was unable to work after the trial, even at proofreading. Fortunately, his brother in Chicago stepped forward with $25,000 in cash bail. But Reinecke's morale remained strong, as did the union's, he thought.[52] Fortunately, the defendants' substantial political support meant that they were soon freed; after they had spent a few days in jail, the wealthy 87-year-old sculptor Julius Rosenstein, a Honolulu resident since 1899, posted bond[53]—and in return a doctor later refused to treat him, in political retaliation.[54] Territorial senator J. B. Fernandes, evidently had little concern about the impact on his electoral fortunes when he posted personal property as surety for Jack Hall.[55] Ray Jerome

Baker confided that he joined the senator and provided his valuable property in Honolulu "for bonding the [Hawaii] 7 during the appeal."[56]

Defense lawyers could not be indifferent to the knowledge that defending reputed Communists was not the ideal way to build a law practice during the apex of the Red Scare. During the 1949 CP trial in which Gladstein participated, after Judge Harold Medina handed out long prison terms to the defendants, he then hit the rambunctious attorneys with contempt citations that led them to prison also.[57] In the wake of the Hawaii Seven trial, Gladstein faced possible disbarment.[58] Speaking at an ILWU rally at Kalama Park in Kihei, Maui, before the trial concluded, Hall reminded those assembled that Judge Wiig had run for political office in 1946 and "his one campaign theme was opposition to so-called radical unions." Well, continued Hall, "we are the only one called radical and the only union of any consequence here, so he must have meant us." He wondered about the harsh treatment accorded to Metzger and pondered why Wiig was not treated similarly—and perhaps he would have been if he had been willing to rule democratically, Hall suggested.[59] Still, though he had conferred with the ferociously anticommunist Judge Medina, generally Judge Wiig did not conduct himself in a similarly confrontational manner; only twice did he have to gavel, using a glass paperweight[60]—except when it came to Bouslog.

While addressing ILWU members shortly after the trial began, Bouslog derided the trial of which she was a part, which was understandable. She was grilled in court about these remarks, but she did not back down, arguing that "apparently [the prosecutor] is not satisfied to try my clients" and now "he desires to try me." The judge intervened, informing her brusquely, "I am not satisfied with your explanation to the Court," and adding, "I am going to instruct the US Attorney to make a further investigation." Bouslog found it "unfortunate that the Court refers it to the prosecution whose conduct I was criticizing." This subsequent serpentine investigation caused Bouslog herself to hire counsel, and she barely escaped disbarment—or worse.[61] During her controversial remarks, Bouslog had spoken eloquently of the "unlawful conducts of the FBI here in Hawaii": "We know and can prove that they have placed Dictaphones in homes, have unlawfully tapped telephones, [and] have seized personal books and papers without search warrants."[62]

That Bouslog was fingered as a Red as this process was unfolding did not aid her case.[63] The intimidation she felt was not unique to her.[64] Others were ensnared as well,[65] as the business of political surveillance boomed.[66]

The perception that Hawai'i—this unsinkable aircraft carrier in the Pacific—was essential to national security was evident in the apparent increase of FBI agents patrolling Honolulu,[67] a presence that was reflected in dramas involving the airwaves.[68] In a direct challenge to McElrath's union-oriented radio broadcasts, IMUA (meaning "moving forward" in the language of indigenes)—a "fascist outfit," as Ray Jerome Baker described it—had begun a program immediately following McElrath's, its antithesis, and basically sought to refute his every word.[69]

Yet while the US authorities were investing heavily in surveillance and trials (and their citizen counterparts, in radio programs), an even more notorious electronic initiative was put forth—a plot intended to compel Jack Hall to defect from the ranks of the ILWU. McElrath was slated by the FBI as the conduit for the plan, and thus he invited the FBI to talk things over. They met near the Kaimukī fire station near 14th Avenue in Honolulu. But the hunter was captured by the prey; as the wily McElrath recalled it later, "[We] drilled a puka [hole] through the floor and put a microphone where the speaker was supposed to be [in] Dave [Thompson's] console radio. And the furniture was arranged so that when they talked, they talked into the microphone. And we're upstairs." Thus, "when we heard [the agents] walking up the driveway, Teddy [Kreps] and I went downstairs. When we closed the door it squealed. So we knew if we went out to pee, it would squeal." The discussion focused on separating Hall from his codefendants and guaranteeing he would be spared jail time. Instead the tapes of this subterfuge exposed government machinations.[70]

This was not the first time there had been an attempt to entice radical leaders. Ariyoshi recalled when John Burns visited him just before his arrest, he was accompanied by Mitsuyuki Kido, who proposed a similar plan.[71]

The attempts to co-opt Hall and Ariyoshi suggested how vulnerable local elites felt in the face of the radical challenge. They had held hearings to investigate the Reineckes, controversial statehood hearings, and House Un-American Activities Committee hearings; compelled union officials to sign non-Communist affidavits; engaged in various forms of harassment; and sought to place union leaders behind bars. And yet radicals and those who followed them refused to bend to their will. After the trial and conviction of the Hawaii Seven, the Big Five found that the ILWU, instead of being on the defensive, had upped the ante.

Perhaps 20,000 workers walked out after Hall's conviction. This marked the first time that local ILWU workers walked out in protest against a trial court decision, though in August 1950 thousands of workers had chosen not to work to protest the jailing of Harry Bridges. And in September 1952, when a federal court upheld Bridges' perjury conviction, 20,000 ILWU members quit work in a one-day protest. Mainland ILWU members joined in the 1952 protest but remained on the job during the 1950 and 1953 walkouts.[72] Surprise was expressed that the June 1953 walkout dwarfed that of 1950, suggesting that instead of being intimidated by the Red Scare, as was the case on the mainland, workers were emboldened.[73] Some thought that the defense had seemed noticeably nonchalant in the face of the trial and possible imprisonment, for it was during this period that Gladstein started ukulele lessons on the side,[74] and Reinecke doodled calmly in Japanese during court sessions.[75] Those who put the Hawaii Seven on trial may have wondered who precisely had lost when the defendants were convicted.

This climate of revolt obtained even when, during the midst of the trial, Hollywood megastar John Wayne arrived in Honolulu, along with future television hero James Arness, to make a film bashing Communists in Hawaiʻi. Strikingly, one of the loudest voices of condemnation of this production emerged from those who were coming to symbolize the fealty of Americans of Japanese Ancestry to the United States—the combat veterans from the war against Tokyo. Given the prominence of Ariyoshi, Fujimoto, Jack Kimoto, and many other leaders of the Left, the veterans were coming to be seen as their antipode, yet when they too denounced the embodiment of the anticommunist consensus—John Wayne—it was evident that not only did Hawaiʻi differ from the mainland but, as well, hammering the archipelago into line would be more than a notion.

This lurid film began with actual HUAC members on-screen with Wayne, who was playing one of their investigators, in their hearing room. During the course of the film a CP leader recommends murder of a fellow leader, and another suffers a nervous breakdown. The character played by Wayne—"Big Jim McClain," also the title of this extravaganza—visits a leper colony and then inquires if the spouse of yet another leader is a leper. Dan Liu, chief of police in Honolulu, played himself—though his acting skills were painfully deficient. Wayne's sidekick, played by Arness, is killed by Communists. The film dances daintily into the sensitive realm of race, as almost all the Communists are Euro-American (defying the prominent role in actuality played by Kimoto, Ariyoshi, Fujimoto, et al.), as if it would be too difficult to shed light on why those subjected to racism might turn to radicalism. A denouement of the film occurs when a raid takes place on a CP meeting and its leader contemptuously informs the Wayne character that "chopping cotton is for white trash and niggers"; the outraged HUAC investigator, incensed by this display of racism, promptly thrashes him violently, the message being that Communists were the vectors of a now discredited racism, and the HUAC the vindicator of anti-racism. After a routine attack on the Fifth Amendment protection against self-incrimination—thought to provide a cloak behind which Reds hid—the credits rolled, which included a grateful acknowledgment of the HUAC's cooperation. In sum, this was a gangster film with the Reds recast as the outlaws and the HUAC as the good guys.[76]

Every Communist in this film—as was typical of the era—was either a humorless tyrant, a psychologically corrupt individual, or just plain weird. Yet the movie was a solid hit with fandom, ranking 27th on the list of top-grossing films of 1952, though *Time* magazine was not impressed.[77] Filmed as the arrests of the defendants were grabbing headlines and screened as they were going to trial, this movie was a crude attempt to influence public opinion in Hawai'i and, more specifically, the jury pool.[78] It was the "strangest coincidence," said the *Honolulu Record*, that the film opened just as the Smith Act trial was beginning.[79] The movie, McElrath assayed, was designed to "hang Jack Hall and the other defendants to the sour apple tree alongside the body of John Brown."[80]

But, again, what may have been most remarkable in the long run about this otherwise forgettable film was its representation of racism, ignoring radicals of Japanese ancestry (of course, portraying these politicos would have meant hiring Asian-American actors, not exactly a Hollywood priority then).[81] Not only did the Communist employ racist epithets, but he also claimed class privilege, asserting, "I'm from the country club set." So at once, Red weapons of antiracism and sympathy for the downtrodden were turned against the usual wielders.[82]

Big Jim McClain did not play very well in San Francisco, the headquarters of cosmopolitanism, where the ILWU was founded.[83] More islanders were probably interested in it, since the production boosted Hawai'i's economy, providing a rare glimpse of the enchanting beaches and stunning vistas there. By one account there were thousands of islanders in the movie as background scenery and extras.[84] Thus an observer remarked that the movie was shown to crowded houses in the islands.[85] John Wayne made a cash contribution to IMUA, the vanguard of anticommunism in Hawai'i, and tourism was bolstered. Art Rutledge, the crusty AFL leader, snared a cameo role,[86] as did Vernon "Red" McQueen, sports editor of the *Honolulu Advertiser*[87]—certainly such glamorous exposure could not have hurt ongoing efforts to woo this important union federation or the mainstream press.[88] As for Wayne himself, after departing Honolulu, he became enmeshed in a nasty divorce punctuated by headlines that he "admitted that he was bitten by a strip-tease dancer [in Hawai'i] and charged his wife with acting like a streetwalker."[89]

The 442nd Veterans Club, during the height of the commotion about the arrests of Ariyoshi and his comrades, debated a resolution denouncing Wayne's movie, terming it by a comfortable majority a "libel on the people of Hawaii." Not at all seduced by this update of a cops-and-robbers plot, the film was said to have been "timed to appear when it was thought it might be helpful to the prosecution in this frame-up." Only the failure to garner two-thirds of the votes of those assembled barred this resolution from being acted upon.[90] Akira Fujiki, executive secretary of the group, testified at the Smith Act trial, and he confirmed that one of the chapters of the 442nd did assail the Wayne movie.[91]

In a sense, this resolution and subsequent testimony were not that surprising, given Ariyoshi's prominence as a war hero and the overall atmosphere in the islands, where increasingly anticommunism was being viewed as the last refuge of the haole elite.[92] The 442nd itself previously, at Fujiki's behest, had invited Hall to address its ranks on the pressing question of unemployment.[93] Richard S. Imada, known as "Open the Door," was a University of Hawai'i graduate and now a real estate man, but he was apparently not sufficiently concerned about his reputation to worry about testifying on behalf of a Communist, Ariyoshi, whom he had known "since my barefoot days."[94] Quite remarkable was the solid support that Japanese-American Communists received from those not so inclined ideologically. "No, I am not a Communist," said Russell K. Kono, who had been born on the Big Island and was a lawyer with a degree from the University of Michigan. He had met Ariyoshi in the military. "I knew him quite well," he said, and he viewed him quite positively.[95]

Yet even with this favorable sentiment toward defendants like Ariyoshi, the fact remains that this movie was not helpful to the defendants' cause, as it showed what emoluments could flow to those who played along with the anti-communist crusade.[96] How could such a mainland production not influence those like Judge J. Frank McLaughlin—and other jurists—who repeatedly made rulings adverse to the union's interests?[97] "We know that McLaughlin spoke to IMUA,"[98] said Hall. On the record, Hall was dumbfounded by McLaughlin's purported statement that Hawai'i was "at the mercy of a single labor union,"[99] a prejudicial comment[100] that mirrored those of Judge Wiig.

Serendipitously, Judge McLaughlin withdrew from the case in favor of Judge Wiig, a decision that ILWU leader Saburo Fujisaki termed a "big victory for us and a real break," since Wiig was seen as less retrograde. Whatever the case, Fujisaki's prodigious organizing was highly effective. By early 1952 there had been, he announced, testimonial picnics or dinners honoring Jack Hall, McCarran Act victim Simeon Bagasol, and their families on three islands. The latest was a buffet luncheon held in the new ILWU building in Honolulu—the building itself was a further testament to the union's staying power; and a picnic held on Kaua'i drew 1,500 persons, a huge percentage of the island's population.[101] The day after Labor Day in 1952, McElrath happily reported on radio that parades marking this occasion were attended by record turnouts of ILWU members and their families. On the island of Kaua'i, more people marched in the parade than there were members in the union. Between 4,000 and 5,000 members and their wives and children marched down the streets of Lihu'e, while on Maui and the Big Island there were record-setting crowds. In Honolulu approximately 5,000 people gathered on the grounds of city hall to hear Jack Hall.[102]

Hall had been quite busy, taking valuable time away from his union duties to drum up support on the mainland for the Hawaii Seven defense.[103] Bouslog intently studied the Smith Act defense in Los Angeles and brought home valuable lessons, along with legal memoranda and motions from that trial.[104] She was also in touch with a range of left-leaning lawyers on the mainland, including such legal wizards as Ben Margolis in Los Angeles, Frank Donner in New York, Aubrey Grossman in San Francisco, and Hy Schlesinger in Pittsburgh.[105]

Such efforts bore fruit when in Southern California a benefit luau was organized with proceeds to go to the defense.[106] This Polynesian affectation was effective in attracting many to the union's banner, as exemplified by one particularly successful fund-raiser featuring Bridges that included palm fronds, flowers, hula dancers, Hawaiian music, kalua pig, lomi salmon, chicken long rice, poi, beer, orchid leis, and other island features.[107]

Shortly after Labor Day, the union showed that it was hardly intimidated, when a territory-wide ILWU walkout began in response to a federal court decision upholding the conviction of Harry Bridges, J. R. Robertson, and Henry Schmidt. "All but one organized sugar plantation is completely shut down," McElrath exclaimed, noting that "practically all field divisions of the pineapple companies are down," while "the docks are idle." Threateningly, he added, "The stoppage will end at midnight tonight—unless some employer gets the idea to discipline the workers who failed to show up this morning." Employers and their allies did seem to have a steep learning curve, apparently forgetting that just after the 1949 strike began, Bridges was indicted and US attorney general Tom Clark reportedly had said that this charge would "straighten out the situation in Hawaii," but what actually occurred was another victory for the union.[108] Clearly irked by the present walkout, one editorialist wondered with sarcasm, "It just occurred to us: will the ILWU leadership call for a sympathy walkout of the rank and file on the day of Stalin's funeral?"[109]

If the idea behind the trial of the Hawaii Seven was to intimidate the union into retreat, it boomeranged, for what occurred instead was a heightened sense in the union's ranks that their gains would be jeopardized unless they accelerated their organizing. Thus, the frequency of ILWU radio broadcasts increased, with a focus on the trial, while a weekly summary of the proceedings was mailed to a list of 3,000. At the workplace there was a routine to ensure that the trial was discussed regularly, with a worker assigned to make a report on the trial. O'ahu workers regularly showed up at the trial, while those of the two huge sugar units—Honokaa and Ookala—did too. Four workers from Pa'auilo chose to spend their vacations at the trial, while the port of Māhukona chipped in with two.[110] Hall's colleague Theodora Kreps was among those who were overwhelmed by the support.[111] "Sometimes I wonder whether I'm worth it," Hall said only half-jokingly, referring to the expenses well in excess of $100,000[112] that went to defense efforts. (Before the trial started, defense attorney Myer Symonds had told Hall that the lawyers' fees would be $50,000—A. L. Wirin had asked for a $10,000 fee plus expenses, as did Gladstein.[113]) This was the outward cost of a debilitating trial of a union that challenged the Big Five.[114]

Yet the war and the trial, as destructive to the union's fortunes as they were, did not destroy it.[115] A few months after the sentences had been delivered, Hall addressed cheering and applauding members of Local 142, and unlike his counterparts on the mainland in analogous circumstances, he hardly seemed like a leader of a union in a deep defensive crouch. As if he were poking a finger in the eye of his antagonists, he first hailed his members who toiled at the *Star-Bulletin*, who had "one of the dirtiest jobs in Hawaii," since "they have to sell a newspaper which is busy attacking us more than any other force." But just as the trial may have perversely strengthened the union, the war might have had a similar impact. "The war economy [has] supplied in the last three years almost one-half of the dollars that have fed people and kept the wheels turning in this territory," Hall observed. "Prior to the start of that adventure, we had some 40 thousand unemployed in this territory—almost one worker out of four." But now, he argued, there were "at least ten thousand unemployed in this territory," a sharp change from the past. Despite the pounding the ILWU had absorbed, "all sections of our union are in better shape than they were a year ago," he said. Indeed, "the degree of organization is higher today," he claimed, "than it's ever been." It was not as if there were no storm signals; union membership was heading downward because of mechanization, speedup, and jobs being eliminated, and similarly unhelpful was ongoing hostility from the AFL. Nevertheless, it continued to be true that a chief victim of these negative trends—stevedores—enjoyed by far the highest wage rates, the best conditions, the best pensions, and an excellent medical plan in comparison with those of other workers in the archipelago. But there was a reason that the union was so enmeshed in politics, since many stevedores had lost their jobs precisely because the military had turned to civil service workers, which was national policy. "Another year," he said, "will see the introduction of bulk sugar in Honolulu as it already has seen bulk loading of sugar on the outside islands and perhaps another one hundred job opportunities will be lost."[116] Still, the union continued to hold certain advantages due to its own nimbleness.

This ability of the union to absorb the weightiest blows from its opponents and not only remain standing but punch back forcefully was enraging its foes.[117] Denouncing McElrath, a dyspeptic correspondent boasted, "First [I'm] a *white* man, pure white, clean and NOT a Communist,"[118] unlike the man he condemned. It was unclear if this angry man was involved when containers of red paint were splashed on the exterior of the recently opened ILWU headquarters in Honolulu and the Bouslog-Symonds law offices.[119]

Of the sprawling territory under the US flag, Hawai'i was a glaring anomaly, a seeming Red outpost in a nation immersed in anticommunism, a territory that was seemingly benefiting—in an exhibition of irony—from the conflict in Korea, as it continued to display a more determined antiwar attitude than the 48 states. Inexorably Hawai'i captured the attention of a gaggle of writers. Foremost among them were Jack Lait and Lee Mortimer, whose lurid accounts were monitored by the powerful Hawaiian Sugar Planters' Association. These two popular writers specialized in exposing the underside of various cities and regions, and when they turned their typewriters toward Hawai'i, it was a signal that the archipelago had arrived, establishing a firm foothold in the national consciousness.

Not all that Lait and Mortimer had to say was misguided. The rise of the air age did erode the islands' isolation while disintegrating the monopoly held by shipping, to the detriment of the Big Five, which were already under siege by the ILWU. By the time of the Smith Act convictions and appeal, three scheduled airlines were flying more passengers in a day to Hawai'i than ships carried in a month. This helped bring mainland underworld money for investment in hotels, as well as less pleasant entities. According to the writers, these planes were also bringing more Negroes—which in turn heightened the fears of the local elite, already heightened by the challenge from the ILWU. "The Negro influx is Hawaii's great tragedy," it was reported, made all the more complex since Negroes were "able to pass as Tahitians or Samoans," a trait that facilitated their seizing "most of the islands' vice"—an exaggeration at best but suggestive of the apprehensions engendered by arriving African-Americans. For it was evident that Negroes did not control what was termed "one of the most notorious red light districts in the world" or the proliferating gambling, which encompassed even "high school games" in Honolulu—"the only city in the U.S. where fixing high school games is major business" and "the only town where fixing of pro football games has been proven." According to these intrepid journalists, Honolulu was also becoming a center for a precursor of a gay and lesbian community—"Waikiki is the hangout of the mahus (fairies) who meet their soldier sweethearts there."[120]

This assault on Hawai'i by these writers was of a piece with the Smith Act trial and the rising concern on the mainland about the fate of what had become a troublesome colony. Yet McElrath was not alone in questioning the authors' emphasis on the purported tie between Negroes and crime, misguided at best, for when he mentioned the names of Honolulu's "vice kings" on the air, he said he received "two threatening phone calls."[121] Things had gotten so bad that Local 142 of the Hawai'i union passed a resolution decrying the archipelago's devolution into a "swindler's paradise"—"fleecers and swindlers of all kinds have had a field day," it was said with disgust, and this hardly was the fault of Negroes. But this allegation was part of the conservative atmosphere brought by the trial and convictions.[122]

Frank Marshall Davis was uniquely situated to analyze these developments, given his political leanings and sensitivity to the small but targeted African-American community. "The issue of communism is a smokescreen," Davis said, since "the solid core of the opposition is racism and the fear by white supremacists that those elected to Congress from Hawaii would back civil rights legislation."[123] As Davis saw things, the central issue was racism—masked by anticommunism[124] imported from the mainland.[125]

Seemingly, Davis' sensitivity to racism—which appeared to be more attuned to realities under the US flag than that of some islanders—was spreading. That was the impression left by Yasuki Arakaki after his trip to Chicago,
Davis' former home. "If you made a comparison with the Hawaiian sugar
workers at home, our conditions are very bad but I saw something worse [in
Chicago]," he said. "People live in destitution. And are they white people?
No, they are Negroes." He had witnessed a "a mob of about thirty whites"
seeking to rout Negroes who had just moved into their neighborhood. The
undaunted Arakaki, accustomed to facing down mean bosses, went out on
the porch of the home in which he was staying. "They said: 'where do you
come from?' I said: 'Hawaii.'" People in the mob asked, "'Do you have niggers
in your neighborhood?'" and he responded, "'We have a few, not many.'" Not
pleased when he refused to condemn miscegenation, they told him, "'Go
back where you come from.'" He left the next day but later found out that the
mob attacked the house in which he was staying. "That is the kind of treatment that Negroes are having in America," he concluded. "If we help Negroes we will help all the minority groups all over the United States." His
words were in the context of a lengthy debate at an ILWU convention, which
backed Paul Robeson and W. E. B. Du Bois as they faced persecution by the
authorities[126]—the point being that the anticommunist climate was bolstering Jim Crow, all to the disadvantage of the ILWU.

Thus, Ewart Guinier, one of the nation's top African-American trade
union leaders, was a union defender,[127] as was Coleman Young, a future Detroit mayor. Together with Harry Bridges, Young had sought funding from
Jack Hall for the cause of "Negro freedom"; and both Guinier and Young led
the National Negro Labor Council, which the ILWU in turn backed.[128]

On one point, Davis and his most determined detractors agreed: Hawai'i
was at a turning point in the wake of the defendants' conviction. Though
some appreciated the humor of the suggestion that the ILWU might stage a
sympathy strike to coincide with Stalin's funeral, others failed to see what
was funny about admitting into the hallowed union a land where the nation's
most dedicated enemies—Communists—seemed to be riding high and
thumbing their nose at what Washington held dear. Senator Ben Dillingham
of the territorial legislature—he of the fabulously wealthy family—was now
espousing the line that was to prevail by 1959, i.e., that statehood was needed
in order to foil the Reds. Speaking in Washington before the US Senate, as
the conflict in Korea was winding down, he gravely informed his fellow solons of this grim reality.[129] More voices were beginning to echo the line that
rejecting statehood for Hawai'i would be seen as racism, pure and simple, in
the pivotal battleground that was Asia.[130] Paul Crouch, the presumed reign-
ing expert on the Reds of Hawai'i, sobered the hearing, presided over by
Senator George Smathers of Florida, when he informed the no doubt stunned

legislators that "Red strength in Hawaii is '20 times' greater than in the U.S. mainland,"[131] an opinion that was echoed by others.[132]

But there was no unanimity in elite circles on how best to blunt the stiff challenge presented by the CP and the ILWU. Walter F. Dillingham, the godfather of what the Left called the "boss haole elite," still balked at statehood,[133] an opinion increasingly accepted.[134] Dillingham found it hard to accept that he had sunk his fortune into islands that were listing to the port side, a view he repeated at the time of the trial.[135] If a front-page *New York Times* headline from the same time were to be believed, however, Walter Dillingham had lost out to Ben Dillingham, for, referring to Hawai'i, it trumpeted: "Senators Forecast Statehood at an Early Date."[136] One problem for Walter Dillingham's side was that Senator Hugh Butler could not help but notice that there were "very few names from Hawaii of persons who oppose statehood that have gone in the record." He complained that "it makes it a little difficult to present a case,"[137] though these silent opponents argued that they feared harassment if they went public.

Still, opponents of statehood had a hard time understanding how absorbing Hawai'i into the Union would solve the Red problem. Leading GOP senator Arthur Watkins of Utah, who thought he knew a thing or two about the region since he had been born in the strategically significant island of Midway, wondered precisely what was going on in Honolulu and demanded a thorough investigation of Ingram Stainback because of his appointment of Jack Hall years earlier to the city's police commission and his appointment of the union's Ernest Arena to another high-level post.[138]

Senator Butler retained a clipping of a Davis column on which was scribbled, "This coon is working to stir up Japanese hatred of whites and is having quite a lot of success. . . . [S]tatehood now would put Hawaii at the mercy of the most vicious bunch of radicals in the world."[139] The Nebraska legislator was seeking protection from the FBI's J. Edgar Hoover for one of his island informants, Alfred Yap, who was facing a "very serious situation," apparently because his cover had been blown.[140]

This may have been true about Yap, but the audacious informant was still monitoring the local scene carefully, notably the busy intersection where race seemed to meet radicalism. Thus he found himself at Ala Moana Park in Honolulu at a three-day celebration of the Bon Dance, a Buddhist ritual conducted by war veterans, with a daily average of 30,000 attending, overwhelmingly from the population of Japanese descent. "Japanese supremacy has arrived at a stage where the local people are accepting it as a matter of fact" was Yap's contention, and it was a bar to statehood, he said.[141]

Leon Sterling Jr. of Hawai'i—a graduate of Oregon State University who worked for the Hawaii Employers Council, an ILWU antagonist—had concerns that paralleled Yap's and that he too shared with Senator Butler,[142] as did Emma Richey, a landlord in the archipelago.[143] William Tilley concurred, adding that "they use the labor organizations [which] are composed of non-Anglo-Saxons to strike against the haole owned businesses" and thus "many haole businesses are being taken over by Orientals." The "aim of statehood," he indicated, was "to quicken the process," as it "would mean that we would have a Japanese and/or Oriental state with a few white men with rings in their noses doing their bidding." He knew of what he spoke, as he was now contesting his "ouster from the Civil Service"; "this is one haole they are afraid of," he exhorted.[144]

But it was Yap who was the most insistent on this matter of racial privilege, telling the senatorial guardian of this dispensation that he could not comprehend why "a Caucasian [can't] be appointed" to certain posts. "Is the territory not Caucasian organized?" he asked,[145] making an apparently persuasive point that attracted the attention of a Mississippi defender of Jim Crow, Senator John Stennis.[146]

Butler's staff was concerned with the "large number of Japanese language motion pictures" exhibited in the islands—"they play to full houses," it was said.[147] The ever busy Yap was angered when "the largest theatre at Waikiki" held a world premiere of a war picture entitled *Go for Broke*, which he said had been financed by a "bunch of Jews in Hollywood, whose God is the almighty dollar." It was a "big fan-fare," with Van Johnson, the movie's star, as well as the governor, the mayor of Honolulu, and other luminaries, present for a film that he thought was insufficient in its castigation of Tokyo.[148] Like others in the isles, Yap did not seem to realize that a Cold War was in sway and Japan was no longer the top foe but, instead, had been enlisted in this new conflict and had to be treated accordingly. Still, for whatever reason, Senator Butler also maintained a "list of persons with Communist relationships who were in possession of firearms," with about 50 mostly Asian-surnamed persons counted.[149]

Rather than worrying about movies and guns, others in the islands were concerned about the national pastime. Jonathan Lee told Butler that he was appalled that "right in our midst a Japanese baseball team in the Hawaiian Baseball League [is] wearing the emblem of Japan, a rising sun on their caps." This logo had "been displayed by the Red Sox baseball team in the [HBL] since the end of World War II," unsurprisingly since "our local Jap citizens here have quietly contributed annually towards building up Japan's foreign exchange by regular U.S. remittances to Japan and by continuing their annual mass migration to Japan every spring to see those wonderful cherry blossoms." To Lee, this was inexplicable. "Why not go see the cherry blossoms on the banks of the Potomac[?]" he asked querulously of the "2,000 each year making this trek to Japan."[150] William Tilley, writing to Butler from Billings, Montana, had resided in the isles and had a similar complaint.[151]

Bill Borthwick continued to smart over the union's past opposition to his electoral bid.[152] Still upset, he now told Senator Butler that "it looks more and more to me like it will be very doubtful if the Republicans could elect two Senators from the state of Hawaii" and "they may not elect one." It was unclear to Borthwick why the GOP should add two Democratic senators to Congress, a growing consensus among the local elite now turning against statehood.[153] Borthwick also delivered this concern to the doorstep of the beacon of GOP conservatism, Senator Robert Taft of Ohio, telling him that Butler did not favor statehood and that Butler remained the only senator who had ever made an independent survey of the local situation. Senator Taft was informed that "the radical element here has elected our Mayor for four consecutive terms," while the now reviled Judge Metzger received more than 40,000 votes in the recent elections[154]—a concern that was receiving reinforcement from others.[155]

Senator Butler, attuned to developing national trends, told Senator Eugene Millikin of Colorado that it "seemed best to me [to] concentrate hard on one issue where we undoubtedly have public opinion on our side—namely, Communism—rather than lay ourselves open to possible criticism by bringing in other issues on which sentiment is divided, such as the race question"[156]— thereby confirming Frank Marshall Davis' suppositions. But Borthwick insisted that this approach was folly; he wanted a sharp focus on the "race question," notably with regard to those of Japanese ancestry—and others. "ILWU keeps 2 Jew lawyers who constantly stir up trouble," he said, a slighting reference to Bouslog and Symonds.[157]

But it was not only Senators Butler and Stennis who were getting an earful from constituents about the prospect of a supposedly Red-dominated Hawai'i entering the sacred Union. A concerned resident suggested to Senator John Sparkman of Alabama, "As a southerner and a white man, there must be some way that you can keep Hawaii from becoming a state[;] don't we have enough colored in this country now[?]" As this onlooker saw things, Hawai'i statehood meant "interracial marriage" and "racial intermingling," both dreaded prospects. "We also have Mexicans and Puerto Ricans," he cried. "Isn't there something that can be done to keep them from coming in?"[158] Edward Lewis of Winnetka, Illinois, felt similarly, alleging that there were "21,000 of second generation of Japanese of draft age who failed to enlist."[159]

On March 10, 1953, Senator Taft was informed by Hudson de Priest of Miami that "today was a black day in our history, if the House's vote to admit the Mongolian territory of Hawaii as a state goes on through the Senate." The perturbed supporter wailed, "I feel as sick over its action as if the Russians had landed in San Francisco for an invasion. We could repel the invaders, but we can never repel the Oriental invasion via Hawaii if we admit it as a state." Outraged, he stressed, *"Never before have we admitted a state until enough white americans had moved into it to ensure its continued Americanism."*[160]

There was good reason to protest in anti-statehood circles, for Senator Butler—the leader of these forces—switched sides. "I changed my position," he said in December 1952, attributing his decision to the legal pressure placed upon Bridges and the onset of the Smith Act trial.[161] "In the past I have felt that the Communist problem [made] statehood undesirable," he said, "but now the Hawaiian residents seem to have this problem under control and I do not believe there is any legitimate ground on which we can deny them statehood any longer."[162] Opponents of Butler's new position had grounds to think that the premise on which the senator had based his switch—the taming of the radical Left—was sorely wanting and seemed more like a tacit acceptance of Ben Dillingham's viewpoint that statehood was the optimal way to contain the CP and the ILWU—and to reassure Asia.

CHAPTER 15

Upheaval

It was a blowout by the Democrats. It was November 1954, the first election in Hawai'i after the Smith Act convictions and its aftermath, when the anticommunist declaration was underlined that Moscow controlled the CP, which in turn controlled the ILWU, which controlled the Democratic Party—and therefore meant that it too was directed from the Kremlin. Yet despite this propaganda barrage, it was during this election that the Democrats established a stranglehold over Hawai'i's politics that has continued to this very moment, in stark defiance of the local elite. Correspondingly, the GOP was the big loser in 1954—and thereafter. The reason for this was simple, said the *Honolulu Record:* the dominant party in the archipelago since the ouster of indigenous rule had banked on Red-baiting and "labor baiting" and was rejected by the electorate.[1]

An ILWU journal roared that fifty-two years of GOP domination had ended, as for the first time in the history of the territory the Democrats gained working majorities in both houses of the legislature and control of three of the four county governments. The GOP, it said teasingly, was "acting like a groggy prize fighter who didn't 'see it coming.'"[2] Robert McElrath observed that from the US takeover of the islands in the 1890s until 1954, the GOP was in power. But in one fell swoop, a GOP majority of 19–11 in the legislature had been transformed into a Democratic majority of 22–8.[3]

While the Democrats on the mainland were in full flight from the spurious charge that they were close cousins of the now hated Reds, in the islands this party took a different approach, which was possible not least because the demographic makeup of Hawai'i was different. That is, the existence of an apartheid-like system, with what Koji Ariyoshi routinely called the "boss haole elite"[4] at the top of the pyramid, made it difficult for the Asian-Pacific electoral majority to swallow the bitter pill that those who had rescued them from misery—Jack Hall and his comrades—were the villains.

Attaining the level of myth was the dramatic episode during the campaign when a politically influential haole—Samuel King—burst into a political meeting, grabbed the microphone, and delivered an extemporaneous tirade about alleged Communist infiltration of the Democratic Party and the islands generally—remarks that were interpreted as challenging the loyalty of the candidates themselves. When he had finished, Daniel Inouye, who possessed an impressively stentorian voice, rose and with much dignity and feeling said that he had lost one arm in Italy fighting Nazis and that he would willingly relinquish his remaining limb fighting Communists if his nation so requested.[5]

A not so subtle message was sent by these transforming elections. As the *Record* headline put, "30 Out of 33 AJA Victors Ran on Democratic Ticket," while "19 Out of 21 AJA Losers [Ran] on GOP Ticket." This headline summarized the lesson to be drawn by alert Americans of Japanese Ancestry—i.e., that the Republicans with their Red-baiting and thought-control trials were the party of the past. After World War II, the elite minority on Oʻahu, especially in the fourth district, went all out to eliminate Chinese American candidates by smearing them as war slackers. Now this same elite was complaining about alleged bloc voting by the majority—though its own routine bloc voting did not grace its concern.[6] Union foe Frank Fasi triumphed over union friend John Wilson as the Democratic nominee for mayor of Honolulu. "Switch-voting of from 10,999 to 15,000 Republicans" in the Democratic primary tipped the scales in Fasi's favor, with virtually all of these switchers being white. "Haole GOP precincts bloc vote," the *Record* contended, as it cited one observer's assertion that "'the one point in which the Chinese and Japanese agreed was in the belief that the greatest amount of bloc voting is done by the haoles.'"[7]

Sour grapes could not obscure the reality that the GOP had been swept from control of the territorial legislature.[8] And the union was credited with bringing "political liberty" to Hawaiʻi,[9] a point endorsed by Hall.[10]

The *Star-Bulletin*, which had a flirtation with those to its left before being hounded back into line (as early as 1950 Hall termed its owner, Joseph Farrington, "anti-union"),[11] also sought to answer the question of the day—if not the era: "Why did the local elections go overwhelmingly Democrat? That's a question that is being asked on every street corner in Honolulu and all over the territory for that matter."[12] It was also a query being posed in the corporate suites and boardrooms where GOP rule was viewed as a precondition to statehood, with implications for the electoral college and the White House—but now that had to be rethought fundamentally. "Dazed is the word to describe the present condition of Hawaii's Republican Party," it was reported accurately. "Bruised and badly shaken from the terrific beating it took," the party remained "stunned" for some time to come. Unlike the GOP leadership, this journal did recognize that "another cause for the big switch was the Republican's use of the Big Smear": "When Democratic candidates talked issues, the Republicans yelled Red! When Democrats talked about such things as taxes, unemployment and land, the Republicans screamed

Communist!" More than this, the *Star-Bulletin* reported, "the ILWU, the Hawaii Government Employment Association, the United Public Workers and many unions of the American Federation of Labor went all out for the Democrats," exemplifying what was to become a decades-long pattern, established successfully in 1954 in reaction to anticommunist[13] upheaval.[14] Startlingly, after the agony of the Smith Act fiasco, the Left, rather than being marginalized and isolated, had seized power instead.[15]

The CIO, which the ILWU had helped propel, had spent an inordinate amount of time in expelling the ILWU in 1950,[16] but as it turned out, this was a self-inflicted wound. This once-proud federation felt compelled to enter a shotgun marriage with the AFL, just as the Hawai'i workers they shunned were registering one of labor's most significant triumphs during the Red Scare.

Still, those paying close attention should not have been surprised by this dramatic turn of electoral events. In early 1953 the ILWU was not sufficiently tied down by the trial; it found the time to announce that it was reviving its political action committee and stocking a war chest for the 1954 elections.[17] In Kaua'i, where the ILWU's heft was thought to be strongest, Democrats backed by the union were in firm control, holding the chairmanship and all but one board seat in the county. All four territorial house members were Democrats. Maui was similarly inclined.[18] The existence of the *Honolulu Record* was at issue at the Smith Act trial; yet a scant year after this proceeding ended, its sixth anniversary edition weighed in at a hefty 72 pages, full of congratulatory advertisements from local businesses.[19] Months before the 1954 election, John Burns, who had become the rallying point for labor and the Left, won handily over his internal Democratic Party opponents. The latter included staunch anticommunists, Big Five fans, and supporters of IMUA (Moving Forward), a group that had galvanized the most determined opponents of the CP and the ILWU. Such a lineup on the mainland would have easily predominated, but in Hawai'i they failed soundly in their attempt to oust Burns from his post as chairman of the party's Central Committee.[20]

Those of Japanese origin in Hawai'i had suffered mightily over the years, and as late as the spring of 1954, property was still being seized from them by the authorities—particularly buildings, housing, and language schools—which the *Honolulu Record* regarded as "little more than stealing behind a façade of legality."[21] Meanwhile, GOP leaders like Farrant Lewis Turner signaled that they must have thought they were living in Mississippi and not Hawai'i; Turner himself contended that his Democratic opposite numbers "wanted to restore [the queen of Hawai'i] to power."[22] The 1954 election was also a referendum on this odious approach.

It was true that the *Record* conceded at one point that the islands had a "colonial status,"[23] but it was also true that the left wing, which this journal represented, remained a firm advocate of statehood. (Perhaps if it had stressed anticolonialism, the Democrats would not have prevailed.) The GOP sought to suggest that the Democrats were playing upon the more than latent anti-haole bias, but this was inaccurate also. The ILWU, referring to Mayor John Wilson, bewailed that "one of the greatest friends the Japanese people have had in Hawaii" was defeated; a "knife was plunged into [his] back," it was said, and "the killers are top leaders and members of the Republican Party of Oahu."[24]

The GOP defeat was all the more bracing, given that the party had gone to extraordinary lengths to win, going so far as to bring Vice President Richard Nixon to the distant outpost that was Hawai'i, but even he could not save them.[25]

The ILWU promised to make the Big Five backers of the GOP pay for their perceived backing of the Smith Act trial, and this proved not to be an empty promise. Hours after the convictions, an emergency ILWU convention was held, filled with angry talk and bitter threats. Louis Goldblatt set the tone when he declared that "the bosses made a mistake" in acquiescing to, if not backing, the trial, "and it's going to cost them money." Wearing a bright aloha shirt and twirling his dark glasses in his hand as he spoke, Goldblatt brought the workers to their feet repeatedly in throaty cheers, as did Jack Hall and Harry Bridges, who were attired similarly.[26]

Labor as a whole did not seem to be particularly intimidated by the trial. AFL workers at the Honolulu Gas Company went on strike in the spring of 1953,[27] bus drivers continued to be typically restive too,[28] and when workers at Honolulu's three largest tourist hotels walked off their jobs at the behest of Art Rutledge the same year that the trial began, it was apparent that it would take more than the Smith Act to keep labor in line in the islands.[29] When the ILWU moved into its spanking-new headquarters in Honolulu as the hospitality workers were demonstrating, the event stood as a resonant symbol of the union's ability to persevere.[30] On this festive occasion, the acting governor was expected to attend, and the Royal Hawaiian Band was slated to present a half-hour concert, belying any notion that the ILWU was isolated.[31]

The ILWU long had been interested in building construction—unsurprising in light of the shacks workers often resided in—and as early as 1946 was talking in large terms about a housing project for the Hawaiian Islands and even developing a housing material industry there.[32] That the ILWU was setting an example became evident when Hall observed that other affiliates of the union had become "building conscious" in emulation of Hawai'i. Ultimately, the ILWU, which had built up a tremendous fund in anticipation of strikes, was able to lend money to mainland affiliates so they too could exit from the business of renting headquarters.[33]

The AFL and the ILWU continued on separate tracks, however, but that did not prove fatal to labor's prospects. Even in 1951, days after the arrests of union activists, virtually every ILWU unit on O'ahu joined together to form a line of march a quarter mile long; many Filipinos marched in their indigenous attire, while flower-decked floats and labor stalwarts on foot were interspersed with others waving signs denouncing the Smith Act. The AFL assembled a respectable 3,000 marchers as hundreds more watched,[34] outstanding numbers for the mainland—but this was the islands.[35] In 1952, weeks before the trial of the Hawaii Seven, the unions sponsored separate Labor Day marches, but with 20,000 participating overall, what they accomplished dwarfed what was occurring in mainland cities of comparable—or larger—size. Of course, ILWU workers had won this paid holiday as a result of recent negotiations.[36]

McElrath conceded that the hotel workers Rutledge had organized under AFL auspices had "better conditions than the ones on the mainland."[37] Rutledge had grown close to the local press that had once advocated his deportation but now saw him as a reasonable alternative to Jack Hall. In the past, Rutledge had been derided as "that Jew agitator," as McElrath recalled, but now was viewed as a labor statesman (though he would have been routed on the mainland). But in contrast to the AFL, the ILWU membership could elect its leaders and could remove them too by petition of a mere 15 percent of the members. Thus, the ILWU downplayed Rutledge's threat to raid the ILWU and organize the growing sector of hotel and bar workers under the AFL umbrella.[38]

Yet in late 1953 a gang of glowering stevedores in Honolulu, some of them armed with vicious-looking cargo hooks, kept a vigil near a passenger freight ship in order to prevent the vessel from sailing with a rival AFL crew aboard. Deadly tension gripped the waterfront as scores of police officers patrolled the area, alert to the possibility of an outbreak of violence. This confrontation was the fruit of a struggle between the Left-led National Union of Marine Cooks and Stewards, backed by the ILWU, and their AFL challengers.[39] Earlier the voyage of a luxury liner had been canceled because of this toxic jurisdictional dispute. Those who could took planes instead, which probably was further evidence of the death knell sounded for the old way of transport.[40] For as this clash was sharpening, Matson Navigation, which had interests throughout the region, including Fiji and Australia, was lamenting a disappointing balance sheet; the company attributed the downturn to a 66-day maritime strike in 1952, which had necessitated the cancellation of 31 voyages and the loss of some 436,000 tons of cargo.[41]

Nonetheless, at first it seemed that the Smith Act trial and convictions had served their purpose in distracting the ILWU from the negotiating table and picket lines and into a courtroom swamp. Weeks after Judge Wiig handed down his sentences, more than 500 workers at the pineapple cannery of Honolulu's Libby, McNeill and Libby were laid off, purportedly because of a six-day-old strike at the company's Molokai plantation. These field workers had stormed off the job after management split work gangs into all-Hawaiian and all-Filipino components in order to make for a "better-balanced" labor force. The ILWU, understandably sensitive to how this kind of segregation had thwarted class cohesion in the past, charged angrily that the purpose was to get these two groups to work against each other in the interest of a speedup.[42] The union prevailed in this confrontation, though not wholly, as the workers were disciplined by the company for their walkout, perhaps providing management with optimism about handling future scrapes.[43]

Management seemed to be challenging the mettle of the union, probing for weaknesses that could be exploited. Thus, work at Waialua Agricultural Company, which had been operating at only 25 to 40 percent of normal production because of a wage dispute, came to a virtual halt in the spring of 1953 following the suspension of a number of employees,[44] an indicator that militancy had not been squashed.[45]

Belying stereotypes about how a Left-led union should conduct itself, the ILWU displayed admirable malleability. Days after the Smith Act verdict, the union was negotiating with the Seventh-day Adventist Church, whose staff it represented, on the issue of these workers having Saturday off to attend religious services, while working instead on Sunday.[46] Showing further flexibility, the union allowed members of this denomination to contribute to the ILWU Memorial Association the same amount of dues that were paid by ILWU members to Local 142, since it was against the stated policy of this faith to join a union.[47] Subsequently the union contacted officials of the Jehovah's Witnesses, seeking to entice this group to allow its members to join the ILWU.[48] Even on the union's radio broadcasts, it was said that "thanking the Lord should be the first consideration before anybody else because he is the source of all strength of any living being on earth"—which was the message sent by a union ally, the Wahiawa Christian Church.[49]

During the same period, union members at the Honolulu Pork Center, which was a subsidiary of CQ Yee Hop and Company (makers of Ho-Min ice cream), went on strike. The ice cream workers had been ILWU members, but management had succeeded in ousting them from the workplace. The Taft-Hartley law made it inadvisable for the union to engage in a secondary boycott against CQ Yee Hop's ice cream, so it opted for a letter-writing campaign[50] instead.[51]

The union leadership had good reason to believe that management was seeking to leverage the defeat of the Left in the courtroom in order to weaken labor's gains at the workplace and negotiating table, something the union had sensed from the first Smith Act arrests of August 1951 to the aftermath of the convictions two years later. Consider that amidst the hullabaloo of the trial, Local 155 in Hilo, with a membership of 357 men in five manufacturing and service units on the Big Island, voted unanimously to bolt from the ILWU; this local had been in disfavor with top leaders of the union since it refused to contribute to the defense funds for Bridges and Hall or to the fund to construct the union headquarters in Honolulu.[52] Of course, management was hardly cooperative either, complicating the picture even more. By the end of 1953, Goldblatt was confessing to Bridges, "The union is compelled to face perhaps the most difficult bargaining situation we've run into in many a year. We've never tackled a contract issue in Hawaii where the employers have been so elusive."[53]

Management felt that the political winds were in its sails and that the union's ship had stalled, and it responded accordingly. A journalist with access to the bosses reported that Goldblatt's antennae had picked up the proper signals, for they didn't envision a sugar strike; they thought that having to contend with both the Smith Act conviction and the new deportation proceedings Bridges was facing would drain and deplete the union's energy and treasury, rendering it unable to confront management effectively.[54]

Thus, when the parties met in the boardroom of the sugar planters at ten o'clock on a Friday morning in late 1953, Hall noted that things were proceeding slowly, as if the managers had all the time in the world. He sought to get their attention and remind them of the high stakes by pushing for "stop work meetings" where the members would be briefed on the negotiations.[55] Management perceived that the ILWU wanted peace at any price—and acted accordingly.[56]

The union found ominous signs that tactics used against sugar workers were also infecting talks with pineapple workers, which suggested a coordination of employer strategy between the two industries. Management was thought to be seeking to provoke pineapple workers into an ill-conceived action that would enervate the union's "weakest division and foul up the strength of the union in sugar where any battle, if it must be fought[,] should take place." Hence, the union provided stirring advice to its members: "Start your strike gardens at once."[57]

The union, however, had inherent advantages over the minority elite it confronted. Jack Hall took to the airwaves regularly, briefing members on the progress of negotiations, and his words were translated into Ilocano, Visayan, and Japanese.[58] Workers were told about attempts to improve their pensions and medical benefits, the move toward a 40-hour week, and the contrasting revelation that cane workers in Louisiana were still putting in a "54 hour straight time week."[59] ILWU members were informed that "no group of workers anywhere in the United States now has a better and more comprehensive medical plan for the protection of themselves and their families"; in contrast to unions that had endured anticommunist purges, sugar workers in Hawai'i on retirement from their jobs had better pension plans than those who had been employed in the basic industries of the nation such as steel, auto, rubber, meatpacking, and so on.[60]

Thus management may have been surprised when Kahuku sugar workers voted 304 to 21 to give their ILWU negotiators the power to call a strike.[61]

Management may have also been taken aback when workers overall voted to strike by a margin higher than 9 to 1.[62] The union's antagonists may not have been listening closely to the radio when McElrath initiated his "Radio School of the Air on Labor and Collective Bargaining," which held classes each Friday evening. Hall appeared at times as a guest lecturer, once pointing out that while the union had tried to open negotiating sessions to the public and the press, management had blocked that proposal, so this radio program would serve as a substitute, allowing all to get a glimpse of whose positions were reasonable—and whose were not. Hall said he wanted to make every member an expert on the contract, which was no minor matter, given that the existing agreement was 60 pages of tightly written provisions.[63] Being informed that the salaries of Hall and McElrath were paid from ILWU headquarters in San Francisco, local workers could feel reassured about how their dues were spent.[64]

The Aloha Network, which had islands-wide reach, carried its broad-casts in various Filipino languages.[65] Its 15-minute broadcast in Japanese aired every Sunday evening[66] and eventually[67] was well received.[68] It was re-markable that these radicals had captured a portion of the airwaves, which, too, distinguished them from their mainland comrades.[69] Radio proved to be one of the ILWU's most powerful and enduring weapons.[70]

As the union saw things, it was no accident that Hall was arrested while embroiled in negotiations. The sugar industry was run basically by those who employed the stevedores—i.e., Castle and Cooke, C. Brewer, Alexander and Baldwin, and American Factors. (The exceptions in this regard were Theo H. Davies and F. A. Schaefer, who were involved in sugar but not the docks.)[71] Still, the long-term trends did not seem to benefit the workers, and not just because the escalating production of corn and high-fructose corn syrup would ultimately eat into markets theretofore dominated by sugar.

Moreover, every year, beginning in 1947, the total wage payout of the industry had declined steadily, and every year the tons of sugar produced per worker had increased. In 1947 each worker produced an average of 100 tons of raw sugar, but by the time of the arrests, this average had increased to 137 tons—yet wages had not risen correspondingly.[72] "One sugar worker today does what 9 did 20 years ago," claimed one left-wing journalist in early 1954.[73] Meanwhile, Kekaha Sugar Company, not atypically, was viewed by a local journalist as a "gold mine . . . what with its 43 and three quarters square miles, its assets worth seven and three-quarters of millions, and its more than 700 employees."[74]

Despite this increased production and wealth, there was no improvement in the basic living conditions of the workers. On the Big Island, workers at Onomea Sugar resided in termite-eaten, rickety old shacks that a careless ciga-rette smoker could send up in flames quite easily—yet fire protection was prac-tically nonexistent. Water pressure was so low that once the fire department's tank truck emptied, the firefighters practically had to stand by and watch a fire burn.[75] Visiting a plantation in the spring of 1954, Koji Ariyoshi found retired Chinese workers residing in the most tragic conditions; these single men were generally housed in far-off camps, in bare shacks needing repair.[76] Land was so precious on the islands that selling it by the square foot was not unknown.[77]

Workers in the fields were subjected to dangerous chemicals like parathion, necessitating the wearing of plastic hats and capes, goggles, and rubber gloves,[78] none of which could altogether save them from debilitating ailments.[79] Repeatedly, McElrath complained that workers—especially those at Libby's Waipio plantation on Oʻahu—were human guinea pigs insofar as they were being subjected to insecticides, such as Malathion.[80] This was the price paid for a job in a context of oversupply of sugar, dwindling pineapple sales—and mechanization of the docks.[81]

The workers had confidence that if they stuck by their union and stayed focused on better wages and improved working conditions rather than diverting their already taxed energies into the Red Scare, they could advance. This was precisely the worry of those with concern about the CP's continuing influence, particularly as the road to statehood became seemingly smoother. Ironically, as this new trend was unwinding, some on the Left were becoming more pessimistic.[82] Just before the 1954 election, Jack Hall was said to have raised the question of commonwealth status—à la Puerto Rico—as a substitute for Hawaiʻi statehood.[83] If that is an accurate report, this would have been a striking turnabout for Hall, who had backed statehood unrelentingly and in his important Labor Day address of 1947 exhorted, "Never forget for a second that statehood for Hawaii is our most important political objective. We ache for statehood"—though adding, remarkably, that he too favored "self-determination" for the archipelago.[84] McElrath asserted that "there can be no factual defense for being anti-statehood"—ignoring self-determination for indigenes in the process.[85] All the while, these advocates of closer union with Washington were kept under unremitting surveillance by the authorities—interestingly, Ray Jerome Baker found it worth noting that most of the FBI agents were Catholic.[86]

The dramatic election of 1954, in sum, had not quelled the concern of those upset by the victory of the Democrats, which was seen as a victory for the ILWU and therefore a victory for the CP and the Kremlin alike. Baker had been a friend of Governor Oren Long's brother—"He is interested in Hawaiian history, which I also am," Baker noted. But with the frostier climate brought by the trial, Baker observed, "He continues to be courteous when he sees me, but kind of shies away from me." The overall mood was not helped by the downturn in sugar and pineapple, which increased tourism did not allay.[87]

Baker's growing concern about the fate of Hawaiʻi was mirrored paradoxically by his polar opponents on the right, particularly on the increasingly fraught matter of statehood. In the period preceding this earthquake of an election in 1954, Paul Crouch—the nemesis of the island Left—was as busy as ever. He was demanding public hearings in Honolulu "and on the three other major islands where Communist power is especially great—Kauai, Maui and Hawaii." He was worried that through the ILWU the Communist Party would pick the candidates to be nominated for the November elections by the Democrats. Contrary to the national trend, CP influence seemed to be spreading, he thought, since the Republican newspaper editor Ray Coll had had the temerity to work alongside McElrath in selecting winners of an ILWU scholarship in honor of W. K. Bassett (thought to be a Red). Crouch believed that daily developments in Indochina made Communist power in Hawai'i an even more vital matter of national security. Hawai'i, he said, embodied Communist power where it was "most dangerous to our nation."[88] Yet Crouch's fervent desire for more hearings on Hawai'i was challenged by Governor Oren Long, who reminded Senator Lyndon B. Johnson months after the Smith Act arrests that "nine separate congressional investigations of Hawaii have been made during the past fifteen years"[89]—and the reality of Red influence had hardly waned.

Moreover, there were others who seized precisely on the issue that fixated Crouch—and arrived at an opposing conclusion. For it was during that same instrumental year of 1954 that Senator Thomas Hennings of Missouri was told that "in our relations with nations other than Europe and Canada, one of our most vulnerable points is that of our supposed discrimination against those of other than white European origin," which could become a "fatal wound" during the Cold War. This correspondent, Arthur Compton of Washington University in St. Louis, blanched at the thought of having to "face in the Orient again this winter the question put to me in all good faith by my Asiatic friends": "Was not the atom bomb used against the Japanese instead of the Germans because they were considered an inferior type of people?"[90]

And if Hawai'i were rejected as a state, would not that be a Cold War problem in Asia? The future US president Lyndon B. Johnson was instructed that it would be "insulting the entire Orient"—i.e., "refusing to accept our gallant Hawaiian Niseis as equals"—if statehood were to be denied.[91] Hawai'i was being viewed as the gateway to the planet's most populous continent—Asia—where wars in Korea and Vietnam were to occupy the nation for years to come. It was during this time that the Rockefeller Foundation proposed a race relations conference in Honolulu, on the premise that "one of the most effective arguments utilized by the Communists in their propaganda war against the democracies, especially among the peoples of Asia and Africa, is the racial discrimination."[92]

Though Bridges' legal problems and the Smith Act convictions may have reassured Senator Butler, the same could not be said for others. Senator James Eastland of Mississippi, perhaps the most conservative—and racist—member of that august body—filed away a newspaper clipping that said that in Hawai'i the "Caucasian population [was] off 111,019 since July 1948" and "conversely the population of Japanese ancestry has grown proportionately"; indeed, according to the article, "all racial elements of population except Caucasian have been growing in the past five years." Scribbled in the blackest of black ink on this news was the message, "Why are whites leaving?"[93] But the implication was clear: was this the kind of territory that should be admitted to the Union?[94]

Senator Eastland also paid close attention to ILWU radio broadcasts, suggesting their potency. The "Filipino Communist Broadcast" was a source of alarm particularly; again, underlined was the matter of the growing numbers of Communists.[95]

Ariyoshi seemed to be a conspicuous target of Senator Eastland's informants, embodying as he did their twin concerns of race and radicalism. They found it hard to believe that in 1952, after Ariyoshi was indicted, the *Honolulu Record* nonetheless carried paid advertising from 330 island business firms, though these companies "definitely knew that they were helping to finance a publication controlled by the Communist Party."[96] Senator Eastland's focus on Hawai'i zeroed in sharply on the matter of "race" and the possibility that the United States would be altering its character by enveloping the archipelago.[97]

But that matter was entangled with radicalism, as the Reds were accused of controlling Honolulu's government, via W. K. Bassett.[98] Bassett, it was noted with revulsion, had come to the islands from Carmel, California, "where he was a close friend of Lincoln Steffens, Ella Winter and other California Reds"; worse, "Bassett told newspaper men that he and Harry Bridges had been close friends for thirty years."[99] Tragically and remarkably, just after this assault, Bassett was taking his regular evening walk when he was struck down by a speeding automobile—and killed. The impact was so great that he was hurled eight feet in the air; the driver, a soldier, was not charged,[100] another curious coincidence akin to the immolation of Frank Marshall Davis' business.

After accumulating and absorbing this mass of material on the radicalism and racial makeup of Hawai'i, Senator Eastland moved swiftly into the vacuum created after Senator Butler abandoned the anti-statehood crusade. Such a development long had been of concern to statehood advocates within the ILWU. Again, it seemed as if the 1954 elections were a catastrophic victory, as conservatives whipped up hysteria about the results, a reaction that ILWU leaders had envisioned since 1946.[101] Soon the ubiquitous Paul Crouch began working day and night with Senator Eastland and other Dixiecrats, fueling the anti-statehood fires.[102]

So briefed, Senator Eastland grumbled that the territory's admission would mean two solid "votes for socialized medicine," "two votes for government ownership of industry," and, perhaps most important in his mind, "two votes against all racial segregation." This staunch defender of Jim Crow figuratively mounted the barricades and bellowed, "I shall fight Hawaiian statehood with every resource at my command"; he threatened the dreaded filibuster, warning bluntly, "It may be necessary to talk for days and this the South must do."[103] Speaking to the press, the influential Eastland asserted that that if statehood was granted, the Honolulu government "would be under the control and domination of Moscow" since the CP was "stronger, more influential and more powerful today" there "than was the Communist Party in the average satellite state of Central or Eastern Europe at the time they were taken over." He was in his region's mainstream, he thought, since "Southerners generally have opposed" statehood.[104] He was not altogether wrong.[105]

Senator Lyndon B. Johnson was told by an interlocutor that he had not found "a single substantial Anglo-Saxon businessman [who] favored statehood," arguing that this status "should be long deferred."[106] As the United States, in the face of global pressure, began to retreat from the more egregious aspects of de jure Jim Crow, many Dixiecrats were coming to see admission of a "majority minority" state to the Union as the thin edge of the wedge of a horrid antiracism. Senator Willis Robertson of Virginia spoke for many of his regional comrades when he expressed his opposition to statehood, comparing it to "a law of the Medes and Persians": "You can't subsequently change it if it works out badly"[107]—or worse.[108] That statehood for Hawai'i was equivalent to the Moscow politburo's having two votes in the US Senate became the charge of the day.[109]

The Mississippi legislature passed a resolution condemning the possibility of statehood.[110] Alfred Yap—perhaps, like Crouch, seeking another patron after Senator Butler's defection—informed Senator Olin Johnston of South Carolina that he should remember that Honolulu was "the only city on American soil where you can be arrested by a Jap policeman, booked by a Jap clerk, prosecuted by a Jap prosecutor, judged, fined and be sentenced by a Jap judge."[111] The peripatetic Yap also lobbied the high-ranking Congressman Sam Rayburn of Texas,[112] who then assured him that "Hawaii should not become eligible for statehood."[113]

Senator Johnston himself pondered, "Will the haoles disappear?" The supposed "fast breeding groups" were outpacing the supposed master race. Citing the eminent educator Nicholas Murray Butler, he concurred that statehood "might easily be the first step in bringing to an end the United States of America as established by the Founding Fathers and as we have known it,"[114] as ideas about alleged race suicide rose[115] along with fears of institutionalized anti-haole bias.[116]

Senator Clyde Hoey of North Carolina was being fed this same diet.[117] Congressman Howard Smith of Virginia was similarly outraged, as he found that "one Chinaman in Hawaii would have the same power in the election of Senators" as "31 American citizens in the great state of New York," if statehood arrived.[118]

The rabidly reactionary and wondrously wealthy Dallas oilman H. L. Hunt, after courteously providing "regards to Mrs. Eastland," arrived at the business at hand, inquiring about profuse dissemination of anti-statehood propaganda.[119] A Democratic Party leader from Texas, William Michels was querulous: what's next, he asked, admission of "coral atolls, islands, zones, territories and possessions?"[120]

This was becoming a theme in anti-statehood discourse: if noncontiguous Hawai'i could become a state, what was the limit? A dumbfounded John T. Barker of Kansas City asked if Israel would be next, since "we peopled Israel—we financed Israel—we support Israel—we have agreed to defend Israel—Israel is our country." The man to whom he addressed these surprising words, the erudite Democratic senator from Arkansas, J. William Fulbright, responded, "I think your questions are very well taken."[121]

Writing from the conservative redoubt of Pasadena, California, Early Van Deventer was so exercised about the prospect of statehood that he stressed the previously unthinkable—"GIVE THEM INDEPENDENCE BUT NEVER STATEHOOD," he emphasized.[122] The closer Hawai'i crept toward statehood, the more the idea of independence seemed to emerge—except from the Left.[123] Leon Rice of South Carolina asked why, if the British Empire "recedes, we start to expand"; the remedy for Hawai'i, he said, was to "set her free, as we did the Philippines."[124] A self-described "transplanted Brooklyn boy" in Hilo also asked why Hawai'i could not be an "independent" and "sovereign nation."[125]

This increasing call for Hawai'i sovereignty coming from the Right may have lulled the Left into thinking that statehood was needed more than ever. Even the mossback conservative Senator Hoey of North Carolina indicated that he was willing to entertain independence, since Hawai'i was "Communist infested."[126] His fellow racist George Lehleitner of New Orleans sought to reassure Hoey, informing him that "Hawaii's Negro population is a negligible three-tenths of one percent!"[127] But the senator from Tobacco Road refused to be distracted by this statistic.[128]

Charles Campbell stated the obvious when he acknowledged that it was not to be expected that "one of the largest flag makers in the country is opposed to statehood"—but he was against statehood, even though it would mean a "consequent great increase in our business" due to massive flag replacement orders. Why was he opposed? Communists, he said.[129] Statehood for Hawai'i and its prospective twin, Alaska, was favored by a wide majority of US citizens, according to polls—but support for statehood for what was to become the largest state was much stronger.[130]

How could the US Congress countenance admission of Hawai'i as a state particularly at a time—1954—when it seemed that Communists were in the process of consolidating their power? It was during that year that Ingram Stainback was summoned to Washington to discuss this matter in hearings

before the Senate Committee on Interior and Insular Affairs. There he recalled a jaunty Harry Bridges, who "sat in my office with his feet cocked on
my desk," telling him—the governor—the facts of life. "Once you have given
statehood," he warned, "it cannot be undone. It is like death, it is so very
final." So think it over carefully, he advised.[131]

Senator Smathers was infuriated. Wielding a copy of the *Honolulu Record*
like a truncheon, he asked Stainback about the 500 business firms that had
offered congratulations in its anniversary issue. Why, he stammered, "the
Communist 'Daily Worker' does not have that many advertisements in it, so
far as I know"—though since he was "not a regular reader," he could not be
too sure. This ignited the debate of the day—was Hawai'i more dangerous as
a territory or a state?—with the consensus seeming to find the status quo no
longer acceptable. A furious debate ensued as to whether the Senate should
admit to its ranks an elected Red.[132]

But when Stainback declared that ILWU influence on that day was "un-
questionably" greater than it had been during the time of the 1949 strike, one
could almost envision the legislators collectively leaping from their seats in
horror. He reminded those before him of the "strange situation" that had obtained at the Smith Act trial when the powerful were reluctant to testify against
the defendants for fear of ILWU retribution. This was a "rather remarkable
setup," he suggested. "I do not think there is a state in the union that can compare with Hawaii for political domination" by Reds, he said, and "their power
seems to be growing," for the ILWU "practically controls the island of Kauai."
Their representative in the legislature was told "you support Jack Hall's bond
[after conviction]" or you will be ousted, Stainback reported. The air was left
heavy with the idea that Hawai'i, with one-fourth of the population of Mississippi, paid as much to Washington in taxes as that state did: $140 million.

Senator George Malone of Nevada compared Hawai'i as a state to Alge-
ria being deemed to be part of France—not too comforting a thought, given
the turmoil that colonial relationship had brought to Paris. Another legislator made an analogy with Great Britain and Northern Ireland, also not very
cheering. Yet since Hawai'i was distant from the mainland, the consensus
seemed to be developing that whatever radical contagion it possessed could
be contained, and given the other factors involved—the Cold War in Asia in
particular—the archipelago seemed to be a step closer to statehood as Stainback winged his way back to Honolulu.[133]

Utah's senator Wallace Bennett, a bellwether of hegemonic conservative
opinion, was pro-statehood, he said, because "it would give a spiritual lift" to
"anxious men around the whole Pacific area—the Japanese, the Chinese, the
Koreans, the people of the Philippines." While "to deny statehood would
injure our stand there," he added, "to confirm it would greatly strengthen
our position."[134]

The ILWU's man in Washington, Jeff Kibre, was unimpressed with Stainback.[135] Yet even Stainback, as despised as he was by the ILWU and the broader Left, earlier had backed congressional action to remove the factor of race as a qualification for citizenship, since it would "deprive the subversive element of one of its favorite arguments—racial discrimination."[136] His support of that proposal suggests that even isle conservatives were less conservative than their mainland counterparts.

Stainback's successor, Governor Samuel Wilder King, did not seem to be pleased that Stainback's concern about Reds was causing him to reconsider statehood. "There are over 50,000 veterans in Hawaii, comprising one in six of our entire adult population," he said, and they were a mighty bulwark against a Moscow takeover. Besides, he said, reflecting the anxiety about Asia, "no man from Hawaii was among the 21 who turned their backs on the United States to adopt Communism at Panmunjon [Korea] just a few weeks ago."[137] Burns responded by bringing a pro-statehood delegation to Washington, which included 8 war veterans. They shared dinner with Senator Russell Long and Congressman Otto Passman, both of Louisiana, and found it necessary to disabuse them of their misconceptions about the religious faith of the Nisei, who, they were told, were Buddhists. Burns added quickly, though, that they were "predominantly of the Christian faith."[138]

But that was not the end of the constant congressional probing of Hawai'i. Paul Crouch—again—turned up in Washington before a hearing chaired by Senator Eastland. Crouch had traveled a lengthy distance from his residence at 1565 Saint Louis Drive in Honolulu, and he justified his journey by bringing along bombshells about an impending Red takeover of the colony. Yes, "actual membership of the Communist Party is only from fifty to seventy-five," he said in early 1954—but "Jack Hall could, if he wished, sign up 500 new members of the Communist Party any day in the islands,"[139] particularly in Kaua'i.[140] These hearings left many islanders embittered—and solons anxious[141]—about the intertwined issues of "race" and radicalism,[142] particularly the growing idea of an unnamed US senator who asserted that Hawai'i could become "the first Communist state in the union."[143]

Washington found that Hawai'i had become a kind of tar-baby colony, paying dividends—yes—but also quite troublesome. More than other regions under the US flag, Hawai'i was implicated directly in matters of national security, given its peculiar demographic makeup, its proximity to Asia, and its role as an unsinkable aircraft carrier in the Pacific. The problem was that the rise of left-wing radicalism with ties to Moscow, at a time when Moscow was being viewed as the citadel of the "evil empire," was a matter of grave concern in Washington. That the Left was strong in both Japan and the Philippines was of similar concern,[144] especially considering that many in the isles hailed from regions where the Japanese Communist Party was strong. Given the composition of the

ILWU membership, it was not surprising that ILWU staffer Lincoln Fairley spoke warmly of the union's "friends in Japan."[145] Just as Ariyoshi had been with Mao Zedong in China, the Filipino wife of one ILWU leader had fought beside the heroic Huks.[146] (Perhaps the union's closeness to the struggle in the Philippines explains why Stainback charged that Hall was intimately involved with these guerrillas.)[147]

On the other hand, the US consul in Manila fretted that some of the Filipinos who had migrated to Hawai'i from Ilocos Sur "may have been involved in active collaboration with the Japanese during the Japanese occupation."[148] Ordinarily this would have seemed like good conservative news, but the idea that these collaborators might not be prone to join the anti-Nippon crusade in the isles was worrying. Similarly worrisome to Stainback was that there was a tendency for migrants to bring their relatives to Hawai'i or for those from areas like the frequently inflamed Ilocos Sur to come there (after hearing stories about the streets paved with platinum in Honolulu).[149] The union, given the composition of its membership, paid careful attention to trends in the Philippines. It encouraged all locals to "wholeheartedly and actively support" Filipino holidays, particularly in view of "certain dangerous elements" who sought to "split our ranks through appeals to narrow Filipino nationalism and vicious innuendoes that the ILWU is 'dominated' by Japanese and other Filipinos"[150]—a gnawing concern among some haoles.[151]

Honolulu stevedores had marched in support of independence for the Philippines in 1946.[152] The ILWU also expressed solidarity with similarly situated sugar workers in the Philippines and their neighbors in Indonesia as well, for, Goldblatt was instructed, unless "these two sugar exporting areas" were "integrated some way," then "potentially the key to breaking" the ILWU in Hawai'i was at hand.[153] Even before this insight became clear shortly after the conclusion of the Pacific War, the ILWU protested the use of US ships to load troops and ammunition that would be used against Indonesians in their conflict with the Dutch.[154] Simultaneously, the union joined with the National Maritime Union and other allies in railing against "smashing the people of Java" with US aid.[155]

The ILWU, in short, did little to allay Washington's concerns by maintaining a robust foreign policy, which paid off in generating global pressure when union leaders were under fire. It seemed that the union's most determined opponents despised them as much because of their global ties—particularly to Moscow—as anything else. Early in 1948 Jack Hall mused, "All we have to do [is] to support the Marshall Plan and the 'cloud of doubt [that] surrounds our union' would be dissipated."[156] Besides, unlike their mainland counterparts, the authorities in Honolulu had to file regular reports with the United Nations on the status of the archipelago.[157]

Thus the Hawai'i Left had much more direct engagement with the rest of the world than its typical mainland counterparts—this also meant it was harder for the leftists in the islands to accept that the obtaining climate in the United States was all there was to the world.[158] The union bought Israeli bonds,[159] exchanged intelligence with Italian workers on collective bargaining agreements,[160] and (in league with Caribbean unions) conferred with union leaders in Mexico;[161] it reported on the epochal 1954 coup in Guatemala, which was tied to the same agricultural interests that were dominant in Hawai'i and that wielded the same weapon: anticommunism.[162] The union may have been the earliest critic of US meddling in Vietnam, denouncing it in May 1954.[163]

But perhaps the union's closest relationship was with Cuba, which had come under the ambit of Washington near the same time that Hawai'i did.[164] This Antillean jewel too was a sugar producer, and by 1946, Goldblatt was told, imports from Cuba represented over 50 percent of the total supply of raw cane sugar in the United States; thus the delivered price of Cuban sugar in New York normally set the market price for all raw cane sugar in the United States as a whole.[165] ILWU representatives were often to be found in conference in Havana.[166]

In turn, Caribbean unions relied upon the ILWU's contacts in Washington in their mutual confrontations there.[167] The sugar industry was studded with quotas and tariffs; that meant that Washington was highly susceptible to arm-twisting, thus making all the more important, for sugar workers in Hawai'i and elsewhere, the ILWU's coterie of delegates in the nation's capital. As the global political climate dipped toward frigidity, the ILWU sought to convene a global conference of sugar workers. As it had previously, the union sought to make sure that no sugar was sold in the United States that was produced by workers making less than $5 a day; this wage floor would benefit workers in Hawai'i, Cuba, and elsewhere.[168]

Seeing similar problems thousands of miles away provided useful perspective for the ILWU—and further reason for global solidarity. At one Havana meeting, Goldblatt pointed to the real difficulty in resisting mechanization and counseled that unions should "adapt creatively" instead. Thus he advised that they should all engage in "organized common action," including "joint publicity, joint action before the Congress of the U.S., joint preparation of material for wage determination hearings," and "collective bargaining negotiations."[169] That same year, 1947, the ILWU had invited its Cuban and Mexican counterparts to confer in San Francisco with the stated goal that "all groups aim at a minimum fixed dollar wage below which no sugar [union] will move,"[170] an initiative also pursued in Puerto Rico.[171] At one point 102,000 sugar workers in Puerto Rico contemplated affiliation with the ILWU, which would have given this union even more influence as it was facing its most severe trials.[172] The union also shared intelligence with its counterparts in Jamaica.[173]

As Cuba moved toward revolution in 1959, the archipelago moved toward statehood in the same year. Both processes were complex, and union leaders often found it necessary for the union to insinuate itself into the affairs of Cuba. "Severe shock" was Hall's reaction at the 1948 assassination of Jesus Menendez, the sugar workers' leader—and a Communist—which served to radicalize Cuba further.[174] This was heartfelt on the union's part, since earlier Menendez' union had donated $2,000 to the ILWU at the time of the trail-blazing 1946 strike,[175] just as the ILWU made substantial donations to unions in the Philippines and Cuba as a result of Paul Robeson's concert tour of Hawai'i.[176]

The ILWU's work in Cuba was an eye-opener.[177] The union in Cuba was illegal and, said its visiting delegate, "their buildings have been seized, their bank accounts taken over and a steady policy of police and government harassment" reigned. There were "shootings and assaults," and meetings were "broken up" by management guards, while it was "accepted practice for all union officials to go armed."[178]

The practice of global solidarity was not just charity on the ILWU's part, for if it were able to fortify workers in Cuba, it reduced the possibility of Hawai'i's planters fleeing for more exploitable climes in the Caribbean.[179]

An early signal that the ILWU and the CIO were not in sync came when the latter stood mute in the face of Cuban turmoil. While Goldblatt was busily raising funds for the bereft Menendez family, he was disgusted at the "complete subservience to the State Department" of the once-militant CIO.[180] But at least the CIO did not emulate the AFL, which was backing those who were attacking Menendez and his comrades. Goldblatt was told that Cuba "has about the strongest left and progressive movement in the Western Hemisphere," yet they were "fighting a combination of the State Department and the AFL[, both] with plenty of dough."[181] The Menendez murder was followed by the assassination of the leader of Cuban stevedores, Iglesias Dias, which the union protested directly to Secretary of State George Marshall.[182]

Similarly, Harry Bridges, who seemed to be perpetually under threat of deportation or incarceration, benefited from the protests abroad that greeted his plight.[183] Via various Communist and labor networks, Bridges' case ignited a firestorm of protest globally, particularly in South America.[184] The secretary-general of the powerful General Confederation of Labor in France was among those from abroad who had objected strenuously to the Smith Act prosecution,[185] just as workers in Cuba were buoyed by ILWU successes.[186] The lesson inferred was that if the ILWU could prevail against US nationals, perhaps Latin America could prevail against US allies.[187]

Even as Hall was marching off to be tried in federal court, the ILWU was heartily protesting repression in the Philippines,[188] something it did[189] frequently.[190]

Thus, isolating Hawai'i radicals was no simple feat, given their entrenchment in a dense network of global contacts and given the isles' importance in fighting the Cold War in Asia. Consideration of Hawai'i as a state had emerged when the GOP was paramount in the islands, and now, as a result of the 1954 election upheaval, it was in decline, thereby complicating national and congressional politics. But backing out of the course toward statehood was not easy and ran the risk of squandering goodwill in the Pacific basin. Above all, despite trials and convictions and deportation proceedings, tragic automobile accidents, and more, Hawai'i radicalism showed few signs of imminent collapse.

CHAPTER 16

Radicals Advance—and Retreat

It was early December 1956, and as was their wont, a goodly number of US legislators and their staffs escaped the chilly weather on the mainland for the expected pleasurable warmth of Hawai'i. "Investigating Hawaii seems to have [become] a racket," growled Ray Jerome Baker. "Every time some Congress[man] wants an excuse to take a trip," said the increasingly exasperated leftist, he "get[s] on some committee to investigate Hawaii."[1]

In that spirit, instead of being greeted by swaying and smiling hula dancers eager to drape leis around their pasty necks, these visitors were met at 'Iolani Palace—former headquarters of the regime deposed by Washington decades earlier—by chanting and raucous stevedores and farmworkers. ILWU members had marched through Honolulu to this site, though the skies opened and rain drenched them, along with their intended targets, only some of whom were huddled safely inside. The chief target of their ire—Senator James Eastland—was not present when they arrived, as he had skedaddled away hurriedly and unobtrusively by a rear entrance as they were approaching. The demonstrators crowded into the palace and mingled with their lawyers and others who had arrived for the latest legislative spectacle from Washington, one that by now had become an almost normalized part of the landscape. The demonstrators were quite a sight. One of their number was clothed in a white robe with a pointed hood—a replica of the outfit of the terrorist Ku Klux Klan—and carried a sign bearing a skull and crossbones insignia on a black field, along with the words "Eastland is Our Leader—White Supremacy."

Shortly before that, some 3,000 ILWU members had gathered in the Honolulu Civic Auditorium for a briefing on the march led by Harry Bridges, resplendent in a bright aloha shirt. The *Honolulu Star-Bulletin* journalist who covered Bridges' pointed remarks added, "Hardly any of the ILWU demonstrators had white skins"[2]—in stark contrast to the solons and their well-paid staffs.

The workers at Kahuku plantation, replete with Filipinos, indigenes, and those of Japanese ancestry, were among the ILWU contingents who amassed, boarding buses at 7 a.m. for a three-hour ride. They were among the heartiest singers of poignant words put to the tune of an old hymn—"We are fighting Jim Crowism and the Victory is here."[3]

Both Bridges and the journalist covering the event were responding to a new environment in the United States brought by its Supreme Court, which had ruled that Jim Crow was unconstitutional, and by the Montgomery Bus Boycott, led by a young minister, Dr. Martin Luther King Jr., which was triumphing and inaugurating a new era in the nation just as Senator Eastland was in full flight. What came to be known as the civil rights movement liberalized the political atmosphere, as it led directly to the enfranchisement of millions of new voters—particularly African-Americans—who leaned leftward. Their favorable attitude toward an expansion of civil liberties was incompatible with the prevailing anticommunist drift and thus undermined it, to the benefit of the ILWU. In addition, these developments made problematic the option of denying statehood for Hawai'i on racist and anticommunist grounds. This new conversation about racism boosted the ILWU, whose members had been historic victims of this ghastly phenomenon, and, correspondingly, it placed on the defensive those who had been its beneficiaries—a category that decisively included the haole elite in Hawai'i. Yet, paradoxically, as the atmosphere on the mainland liberalized and the ILWU gained in power and influence and was accepted in Hawai'i, there seemed to be less of a perceived need for a confrontational radicalism that had characterized the archipelago in the prelude to the watershed 1954 elections; this change served to undermine Koji Ariyoshi's *Honolulu Record*, Robert McElrath's militant radio broadcasts, and other ventures of that stripe. In other words, ironically, acceptance of the ILWU may have brought a softened, less militant ILWU.

Moreover, the Smith Act trials had taken their toll and accomplished their purpose. Whatever its flaws, the CP had provided a venue for coordination of radical activity in various spheres and a venue for the criticism of white supremacy. However, the convictions of the leading leftists eroded the will of many to continue working with this organization, which concomitantly eroded the Left itself. That is to say, the organized Left was in retreat even though it seemed to be advancing. It was as if the radicals had leapt from a plane with a parachute, and as the ripcord was pulled, they seemed to be heading upward when instead they were heading downward at a less rapid rate. "The local Redbaiting has eased up considerably," said Ray Jerome Baker in 1957, and the Hawaii Seven "no longer talk of going to jail."[4] Nonetheless, Howard Hoddick, the Harvard alumnus who had prosecuted the Hawaii Seven, admitted that his handiwork meant a "decided drop in known members of the party."[5]

Still, instead of fleeing in the face of the visiting inquisitors of the US Senate's Internal Security Subcommittee, the ILWU protested vigorously. Hilo stevedores greeted them with a one-day work stoppage.[6] This was followed by a protest of 6,200 ILWU members at eight plantations on the Big

Island and five on Kaua'i and on the waterfront there.[7] As Eastland and his minions were settling into their commodious hotels, an estimated 13,000 of the union's 23,000 members were taking part in work stoppages of various sorts in his honor.[8]

Conservative opinion was predictably enraged.[9] Leading anticommunist Dr. Fred Schwarz, whose roots were in Australia, joined the outcry.[10] Speaking to a group of worried Rotarians and Kiwanis Club members in Honolulu—mostly haoles—Schwarz expressed astonishment that the legislature had chosen to slash funding for the Territorial Subversive Activities Board, which practically made it defunct, at a time when Red influence had yet to be extirpated.[11]

One side argued that the Senate subcommittee's hearings were about radicalism; the other—just as insistently—cried that the issue was racism.[12] That the latter was easier for the isles' majority to accept—given the archipelago's unique demography—than the former neatly summarizes how Hawai'i was different than the mainland and why radicalism was able to take root there at a level at odds with what was occurring elsewhere under the US flag.

Signaling the importance of what was occurring in the islands, the top CP leader, Eugene Dennis, made an official statement on behalf of his organization, claiming that there were "no Communist Party members in Hawaii." If there were, he added puckishly, "they must be tourists."[13] The CP had 23,000 members in the United States, he reiterated, but none in Hawai'i or Alaska.[14] This may—or may not—have been true, but it elided a larger point: the political atmosphere in Hawai'i was radically different from that in what were soon to be its fellow states.

A combative tone was to characterize the union's approach to Senator Eastland. Comforted by the electoral rebuff of the conservatives in November 1954, the union aggressively confronted their presumed surrogates. This trend was bolstered in the November 1956 election, when the Democrats picked up three additional members in the territorial senate, with the ILWU playing a strong role in their win. On the Big Island, the formerly GOP-dominated Board of Supervisors switched to Democratic control. Perhaps the union's closest ally in the Democratic Party—John Burns—was sent to Washington as the archipelago's representative in the US House.[15] So prompted, Daniel Inouye condemned Eastland's visit in no uncertain terms, claiming, "Everything he stands for, I'm against."[16] To Frank Marshall Davis, the message was clear: the electorate had revolted against the idea that a "notorious white supremacist" had been dispatched to intimidate them.[17] To Davis, Eastland's backers in the islands were "our local lunatic fringe, composed primarily of haoles," which was "overjoyed at having its high priests of white supremacy in its midst."[18] Unlike on the mainland, in Hawai'i the GOP faced a "dark future," said the *Honolulu Record*.[19]

The Left was hardly in a mood for compromise. With sarcasm dripping, Bridges averred that "the people of our union have the right to vote for their union officials—and that is not true of Mississippi,"[20] while Jack Hall's riposte was, "I can get more votes in Hawaii than [Eastland] can get in Mississippi if everyone has a chance to vote in Mississippi,"[21] which decidedly was not the case.[22] Besides, those of Eastland's persuasion were afraid of potential ILWU strength in the southern ports, such as Biloxi, Mobile, Pensacola, and the like.[23] Frank Marshall Davis agreed, asserting that "one of the hidden reasons for the hearings was an attempt by Southern shipping interests to prevent the ILWU from extending its influence to Dixie ports where Negro longshoremen are paid less."[24]

Bridges and the union leadership had helped orchestrate this rebuff of the leading Dixiecrat. The top ILWU leader saw the opportunity to turn the tables on the anticommunists by linking them tightly to Eastland's white supremacy, which was increasingly discredited. He associated the Mississippi legislator with management and IMUA, which placed all three on the defensive.[25] Days before the demonstration at 'Iolani Palace, the union had produced and distributed 60,000 copies of a leaflet titled "Senator Eastland vs. the People of Hawaii," with most copies circulated in O'ahu.[26]

Shortly after the Thanksgiving holiday, Bridges himself touched down in Honolulu on a Pan American Airways flight, looking as if he was spoiling for a fight. He spared not a moment in instantly launching a blistering verbal assault against Eastland, sprinkled liberally with rococo bursts of profanity aimed at the paunchy, glowering, balding, cigar-chomping senator. Using words that resonated strongly with ILWU members, he added, "I don't think anything but a white America and a white Hawaii would divert Eastland."[27] Speaking earlier at a 900-person tribute to Hall in Honolulu, Bridges received stormy applause as he condemned Eastland's race-baiting. At the head table with him were former judge Delbert Metzger, the widow of Mayor John Wilson, future congresswoman Patsy Mink—and even the territorial attorney general, Edward Sylva.[28] Shortly thereafter, the chief legal officer of the islands was fired unceremoniously,[29] though the ILWU did not relent in response.[30]

"Eastlandism is a blood relative of Hitlerism" was the slogan of the ILWU. It was pointed out that sailors from Hawai'i had been victimized by "Eastlandites" while their ships docked in southern ports and that the senator's visit was part of a counterattack against equality. In a poster, the union added in a jab at its local opponents—"P.S. The Honolulu Star-Bulletin refused to publish this as a paid advertisement."[31]

Mobilizing adeptly, the ILWU held a meeting to plot against Eastland. The point stressed was that the senator's arrival was part of an employer offensive meant to place the union in retreat, as evidenced by the participation of employers in IMUA and their joint attempt to facilitate this hearing. Irked,

Bridges thought that management had sought to tie the union's hands with long-term contracts, then frame the leaders on spurious charges brought by Washington. The members, as was their wont, posed a blizzard of questions to Hall and Bridges, with one asking the latter about his political affiliations. Bridges responded that in 1934, when he was leading the General Strike in San Francisco, he was accused of being a British agent—now he was allegedly a Soviet agent. Asked about the relationship between the CP and the ILWU, Bridges replied, "I'll be darned if I know," since "as the President of the International, I have enough trouble with our own union"; for in the ILWU, he said, "people can be what they like" since "you have no union shop, closed shop and every member of this union was put on the job by the employer." Thus, he added, "if they're Communists, [Democrats, or] Republicans [we] didn't put them there," as "we're not a political party."[32]

The ILWU rapidly capitalized upon the turn represented by court-ordered desegregation, stressing how it benefited members.[33] The American Legion—and white war veterans generally—had been a bulwark of support for conservatism in Hawai'i, but now they too were being placed on the defensive as McElrath skewered them for their restrictions on admitting members with "colored skins," a practice he deemed "un-American."[34] McElrath underscored the anti-Asian crusades led in the past by unions as he scorned Bret Harte and Jack London for their racist sins in the process, while emphasizing that the ILWU's record was decidedly different—a point that could not hurt its already stunning popularity with a mostly Asian-Pacific working class.[35]

Of course, the ILWU did not have to look eastward in order to find examples of segregation. "The estates still maintain color bars in certain residential areas," according to Frank Marshall Davis. "On the Windward side, certain sections of Kailua, parts of Kaneohe Bay Drive and Mahalani Circle on the water in Kaneohe and Kawela Bay near Kahuku are restricted to haoles only."[36]

In the midst of sugar negotiations, McElrath made a radio broadcast about a Negro minister who had been convicted of the crime of "conspiring with other colored people to demand their being treated as human beings." The reference was to Dr. Martin Luther King Jr. and the "foul record of human oppression below the Mason-Dixon line." The union demanded that the constitutional proviso that mandated reducing congressional representation in the South—passed during the Reconstruction era—be enforced.[37]

The *Honolulu Record* charged that only haoles were allowed to visit ships of the American President Lines[38] without a pass.[39] "I have talked with other servicemen and merchant seamen," said Davis, "who swear that Honolulu is one of the most prejudiced places against Negroes that they have ever seen. Many cafes and entertainment places, both downtown and in Waikiki have consistently refused to serve Negroes," he contended. "Still others may accept colored patronage one night and then refuse to admit the same individuals the following evening," while "many Negroes live in Kailua, Ewa or Nanakuli," due to residential segregation.[40] Richard Drake, a former disk jockey then toiling as a chef in Waikīkī—and a Negro—had his application rejected when he sought to join the Honolulu Police Department. This occurred, said Davis, though Drake was far lighter in complexion than many members of the police force and though there were no known Negroes employed by this body.[41]

In such a climate, it became easier for Bridges to place anticommunists on the defensive by hammering Eastland for racism, an ideology once hailed but rapidly becoming discredited.[42] The union's opponents were reduced to maintaining that the ILWU was bent on stirring up racial antagonisms, "particularly against haoles," as one anticommunist leader put it—but this argument was hard to accept, given the union's vanguard antiracist crusade (and Bridges' leadership).[43]

"Those backing the probe are mostly conservative white Republicans," Davis said of the Senate Internal Security Subcommittee, and "out here" Redbaiting "no longer [has] much meaning," being perceived widely as "the equivalent of what we on the mainland call 'more white folks' foolishness.'" Davis—being black and Red—was often attacked on the radio, but this hardly seemed to affect his standing. "Officials of the Chinese bank where I do business will sometimes keep me for an hour or so just talking about the race question; prominent Japanese lawyers and businessmen stop me on the street to congratulate me about something I wrote," he mused. As Davis saw it, "Most of the island people actually hate whites, who generally consider themselves superior[,] and like me because I've got the 'guts' to say what they want to say." Putting his finger on a central difference between Hawai'i and the mainland, he sagely observed that "in Japan and China where many Oriental people still have strong family ties, many of these families are now avowed Communists." They recognized that the charges "being hurled and primarily by whites [are] a weapon to weaken labor unions."[44] At the same time, race relations in Hawai'i were of such a nature that Davis claimed he was embraced—his politics aside— because most islanders "feel close to me since I'm about the same color," while these same folks were "knocked out" by his Euro-American spouse because "it was the first time a 'haole' [woman] had ever worked and waited on them!"[45]

In such an environment, bringing Eastland to Honolulu in 1956 to warn of the danger said to be represented by Communists was like bringing Benedict Arnold to the thirteen colonies in 1779 to warn of the dangers of revolt. Certainly the Left was not terrorized at the prospect of Eastland's imminent arrival.[46] Instead of fleeing, the Left went on the offensive.[47]

For his part, Senator Eastland, after glimpsing what was in store, had a low-key stay in Honolulu. Resembling a prosperous midwestern hardware dealer and clad in a business suit—instead of string tie and slouch hat, as his stereotype might have dictated—this tall man, weighing in at 200 pounds, had shoulders that seemed to droop, perhaps because of the burdens that he carried, perhaps because of poor posture. An onlooker thought he looked like former President Truman. Certainly he seemed on edge upon his arrival, possibly having been briefed about what he should expect.[48]

Eastland's mood was not improved by what he heard during the course of his obstreperous hearings—or, perhaps, what he did not hear. Though he and his fellow solons were reportedly struck by the umbrella-like spread of the Reds over the islands, they were not pleased when 20 out of 30 witnesses called to testify invoked their right to remain silent under the Fifth Amendment.[49]

Like the 1950 hearings, these too were broadcast over the radio. During the course of this human drama, Myer Symonds strolled over to the basement of the palace to meet Senator Eastland. The confident legislator had both his feet up on the desk, Symonds recalled later, and "had a big cigar in his mouth with a big hat parked on his cranium"—"he never [at] one time acknowledged I was in the room," Symonds noted. "[He] just kept smoking his cigar and looking down. He just completely ignored me as a person, and then I sat down."[50] Symonds knew that his law firm was one of the visitor's chief targets, along with the ILWU, the United Public Workers, and the *Record*.[51]

The ILWU was pleased with its anti-Eastland offensive. Jeff Kibre, its tough-minded Washington representative, was gloating about the lack of press coverage of the hearings. Although radicals nationally were hiding or converting opportunistically to liberalism, Kibre advised, "We have to mount a very definite counterattack," as he envisioned "writing the final chapter on the Eastland hearing."[52]

The union was largely successful in this initiative, demonstrating to the mainlanders how anticommunism could be put in helter-skelter retreat. A resonant metaphor emerged when Eastland's research director, Benjamin Mandel, nearly drowned at Waikīkī while swimming. He was pulled unconscious from the water as his skin was turning blue, and he was almost given up for dead. Like many inexperienced tourists, he found himself in deep water in a spot where usually it was only waist high, and then he began to swim hurriedly for shore.[53] He finally made it but, like his committee, was battered and almost expired in the process.

On the other hand, Eastland's stooped posture may have been induced by the weight and potency of what he had heard just before getting on a westward plane. The irascible Lieutenant General John W. O'Daniel—otherwise known as "Iron Mike"—had commanded the US Army in the Pacific from September 1952 to April 1954, at a time when the ILWU was reeling from Hall's prosecution and conviction. From O'Daniel's viewpoint, the union hardly seemed to be on the defensive, and this is precisely what he conveyed to Eastland's Internal Security Subcommittee of the US Senate. In fact, he told a hushed audience, he expected the worst if his country had entered a shooting war in the mid-Pacific: "I visualized an uprising in the islands si-multaneous with an attack from the outside"—spearheaded by Hawai'i's no-torious corps of Communists—he confided.[54] General O'Daniel conducted practice alerts every 90 days while in the islands, and, indicative of the seri-ousness with which he viewed the CP, one phase of the exercises simulated this purported Red uprising. The important Hawai'i politico Oren Long was not alone in saying that this was "the most amazing statement about Hawaii that I have heard during my 40 years [of] residence in the territory."[55]

Influential columnist Victor Riesel did not disagree. "Only the Army, Navy and Air Force can match the power wielded" by Bridges in Hawai'i, he opined. "The pro-Commie union," meaning the ILWU, "has about $1,000,000 in assets, provides doctors, medicine, legal advice and domestic counseling" to its grateful members, and also helps them to "buy furniture and household appliances at cut rate prices"; even high-ticket items like automobiles were purchased by members with union assistance, binding them further to the ILWU, Riesel asserted. "If we want the western world to survive," he added ominously, "we'd better take some time out and do a little more for the peoples of the Eastern world. Right now they aren't exactly fond of us," he said—though how routing the ILWU would change this was left unclear.[56] Riesel had become the chief journalistic adversary of the union, launching hysteri-cal attacks on the ILWU in his testimony before Congress,[57] then repeating the same charges with added relish in his columns.[58]

It seemed that anticommunists did not know how to accept victory. Eu-gene Dennis may have been exaggerating in claiming that the only Reds in Hawai'i were tourists, but the thrust of his statement—pooh-poohing Com-munist strength in the archipelago—was not far wrong. Once there had been a few hundred Reds in the islands, but when Dr. Lyle G. Phillips, the leader of the anticommunist IMUA—which seemed to be rising as the CP was declining—embarked on a cross-country speaking tour after Eastland's de-parture, he claimed that there were fewer than 50 Reds in Hawai'i.[59]

Congressman Carroll Reece of Tennessee, who was of like mind, as-serted that by May 1950 there were no more than 90 Reds in Hawai'i and that J. Edgar Hoover himself had confirmed that two years later this number had dipped to 56—and had declined since.[60] By early 1956, Governor Samuel Wilder King said there were 36 Reds in Hawai'i—but he hastened to pro-claim that "numbers alone do not give an accurate picture of the extent of the Communist influence in Hawaii."[61] In an analysis of the ILWU's leaders and staff by a leading anticommunist body in Honolulu, it was ascertained that about 50 percent of them were "either identified Communists or known alumni of the Communist California Labor School."[62]

Thus, as the union's opponents perceived matters, when union-friendly John Burns set off for Washington to represent the archipelago in Congress, it was tantamount to V. I. Lenin's arrival at the Finland Station a few decades earlier.[63] Even the *New York Herald Tribune*, which traditionally paid as much attention to Hawai'i as it did to Bhutan, began to express concern about trends in the islands.[64] In sum, though the CP had been weakened seriously, radical-ism had yet to disappear from Hawai'i—but blocking the territory's ascension to statehood was increasingly seen as contrary to Cold War mandates.

That radicalism was alive and well was reflected in the 1955 anniversary edition of the *Honolulu Record*—studied by some as if it were the lineup of So-viet leadership on May Day in Red Square. The issue featured, according to one distressed account, advertisements from "a total of 21 public office holders, the chairman of the Democratic Party and 58 ILWU units and divisions"—not to mention one from John Burns.[65] This fed the ongoing campaign to frighten away the journal's advertisers,[66] notably by raising the cry that the *Record* was tied to "Communist China."[67]

In the prelude to Senator Eastland's visit, the legislature in Honolulu was wrestling for hours on end with the question of alleged subversion by Reds and held secret sessions devoted to ascertaining who had leaked a report on this burdened matter. The debate focused on allegations that leading members of the Democratic Party were actually Communists. McElrath himself was sum-moned to testify before the subcommittee. Interrogated by Daniel Inouye, the union leader disclaimed any knowledge of the purloined report.[68]

Yet the legislature's lack of success in preserving the local version of the Un-American Activities Committee or even keeping private its secrets was an indication of how anticommunism—still riding high on the mainland—was in retreat in Hawai'i. The minority elite was adjusting to the new realities: McElrath noticed that previously the vast majority of chamber of commerce and Merchant Street lobbyists were haole lawyers or haole executives, but "now we find numerous Japanese-Americans carrying the ball for the big boys" since "some people believe that Japanese members of the legislature will be more likely to listen with greater sympathy to lobbyists of Japanese ancestry."[69] In short, to better confront radical success in the isles, the haole elite had to en-gage in racial integration—which, in turn, undermined conservatism.

On the mainland, reputed Communists were in prison when not under-ground or silenced. McElrath—by way of contrast—had to deny that the territorial legislature was "dominated by the ILWU" and "that whenever Jack Hall cracks the whip, things began to happen up at Iolani Palace."[70] This was not true, he declared—though his opponents doubted the veracity of his denial.

Certainly local senator Ben Dillingham disbelieved McElrath. He ac-cused the upper house, where he sat, of being dominated by the ILWU. Yes, this body had raised the minimum wage, McElrath responded, which would benefit thousands of waitresses, clerks, janitors, and laborers, and, yes, a real property exemption had been secured, which was an ILWU proposal—but this hardly meant union domination.[71] In response, the GOP demanded re-apportionment of the legislature, seeking to slash representation beyond the cozy confines of Oʻahu.[72]

As Hawaiʻi crept closer to statehood, sour apprehension about the nature of its political makeup grew accordingly. This skepticism was endemic among Dixiecrats. The problem was that, with the rise of the civil rights movement, their core ideas were losing popularity—particularly racism, which rested close to their opposition to statehood.[73] A white southerner sarcastically argued that the name of the nation should be changed to "United Nations of the Western Hemisphere" or even the "United States of the World." Drew Smith, yet another disgruntled Euro-American, contrasted the United States with the now declining British Empire, where "colonials of Africa and elsewhere do not sit in the English Parliament." Irate, he proclaimed that "never before in the history of our nation, have we been confronted with the addition of a new state where the native white inhabitants are being displaced by other races." The "Caucasian race cannot compete in breeding capacity with the Mongolian peoples of the world," he cried. "Just as the Japanese absorbed the white Ainu in Hokkaido, the Orientals will obliterate the white Americans in Hawaii."[74]

Summarizing the viewpoint of a growing body of elite opinion, the *Hilo Tribune-Herald* acknowledged that statehood "can never be divorced, unfortunately, from the South's battle against equal rights for the Negro" for "the South regards Hawaii as a natural enemy who would only weaken the South's position in Congress." Thus, Eastland's hearings, it was said, "have done Hawaii's chances for statehood very serious damage."[75]

Republican patriarch Walter Dillingham was cited for the notion that the ILWU was so strong that Hawaiʻi would be a Pacific version of Finland during the Cold War, implying that the islands would be unable to counter or confront Communists effectively because of the party's local strength.[76] Territorial senator Ben Dillingham had a similar concern but a different approach, for he appealed for statehood as a means to thwart the Reds.[77] As it turned out, the argument of the latter won out.

Radical potency had spread from the docks and the fields to government offices—or so it was thought—thereby increasing anxieties about statehood. The United Public Workers were organized in 1946 (with ILWU aid) and in less than a decade had a membership of about 2,000, consisting mostly of hospital, culinary, and service workers. The new union was led by a suspected Communist, Henry Epstein, who had arrived in Hawaiʻi in May 1947.[78]

Moreover, Eastland was being told that Alaska—once thought to be reliably conservative—might be evolving in Hawaiʻi's direction. A dangerous situation existed in Anchorage, since "there are enough Negroes [there] alone to carry a ticket if they all get behind a candidate and vote," said his correspondent, Sherman Clemmons. "The same is true of Fairbanks[,] our next largest town. Between the two there are approximately 15,000 Negroes[,] all of whom have come to this country within the past ten years." Alaska too was becoming a "threat to the white race," he added, "and the South should be frightened at the prospect of statehood for Alaska."[79] How to attain statehood for a territory that seemed to be crawling with Communists was a question that elite opinion found difficult to answer.[80]

McElrath sensed that "advocates of master race theory" were losing popularity in the new environment. and thus anti-statehood proponents were reduced to telling "Communist menace fairy tales,"[81] though such tales remained powerful.[82] "This union and its leaders are realistic," McElrath confided in April 1956, "and have recognized that statehood for Hawaii is so remote a possibility that it's about time to do something [else]," suggesting an arrangement akin to the commonwealth status then endured by Puerto Rico.[83] Statehood "seems to be far and away into the future," Ray Jerome Baker said in 1956. "There seems to be no possibility of getting it now or in the foreseeable future."[84] Soon-to-be-defrocked Hawaiian attorney general Edward Sylva asserted that statehood was a "dead duck, as long as Southern bigotry continues to flourish and grow."[85]

The San Francisco–based leadership of the ILWU moved toward backing commonwealth status, as Bridges concluded that statehood was remote. Hall intervened to disagree, but Bridges' sentiments seemed more realistic.[86] Even Governor King sensed a letdown in the enthusiasm for statehood,[87] as did others.[88]

In the midst of building the Democratic Party, plumping for statehood, and foiling visiting senators, the ILWU was also embroiled in negotiations for contracts for its membership. The union continued to display contempt for US officials in a manner that was alien to radicals on the mainland. When President Eisenhower's labor secretary, James Mitchell, arrived in Honolulu, he promptly denounced Hall as unfit, and just as promptly the union suspended both sugar and pineapple negotiations until he left town.[89] Such lèse-majesté did little appreciable harm to the union, which could depend reliably on unceasing hostility from the GOP in any case. Shortly after Mitchell's departure, McElrath announced proudly that pineapple workers—in the islands' second-largest industry—"for the first time in the history of American agriculture" had signed a contract that provided for severance pay for field workers—in addition to an across-the-board pay boost.[90] Just before Eastland's arrival, the ILWU announced that Hawaiian stevedores had attained parity in many respects with their counterparts in California, achieving a long-standing union demand.[91] It was not easy for workers in Hawai'i to join the anticommunist bandwagon when the target of conservative ire—their union, the ILWU—was improving workers' very lives.

As Senator Eastland began to contemplate his 5,000-mile journey westward, dilapidated and blighted plantation houses at Ewa, surrounded by open
sewers, outhouses, and poor drainage, were being transformed by the addition of green lawns, flower beds, and bushes, as well as general upgrading.[92]
Not so long ago, workers had complained bitterly that rats bit their behinds
as they sat nervously in collapsing outhouses, but by the time of the Eastland
hearings, they were residing in new or remodeled three-bedroom houses
with spacious yards[93]—another marker as to why these hearings failed.

Still, despite its evident gains, labor had much to worry about. Speaking on
Labor Day in 1955 at 'A'ala Park in Honolulu, Jack Hall lamented that as a result
of mechanization the number of sugar workers had declined in the previous
eight years from 22,743 to 16,733—and 700 more workers were slated to be
dropped from the payrolls in coming months. This reduction was occurring
even though the average return on investment in this industry was a comfortable 22.4 percent and dividends continued to rise annually at a rate of 14.5 percent.[94] Ray Jerome Baker said that the millions of tons of sugar were produced
with a workforce of about one-third the number of men that had been required
to produce the last million-ton crop, which was before the war. Speaking in
1956, he thought 1,000 more men would lose their jobs through additional automation within the next two years.[95] In 1956 the sugar crop in Hawai'i was worth
$147 million, which was about $1.5 million more than the value of the 1955
crop—but $1 million less than the record 1953 crop.[96] Plantation profits totaled
a handsome $11.9 million in 1956, and the Big Five—or the "cream separators,"
as one economist termed them—made a net profit in 1956 of $7.2 million, most
of it coming from sugar. It cost less in wages to produce a ton of sugar in Hawai'i
than anywhere else under the US flag, including Puerto Rico.[97] Hawai'i was
leading the world in efficiency of cane production, the record there being 2.63
man-days of field work per ton, which compared favorably against Florida's 4.3.[98]

In early 1956 Ray Jerome Baker remarked that sugar plantations anticipated that "within the next two years about a thousand more men will be lopped
off their jobs," a development that had complicated negotiations about severance pay.[99] Hence, Henry Walker Jr., whom the union deemed to be an important member of the minority elite, was probably correct when he argued years
later that both sugar and pineapple were commodities that could be grown in
many sites and that it was inevitable that instead of bringing Filipinos to Hawai'i
to work in the fields, these laborers could work more profitably in the fields of
their homeland. "The union didn't kill sugar or pineapple" in Hawai'i, he
said[100]—but surely what was to be called "globalization" had wounded it. Certainly the radicalism of the ILWU was an incentive for planters to find a production site other than Hawai'i, labor's productivity there notwithstanding.

California's tremendously wealthy Henry Kaiser had begun to eye the
islands, but even he did not necessarily view them as an investment paradise.

By the mid-1950s he had a home in Kāhala, worth a then lofty $187,500, and his companies worldwide did business to the tune of hundreds of millions of dollars annually.[101] "Between the two of us," Lorrin Thurston, a member of one of Honolulu's oldest haole families, told "my dear Henry," "I think we could develop something which would have absolutely no equal in the territory of Hawaii."[102] But Kaiser had reason to believe that the global market in sugar was becoming increasingly competitive and that pineapple was trending in a similar direction, while Kaiser's preferred field of investment—tourism—was deemed by one expert to be "essentially hazardous."[103]

Moreover, the union's adversaries had not disappeared. AFL unions, instead of joining with the ILWU against the IMUA and the anticommunists, instead collaborated with the latter, assisting them with their fund-raising.[104] The Teamsters, which Art Rutledge considered to be the backbone of anticommunism in Hawai'i,[105] was particularly energetic in this sphere,[106] becoming a master in poaching members from other unions.[107]

Symptomatic of the internecine warfare that had erupted was that the ILWU took the extraordinary step of crossing AFL picket lines thrown up at Foodland, as Hall deemed their efforts "not legitimate;"[108] the ILWU bested its rivals by receiving 61 percent of the workers' votes on the right to bargain on their behalf,[109] an extraordinary victory.[110] Ray Jerome Baker felt that Rutledge was part of a corrupt axis of gangster unions and greedy bosses.[111] Ben Dillingham admitted that when Rutledge had problems with his immigration status and faced possible deportation, he assisted him, since this labor leader had helped to "offset the very real threat of one-union control"—meaning ILWU control—in Hawai'i.[112] Like a boxer nonchalantly pummeling an outmatched opponent, Hall commented casually that "after all [we] are twice the size of the AFL-CIO in Hawaii" and magnanimously "turned over our membership in utilities" to one of their affiliates, "even though they were unable to take them over in raiding attempts"[113]—suggesting why it was so necessary for some to maintain Rutledge's viability.

Nevertheless, it seemed that the AFL perceived the ILWU as a larger obstacle to its advance than the employers who hired—and fired—its members.[114] While the ILWU was in a virtual death match with the fire-breathing journalist Victor Riesel, the AFL was lobbying a local newspaper to carry his column regularly.[115] Earlier the AFL had informed the US Department of the Interior that it backed the department's choice to be the colony's governor precisely because of his "vigorous fight against Communists,"[116] with whom the ILWU was thought to be associated.

From the AFL's viewpoint, it had good reason to derail the ILWU. Having survived the Smith Act trial, Jack Hall was now attempting to expand his union by seeking to organize workplaces directly contiguous to the waterfront, such as trucking, thereby augmenting contracts the ILWU already had with two major automotive operations. There was "no question that the vast majority of people in the hotel industry are sympathetic to us," he thought, and organizing there would bring an inevitable confrontation with the AFL, as would the ILWU plans to organize the carpenters and other construction workers. Hall thought that on Kaua'i, for example, "some of the larger contractors of Japanese ancestry are quite friendly" with the ILWU and that a "union establishing a basic minimum wage will be a stabilizing factor in the industry,"[117] which could impel his union to organize further. This plan was ambitious—and guaranteed to foment bitter feelings within the AFL.

ILWU leaders were heartened, however, when they met in Manhattan with packinghouse workers—the International Longshore Association, their direct AFL competitor—and a number of other unions, with sugar being high on the agenda. Mob boss Albert Anastasia was there, and the fact that he seemed to be headed for an open war with the ILA certainly would have distracted this competitor from attacking the ILWU.[118]

Similarly, as the AFL and CIO were merging—or more accurately, the latter was surrendering to the former—the ILWU was consolidating.[119] Yet the union was nagged by its failure to diversify at the highest level. Thus Matsuki Arashiro—a war veteran, an ILWU member, and later a senator from Kaua'i— remained angry with Hall years later, still resenting this top leader's backing of businessman Tony Baptiste over himself in the pivotal 1954 elections. Hall's decision, he said, was made "because of the racial question" since "those were the days when race meant a lot."[120]

The fractiousness that had bedeviled the ILWU also continued, perhaps an inevitable result of the pressures it faced. Louis Goldblatt was ready to oust McElrath, accusing him of haphazard work habits that were leading to "nervous breakdowns and maybe loss of life" among his comrades. "I've raised hell about this so often," he said.[121] J. R. Robertson, no friend of Hall's, also was highly critical of McElrath, accusing him of overcompensating aggressively because of his height—"he's a very small man in stature," he said.[122] Rachel Saiki, a union stalwart for years, recalled later that although McElrath used to visit her home "frequently for supper . . . he never once said 'Hello, goodbye, thank you' to my parents." Still miffed years later, she declared, "I never forgave Bob for not being a little more courteous [toward] my parents."[123] Saiki had been involved in strikes since 1938—"I've been in many picket lines," she admitted modestly, though accurately—and she resented Hall.[124] Mitsuo "Slim" Shimizu, recalled a settlement of pineapple negotiations in 1956 in Kaua'i that he found unsatisfactory; when he called Hall to complain, he was told, "If you don't like it, fuck you."[125]

The bitterness that often arises when strong-willed men and women work together under tense conditions had not disappeared. Over Bridges' objection, Eddie Tangen was brought over from the mainland to take a high-level post in the ILWU, and McElrath was named regional director even though the union remained verbally committed to promotion of non-haole leadership: the seeming contradiction in these appointments roiled the waters.[126] In the ultimate indignity, management negotiator Philip Maxwell asserted that "one of the basic weaknesses in the ILWU, in my opinion, is their failure to promote secondary leadership," as "they keep electing these same nonentities" when "they ought to be able to find a Filipino."[127] Ariyoshi became terribly upset when the union brought over yet another mainland haole to run a newspaper that the ILWU had initiated. The relations between Hall and his colleague in union leadership, Newton Miyagi, had become so bad that although their offices were adjacent, the Japanese-American admitted that "we started writing each other written memos" in order to communicate.[128]

Even Hall, who had worked alongside McElrath profitably for years, was now seeking a "reappraisal" of his comrade's signature effort: the radio broadcasts. "Both the Filipino and English programs [have] lost listening audiences," Hall objected. Yet this reduction in listeners might have had something to do with the enhanced status of the union and its apparent acceptance by employers, for Hall added that "in line with our policy of toning down because of our understanding with the employers, we have turned the program over primarily to community use." Ironically, Hall indicated the value of these broadcasts as he moved to eliminate them, suggesting that employers knew that because of McElrath's initiative "deliberate lies and deliberate misrepresentations of facts can be answered."[129]

Hall prevailed on the issue of radio programming, and thus the union removed one of its most valuable pieces off the chessboard in return for a less confrontational stance by management. The acceptance of the union meant that now Hall was getting closer to those with whom he negotiated. Wendell Carlsmith was one of these men. Hall became "our frequent visitor" at his family's palatial estate, this epitome of the haole elite recalled later. "I was probably closer to [Hall] than any other person . . . at the time of his death," the Stanford alumnus claimed.[130]

It was probably unavoidable that after spending so much time negotiating—and boozing—that representatives of management and labor would become closer. Likewise, as employers came to realize that their most strenuous efforts would not destroy the ILWU, they switched—as in the children's tale—from unleashing hurricane force winds to exuding warm sunshine. This was disarming. Even Maxwell recognized that in the larger scheme of things, the ILWU was a boon to Hawai'i, not least since its efforts gave workers greater purchasing power, which meant more sales of "refrigerators, tv sets and furniture," to the ultimate benefit of merchants.[131] More realistic members of the elite had reason to seek accommodation with the union.

This was part of the transformation of Hawai'i wrought by the ILWU, of which November 1954 was only a part. Thus it was in 1956, when all eyes were trained on Senator Eastland, that the union quietly entered the insurance field; this involved an initiative to provide automobile insurance at the lowest possible rates, which led to a general fall in premiums in the archipelago. Higher wages for sugar workers, historically the lowest-paid of all, produced great pressure to raise all other wages in Hawai'i. Consequently, employers bent on maintaining a union-free environment still had to yield to the ILWU's competitive pressure and raise wages; often this was done at the express behest of the Hawaii Employers Council. Also in 1956, Labor Secretary Mitchell announced that family income in Hawai'i had climbed to a point that the territory now ranked above all states except Connecticut, New Jersey, Nevada, and the District of Columbia, and the islands' per capita income was topped by only 13 states.[132]

The union had delivered benefits to its members, which complicated enormously the ability of Senator Eastland to win them over. During the same year that the Mississippian arrived in the islands, *Business Week* seemed taken aback when the ILWU negotiated with pineapple growers what they believed to be the first unemployment compensation plan for US agricultural workers, a sector of the labor force traditionally given short shrift on the mainland. This new development was "sure to get a close reading," said the pro-employer journal.[133]

The 1954 electoral triumph was the tipping point that set in motion events that were to create modern Hawai'i as the closest thing to a social democracy under the US flag. Ray Jerome Baker predicted confidently—and accurately—that a renewed, post-1954 tax structure was now in store "with less favoritism toward the big shots." Wages for government workers and teachers were scheduled for a raise. Appropriations for investigations of purported subversive activities were predictably scheduled for severe downsizing.[134] The University of Hawai'i campus, traditionally neglected, received upgrading. Baker thought that the propertied class had never been sold on the university, because "so many of the students have come from the ranks of what were supposed to be servile, Oriental workers."[135] That too began to change, as an outgrowth of the ILWU induced electoral triumph.

Whereas before, Washington representatives like the Farringtons had—at best—supped with the ILWU with a long spoon, their replacement, John Burns, had no compunctions about sitting closely alongside the union at the same table.[136] This warm relationship was indicative of the union's enhanced profile on the islands. Hall felt that the Eastland hearings had been a disaster for the union's opponents (particularly the Republicans), chortling that the GOP—once seen as leading the archipelago to statehood, which was backed by many on that premise—was now "about as ineffective as the pre-1946

Democratic Party and we are back practically to a one-party system again." Hall felt that "if it were not for the ILWU support of the Republican House members, the Democrats would have overwhelming veto over-riding power in the House as well as the Senate and they [Republicans] would have lost the two county administrations they still retain."[137] The ILWU seemed to be wielding so much power that an alarmed Ben Dillingham claimed that the employers had become "weak-kneed" in dealing with them.[138]

As the movement symbolized by Dr. King gained traction, more African-Americans began to speak out more vigorously in support of the union. The leading Negro newspaper in San Francisco argued that the ILWU was "one of the few labor organizations in the entire United States that welcomed [Negroes] as brothers" and had created a situation where "in terms of pure wages" waterfront workers on the West Coast were "the elite of all Negro workers." This glowing description had once been affixed as well to the ILWU's ally, the Marine Cooks and Stewards Union, but after Harry Lundberg of the Sailors' Union of the Pacific began to raid its ranks—with the aid of the NAACP— "Negro seamen are now being replaced as fast as Lundberg can do it," said this journal. "Ask Negroes who sail the seas to tell you their sad stories, and you will be truly amazed."[139] Thus the attacks on the unions had caused certain allies among Negroes to cling even more closely to the ILWU, boosting its resolve.

There were other troubling indications that despite the strength of the Left, its continued good health was not necessarily ineluctable. In the summer of 1956 the Left's old friend John H. Wilson, the longtime mayor of Honolulu, passed away. He had been born to a blacksmith father of Scotch-Tahitian heritage, who was also a part-time firefighter and a close friend of Queen Lili'uokalani. John Wilson had attended Stanford University, where he was termed derisively "Kanaka Jack."[140] His close relationship to radicals did not appreciably dampen the outpouring of grief that accompanied his funeral. A 44-car, seven-block-long procession inched its way to the cemetery, and 1,000 persons watched the burial rites. All along the line of march the ordinary workers stopped to pay homage. Men in jeans jerked off their hats and stood awkwardly at attention, as women leaned from second-story windows and watched silently, or turned their heads and sobbed uncontrollably and inconsolably. The presence of five Buddhist priests in robes and religious insignia were further indication—if any were needed—that this was Hawai'i, an archipelago with a different history and tradition from those that marked the mainland.[141]

The loss of this ally could not have happened at a worse moment, for it was then that Congressman Francis Walter of the House Un-American Activities Committee asked the US attorney general to rule that the ILWU was subversive. "Should the Attorney General do so," he said, "this would mean that an employer is not required to recognize the union as bargaining agent for its employees."[142] When Bridges arrived in Honolulu just before statehood, he reported glumly that "a couple of days before I left the mainland, we received two letters from Internal Revenue, Department of the Treasury," whose agents had been rooted in his San Francisco offices for almost a year, "going over all the books of this union."[143] Bridges had good reason to worry: a recommendation had been made that the ILWU's tax-exempt status be revoked.[144]

As Hawai'i moved closer to statehood, conservative congressmen began to ponder more profoundly the meaning of its admission to the Union.[145] The "Red Termites," said the *Star-Bulletin*, were "still boring away."[146] Newton Miyagi, a rising leader of the union, was coming under closer inspection, and it was said in his defense that he had "never been formally accused, indicted, tried or convicted as a Communist." Well, "neither have Khrushchev, Bulganin, [nor] Molotov," huffed the *Maui News*. "Nor were Stalin and Lenin."[147] The union retained the support of its members, but Hawai'i was still ruled from Washington and thus was buffeted by what was influencing the United States as a whole.

Hungary erupted in anticommunist riots just as Senator Eastland was arriving in Honolulu, which prompted the *Star-Bulletin* to observe that the United States was "going through a sort of horrified realization of what communism can mean"—which raised further questions about the ILWU in the opinion of this journal.[148] Lest the union think that Hawai'i was—somehow—liberated territory, the authorities in Hilo refused to grant it permission to use a school auditorium in order to screen the now classic pro-labor movie *Salt of the Earth*.[149] To do so, said one official, would be tantamount to "endorsing Communist propaganda" that "furthered Communist aims."[150]

But it was not only the loss of Wilson and the skepticism of the Left brought by Hungary that dealt a vigorous body blow to the union. The Communist Party had been essential to the union's launch in the islands, and now it was reeling from Smith Act prosecutions from the Pacific to the Atlantic. Falling like dominoes were CP-oriented institutions, foremost among them the California Labor School in San Francisco, where many an ILWU leader had taken classes. Once students could take courses there pursuant to the GI Bill of Rights, indicative of its popular support, and overall a total of 75,000 students took courses there. But by 1957[151] it was defunct, ending a reign that had begun in 1942 and that had once offered courses from Sacramento to San Jose.[152] The ILWU also had benefited from its ties to the dwindling number of radical-led unions like itself, uppermost among them being the Mine, Mill and Smelter Workers Union—but soon this once-strapping union too was defunct.[153]

In 1955 at Jack Hall's Labor Day address—which for Hawai'i was the yearly equivalent of the US president's State of the Union remarks—he complained about the wages of stevedores. Even the good news seemed to bear a glimpse of cloudiness; thus Hall recognized that it was in sugar that "our members have made the greatest gains," as the ILWU—in collaboration with

management—was able "to completely mechanize a primarily hand operation with a union around and almost cut its work force in half without opposition."[154] But this union goodwill meant reduced dues payments too and,
in the long run, a weakened union.

There were other ominous signs. The price of sugar was basically set by
the federal government, and despite the sugar barons' influence in Washington, it did not require a seer to suspect that the more devious congressmen
might decide that undermining the sugar industry could be the best way to
undermine sugar workers. In any event, the deployment of mechanical cane
cutters was spreading significantly already, which had the potential to do away
with thousands of what McElrath referred to as "cut cane men and hapai ko
[loading cane] men."[155] Moreover, despite the widespread acceptance of the
ILWU, Ray Jerome Baker sensed in 1956 that the planters hoped, "with the aid
of Brownell's gang and the Republican administration[,] to force a strike of the
sugar workers and, if possible, to bust the union." Management "practically
told the men to take" what it was offering the union "or lump it," he said.[156]

CHAPTER 17

Toward Statehood

Jack Hall was barefoot and relaxed. His hair was closely cropped, and he had lost a few pounds, which was evident in the way he filled out his shirt and pants. Charles Fujimoto, on the other hand, looked about 20 pounds heavier; perhaps this was due to the enforced sitting that came with his newest initiative: running a small television and radio repair business. He was accompanied by his spouse, Eileen, now a secretary at the ILWU. Jack Kimoto was there too, still cricket slim, still blinking his eyes rapidly when he talked. Dwight Freeman was espied, now doing well in the construction business. John Reinecke and Koji Ariyoshi continued to work long hours for the *Honolulu Record*—nothing new there. Steaks were broiling over the charcoals, drinks were flowing, mirth was rising. There were repeated toasts at this celebration at Hall's abode on Paula Drive in Kāhala Heights in Honolulu, for the Hawaii Seven had heard only recently that their Smith Act convictions had been reversed, yet another setback for their anticommunist antagonists.[1]

The costs had been high. Jeff Kibre estimated that simply carrying the case to the US Supreme Court involved a $10,000 expenditure, plus an additional amount of about $1,400 to cover the printing of the record, briefs, and so on.[2] The case had been before the Ninth Circuit Court of Appeals for four years, as the judges seemed paralyzed at the prospect of ruling, causing Senator John Butler of Maryland to threaten an investigation of this "inordinate and shocking delay."[3] There were other nicks in the armor of the radicals. Kimoto had to fight a charge of fraudulent real estate dealings based on the allegation that he had transferred property to his wife days before he was indicted on Smith Act charges.[4] Reinecke was deemed ineligible to receive unemployment compensation, because of the conviction he had suffered.[5] Sensing the broader implication of this penalty, Hall enlisted the union to support Reinecke, as Hall thought such a legal precedent could lead to routine denial of government benefits on political grounds. "We should go all out on this matter," he counseled.[6] Honolulu firefighter Stephen Kong was convicted of attempting to influence a juror during the Smith Act trial and was sentenced to three years in

Jack Hall, the top leader of the ILWU in Hawai'i, was accused of being a Communist Party member. Courtesy of Anne Rand Library, ILWU–San Francisco.

prison; the conviction was based upon a brief conversation with juror Samson Peneku, who testified that Kong asked him to vote not guilty—an allegation adamantly denied.[7] But these costs were relatively minor in comparison with the benefits accrued to the Hawaii Seven—and those they represented.

The opponents of these radicals were upset that the majority in Hawai'i had not seen fit to isolate and marginalize these leftists as a condition precedent to admission to the revered Union, but they need not have worried, at least not unduly. In a culminating report to the territorial legislature, the territory's official body charged with ferreting out information about the Left noted that the Communist Party, which had arisen in the islands in late 1937 or early 1938, was dormant during the war before reactivating in 1945, and reached its peak shortly before the war in Korea, when its membership approached 200, now may have had a mere 15 "hard-shell formal members"—and this may have been an exaggeration. In the year of statehood it was reported elatedly that "there is now no formally organized and effective Hawaii section of the Communist Party." The purported Red Menace had been beaten back—but its lasting legacy had not. Its primary offspring, the ILWU, now had a reported 70,000 members (amid the territory's population of more than 500,000) in 83 locals, with Local 142 containing 22,000, or about 31 percent of the total membership.[8]

Despite this apparent disappearance of the CP, this organization, like the phantom pain felt in an amputated arm, continued to be hunted and hounded; it was as if the party were on the verge of seizing power. A scant year before the Smith Act reversal, Robert McElrath was offered immunity by Senator James Eastland in return for testifying in Washington about the CP. "I can honestly say that I am not a party member," he responded, but disbelief was the response in return.[9] Anticommunists insisted that the reason the CP could not be detected was that it operated in a semiclandestine manner; they seemed angry that, of the roughly dozen unions expelled by the CIO because of varying ties to Communists, only the ILWU remained virtually unaffected by the expulsion.[10]

When rising ILWU leader Newton Miyagi claimed, as statehood approached, that he had not been a Communist Party member since 1950[11]—while praising increasingly radical Cuba in the process[12]—IMUA tempers were not cooled. Even the Eisenhower administration took note when Miyagi was appointed to the board of the local Red Cross, though he had taken the Fifth Amendment during the Eastland hearings.[13] IMUA members might have been even more outraged if they had known that Myer Symonds had been by the office of the colony's chief justice to help rewrite what the ILWU lawyer termed "the archaic territorial rules of Criminal Procedure"; if they had known that he asked Ben Margolis (Los Angeles' leading radical lawyer) and Norman Leonard (his San Francisco counterpart) for advice, it would have solidified their fear that Reds truly had established a beachhead in Hawai'i that could be used for further assaults on the mainland.[14] Passions were hardly cooled when in 1976, years after statehood and years after the drama of an earlier era had diminished, Reinecke acknowledged, "I never agreed wholly with the Communist Party when I was in it and I still don't know that I'm out of it."[15]

But Dr. Lyle G. Phillips, IMUA's leader, denied that he was chasing phantoms; in fact, he alleged that the "ILWU Communist clique" had taken control of the Democratic Party. Of 811 precinct club officers monitored in the period just before statehood, he maintained, 175 were either Communist members, Communist sympathizers, or persons directly subject to Communist influence. Dejectedly, he added, in Hawai'i the "Communist conspiracy has gone further toward accomplishment of its primary aims than anywhere else in the United States."[16]

What irked the enemies of the ILWU was that they thought they perceived the purported pestilence of this body better than most. "Management in Hawaii," said McElrath, "makes it a point to know what's going on within even the most private councils of this union," as a result of "espionage activity within the ranks of trade unions." Sensing radical influence and being unable to squash it seemed to induce a cascade of anger among the anticommunists.[17] Frank Marshall Davis neatly summarized the intractable dilemma they faced in the isles. As long as anticommunism was centered disproportionately among the haole minority, it was inevitable that they—instead of their targets[18]—would be the ones isolated and marginalized.[19] What made this Hawaiian dilemma even more maddening was that the clout exercised by Hawai'i's elite seemed to hardly move those in the isles. When President Eisenhower visited the islands, the first question he posed upon alighting from his flight was, "'Where's Walter?'"[20]—but Dillingham's influence with the occupant of the White House did not seem to faze islanders.

In any case, the growing numbers of ILWU members hinted at a wider metamorphosis of the islands. Hawai'i was about to become part of the United States as a progressive anchor, contrary to the wishes of those who had touted statehood in the first instance. This was a fundamental truth.

Another fundamental truth also existed in Hawai'i, said Louis Goldblatt in early 1958: sugar had built Hawai'i. Yes, the Big Five had made a tidy sum in the nineteenth century in whaling, and it was true that in recent years Henry Kaiser had invested in tourism in the islands. But as Goldblatt surveyed the beautiful office buildings, the sumptuous hotels and attractive department stores, the lovely homes, the lush parks, and the other accoutrements that captured the eye of a growing flood of tourists, he argued that it all was based on sugar fields, or, more specifically, the labor of sugar workers whom the ILWU represented.[21]

Consequently, though the union had demonstrated time and time again that it was no force to be trifled with—as Senator Eastland could well attest—sugar negotiations were notably contentious during this year before statehood.

At one typical morning session in January 1958, the employer gruffly inquired about giving leaves for more than six months. "I presume it is intended primarily for those Filipinos who go back to the Philippine Islands," he said. Hall replied, "Yes, it's primarily for the Filipino members who came in 1946, so that they can have enough time for courting to catch a bride. Six months is not enough." In remarks deemed insensitive to the often lonely plight of these men, the employer responded, "What makes you think that if you can't catch a bride in six months you can catch one in 12 months?" He punctuated this outburst by adding, "The six months' leave of absence is a very liberal policy and we are opposed to extending it further."[22] It was such stubbornness that virtually guaranteed that the ILWU would sweep into statehood with yet another victory over its leading antagonists—the sugar barons—and thus would help set the tone for what was to come.

The union, in any case, had long aided its Filipino members in repatriating after they had become pensioners.[23] According to union attorney Harriet Bouslog, somewhere between 50 and 60 percent of plantation workers in Maui were Filipino as of 1947, and their preponderance in the union was hardly less elsewhere in the archipelago.[24] Thus these were not minor matters for the union. As one ILWU member put it, "The status of the Filipino[s] in many ways was infinitely worse than [that of] the blacks. The Filipinos were totally excluded from every union in Seattle except our union." Consequently, the union scooped up some of its most fervent and devoted members when it spoke up in avid defense of this marginalized minority.[25] Cebu-born Ricardo Labez, a gnome-faced man who was a leader of Filipinos in the union, has argued persuasively that "without the Filipino involvement we'd have no union."[26]

What managers in Honolulu apparently did not realize was that they had touched an acutely sensitive nerve, at once hitting crudely on a fragilely vulnerable aspect of the most deeply personal part of the workers' lives and driving them closer to the union that had risen to their support. For not only did a preponderance of the union have roots in this archipelago due west of Hawai'i, but about 8,000 of them were "aliens." They constituted the largest single "alien" group then in Hawai'i, surpassing the Japanese in the wake of the passage of the McCarran-Walter Act, which had made them eligible for citizenship.[27] Their delicate legal status was not assuaged by the lack of personal companionship. With such maladroit tactics, it was virtually preordained that management—once again—would wind up on the losing side of a titanic struggle.

Managers sought to compensate for its shortfall in effective tactics by resorting to other means. They pushed to the forefront Hilario C. Moncado, who—according to Ray Jerome Baker—"said he was the third representative of God, after Christ and Rizal," though "charges were made that [he] had collaborated in the Philippines with the Imperial Japanese Army." Nonetheless, the

Honolulu Chamber of Commerce swallowed its patriotism and accepted him as a member, largely because he advised his followers not to join the sugar workers union. But this was to little avail since "for many years now," said Baker, "his appeal to Filipinos has been declining,"[28] as this group formed the heart of a union that seemed to be unstoppable.

Nevertheless, even with a firm grip on the loyalties of the Filipino membership, rarely was there a good time to call a strike—not least in a strategic industry like sugar. This was particularly so in the period before statehood, when mechanization and layoffs were decimating the labor force and when wages annually paid by the sugar industry were smaller than they had been in the late 1940s, even though productivity had gone up—along with profits.[29] "Mechanization took place drastically from the year 1953 to 1954," said Yasuki Arakaki, and then it accelerated drastically thereafter.[30] For workers to sacrifice their paychecks and to picket and agitate instead did not seem like a fair bargain on its face. Yet, unlike many workers, those of the ILWU had a more advantageous climate in which to conduct such a struggle, as it was not they but their opponents who were smarting from recent setbacks.

Thus it was not accidental that in 1958 Goldblatt had chosen this moment to muse on the fortunes of the sugar industry, for it was then that, in a replay of its pathbreaking 1946 strike, once more the ILWU found itself on strike. By mid-March 1958 the strike was already at the 46-day mark and had cost the islands more than 10 times as many man-days of work as had been lost in various strikes of the previous two years.[31] Yet, forged in the furnace of struggle, the union found not a single scab among the 13,000 reported to be on strike.[32]

Befitting the centrality of sugar in Hawai'i's economy, there was virtually no segment of the Big Island's economy that was not adversely affected by this job action. Without sugar to cart to California, Matson, for example, was sustaining heavy losses by simply maintaining weekly calls at the Hilo port.[33] By mid-April, Big Island county supervisor James Kealoha was moaning that the sugar strike would be hurting Hilo for years to come. There had been a sharp fall in sales, with appliance dealers' sales down by half, supermarkets' by 10 percent—and even parking meter revenue down by 14 percent.[34]

This was nothing new. The very threat of a strike in 1956 caused a veritable freeze in purchases of the latest consumer necessity—televisions. Before the threat, the leading television wholesaler shipped about 200 units to Maui and the Big Island, but after the alarming prospect of a walkout, the number supplied dwindled to 6 in the Valley Island alone, with sales falling just as precipitously. Even after employers in retaliation refused to extend the agreement allowing an automatic payroll deduction for union dues, the ILWU was able to demonstrate further its strength by cumbersomely collecting dues on an individual basis.[35] Valley Isle merchants were stung further when some of the most significant work stoppages in protest of the Eastland hearings hit Maui Pineapple Company.[36]

There were other losses. Sugarcane was getting tinder-dry by late April, and cane fires were erupting crazily, burning more than 18 acres of the valuable commodity.[37] Naturally, arson was suspected, but even if this were not so, the fact that it was being seriously bruited was one more psychological weapon the union seemed to wield against the employers, who were coming to resemble a pitiful and helpless giant. By late June 1958 the 126-day sugar strike had come to an end with a smashing victory for the union, further confirmation that the ILWU was not to be easily dislodged from its preeminent position within Hawai'i's constellation.[38] Typically, Ray Jerome Baker sensed what was unfolding. "The bosses sacrificed more by prolonging the strike that it would have cost them to pay the workers' increase for years to come," he suggested accurately.[39]

"The Sugar Strike of 1958 was a complete victory for us and decisive defeat for the employers," was the view of the ILWU leadership. Bosses, it was said, had badly misjudged the temper and maturity of the sugar workers and had badly miscalculated, perhaps as a result of being part of a nation where unions were becoming ever more powerless but living in an archipelago where this was not so. The ILWU won a breakthrough in gaining a union shop, which, they thought, made union security all but automatic for most, just as the Smith Act victory meant that the union could devote less funds and staff time to defending its right to exist.[40]

Speaking at a local hotel in Honolulu to a gathering of accountants, Hall upbraided management for its clumsy tactics, charging that the strike it helped induce had cost the sugar companies $50 million—which "need not have occurred." To call management's performance inept, he said, was much too kind. Exuding confidence that had been formed in struggle and triumph, Hall proclaimed, "One thing [is] for sure[;] we won the strike and don't intend to pay for it by forgoing wage increases."[41] Management had made a stupid mistake, agreed Harry Bridges. "They walked into that one," he said, speaking of a strike that "could have been avoided."[42] An indicator of how the mighty had fallen was suggested when in the midst of this strike, it was management that cried out for arbitration, something even Philip Maxwell—who negotiated on the bosses' behalf—conceded was a weapon of the weak.[43]

The triumph in sugar led Hall to believe that a similar result could be obtained in pineapple, an industry that had bested the union infamously in 1947. It was not terribly relevant that pineapple employers were pleading poverty—"because when they are in a weak position, they don't want to take a strike,"[44] said the confident Hall. Apparently impressed by the union's fortitude during the strike in sugar, the pineapple barons made serious efforts at bargaining with the union as equals, not with contempt as in previous years.[45]

Still, the pounding the union had absorbed—the Smith Act trials, the theatrical though pulverizing congressional hearings, the racist attacks on statehood—had taken its toll. Ironically, shortly after the sugar strike ended, so did the *Honolulu Record*. The paper departed in flames of glory, hailing the workers' performance in what was termed a decisive battle in Hawaiian history, which signaled the momentous as statehood loomed: "the hegemony of the Big Five has ended," the *Record* declared.

This statement was true in the sense that the archipelago had been on a long journey since the ILWU first arrived on the scene and Hawai'i's days as a feudal apartheid-like outpost had ended, fortuitously just before statehood. Yes, Hawai'i had progressed, had changed and was changing, as was said. The Big Five need not go to their Elba, which was equally true—this was US territory at the end of the day—and yes, there remained "a need for a change of attitude" on their part. But the reality was that, not least due to the ample ministrations of the ILWU, a conservative citadel had become a liberal bastion.[46]

Sadly, the journal that Ariyoshi had nursed from infancy was unable to enter this new era. As late as June 1958 it did not seem this would be the case. "Not too long ago," he said then, "we were called derisively the 'Pravda of the Pacific,'" and the paper's imminent demise was said to be nigh. Yet, he claimed—wrongly—the journal was in hail good health.[47]

Unfortunately, this journal was not alone in going under. The *Hawaiian Chinese Journal* suspended publication in January 1958, though it planned to resume publication. What was occurring, according to Ariyoshi, was that the "boss-haole elements" were engaged in a two-pronged offensive—against the organized Left and against the organized Asian-Pacific community—and though it had stalemated against the ILWU, it had prevailed in its confrontation with the CP and the press. They "constantly say," asserted the former Smith Act defendant, "that Japanese, Chinese and Filipino organizations should cease to operate"; well, he responded stubbornly, when such discrimination that caused them to come into being "disappears, we will have less emphasis on racial and ethnic organizations."[48]

Ariyoshi's perception was foreshadowed when, in the halls of Congress, Senator George Smathers of Florida asked then governor Oren Long "why there should be a United States Chamber of Commerce and [a] Japanese Chamber of Commerce" in Hawai'i.[49] That some on the Left also had doubts about ethnically based entities made it easier to pick them all off.

Thus, instead of being exiled to Elba, the Big Five and their supporters instead had helped banish one of their chief tormentors—the *Record*—to a permanent purgatory. In the paper's final issue, published in July 1958, Ariyoshi admitted that he and his colleagues had considered suspension in the previous year. IMUA crusades had worn them down or, more precisely, had worn down their advertisers, as their detractors had made door-to-door calls on businesspeople in Hilo to frighten them—successfully. And so it was to the newspaper cemetery for the *Record*, though the ILWU—which Ariyoshi accused of being insufficiently supportive of his journal—was to publish a similar periodical.[50]

An irate Reinecke agreed that the ILWU had given insufficient support to the trailblazing *Record*, perhaps because of the perception that Ariyoshi was hard to control.[51] The successor journal, the union-backed *Hawaii Reporter*, called itself liberal,[52] unlike the *Record*, which had proudly and defiantly stood to the left of liberalism. Thus there was no Frank Marshall Davis gracing the pages of the *Reporter*, which, as a testament to the gap it was allegedly filling, lasted for little more than a month.[53]

This burial had been preceded by that of the ILWU's regular radio broadcasts, which had been quite effective but were dropped in part because the employers' acceptance of the union precluded the kind of no-holds-barred assaults on management that had characterized McElrath's pet project.[54] In some ways, this loss may have been even more grievous than that of the *Record*. McElrath's prickly broadsides had become a fixture, coming into homes in the islands five nights a week in English—with other broadcasts in Japanese and Filipino languages. So waspish was the invective spewed forth that employers were often left hurting in every nerve. The cost was high—$20,000 per year—but the loss of these programs was even more significant.[55] For example, as the notorious Senator Joseph McCarthy came under fire, the ILWU had devoted a one-hour program to his misadventures, in fiery words that reached Honolulu, Kaua'i, Maui, and the Big Island.[56]

Admittedly, the union had a problem after its broadcast vehicle, KHON, changed ownership and the newly installed management was not as friendly as its predecessor.[57] The problem was exacerbated when the leadership found that many members were not listening to these broadcasts.[58] (Once the union had considered purchasing time for television broadcasts, but the technical and financial requirements seemed daunting at the time.[59]) Still, this loss was even more critical, since the ILWU's adversaries in IMUA were heard throughout the colony and, as statehood approached, had reached the milestone of 700 consecutive broadcasts,[60] not including special programming targeting women.[61] "We doubt very much if anyone listens to it," sniffed McElrath, "other than a few dues-paying fanatics and enemies of the ILWU." This may have been true, but that made all the more troubling the union's unilateral disarmament in the face of such a determined foe.[62]

For example, the union's liaison with Filipinos, the Reverend Emilio C. Yadao, who came to the islands in 1927, provided radio commentaries that not only were the sole source of information for thousands of ILWU members during the 1958 strike but also were monitored and translated daily by the employers—which sheds light on why they were so gleeful when the union abandoned the airwaves.[63]

The union's relinquishing of its megaphone did not induce a cease-fire by its opponents. Months before statehood arrived, Ray Jerome Baker groused about the notorious *Advertiser* and *Star-Bulletin*, whose press coverage, slanted to the most retrograde elements among haoles, had hardly dented the armor of radicalism. "They publish hate editorials about Russia [and] labor unions and run the pieces of the most reactionary columnists." According to these papers, he said, "wage increases are always Communist plots," while "crime, murders and accidents are always featured on the front page." Peccadilloes by the elite were ignored, whereas "if one criticizes our foreign policy or mentions unfavorably the military, his letter is not published, [but] it is turned over to the FBI."[64] The *Star-Bulletin* felt particularly aggrieved, since the union had a contract representing the paper's mailing and distribution divisions of the circulation department.[65]

Thus Hawai'i was stumbling into statehood at a time when the left-wing press, which could have provided needed clarity to these tumultuous and transformative events, was slipping into remission and the mainstream press was wallowing in a combination of distortion and obliviousness. Not least because of how the ILWU had altered the political economy, Hawai'i, as statehood loomed, was enduring significant change that too could have benefited from sharper analysis. The number of registered vehicles doubled in a six-year period following 1947 and accelerated thereafter,[66] and an inevitable outgrowth was more accidents; but this had a political twist that the mainstream organs had difficulty reporting. According to Baker, "car wrecks from drunk driving in the early hours of the morning and killing on the highways can be [attributed] to service men," for they seemed to think that "they can do as they please in this far outpost."[67] Land was becoming so expensive in O'ahu—a plaint for some time—that people of modest means were being priced out of the market.[68] The availability of potable water was becoming an unceasing problem—ironically enough in the middle of an ocean.[69] Tourism and nightlife were increasing, turning a sleepy island paradise into something approaching Las Vegas in the Pacific. Baker recalled a time when Honolulu had little in the way of street lighting and no nightclubs, taverns, or cocktail lounges, only "saloons." One or two of them catered to high-class trade, but most of them were frequented by waterfront bums, castaways, or perhaps "an occasional Hawaiian whose wife was giving him a bad time"—but now that moguls like Henry Kaiser were taking an interest in the islands, this was changing.[70]

Thus, between 1950 and statehood, tourist spending jumped 350 percent, from $24 million to $109 million annually, while the number of tourists increased from 34,000 in 1945 to 243,000 in 1959.[71] The press baron of Los Angeles, Norman Chandler, was frequenting the islands nowadays, according to Honolulu mogul Lorrin Thurston, who was now enticing J. B. Stoddard: "[He] has a fabulous oil income," Thurston gushed, and was "seeking investments"—Hawai'i seemed as inviting as anywhere else, it was thought.[72]

The increased tourist traffic, combined with the more forgiving climate delivered by the rise of radicalism, had brought social change along with it. In the months preceding statehood, it appeared that a nascent homophile trend had been unveiled in Honolulu: "A couple of bars downtown have been known for several years to flourish on the 'swish' trade," as the *Record* indelicately put it,[73] though this journal also gave prominent coverage to lesbian life in Honolulu.[74] For his part, Ariyoshi noticed a proliferation of "nude parties on the beaches of paradise."[75] A colleague of his reported that "teenage nudity has become an added attraction for tourists at Waikiki."[76]

On the other hand, the union might have felt that given what seemed to be its impregnable position in the islands, it could afford to assuage statehood opponents by dispensing with some of the more powerful weapons in its formidable arsenal. A weapon it did not dispense with, however, was one that had proven to be remarkably effective: global solidarity. Since Hilo was closer to Kobe than to Bangor and since so many of its members had roots in the Asia-Pacific region, it stood to reason that the union would have more friends and allies outside the United States than most of its counterparts on the mainland did. Since the leftists believed sincerely in transnational solidarity, their opponents sought to turn this back against them by arguing that leftism was not a national movement but, instead, was dependent on the goodwill and wishes of foreigners. This charge was wielded repeatedly against the *Record*, particularly after Washington charged that tens of thousands of pieces of propaganda from socialist bloc countries came to the isles by mail. With exasperation, the journal admitted that it had subscribers in China, Hong Kong, India, Canada, the Philippines, and Czechoslovakia.[77]

At the time, there were also pressing regional matters that occupied the grave attention of the archipelago generally. For at that juncture France was exploding nuclear devices in the South Pacific, frighteningly close to Hawai'i's shores. The awesome and deadly mushroom cloud was seen by residents of Honolulu as the sky was lit hellish red: how could the union ignore foreign policy or the world beyond the United States, given such threats?[78]

Because of the diversity of its membership, the union had to be alert to the exchange rate of the dollar with the yen and the Filipino peso.[79] Unsurprisingly, Miyagi was trying to establish closer ties with Asian unions, a matter that was facilitated by the fluency of certain members in Japanese and other languages.[80] Still hanging fire as statehood approached was the question of whether union stevedores would be allowed to unload military materiel destined for foreign battlefields—450 tons of dynamite was the explosive matter at issue in late 1957.[81]

As Bridges faced the legal difficulties that had caused him to be jailed and considered for deportation, he continued to find support abroad. "Feeling runs very high within that union," said a US diplomat in his hometown of Melbourne, referring to protests by Australia's Seamen's Union over Bridges' parlous position.[82] After Moscow-Washington relations began to thaw, Bridges cultivated these ties with travels abroad: a factor that facilitated global solidarity was that waterfront workers—perhaps because of the internationalism spawned by their role in handling exports and imports—were often overjoyed to greet him. The year of statehood found him in Genoa[83] and then Prague, where a US diplomat was taken by his "allegedly unfavorable comparison of American conditions with those of Czechoslovakia."[84]

Continuing a long-standing pattern, the ILWU's most significant global engagement was with Cuba. Shortly after the Cuban Revolution—and just before statehood—Jeff Kibre was seeking a meeting with sugar workers there, but nothing jelled, he reported. "Castro is moving in several different directions at once," he said, "apparently trying to appease our State Department while at the same time pushing for domestic reforms."[85] Just before that, the ILWU had displayed its solidarity with those seeking to dislodge the US-backed regime when it refused to confer with a Cuban sugar agent in Hawai'i; the agent was affiliated with a firm that McElrath described as having "the largest holdings of sugar in the western hemisphere"—yet the union, he said, "could not and would not rub shoulders with Cuban sugar."[86]

Though the ILWU was castigated by its detractors as being in a relationship of ventriloquism with Moscow, this accusation hardly jibed with what the *Record* had to say at the time of the 1956 uprising in Budapest; unlike many Communist parties globally, Ariyoshi's journal was quite critical of the Soviet intervention.[87] Frank Marshall Davis reacted similarly, though inevitably he could not help but mention that "my heart cannot bleed for the dead in Hungary without bleeding just as generously for the dead in Egypt,"[88] a nation then under attack during the Suez War.

Of course, the Left's focus on global events centered mostly not on Europe but on Asia. A writer who dwarfed the influence exerted by Davis and Ariyoshi said as much. James Michener became an outspoken advocate of statehood in the postwar era, just as his writings about the South Pacific set the tone for a renewed interest in this region and its diversity. He met the Dixiecrats head-on, constructing the isles as a positive symbol of multiracialism that were an alternative to the messiness of Little Rock. As he saw it, statehood would reassure Asians about the racial bona fides of Uncle Sam; further, he saw Hawai'i as helping to heal his homeland's nasty racial sores, as mediators between those defined as black and white.[89]

Michener's remarks reflected the fact that Hawai'i had become the bridge between "East and West," something that was noticeably evident with the advent of the conference of mostly Asian and African nations held in Bandung, Indonesia, in the years preceding statehood. Sukarno, the leader of this most populous predominantly Muslim nation, passed through Honolulu shortly after this gathering. Baker thought that Sukarno might have been beckoned as a recuperative measure in reaction to the awkward US presence in Bandung, which he found to be both arrogant and snooty, with "contempt for the 'gooks.'" Sukarno's presence, Baker said, suggested "how sensitive Uncle Sam now is over relations in the Far East," a concern that opponents of statehood would not be allowed to dislodge.[90] Baker knew rather well Syngman Rhee, South Korea's strongman, during the "many years ago when he lived in Hawaii,"[91] one more indication of the strategic location of Hawai'i—and its Left.

The sensitivity to the feelings of those on this strategic continent was exposed when, at an annual gathering of dental hygienists in Texas, a decision was made to construe inclusively (and bizarrely) those of Asian origin as "Caucasian"—while still maintaining a bar against Negroes.[92] Michener's dream for Hawai'i may have been overambitious, since embracing a powerful Asia did not necessarily mean much for African-Americans. Just as the dental hygienists were seeking to sanitize partially their racial record, Frank Marshall Davis was complaining about minstrel shows—the traditionally popular disparaging entertainment featuring Negroes—broadcast on local television stations in order to raise funds for charities in Kaua'i.[93]

Yet it seemed that the ILWU had to reassure the doubting who feared that admitting Hawai'i into the sacrosanct Union would be akin to giving the Kremlin the keys to the federal car—and the way to provide such reassurance was to make concessions as a sign of good faith as the union's long-pursued goal of statehood loomed ever closer. Opponents of statehood on the mainland, particularly in the former slave South, were in a similar quandary. Rejecting Hawai'i as a state was viewed widely as a Cold War faux pas, designed to offend Asians, but accepting the archipelago was viewed not only as a gift to the Kremlin, which was thought to dominate Honolulu, but more importantly as an act that would bring two anti–Jim Crow senators to Washington, at a time when massive resistance to desegregation was rising.

As statehood approached in 1959, profound regret at the prospect of Hawai'i statehood increased accordingly. At this point, the powerful majority leader of the US Senate, Lyndon B. Johnson of Texas, was pondering the prospect of making a race for the White House and hardly needed the racial and political briar patch that Hawai'i was becoming. He was not passionate about statehood, according to journalist William S. White; in fact, he was not very keen on it at all. The hawkish segregationist Senator Richard Russell of Georgia would harangue the Texan about the "unwisdom" of it—but Johnson had to consider the impact that blocking Hawai'i would have on his presidential ambitions.[94]

It was unclear how some of Johnson's flaws affected his view of state-hood. For example, his aide George Reedy felt that the senator was "very unsophisticated about labor" and "had literally no understanding of the vari-ous unions and how they operated"[95]—which may have led him to misunder-stand the wailings about the impact of the ILWU. Yet in Johnson's home state, said Reedy, "if anybody wanted to win an election, the easiest way was to come out against the unions in Texas."[96] On the other hand, in Texas, Reedy recalled, the "anticommunist hysteria reached real heights," though—he added with a hint of yeast—"they'd never seen a Communist."[97]

Reedy, who worked closely with Johnson, said the statehood battle was replete with complexity, since Alaska was initially perceived as being ori-ented toward the Democratic Party and Hawai'i toward the GOP and "you couldn't get one without the other." Then the archipelago switched, but so-lons found it difficult to reject it for admittance, for fear of seeming insensi-tive to Asians during the Cold War. "And you had the extra problem of civil rights," said Reedy—a movement that was rising on the national scale, to the detriment of the Dixiecrats.[98] Thus, in visiting Hawai'i after statehood was a fait accompli, Johnson seemingly had a hard time accepting the isles as part of the United States, having to be reminded continually, according to an aide, that "this is not a foreign country."[99]

Hence, President Eisenhower had become extremely concerned over what he should do if Congress approved statehood for Alaska and not for Hawai'i, though an aide recognized that "politically, Republicans are in a better situation currently in Alaska than in Hawaii."[100] As it turned out, the political party switch of these two twin outlying states eased their dual ad-mission to statehood. Consequently, said California senator Thomas Kuchel, Alaskan statehood was handled first because of Hawai'i's intricacies and be-cause of the "overtones of racism" involved in the latter.[101]

Yet Johnson and even Eisenhower had ties to Texas, and this rapidly grow-ing and increasingly important state harbored determined constituents who were adamantly opposed to Hawai'i statehood. Lillian Coltzer of Galveston warned him that a "handful of Communists stand in practical mastery" of the islands. "And when I say Communists," she clarified, "I don't mean 'pinkos': I mean convicted Communists," singling out Hall.[102] This irked opinion was shared by others[103] who expressed grave trepidations.[104] Austin Burges and his spouse, both of Dallas, thought that admitting Hawai'i would mean a "flood of Oriental immigration" and, perhaps worse, would lead to statehood applica-tions by Cuba, Puerto Rico, "Greenland or some European, Asian or African country." The couple asked, "On what basis can we say no?"[105]

J. R. English of Little Rock had similar thoughts; why not "change . . . the name of our country" to "'United States of America and Some Small Specks Far West?'" he asked sarcastically.[106] Reverend Donald J. Ely of Baltimore was of like mind. If Hawai'i were to be crowned a state, then why not "Guam, the Virgin Islands and even South Vietnam"; Oregon was bad enough, he thought, he said, with its "two leftists" in the "Upper Chamber"—"I wish it could be sunk in the South Pacific," he scoffed. And Hawai'i would just contribute to this mess, he said, informing Senator J. Strom Thurmond of South Carolina that "if everyone would take a firm [stand] against so-called civil rights (actually special privileges for Negroes), as you do, we would not be having the trouble we do today."[107]

Foes of statehood had a hard time deciding if the basis for their opposition was Hawai'i's Asian-Pacific majority—or the territory's profusion of radicals. This evident dilemma was captured by Stanley Morse of South Carolina, who railed against what he termed dismissively as the "Red Racial Revolution" unfolding in the islands.[108]

William Rickard of St. Louis was of like mind, reminding his senator, "Some day on your day off take a walk thru Harlem or the Puerto Rico section of New York (that is, [if] you are not afraid of having your throat cut) and judge for yourself if we need any more of this kind of citizen."[109] Hicklin A. Harrel, who was sympathetic to racism, told House Speaker Sam Rayburn, a similarly influential Texan, that when he first arrived in Honolulu, he was pro-statehood, but now, as this prospect approached, he had severe doubts. "I reminded a Japanese, U.S. veteran [that] he is an American," and to Harrel's dismay, he replied, "'I am a Japanese, first, last and always.'"[110] Senator Thurmond was informed that the numerous indigenes—"they call themselves natives" but resembled Negroes—were the reason statehood should be opposed.[111]

Senator Smathers was also told that native Hawaiians, now thoroughly angry about statehood, were organizing, and that "fear [was] spreading among Japanese that the hordes of haoles rushing in from the mainland will smother their political power." The prospect of statehood, in short, was exacerbating tensions, not alleviating them.[112]

Thus a man with a distinguished pedigree in elite politics in Hawai'i—former governor Ingram Stainback—launched a last-ditch personal crusade against statehood in 1959. He linked Reds and racism, as he believed that many Japanese-Americans "'connected the white race and its government with tyranny and oppression,'" making them susceptible to the blandishments of the Communist Party[113]—which suppressed anti-statehood dissent.[114] This "fanatical pursuit of statehood" was proving to be disastrous, he told Senator Olin Johnston of South Carolina, advocating commonwealth status[115] instead.[116]

Stainback's outreach to Dixie was a reflection of a developing trend: haoles bypassing the thicket of Hawaiian politics and reaching across the ocean directly to the like-minded on the mainland—in order to influence Hawai'i. Senator Johnston hardly needed prompting, however, as he (along with almost

US President Dwight D. Eisenhower exults in 1959 as he signs the bill mandating Hawaiian statehood, in culmination of a process that had begun roughly six decades earlier with the violent overthrow of the legally constituted government of Hawai'i. Courtesy of Dwight D. Eisenhower Library, Abilene, Kansas.

all those concerned about preserving Jim Crow) voted against statehood,[117] along with his fellow South Carolinian Thurmond. "I opposed most vigorously the admission of Alaska into the union," Thurmond thundered, adding with relish, "My feelings about Hawaii are even stronger."[118] The spouse of Emmitt Wieruscheske—whose brother served as president of Hawaiian Airlines—tried to assure the doubting by saying, "I don't think that Hawaii's admission would weaken the South's position on integration."[119] But this was not enough to sway the segregationists.

In any event, Hawai'i entered the Union, and Jim Crow was weakened—though there was not a mandatory connection between the two. Previously, the British embassy had exposed the maneuvering on statehood by Dixiecrats, spurred by fear of the fate of Jim Crow and the concomitant reluctance to reveal this openly, noting that "the Southerners have not [admitted] publicly that this is their motive."[120] Of course, after statehood, this motive was hardly discussed—openly or otherwise. As for the other roadblock to statehood—the question of Communists and the Cold War—former president Truman had backed statehood, as he thought it would aid the US image in Asia; it is unclear if it did, though admission probably did not harm Washington's profile.[121]

In summing up the fierce—and elongated—debate, a Senate report acknowledged that "the question of admitting Hawaii to statehood has been longer considered and more thoroughly studied than any other statehood proposal that has ever come before Congress."[122] This was true, for the archipelago, which had begun its trek to statehood in a different era of GOP dominance and apartheid-like rule, then entered the Union as a liberalizing bastion with an overflow of minorities of a sort that struck fear in the hearts of Dixiecrats. Inexorably, this turn of events brought prolonged contestation and anxiety.

"The day of full-fledged statehood is indeed a great day for Hawaii but an even better day for the United States," enthused Vice President Richard M. Nixon in August 1959.[123] Statehood advocates felt vindicated when the predictable occurred and Hawai'i began to send non-haoles to the US Senate. President Eisenhower may have been heartened when C. H. Kwock, editor of the *Chinese World* in San Francisco, told him that "Communist-threatened Asian countries have taken note of Senator [Hiram] Fong's election to Congress and hailed it as a further demonstration of democracy at work."[124] Advocates of white supremacy learned to accept having a colleague, Fong, whose face had the color and texture of mahogany,[125] and they did so without evident signs of distress. When Fong retired from the Senate in 1976, commendations poured in from such die-hard racists as Jesse Helms of North Carolina, Strom Thurmond of South Carolina, and James Eastland of Mississippi, suggesting that—at least—they had evolved to a degree.[126]

* * *

Management in Hawai'i had learned a bitter lesson in its confrontation with the ILWU. Perhaps not coincidentally or conspiratorially, the long-term trend of reduction of the number of sugar workers continued after statehood—which simultaneously reduced the membership and strength of the ILWU. The number of sugar workers dropped from 50,000 in 1932 to about 23,000 in

1947 and 4,888 in 1990. The statewide stevedore workforce slipped from 2,066 in 1947 to 1,202 by 1970, then to 740 in 1990. Separation pay and repatriation allowances enabled older workers who were nationals of the Philippines to return home, which was good for them—perhaps not so good for the union.[127] The union's determined antagonist, Matson, which had grown from a single ship in Hawai'i in 1882 to a sprawling conglomerate, entered the container era in August 1958, and a few months later the world's first container crate went into operation; one 40,000-pound box was loaded every three minutes, dwarfing—by a factor of 40—the average productivity of a longshore gang using shipboard winches. Container crates were in place in Honolulu by 1960, somewhat vitiating the force of the ILWU. That same year, Bridges negotiated a contract that allowed unlimited automation of the docks and, according to some critics, gravely underestimated the speed with which containers would alter work on the docks. Nonetheless, by 1970 Matson relinquished its global ambitions, selling its ships and abandoning its earlier attempt to make Honolulu a hub of the Pacific.[128]

The ILWU did not go away meekly, however, as it stunned management on May Day in 2008 by shutting down the ports in the western United States in protest of the war in Iraq.[129] The day before the ILWU's startling walkout, which evoked memories of the union's past in Hawai'i, another decades-old story emerged that shed light on the statehood process. It was reported that concerns in 1958 about the Cold War in Asia had been more serious than even the doomsayers had imagined: President Eisenhower had been seriously considering using 10- to 15-kiloton nuclear bombs against targets in China as tensions in the Taiwan Straits escalated.[130] Back then, the ILWU had chosen to endure the severe headwinds at a time when calls for engagement with "Red China" routinely brought derision at best. Just before statehood, Louis Goldblatt was arranging a delegation to China for the purpose of exploring the possibilities of trade in nonstrategic goods.[131]

Frank Marshall Davis continued his often lonely crusade against racism in Hawai'i. In his unjustly neglected memoir, he recalled a time when "by far the biggest beefs [were] between island gals and haole youths": "In some instances, island boys have jumped into fights between white and black servicemen on the side of the blacks. I have known a few Orientals who are so belligerent they will go to a bar hoping to pick fights with haoles." Bedazzled by it all, Davis grandly concluded that Hawai'i was "developing a new civilization of its own."[132]

Davis also continued to attract the irritated attention of advocates of Jim Crow and anticommunism. Just before statehood, a public hearing in Tallahassee concluded that "the Communists have organized and promoted a succession of united fronts and fronts designed especially for winning Negroes to Communism," as it warned against the proclivities of "the so-called Negro intellectuals" whose alarming role in these efforts was deemed worthy of consideration.

If these investigators had turned their attention westward, no doubt they would have pointed to Davis as an exemplar of what they found disturbing.[133]

For Davis had become integrated into the islands. "I find myself using the island inflection quite often, as well as a smattering of pidgin and Hawaiian phrases," he observed in a letter to a friend. "Often it's the only way I can make myself understood. Instead of saying I'm sold out of an item, I'll say, 'Pau already.'"[134] Davis had good reason to learn this phrase, since by the year of statehood he had started an import-export business, bringing in items directly from Japan, Thailand, and Hong Kong. He added enthusiastically that he was "establishing contact for other Asian areas."[135] His unflagging support for the ILWU was bolstered when one analyst of Bridges' tenure said that the ILWU leader "personally believed that [if] work ever slowed to the point that there were only two workers left on the docks, . . . one should be black"[136]—a dramatic contrast to the haole job trusts that so many other unions resembled.

As statehood approached, the voluble and gregarious Davis befriended a family with Kansas roots similar to his own that too had decided to take up residence in Honolulu, and months after statehood, a student who hailed from Kenya arrived to study at the University of Hawai'i.[137] Davis later became something of a male role model and substitute father figure for an offspring of this fated union between Kansas and Kenya: his name was Barack Obama.[138]

Things were not going smoothly for the NAACP, the organization that Davis had helped build in the isles before it succumbed to a tidal wave of anticommunism. Just after statehood, association leader Gloster Current was told that his group was being attacked in newspaper articles, while Daniel Inouye was complaining that the group had snubbed him and otherwise treated him badly. Some associated with the group in Honolulu were, amazingly, stating that the NAACP "was not needed in Hawaii," which was a bad public relations situation indeed. Current's interlocutor concluded that the "prognosis is not good that we will have a strong ongoing branch," indicating that the purges of yore hardly revivified the battle against racism in the archipelago. The statement by Current's correspondent that "the Orientals run Hawaii and discriminate against Hawaiians and the 'howies' [haoles]" did not suggest any particular acuity or indicate that the prognosis for the chapter would be altered anytime soon.[139]

Senator Johnson had become US president in 1963 and had indicated his interest in Hawai'i by seeking to construct an "East-West Center" in order to solidify the new state's role as a bridge to Asia. Simultaneously, however, the need for a new NAACP chapter was equally solidified when his aides contemptuously referred to this institute as "Coolie College."[140]

Though the ground was eroding beneath his feet as ILWU membership dwindled, Jack Hall continued to be a major player in Hawai'i. Sanford Zalburg, his biographer, recalls that it was not unusual when Hall summoned other

leading figures like John Burns, Art Rutledge, and Daniel Inouye to his abode
and "laid down the law to them." When presidential candidate Richard Nixon
arrived in Honolulu in 1960, he met with Hall in Kapiolani Park. "I know," said
Hall's spouse. "I drove him up there. I was laughing all the way. It was just like
cops-and-robbers," she recalled, recounting their dodging the press. "He
wanted me to take the most devious route."[141] Nixon, a renowned anticommunist, was chagrined about feeling compelled to kiss the ring of a reputed Red,
which explained why Yoshiko Hall delivered her husband to him via a circu-
itous route. Her intentional misdirection was not unique to her. Typically, the
union wrong-footed its opponents; for example, in 1956 Bridges registered as a
Republican, which "really confused and confounded a lot of people out of our
ranks," a pleased Hall wrote to Goldblatt, adding: "Good Stuff."[142]

Some were not as mirthful about Burns' ties to Hall. One suspicious individual wondered if what was devious was the union's backing of the man who
served as governor from 1962 to 1974, after his tenure as the isles' representative in Washington. "Does anyone believe that the ILWU gives this kind of
support without expecting—and getting—something in return?" it was asked
with suspicion.[143] Another person demanded that Burns resign as leader of the
Democratic Party if he continued "to work with and be used by Communists in
Hawaii"[144]—words that were ignored. Other adversaries of Burns thought he
had handicapped himself by being perceived as too close to Americans of Japanese Ancestry. Reportedly, this was the cause given by Frank Fasi for Burns'
earlier defeat in a gubernatorial race—though Burns' evident success as a
founding father of modern Hawai'i tends to belie this assertion too.[145]

Burns, a Catholic born in Montana in 1913, remained defiant, asserting
shortly after he stepped down as the state's governor, "Frankly, I never had
any period that I wouldn't be seen talking to Jack Hall. I think that being
seen talking to him did cost. But so what?" Hall, he said, was a "great man for
any time": "He could have been a damn fine outstanding leader in any kind of
business, he could have gone in for. He was a leader. He was a leader who
placed the interests of his fellow man above his own interest."[146]

"The man to see in Honolulu is Jack Hall," said the profoundly anticommunist journalist A. M. Rosenthal two years after statehood, describing him
to readers of the *New York Times* as a "power in the industry and politics of
the newest state." Rather modestly, Hall disclaimed these compliments,
though he added tellingly, "I think race consciousness is the most important
single thing. But you could say we [ILWU members] are the most cohesive
factor." Hall believed that his union bridged racial divides that too often led
to painful rifts on the mainland. "If we don't put out a full union ticket," he
said, "our men are likely to vote on the basis of race."[147]

As time passed, an entente of sorts developed between the union and the
mainstream press, its onetime mortal combatant. In 1965 Hall found the press'

treatment of union affairs to be "excellent," noting, "It is far superior to anything I've seen elsewhere in the country. We get coverage in depth here." He continued to disdain the ascending anticommunist liberal press of the mainland, however. Speaking of Americans for Democratic Action, a group that symbolized this ideological tendency, Hall told a reporter, "I don't dig that ADA crowd." Hawai'i continued to be a fountainhead of progressivism, with Hall admitting as early as 1965 that he opposed the conflict in Vietnam, which at this date still enjoyed more than a modicum of support on the mainland.[148]

Hawai'i's progressivism was certified when Hall got into trouble in early 1968 by admitting, "I once wanted socialism but I don't any more. It isn't practical." He confessed, "When I was young, I believed socialism was the answer to unemployment, depression and poverty. I don't believe that any more."[149] But this was Hawai'i—not the mainland, where such comments would have been deemed almost anodyne—and Hall found he had to retreat, adding the clarification that "it has been and still is my belief that socialist organization of their economy is the only real hope for the impoverished working people in the underdeveloped countries of Asia, Africa and Latin America"[150]—conspicuously omitting North America and Europe.

The difference that Hawai'i provided may help explain why Hall decided to abandon the isles shortly after these controversial remarks and move to the Bay Area. "He was bored," said Harriet Bouslog, speaking from Honolulu. "He was bored here. He was bored with his home life. He was bored with his office life. He was bored with the people he was surrounded with." Of course, Bouslog and Hall were not exactly buddies, and friends of his friends were suspicious when—by her own admission—"Stainback got to be very fond of me," thereby tempering the thrust of her assessment. Later she had a bad accident that she barely survived. "Every bone in my face [was] fractured," she said morosely. This decomposition mirrored what was happening to her political viewpoints. Like Hall, she seemed to be mellowing—or, as some might have it, moving away from her previous radical commitments. "I've given up hope that I once had as a young crusader to be able to see any change," she confessed in 1976.[151] Things had changed since the time in 1948 when her law partner, Myer Symonds, claimed that the chief justice had told him directly that "if I was a member of the Communist Party I could not practice law" in Hawai'i.[152]

She had been preceded in this ennui by Jack Kawano, the man who had helped set in motion the enormous changes that had transformed Hawai'i. By the time he died in virtual anonymity in 1984 in California—where he had moved to work for the major merchant of death, Lockheed—his name remained mud in the left-liberal circles that continued to prevail in Hawai'i.[153] By way of contrast, Thomas Yagi, who had begun his life as a laborer at Wailuku Sugar Company in 1939 and went on to become Maui division director of Local 142, was celebrated when he passed away in 1995. When the man once accused by a Catholic priest of being a devilish Communist died, messages poured in from the state's governor, congressional representatives, and members of the local legislature.[154] Juxtaposed with the way Kawano was treated in death, it seemed that, at least in Hawai'i, anticommunism had yet to gain the traction it displayed so effortlessly and unremittingly on the mainland. The union's wider significance was signaled when former staffer Ricardo Labez passed away in 1993 at the age of 79. He had come to Kaua'i at the age of two and had risen rapidly in the ranks of the union. He returned to his homeland in the 1950s to toil as an aide to President Ramon Magsaysay, then returned to Honolulu in the 1960s to work for Burns.[155]

Indicative of the contradictions involved when radicals sank roots in the region, Hall was denied a visa by Manila in 1959 because of his supposed "redline activities"—though one of his closest colleagues had worked alongside the leader of the Philippines.[156] In a like manner, Hall, a jazz aficionado who collected the records of Fats Waller, was refused membership in Honolulu's Hot Jazz Society—some members resigned upon his joining, then the board rejected him[157]—though he was close to John Burns, and Richard Nixon rushed to greet him.

Despite such slights, the ILWU had chosen not to veer away from its radicalism. In 1988 Goldblatt visited Havana—almost thirty years after a revolution that had led to dispiriting relations with Washington—and immediately went to see his old friend Ursino Rojas, then on the Central Committee of the Cuban Communist Party. Rojas said that Cuban sugar workers felt more confident because of ILWU victories in the United States.[158]

Hall's move to the mainland did not seem to rescue him from the discontent that Bouslog claimed had ensnared him, for there his tensions with Bridges had further opportunity to flourish.[159] The two had been adversaries, according to Sanford Zalburg, and became enemies.[160] Bill Bailey, the stevedore who had resided both in Hawai'i and San Francisco and was a friend of both men, thought Bridges was "paranoid" about Hall, perhaps believing that the islander desired his job.[161] In the Bay Area, Hall also had the opportunity to renew hostilities with John Elias, a stevedore born in Kaua'i in 1912. Elias had had many an argument with Hall in Hawai'i, he recalled later, which caused him to move to San Francisco. He thought Hall was a "dictator."[162]

It needs to be emphasized that the pressure cooker in which the union operated gave rise almost effortlessly to internecine conflict. Even the otherwise mild-mannered John Reinecke was not immune, once deriding union staffer Theodora Kreps as being "pasty faced" and "difficult." She "always seemed to be on the defensive," he remarked. "I think she felt white women were discriminated against [and] distrusted by white men."[163]

Possibly falling victim to such tensions, Hall, rarely in good health, passed away in 1971, two years after moving to the mainland, as he apparently did not find the contentment for which he yearned. A few years after his death, an unrepentant J. R. Robertson asserted, "People in the islands—and especially the ILWU people—yes, and all of them in the leadership now . . . expressed great love and devotion for Jack Hall but they hated his goddamned guts"; in fact, Robertson said, "when he died, they were the most—they were happy over this." Heroic figures like Joe Blur, he says, were "never given the opportunity to come above a certain rung in the leadership level." The salty, dyspeptic Robertson also was hard on both McElrath and Goldblatt, so his views can be discounted to a degree—but what his opinions do illuminate is that one does not have to love a comrade in order to advance the cause for which both are working.[164]

Hall's old comrade McElrath passed away in 1995 at the age of 78. The tireless reporter Sanford Zalburg was among those who mourned his demise, not least since he had been so helpful to Zalburg in reconstructing the history of the labor movement that the journalist chronicled. McElrath had a "fantastic memory," Zalburg said. "An incredible memory, really. . . . [H]e gave me more time than any other single person."[165]

Still, it did seem that as this goal of statehood appeared to be within reach, there was a kind of buyer's remorse among some on the Left who rarely seemed to think through carefully the implications of acceding to the brutal overthrow of indigenous rule in the archipelago. Thus Ben Dillingham, a man whose very name represented this coup, recalled a telling conversation with Bridges as statehood approached. With thinning curly hair, this huge man who smoked incessantly—cigars followed by cigarettes—recalled speaking to the ILWU leader at the Ala Moana Tropics, where Bridges responded to the charge that he was a Red by requesting that his interlocutor simply look at his paterfamilias. "What did he do?" asked the stunned Dillingham. Well, replied Bridges, "I've never been charged with heading an insurrection against established rulers. Your father raised arms against the Queen. Your father bore arms."[166]

Bridges may have been moved to this assertion by the isle controversy that erupted when Daniel Inouye and 19 members of the lower house in Honolulu signed a statement saying that Washington should acknowledge that Hawai'i had been stolen from the indigenes.[167] Before expiring, the *Record* rejected "American colonialism,"[168] though it did not deign to mention Hawai'i; however, the newspaper did argue that "they stole Hawaii!" suggesting an evolution of sorts.[169] Again in 1957 the rising symbol of Democratic Party liberalism, Daniel Inouye, introduced a resolution in the local legislature requesting Congress to return crown lands to indigenes.[170] Even the union, which may have been the most effective proponent of statehood, took to the radio airwaves to defend Queen Lili'uokalani. In the broadcast, the union contended, "Her crown was stolen from her because annexation to the United States meant a two cent increase in the price of sugar. That is a matter of historical record."[171]

Remarkably, John Burns argued passionately in 1959 that it was the ILWU that had laid the foundations for democracy in Hawai'i. "[No] honest man—any objective person—possessing more than a cursory knowledge of Hawaii," he argued, "would be willing to say that democracy was practiced" in the isles prior to the union's arrival. "Let's even extend the time to the middle of [the] 40s," he added. He continued by noting that at the 27 June 1959 plebiscite that preceded statehood, "1 out of 5 in certain Oahu precincts voted against statehood contrary to the 19 and 23 to 1 majorities in the communities from which [ILWU members] primarily come."[172] Thus, radicals had made the ironic contribution of rescuing Hawai'i from apartheid-like exploitation and delivering it to a statehood that—in a prima facie sense—had paid short shrift to the bedrock principle of self-determination for indigenes. Such was the paradoxically racial route of radicals in the terrestrial paradise that Hawai'i was said to be.

Notes

Introduction

1. *Honolulu Star-Bulletin*, 20 June 1953.
2. "On the Beam," n.d., box 7, Harry Bridges Papers, Labor Archives and Research Center, San Francisco State University (hereafter cited as Bridges Papers, San Francisco).
3. *Honolulu Advertiser*, 21 June 1953.
4. *Honolulu Star-Bulletin*, 22 June 1953.
5. *Honolulu Star-Bulletin*, 8 September 1952.
6. Dyna Nakamoto, interview, 29 May 1996, transcript, University of Hawai'i–West O'ahu, Center for Labor Education and Research.
7. *New York Times*, 26 January 2007.
8. Moon-Kie Jung, *Reworking Race: The Making of Hawaii's Interracial Labor Movement* (New York: Columbia University Press, 2006), 2.
9. Transcript of radio broadcast, 9 September 1954, University of Hawai'i at Mānoa, Special Collections.
10. *Labor Today* 5, no. 5 (October–November 1966): 1, Library and Archive, ILWU Headquarters, San Francisco.)
11. *Honolulu Beacon*, September 1964.
12. *Honolulu Star-Bulletin*, 20 February 1973.
13. Kevin Phillips, *The Emerging Republican Majority* (New Rochelle, NY: Arlington House, 1969); Dan T. Carter, *From George Wallace to Newt Gingrich: Race and the Conservative Counterrevolution, 1963–1994* (Baton Rouge: Louisiana State University Press, 1996); Thomas Frank, *What's the Matter with Kansas? How Conservatives Won the Heart of America* (New York: Metropolitan Books, 2004).
14. Captain Anthony Gelardi to Fred Kilguss, administration assistant, 7 October 1947, box 26, J. Howard McGrath Papers, Harry S. Truman Papers, Harry S. Truman Library and Museum, Independence, Mo.
15. *Hawaii Sentinel*, 26 August 1937, Labor Archives and Research Center, San Francisco State University.
16. Gwenfread Allen, *Hawaii's War Years, 1941–1945* (Honolulu: University of Hawai'i Press, 1950), 183.
17. See report by Edward J. Eagen, March 1937, and report by House Committee on Labor, 3 May 1940, notebook 14, Sanford Zalburg Papers, University of Hawai'i at Mānoa, Archives and Manuscripts (hereafter cited as Zalburg Papers).
18. Governor Oren Long to James P. Davis, Director, Office of the Territories, Department of Interior, 29 August 1951 (see the attached memorandum), 10-8,

Governor Oren Long Papers, Hawaiʻi State Archives, Honolulu (hereafter cited as Long Papers).

19. Ronald B. Jamieson to Governor Oren Long, 7 May 1951, 10-8, Long Papers.

20. Allen, *Hawaii's War Years*, 183.

21. *Honolulu Star-Bulletin*, 31 January 1953. At this juncture, ILWU membership on the "Big Island," the island known as Hawaiʻi. was 6,276; on Maui, 6,216; on Oʻahu, the most populous island and home of Honolulu, 6,678; and on Kauaʻi, one of the smaller islands but in some ways the most radical, 4,466. There were 17,143 sugar workers, 4,163 pineapple workers, and 1,804 stevedores, with about 526 members scattered in other unions, making it "by far the largest union in the Territory."

22. A summary of the principal strikes would include the 87-day sugar strike on Maui in 1937; the 77-day longshore strike in Port Allen and Kauaʻi in 1940–1941; the 77-day territory-wide sugar strike in 1946; the 121-day Pioneer Mills sugar strike in 1946; the 5-day territory-wide pineapple strike in 1947; the 66-day Olaa sugar strike in 1948; the 1949 territory-wide longshore strike of 178 days; the 1951 pineapple strike in Lanaʻi of 201 days; the 128-day Hutchinson sugar strike in 1954; and the 126-day territory-wide sugar strike in 1958. See Summary, notebook 12, Zalburg Papers.

23. Robert W. Cherny, "The Making of a Labor Radical: Harry Bridges, 1901–1934," *Pacific Historical Review*, 1995, box 4, Bridges Papers, San Francisco. Bridges' lawyer, the leonine Vincent Hallinan, objected strenuously to such allegations. See Vincent Hallinan to Frank Hennessy, 27 December 1949, box 12, folder 26, Harry Bridges Papers, Southern California Library for Social Studies and Research, Los Angeles (hereafter cited as Bridges Papers, Los Angeles).

24. Noriko "Nikki" Bridges, interview, 29 June 1975, Zalburg Papers. Ms. Bridges, the leader's second wife, married him in December 1958 when she was 32 and he was 57 years of age.

25. Remarks of Robbie Bridges in Griffin Fariello, ed., *Red Scare: Memories of the American Inquisition* (New York: Norton, 1995), 58–63.

26. *PM*, 25 and 26 August 1941, box 6, folder 6, Bridges Papers, Los Angeles.

27. *Honolulu Record*, 25 October 1956.

28. US Senate, *Statehood for Hawaii . . . Communist Penetration of the Hawaiian Islands*, 80th Cong., 2nd sess., 21 June 1949 (Washington, D.C.: Government Printing Office, 1949), University of Hawaiʻi at Mānoa, Special Collections.

29. *Honolulu Record*, 26 February 1953.

30. Samuel Wilder King to Senator Pat Harrison, 29 April 1937, Special Collections, University of Virginia, Charlottesville.

31. See, e.g., Gerald Horne, *The White Pacific: U.S. Imperialism and Black Slavery in the South Seas after the Civil War* (Honolulu: University of Hawaiʻi Press, 2007). In 1955, ILWU leader Robert McElrath reported that 40 percent of Hawaiʻi's population consisted of Japanese-Americans; 20 percent were indigenous; 15 percent were white, 13 percent were Filipino, 2.3 percent were Puerto Rican, 1.6 percent were Korean, 6.8 percent were Chinese, and others—including African-Americans—were about 0.9 percent. See ILWU Radio Transcripts, 1 June 1955, University of Hawaiʻi at Mānoa, Special Collections.

32. Louis Goldblatt, "Working Class Leader in the ILWU, 1935–1977," oral history transcript, Regional Oral History Office, Bancroft Library, University of California, Berkeley, 351.

33. Grover Johnson, interview, n.d., notebook 30, Zalburg Papers.

34. *New York Times,* 12 July 2005.

35. See, e.g., William Pomeroy, *The Philippines: Colonialism, Collaboration, and Resistance* (New York: International Publishers, 1992).

36. Sen Katayama, "Hawaii, the Strategic Knot of the Pacific," *Communist International* (1933), box 3a, *United States v. Charles Fujimoto et al.*, RG 21, case #10495, compartment 1069B, National Archives and Records Administration, San Bruno, Calif. (cited hereafter as *US v. Charles Fujimoto et al.*).

37. Article by Michael Carey, 1 August 1950, box 95, Hugh Butler Papers, Nebraska State Historical Society, Lincoln (hereafter cited as Butler Papers).

38. James Coke to Senator Hugh Butler, 27 April 1950, box 101, Butler Papers.

39. Yasuki Arakaki, oral history transcript, 19 March 1991, University of Hawaiʻi–West Oʻahu, Center for Labor Education and Research.

40. Jack Kimoto, interview, 15 December 1974, notebook 23, Zalburg Papers.

41. Alice M. Beechert and Edward D. Beechert, eds., *From Kona to Yenan: The Political Memoirs of Koji Ariyoshi* (Honolulu: University of Hawaiʻi Press, 2000).

42. Koji Ariyoshi, interview, 18 January 1976, notebook 28, Zalburg Papers.

43. Sanford Zalburg, *A Spark Is Struck! Jack Hall and the ILWU in Hawaii* (Honolulu: University of Hawaiʻi Press, 1979), xiv.

44. Ibid., xiii, xiv, xv.

45. Yoshiko Hall, interview, 24 November 1975, notebook 12, Zalburg Papers.

46. Conversation between David Thompson and FBI agents, n.d., ca. 1951, file Smith Act Case—Hall, ILWU Headquarters, Honolulu.

47. David Thompson, interview, 12 June 1975, notebook 6, Zalburg Papers.

48. John F. Murphy, interview, 29 July 1975, notebook 30, Zalburg Papers.

49. Charles P. Larrowe, *Harry Bridges: The Rise and Fall of Radical Labor in the United States* (Westport, Conn.: Lawrence Hill, 1972), 268.

50. O. Vincent Esposito, interview, 19 November 1974, notebook 21, Zalburg Papers.

51. Yoshiko Hall interview, 24 November 1975.

52. John Burns, interview, 24 August 1973, notebook 20, Zalburg Papers.

53. Koji Ariyoshi, interview, 20 August 1974, notebook 28, Zalburg Papers.

54. *Honolulu Advertiser,* 7 July 1955.

55. Marc Levinson, *The Box: How the Shipping Container Made the World Smaller and the World Economy Bigger* (Princeton, N.J.: Princeton University Press, 2006), 26.

56. Howard Kimeldorf, *Reds or Rackets? The Making of Radical and Conservative Unions on the Waterfront* (Berkeley: University of California Press, 1988).

57. Transcript of radio broadcast, January 1952, file ILWU Radio Program, January 1952, ILWU Headquarters, Honolulu.

58. Philip Maxwell, interview, 20 November 1973, notebook 24, Zalburg Papers.

59. C. Wendell Carlsmith, interview, 26 February 1975, notebook 21, Zalburg Papers.

60. *Honolulu Advertiser*, 4 October 1951.

61. Senate Committee on Labor and Public Welfare, 81st Cong., 1st sess., 12 July 1949, notebook 11, Zalburg Papers.

62. Testimony of Aiko T. Reinecke, 16 September 1948, Reinecke file, 318-2-3, Corr.: Commissioner, DPI Hearing Transcript, box 1, Hawai'i State Archives, Honolulu (hereafter cited as Reinecke file, 318-2-3).

63. *Honolulu Record*, 30 August 1956.

64. *Honolulu Record*, 14 February 1957.

65. Transcript of radio broadcast, 26 February 1949, file ILWU Radio Program, February 1949, ILWU Headquarters, Honolulu.

66. *Honolulu Record*, 2 December 1948.

67. *Honolulu Record*, 4 August 1949.

68. *Honolulu Record*, 24 May 1951.

69. *Honolulu Record*, 27 March 1952.

70. *Honolulu Record*, 27 October 1955.

71. *Honolulu Record*, 27 November 1952.

72. Susanna Moore, *Light Years: A Girlhood in Hawai'i* (New York: Grove Press, 2007), 83, 84.

73. Testimony, 14 April 1953, box 9, *US v. Charles Fujimoto et al.*

74. Testimony of John Reinecke, 10 September 1948, Reinecke file, 318-2-3.

75. Lucile Paterson to Senator Hugh Butler, 19 November 1947, box 101, Butler Papers.

76. Testimony of Francis D. Houston, "Stenographic Transcript of Hearings before the Committee on Interior and Insular Affairs," US Senate, 1–5 November 1948, "Confidential Interviews," box 97, Butler Papers (hereafter cited as "Stenographic Transcript of Hearings").

77. Testimony of Arthur Bauckham and of Joseph Whitfield, "Stenographic Transcript of Hearings"; J. E. Clark to Senator Guy Cordon, 26 January 1948, box 97, Butler Papers.

78. Testimony of Martin E. Alan, "Stenographic Transcript of Hearings."

79. Minutes of Special Meeting, 7 December 1941, box 1, Edna E. Jenkins Papers, Maui Historical Society, Wailuku, Hawai'i.

80. Allen, *Hawaii's War Years*, 46.

81. Statement by Senator Olin Johnston, uncertain provenance, box 41, Olin D. Johnston Papers, South Caroliniana Library, University of South Carolina, Columbia.

82. J. Strom Thurmond to Daisy Harvey, 24 July 1958, Subject Correspondence, 1958, Federal Government, Statehood, J. Strom Thurmond Papers, Clemson University, Clemson, S.C.

83. Daniel Inouye, oral history transcript, 18 April 1969, Lyndon Baines Johnson Library, University of Texas at Austin.

84. Richard M. Nixon to Myrtle Wilkins, 17 March 1959, LN Collection, ser. 320, folder Hawaii, Richard Nixon Presidential Library, Yorba Linda, Calif.

85. Letter from Henry A. White, 28 December 1946, folder 6340, Forrest Donnell Papers, Western Historical Manuscript Collection–Columbia, University of Missouri.

86. Ray Jerome Baker to Carl Christensen, 11 May 1952, box 33, Ray Jerome Baker Papers, Bishop Museum, Honolulu (hereafter cited as Baker Papers).

87. Ray Jerome Baker to W. R. Tosh, 24 November 1952, box 33, Baker Papers.

88. Harry Bridges, interview, 1 June 1975, notebook 22-A, Zalburg Papers.

89. Stephen Murin, interview, 27 July 1975, notebook 30, Zalburg Papers.

90. Memorandum, October 1945, notebook 1, Zalburg Papers.

91. But see Dyna Nakamoto interview, 29 May 1996.

92. Testimony of Robert Kempa, box 5, *US v. Charles Fujimoto et al.*

93. Testimony of John Reinecke, 13 September 1948, Reinecke file, 318-2-3.

94. "On the Question of Hawaii," Communist Party document, n.d., ca. early 1950s, box 2, Celeste Strack Papers, Southern California Library for Social Studies and Research, Los Angeles.

95. Officers' Report, part 1, ILWU Local 142, file Proceedings, Third National Convention, ILWU Local 142, Honolulu, Hawai'i, 25–28 September 1959, ILWU Headquarters, Honolulu.

Chapter 1. Confronting Colonial Hawai'i

1. Bill Bailey, interview, 27 June 1973, notebook 28, Sanford Zalburg Papers, University of Hawai'i at Mānoa, Archives and Manuscripts (hereafter cited as Zalburg Papers).

2. Bill Bailey, *The Kid from Hoboken: An Autobiography* (San Francisco: Circus Lithographic, 1993), 302, 303.

3. Bill Bailey interview, 27 June 1973.

4. Senator Hiram Johnson to Harold Ickes, 15 July 1934, Official File, OF407b, box 11, Franklin D. Roosevelt Library, Hyde Park, N.Y. (hereafter cited as FDR Library).

5. Frank Merriam, Acting Governor of California, to President Roosevelt, 18 July 1934, Official File, OF407b, box 11, FDR Library.

6. Jack Hall, interview by Edward Beechert, 1 August 1966, notebook 12, Zalburg Papers.

7. Gerald Horne, *Powell v. Alabama: The Scottsboro Boys and American Justice* (New York: Franklin Watts, 1997).

8. David E. Stannard, *Honor Killing: How the Infamous "Massie Affair" Transformed Hawai'i* (New York: Viking, 2005).

9. *Liberator*, 2 June 1932.

10. Interview subject, n.d., transcript, box 12, Robert E. Park Papers, Special Collections Research Center, University of Chicago.

11. William Armstrong, journal, 5 December 1880, box 5, William Nevins Armstrong Papers, Manuscripts and Archives, Yale University Library, New Haven, Conn.

12. Ibid., 6 March 1881.

13. Karl Yoneda, "Brief History of Japanese Labor in Hawaii," *Hawaii Pono Journal* 1, no. 2 (February 1971): 1–9, 3, VF, PF, Tamiment Library, New York University.

14. Clipping, ca. 1901, publication unknown, in Aiken Scrapbook, Maui Historical Society, Wailuku, Hawai'i.

15. Ichiro Izuka, "Directed Research 799: The Labor Movement in Hawaii (1934–1949)" (University of Hawai'i, 11 April 1974), University of Hawai'i at Mānoa, Special Collections.

16. Rotary Club, "To You Defenders of Maui, USA," 20 May 1942, box 1, Edna E. Jenkins Papers, Maui Historical Society.

17. Hawaii Sugar Planters' Association, *Story of Sugar in Hawaii* (1926), at J. Porter Shaw Maritime Library, San Francisco.

18. W. Somerset Maugham, *South Sea Stories* (Garden City, N.Y.: Doubleday, 1956; first published 1921), 62.

19. See Horne, *White Pacific*.

20. Edwin R. Embree to Raymond B. Fosdick, 27 April 1926, RG 1.1, ser. 214, box 1, Rockefeller Foundation Archives, Rockefeller Archives Center, Sleepy Hollow, N.Y. (hereafter cited as Rockefeller Foundation Archives).

21. Memorandum from R. N. Dean, 13 April 1926, RG 1.1, ser. 214, box 1, Rockefeller Foundation Archives.

22. Minutes of Rockefeller Foundation grant to the University of Hawai'i, 9 October 1931, RG 1.1, ser. 214, box 1, Rockefeller Foundation Archives.

23. Listing, n.d., folder 11, box 94, C. Brewer Records, Lyman Museum, Hilo, Hawai'i.

24. Yoneda, "Brief History," 8.

25. *Butte Bulletin*, 11 November 1921, reel 31, vol. 226, American Civil Liberties Union Papers, Princeton University, Princeton, N.J. (hereafter cited as ACLU Papers).

26. Josephine Fowler, "'To Be Red and "Oriental"': The Experience of Japanese and Chinese Immigrant Communists in the American and International Communist Movements, 1919–1933" (PhD diss., University of Minnesota, 2003), 112, 226, 379; *Western Worker*, 2 October 1934.

27. Karl Yoneda, interview, 7 November 1983, transcript, Oral History of the American Left, New York University.

28. Michael Carey, "The Japanization of Hawaii: The Japanese-Communist Master Plan," 1 August 1950, box 95, Hugh Butler Papers, Nebraska State Historical Society, Lincoln.

29. George Wright, President, Central Labor Council, and Vice President, English Language Department of United Workers of Hawaii, to "Dear Comrade Milner," 18 February 1922, reel 31, vol. 226, #307, ACLU Papers.

30. Jan Valtin, *Out of the Night* (London: Heinemann, 1941), 107.

31. 13th Plenum Executive Committee of Communist International, *Revolutionary Struggle of the Toiling Masses of Japan: Speech by Okano* (New York: Workers Library, 1934), at University of Kansas, Lawrence. See also T. A. Bisson, *Shadow over Asia: The Rise of Militant Japan* (New York: Foreign Policy Association, 1941); and Pan-Pacific Trade Union Secretariat, *The Class Trade Unions of Japan: Their Revolutionary Role and Tasks* (New York: Workers Library, 1934), at University of Kansas, Lawrence.

32. Material on Paul Crouch, reel 52, vol. 299, p. 446, ACLU Papers.

33. Material on Paul Crouch, n.d., box 11, folder 20, Harry Bridges Papers, Southern California Library for Social Studies and Research, Los Angeles.

34. *Report of the Commission on Subversive Activities to the Legislature of the Territory of Hawaii* (March 1951), University of Hawai'i at Mānoa, Special Collections.

35. *Daily Worker*, 20 May 1925.

36. *Daily Worker*, 6 August 1928.

37. *Honolulu Advertiser*, 22 December 1949.

38. Paul Crouch, "Moscow's Supervision of Communist Activities in Hawaii," n.d., James Eastland Papers, University of Mississippi, Oxford.

39. Felipe Lariosa, interview, 16 June 1995, University of Hawai'i–West O'ahu, Center for Labor Education and Research.

40. A. Q. McElrath, interview, n.d., transcript, University of Hawai'i–West O'ahu, Center for Labor Education and Research.

41. *Voice of Labor*, 21 October 1937, ILWU Headquarters, Honolulu.

42. Pablo Manlapit, President, Hawaii Federation of Labor, to President of the US, 28 March 1934, 8-21, Governor J. B. Poindexter Papers, Hawai'i State Archives, Honolulu (hereafter cited as Poindexter Papers).

43. Ines Cayaban, *A Life History as Told to Yvonne Yarber* (Honolulu: Department of Education of Hawai'i, 1991), at Hawai'i State Library, Honolulu. See also Ines Cayaban, *A Goodly Heritage* (Wanchai, Hong Kong: Gulliver, 1981), 124–136.

44. Grover Johnson to Sanford Zalburg, n.d., notebook 30, Zalburg Papers.

45. Curtis Cosmos Aller Jr., "The Evolution of Hawaiian Labor Relations: From Benevolent Paternalism to Mature Collective Bargaining" (PhD diss., Harvard University, 1958), 98.

46. Hideo Okada, interview, 14 October 1974, notebook 24, Zalburg Papers.

47. Doc Hill, interview, 25 February 1970, notebook 29, Zalburg Papers.

48. Mrs. L. McCandless to James Farley, 5 December 1934, Democratic National Committee, Women's Division, box 71, FDR Library.

49. Bailey, *Kid from Hoboken*, 303–304.

50. Manuel Jardin, Treasurer, CLC, to Frank Morrison, AFL, Washington, D.C., 27 December 1927, files of Hawaii's Old Central Labor Council, University of Hawai'i–West O'ahu, Center for Labor Education and Research.

51. Louis Goldblatt, "Working Class Leader in the ILWU, 1935–1977," oral history transcript, Regional Oral History Office, Bancroft Library, University of California, Berkeley, 265.

52. Aller, "Evolution of Hawaiian Labor Relations," 226–227.

53. *Daily Worker*, 5 February 1936.

54. Resolution signed by Willie Crozier and Charles M. Kekoa, 8 December 1936, 8-27, Poindexter Papers.

55. William J. Puette, *The Hilo Massacre: Hawaii's Bloody Monday, August 1st, 1938* (Honolulu: University of Hawai'i–West O'ahu, Center for Labor Education and Research, 1988), 3. See also Bernard Stern, *The Aloha Trade: Labor Relations in Hawaii's Hotel Industry, 1941–1987* (University of Hawai'i–West O'ahu, Center for Labor Education and Research, 1988); and Bernard Stern, *Rutledge Unionism: Labor Relations in the Honolulu Transit Industry* (Honolulu: University of Hawai'i–West O'ahu, Center for Labor Education and Research, 1986).

56. Fred Luning, Corresponding Secretary, to Harry Kamoku, Hilo Branch of International Longshoremen's Association, 18 December 1935, ILWU Headquarters, Honolulu.

57. Harry Kamoku, Hilo, to Honolulu Longshoremen, 22 August 1936, ILWU Headquarters, Honolulu.

58. *Longshoreman: A Rank and File Trade Union Paper* 1, no. 1 (21 November 1935), ILWU Headquarters, Honolulu.

59. William G. Craft, ILA District Organizer, Pacific Coast District, to Joseph P. Ryan, 28 October 1936, ILWU Headquarters, Honolulu.

60. Minutes of "Regular Business Meetings of the Wharf and Warehousemen's Association of the HLA Held at 1838 Kamehameha Avenue . . . ," 29 May 1937, file Applications, ILWU Headquarters, Honolulu.

61. Telegram from Governor J. B. Poindexter, 21 December 1936, 8-27, Poindexter Papers.

62. Randolph Sevier, Castle and Cooke, to Frank Thompson, 12 December 1937, 8-26, Poindexter Papers.

63. Mildred G. Smith, Secretary, Zonta Club of Honolulu, to Governor Poindexter, 11 February 1938, 8-26, Poindexter Papers.

64. Honolulu Japanese Poultrymen to Governor Poindexter, 1 December 1936, 8-26, Poindexter Papers.

65. Governor Poindexter to Ernest Gruening, 2 December 1936, 8-26, Poindexter Papers.

66. C. J. Fern, President of Kauai Chamber of Commerce, to Governor Poindexter, 30 November 1936, 8-26, Poindexter Papers.

67. Gordon Scruton, Executive Secretary of Hilo Chamber of Commerce, to Governor Poindexter, 25 November 1936, 8-26, Poindexter Papers.

68. Lyle G. Phillips, President of Territory of Hawaii Medical Association, to Governor Poindexter, 20 January 1937, 8-27, Poindexter Papers.

69. Memorandum, 28 November 1936, RG 126, Office of the Territories, Classified Files, 1907–1951, box 659, National Archives and Records Administration, College Park, Md.

70. Memorandum from "PMS," 6 November 1936, 8-27, Poindexter Papers.

71. Robert Bodie, Honolulu Longshoremen's Association, to Harry Kamoku, 14 December 1936, ILWU Headquarters, Honolulu.

72. Chair and Secretary of Strike Committee of Hilo Longshoremen to ILWU, 8 August 1937, file Port Allen Strike, 1937, ILWU Headquarters, Honolulu.

73. Governor J. B. Poindexter to Ruth Hampton, Department of Interior, Washington, D.C., 9 June 1937, 8-27, Poindexter Papers.

74. Bill Bailey to Harry Bridges, 26 April 1937, file Vibora Luviminda, ILWU Headquarters, Honolulu.

75. William Bailey to Harry Bridges, 27 April 1937, file Vibora Luviminda, ILWU Headquarters, Honolulu.

76. Hawaii Island Poultry Association to Governor Poindexter, 12 August 1938, 8-27, Poindexter Papers. See also the report by John Reinecke titled "Inter-Island Strike, May 28 to September 27, 1938," notebook 26, Zalburg Papers.

77. Edward Berman to Calixto Piano, 7 October 1938, file 1938 Shooting, ILWU Headquarters, Honolulu.

78. "Delegate Reports," Local 1-36, Hilo, n.d., ILWU Headquarters, Honolulu.

79. Resolution by Hilo Industrial Union Council, 28 September 1938, notebook 1, Zalburg Papers.

80. Attorney General J. V. Hodgson to Governor Poindexter, 9 September 1938, notebook 14, Zalburg Papers.

81. Report by J. V. Hodgson on "Bloody Monday," 9 September 1938, ILWU Headquarters, Honolulu.

82. Bert Nakano, interview, 6 September 1973, notebook 24, Zalburg Papers.

83. Attorney George Anderson to CIO, San Francisco, 26 October 1938, ILWU Headquarters, Honolulu.

84. Attorney General J. V. Hodgson to Governor Poindexter, 4 August 1938, 8-27, Poindexter Papers.

85. Sheriff Henry K. Martin to Governor Poindexter, 1 August 1938, 8-27, Poindexter Papers.

86. Edward Berman, interview, 29 April 1974, Zalburg Papers.

87. Maxie Weisbarth, interview, 20 August and 1 September 1975, Zalburg Papers.

88. Harry Kamoku to Maxie Weisbarth, 8 July 1936, file Honolulu Longshoremen's Association Correspondence with Hilo, L.A., 1935–1937, ILWU Headquarters, Honolulu.

89. Paul Kalina to Harry Kamoku, 24 August 1937, ILWU Headquarters, Honolulu.

90. See report by Maxie Weisbarth, Chairman, Board of Directors, HLA, to "all membership and officers," re "pending affiliation with American Federation of Labor," 22 June 1937, ILWU Headquarters, Honolulu.

91. Jack Kawano, interview, 4 September 1974, notebook 23, Zalburg Papers. Emphasis in original.

92. Communist Party—Santa Barbara, to Governor Poindexter, 4 August 1938, 8-27, Poindexter Papers.

93. Ray Jerome Baker to Governor Poindexter, 2 August 1938, 8-27, Poindexter Papers.

94. L. H. Michener, CIO Industrial Council of Los Angeles, to Senate Civil Liberties Committee, 10 October 1938, file Bloody Monday—August 1st, ILWU Headquarters, Honolulu.

95. William Kaluhikau, Acting Secretary, to "All Organizations," 28 September 1938, file Local 136 (137), Correspondence with Hilo Local 136, 1938–1941, ILWU Headquarters, Honolulu.

96. Report by Acting Health Officer, Hilo, 2 August 1938, 8-27, Poindexter Papers.

97. House Committee on Un-American Activities, "Hearings Regarding Communist Activities in the Territory of Hawaii—Part 1," 1951, University of Hawai'i at Mānoa, Special Collections.

98. Bailey, *Kid from Hoboken*, 305, 318, 321.

Chapter 2. An Apartheid Archipelago?

1. Regular Hilo Longshoremen's Business Meeting Minutes, 21 July 1936, ILWU Headquarters, Honolulu. See also Andrew Lind, *Hawaii's Japanese: An Experiment in Democracy* (Princeton, N.J.: Princeton University Press, 1946).

2. *Voice of Labor*, 22 September 1938, ILWU Headquarters, Honolulu.

3. House Committee on Un-American Activities, "Hearings Regarding Communist Activities in the Territory of Hawaii—Part 1," 6 July 1951, at University of Hawai'i at Mānoa, Special Collections.

4. *Report of the Commission on Subversive Activities to the Legislature of the Territory of Hawaii* (March 1951), University of Hawai'i at Mānoa, Special Collections.

5. *Democrat*, 15 June 1938, Labor Archives and Research Center, San Francisco State University.

6. Comments by Sanford Zalburg, 15 December 1974, notebook 23, Sanford Zalburg Papers, University of Hawai'i at Mānoa, Archives and Manuscripts (hereafter cited as Zalburg Papers).

7. *Democrat*, 18 May 1938.

8. *Hawaii Sentinel*, 26 August 1937, Labor Archives and Research Center, San Francisco State University.

9. "Black Persons Living in Hawaii," 12 April 1933, box 512, Langston Hughes Papers, Yale University, New Haven, Conn.

10. *Democrat*, 20 July 1938.

11. *Democrat*, 12 October 1938.

12. *Hawaii Sentinel*, 10 June 1937.

13. *Hawaii Sentinel*, 25 November 1937.

14. "On the Question of Statehood," Communist Party document, n.d., ca. 1948, box 2, Celeste Strack Papers, Southern California Library of Social Studies and Research, Los Angeles. Emphasis in the original.

15. *Voice of Labor*, 21 October 1937.

16. VF, BF, Hall, Jack, "Jack Hall—ILWU" (Honolulu: ILWU, 1952), at New York University. See also Stephen E. Marsland, *The Birth of the Japanese Labor Movement: Takano Fusatarō and the Rōdō Kumiai Kiseika* (Honolulu: University of Hawai'i Press, 1989); Robert Scalapino, *The Early Japanese Labor Movement: Labor and Politics in a Developing Society* (Berkeley: Center for Japanese Studies, University of California, Berkeley, 1983); Iwao F. Ayusawa, *A History of Labor in Modern Japan* (Honolulu: East-West Center Press, University of Hawai'i, 1966); and Milton Murayama, *All I Asking for Is My Body* (Honolulu: University of Hawai'i Press, 1988).

17. "Labor Problems in Hawaii: Does Hawaii Need Chinese?" *American Federationist* (1923), carton 1, Paul Scharrenberg Papers, Bancroft Library, University of California, Berkeley.

18. Edward Berman, interview, 29 April 1974, Zalburg Papers.

19. *Hawaii Observer*, 10 November 1976.

20. *Kauai Herald*, 2 June 1941, ILWU Headquarters, Honolulu.

21. *Kauai Herald*, 20 October 1941.

22. Samuel King to D. P. Lopes, Secretary, Central Labor Council, 3 April 1941, University of Hawai'i–West O'ahu, Center for Labor Education and Research.

23. George Cass to Ruben Ortiz, 29 August 1941, University of Hawai'i–West O'ahu, Center for Labor Education and Research.

24. Alice M. Beechert and Edward C. Beechert, eds., *A Man Must Stand Up: The Autobiography of a Gentle Activist* (Honolulu: University of Hawai'i Press, 1993), 22. See also William H. Dorrance, *Sugar Islands: The 165-Year Story of Sugar in Hawaii* (Honolulu: Mutual, 2000), vii.

25. Bobette Gugliotta, *Nolle Smith: Cowboy, Engineer, Statesman* (New York: Dodd, Mead, 1971), 88, 96, 102.

26. *Honolulu Record*, 9 August 1950.

27. Bill Eubanks, interview, 30 May 1946, transcript, box 16, folder 29, Romanzo Adams Social Research Laboratory Collection, University of Hawai'i at Mānoa, Archives and Manuscripts (hereafter cited as Adams Collection).

28. "Foremost Negro in Hawaii," *Ebony*, March 1948, box 16, folder 29, Adams Collection.

29. Testimony of Nolle Smith, 7 May 1953, box 10, *United States v. Charles Fujimoto et al.*, RG 21, case #10495, compartment 1069B, National Archives and Records Administration, San Bruno, Calif. (cited hereafter as *US v. Charles Fujimoto et al.*).

30. "The Negro in Hawaii," n.d., box 16, folder 25, Adams Collection.

31. Frank Marshall Davis, articles, 16 March and 16 April 1949, in John Edgar Tidwell, ed., *Writings of Frank Marshall Davis: A Voice of the Black Press* (Jackson: University Press of Mississippi, 2007), 173, 176, 177.

32. Frank Marshall Davis, *Livin' the Blues: Memoirs of a Black Journalist and Poet* (Madison: University of Wisconsin Press, 1992), 313, 314, 315, 317, 320.

33. *Honolulu Record*, 10 March 1949.

34. *Honolulu Record*, 2 December 1954.

35. Romanzo Adams, "The Peoples of Hawaii," VF, Tamiment Library, New York University.

36. Frank Marshall Davis, *I Am the American Negro* (Chicago: Black Cat Press, 1937), 7.

37. *Honolulu Record*, 15 November 1956.

38. Kathryn Waddell Takara, "The Fire and the Phoenix: Frank Marshall Davis (an American Biography)" (PhD diss., University of Hawai'i, 1993), 361.

39. Wilbur Wood, interview, 28 June 1946, transcript, box 16, folder 29, Adams Collection.

40. Richard Masuda, "Specific Attitudes toward the Negroes in Hawaii," June 1946, box 16, folder 27, Adams Collection.

41. *Honolulu Star-Bulletin*, 28 August 1951.

42. Alice M. Beechert and Edward D. Beechert, eds., *From Kona to Yenan: The Political Memoirs of Koji Ariyoshi* (Honolulu: University of Hawai'i Press, 2000), 12, 33, 34, 35, 40, 193.

43. Edwin Embree to Dr. Arthur Dean, University of Hawai'i, 6 October 1926, RG 1.1, ser. 214, box 1, Rockefeller Foundation Archives, Rockefeller Archive Center, Sleepy Hollow, N.Y.

44. Testimony of Aiko T. Reinecke, 16 September 1948, Reinecke file, 318-2-3, Corr.: Commissioner, DPI Hearing Transcript, box 1, Hawai'i State Archives, Honolulu.

45. Jim Sharp to "Dear George," 27 May 1937, box 13, Carey McWilliams Papers, University of California, Berkeley.

46. *Hawaii Sentinel*, 9 September 1937.

47. US Department of Labor, Bureau of Labor Statistics, *Labor Conditions in the Territory of Hawaii, 1929–1930*, Bulletin of the US Bureau of Labor Statistics 534 (Washington, D.C.: Government Printing Office, 1931), at Lyman Museum, Hilo, Hawai'i. See also J. A. Mollett, *The Sugar Plantation in Hawaii: A Study of Changing Patterns of Management and Labor Organization*, Agricultural Economics Bulletin, Hawaii Agricultural Experiment Station, University of Hawai'i (n.d.), at Lyman Museum, Hilo, Hawai'i.

48. *Honolulu Star-Bulletin*, 31 August 1990. See also James H. Shoemaker, *Labor in the Territory of Hawaii, 1939* (Washington, D.C.: Government Printing Office, 1940), at University of Hawai'i–West O'ahu, Center for Labor Education and Research.

49. *Seventy Five Years a Corporation: 1900–1975* (Alexander and Baldwin, 1975), at J. Porter Shaw Maritime Library, San Francisco.

50. Louis Goldblatt, "Working Class Leader in the ILWU, 1935–1977," oral history transcript, Regional Oral History Office, Bancroft Library, University of California, Berkeley, 266, 298.

51. Louis Goldblatt, interview, 18 September 1975, notebook 22-B, Zalburg Papers.

52. Harold Ickes to President Roosevelt, 7 November 1936, Official File, OF407b, box 11, Franklin D. Roosevelt Library, Hyde Park, N.Y.

53. Undated document on Waialua case, box suppl. 1, Norman Leonard Collection, Labor Archives and Research Center, San Francisco State University. See also Melissa C. Miller, comp., and Linda K. Menton, ed., *Pineapple in Hawaii: A Guide to Historical Resources* (Honolulu: Hawaii Historical Society, 1990).

54. Robert Cherny, "Labor and Vertical Integration: The Hawaiian Sugar Industry and San Francisco Labor, 1900–1946," box 4, Harry Bridges Papers, Labor Archives and Research Center, San Francisco State University.

55. Report by Edward Eagen, Regional Director of NLRB, Seattle (1940), notebook 15, Zalburg Papers.

56. *Honolulu Beacon*, September 1964, notebook 24, Zalburg Papers.

57. *Honolulu Star-Bulletin*, 28 August 1951.

58. Joyce Lea Walker, "A Rhetorical Analysis of the Epideictic Speeches of Jack Hall, Regional Director of the ILWU for Hawaii" (MA thesis, University of Hawai'i, 1961), 17.

59. Gerald Horne, *Red Seas: Ferdinand Smith and Radical Black Sailors in the United States and Jamaica* (New York: New York University Press, 2005).

60. Jack Hall, interview, 1 August 1966, notebook 12, Zalburg Papers.

61. Edward Berman, interviews, 29 April 1974, 2 February 1973, Zalburg Papers.

62. Sanford Zalburg, *A Spark Is Struck! Jack Hall and the ILWU in Hawaii* (Honolulu: University of Hawai'i Press, 1979), xiv, 14.

63. George Goto, interview, 1 February 1976, notebook 29, Zalburg Papers.

64. See Louis Goldblatt interview, 18 September 1975.

65. Revels Cayton, interview, 21 May 1975, notebook 28, Zalburg Papers. Hall's spouse confirmed Cayton's role in dispatching the future ILWU leader to the islands. See Yoshiko Hall interview, 24 November 1975, notebook 12, Zalburg Papers.

66. Robert McElrath, interview, 28 March 1975, notebook 25, Zalburg Papers.

67. John F. Murphy, interview, 18 July 1975, notebook 30, Zalburg Papers.

68. Rachel Saiki, interview, 1 February 1976, notebook 31, Zalburg Papers.

69. Yoshiko Hall interview, 24 November 1975.

70. Testimony of William Norwood, 7 April 1953, box 9, *US v. Charles Fujimoto et al.*

71. A. Q. McElrath interview, n.d., transcript, University of Hawai'i–West O'ahu, Center for Labor Education and Research.

72. Testimony of John B. Fernandes, 24 March 1953, box 8, *US v. Charles K. Fujimoto et al.*

73. Zalburg, *A Spark Is Struck!* 46.

74. Testimony of William Crozier Jr., 26 March 1953, box 8, *US v. Charles K. Fujimoto et al.*

75. Testimony of Paul Crouch, 20 November 1952, box 3b, *US v. Charles K. Fujimoto et al.*

76. Testimony of Robert McBurney Kempa, 22 January 1953, box 4, *US v. Charles K. Fujimoto et al.*

77. Testimony of Ichiro Izuka, 20 November 1952, box 3b, *US v. Charles K. Fujimoto et al.*

78. Testimony of Jack Kawano, 2 February 1953, box 6, *US v. Charles K. Fujimoto et al.*

79. Testimony of Emil Muller, 5 December 1952, box 3c, *US v. Charles K. Fujimoto et al.*

80. Irving N. Ninnell, US Consul-General, Canton, to Governor Joseph B. Poindexter, 17 January 1939, 8-21, Governor J. B. Poindexter Papers, Hawai'i State Archives, Honolulu (hereafter cited as Poindexter Papers).

81. *Montgomery (Ala.) Advertiser,* 1 December 1940, 8-3, Poindexter Papers.

Chapter 3. The Race of War

1. Dan Gilbert, *What Really Happened at Pearl Harbor?* (Grand Rapids, Mich.: Zondervan, 1948), 7. See also Rear Admiral Robert A. Theobald, US Navy, retired, *The Final Secret of Pearl Harbor: The Washington Contribution to the Japanese Attack* (New York: Devin-Adair, 1954); Owen Roberts et al., comps., *"Asleep": The Complete Official Story of What Happened at Pearl Harbor* (Girard, Kans.: Halden-Julius, 1942).

2. Editors of the "Army Times," *Pearl Harbor and Hawaii: A Military History* (New York: Bonanza, 1971), 130. See also, e.g., Hartford Van Dyke, *The Skeleton in Uncle Sam's Closet* (Vancouver, Wash.: HVD, 1973); Bruce Bartlett, *Cover-Up: The Politics of Pearl Harbor, 1941–1946* (New Rochelle, N.Y.: Arlington House, 1978); and Husband E. Kimmel, *Admiral Kimmel's Story* (Chicago: Regnery, 1955).

3. *Kauai Herald,* 9 April 1941, ILWU Headquarters, Honolulu.

4. Robert McElrath, interview, 28 March 1975, notebook 25, Sanford Zalburg Papers, University of Hawai'i at Mānoa, Archives and Manuscripts (hereafter cited as Zalburg Papers).

5. *Washington Post,* 26 December 1942.

6. *Honolulu Star-Bulletin*, 17 March 1967.

7. *Honolulu Star-Bulletin*, 6 December 1975.

8. Letter to Harry Bridges, 19 December 1940, file Local 136 (137), Correspondence with Hilo Local 136, 1938–1941, ILWU Headquarters, Honolulu.

9. Jack Kawano to Bert Nakano, 3 February 1941, file Local 136 (137), Correspondence with Hilo Local 136, 1938–1941, ILWU Headquarters, Honolulu.

10. *Kauai Herald*, 2 June 1941.

11. Koji [Ariyoshi] to Jack Kawano, 2 September 1941, unnamed file, ILWU Headquarters, Honolulu.

12. Koji [Ariyoshi] to Fred Kamahoahoa, 4 November 1941, unnamed file, ILWU Headquarters, Honolulu.

13. Curtis Cosmos Aller Jr., "The Evolution of Hawaiian Labor Relations: From Benevolent Paternalism to Mature Collective Bargaining" (PhD diss., Harvard University, 1958), 249, 292.

14. Ichiro Izuka to Jack Hall et al., 27 November 1942, University of Hawai'i at Mānoa, Special Collections.

15. Alice M. Beechert and Edward D. Beechert, eds., *From Kona to Yenan: The Political Memoirs of Koji Ariyoshi* (Honolulu: University of Hawai'i Press, 2000), 45.

16. Memorandum from Joseph Farrington, 7 November 1945, box 30, Joseph Farrington Papers, Hawai'i State Archives, Honolulu (hereafter cited as Farrington Papers).

17. Alice M. Beechert and Edward C. Beechert, eds., *A Man Must Stand Up: The Autobiography of a Gentle Activist* (Honolulu: University of Hawai'i Press, 1993), 39.

18. *Garden Island* (Kauai), 17 November 1942.

19. *Kauai Herald*, 9 March 1942.

20. *Kauai Herald*, 16 March 1942.

21. *Congressional Record*, 3 February 1943, M-481, box 23, Farrington Papers.

22. *Congressional Record*, 15 April 1943, M-481, box 23, Farrington Papers.

23. Testimony of Earl M. Finch, "Stenographic Transcript of Hearings before the Committee on Interior and Insular Affairs," US Senate, Honolulu, 1–5 November 1948, box 97, Hugh Butler Papers, Nebraska State Historical Society, Lincoln (hereafter cited as "Stenographic Transcript of Hearings").

24. Ray Jerome Baker, diary, 21 June 1944, box 13, Ray Jerome Baker Papers, Bishop Museum, Honolulu (hereafter cited as Baker diary).

25. Untitled, undated 63-page memorandum, box 50, file 1, Walter F. Dillingham Papers, Bishop Museum, Honolulu.

26. James R. Young, *Our Enemy* (Philadelphia: David McKay, 1942), 52, 109. See also John L. Spivak, *Honorable Spy: Exposing Japanese Military Intrigue in the United States* (New York: Modern Age Books, 1939); and T. A. Bisson, *Shadow over Asia: The Rise of Militant Japan* (New York: Foreign Policy Association, 1941).

27. *Kourier* 6, no. 4 (March 1930): 21, at University of Kansas, Lawrence.

28. *Kourier* 12, no. 10 (September 1936): 2.

29. Emma Richey to Senator Hugh Butler, 31 January 1948, box 100, Butler Papers.

30. "Stenographic Transcript of Hearings."

31. Clipping, n.d., publication unknown, box 97, Butler Papers.

32. *Honolulu Star-Bulletin*, 25 August 1944.

33. *Honolulu Advertiser*, 7 August 1943.

34. "Stenographic Transcript of Hearings."

35. Alfred Yap to Senator Hugh Butler, 5 May 1951, box 101, Butler Papers.

36. *Christian Science Monitor*, 16 September 1943.

37. *Christian Science Monitor*, 21 August 1943.

38. Memorandum on Military Control of Hawaiian Labor, n.d., ca. 1943, box 14, folder 7, Romanzo Adams Social Research Laboratory Collection, University of Hawai'i at Mānoa, Archives and Manuscripts (hereafter cited as Adams Collection).

39. Gwenfread Allen, *Hawaii's War Years, 1941–1945* (Honolulu: University of Hawai'i Press, 1950), 134, 139, 288, 305, 351, 377.

40. Baker diary, 19 February 1943, box 31.

41. Ibid., 25 August 1944.

42. Ray Jerome Baker to Jessie Greenwood, 11 October 1945, box 21, Ray Jerome Baker Papers, Bishop Museum, Honolulu.

43. Noriko Asato, *Teaching Mikadoism: The Attack on Japanese Language Schools in Hawaii, California, and Washington, 1919–1927* (Honolulu: University of Hawai'i Press, 2006).

44. Testimony of John Reinecke, 10 September 1948, Reinecke file, 318-2-3, Corr.: Commissioner, DPI Hearing Transcript, box 1, Hawai'i State Archives, Honolulu (hereafter cited as Reinecke file, 318-2-3). Reinecke added: "I can no longer describe myself as an anti-clerical, [for that] change took place approximately in 1936 to [193]8 or 9." See also *Honolulu Advertiser*, 22 October 1940, wherein Reinecke comments on "Shinto Temples."

45. Art Rutledge to H. A. Millis, National Labor Relations Board, 13 October 1943, files of "Hawaii's Old Central Labor Council," University of Hawai'i–West O'ahu, Center for Labor Education and Research.

46. Letter from Korean National Front Federation and Sino-Korean People's League, 12 May 1943, M-481, box 23, Farrington Papers.

47. Kilsoo K. Haan to Ruth Hampton, 19 June 1942, RG 126, Office of the Territories, Classified Files, 1907–1951, box 723, National Archives and Records Administration, College Park, Md.

48. Headquarters, Maui District, Civil Regulation 39, 24 February 1942, box 1, Edna E. Jenkins Papers, Maui Historical Society, Wailuku, Hawai'i.

49. Gary Y. Okihiro and Joan Myers, *Whispered Silences: Japanese Americans and World War II* (Seattle: University of Washington Press, 1996), 163.

50. Louis Goldblatt, interview, 18 September 1975, notebook 22-B, Zalburg Papers.

51. Allen, *Hawaii's War Years*, 145.

52. Testimony of Martin E. Alan, "Stenographic Transcript of Hearings."

53. Dan Gilbert, *The Yellow Peril (Japan) and Bible Prophecy* (Grand Rapids, Mich.: Zondervan, 1943), 7.

54. Testimony of John Reinecke, 10 September 1948, Reinecke file, 318-2-3.

55. Judy Kutulas, *The American Civil Liberties Union and the Making of Modern Liberalism, 1930–1960* (Chapel Hill: University of North Carolina Press, 2006).

56. James H. Okahata and United Japanese Society of Hawaii, eds., *A History of Japanese in Hawaii* (Honolulu: UJSH, 1971), 265.

57. Roy Wilkins to Henry Stimson, 18 April 1941, box IIB89, NAACP Papers, Library of Congress, Washington, D.C. (hereafter cited as NAACP Papers). See also *Honolulu Advertiser*, 5 April 1941.

58. Walter White to President Roosevelt, 10 September 1942, box IIB89, NAACP Papers.

59. Beth Bailey and David Farber, *The First Strange Place: The Alchemy of Race and Sex in World War II Hawaii* (New York: Free Press, 1992), 134, 143, 152, 155, 158.

60. *Maui News*, 7 May 1983.

61. *Honolulu Star-Bulletin*, 13 December 1959.

62. Hawaii Social Research Laboratory, University of Hawaiʻi, *What People Are Saying and Doing*, Report 4 (1 August 1944), at University of Hawaiʻi at Mānoa, Special Collections.

63. William Pickens to Clarence Muse, 4 January 1936, box IG46, NAACP Papers.

64. William Pickens to "The Crisis," 4 January 1936, box IG46, NAACP Papers.

65. Press release, n.d., ca. June 1932, box IC305, NAACP Papers.

66. Walter White to Hon. Charles Francis Adams, Secretary of the Navy, 15 January 1932, box IC305, NAACP Papers.

67. Art Rutledge to "The Catering Industry," Cincinnati, 31 July 1943, box 14, folder 7, Adams Collection.

68. Roy Wilkins to William Pickens, 15 April 1941, box IIC42, NAACP Papers.

69. William Pickens to Jacob Prager, 14 May 1941, box IIC42, NAACP Papers.

70. Jacob Prager to Joel Spingarn, 2 May 1941, box IIC42, NAACP Papers.

71. Jacob Prager to NAACP, 20 September 1941, box IIC42, NAACP Papers.

72. Jacob Prager to William Pickens, 28 July 1941, box IIC42, NAACP Papers.

73. L. Black to Miss Randolph, 25 March 1941, box IIC42, NAACP Papers.

74. Clipping, n.d., ca. 1942, publication unknown, box IIC42, NAACP Papers.

75. "Conversation Concerning Interracial Reaction at USO Centers," February 1944, box 16, folder 24, Adams Collection.

76. "Special Staff Meeting[,] Department of Public Welfare," 22 April 1943, box 16, folder 24, Adams Collection.

77. Bill Eubanks, interview, 30 May 1946, transcript, box 16, folder 29, Adams Collection.

78. Memorandum, 10 July 1944, box 16, folder 24, Adams Collection.

79. Letter from unidentified person, n.d., box 16, folder 25, Adams Collection.

80. Letter from Walter White, box 7, sec. 1, ser. 1, folder 219, Walter White Papers, Yale University, New Haven, Conn.

81. Letter from unidentified person, January 1945, box 16, folder 25, Adams Collection.

82. Okihiro and Myers, *Whispered Silences*.

83. Richard Masuda, "Specific Attitudes toward the Negroes in Hawaii," June 1946, box 16, folder 27, Adams Collection.

84. Testimony of Aiko Reinecke, 16 September 1948, Reinecke file, 318-2-3.

85. Baker diary, 30 January 1945, box 13.

86. Ibid., 10 September 1945.

87. Ibid., 18 October 1944, box 6, folder 4.

88. Frank Thompson to Louis Goldblatt, 26 November 1945, box 6, Organizing Files, ILWU Headquarters, San Francisco.

89. Arthur Rutledge, interview, 25 August 1973, notebook 17, Zalburg Papers.

90. John Reinecke to "Dear Friends," 25 December 1943, box 14, folder 7, Adams Collection.

91. *Hawaii Herald*, August 1943, box 14, folder 7, Adams Collection.

92. Art Rutledge to "The Catering Industry Employee," Cincinnati, 31 July 1943, box 14, folder 7, Adams Collection.

93. Art Rutledge to Governor Ingram Stainback, 25 September 1943, Gov. 9, box 34, Governor Ingram Stainback Papers, Hawai'i State Archives, Honolulu (hereafter cited as Stainback Papers).

94. Testimony of John Reinecke, 10 September 1948, Reinecke file, 318-2-3.

95. J. A. Balch, "Shall the Japanese Be Allowed to Dominate Hawaii?" n.d., ca. 1942, vertical file, Franklin D. Roosevelt Presidential Library, Hyde Park, N.Y.

96. Frank Knox to FDR, 25 February 1942, box 118, John Toland Papers, Franklin D. Roosevelt Presidential Library, Hyde Park, N.Y. (hereafter cited as Toland Papers).

97. Cecil Henry Coggins, "The Japanese-Americans in Hawaii," n.d., box 118, Toland Papers.

98. Shiho Imai, "Creating the Nisei Market: Japanese American Consumer Culture in Honolulu, 1920–1941," PhD diss., Brown University, 2005.

99. Governor Ingram Stainback to Art Rutledge, 27 September 1943, Gov. 9, box 34, Stainback Papers.

100. Jack Reinecke to "Dear Friends," 25 December 1943.

Chapter 4. The Labor of War

1. Frank Thompson to Louis Goldblatt, 11 July 1944, box 6, Organizing Files, ILWU Headquarters, San Francisco (hereafter cited as ILWU Organizing Files).

2. Frank Thompson to Louis Goldblatt, 31 July 1944, box 6, ILWU Organizing Files.

3. Report on Yoshito Watanabe, 2 September 1944, unclear provenance, box 5, ILWU Organizing Files.

4. Report from Frank Thompson, n.d., box 6, ILWU Organizing Files.

5. Frank Thompson to Louis Goldblatt, 5 February 1945, Regional Office Organization Reports to San Francisco from Frank Thompson, 1944–1946, ILWU Headquarters, Honolulu (hereafter cited as ILWU Regional Reports).

6. Frank Thompson to Louis Goldblatt, 30 January 1945, box 6, ILWU Organizing Files.

7. Frank Thompson to Louis Goldblatt, 16 October 1945, ILWU Regional Reports.

8. Louis Goldblatt to Jack Hall and Frank Thompson, 15 March 1945, ILWU Regional Reports.

9. Jack Kawano, interview, 4 September 1974, notebook 23, Sanford Zalburg Papers, University of Hawai'i at Mānoa, Archives and Manuscripts (hereafter cited as Zalburg Papers).

10. John J. Swissler Jr., "Sabotaging 'Soviet' Hawaii: The 'Honolulu Advertiser,' Anti-Communism and Statehood for Hawaii" (Department of History, University of Hawai'i, 1977), University of Hawai'i at Mānoa, Special Collections.

11. Jack Hall to J. R. Robertson and Louis Goldblatt, 14 December 1944, box 6, Officers' Correspondence, 1934–1977 (hereafter cited as ILWU Officers' Correspondence, 1934–1977), Individuals, Jack Hall, ILWU Headquarters, San Francisco.

12. *Dock Bulletin* (newspaper), 23 January 1941, file Local 136, Oahu Membership Meetings, 1944–1948, ILWU Headquarters, Honolulu.

13. *Voice of Labor*, 18 August 1938, ILWU Headquarters, Honolulu.

14. Minutes of Joint Executive-Trustee Meeting, 28 April 1943, file Local 136, Oahu Membership Meetings, 1944–1948, ILWU Headquarters, Honolulu.

15. Jack Kawano to Harry Bridges, 28 January 1944, file Local 136 (137) Correspondence with International Unions, 1941–1944, ILWU Headquarters, Honolulu (hereafter cited as file Local 136 (137) Correspondence).

16. Jack Kawano to Harry Bridges, 26 January 1944, file Local 136 (137) Correspondence.

17. J. D. Daves, International Union of Operating Engineers, Local 635, Honolulu, to John Owens, 16 December 1943, University of Hawai'i–West O'ahu, Center for Labor Education and Research.

18. John Owens to Frank Fenton, AFL, 8 September 1941, University of Hawai'i–West O'ahu, Center for Labor Education and Research.

19. Arthur A. Rutledge to Governor Stainback, 28 September 1943, Gov. 9, box 34, Governor Ingram Stainback Papers, Hawai'i State Archives, Honolulu.

20. Yasuki Arakaki, interview, 19 March 1991, transcript, University of Hawai'i–West O'ahu, Center for Labor Education and Research.

21. Notes on Jack Kimoto interview, 15 December 1974, notebook 23, Zalburg Papers.

22. Jack Hall to Judge J. Frank McLaughlin, Chairman, Distinguished Service Award Committee, Junior Chamber of Commerce, 14 January 1946, Regional Office, Correspondence of Governmental Agencies, 1945–1954, ILWU Headquarters, Honolulu.

23. Bert Nakano, interview, 6 September 1973, notebook 24, Zalburg Papers.

24. Carol King to "Dear Lou," 25 May 1942, file ILWU History, Minorities, Japanese-Americans, 1942–, ILWU Headquarters, San Francisco (hereafter cited as file ILWU History).

25. Statement by Louis Goldblatt, 23 February 1942, file ILWU History.

26. Louis Goldblatt to Carol King, 22 May 1942, file ILWU History.

27. Bert Nakano to Jack Kawano, 17 July 1942, unnamed file, ILWU Headquarters, Honolulu.

28. Jack Kawano to Harry Bridges, 13 March 1940, file Local 136 (137) Correspondence.

29. Alice M. Beechert and Edward D. Beechert, eds., *From Kona to Yenan: The Political Memoirs of Koji Ariyoshi* (Honolulu: University of Hawai'i Press, 2000), 47.

30. Karl G. Yoneda, *Ganbatte: Sixty-Year Struggle of a Kibei Worker* (Los Angeles: Asian American Studies Center, UCLA, 1983), 151.

31. Beechert and Beechert, *From Kona to Yenan*, 81.

32. Soichi Yonemori to Jack Hall, 9 January 1945, Regional Office Correspondence, Local 142, Sugar, Oahu Division, ILWU Headquarters, Honolulu.

33. Edward Berman, "Report on the Hawaiian Labor Movement," 30 August 1937, box 5, ILWU Organizing Files.

34. Roy Gutsch to "Brother Bridges," 11 February 1944, box 5, ILWU Organizing Files.

35. Testimony of Jack Kawano, 4 February 1953, *United States v. Charles K. Fujimoto et al.*, RG 21, case #10495, compartment 1069B, National Archives and Records Administration, San Bruno, Calif. (cited hereafter as *US v. Charles Fujimoto et al.*).

36. "Running Story, Hawaii Smith Act Trial," 20 November 1952 (published by ILWU), at University of Hawai'i at Mānoa, Special Collections.

37. Testimony of Jack Kawano, House Committee on Un-American Activities, "Hearings Regarding Communist Activities in the Territory of Hawaii—Part 1," 6 July 1951, University of Hawai'i at Mānoa, Special Collections.

38. Ibid.

39. Testimony of Jack Kawano, 16 February 1953, *US vs. Charles Fujimoto et al.*

40. Jack Hall to Louis Goldblatt, 15 June 1944, box 6, ILWU Officers' Correspondence, 1934–1977, Individuals, Jack Hall.

41. *Honolulu Advertiser*, 5 August 1943.

42. *ILWU Dispatcher*, September 2006, ILWU Headquarters, San Francisco.

43. A. Q. McElrath, interview, n.d., transcript, University of Hawai'i–West O'ahu, Center for Labor Education and Research.

44. Steve Sawyer and Harriet Bouslog, interview, n.d., transcript, University of Hawai'i–West O'ahu, Center for Labor Education and Research.

45. Anna Duvall, interview, 11 July 1996, transcript, University of Hawai'i–West O'ahu, Center for Labor Education and Research.

46. Minutes of Local 137, Joint Board Meeting, 16 October 1945, file Local 136 Correspondence, ILWU Headquarters, Honolulu.

47. Frank Thompson to Louis Goldblatt, 8 January 1945, notebook 6, Zalburg Papers.

48. Frank Thompson to Louis Goldblatt, 20 February 1945, notebook 6, Zalburg Papers.

49. Frank Thompson to Louis Goldblatt, 8 January 1945, notebook 6, Zalburg Papers.

50. Frank Thompson to Louis Goldblatt, 14 December 1945, notebook 6, Zalburg Papers.

51. Louis Goldblatt to Frank Thompson, 18 January 1945, notebook 6, Zalburg Papers.

52. Jack Kawano interview, 4 September 1974.

53. John and Aiko Reinecke, interview, 9 March 1975, notebook 26, Zalburg Papers.

54. Note by Sanford Zalburg in Frank Thompson, interview, 8 September 1974, notebook 5, Zalburg Papers.

55. Saburo Fujisaki to Bob Robertson, 20 December 1945, notebook 6, Zalburg Papers.

56. Saburo Fujisaki to ILWU, January 1946, notebook 6, Zalburg Papers.

57. Comment by Sanford Zalburg on Fujisaki letter, notebook 6, Zalburg Papers.

58. Saburo Fujisaki to ILWU, January 1946.

59. Letter from Matt Meehan, 21 April 1944, notebook 1, Zalburg Papers.

60. Frank Thompson to Louis Goldblatt, 22 January 1945, notebook 6, Zalburg Papers.

61. Frank Thompson to Louis Goldblatt, 18 February 1946, notebook 6, Zalburg Papers.

62. Jack Kimoto, interview, 15 December 1974, notebook 23, Zalburg Papers.

63. Louis Goldblatt, interviews, 17–18 September 1975, notebook 22-B, Zalburg Papers.

64. Ibid.

65. Frank Thompson to Louis Goldblatt, 9 September 1945, notebook 6, Zalburg Papers.

66. Letter from Koji Ariyoshi, 9 September 1941, unnamed file, ILWU Headquarters, Honolulu.

67. *ILWU Reporter*, 15 November 1944.

68. Yasuki Arakaki, interview, 9 September 1973, notebook 28, Zalburg Papers.

69. Yasuki Arakaki, interview, 19 March 1991, transcript, University of Hawai'i–West O'ahu, Center for Labor Education and Research.

70. John Reinecke, interview, 9 March 1975, notebook 26, Zalburg Papers.

71. Jack Kawano interview, 4 September 1974.

72. Jack Hall, interview, 1 August 1966, notebook 12, Zalburg Papers.

73. Louis Goldblatt, interview, 17 September 1975, notebook 22-B, Zalburg Papers.

74. Bert Nakano interview, 6 September 1973.

75. Louis Goldblatt to Jack Hall, 20 August 1945, notebook 1, Zalburg Papers.

76. Memorandum, October 1945, notebook 1, Zalburg Papers.

77. Letter from Louis Goldblatt, 23 January 1945, notebook 1, Zalburg Papers.

78. Jack Hall to Shigeo Takemoto, President, ILWU Local 144, Unit 3, Wailuku, Maui, 19 December 1946, Regional Office Correspondence, Maui Division, 1944–1946, ILWU Headquarters, Honolulu.

79. Louis Goldblatt interview, 18 September 1975.

80. Hideo Okada, interview, 14 October 1974, notebook 24, Zalburg Papers.

81. Robert McElrath, interview, 28 March 1975, notebook 25, Zalburg Papers.

82. Harry Bridges, interview, 1 June 1975, notebook 22-A, Zalburg Papers.

83. Matt Meehan to Louis Goldblatt, J. R. Robertson, et al., 21 April 1944, box 6, ILWU Organizing Files.

84. Letter from Matt Meehan, 21 April 1944.

85. Zalburg's comment can be found in the interview with Robert McElrath, 28 November 1975, notebook XXV, Sanford Zalburg Papers.

86. John and Aiko Reinecke, interview, 9 March 1975.

87. James R. "Bob" Robertson, interview, 26 September 1974, notebook 26, Zalburg Papers.

88. Jack Kawano interview, 4 September 1974.

89. E. A. Coffi, Captain, District Coast Guard Officer, to Jack Hall, 26 July 1945, Regional Office, Correspondence of Governmental Agencies, 1945–1954, ILWU Headquarters, Honolulu.

90. Jack Hall to Commanding General, Army Port and Service Command, 26 March 1945, Regional Office, Correspondence of Governmental Agencies, 1945–1954, ILWU Headquarters, Honolulu.

91. Isami Uwaine to Thomas Clark, Personnel Director, Area No. 2, US Engineering Department, Construction Service, Central Pacific Base Command, Honolulu, 18 June 1945, ILWU Hawaii, History Files, 1945, Barring AJAs from Waterfront, ILWU Headquarters, Honolulu.

92. Jack Hall to Takumi Akama, Secretary of ILWU Local 149, Lihue, Kauai, n.d., Regional Correspondence, Kauai Division, 1944–1947, ILWU Headquarters, Honolulu.

93. Memorandum from Virginia Woods, 15 May 1946, box 6, ILWU Officers' Correspondence, 1934–1977, Individuals, Jack Hall.

94. J. R. Robertson to Mayor's Committee for Civic Unity, 22 September 1945, file ILWU History Minorities (General), ILWU Headquarters, San Francisco.

95. Evelyn Bascom to Louis Goldblatt, 12 December 1945, box 18L, ILWU Officers' Correspondence, 1934–1977, ILWU Locals, Local 142, ILWU Headquarters, Honolulu.

96. Raymond Bascom, Executive Secretary, Local 904, Gasoline and Oil Drivers, Warehousemen and Helpers, AFL, to Louis Goldblatt, 14 December 1945, box 18L, ILWU Officers' Correspondence, 1934–1977, ILWU Locals, Local 142.

97. *Honolulu Star-Bulletin*, 24 March 1950.

98. Wilfred Oka, interview, 14 April 1975, notebook 24, Zalburg Papers.

99. Maxie Weisbarth, interview, 20 August 1975, notebook 17, Zalburg Papers.

100. Myer Symonds, interview, 31 October 1974, notebook 19, Zalburg Papers.

101. Robert McElrath interview, 28 March 1975.

102. Tokuichi Takushi, interview, 22 October 1974, notebook 31, Zalburg Papers. At the same site in the same collection, see also notebook 23, which contains notes made concerning an interview with Takushi.

103. *Honolulu Star-Bulletin*, 25 February 1975.

104. Robert McElrath interview, 28 March 1975.

105. John Reinecke interview, 9 March 1975.

106. Jack Kimoto interview, 15 December 1974, Notebook 23, Zalburg Papers.

107. *ILWU Dispatcher*, 28 December 1945.

108. *ILWU Dispatcher*, 11 January 1946.

Chapter 5. Sugar Strike

1. Howard Babbitt, interview, 4 May 1976, notebook 18, Sanford Zalburg Papers, University of Hawai‘i at Mānoa, Archives and Manuscripts (hereafter cited as Zalburg Papers).

2. John J. Swissler Jr., "Sabotaging 'Soviet' Hawaii: The 'Honolulu Advertiser,' Anti-Communism and Statehood for Hawaii" (Department of History, University of Hawai‘i, 1977), University of Hawai‘i at Mānoa, Special Collections.

3. Ichiro Izuka, "Directed Research 799: The Labor Movement in Hawaii (1934–1949)" (University of Hawai‘i, April 1974), University of Hawai‘i at Mānoa, Special Collections.

4. P. E. Spalding, President of Hawaii Sugar Planters' Association, to Governor Ingram Stainback, 17 May 1945, Gov. 9, box 34, Governor Ingram Stainback Papers, Hawai'i State Archives, Honolulu.

5. Frank Thompson to Louis Goldblatt, 1 April 1946, box 6, Organizing Files, ILWU Headquarters, San Francisco (hereafter cited as ILWU Organizing Files).

6. Frank Thompson to Louis Goldblatt, 30 September 1944, box 6, ILWU Organizing Files.

7. Lloyd Fisher, Research Director, to Wendell Berge, Assistant Attorney General, Justice Department, Washington, D.C., 16 February 1945, Regional Office, Correspondence of Governmental Agencies, 1945–1954, ILWU Headquarters, Honolulu.

8. Jack Hall to J. R. Robertson, 2 July 1945, box 6, Officers' Correspondence, 1934–1977, Individuals (hereafter cited as ILWU Officers' Correspondence), Jack Hall, ILWU Headquarters, San Francisco.

9. Jack Hall to Governor Stainback, 3 January 1946, file Territorial ILWU Policy Committee, ILWU Headquarters, Honolulu.

10. Minutes of Joint Board Meeting, 13 August 1945, Regional Office Correspondence, Miscellaneous, ILWU Headquarters, Honolulu (hereafter cited as Regional Office Correspondence, Misc.).

11. Jack Hall to Senator J. B. Fernandes, 26 June 1944, Regional Office Correspondence, Misc.

12. Jack Kawano to "All ILWU Locals," 24 July 1945, Regional Office Correspondence, Misc.

13. Frank Thompson to J. R. Robertson, 13 May 1946, Regional Office Organization Reports to San Francisco from Frank Thompson, 1944–1946, ILWU Headquarters, Honolulu (hereafter cited as ILWU Regional Reports).

14. Henry Schmidt to "All Longshore Locals," 3 July 1946, file ILWU Local 137, ILWU Headquarters, Honolulu.

15. Frank Thompson to Louis Goldblatt, 13 May 1946, box 6, ILWU Organizing Files.

16. Frank Thompson to Louis Goldblatt, 9 March 1945, box 6, ILWU Organizing Files.

17. Frank Thompson to Morris Watson, 30 March 1945, box 6, ILWU Organizing Files.

18. Report, February–March 1944, ILWU Organizing Files.

19. Bert Nakano to Jack Hall, 12 September 1945, Regional Office Correspondence, Hawaii Division, 1944–1948 (Sugar), ILWU Headquarters, Honolulu.

20. Robert McElrath, script for radio broadcast on KGMB, 11 September 1946, file ILWU Radio Program, KGMB, 1946, ILWU Headquarters, Honolulu.

21. ILWU Dispatcher, September 2006, ILWU Headquarters, San Francisco.

22. Jack Hall to Louis Goldblatt, 25 July 1946, Regional Office, Reading File, 1946: April–July, ILWU Headquarters, Honolulu (hereafter cited as Reading File, 1946: April–July).

23. Curtis Cosmos Aller Jr., "The Evolution of Hawaiian Labor Relations: From Benevolent Paternalism to Mature Collective Bargaining" (PhD diss., Harvard University, 1958), 226, 249, 340, 451.

24. Harriet Bouslog, *Fear*, ILWU pamphlet (ca. 1952), University of Hawai'i at Mānoa, Special Collections.

25. Frank J. Taylor, Earl M. Welty, and David W. Eyre, *From Land and Sea: The Story of Castle and Cooke of Hawaii* (San Francisco: Chronicle Books, 1976), 211.

26. Swissler, "Sabotaging 'Soviet' Hawaii."

27. Stanley M. Miyamoto to Jack Hall, 28 July 1944, Regional Office Correspondence, Misc.

28. Materials concerning ILWU and *Waialua Agricultural Company v. Ciraco Maaneja et al.*, 1950–1954, n.d., "Stipulation," box suppl. 1, Norman Leonard Collection, Labor Archives and Research Center, San Francisco State University.

29. Elinor Kahn to Jack Hall, Louis Goldblatt, and Lloyd Fisher, 2 August 1945, box 18L, ILWU Officers' Correspondence, ILWU Local 142 (Hawaii).

30. Thomas Yagi, interview, 9 November 1989, transcript, University of Hawai'i–West O'ahu, Center for Labor Education and Research.

31. Jack Hall to Charles Hackler, National Labor Relations Board, 4 June 1946, Reading File, 1946: April–July.

32. Eddie Lapa, interview, 16 May 1996, transcript, University of Hawai'i–West O'ahu, Center for Labor Education and Research.

33. Ibid.

34. Ibid.

35. Joe "Blur" Kealalio, interview, 11 September 1996, transcript, University of Hawai'i–West O'ahu, Center for Labor Education and Research. Kealalio's nickname emerged early on when, in a dark theater, he accidentally stepped on the toes of a fellow patron and said, "'It's blurry in here.'"

36. George Kruse, interview, n.d., transcript, University of Hawai'i–West O'ahu, Center for Labor Education and Research.

37. Martha Kruse, interview, n.d., transcript, University of Hawai'i–West O'ahu, Center for Labor Education and Research.

38. Tony Bise, interview, n.d., transcript, University of Hawai'i–West O'ahu, Center for Labor Education and Research.

39. A. Q. McElrath, interview, n.d., transcript, University of Hawai'i–West O'ahu, Center for Labor Education and Research.

40. Flowchart, n.d., ca. 1946, unnamed file, ILWU Headquarters, Honolulu.

41. Yasuki Arakaki, interview, 19 March 1991, transcript, University of Hawai'i–West O'ahu, Center for Labor Education and Research.

42. Avelino "Abba" Ramos, oral history transcript, 9 May 1996, Labor Archives and Research Center, San Francisco State University.

43. Dave Thompson to Charles Saka, 23 January 1947, notebook 2, Zalburg Papers.

44. Frank Thompson to Louis Goldblatt, 26 November 1945, box 6, ILWU Organizing Files.

45. Frank Thompson to Louis Goldblatt, 29 July 1946, ILWU Regional Reports.

46. Jack Hall to Louis Goldblatt, 8 April 1946, Reading File, 1946: April–July.

47. Frank Thompson to Louis Goldblatt, 2 April 1946, box 6, ILWU Organizing Files.

48. Sadao Kobayashi, interview, n.d., transcript, University of Hawai'i–West O'ahu, Center for Labor Education and Research.

49. Letter to "Bob and Harry," 23 September 1946, box 37, Research Department, Local Files, Local 142, Case Files, Sugar, 1945–1947, ILWU Headquarters, San Francisco (cited hereafter as Local 142, Case Files, Sugar).

50. "Communications Report," 3 September 1946, box 37, Local 142, Case Files, Sugar.

51. Harry L. Kamoku, President of ILWU Local 136 to Morris Watson, 29 October 1946, box 37, Local 142, Case Files, Sugar.

52. Ricardo Labez, script for radio broadcast on KGMB, 26 August 1946, file ILWU Radio Program, KGMB, 1946, ILWU Headquarters, Honolulu.

53. *ILWU Dispatcher* (Hawaiian edition), 6 September 1946.

54. Louis Goldblatt to Frank Thompson, 20 May 1946, box 6, ILWU Organizing Files.

55. Memorandum from R. T. Simmons, 27 August 1946, notebook 11, Zalburg Papers.

56. Louis Goldblatt, interview, 18 September 1975, notebook 22-B, Zalburg Papers.

57. *ILWU Dispatcher*, September 2006.

58. Frank Thompson, interview, 8 September 1974, notebook 5, Zalburg Papers.

59. Jack Hall to Vice Admiral E. S. Land, War Shipping Administration, 29 November 1945, ILWU Hawaii, History Files, Filipino Importation, 1945–1946, ILWU Headquarters, Honolulu.

60. Jack Hall to Governor Ingram Stainback, 28 May 1945, ILWU Hawaii, History Files, Filipino Importation, 1945–1946, ILWU Headquarters, Honolulu.

61. Jack Hall, quoted in 1956, notebook 13, Zalburg Papers.

62. Yasuki Arakaki, interview, 2 September 1980, transcript, Labor Archives and Research Center, San Francisco State University.

63. Memorandum from Marshall McEuen, 22 October 1946, attached to 22 September 1946 radio commentary by John Jordan, box 30, M-473, Joseph Farrington Papers, Hawai'i State Archives, Honolulu (hereafter cited as Farrington Papers).

64. Wilton B. Persons to Joseph Farrington, 7 October 1946, box 39, Farrington Papers.

65. Report on Negotiations, 28 August 1946, notebook 11, Zalburg Papers.

66. Henry Walker, interview, 22 August 1996, transcript, University of Hawai'i–West O'ahu, Center for Labor Education and Research.

67. *Report of the Commission on Subversive Activities to the Legislature of the Territory of Hawaii* (March 1951), University of Hawai'i at Mānoa, Special Collections.

68. Jack Kawano, 3 February 1953, *United States v. Charles Fujimoto et al.*, RG 21, case #10495, compartment 1069B, National Archives and Records Administration, San Bruno, Calif. (cited hereafter as *US v. Charles Fujimoto et al.*).

69. Testimony of Jack Kawano, 4 February 1953, *US v. Charles Fujimoto et al.*

70. David Jenkins to Harry Bridges, 10 July 1946, box 19, Correspondence with Organizations—California Labor School, ILWU Officers' Correspondence, 1934–1977.

71. "Building the ILWU Road to Higher Wages, Better Living: A Report on the Training Program and a Study Manual for Hawaii's Unionists," February–April 1946, B/F, Labor Archives and Research Center, San Francisco State University.

72. Thomas Yagi interview, 9 November 1989.

73. Materials on California Labor School, 1946, 1949, VF, Tamiment Library, New York University.

74. Yasuki Arakaki interview, 2 September 1980.

75. Harry Bridges, interview, 1 June 1975, notebook 22-A, Zalburg Papers.

76. Jack Hall to Harry Bridges, 22 October 1946, Regional Office Correspondence, Joseph R. Farrington, ILWU Headquarters, Honolulu.

77. Ibid.

78. Ray Jerome Baker, diary, 5 October 1946, box 13, Ray Jerome Baker Papers, Bishop Museum, Honolulu.

79. Jack Kawano testimony, 4 February 1953.

80. *Garden Island* (Kaua'i), 12 November 1946.

Chapter 6. Red Scare Rising

1. Reinecke letter, 26 December 1947, box 8, folder 9, Romanzo Adams Social Research Laboratory Collection, University of Hawai'i at Mānoa, Archives and Manuscripts.

2. Ibid.

3. Ibid.

4. Ibid.

5. Ray Jerome Baker to Warren Smith, 24 March 1946, box 32, Ray Jerome Baker Papers, Baker Museum, Honolulu (hereafter cited as Baker Papers).

6. Ray Jerome Baker, diary, 1 January 1947, box 32, Baker Papers.

7. Ray Jerome Baker to Donald Anderson, 4 June 1947, box 32, Baker Papers.

8. Curtis Cosmos Aller Jr., "The Evolution of Hawaiian Labor Relations: From Benevolent Paternalism to Mature Collective Bargaining" (PhD diss., Harvard University, 1958), 95.

9. *Honolulu Star-Bulletin*, 11 July 1947.

10. Jack Hall to Louis Goldblatt, 25 February 1947, Regional Office, Reading File, 1947: January–March, ILWU Headquarters, Honolulu (hereafter cited as Reading File, 1947: January–March).

11. Jack Hall to Louis Goldblatt, 12 May 1947, Reading File, 1947: January–March.

12. Robert McElrath to Virginia Stevens, 31 March 1947, Reading File, 1947: January–March.

13. Oren Long to Governor Stainback, 14 July 1947, Gov. 9, box 34, Governor Ingram Stainback Papers, Hawai'i State Archives, Honolulu (hereafter cited as Stainback Papers).

14. Rhoda V. Lewis to Governor Stainback, 21 July 1947, Gov. 9, box 34, Stainback Papers.

15. Letter to Acting Governor Oren Long, 15 July 1947, Gov. 9, box 34, Stainback Papers.

16. Curtis Sylva, Detective, District II, to Andrew S. Freitas, Assistant Chief of Police, 23 May 1947, box 150, RG 233, Records of the US House of Representatives, House Committee on Un-American Activities, National Archives and Records Administration, Washington, D.C. (hereafter cited as Records, House Committee on Un-American Activities).

17. H. M. Tavares, Captain of Police, to Andrew S. Freitas, 28 May 1947, box 159, Records, House Committee on Un-American Activities.

18. Louis Goldblatt radio broadcast, 21 June 1947, transcript, file ILWU Radio Program, KPOA, ILWU Headquarters, Honolulu.

19. Press release, 14 July 1947, box 35, Research Department, Local Files, Local 142, Case Files, Pineapple, Sugar, 1946–1977, ILWU Headquarters, San Francisco.

20. Jack Hall, interview, 1 August 1966, notebook 12, Sanford Zalburg Papers, University of Hawai'i at Mānoa, Archives and Manuscripts (hereafter cited as Zalburg Papers).

21. Jack Hall to William Hoopai, Honolulu Police Department, 29 August 1947, Regional Office, Reading File 1947: April–August, ILWU Headquarters, Honolulu (hereafter cited as Reading File 1947: April–August).

22. *Honolulu Star-Bulletin*, 9 August 1947.

23. Dwight C. Steele to Louis Goldblatt, 18 September 1947, box 37, Research Department, Local Files, Local 142, Case Files, Sugar, 1945–1947, ILWU Headquarters, San Francisco.

24. Dwight Steele, interview, 16 September 1974, notebook 12, Zalburg Papers.

25. Notes on interview with Yoshiko Hall, 24 November 1975, notebook 12, Zalburg Papers.

26. Dwight Steele interview, 16 September 1974.

27. Howard Babbitt, interview, 4 May 1976, notebook 18, Zalburg Papers.

28. ILWU Negotiating Committee to Harry Bridges, 22 May 1947, Reading File, 1947: January–March.

29. Zalburg commentary, n.d., notebook 12, Zalburg Papers.

30. Harry Bridges, interview, 1 June 1975, notebook 22-A, Zalburg Papers.

31. James R. "Bob" Robertson, interview, 26 September 1974, Zalburg Papers.

32. *Honolulu Star-Bulletin*, 17 July 1947.

33. *Honolulu Advertiser*, 3 July 1947.

34. *ILWU Dispatcher*, October 2006, ILWU Headquarters, San Francisco.

35. Jack Hall to Regional Office, Department Heads, Local and Unit Officers, 4 February 1947, Regional Office Circulars, 1947, ILWU Headquarters, Honolulu.

36. Aller, "Evolution of Hawaiian Labor Relations," 581.

37. *Honolulu Advertiser*, 3 July 1947.

38. *Honolulu Advertiser*, 28 May 1947.

39. Petition, 11 June 1947, Gov. 9, box 34, Stainback Papers.

40. Testimony of John Reinecke, 13 September 1948, Reinecke file, 318-1-1, Corr.: Commissioner, DPI Hearing Transcript, box 1, Hawai'i State Archives, Honolulu.

41. Ray Jerome Baker to Mr. and Mrs. Samuel Reisbord, Los Angeles, 1 October 1947, box 32, Baker Papers.

42. *Honolulu Advertiser*, 25 May 1947.

43. Henry Schmidt, ILWU, to John Owens, AFL, Honolulu, 29 May 1947, Reading File 1947: April–August.

44. Jack Kawano to D. K. Hirahara, 2 June 1947, file ILWU Council, Island of Oahu, ILWU Headquarters, Honolulu.

45. Robert McElrath to Louis Goldblatt, 29 May 1947, box 18L, Officers' Correspondence, 1934–1977, ILWU Locals, Local 142, Hawaii, ILWU Headquarters, San Francisco.

46. Harry Bridges to Jack Hall et al., 13 May 1947, unnamed file (seemingly intra-union), ILWU Headquarters, Honolulu.

47. *Honolulu Advertiser*, 6 June 1947.

48. Frank Thompson, interview and memoranda, July 1946, notebook 5, Zalburg Papers.

49. *Honolulu Advertiser*, 8 July 1947.

50. Jack Kawano, interview, 4 September 1974, notebook 23, Zalburg Papers.

51. *Honolulu Advertiser*, 22 June 1947; *Honolulu Star-Bulletin*, 22 June 1947.

52. *Business Week*, 10 May 1947.

53. *Newsweek*, 7 April 1947.

54. *People's World*, 24 September 1947.

55. *Honolulu Advertiser*, 26 June 1947.

56. Robert McElrath to Marvin D. Loughbom, Los Angeles, 13 June 1947, Reading File 1947: April–August.

57. Memorandum from C. C. Cadagan, 28 January 1946, Gov. 9, box 34, Stainback Papers.

58. Ichiro Izuka, *The Truth about Communism in Hawaii* (1947), University of Hawai'i at Mānoa, Special Collections.

59. Jack Kimoto, interview, 15 December 1974, notebook 23, Zalburg Papers.

60. Chuck Mau, interview, 11 November 1974, Zalburg Papers.

61. Minutes of Executive Board Meeting, 8 October 1946, file Local 136 Correspondence, ILWU Headquarters, Honolulu.

62. Jack Hall to J. A. Krug, 28 May 1946, notebook 1, Zalburg Papers.

63. John J. Swissler Jr., "Sabotaging 'Soviet' Hawaii: The 'Honolulu Advertiser,' Anti-Communism and Statehood for Hawaii" (Department of History, University of Hawai'i, 1977), University of Hawai'i-Mānoa, Special Collections.

64. Testimony of Robert McBurney Kempa, 22 January 1953, box 5, *United States v. Charles Fujimoto et al.*, RG 21, case #10495, compartment 1069B, National Archives and Records Administration, San Bruno, Calif. (cited hereafter as *US v. Charles Fujimoto et al.*).

65. Robert McElrath, interview, 28 March 1975, notebook 25, Zalburg Papers.

66. *Honolulu Advertiser*, 4 January 1948.

67. Report on Territorial Sugar Conference, 3 January 1948, Hilo Armory, Local 142, unnamed file, ILWU Headquarters, San Francisco.

68. *Garden Island* (Kaua'i), 25 November 1947.

69. John F. G. Stokes to Senator Hugh Butler, 30 November 1947, box 100, Senator Hugh Butler Papers, Nebraska State Historical Society, Lincoln.

70. Jack Kimoto interview, 15 December 1974.

71. Yasuki Arakaki, interview, 9 September 1973, notebook 28, Zalburg Papers.

72. Koji Ariyoshi, interview, 18 January 1976, notebook 28, Zalburg Papers.

73. Testimony of Ichiro Izuka, 24 November 1952, box 3C, *US v. Charles Fujimoto et al.*

74. Testimony of Jack Kawano, 4 February 1953, box 6, *US v. Charles Fujimoto et al.*

75. Ichiro Izuka, interview, 14 August 1975, notebook 29, Zalburg Papers.

76. Jack Kawano interview, 4 September 1974.

77. Testimony of Jack Kawano, 4 February 1953.

78. Saburo Fujisaki, Corresponding Secretary, Local 148, Olaa, to ILWU, notebook 6, Zalburg Papers.

79. Yasuki Arakaki, interview, 23 April 1996, transcript, University of Hawai'i–West O'ahu, Center for Labor Education and Research.

80. Minutes of Hilo ILWU Local 142, 14 December 1947, ILWU Hawaii, History Files, 1948, Ignacio Revolt and UHW Material, ILWU Headquarters, Honolulu.

81. *Maui News*, 17 December 1948.

82. *Hilo Tribune-Herald*, 3 January 1948.

83. John Reinecke, interview, 9 March 1975, notebook 26, Zalburg Papers.

84. Amos Ignacio, interview, 7 September 1973, notebook 29, Zalburg Papers.

85. A. Q. McElrath to Morris Watson, 21 September 1948, Reading File, 1948, ILWU Headquarters, Honolulu.

86. Yasuki Arakaki, interview by Sid Rogers, 2 September 1980, transcript, Labor Archives and Research Center, San Francisco State University.

87. Frank Thompson to Louis Goldblatt, 28 December 1945, box 6, ILWU Organizing Files, ILWU Headquarters, San Francisco.

88. Robert McElrath interview, 28 March 1975.

89. Jack Hall to Harry Bridges et al., 22 December 1947, box 6, Officers' Correspondence, 1934–1977, Individuals, Jack Hall, ILWU Headquarters, San Francisco.

90. *Hawaii Tribune-Herald*, 29 October 1972.

91. *Honolulu Star-Bulletin*, 6 January 1949. See also press release from Sugar Workers Local 142, 22 December 1947, file ILWU Hawaii, History Files: 1948 Unity Conference, Referendum on Affiliation Vote, ILWU Headquarters, Honolulu: Revolt "crumbling": "Pepeekeo Sugar . . . membership voted overwhelmingly to support the ILWU. . . . Amos' home unit . . . Kaiwiki Sugar . . . voted to stick with the ILWU. . . . Hamakua Mill . . . membership unanimously voted to stick with the ILWU. . . . Olaa Sugar Company. Membership voted unanimously voted . . . to stick with the ILWU. . . . Hilo Sugar . . . membership unanimously voted . . . to stick with the ILWU. . . . Hawaiian Agricultural Co. The Executive Board is solidly on record in support of the ILWU. . . . Waiakea Mill Co. . . . unanimously voted to stick with the ILWU."

Chapter 7. Purge

1. Jack T. Osakoda, General Organizer, Local 137, to "Gentlemen," file Organization Correspondence, ILWU Headquarters, Honolulu.

2. Minutes of Special Meeting of Territorial ILWU Conference, 29 June 1947, file CIO Unions, ILWU Headquarters, Honolulu.

3. Testimony of Masaru Shimonishi, 24 March 1953, box 8, *United States v. Charles Fujimoto et al.*, RG 21, case #10495, compartment 1069B, National Archives and Records Administration, San Bruno, Calif. (cited hereafter as *US v. Charles Fujimoto et al.*).

4. Ray Jerome Baker, diary, 25 November 1947, box 13, Ray Jerome Baker Papers, Bishop Museum, Honolulu (hereafter cited as Ray Jerome Baker diary).

5. Ibid., 11 November 1947.

6. Morris Watson, Editor, "The Dispatcher," to Jack Hall, 9 September 1947, Regional Office Correspondence, Inter-Office, San Francisco, 1944–1957, ILWU Headquarters, Honolulu.

7. Alice M. Beechert and Edward C. Beechert, eds., *A Man Must Stand Up: The Autobiography of a Gentle Activist* (Honolulu: University of Hawai'i Press, 1993), vii, xv.

8. Ray Jerome Baker diary, 9 December 1947.

9. Ellis Harris, Editor, Aloha Network News, to Alexander Smith, Department of Public Instruction, 5 December 1947, Reinecke file, 318-1-1, DPI Hearing Transcript, box 1, Hawai'i State Archives, Honolulu.

10. Ray Jerome Baker diary, 10 June 1944.

11. Ibid., 26 June 1944.

12. "Hawaiian Diary," n.d., box 2, Celeste Strack Papers, Southern California Library for Social Studies and Research, Los Angeles (hereafter cited as Strack Papers).

13. Koji Ariyoshi, interview, 18 January 1976, notebook 28, Sanford Zalburg Papers, University of Hawai'i at Mānoa, Archives and Manuscripts (hereafter cited as Zalburg Papers).

14. John Reinecke to Celeste Strack, 17 November 1948, box 2, Strack Papers.

15. Celeste Strack to John Gates, 14 September 1948, box 2, Strack Papers.

16. Celeste Strack to "Dear Al," 14 September 1948, box 2, Strack Papers.

17. "Hawaiian Diary."

18. Ray Jerome Baker to Bessie Pick, 3 October 1948, box 32, Ray Jerome Baker Papers, Bishop Museum, Honolulu (hereafter cited as Baker Papers).

19. Richard Gladstein to Myer Symonds, 11 September 1948, box 2, folder 20, Richard Gladstein Collection, Southern California Library for Social Studies and Research, Los Angeles.

20. Memorandum from George Yamamoto, 6 January 1948, box 5, folder 11, Romanzo Adams Social Research Laboratory Collection, University of Hawai'i at Mānoa, Archives and Manuscripts (hereafter cited as Adams Collection).

21. "Hawaiian Diary."

22. Report by Oscar Iden, ca. August 1948, box 97, Hugh Butler Papers, Nebraska State Historical Society, Lincoln (hereafter cited as Butler Papers).

23. Testimony of Ichiro Izuka et al., August–September 1948, Reinecke file, 318-1-1, Corr.: Commissioner, DPI Hearing Transcript, box 1, Hawai'i State Archives, Honolulu (hereafter cited as Reinecke file, 318-1-1).

24. *Honolulu Advertiser*, 24 August 1948.

25. Ichiro Izuka, interview, 14 August 1975, notebook 29, Zalburg Papers.

26. Koji Ariyoshi interview, 18 January 1976.

27. Testimony of John Reinecke et al., August–September 1948, Reinecke file, 318-1-1.

28. *Honolulu Star-Bulletin*, 11 June 1948.

29. Dave Thompson to Jack Hall, 5 December 1947, notebook 5, Zalburg Papers.

30. Jack Hall to J. R. Robertson, 4 December 1947, box 6, Officers' Correspondence, 1934–1977, Individuals, Jack Hall, ILWU Headquarters, San Francisco.

31. Jack Hall to All Locals and Units, 30 October 1946, box 37, Research Department, Local Files, Local 142, Case Files, Sugar, 1945–47, ILWU Headquarters, San Francisco.

32. Testimony of Aiko Reinecke et al. and exhibits, August–September 1948, Reinecke file, 318-1-1.

33. Ray Jerome Baker diary, 3–4 August 1948.

34. Minutes of Membership Meeting, 2 September 1948, file Local 136, Oahu Membership Meetings, 1944–1948, ILWU Headquarters, Honolulu.

35. Ray Jerome Baker to Millard Mundy, 2 September 1948, box 32, Baker Papers.

36. Ray Jerome Baker to the Smiths, 3 October 1948, box 32, Baker Papers.

37. Ibid.

38. John Reinecke, interview, 9 March 1975, notebook 26, Zalburg Papers.

39. Ray Jerome Baker diary, 8 December 1946.

40. Memorandum from Ronald Jamieson, 22 September 1948, box 464, American Civil Liberties Union Papers, Princeton University, Princeton, N.J.

41. *Honolulu Advertiser*, 4 December 1949.

42. *Honolulu Advertiser*, 20 March 1947.

43. *Honolulu Star-Bulletin*, 1 July 1948.

44. *Honolulu Star-Bulletin*, 21 September 1948.

45. *Honolulu Star-Bulletin*, 27 September 1948.

46. *Honolulu Star-Bulletin*, 15 October 1948; *Honolulu Advertiser*, 15 October 1948.

47. Testimony of Jack Kawano, 3 February 1953, box 6, *US vs. Charles Fujimoto et al.*

48. Ray Jerome Baker diary, 23 December 1947.

49. Ibid., 2 September 1948.

50. Ibid., 10 April 1946.

51. Ray Jerome Baker to "Honolulu Star-Bulletin," 19 January 1948, box 32, Baker Papers.

52. Ray Jerome Baker diary, 20 February 1948.

53. Marion Holmes to Ray Jerome Baker, 27 May 1943, box 4, Baker Papers.

54. Marion Holmes to Ray Jerome Baker, 29 May 1943, box 4, Baker Papers.

55. *Honolulu Record*, 30 September 1948.

56. *Honolulu Record*, 14 October 1948.

57. Frank Marshall Davis, *Livin' the Blues: Memoirs of a Black Journalist and Poet* (Madison: University of Wisconsin Press, 1992), 311.

58. Claude A. Barnett to Michel Fabre, 11 May 1963, part 2, reel 5, Claude Barnett Papers, Columbia University, New York (hereafter cited as Barnett Papers).

59. Frank Marshall Davis, oral history transcript, 11 August 1987, University of Hawai'i–West O'ahu, Center for Labor Education and Research.

60. Frank Marshall Davis to Jack Hall, 27 July 1948, Regional Office Correspondence, Miscellaneous, 1948–1957, ILWU Headquarters, Honolulu.

61. Frank Marshall Davis to Langston Hughes, 10 August 1948, box 8, folder 196, Langston Hughes Papers, Yale University, New Haven, Conn. Hughes had his own interest in Hawai'i, e.g., writing the lyrics to "Honolulu Yaka-Hula Dixie" during the war. In the same collection, see box 394.

62. Frank Marshall Davis to Malcolm B. Smith, 28 May 1947, part 2, reel 5, Barnett Papers.

63. Claude Barnett to Frank Marshall Davis, 29 December 1948, part 2, reel 5, Barnett Papers.

64. Davis, *Livin' the Blues*, 311.

65. Frank Marshall Davis to Claude Barnett, n.d., part 2, reel 5, Barnett Papers.

66. Frank Marshall Davis to Claude Barnett, 29 December 1948, part 2, reel 5, Barnett Papers.

67. Frank Marshall Davis to Claude Barnett, 4 January 1949, part 2, reel 5, Barnett Papers.

68. Frank Marshall Davis to Claude Barnett, 11 January 1949, part 2, reel 5, Barnett Papers.

69. Frank Marshall Davis to Claude Barnett, 26 January 1949, part 2, reel 5, Barnett Papers.

70. Claude Barnett to Frank Marshall Davis, 18 January 1949, part 2, reel 5, Barnett Papers.

71. Roy Wilkins to Frank Marshall Davis, 21 April 1949, box IIC42, NAACP Papers, Library of Congress, Washington, D.C. (hereafter cited as NAACP Papers).

72. Frank Marshall Davis, oral history transcript, 11 August 1987.

73. Davis, *Livin' the Blues*, 312, 318–319.

74. Gerald Horne, *Communist Front? The Civil Rights Congress, 1946–1956* (London: Associated University Presses, 1988).

75. Robert Greene to Jack Hall, 15 February 1949, Regional Office Correspondence, Miscellaneous, 1948–1957, ILWU Headquarters, Honolulu.

76. *Honolulu Record*, 28 October 1948.

77. Minutes of meeting of Hawaii Civil Liberties Committee, 4 October 1948, box 8, folder 10, Adams Collection.

78. Report by Oscar Iden, ca. 1948, box 97, Butler Papers.

79. *Honolulu Record*, 27 January 1949.

80. Frank Marshall Davis column, 2 February 1949, in John Edgar Tidwell, ed., *Writings of Frank Marshall Davis: A Voice of the Black Press* (Jackson: University Press of Mississippi, 2007), 167.

81. *Honolulu Record*, 13 January 1949.

82. Frank Marshall Davis column, 23 February 1949, in Tidwell, *Writings of Frank Marshall Davis*, 169.

83. Oscar Brown to NAACP, 4 January 1944, box IIC42, NAACP Papers.

84. Harry Davis to Walter White, 10 July 1944, box IIC42, NAACP Papers.

85. Statement by Honolulu Branch of NAACP, n.d., ca. 1945, box IIC42, NAACP Papers.

86. Memorandum from Madison Jones, n.d., box IIC42, NAACP Papers.

87. Katherine Lackey to NAACP, 14 August 1945, box IIC42, NAACP Papers. See also Katherine Lackey to Ella Baker, NAACP, 14 August 1945, box 4, folder 16,

Ella Baker Papers, Schomburg Center, New York Public Library (cited hereafter as Ella Baker Papers): "I have been asked to serve as the first President of the Hawaii Branch."

88. *Ebony*, March 1948, box 16, folder 19, Adams Collection.

89. Katherine Lackey to NAACP, 14 August 1945, box 4, folder 16, Ella Baker Papers.

90. Katherine Lackey to NAACP, 4 December 1945, box IIC42, NAACP Papers.

91. Katherine Lackey to NAACP, 4 December 1945, box 4, folder 16, Ella Baker Papers.

92. Ibid.

93. Katherine Lackey to Ella Baker, 14 August 1945, box 4, folder 16, Ella Baker Papers.

94. *Ebony*, March 1948.

95. "Hawaiian Diary."

96. *Ebony*, December 1947, box 16, folder 19, Adams Collection.

97. Katherine Lackey to Kenneth Sano, 14 August 1946, box 4, folder 16, Ella Baker Papers.

98. Remarks by Katherine Lackey, 17 February 1946, box IIC42, NAACP Papers.

99. Memorandum from Madison Jones, 29 July 1946, box IIC42, NAACP Papers.

100. 1947 NAACP stationery, box IIC42, NAACP Papers.

101. Fleming Waller, President, NAACP Branch, to Robert Carter, 18 July 1946, box IIC42, NAACP Papers.

102. Claude Barnett to Frank Marshall Davis, ca. 1948, part 2, reel 5, Barnett Papers.

103. Frank Marshall Davis to Claude Barnett, 2 March 1949, part 2, reel 5, Barnett Papers. See also *Honolulu Advertiser,* 14 February 1948.

104. Gloster Current to Honolulu Branch, 5 February 1949, box IIC42, NAACP Papers.

105. Gerald Horne, *Black and Red: W. E. B. Du Bois and the Afro-American Response to the Cold War, 1944–1963* (Albany: State University of New York Press, 1986).

106. Memorandum of telephone conversation between Gloster Current and Morris Freedman, 7 February 1949, box IIC42, NAACP Papers.

107. Gloster Current to Alfred Stacy, 3 March 1949, box IIC42, NAACP Papers.

108. Catherine Christopher to Gloster Current, 28 April 1949, box IIC42, NAACP Papers.

109. Charles S. Bouslog to Roy Wilkins, 27 September 1949, box IIC42, NAACP Papers.

110. Dan Lie, Deputy Chief of Police, to Gloster Current, 7 July 1948, box IIC42, NAACP Papers.

111. William Green to Mrs. Penman, 31 March 1948, box IIC42, NAACP Papers.

112. Newton R. Holcomb, interview, 3 July 1946, transcript, box 16, folder 26, Adams Collection.

113. Lincoln Fairley to Robert Dunn, Labor Research Association, 5 December 1946, file Minorities—Blacks, ILWU History, Membership Statistics, Negroes, ILWU Headquarters, San Francisco.

114. "Mr. White" to Gloster Current, Thurgood Marshall, and Roy Wilkins, 19 October 1949, box IIC42, NAACP Papers.

115. Fleming Waller to Gloster Current, 29 August 1947, box IIC42, NAACP Papers.

116. Alfred Stacy to Gloster Current, 10 February 1949, box IIC42, NAACP Papers.

117. Frank Marshall Davis to Roy Wilkins, 17 February 1949, box IIC42, NAACP Papers.

118. *Cleveland Herald*, 14 March 1949.

119. Edward Berman to Roy Wilkins, 26 September 1949, box IIC42, NAACP Papers.

120. Frank Marshall Davis to Roy Wilkins, 7 April 1949, box IIC42, NAACP Papers.

121. Charles Bouslog to Roy Wilkins, 27 September 1949.

122. Roy Wilkins to Catherine Christopher, 20 June 1949, box IIC42, NAACP Papers.

123. Frank Marshall Davis to Roy Wilkins, 20 April 1950, box IIC42, NAACP Papers.

Chapter 8. Surge?

1. Leaflet, 27 September 1948, file Local 136: Leaflets, Oahu Division, Publicity, ILWU Headquarters, Honolulu.

2. Jack Hall to Louis Goldblatt, 22 August 1944, box 6, ILWU Headquarters, San Francisco.

3. Frank Thompson to David Thompson, 17 January 1947, Regional Office Correspondence, Trade Unions and Auxiliaries, 1944–1959, ILWU Headquarters, Honolulu.

4. Jack Hall to Louis Goldblatt, 15 June 1944, box 6, ILWU Headquarters, San Francisco.

5. Ray Jerome Baker, diary, 9 November 1946, box 13, Ray Jerome Baker Papers, Bishop Museum, Honolulu (hereafter cited as Ray Jerome Baker diary).

6. William A. Wheeler to Louis J. Russell, 16 January 1950, RG 233, box 122, Records of US House of Representatives, Committee on Un-American Activities, National Archives and Records Administration, Washington, D.C. (hereafter cited as Records of House Un-American Activities Committee).

7. Testimony of Jack Kawano, 5 February 1953, box 6, *United States v. Charles Fujimoto et al.*, RG 21, case #10495, compartment 1069B, National Archives and Records Administration, San Bruno, Calif. (cited hereafter as *US v. Charles Fujimoto et al.*).

8. Testimony of Jack Kawano, 3 February 1953, box 6, *US v. Charles Fujimoto et al.*

9. Clipping, 3 October 1948, ser. 4, file G-50, ser. 4, file I-52, Romanzo Adams Social Research Laboratory Collection, University of Hawai'i at Mānoa, Archives and Manuscripts (hereafter cited as Adams Collection).

10. *Honolulu Star-Bulletin*, 21 February 1948.

11. Ibid.

12. *Hilo Tribune-Herald*, 18 April 1948.

13. Ray Jerome Baker to J. E. Snyder, 3 October 1948, box 32, Ray Jerome Baker Papers, Bishop Museum, Honolulu (hereafter cited as Baker Papers).

14. Minutes of Local 142, 18–19 September 1948, file Local 142, Meetings, General Executive Board, 1948, ILWU Headquarters, Honolulu.

15. Ray Jerome Baker diary, 24 September 1948.

16. *Honolulu Advertiser*, 3 March 1948.

17. *Honolulu Star-Bulletin*, 15 June 1948.

18. *Valley Isle Chronicle*, 5 March 1948.

19. Sanford Zalburg, *A Spark Is Struck! Jack Hall and the ILWU in Hawaii* (Honolulu: University of Hawai'i Press, 1979), 223.

20. Jack Kawano to J. R. Robertson, 3 June 1948, file Local 136, Organization, Reports—President, ILWU Headquarters, Honolulu.

21. Mitsuyuki Kido, interview, 28 October 1974, notebook 23, Sanford Zalburg Papers, University of Hawai'i at Mānoa, Archives and Manuscripts (hereafter cited as Zalburg Papers).

22. Koichi Imori, Local 144, Processing, Distribution to J. R. Robertson, Jack Hall, Dave Thompson, Robert McElrath, 29 June 1948, box 5, ILWU Headquarters, San Francisco.

23. Koichi Imori, interview, 8 February 1976, notebook 29, Zalburg Papers.

24. *Honolulu Star-Bulletin*, 26 May 1947.

25. *Honolulu Star-Bulletin*, 15 April 1950.

26. *Honolulu Star-Bulletin*, 13 April 1950.

27. *Honolulu Star-Bulletin*, 15 June 1948.

28. *Valley Isle Chronicle*, 15 June 1948.

29. Victor Riesel to Governor Stainback, 4 May 1948, Gov. 9, box 32, Governor Ingram Stainback Papers, Hawai'i State Archives, Honolulu (hereafter cited as Stainback Papers).

30. Governor Stainback to Victor Riesel, 22 October 1948, Gov. 9, box 32, Stainback Papers.

31. Paul Crouch, "Moscow's Supervision of Communist Activities in Hawaii," n.d., James Eastland Papers, University of Mississippi, Oxford (hereafter cited as Eastland Papers).

32. Governor Stainback to Victor Riesel, 17 May 1948, Gov. 9, box 32, Stainback Papers.

33. *Honolulu Advertiser*, 12 May 1948.

34. *Saturday Evening Post*, 28 June 1947.

35. Testimony of Victoria K. Holt, "Stenographic Transcript of Hearings before the Committee on Interior and Insular Affairs," US Senate, 1–5 November 1948, "Confidential Interviews," box 97, Hugh Butler Papers, Nebraska State Historical Society, Lincoln (hereafter cited as "Stenographic Transcript of Hearings").

36. Testimony of Martin E. Alan, "Stenographic Transcript of Hearings."

37. *Honolulu Advertiser*, 24 August 1948.

38. J. Harold Hughes to Tom Clark, Attorney General, 4 February 1948, box 26, J. Howard McGrath Papers, Harry S. Truman Library, Harry S. Truman Library and Museum, Independence, Mo.

39. J. Harold Hughes to J. A. Krug, Secretary of the Interior, 31 March 1948, RG 126, Office of the Territories, Classified Files, 1907–1951, box 659, National Archives and Records Administration, College Park, Md. (hereafter cited as Office of the Territories, Classified Files).

40. Governor Stainback to Oscar Chapman, 26 February 1948, Office of the Territories, Classified Files, box 659.

41. Governor Stainback to J. A. Krug, 15 September 1947, Office of the Territories, Classified Files, box 659.

42. Governor Stainback to Harold Ickes, 5 November 1945, Office of the Territories, Classified Files, box 657.

43. *Honolulu Star-Bulletin*, 9 August 1947, box 100, Hugh Butler Papers, Nebraska State Historical Society, Lincoln (hereafter cited as Butler Papers). Emphasis in original.

44. Testimony of John Wilson, 8 April 1953, box 9, *US v. Charles Fujimoto et al.*

45. Testimony of Ingram Stainback, 30 April–1 May 1953, box 10, *US v. Charles Fujimoto et al.*

46. *Maui News*, 4 August 1948.

47. Jack Hall to Louis Goldblatt et al., 23 October 1948, box 6, ILWU Headquarters, San Francisco.

48. Louis Goldblatt to Jack Hall, 4 November 1948, box 6, ILWU Headquarters, San Francisco.

49. Ray Jerome Baker to John and Lena Snyder, 21 July 1948, box 32, Baker Papers.

50. Louis Goldblatt to Jack Hall, 7 October 1948, box 6, ILWU Headquarters, San Francisco.

51. Jack Hall to Louis Goldblatt et al., 5 November 1948, Reading File, 1948, ILWU Headquarters, Honolulu (hereafter cited as Reading File, 1948).

52. Jack Hall to Louis Goldblatt et al., 8 November 1948, Reading File, 1948.

53. Ray Jerome Baker diary, 1 July 1948.

54. Jack Hall to J. R. Robertson, 4 December 1947, Regional Office, Reading File, 1947: September–December, ILWU Headquarters, Honolulu (hereafter cited as Reading File, 1947: September–December).

55. *Hilo Tribune-Herald*, 27 March 1948.

56. Letter to Louis Goldblatt, 7 August 1947, box 42, Norman Leonard Collection, Labor Archives and Records Center, San Francisco State University.

57. Jack Hall to Manuel Asue, 15 September 1947, Reading File, 1947: September–December.

58. Ray Jerome Baker diary, 22 February 1947.

59. Jack Kawano, interview, 4 September 1974, notebook 23, Zalburg Papers.

60. Archie Brown, interview, 9 May 1975, notebook 28, Zalburg Papers.

61. Jack Kimoto, interview, 15 December 1974, notebook 23, Zalburg Papers.

62. Testimony of Robert McBurney Kempa, 26 January 1953, box 6, *US v. Charles Fujimoto et al.*

63. Robert McElrath, interview, 28 March 1975, notebook 25, Zalburg Papers.

64. Jack Kawano interview, 4 September 1974.

65. Ibid.

66. John Reinecke, interview, 9 March 1975, notebook 26, Zalburg Papers.

67. Ernest Arena, interview, 3 July 1973, notebook 28, Zalburg Papers.

68. Koji Ariyoshi, interview, 18 January 1976, notebook 28, Zalburg Papers.

69. T. Oshiro, Secretary-Treasurer, Pineapple and Cannery Workers, ILWU, Local 152, to Harry Bridges et al., 21 December 1948, notebook 2, Zalburg Papers.

70. Philip Maxwell, interview, 20 November 1973, notebook 24, Zalburg Papers.

71. Roy Gutsch to Harry Bridges, 11 February 1944, box 5, Organizing Files, ILWU Headquarters, San Francisco.

72. Minutes of ILWU Local 137, Joint Board Meeting, 11 December 1945, Regional Office Correspondence, Miscellaneous, ILWU Headquarters, Honolulu.

73. Minutes of ILWU Local 137, Executive Board, 23 January 1946, Regional Office Correspondence, Miscellaneous, ILWU Headquarters, Honolulu.

74. S. Fujisaki to J. R. Robertson, 26 November 1947, box 6, Organizing Files, ILWU Headquarters, San Francisco.

75. Jack Hall to Louis Goldblatt, 12 August 1946, box 37, Research Department, Local Files, Local 142, Case Files, Sugar, 1945–1947, ILWU Headquarters, San Francisco.

76. Robert McElrath interview, 28 March 1975.

77. A. Q. McElrath to Jack Hall, 13 July 1948, Reading File, 1948.

78. T. Oshiro, Secretary-Treasurer, Local 152, Pineapple and Cannery Workers, to Harry Bridges et al., 16 June 1948, box 5, Organizing Files, ILWU Headquarters, Honolulu.

79. T. Oshiro to J. R. Robertson, 16 September 1948, Organizing Files, ILWU Headquarters, Honolulu.

80. See letter from Steve Murin and clipping, 15 September 1948, box 464, American Civil Liberties Union Papers, Princeton University, Princeton, N.J. (hereafter cited as ACLU Papers).

81. Allan F. Saunders to Roger Baldwin, 20 September 1948, box 464, ACLU Papers.

82. Charles Fujimoto, text of radio remarks, 29 October 1948, box 2, folder 4, Celeste Strack Papers, Southern California Library for Social Studies and Research, Los Angeles (hereafter cited as Strack Papers).

83. Ray Jerome Baker diary, 30 October 1948.

84. Testimony of Adam Smyser, 2 February 1953, box 5, *US v. Charles Fujimoto et al.*

85. David Jenkins to Louis Goldblatt, 17 September 1947, box 19, Correspondence with Organizations—California Labor School, ILWU Officers' Correspondence, 1934–1977, ILWU Headquarters, San Francisco.

86. "Listing of Students in the Course," April 1947, box 19, ILWU Headquarters, San Francisco. Attendees included Tadashi Ogawa, Local 145-1, Waipahu, O'ahu, a "Member of the Executive Board, employed as pan man in sugar mill"; Frank G. Pereira, Local 149–1, Hanamā'ulu, Kaua'i, "Member of the Executive Board, employed as mechanic in sugar industry"; Joseph Morita, Local 145-7, Waialua, O'ahu, "Member of

the Executive Board, employed as auto mechanic in the sugar industry"; James G. No-gami, Local 149–1, Lihu'e, Kaua'i, "shop steward, employed as clerk in the sugar indus-try"; Gil L. Gajo, Local 149, "Halaula, Hawaii, Second Vice-President of his local, employed as a warehouse clerk in the sugar industry."

87. See thick booklet *Building the ILWU Road to Higher Wages and Better Living in Hawaii: Report on the Leadership Training Program Given for the Hawaiian Unionists by the International Officers and Staff of the ILWU and the Teaching Staff of the California Labor School, San Francisco, February–April 1946*, box 19, ILWU Headquarters, San Francisco.

88. Report, ca. 1948, box 146, J. B. Matthews Papers, Duke University, Durham, N.C.

89. *Report of the Commission on Subversive Activities to the Legislature of the Territory of Hawaii* (March 1951), James Eastland Papers, University of Mississippi, Oxford (hereafter cited as Eastland Papers).

90. Minutes of Meeting of ILWU Council of Hawaii, 23 May 1948, file Hawaii ILWU Council, ILWU Headquarters, Honolulu.

91. Report, ca. 1948, Files and Reference Section, Records of House Un-American Activities Committee, box 150.

92. Testimony of Robert McBurney Kempa, 26 January 1953.

93. Testimony of Jack Kawano, 16 February 1953, box 6, *US v. Charles Fujimoto et al.*

94. William A. Wheeler to Louis J. Russell, 23 January 1950, Records of House Un-American Activities Committee, box 122.

95. Testimony of Jack Kawano, 3 February 1953, box 6, *US v. Charles Fujimoto et al.*

96. "On the Question of Hawaii," Communist Party document, n.d., ca. early 1950s, box 2, Strack Papers.

97. John F. G. Stokes to Senator Hugh Butler, 30 November 1947, box 100, Butler Papers.

98. Testimony of Henry S. Toyama, 29 January 1953, box 6, *US v. Charles Fujimoto, et al.*

99. Testimony of Jack Kawano, 5 February 1953. See also Gerald Horne, *Red Seas: Ferdinand Smith and Radical Black Sailors in the United States and Jamaica* (New York: New York University Press, 2005).

100. Ibid.

101. Ibid.

102. Jack Kawano interview, 4 September 1974.

103. Jack Hall to Samuel B. Kemp, Chief Justice, Hawai'i Supreme Court, 10 January 1948, Reading File, 1947: September–December.

104. "In the District Court of Honolulu, City and County of Honolulu, Territory of Hawaii," "Transcript of Testimony," Violation of Section 11450 RLH/45, file ILWU Local 137, ILWU Headquarters, Honolulu.

105. Ray Jerome Baker diary, 24 September 1948.

106. Ibid.

107. *Honolulu Advertiser*, 29 December 1948.

108. Undated material, notebook 18, Zalburg Papers; *Honolulu Star-Bulletin*, 30 October 1951.

109. Edward Berman, interview, 29 April 1974, notebook 18, Zalburg Papers.

110. Testimony of Tsuneto Kunimura, September 1948, Reinecke file, 318-1-8, Corr.: Commissioner, DPI Hearing Transcript, box 1, Hawai'i State Archives, Honolulu.

111. ILWU radio broadcast, 13 September 1946, transcript, file ILWU Radio Program, KGMB, 1946, ILWU Headquarters, Honolulu.

112. Frank Marshall Davis to Jack Hall, 5 October 1948, Regional Office Correspondence, Miscellaneous, 1948–1957, ILWU Headquarters, Honolulu.

113. Louis Goldblatt, "Working Class Leader in the ILWU, 1935–1977," oral history transcript, Regional Oral History Office, Bancroft Library, University of California, Berkeley, 523.

114. A. Q. McElrath to Harry Bridges, 1 March 1948, Reading File, 1947: September–December.

115. Memorandum from A. Q. McElrath, 16 March 1948, Reading File 1948.

116. *Honolulu Star-Bulletin*, 6 March 1948.

117. Jack Hall to Louis Goldblatt, 18 March 1948, Reading File 1948.

118. Ray Jerome Baker diary, 9 March 1948.

119. Ray Jerome Baker to Marion Holmes, 19 March 1948, box 32, Baker Papers.

120. Clipping, n.d., ILWU Hawaii, History Files, 1948, Robeson Concert Tour (March 1948), ILWU Headquarters, Honolulu.

121. *Report of the Commission on Subversive Activities to the Legislature of the Territory of Hawaii* (March 1951) University of Hawai'i at Mānoa, Special Collections.

122. Testimony of Jack Kawano, 4 February 1953, box 5, *US v. Charles Fujimoto et al.*

123. Testimony of Jack Kawano, 5 February 1953.

124. *Report of the Commission on Subversive Activities to the Legislature of the Territory of Hawaii* (March 1951), Eastland Papers.

125. Dan Moulder to Morgan Moulder, 10 October 1949, Records of House Un-American Activities Committee, box 11.

126. Testimony of Harold Shin, 8 April 1953, box 9, *US v. Charles Fujimoto et al.*

127. US Senate, *Report of the Subcommittee to Investigate the Administration of the Internal Security Act and Other Internal Security Laws of the Committee on the Judiciary, United States Senate*, 84th Cong., 2nd sess. (1956; Washington, D.C.: Government Printing Office, 1957), at University of Hawai'i at Mānoa, Special Collections.

Chapter 9. State of Anxiety?

1. Senate Committee on Interior and Insular Affairs, *Statehood for Hawaii: Communist Penetration of the Hawaiian Islands*, 80th Cong., 2nd sess. (1948; Washington: Government Printing Office, 1948), University of Hawai'i at Mānoa, Special Collections.

2. O. R. Watkins to Senator Guy Cordon, 8 December 1947, box 97, Hugh Butler Papers, Nebraska State Historical Society, Lincoln (hereafter cited as Butler Papers).

3. Hugh Butler to Arthur Nelson, 8 August 1949, box 97, Butler Papers.

4. Hugh Butler to Douglas MacArthur, 23 June 1949, box 97, Butler Papers.

5. Ralph L. Boone to Senator Guy Cordon, 27 January 1948, box 97, Butler Papers.

6. Edward Silva to Senator Guy Cordon, 25 August 1947, box 97, Butler Papers.

7. Joseph Whitfield to Senator Guy Cordon, 27 January 1948, box 97, Butler Papers.

8. Testimony of Calvin C. McGregor, "Stenographic Transcript of Hearings before the Committee on Interior and Insular Affairs," US Senate, 1–5 November 1948, "Confidential Interviews," box 97, Butler Papers (hereafter cited as "Stenographic Transcript of Hearings").

9. Testimony of Samuel Pailthorpe King, "Stenographic Transcript of Hearings."

10. Testimony of Robert Park Lewis, "Stenographic Transcript of Hearings."

11. Testimony of Harry I. Kurisaki, "Stenographic Transcript of Hearings."

12. *Honolulu Record*, 11 November 1948.

13. Lucile Paterson to Senator Hugh Butler, 19 November 1947, box 101, Butler Papers.

14. Testimony of John F. G. Stokes, "Stenographic Transcript of Hearings."

15. Testimony of James Coke, "Stenographic Transcript of Hearings."

16. Testimony of Ruby Thelman, "Stenographic Transcript of Hearings."

17. Alfred Yap to Senator Guy Cordon, 15 February 1948, box 97, Butler Papers.

18. Unsigned, undated letter to Senator Hugh Butler, box 97, Butler Papers.

19. "Confidential Memorandum," 7 May 1948, box 100, Butler Papers.

20. Testimony of William H. Tilley, "Stenographic Transcript of Hearings."

21. Testimony of Lucille Martin, "Stenographic Transcript of Hearings."

22. Testimony of Ralph E. Woolley, "Stenographic Transcript of Hearings."

23. Testimony of Richard Kellett, "Stenographic Transcript of Hearings."

24. A. M. Wilson to Senator Hugh Butler, 26 January 1948, box 98, Butler Papers.

25. Bill Ritchie to Hugh Butler, 9 September 1948, box 100, Butler Papers.

26. Andrew Kalinchak to Hugh Butler, 27 January 1948, box 98, Butler Papers. Emphasis in original.

27. Roman V. Ceglowski to Hugh Butler, 3 June 1948, box 98, Butler Papers.

28. Testimony of Bill Du Bois, "Stenographic Transcript of Hearings."

29. Ibid.

30. Testimony of Dr. Guy Milnor, "Stenographic Transcript of Hearings."

31. Testimony of Dr. Virgil Harl, "Stenographic Transcript of Hearings."

32. William Stryker to Senator Butler, n.d., box 101, Butler Papers.

33. *Honolulu Record*, 5 August 1948.

34. Ernest Greuning to Senator Hugh Butler, 6 December 1947, RG 126, Office of the Territories, Classified Files, 1907–1951, box 723, National Archives and Records Administration, College Park, Md. (hereafter cited as Office of the Territories, Classified Files).

35. Hugh Butler to Esther Van Orsdel, 15 July 1947, box 101, Butler Papers.

36. Esther Van Orsdel to Hugh Butler, n.d., box 101, Butler Papers.

37. Hugh Butler to Esther Van Orsdel, 15 July 1947.

38. Clipping from unknown publication, September 1948, box 101, Hugh Butler Papers.

39. Knight Woolley to Robert Lovett, Under-Secretary of State, 3 June 1948, Office of the Territories, Classified Files, box 728.

40. *Honolulu Record*, 30 June 1949.

41. Memorandum, n.d., FO371/68068B, National Archives (UK), London.

42. Report from British Embassy, Washington, D.C., 20 October 1947, FO371/61100, National Archives (UK), London.

43. Mayor John Wilson to Hon. Adolph J. Sabath, 3 July 1947, DCN43, F69, J. William Fulbright Papers, University of Arkansas, Fayetteville.

44. Robert McElrath to Morris Watson, 3 January 1946, Regional Office Correspondence, Inter-Office, San Francisco, 1944–1947, ILWU Headquarters, San Francisco.

45. *Honolulu Advertiser*, 22 March 1948.

46. A. Q. McElrath to Lois Altman, 6 May 1948, Reading File, 1948, ILWU Headquarters, Honolulu (hereafter cited as Reading File, 1948).

47. Jack Hall to Governor Stainback, 3 January 1946, unnamed file, ILWU Headquarters, Honolulu.

48. Jack Hall, "Hawaii's Case for Statehood," September 1946, file ILWU, Hawaii, Labor Archives and Research Center, San Francisco State University.

49. US House of Representatives, *Hearings before the Subcommittee of the Committee on the Territories*, 70th Cong., 2nd sess., 8 January 1946, in notebook 4, Zalburg Papers.

50. Transcript of radio broadcast, 11 January 1949, file ILWU Radio Program, KPOA, 1949 Special Broadcasts, ILWU Headquarters, Honolulu.

51. Frank Thompson, ILWU, Hawaii, to Abram Flaxer, 19 February 1946, Regional Office Correspondence, Trade Unions and Auxiliaries, 1944–1959, ILWU Headquarters, Honolulu.

52. Transcript of radio broadcast, n.d., file ILWU Radio Program, 1949 and 1950, Undated Scripts to Be Checked with HEC Summaries, ILWU Headquarters, Honolulu.

53. Harold Dillingham to President Roosevelt, 30 June 1937, President's Personal File, 438, Franklin D. Roosevelt Presidential Library, Hyde Park, New York (hereafter cited as FDR Library).

54. President Roosevelt to "Dear Walter," 4 August 1944, President's Personal File, 438, FDR Library.

55. Jack Hall to Harriet Bouslog, 28 May 1946, Reading File, 1946: April–July, ILWU Headquarters, Honolulu.

56. *Hartford (Conn.) Times*, 30 June 1949.

57. *Tampa Tribune*, 27 June 1949. There was a split of opinion among editorial columns concerning statehood. See *Waterbury (Conn.) American*, 24 June 1949; *Boston Herald*, 25 June 1949; *St. Louis Globe-Democrat*, 28 June 1949; and *Omaha Morning Herald*, 30 June 1949.

58. *Monmouth (Ill.) Review Atlas*, 1 June 1949, Office of the Territories, Classified Files, box 728.

59. "Hawaii Information on the Territory of Hawaii Transmitted by the United States to the Secretary-General of the United Nations Pursuant to Article 73 (e) of the Charter," June 1947, Office of the Territories, Classified Files, box 723.

60. Alger Hiss, State Department Director, Office of Special Political Affairs, to Edward R. Stettinius Jr., S-9539, box 4, file 2, United Nations Archives, United Nations, New York (hereafter cited as UN Archives). See also R. H. Simpson, Acting Secretary, Interior Committee on Headquarters to Governor Stainback, 15 January 1946, S-9539, box 4, file 2, UN Archives: "Thank you warmly for your courteous and valued proffer of a site" but the decision to "recommend" the headquarters be sited "in areas immediately adjacent to the cities of New York or Boston makes it impossible" to select Honolulu, "with a view to the convenience of all members throughout the world."

61. Curtis D. Stringer to Governor Stainback, 14 June 1945, Gov. 9, box 3, Governor Ingram M. Stainback Papers, Hawaiʻi State Archives (hereafter cited as Stainback Papers).

62. Remarks introduced by Hon. Frederick Coudert, *Congressional Record*, 12 March 1947, Gov. 9, box 3, Stainback Papers.

63. Senator Henry Cabot Lodge to Senator Hugh Butler, 25 May 1948, Gov. 9, box 5, Stainback Papers.

64. Senate Committee on Interior and Insular Affairs, *Statehood for Hawaii.*

65. Lt. Governor Arthur W. Coolidge to Governor Stainback, 25 February 1948, Gov. 9, box 32, Stainback Papers.

66. Captain Anthony Gelardi to Fred Kilgus, 7 October 1947, box 26, J. Howard McGrath Papers, Harry S. Truman Papers, Harry S. Truman Library and Museum, Independence, Mo.

67. Transcript of radio broadcast, 26 February 1949, file ILWU Radio Program, February 1949, ILWU Headquarters, Honolulu.

68. Theodora Kreps to Lincoln Fairley, 1 June 1948, Reading File, 1948.

69. Dave Thompson to J. R. Robertson, Jack Hall, 26 August 1948, box 6, Organizing Files, ILWU Headquarters, San Francisco (hereafter cited as ILWU Organizing Files).

70. J. R. Robertson to William Lawrence, ILWU, Los Angeles, 18 February 1948, Regional Office, Reading File, 1947: September–December, ILWU Headquarters, Honolulu.

71. Transcript of radio broadcast, 9 October 1948, file ILWU Radio Program, KULA, 1948, ILWU Headquarters, Honolulu.

72. Jack Hall to Louis Goldblatt, 20 October 1948, Reading File, 1948.

73. Jack Hall to J. R. Robertson, 16 August 1948, Reading File, 1948.

74. S. Fujisaki, Local 142, Secretary-Treasurer, to J. R. Robertson, 23 October 1948, ILWU Organizing Files.

75. Transcript of radio broadcast, 8 December 1948, file ILWU Radio Program, KIPA, 1948, ILWU Headquarters, Honolulu.

76. Jack Hall to Louis Goldblatt, 1 December 1948, Reading File, 1948.

77. Clipping, October 1948, publication unknown, ser. A, file I-71, 1948a, Romanzo Adams Social Research Laboratory Collection, University of Hawaiʻi at Mānoa, Archives and Manuscripts (hereafter cited as Adams Collection).

78. To All Locals from Ricardo Labez, 5 March 1947, Regional Office Circulars, 1947, ILWU Headquarters, Honolulu.

79. Jack Hall to All Locals and Units, 20 March 1947, Regional Office Circulars, 1947, ILWU Headquarters, Honolulu.

80. Article by Jared Smith, ca. 1948, ser. A, file I-71, 1948a, Adams Collection.

81. Clipping, October 1948, Adams Collection.

82. *Honolulu Advertiser*, 5 November 1948.

83. Ray Jerome Baker to Bessie Pick, 3 October 1948, box 32, Ray Jerome Baker Papers, Bishop Museum, Honolulu (hereafter cited as Baker Papers).

84. Ray Jerome Baker to J. E. Snyder, 3 October 1948, box 32, Baker Papers.

85. *Honolulu Advertiser*, 19 March 1949.

86. *Annual Report of Matson Navigation Company for the Fiscal Year Ended 31 December 1948*, box 43, Norman Leonard Collection, Labor Archives and Research Center, San Francisco State University (hereafter cited as Leonard Collection).

87. Jack Hall to Harriet Bouslog, 28 May 1946.

88. Jack Hall to Bernie Lucas, Warehouse and Distribution Workers, Chicago, 16 November 1948, Regional Office Correspondence, Trade Unions and Auxiliaries, 1944–1959, ILWU Headquarters, Honolulu.

89. Ray Jerome Baker to W. L. Smith, 9 February 1948, box 32, Baker Papers.

90. *Valley Isle Chronicle*, 5 March 1948.

91. Ray Jerome Baker, diary, 9 March 1948, box 13, Baker Papers.

92. Theodora Kreps to Jean Bruce, 14 July 1948, Reading File, 1948.

93. Jack Hall to Ruth Ozaki, 19 March 1949, Regional Office, Reading File, 1949: January–June, ILWU Headquarters, Honolulu.

94. Ray Jerome Baker to John and Lena Snyder, 21 March 1949, box 32, Baker Papers.

95. Minutes of Local Officers Meeting, 12 May 1948, file Local 142, Meetings, Local Officers, ILWU Headquarters, Honolulu.

96. Dave Thompson to J. R. Robertson, Jack Hall, 31 March 1948, ILWU Organizing Files.

97. J. R. Robertson to Louis Goldblatt, 18 February 1948, Reading File, 1948.

98. Kenji Omuro, Acting Vice-President, Hawaii Division, ILWU, to Antonio Rania, 18 May 1948, Regional Office Correspondence, Hawaii Division, Local 142, Progress Reports, ILWU Headquarters, Honolulu.

99. "Rank-in-Filer" to Jack Hall, 1 December 1947, National Office, Maui Division, 1947–1952, ILWU Headquarters, Honolulu.

100. Jack Hall to Louis Goldblatt, 18 March 1948, Regional Office, Reading File, 1947: September–December, ILWU Headquarters, Honolulu.

101. Jack Hall to J. R. Robertson, 1 November 1948, Reading File, 1948.

102. Minutes of Local Officers, 16 June 1948, file Local 142, Meetings of Local Officers and Regional Office Staff, 1948–1949, #1, ILWU Headquarters, Honolulu.

103. Jack Hall to Harry Bridges, J. R. Robertson, 17 February 1948, Reading File, 1948.

104. *Congressional Record*, 18 May 1949.

105. Memorandum on "Communism in Hawaii," 23 May 1948, FO371/68068B, National Archives (UK), London.

106. "Stenographic Transcript of Hearings before the Committee on Education and Labor," US House of Representatives, 22 October 1948, box 330, Norman Leonard Collection.

107. Anne Rand to Milton Wells, 5 March 1948, file Minorities—Blacks, ILWU History, Membership Statistics, Negroes, ILWU Headquarters, San Francisco.

108. *Washington Post*, 27 May 1949.

Chapter 10. Stevedores Strike

1. Testimony of Mamoru Yamasaki, Business Agent of ILWU and Secretary of Territorial Strike Strategy Committee in 1949, 24 March 1953, box 8, *United States v. Charles Fujimoto et al.*, RG 21, case #10495, compartment 1069B, National Archives and Records Administration, San Bruno, Calif. (cited hereafter as *US v. Charles Fujimoto et al.*). See also *Honolulu Star-Bulletin*, 6 October 1949.

2. Louis Goldblatt, "Working Class Leader in the ILWU, 1935–1977," oral history transcript, Regional Oral History Office, Bancroft Library, University of California, Berkeley, 512, 516.

3. *Honolulu Star-Bulletin*, 24 October 1949.

4. *Honolulu Star-Bulletin*, 11 August 1949.

5. *Honolulu Advertiser*, 7 August 1949.

6. *Congressional Record*, 8 June 1949.

7. Harry Bridges, interview, 1 June 1975, notebook 22-A, Sanford Zalburg Papers, University of Hawai'i at Mānoa, Archives and Manuscripts (hereafter cited as Zalburg Papers).

8. *Honolulu Star-Bulletin*, 1 September 1971.

9. *ILWU Dispatcher*, October 2006, ILWU Headquarters, San Francisco.

10. Myer Symonds to Jack Hall, 29 July 1949, box 42, Norman Leonard Collection, Labor Archives and Research Center, San Francisco State University (hereafter cited as Leonard Collection).

11. *Honolulu Star-Bulletin*, 20 June 1949.

12. Transcript of radio broadcast, 30 May 1949, file ILWU Radio Program, May 1949, ILWU Headquarters, Honolulu.

13. Frederick Tam Low, interview, 5 September 1973, notebook 30, Zalburg Papers.

14. Frederick Tam Low to PTA, 29 April 1949, Regional Office, Reading File: 1949, January–June, ILWU Headquarters, Honolulu.

15. Minutes of Longshore Negotiations, 9 March 1948, file Local 148, Strike Strategy Committee Minutes, ILWU Headquarters, Honolulu.

16. Hawaii Economic Foundation, *A Study of Ownership of Corporations in Hawaii* (University of Virginia, Charlottesville, 1948).

17. Walter Dillingham to Joseph Farrington, 23 May 1946, box 30, Joseph Farrington Papers, Hawai'i State Archives, Honolulu.

18. Philip Maxwell, interview, 20 November 1973, notebook 24, Zalburg Papers.

19. *Life*, 20 June 1949.

20. Albert Bean to Senator Forrest Donnell, 21 July 1949, folder 7515, Forrest Donnell Papers, Western Historical Manuscript Collection–Columbia, University of Missouri (hereafter cited as Donnell Papers).

21. *Honolulu Advertiser*, 14 May 1949.

22. *Honolulu Advertiser*, 4 July 1949.

23. J. C. Duran to Spessard Holland, 14 July 1949, Spessard Holland Papers, Special and Area Studies Collections, University of Florida, Gainesville (hereafter cited as Holland Papers).

24. Mrs. C. A. Weil to Senator Forrest Donnell, 29 June 1949, folder 7517, Donnell Papers.

25. H. E. Turpin to Senator Forrest Donnell, 28 June 1949, folder 7517, Donnell Papers.

26. D. J. Biller to Senator Forrest Donnell, 7 July 1949, folder 7515, Donnell Papers.

27. C. Rodriguez to J. Howard McGrath, box 26, J. Howard McGrath Papers, Harry S. Truman Papers, Harry S. Truman Library and Museum, Independence, Mo.

28. A. P. Steele Jr. to Senator Frank Porter Graham, 9 July 1949, box 79, folder 3572, Frank Porter Graham Papers, Southern Historical Collection, Wilson Library, University of North Carolina at Chapel Hill.

29. Roger F. Dykes to Spessard Holland, 15 September 1949, Holland Papers.

30. Hilo Junior Chamber of Commerce to "Dear Jaycees," 1 August 1949, Holland Papers.

31. *Honolulu Star-Bulletin*, 20 May 1949.

32. William H. Soper to J. A. Krug, 9 June 1949, RG 126, Office of the Territories, Classified Files, 1907–1951, box 660, 9-4-55, National Archives and Records, College Park, Md., (hereafter cited as Office of the Territories, Classified Files).

33. Fred Barnett to James P. Davis, 24 May 1949, Office of the Territories, Classified Files, box 660, 9-4-55.

34. *Honolulu Star-Bulletin*, 17 May 1949.

35. Riley Allen to Danton Walker, 8 August 1949, Office of the Territories, Classified Files, box 660, 9-4-55.

36. *Hawaii Herald*, 17 May 1949.

37. *Honolulu Advertiser*, 24 June 1949.

38. *Honolulu Advertiser*, 26 June 1949.

39. *Honolulu Advertiser*, 29 June 1949.

40. *Honolulu Star-Bulletin*, 30 June 1949.

41. *Honolulu Advertiser*, 4 July 1949.

42. *Honolulu Star-Bulletin*, 29 July 1949.

43. Bill Cole to J. A. Krug, 17 May 1949, Office of the Territories, Classified Files, box 660, 9-4-55.

44. *Honolulu Star-Bulletin*, 4 June 1949.

45. *Honolulu Advertiser*, 16 July 1949.

46. Hawaii Sugar Producers' Association, press release, 11 April 1949, file ILWU Radio Program, May 1949, ILWU Headquarters, Honolulu.

47. *Honolulu Advertiser*, 12 May 1949.

48. *Honolulu Advertiser*, 16 July 1949.

49. *Honolulu Star-Bulletin*, 10 September 1949.

50. *New York Times*, 9 October 1949.

51. Oren Long, Acting Governor, to Ingram Stainback, 21 June 1949, Office of the Territories, Classified Files, box 660, 9-4-55.

52. *Honolulu Advertiser*, 14 June 1949.

53. *Honolulu Advertiser*, 6 May 1949.

54. *Honolulu Advertiser*, 4 September 1949.

55. Message from President H. A. White, "Hawaiian Pineapple Company," 8 August 1949, box 43, Leonard Collection.

56. *Congressional Record*, 3 August 1949.

57. Testimony of Ingram Stainback, 30 April 1953, box 10, *US v. Charles Fujimoto et al.*

58. *Honolulu Advertiser*, 7 October 1949.

59. Letter to Senator Butler, 11 February 1950, box 101, Hugh Butler Papers, Nebraska State Historical Society, Lincoln (hereafter cited as Butler Papers).

60. Gregg M. Sinclair to J. A. Krug, Secretary of the Interior, 8 September 1949, Office of the Territories, Classified Files, box 660, 9-4-55.

61. *Congressional Record*, 27 June 1949.

62. *Honolulu Advertiser*, 2 July 1949.

63. *Honolulu Advertiser*, 8 August 1949.

64. *Honolulu Advertiser*, 1 June 1949.

65. *Honolulu Advertiser*, 26 May 1949.

66. *Honolulu Advertiser*, 30 June 1949.

67. Lorrin Thurston, interview, 7 September 1973, notebook 31, Zalburg Papers.

68. *Honolulu Record*, 30 June 1949.

69. *Honolulu Advertiser*, 23 May 1949.

70. *Honolulu Advertiser*, 28 July 1949.

71. Theodora Charmian Kreps, interview, 17 May 1975, notebook 30, Zalburg Papers.

72. Henry Schmidt to J. R. Robertson, 20 July 1949, box 32A, ILWU Headquarters, San Francisco.

73. Henry Schmidt to Howard Bodine, 22 July 1949, file Longshore Strike, Reading File: 1949, May–July, ILWU Headquarters, Honolulu.

74. ILWU, press release, 19 June 1949, box 32, ILWU Headquarters, San Francisco.

75. *Honolulu Advertiser*, 29 May 1949.

76. *Honolulu Advertiser*, 21 July 1949.

77. *San Francisco Chronicle*, 21 June 1949; *New York Times*, 21 July 1949.

78. *Oregonian*, 30 September 1949.

79. *Oregon Journal* (Portland), 30 September 1949.

80. *Honolulu Star-Bulletin*, 31 May 1949.

81. Robert McElrath, interview, 28 March 1975, notebook 25, Zalburg Papers.

82. Yoshiko Hall, interview, 24 November 1975, notebook 12, Zalburg Papers.

83. Eddie Tangen, Secretary-Treasurer, National Maritime Union, San Francisco, to Louis Goldblatt, 8 August 1949, box 32, Research Department, Local Files, Local 142, Longshore, Case Files, 1949, ILWU Headquarters, San Francisco.

84. *Honolulu Advertiser*, 29 June 1949.

85. *Honolulu Advertiser*, 21 June 1949.

86. *Honolulu Star-Bulletin*, 25 June 1949.

87. Ray Jerome Baker, diary, 16 August 1948, box 13, Ray Jerome Baker Papers (hereafter cited as Baker Papers).

88. Ray Jerome Baker to Lt. R. W. Isle, 14 June 1946, box 10, Baker Papers.

89. Ray Jerome Baker to Richard Liebes, 27 June 1949, box 32, Baker Papers.

90. Henry Schmidt to J. R. Robertson, 20 July 1949.

91. *Honolulu Advertiser*, 21 May 1949.

92. *Honolulu Star-Bulletin*, 16 June 1949.

93. *Honolulu Advertiser*, 2 September 1949.

94. J. A. Krug to Governor Ingram Stainback, 8 July 1949, Office of the Territories, Classified Files, box 660, 9-4-55.

95. Governor Ingram Stainback to Victor Riesel, 24 May 1949, box 250, J. B. Matthews Papers, Duke University, Durham, N.C.

96. William R. Tansill, "Hawaii and Statehood," July 1948, box 51, Bryan Dorn Papers, South Carolina Political Collections, University of South Carolina, Columbia.

97. Ibid.

98. Ibid.

99. *Los Angeles Times*, 15 June 1949, box 101, Butler Papers.

100. "School Teacher" to Senator Hugh Butler, 25 June 1949, box 101, Butler Papers.

101. President Harry S. Truman to A. T. Longley, Statehood Commission, Honolulu, 12 March 1949, folder 7517, Donnell Papers.

102. *Honolulu Advertiser*, 11 August 1949.

103. *Honolulu Star-Bulletin*, 20 July 1949.

104. Senator Hugh Butler to Governor Ingram Stainback, 1 March 1949, box 101, Butler Papers.

105. William Glazier to Harry Bridges, Louis Goldblatt, 30 June 1949, box 32, ILWU Headquarters, San Francisco.

106. William Glazier to Harry Bridges, 22 June 1949, box 32, ILWU Headquarters, San Francisco.

107. *The Everlasting Bridges Case* (San Francisco: ILWU, May 1955), VF, Tamiment Library, New York University.

108. Affidavit by Myer Symonds, 12 January 1948, RG 233, box 148, Records of US House of Representatives, Committee on Un-American Activities, National Archives and Records Administration, Washington, D.C. (hereafter cited as Records of House Un-American Activities Committee).

109. Dalton Trumbo, *Harry Bridges* (Los Angeles: Plantin Press, 1941), VF, Tamiment Library, New York University.

110. "In the District Court of Honolulu, City and County of Honolulu Territory of Hawaii," "Transcript of Testimony," Violation of Section 11450 RLH/45, file ILWU Local 137, ILWU Headquarters, Honolulu.

111. Harvey Schwartz, "Harry Bridges and the Scholars: Looking at History's Verdict," *California History* 59, no. 1 (Spring 1980): 66–79.

112. Paul Jacobs, "The Due Processing of Harry Bridges," *Reporter* (8 March 1956), VF, GF, Communist Trials, Tamiment Library, New York University.

113. *New York Post*, 29 January 1945.

114. Harry Bridges Defense Committee, *The Bridges Exile Bill a Blow at Labor* (San Francisco: HBDC, n.d.), VF, Tamiment Library, New York University.

115. Harry Bridges Victory Committee, Annual Report, 1943, VF, Tamiment Library, New York University.

116. David Thompson, interview, 12 June 1975, notebook 6, Zalburg Papers.

117. Jack Hall, interview, 1 August 1966, Notebook 12, Zalburg Papers.

118. Remarks by Harry Bridges at Waiakea Social Settlement Gym, Hilo, 9 August 1948, file ILWU Local 137, ILWU Headquarters, Honolulu.

119. Ibid.

120. Interview with Harry Bridges, 14 August 1949, Records of House Un-American Activities Committee, box 150.

121. Jack Hall to J. R. Robertson, Louis Goldblatt, 5 November 1948, Reading File, 1948, ILWU Headquarters, San Francisco.

122. Jack Burnett to Jack Hall, 20 October 1948, Reading File, 1948, ILWU Headquarters, Honolulu.

123. *Honolulu Advertiser*, 20 August 1949.

124. Senator Hugh Butler to L. C. Denise, 3 August 1949, box 101, Butler Papers.

125. Minutes, Local 142, Annual Convention, 30–31 January, 1 February 1952, file Local 142 Meetings, Conventions (Annual), ILWU Headquarters, Honolulu.

126. Letter from William Glazier, ILWU, Washington, D.C., 5 July 1949, box 32, ILWU Headquarters, Honolulu.

127. Ray Jerome Baker to Norman Flook, 21 September 1958, box 10, Baker Papers.

128. William Glazier to Harry Bridges, Louis Goldblatt, 8 June 1949, box 32, ILWU Headquarters, San Francisco.

129. William Glazier to Jack Hall, 8 June 1949, box 32, ILWU Headquarters, San Francisco.

130. William Glazier to Louis Goldblatt, 10 May 1949, box 32, ILWU Headquarters, San Francisco.

131. *Honolulu Advertiser*, 7 September 1949.

132. John Burns, interview, 24 August 1973, notebook 20, Zalburg Papers.

133. Louis Goldblatt, interview, 18 September 1975, notebook 22-B, Zalburg Papers.

134. Daniel Inouye, interview, 30 August 1975, notebook 23, Zalburg Papers.

135. Robert McElrath interview, 28 March 1975.

136. Jack Kawano, testimony, 9 and 19 February 1953, box 5, *US v. Charles Fujimoto et al.*

137. Mamoru Yamasaki to ILWU Local 150, 30 August 1949, file Longshore Strike, Reading File, 1949: August–November, ILWU Headquarters, Honolulu (hereafter cited as Reading File, 1949: August–November).

138. Henry Schmidt, interview, 1 July 1973, notebook 31, Zalburg Papers.

139. Henry Schmidt to George Boyser, 6 July 1949, Regional Office, Reading File, 1949: July–December, ILWU Headquarters, Honolulu.

140. Jack Hall to Attorney Arthur Miller, Federal Security Agency, 16 August 1949, box 32, ILWU Headquarters, Honolulu.

141. Henry Schmidt to William Gettings, 3 October 1949, file Longshore Strike, Reading File, 1949: August–November.

142. Primitivo Queja, Kauai Division, Local 136, to Yukio Abe, n.d., file Local 136, Kauai Division, Correspondence, 1949–1950, ILWU Headquarters, Honolulu.

143. Joe Blur to "Dear Jack," 15 December 1949, file Local 136 Correspondence, Organization, International Representative, ILWU Headquarters, Honolulu.

144. *San Francisco Chronicle*, 13 August 1949.

145. Henry Schmidt to "Strike Strategy Committee," 15 September 1949, file Local 136, Kauai Division, Correspondence, 1949–1950, ILWU Headquarters, Honolulu.

146. Jack Hall to Louis Goldblatt, 6 June 1949, box 32A, ILWU Headquarters, San Francisco.

147. *Honolulu Advertiser*, 2 July 1949.

148. *ILWU Dispatcher*, 15 August 1949.

149. *Honolulu Advertiser*, 1 September 1949.

150. *Honolulu Advertiser*, 29 September 1949.

151. *Honolulu Advertiser*, 2 September 1949.

152. Minutes of Meeting of Maritime Unions, 1 August 1949, box 32, ILWU Headquarters.

153. Henry Schmidt to F. T. Moore, 6 October 1949, file Longshore Strike, Reading File, 1949: August–November.

154. *New York Times*, 7 October 1949.

155. Harry Bridges interview, 1 June 1975.

Chapter 11. Racism—and Reaction

1. Jack Hall, "The Unemployment Problem in the Territory of Hawaii," 26 October 1949, box 3, *United States v. Charles Fujimoto et al.*, RG 21, case #10495, compartment 1069B, National Archives and Records Administration, San Bruno, Calif. (cited hereafter as *US v. Charles Fujimoto et al.*).

2. *Honolulu Advertiser*, 25 May 1949.

3. *Honolulu Star-Bulletin*, 4 August 1950.

4. *Honolulu Star-Bulletin*, 22 December 1950.

5. *Honolulu Advertiser*, 25 December 1950.

6. *Honolulu Star-Bulletin*, 26 December 1950.

7. Harry Bridges, interview, 1 June 1975, notebook 22-A, Sanford Zalburg Papers, University of Hawai'i at Mānoa, Archives and Manuscripts (hereafter cited as Zalburg Papers).

8. Theodora Kreps to Jean Bruce, 17 July 1948, Reading File, 1948, ILWU Headquarters, Honolulu.

9. Oscar Iden to Senator Butler, 14 May 1950, box 101, Hugh Butler Papers, Nebraska State Historical Society, Lincoln (hereafter cited as Butler Papers).

10. Alfred Yap (also known as "Jonathan Lee") to "Dear Iden," 17 March 1950, box 97, Butler Papers.

11. Bill Borthwick to "Dear Al," 5 August 1950, box 95, Butler Papers.

12. "Decline of the Caucasian Population in Hawaii," n.d., James Eastland Papers, University of Mississippi, Oxford (hereafter cited as Eastland Papers).

13. "Dangerous Factors in Proposed Hawaiian Statehood," n.d., Eastland Papers.

14. *Honolulu Advertiser*, 5 August 1950.

15. Bernhard L. Hormann to Rockefeller Foundation, 27 July 1950, ser. 214, box 490, F3285, RG 2, Rockefeller Foundation Archives, Rockefeller Archives Center, Sleepy Hollow, N.Y.

16. *Honolulu Star-Bulletin*, 22 November 1950.

17. *Honolulu Record*, 7 December 1950.

18. Joseph A. Farrington to Lyndon B. Johnson, 27 November 1950, box 224, Senate, Lyndon B. Johnson Papers, Lyndon Baines Johnson Library, University of Texas at Austin.

19. *Honolulu Record*, 9 November 1950.

20. Frank Marshall Davis to Claude A. Barnett, 29 March 1949, part 2, reel 5, Claude A. Barnett Papers, Columbia University, New York (hereafter cited as Barnett Papers).

21. Frank Marshall Davis to Claude A. Barnett, 2 July 1949, part 2, reel 5, Barnett Papers.

22. Frank Marshall Davis to Claude A. Barnett, 16 August 1949, part 2, reel 5, Barnett Papers.

23. Frank Marshall Davis to Claude A. Barnett, 10 April 1950, part 2, reel 5, Barnett Papers.

24. *Honolulu Record*, 10 March 1949.

25. Frank Marshall Davis to Claude A. Barnett, 24 May 1950, part 2, reel 5, Barnett Papers.

26. Frank Marshall Davis to Claude A. Barnett, 9 August 1950, part 2, reel 5, Barnett Papers.

27. Frank Marshall Davis to Claude A. Barnett, 20 November 1950, part 2, reel 5, Barnett Papers.

28. *Honolulu Record*, 3 February 1949.

29. *Honolulu Record*, 10 February 1949.

30. Gerald Horne, *Black and Red: W. E. B. Du Bois and the Afro-American Response to the Cold War, 1944–1963* (Albany: State University of New York Press, 1986).

31. *Honolulu Record*, 16 February 1950.

32. *Honolulu Record*, 23 February 1950.

33. *Honolulu Record*, 9 March 1950.

34. *Honolulu Record*, 2 March 1950.

35. Bob McElrath to Civil Rights Congress, 6 September 1951, Regional Office, Reading File, 1951: July–December, ILWU Headquarters, Honolulu.

36. *Honolulu Record*, 25 May 1950.

37. Frank Marshall Davis to Claude A. Barnett, 14 October 1949, part 2, reel 5, Barnett Papers.

38. *Honolulu Record*, 29 June 1950.

39. Minutes of Hawaii Civil Liberties Committee, 7 November 1949, box 8, folder 10, Romanzo Adams Social Research Laboratory Collection, University of Hawai'i at Mānoa, Archives and Manuscripts (hereafter cited as Adams Collection).

40. Robert McElrath, transcript of radio broadcast, 14 December 1950, file ILWU Radio Program, December 1950, ILWU Headquarters, Honolulu.

41. *Honolulu Record*, 1 September 1949.

42. *Honolulu Record*, 20 October 1949.

43. *Honolulu Record*, 3 November 1949.

44. *Honolulu Record*, 9 March 1950.

45. *Honolulu Record*, 8 December 1949.

46. *Honolulu Record*, 7 July 1949.

47. *Honolulu Record*, 5 April 1951.

48. Ray Jerome Baker, diary, 24 December 1949, box 14, Ray Jerome Baker Papers, Bishop Museum, Honolulu (hereafter cited as Ray Jerome Baker diary).

49. "On the Question of Hawaii," Communist Party document, n.d., ca. early 1950s, box 2, Celeste Strack Papers, Southern California Library for Social Studies and Research, Los Angeles.

50. Ibid.

51. Ibid.

52. Report to Department of State, 17 January 1950, roll 4, Central Decimal File, 1950–1954, 8603.062/1-1750, LM 96, Records of the Department of State, Internal Affairs of Finland, National Archives and Records Administration (hereafter cited as NARA), College Park, Md.

53. Report to Department of State, 6 January 1950, roll 4, Central Decimal File, 1950–1954, 768.001/1-550, LM 77, Records of the Department of State, Internal Affairs of Yugoslavia, NARA, College Park, Md.

54. Report to Department of State, 24 April 1950, RG 59, Central Decimal File, 1950–1954, box 4871, 844.062/4-2450, Records of the Department of State, NARA, College Park, Md.

55. *Honolulu Star-Bulletin*, 7 August 1950.

56. *Honolulu Advertiser*, 9 September 1949.

57. Report by William F. Doyle, 19 August 1949, FBI, file 97–10, RG 126, Office of the Territories, Classified Files, box 728, NARA, College Park, Md. (hereafter cited as Office of the Territories, Classified Files).

58. Ray Jerome Baker diary, 16 May 1949.

59. Ibid., 15 April 1949.

60. Gerald Horne, *Communist Front? The Civil Rights Congress, 1946–1956* (London: Associated University Presses, 1988).

61. Aubrey Grossman to Claude White, 16 October 1950, part 2, reel 24, no. 908, Civil Rights Congress Papers, Schomburg Center, New York Public Library (hereafter cited as Civil Rights Congress Papers).

62. Claude White to Aubrey Grossman, 28 September 1950, part 2, reel 24, no. 908, Civil Rights Congress Papers.

63. HCLC Minutes, 29 August 1949, box 8, folder 10, Adams Collection.

64. HCLC Minutes, 7 November 1949, box 8, folder 10, Adams Collection.

65. Testimony of Robert McBurney Kempa, 22 January 1953, box 4, *US v. Charles Fujimoto et al.*

66. Testimony of Jack Kawano, 12 February 1953, box 7, *US v. Charles Fujimoto et al.*

67. Jack Kawano, interview, 4 September 1974, notebook 23, Zalburg Papers.

68. Jack Kimoto, interview, 15 December 1974, notebook 23, Zalburg Papers.

69. Koji Ariyoshi, interview, 18 January 1976, notebook 28, Zalburg Papers.

70. James Davis to J. Edgar Hoover, 19 April 1948, Office of the Territories, Classified Files, box 728.

71. Letter from Louis Goldblatt, 1 November 1950, file Local 136 Correspondence, ILWU International, ILWU Headquarters, Honolulu.

72. Remarks by Jack Hall, Labor Day 1950, notebook 10, Zalburg Papers.

73. *ILWU Dispatcher*, 26 May 1950, file Four Locals Joint Conference, Defense of Union Committee Meetings, 2–4 June 1950, ILWU Headquarters, Honolulu.

74. Resolution, International Executive Board Meeting, San Francisco, 10–11 November 1949, file Local 142 Meetings, Local Executive Officers, 1949 January–December, ILWU Headquarters, Honolulu.

75. Transcript of radio broadcast, 31 August 1950, file ILWU Radio Program, August 1950, ILWU Headquarters, Honolulu.

76. Remarks by Harry Bridges at Territorial Conference, 4 June 1950, file Meetings, 1950 Joint Conference, Forrester Hall, ILWU Headquarters, Honolulu.

77. Remarks by Harry Bridges, 21 January 1950, file Meetings, 1950 Joint Conference, Camp Erdman, January 1950, ILWU Headquarters, Honolulu.

78. Ernest Arena, interview, 3 July 1973, notebook 28, Zalburg Papers.

79. Remarks by Ernest Arena at Territorial Conference, n.d., ca. June 1950, file Meetings, 1950 Joint Conference, Forrester Hall, ILWU Headquarters, Honolulu.

80. Theodora Kreps to Edward Johannessen, 8 May 1950, Regional Office, Reading File, 1950: April–June, ILWU Headquarters, Honolulu.

81. Minutes of Special Meeting of Local Officers, 27 February 1950, file Local 142 Meetings, Local Officers and Regional Office Staff, 1950, ILWU Headquarters, Honolulu.

82. J. R. Robertson to Koichi Imori, 30 December 1949, Regional Office Correspondence, Inter-Office, San Francisco, 1949, ILWU Headquarters, Honolulu.

83. *New York Times*, 9 October 1949.

84. Bob McElrath to Harry Bridges, "personal," 29 August 1950, box 6, ILWU Headquarters, San Francisco.

85. Henry Schmidt to Jack Hall, 14 March 1949, Regional Office Correspondence, Inter-Office, San Francisco, 1949, ILWU Headquarters, Honolulu.

86. Transcript of radio broadcast, 26 July 1950, file ILWU Radio Program, July 1950, ILWU Headquarters, Honolulu.

87. Transcript of radio broadcast, n.d., ca. August 1950, file ILWU Radio Program, August 1950, ILWU Headquarters, Honolulu.

88. Transcript of radio broadcast, 21 August 1950, file ILWU Radio Program, August 1950, ILWU Headquarters, Honolulu.

89. "Statement of Policy on the Korean Situation," by Executive Officers of Locals 136, 142, 150, and 152, 25 July 1950, file Local 142 Meetings, Local Officers and Regional Office Staff, 1950, ILWU Headquarters, Honolulu.

90. Ray Jerome Baker diary, 19 May 1949.

91. Ibid., 23 June 1949.

92. Transcript of radio broadcast, n.d., ca. September 1950, file ILWU Radio Program, September 1950, ILWU Headquarters, Honolulu.

93. W. K. Bassett to Oscar Chapman, 1 March 1950, Office of the Territories, Classified Files, box 728. See also *Los Angeles Daily News*, 22 February 1950.

94. *Honolulu Record*, 11 May 1950.

95. *Honolulu Advertiser*, 5 January 1950.

96. *Honolulu Advertiser*, 6 January 1950.

97. *Honolulu Advertiser*, 10 August 1949; *San Francisco News*, 4 August 1949.

98. *San Francisco News*, 2 August 1949.

99. Robert McElrath, transcript of radio broadcast, 1 March 1949, file ILWU Radio Program, May 1949, ILWU Headquarters, Honolulu.

100. Robert McElrath, transcript of radio broadcast, 28 April 1950, file ILWU Radio Program, April 1950, ILWU Headquarters, Honolulu.

101. Letter to William Glazier, writer unclear, 4 April 1950, Regional Office Correspondence, Inter-Office, Washington, 1949–1955, ILWU Headquarters, Honolulu.

102. *Honolulu Advertiser*, 1 May 1950.

103. O. Vincent Esposito, interview, 19 November 1974, notebook 21, Zalburg Papers.

104. *Honolulu Advertiser*, 2 May 1950.

105. Harry Bridges interview, 1 June 1975.

106. Jack Hall to Thomas Yagi, 14 September 1950, file National Office Correspondence, Maui Division, 1947–1952, ILWU Headquarters, Honolulu.

107. Testimony of Helen Kanahele, 7 April 1953, box 9, *US v. Charles Fujimoto et al.*

108. John Wilson to William Boyle Jr., 6 May 1950, Office of the Territories, Classified Files, box 729.

109. *Honolulu Star-Bulletin*, 24 April 1950.

110. *Honolulu Star-Bulletin*, 17 January 1950.

111. Frank S. Tavenner Jr. to William A. Wheeler, 18 November 1949, RG 233, box 11, Records of US House of Representatives, Committee on Un-American Activities, NARA, Washington, D.C. (hereafter cited as Records of House Un-American Activities Committee).

112. "Courtney and Bill" to Frank S. Tavenner Jr., 30 March 1950, Records of House Un-American Activities Committee, box 11.

113. Peter S. Fukunaga to William A. Wheeler, 9 November 1949, Records of House Un-American Activities Committee, box 11.

114. Frank S. Tavenner Jr. to William A. Wheeler, 28 October 1949, Records of House Un-American Activities Committee, box 11.

115. Interview with John Burns, 24 August 1949, transcript, Records of House Un-American Activities Committee, box 146.

116. Ray Jerome Baker diary, 27 May 1949.

117. Ray Jerome Baker to Marie Baker, 30 April 1949, box 32, Ray Jerome Baker Papers, Bishop Museum, Honolulu.

Chapter 12. Strife and Strikes

1. *Honolulu Advertiser*, 3 May 1976.

2. Transcript of radio broadcast, ca. February 1950, file ILWU Radio Program, February 1950, ILWU Headquarters, Honolulu.

3. House Committee on Un-American Activities, "Hearings Regarding Communist Activities in the Territory of Hawaii," 10–12 April 1950, University of Hawai'i at Mānoa, Special Collections.

4. Ibid.

5. Ibid.

6. *Honolulu Advertiser*, 11 April 1950.

7. Daniel Inouye, interview, 30 August 1975, notebook 23, Sanford Zalburg Papers, University of Hawai'i at Mānoa, Archives and Manuscripts (hereafter cited as Zalburg Papers).

8. ILWU Resolution, 3 August 1951, notebook 23, Zalburg Papers.

9. Interview with Mitsuyuki Kido, 28 October 1974, notebook 23, Zalburg Papers.

10. Interview with Chuck Mau, 25 February 1975, notebook 23, Zalburg Papers.

11. *Honolulu Star-Bulletin*, 14 April 1950.

12. Ibid..

13. *Honolulu Star-Bulletin*, 12 April 1950.

14. *Honolulu Star-Bulletin*, 18 April 1950.

15. *Honolulu Star-Bulletin*, 7 June 1950.

16. *Honolulu Star-Bulletin*, 13 April 1950.

17. Note by Sanford Zalburg, 7 March 1976, notebook 25, Zalburg Papers.

18. Transcript of radio broadcast, 17 April 1950, file ILWU Radio Program, April 1950, ILWU Headquarters, Honolulu.

19. *Honolulu Star-Bulletin*, 16 January 1951.

20. *Honolulu Advertiser*, 21 January 1951.

21. Ray Jerome Baker to Warren Smith, 24 February 1951, box 33, Ray Jerome Baker Papers, Bishop Museum, Honolulu (hereafter cited as Baker Papers).

22. John Burns, interview, 24 August 1973, notebook 20, Zalburg Papers.

23. Ray Jerome Baker, diary, 22 April 1953, box 14, Baker Papers (hereafter cited as Ray Jerome Baker diary).

24. Ray Jerome Baker to Frank S. Scudder, 20 March 1948, box 32, Baker Papers.

25. Ray Jerome Baker to Warren Smith, 10 February 1952, box 33, Baker Papers.

26. *Honolulu Advertiser*, 6 August 1951.

27. *Honolulu Advertiser*, 15 June 1950.

28. *Honolulu Advertiser*, 25 April 1950.

29. *Honolulu Star-Bulletin*, 19 April 1950.

30. *Honolulu Star-Bulletin*, 10 April 1950.

31. *Report of the Commission on Subversive Activities to the Legislature of the Territory of Hawaii* (March 1951), University of Hawai'i at Mānoa, Special Collections.

32. Mitsuyuki Kido interview, 28 October 1974.

33. *Hawaii Economic Report for Year 1950*, FO371/90953, National Archives (UK), London.

34. Jack Hall to Louis Goldblatt, 12 May 1947, box 6, ILWU Headquarters, San Francisco.

35. Memorandum from Theodora Kreps, 4 April 1950, Regional Office, Reading File, 1950: April–June, ILWU Headquarters, Honolulu.

36. *Honolulu Advertiser*, 10 April 1950.

37. *Honolulu Star-Bulletin*, 4 December 1956. For more on the Reluctant 39, see press releases, etc., ca. 1950, part 2, reel 21, Civil Rights Congress Papers, University of North Carolina at Chapel Hill.

38. *Honolulu Star-Bulletin*, 19 January 1951.

39. William Grazier to Jack Hall, 7 December 1950, file Contempt Cases, Reluctant 39, 1950–1951, ILWU Headquarters, Honolulu.

40. *Honolulu Star-Bulletin*, 16 January 1951.

41. Ray Jerome Baker diary, 14 January 1951.

42. *Honolulu Star-Bulletin*, 27 January 1976.

43. *Honolulu Star-Bulletin*, 22 April 1950.

44. ILWU leaflet, 19 September 1950, file Un-American Committee Hearings, Renewed Hearings, Attempts, September 1950, ILWU Headquarters, Honolulu.

45. John Williams to Hugh Butler "and/or Bill," 26 September 1950, box 98, Hugh Butler Papers, Nebraska State Historical Society, Lincoln (hereafter cited as Butler Papers).

46. John Williams to Hugh Butler, 28 September 1950, box 98, Butler Papers.

47. John Williams to Hugh Butler, 11 November 1950, box 98, Butler Papers.

48. John Williams to Hugh Butler, 2 December 1950, box 98, Butler Papers.

49. Alfred Yap to Hugh Butler, 3 December 1950, box 98, Butler Papers.

50. Alfred Yap to Hugh Butler, 26 November 1950, box 98, Butler Papers.

51. Michael Carey to Hugh Butler, 15 August 1950, box 98, Butler Papers.

52. Bill Borthwick to Hugh Butler, 2 August 1950, box 98, Butler Papers.

53. Pauline Laurin to Hugh Butler, 17 July 1950, box 98, Butler Papers.

54. Garland Cannon to Hugh Butler, 6 September 1950, box 101, Butler Papers.

55. Thomas Paine Jr. to Hugh Butler, 14 July 1950, box 100, Butler Papers. Emphasis in original.

56. Hudson De Priest to Spessard Holland, 1 July 1950, Spessard Holland Papers, Special and Area Studies Collections, University of Florida, Gainesville (hereafter cited as Holland Papers).

57. *Honolulu Record*, 10 August 1950.

58. *Honolulu Record*, 18 January 1951.

59. *Honolulu Record*, 29 November 1951.

60. Memorandum from Michael Carey, 15 August 1950, box 100, Butler Papers.

61. *Reader's Digest*, November 1951, box 50, file 3, Walter F. Dillingham Papers, Bishop Museum, Honolulu (hereafter cited as Dillingham Papers).

62. Memorandum, unclear provenance, box 50, file 1, Dillingham Papers.

63. Walter F. Dillingham to Knight Woolley, 2 August 1948, box 50, file 1, Dillingham Papers.

64. Walter F. Dillingham to Hugh Butler, 10 August 1950, box 101, Butler Papers.

65. Ray Jerome Baker to Riley Allen, 23 September 1948, box 32, Baker Papers.

66. Ray Jerome Baker to Roy Madden, 23 November 1950, box 32, Baker Papers.

67. Kitty Wintringham, "Hawaii: Paradise of Reaction?" *Frontier* (November 1951), box 2, folder 11, Smith Act Collection, Southern California Library for Social Studies and Research, Los Angeles.

68. Samuel Josephson to Harry S. Truman, 26 November 1951, box 71, Oscar Chapman Papers, Harry S. Truman Presidential Library, Independence, Mo. (hereafter cited as Chapman Papers).

69. Chuck Mau to Oscar Chapman, "personal and confidential," 17 December 1951, box 71, Chapman Papers.

70. Edward Bernays to Frank Porter Graham, 22 September 1950, box 84, folder 3798, Frank Porter Graham Papers, Southern Historical Collection, Wilson Library, University of North Carolina, Chapel Hill (hereafter cited as Graham Papers).

71. *Washington (D.C.) Star*, 15 August 1950.

72. E. R. Burke to John Sparkman, 22 August 1950, file Statehood Commission, John Sparkman Papers, University of Alabama, Tuscaloosa (hereafter cited as Sparkman Papers).

73. C. A. Franklin to Thomas Hennings, 1 February 1952, folder 1749, Thomas C. Hennings Jr. Papers, Western Historical Manuscripts Collection–Columbia, University of Missouri.

74. Ray Jerome Baker to Warren Smith, 24 February 1951.

75. Ray Jerome Baker to V. W. Cazel, 27 December 1950, box 32, Baker Papers.

76. Ray Jerome Baker to Warren Smith, 3 April 1951, box 33, Baker Papers.

77. *Honolulu Star-Bulletin*, 29 July 1950.

78. Jack Hall to George H. Richardson, 27 April 1949, Regional Office, Reading File, 1949: January–June, ILWU Headquarters, Honolulu.

79. George H. Lehleitner to Frank Porter Graham, 20 September 1950, box 84, folder 3798, Graham Papers.

80. George H. Lehleitner to John Stennis, 13 September 1950, file Statehood, Sparkman Papers.

81. George H. Lehleitner to Olin Johnston, 18 July 1950, box 22, Olin D. Johnston Papers, South Caroliniana Library, University of South Carolina, Columbia (hereafter cited as Johnston Papers).

82. George H. Lehleitner to "My Dear Senator," 15 August 1950, file Statehood, Sparkman Papers.

83. Ingram Stainback and Joseph Farrington to Spessard Holland, 28 November 1950, Holland Papers.

84. George H. Lehleitner to John Sparkman, 12 July 1950, file Statehood, Sparkman Papers.

85. William Michels to Olin Johnston, 24 November 1950, box 22, Johnston Papers.

86. George McClane to Forrest Donnell, 7 August 1950, folder 7519, Forrest Donnell Papers, Western Historical Manuscripts Collection–Columbia, University of Missouri.

87. *New York Times*, 30 July 1950.

88. Senate Committee on Interior and Insular Affairs, *Statehood for Hawaii, Together with Minority Views*, 82nd Cong., 1st sess. (8 May 1951), calendar 296, report 314, BCN47, F10, J. William Fulbright Papers, University of Arkansas, Fayetteville.

89. Jack Hall to Louis Goldblatt, 17 July 1950, box 6, ILWU Headquarters, San Francisco.

90. Remarks by Jack Hall, Terminal Building Pier 11, Local 152 Executive Board Meeting, 6 November 1949, file Local 152 Meetings, Executive Board 1949, ILWU Headquarters, Honolulu.

91. Jack Kawano to Eddie Tangen, Secretary-Treasurer, NMCS (National Union of Marine Cooks and Stewards), 9 July 1949, file Local 136, Trade Unions, Correspondence, ILWU Headquarters, San Francisco.

92. Jack Hall to Louis Goldblatt, 8 July 1950, box 6, ILWU Headquarters, San Francisco.

93. Jack Hall to Rear Admiral C. H. McMorris, 31 March 1949, Regional Office, Reading File, 1949: January–June, ILWU Headquarters, Honolulu.

94. Jack Hall to Louis Goldblatt, 22 April 1950, box 6, ILWU Headquarters, San Francisco.

95. Transcripts of radio broadcast, 30 March 1949, file ILWU Radio Program, May 1949, ILWU Headquarters, Honolulu.

96. Myer Symonds to Jack Hall, 25 April 1951, Regional Office Correspondence, Attorneys Bouslog and Symonds, 1947–1951, ILWU Headquarters, Honolulu.

97. Ray Jerome Baker diary, 16 March 1950.

98. Jack Hall to Louis Goldblatt, 31 May 1949, box 6, ILWU Headquarters, San Francisco.

99. Dave Thompson to Jack Hall, J. R. Robertson, Koichi Imori, 13 May 1949, box 6, ILWU Headquarters, San Francisco.

100. Dave Thompson to J. R. Robertson, Koichi Imori, et al., 19 November 1949, box 6, ILWU Headquarters, San Francisco.

101. *Honolulu Record*, 2 August 1951.

102. Dave Thompson to J. R. Robertson, Jack Hall, Koichi Imori, 27 May 1949, box 6, ILWU Headquarters, San Francisco.

103. *Hilo Tribune-Herald*, 5 September 1951.

104. Oren Long to James P. Davis, Director, Office of the Territories, Interior Department, 29 August 1951, 10-8, Governor Oren Long Papers, Hawai'i State Archives, Honolulu (hereafter cited as Long Papers).

105. *Honolulu Star-Bulletin*, 16 March 1951.

106. Memorandum from Pineapple and Cannery Workers Union, ILWU Local 150, Report of Negotiating Committee on the Memoranda of Agreement Reached with Hawaiian Pineapple Company and Maui Pineapple Company, 23 October 1950, box 35, ILWU Headquarters, San Francisco.

107. Frank Thompson to Louis Goldblatt, 29 April 1946, box 6, ILWU Headquarters, San Francisco.

108. Memorandum, n.d., RG 233, box 150, Records of US House of Representatives, Committee on Un-American Activities, National Archives and Records Administration, Washington, D.C.

109. *Hilo Herald-Tribune*, 25 June 1952.

110. Louis Goldblatt, interview, 17 September 1975, notebook 22-B, Zalburg Papers.

111. Note by Sanford Zalburg, ca. 1975, notebook 22-B, Zalburg Papers.

112. Ronald Jamieson to Oren Long, 7 May 1951, 10-8, Long Papers.

113. "Confidential" memorandum from Ronald Jamieson, n.d., 10-8, Long Papers.

114. Transcript of radio broadcast, 28 February 1951, file ILWU Radio Program, February 1951, ILWU Headquarters, Honolulu.

115. *Hawaii Business News*, 29 December 1950, cited in transcript of radio broadcast, 4 January 1951, file ILWU Radio Program, ILWU Headquarters, Honolulu.

116. Ray Jerome Baker to Warren Smith, 24 February 1951.

117. Dave Thompson to J. R. Robertson, Jack Hall, Koichi Imori, 27 May 1949.

118. Minutes, General Council Board, Local 152, Camp Erdman, Oahu, 20 January 1950, file Local 152, Meeting, General Council Board, 1948–1950, ILWU Headquarters, Honolulu.

119. Ibid.

120. Resolution by International Executive Board on Lanai Strike, 27 June 1951, box 5, ILWU Headquarters, San Francisco.

121. US Senate, *Hearings before Committee on Labor and Public Welfare*, 81st Cong., 1st sess. (12 July 1949), University of Hawai'i at Mānoa, Archives and Manuscripts.

122. Interview with Louis Goldblatt, 18 September 1975, notebook 22-B, Zalburg Papers.

123. Theodora Kreps to Katsumi Murakami, 17 April 1951, Regional Office, Reading File, 1951: April–June, ILWU Headquarters, Honolulu.

124. Emilio Yadao to Hon. Jose P. Melencio, Consul General, Philippines, ca. December 1950, Regional Office, Reading File, 1950: October–December, ILWU Headquarters, Honolulu.

125. Ray Jerome Baker diary, 5 April 1951.

126. Ray Jerome Baker to Alfred G. Eddy, 2 April 1951, box 33, Baker Papers.

127. Report of Yukio Abe, 25 April 1951, file Local 142 Meetings, Local Officers and Regional Office Staff, 1951, ILWU Headquarters, Honolulu.

128. Joseph Balalio to Charles Nouchi, President, Local 136, Maui, 26 June 1951, file Local 136, Maui Division, Correspondence, 1947–1951, ILWU Headquarters, Honolulu.

129. *Honolulu Star-Bulletin*, 28 April 1951.

130. *Honolulu Star-Bulletin*, 3 August 1951.

131. *Honolulu Advertiser*, 31 August 1951.

132. Jack Hall to John F. Conway, 17 May 1951, Regional Office, Reading File, 1951: April–June, ILWU Headquarters, Honolulu.

133. Transcript of radio broadcast, 10 May 1951, file ILWU Radio Program, May 1951, ILWU Headquarters, Honolulu.

134. Howard Babbitt, interview, 4 May 1976, notebook 18, Zalburg Papers.

135. *Garden Island* (Kaua'i), 8 August 1951.

136. Oren Long to James P. Davis, 27 August 1951, 10-8, Long Papers.

137. Henry A. White to stockholders, 20 July 1951, 10-8, Long Papers.

138. Ronald Jamieson to Governor Long, 20 July 1951, 10-8, Long Papers.

139. *Honolulu Record*, 6 February 1958.

Chapter 13. Radicalism on Trial

1. Philip Maxwell, interview, 20 November 1973, notebook 24, Sanford Zalburg Papers, University of Hawai'i at Mānoa, Archives and Manuscripts (hereafter cited as Zalburg Papers).

2. Robert McElrath, interview, 7 March 1976, notebook 25, Zalburg Papers.

3. *Honolulu Advertiser*, 29 August 1951.

4. Jack Hall to Louis Goldblatt, 28 May 1951, box 36, ILWU Headquarters, San Francisco.

5. *Honolulu Advertiser*, 2 July 2006.

6. *Honolulu Advertiser*, 29 January 1953.

7. *Honolulu Star-Bulletin*, 19 June 1954.

8. *Honolulu Star-Bulletin*, 3 July 1953.

9. *Honolulu Advertiser*, 5 July 1953.

10. *Honolulu Advertiser*, 2 January 1954.

11. *Honolulu Advertiser*, 29 August 1951.

12. *Honolulu Star-Bulletin*, 29 August 1951.

13. *Honolulu Star-Bulletin*, 30 August 1951.

14. *Honolulu Advertiser*, 24 July 1953.

15. Memorandum from Theodora Kreps, 4 September 1951, Regional Office, Reading File, 1951: July–December, ILWU Headquarters, Honolulu (hereafter cited as Reading File, 1951: July–December) .

16. Jack Hall to ILWU, San Francisco, 5 October 1951, Reading File, 1951: July–December.

17. Jack Hall to Mr. and Mrs. William Chester, 27 November 1951, Regional Office, Reading File, 1951: July–December.

18. William Glazier to Theodora Kreps, 30 August 1951, Regional Office Correspondence, Inter-Office, Washington, 1949–1955, ILWU Headquarters, Honolulu.

19. William Glazier to Harry Bridges and Louis Goldblatt, 24 June 1949, box 32, ILWU Headquarters, San Francisco.

20. *Cleveland News*, 13 September 1951; memorandum from ILWU Local 209, Cleveland, 18 September 1951, box 36, ILWU Headquarters, San Francisco.

21. *San Francisco Sun-Reporter*, 29 September 1951.

22. Walter F. Dillingham to Eugene Meyer, 11 November 1952, box 50, file 3, Walter F. Dillingham Papers, Bishop Museum, Honolulu (hereafter Dillingham Papers).

23. Walter F. Dillingham to Roy Blount, 1 June 1953, box 50, file 3, Dillingham Papers.

24. *ILWU Reporter* (Hawaiian edition), 10 December 1952.

25. *Honolulu Advertiser*, 21 May 1949.

26. *Honolulu Advertiser*, 30 June 1949.

27. Union Defense Weekly Report by Saburo Fujisaki to Executive Officers of ILWU Locals 136, 142, 150, 19 March 1952, file Local 142 Meetings, Local Officers and Regional Office Staff, 1952, ILWU Headquarters, Honolulu.

28. Jack Hall, vertical file, BF, "Jack Hall—ILWU," Honolulu, ILWU, 1952, New York University.

29. *Honolulu Advertiser*, 29 January 1953.

30. *ILWU Dispatcher*, October 2006.

31. Frank Marshall Davis, *Livin' the Blues: Memoirs of a Black Journalist and Poet* (Madison: University of Wisconsin Press, 1992), 324–325.

32. John A. Burns Oral History Project, 1975–1976, Hawai'i State Library, Honolulu.

33. Koji Ariyoshi, interview, 18 January 1976, notebook 28, Zalburg Papers.

34. Memorandum, 27 April 1953, notebook 18, Zalburg Papers.

35. Memorandum, 20 April 1953, notebook 18, Zalburg Papers.

36. Memorandum, 29 April 1953, notebook 18, Zalburg Papers.

37. Memorandum from William Barlow, 18 May 1953, notebook 17, Zalburg Papers.

38. Memorandum, n.d., ca. 1953, notebook 17, Zalburg Papers.

39. Jon Wiig, interview, 17 August 1974, notebook 31, Zalburg Papers.

40. "Resolution on Korea," ILWU Executive Board, 6–7 March 1952, file Local 142 Meetings, Local Officers and Regional Office Staff, 1952, ILWU Headquarters, Honolulu.

41. "Political Recommendations for the ILWU, 1952," file Local 142 Meetings, Local Officers and Regional Office Staff, 1952, ILWU Headquarters, Honolulu.

42. Ray Jerome Baker to Olga Eddy, 15 March 1952, box 33, Ray Jerome Baker Papers, Bishop Museum, Honolulu (hereafter cited as Baker Papers).

43. Speech by Jack Hall, 5 March 1952, notebook 10, Zalburg Papers.

44. Richard Gladstein to Sanford Zalburg, 8 November 1976, notebook 17, Zalburg Papers.

45. Jack Kimoto, interview, 15 December 1974, notebook 23, Zalburg Papers.

46. *Honolulu Star-Bulletin*, 6 February 1953.

47. Note by Sanford Zalburg, ca. November 1975, notebook 12, Zalburg Papers.

48. C. E. Owens to Louis J. Russell, 23 July 1949, RG 233, box 146, Records of US House of Representatives, Committee on Un-American Activities, National Archives and Records Administration, Washington, D.C. .

49. F. McCracken Fisher, Chief, China Division, Office of War Information, to Major General Albert C. Wedemeyer, 10 January 1945, box 3, *United States v. Charles Fujimoto et al.* RG 21, case #10495, compartment 1069B, National Archives and Records Administration, San Bruno, Calif. (cited hereafter as *US v. Charles Fujimoto et al.*).

50. Koji Ariyoshi, interviews, 18 and 24 January 1976, notebook 28, Zalburg Papers.

51. Robert McElrath, interview, 28 March 1975, notebook 25, Zalburg Papers.

52. Ray Jerome Baker, 5–7 September 1950, diary, box 14, Baker Papers.

53. Richard Gladstein to Sanford Zalburg, 8 November 1976.

54. Yoshiko Hall, interview, 24 November 1975, notebook 12, Zalburg Papers.

55. John Reinecke, interviews, 9 March 1975, 23 July 1973, notebook 26, Zalburg Papers.

56. Note by Sanford Zalburg, ca. November 1975.

57. Harriet Bouslog, interview, 11 March 1976, notebook 19, Zalburg Papers.

58. Note by Sanford Zalburg, ca. March 1976, notebook 19, Zalburg Papers.

59. John Reinecke, interview, 9 March 1975.

60. Myer Symonds, interviews, 4 November and 16 December 1974, notebook 19, Zalburg Papers.

61. Harriet Bouslog, interview, 11 March 1976.

62. Note by Sanford Zalburg and O. Vincent Esposito, interview, 19 November 1974, notebook 21, Zalburg Papers.

63. Yoshiko Hall, interview, 24 November 1975.

64. House Committee on Un-American Activities. "Hearings Regarding Communist Activities in the Territory of Hawaii," 10–12 April 1950, University of Hawaiʻi at Mānoa, Special Collections.

65. Transcript, 8 January 1953, box 5, *US v. Charles Fujimoto et al.*

66. Transcript, 28 January 1953, box 5, *US v. Charles Fujimoto et al.*

67. Note by Sanford Zalburg, ca. November 1975.

68. Yoshiko Hall interview, 24 November 1975.

69. Note by Sanford Zalburg, ca. 1975, notebook 18, Zalburg Papers.

70. Note by Sanford Zalburg, ca. September 1975, notebook 22-B, Zalburg Papers.

71. O. Vincent Esposito, interview, 19 November 1974.

72. James R. "Bob" Robertson, interview, 26 September 1974, notebook 26, Zalburg Papers.

73. Jon Wiig, interview, 17 August 1974.

74. Ernestine K. Enomoto, "The Hawaii Smith Act Case of 1951: An Examination of the Japanese Response" (BA thesis, University of Hawaiʻi, 1971), 2, 6.

75. Robert McNamara, "Hawaii's Smith Act Case" (MA thesis, University of Hawaiʻi, 1960), 10.

76. See ILWU, "Running Story, Hawaii Smith Act Trial," 13, 17, and 20 November 1952, University of Hawaiʻi at Mānoa, Special Collections.

77. ILWU, "Running Story, Hawaii Smith Act Trial," 10 March 1953.

78. Transcript of radio broadcast, 16 October 1952, file ILWU Radio Program, October 1952, ILWU Headquarters, Honolulu.

79. Memorandum to Jack Hall, 20 January 1953, box 6, Harry Bridges Papers, Labor Archives and Research Center, San Francisco State University.

80. *Honolulu Advertiser*, 18 November 1952.

81. *Honolulu Advertiser*, 19 November 1952.

82. *Honolulu Star-Bulletin*, 22 November 1952.

83. *Honolulu Advertiser*, 6 January 1953.

84. Transcript, 20 November 1952, box 3b, *US v. Charles Fujimoto et al.*

85. *Honolulu Star-Bulletin*, 21 November 1952.

86. ILWU, "Running Story, Hawaii Smith Act Trial," 20 November 1952.

87. Ibid., 12 March 1953.

88. Ibid., 3 December 1952.

89. Transcript, 10 December 1952, box 3c, *US v. Charles Fujimoto et al.*

90. Ibid.

91. ILWU, "Running Story, Hawaii Smith Act Trial," 8 December 1952.

92. Transcript, 19 and 23 December 1952, box 4, *US v. Charles Fujimoto et al.*

93. ILWU, "Running Story, Hawaii Smith Act Trial," 19 December 1952.

94. Ibid., 16 January 1953.

95. Transcript, 8 January 1953, box 5, *US v. Charles Fujimoto et al.*

96. *Honolulu Advertiser*, 21 January 1953.

97. Transcript, 22 January 1953, box 5, *US v. Charles Fujimoto et al.*

98. *Honolulu Advertiser*, 23 January 1953.

99. ILWU, "Running Story, Hawaii Smith Act Trial," 13 March 1953.

100. Transcript, 20 March 1953, box 8, *US v. Charles Fujimoto et al.*

101. Transcript, 27 January 1953, box 5, *US v. Charles Fujimoto et al.*

102. Transcript, 28 January 1953, box 5, *US v. Charles Fujimoto et al.*

103. Transcript, 29 January 1953, box 5, *US v. Charles Fujimoto et al.*

104. Transcript, 3, 4, 6, 10, 11, 12, 13, 16, and 19 February 1953, boxes 6 and 7, *US v. Charles Fujimoto et al.*

105. ILWU, "Running Story, Hawaii Smith Act Trial," 4 February 1953.

106. Ibid., 24 February 1953.

107. *Honolulu Advertiser*, 13 February 1953.

108. Transcript, 19 March 1953, box 8, *US v. Charles Fujimoto et al.*

109. Transcript, 20 March 1953, box 8, *US v. Charles Fujimoto et al.*

110. Transcript, 8 April 1953, box 8, *US v. Charles Fujimoto et al.*

111. Transcript, 9 April 1953, box 8, *US v. Charles Fujimoto et al.*

112. ILWU, "Running Story, Hawaii Smith Act Trial," 24 March 1953.

113. Ibid., 8 April 1953.

114. *Honolulu Advertiser*, 9 April 1953.

115. Transcript, 24 March 1953, box 8, *US v. Charles Fujimoto et al.*

116. Ibid.

117. Charles Hite to Ingrid Stainback, 27 January 1948, box 2, *US v. Charles Fujimoto, et al.*

118. Transcript, 24 March 1953, box 8, *US v. Charles Fujimoto et al.*

119. Transcript, 25 March 1953, box 8, *US v. Charles Fujimoto et al.*

120. Transcript, 26 March 1953, box 8, *US v. Charles Fujimoto et al.*

121. Transcript, 13 April 1953, box 8, *US v. Charles Fujimoto et al.*

122. Transcript, 31 March 1953, box 8, *US v. Charles Fujimoto et al.*

123. Transcript, 3 April 1953, box 8, *US v. Charles Fujimoto et al.*

124. Transcript, 30 April 1953, box 10, *US v. Charles Fujimoto et al.*

125. Transcript, 4 May 1953, box 10, *US v. Charles Fujimoto et al.*

126. Transcript, 12 May 1953, box 10, *US v. Charles Fujimoto et al.*

127. Transcript, 18 May 1953, box 10, *US v. Charles Fujimoto et al.*

128. Transcript, 19 May 1953, box 11, *US v. Charles Fujimoto et al.*

129. Ibid.

130. Transcript, 14 May 1953, box 10, *US v. Charles Fujimoto et al.*

131. Transcript, 8 May 1953, box 10, *US v. Charles Fujimoto et al.*

132. Transcript, 13 May 1953, box 8, *US v. Charles Fujimoto et al.*

133. ILWU, "Running Story, Hawaii Smith Act Trial," 30 January 1953.

134. *Honolulu Advertiser*, 26 November 1952.

135. *Honolulu Advertiser*, 6 June 1952.

136. *Honolulu Advertiser*, 10 June 1952.

137. *Honolulu Advertiser*, 13 June 1953.

138. *Honolulu Star-Bulletin*, 9 June 1953.

139. ILWU, "Running Story, Hawaii Smith Act Trial," 3 July 1953.

140. *Honolulu Star-Bulletin*, 20 June 1953.

141. *Honolulu Star-Bulletin*, 29 January 1953.

142. *Honolulu Record*, 26 March 1953.

143. *Honolulu Record*, 2 April 1953.

144. *Honolulu Record*, 25 June 1953.
145. *Honolulu Record*, 8 May 1958.

Chapter 14. The Trials of Racism and Radicalism

1. *Honolulu Record*, 26 June 1952.
2. *Honolulu Record*, 10 July 1952.
3. *Honolulu Star-Bulletin*, 27 July 1951.
4. Transcript of radio broadcast, 9 November 1951, file ILWU Radio Program, November 1951, ILWU Headquarters, Honolulu.
5. Transcript of radio broadcast, ca. November 1951, file ILWU Radio Program, November 1951, ILWU Headquarters, Honolulu.
6. Ibid.
7. *Honolulu Advertiser*, 7 May 1953.
8. Transcript, 7 May 1953, box 10, *United States v. Charles Fujimoto et al.*, RG 21, case #10495, compartment 1069B, National Archives and Records Administration, San Bruno, Calif. (cited hereafter as *US v. Charles Fujimoto et al.*).
9. *Honolulu Star-Bulletin*, 8 May 1953.
10. *Honolulu Star-Bulletin*, 7 May 1953.
11. Transcript, 11 May 1953, box 10, *US v. Charles Fujimoto et al.*
12. Ibid.
13. ILWU, "Running Story, Hawaii Smith Act Trial," 16 April 1953, University of Hawai'i at Mānoa, Special Collections.
14. Study, n.d., ca. 1952, box 33, *US v. Charles Fujimoto et al.*
15. Transcript, 7–9 April 1952, box 15, *US v. Charles Fujimoto et al.*
16. Transcript, 26 February 1952, box 13, *US v. Charles Fujimoto et al.*
17. Transcript, 7 April 1952, box 15, *US v. Charles Fujimoto et al.*
18. Transcript, 5 November 1952, box 14, *US v. Charles Fujimoto et al.*
19. Transcript, 28 April 1953, box 9, *US v. Charles Fujimoto et al.*
20. Transcript, 18 February 1952, box 13, *US v. Charles Fujimoto et al.*
21. *Honolulu Star-Bulletin*, 12 February 1952.
22. *Honolulu Star-Bulletin*, 21 February 1952.
23. *Maui News*, 21 February 1952.
24. Ray Jerome Baker to Williams Smith, 14 November 1952, box 33, Ray Jerome Baker Papers, Bishop Museum, Honolulu (hereafter cited as Baker Papers).
25. *Honolulu Record*, 2 July 1953.
26. *Honolulu Star-Bulletin*, 1 July 1953.
27. Ray Jerome Baker to Marshall McEuen, 22 February 1953, box 33, Baker Papers.
28. *Honolulu Star-Bulletin*, 16 May 1951.
29. *Maui News*, 20 June 1951.
30. *Honolulu Star-Bulletin*, 21 October 1948.
31. *Honolulu Advertiser*, 14 May 1953.
32. *Honolulu Star-Bulletin*, 14 May 1953.
33. Robert McElrath to Linus Pauling, 14 March 1951, Regional Office, Reading File, 1951: January–March, ILWU Headquarters, Honolulu.

34. *Hilo Tribune-Herald*, 31 May 1952.

35. *Honolulu Star-Bulletin*, 11 May 1951.

36. *Honolulu Star-Bulletin*, 22 April 1953.

37. Letter from Jack Hall, 27 June 1952, Regional Office, Reading File, 1952: April–June, ILWU Headquarters, Honolulu (hereafter cited as Reading File, 1952: April–June).

38. Andy Salz, ILWU Staff, to Lincoln Fairley, Research Director, ILWU, ca. mid-1952, Reading File, 1952: April–June.

39. Transcript, 27 March 1953, box 8, *US v. Charles Fujimoto et al.*

40. *Honolulu Star-Bulletin*, 27 March 1953.

41. *Honolulu Advertiser*, 5 May 1953.

42. Jack Hall to L. B. Thomas, 8 July 1952, Regional Office, Reading File, 1952: July–December, ILWU Headquarters, Honolulu.

43. *Saturday Evening Post*, 2 February 1952; *Honolulu Advertiser*, 30 January 1952.

44. *Honolulu Advertiser*, 2 February 1952.

45. *Hilo Tribune-Herald*, 17 November 1952.

46. *Honolulu Star-Bulletin*, 25 March 1953.

47. *Honolulu Star-Bulletin*, 17 and 19 June 1953.

48. Koji Ariyoshi, interview, 18 January 1976, notebook 28, Sanford Zalburg Papers, University of Hawai'i at Mānoa, Archives and Manuscripts (hereafter cited as Zalburg Papers).

49. *Honolulu Star-Bulletin*, 20 June 1953.

50. Hearing on Motion to Reduce Bail, 6 July 1953, box 32, *US v. Charles Fujimoto et al.*

51. Koji Ariyoshi interview, 18 January 1976, notebook 31, Sanford Zalburg Papers.

52. Ray Jerome Baker to Richard Liebes, 30 September 1953, box 33, Baker Papers.

53. *Honolulu Advertiser*, 12 July 1953.

54. Ray Jerome Baker to George and Betty Marion, 15 August 1953, box 33, Baker Papers.

55. *Honolulu Star-Bulletin*, 3 September 1953.

56. Ray Jerome Baker to "Dear Julius and Adele," 30 July 1953, box 33, Baker Papers.

57. Gerald Horne, *Black Liberation/Red Scare: Ben Davis and the Communist Party* (Newark: University of Delaware Press, 1994).

58. *Honolulu Star-Bulletin*, 19 May 1955.

59. *Maui News*, 1 April 1953.

60. Jon Wiig, interview, 17 August 1974, notebook 31, Zalburg Papers.

61. Transcript, 16 December 1952, box 4, *US v. Charles Fujimoto et al.*

62. Harriet Bouslog, *Fear* (Honolulu: ILWU, ca. 1952), University of Hawai'i at Mānoa, Special Collections.

63. *New York Times*, 5 May 1953, box 57, Joseph Farrington Papers, Hawai'i State Archives, Honolulu.

64. Transcript, 9 April 1953, box 9, *US v. Charles Fujimoto et al.*

65. Ray Jerome Baker to Roy E. Maddon, 1 May 1952, box 33, Baker Papers.

66. Ray Jerome Baker to Richard Liebes, 30 September 1953.

67. Ray Jerome Baker, diary, 7 March 1952, box 14, Baker Papers.

68. Script from KIKI Radio, 19 February 1952, box 50, file 3, Walter F. Dillingham Papers, Bishop Museum, Honolulu (hereafter cited as Dillingham Papers).

69. Ray Jerome Baker to Marshall McEuen, 22 February 1953.

70. Bob McElrath, interview, 7 March 1976, notebook 25, Zalburg Papers.

71. Koji Ariyoshi, interview, 18 January 1976, notebook 31.

72. *Honolulu Star-Bulletin*, 26 June 1953.

73. *Honolulu Star-Bulletin*, 24 June 1953.

74. *Honolulu Advertiser*, 17 April 1953.

75. *Honolulu Advertiser*, 26 March 1953.

76. Donald Shepherd and Robert Slatzer, with David Grayson, *Duke: The Life and Times of John Wayne* (Garden City, N.Y.: Doubleday, 1985), 246.

77. *Time*, 29 September 1952.

78. Randy Roberts and James S. Olson, *John Wayne: American* (New York: Simon and Schuster, 1995), 377–378.

79. *Honolulu Record*, 4 September 1952.

80. Transcript of radio broadcast, 5 September 1952, file ILWU Radio Program, September 1952, ILWU Headquarters, Honolulu.

81. *Honolulu Star-Bulletin*, 30 August 1952.

82. Richard D. McGhee, *John Wayne: Actor, Artist, Hero* (Jefferson, N.C.: McFarland, 1999), 36. For more on this film, see, e.g., *Honolulu Star-Bulletin*, 29 and 30 April 1952; and *Honolulu Advertiser*, 29 and 30 April 1952, 1 May 1952.

83. *San Francisco Chronicle*, 7 September 1952.

84. *Honolulu Star-Bulletin*, 13 May 1952.

85. "Greetings" from Ray Jerome Baker, 1 January 1953, box 33, Baker Papers.

86. *Honolulu Star-Bulletin*, 30 August 1952.

87. *Honolulu Advertiser*, 8 May 1952.

88. Andy Salz to Les Fishman, 19 June 1952, Reading File, 1952: April–June 1952.

89. *Honolulu Record*, 5 November 1953.

90. Cited in ILWU, "Running Story, Hawaii Smith Act Trial," 18 May 1953.

91. Transcript, 18 May 1953, box 10, *US v. Charles Fujimoto et al.*

92. Transcript, 20 April 1953, box 9, *US v. Charles Fujimoto et al.*

93. Ibid.

94. Transcript, 14 April 1953, box 9, *US v. Charles Fujimoto et al.*

95. Transcript, 9 April 1953, box 9, *US v. Charles Fujimoto et al.*

96. Jack Hall to Regino Colotario, ca. January 1952, Regional Office, Reading File, 1952: January–March, ILWU Headquarters, Honolulu.

97. Jack Hall to Thad Black, ILWU, San Diego, 30 November 1953, Regional Office Correspondence, ILWU Locals (Mainland) and Regional Directors, 1946–1968, ILWU Headquarters, Honolulu.

98. Jack Hall to Harriet Bouslog and Myer Symonds, 9 November 1951, box 6, ILWU Headquarters, San Francisco.

99. *Honolulu Advertiser*, 23 and 27 November 1953.

100. Jack Hall to Myer Symonds, 3 December 1951, box 6, ILWU Headquarters, San Francisco.

101. Saburo Fujisaki to Hal Kramer, 26 March 1952, file Union Defense Correspondence, 1951–1952, ILWU Headquarters, Honolulu.

102. Transcript of radio broadcast, 2 September 1952, file ILWU Radio Program, September 1952, ILWU Headquarters, Honolulu.

103. Hal Kramer, Executive Secretary of Northern California Trade Union Committee to Repeal the Smith Act and Other Anti-Labor Legislation, San Francisco, 5 May 1952, file Union Defense Correspondence, 1951–1952, ILWU Headquarters, Honolulu.

104. Harriet Bouslog to Jack Hall, 8 March 1952, file Union Defense Correspondence, Research Committee, ILWU Headquarters, Honolulu.

105. Harriet Bouslog to Myer Symonds, 12 December 1951, box 6, ILWU Headquarters, San Francisco.

106. Weekly Report of "Union Defense Committee," 19 March 1952, file Local 142 Meetings, Local Officers and Regional Office Staff, ILWU Headquarters, Honolulu.

107. Press release, 22 April 1952, box 39, ILWU Headquarters, San Francisco.

108. Transcript of radio broadcast, 8 September 1952, file ILWU Radio Program, September 1952, ILWU Headquarters, Honolulu.

109. *Garden Island* (Kaua'i), 4 March 1953.

110. Minutes, Steering Committee, 16–19 December 1952, file 1952 Meetings of Local Executive Officers and Steering Committee, ILWU Headquarters, Honolulu.

111. Theodora Kreps to Martha Schiferl, 17 December 1952, Regional Office, Reading File, 1952: January–March, ILWU Headquarters, Honolulu.

112. Minutes, ILWU Local 142, 28–31 January 1953, Afternoon Session, 28 January, file Jack Hall Speeches, ILWU Headquarters, Honolulu.

113. Myer Symonds to Jack Hall, 21 July 1952, box 6, ILWU Headquarters, San Francisco.

114. Ray Jerome Baker to Warren Smith, 14 November 1952, box 33, Baker Papers.

115. Jack Hall to Mildred McIntyre, 22 May 1952, Regional Office, Reading File, 1952: April–June, ILWU Headquarters, Honolulu.

116. Minutes, ILWU Local 142, Annual Local Convention, 15–18 October 1953, file Meetings, 1953, Local Convention (First Biennial), ILWU Headquarters, Honolulu.

117. Anonymous correspondent to Bob McElrath, 7 July 1953, file National Office, Publicity, Radio Program, Crank and Fan Letters, ILWU Headquarters, Honolulu.

118. Anonymous correspondent, 18 December 1951, file National Office, Publicity, Radio Program, Crank and Fan Letters, ILWU Headquarters, Honolulu. Emphasis in original.

119. *Honolulu Star-Bulletin*, 9 July 1953.

120. Memorandum from Hawaiian Sugar Planters' Association re book by Jack Lait and Lee Mortimer, 13 May 1952, University of Hawai'i at Mānoa, Special Collections.

121. Transcript of radio broadcast, 2 October 1951, file ILWU Radio Program, October 1951, ILWU Headquarters, Honolulu.

122. Resolution, January 1952, file Local 142 Meetings, Conventions (Annual), 30–31 January, 1 February 1952, ILWU Headquarters, Honolulu.

123. *Honolulu Record*, 25 June 1953.

124. *Honolulu Record*, 5 November 1953.

125. Jack Hall to Thomas Yagi, 9 May 1955, Regional Office Correspondence, Maui Division, 1955, ILWU Headquarters, Honolulu.

126. Report by Yasuki Arakaki, Proceedings of the Ninth Biennial Convention of the ILWU, 2–6 April 1951, ILWU Headquarters, San Francisco.

127. Ewart Guinier to Harry Bridges, 9 June 1952, box 37, ILWU Headquarters, San Francisco.

128. Coleman Young to Jack Hall, 17 March 1954, box 37, ILWU Headquarters, San Francisco.

129. *Hilo Tribune-Herald*, 2 July 1953.

130. *Honolulu Star-Bulletin*, 3 July 1953.

131. *Honolulu Advertiser*, 4 July 1953.

132. *Honolulu Star-Bulletin*, 7 July 1953.

133. Walter F. Dillingham to John T. Kuntz, 20 January 1953, box 50, Dillingham Papers.

134. Ray Jerome Baker to Warren Smith, 22 May 1952, box 33, Baker Papers.

135. Walter F. Dillingham to Jan Schaafsma, 16 June 1953, box 50, Dillingham Papers.

136. *New York Times*, 6 January 1953.

137. Hugh Butler to "Dear Friends," 9 May 1950, box 95, Hugh Butler Papers, Nebraska State Historical Society, Lincoln (hereafter cited as Butler Papers).

138. Transcript of radio broadcast, 14 June 1951, file ILWU Radio Program, June 1951, ILWU Headquarters, Honolulu.

139. *Honolulu Record*, 15 June 1950, box 99, Butler Papers.

140. Hugh Butler to J. Edgar Hoover, 4 December 1950, box 97, Butler Papers.

141. Alfred Yap to Hugh Butler, 8 August 1951, box 97, Butler Papers.

142. "Stenographic Transcript of Hearings before the Committee on Interior and Insular Affairs," US Senate, 1–5 November 1948, box 97, Butler Papers.

143. Emma Richey to Senator Hugh Butler, 31 January 1948, box 100, Butler Papers.

144. William Tilley to Hugh Butler, 8 March 1952, box 102, Butler Papers.

145. Alfred Yap to Senator John Stennis, 29 September 1951, box 101, Butler Papers.

146. John Stennis to Alfred Yap, 24 May 1951, box 101, Butler Papers.

147. Report by Oscar Iden, date unclear, box 97, Butler Papers.

148. Alfred Yap to Senator John Stennis, 5 May 1951, box 101, Butler Papers.

149. List, 1 August 1948, box 97, Butler Papers.

150. Memorandum from Jonathan Lee, 24 May 1951, box 101, Butler Papers.

151. William Tilley to Hugh Butler, 8 March 1952.

152. William Borthwick to James Eastland, 16 April 1950, box 41, Olin D. Johnston Papers, South Caroliniana Library, University of South Carolina, Columbia.

153. Bill Borthwick to Hugh Butler, 3 January 1953, box 101, Butler Papers.

154. Bill Borthwick to Senator Robert Taft, 3 January 1953, box 101, Butler Papers.

155. James Coke to Hugh Butler, 24 January 1952, box 102, Butler Papers.

156. Hugh Butler to Senator Eugene Millikin, 5 May 1951, box 101, Butler Papers.

157. Bill Borthwick to Hugh Butler, 19 March 1951, box 101, Butler Papers.

158. Jack Hart to Senator John Sparkman, 3 September 1953, file Statehood, John Sparkman Papers, University of Alabama, Tuscaloosa (hereafter cited as Sparkman Papers).

159. Edward Lewis to Senator John Sparkman, 14 March 1953, file Statehood, Sparkman Papers.

160. Hudson De Priest to Senator Robert Taft, 10 March 1953, box 148, Clyde Roark Hoey Papers, Duke University, Durham, N.C. Emphasis in original.

161. Hugh Butler to Captain M. D. Matthews, 30 December 1952, box 94, Butler Papers.

162. Hugh Butler to Edward Lewis, 8 January 1953, box 94, Butler Papers.

Chapter 15. Upheaval

1. *Honolulu Record*, 4 November 1954.

2. *ILWU Reporter*, 24 November 1954.

3. Transcript of radio broadcast (ILWU), 19 December 1955, University of Hawai'i at Mānoa, Special Collections.

4. *Honolulu Record*, 14 April 1955.

5. Transcript of radio program (ILWU), 20 December 1955, University of Hawai'i at Mānoa, Special Collections.

6. *Honolulu Record*, 18 November 1954.

7. *Honolulu Record*, 7 October 1954.

8. *Honolulu Advertiser*, 22 November 1954.

9. *Honolulu Star-Bulletin*, 23 November 1954. Subsequently, Burns denied crediting the ILWU with the Democrats' victory; *Honolulu Star-Bulletin*, 18 December 1954.

10. *Honolulu Advertiser*, 4 November 1954.

11. *Honolulu Advertiser*, 7 November 1950.

12. *Honolulu Star-Bulletin*, 5 November 1954.

13. *Honolulu Star-Bulletin*, 3 November 1954.

14. *Honolulu Star-Bulletin*, 10 November 1954.

15. Clipping, ca. April 1954, publication unknown, box 1, ILWU Headquarters, Honolulu.

16. "Hearings before the Committee to Investigate the Charges against [ILWU]," 17 May 1950, Washington, D.C., transcript, box 2, ILWU Headquarters, Honolulu. See also *Official Reports on the Expulsion of Communist Dominated Organizations from the CIO*, September 1954, RG 46, box 135, Records of the US Senate, Internal Security Subcommittee of the Senate Judiciary Committee, National Archives and Records Administration (hereafter cited as NARA), Washington, D.C.

17. *Honolulu Advertiser*, 3 February 1953.

18. *Honolulu Star-Bulletin*, 25 September 1954.

19. *Honolulu Record*, 5 August 1954.

20. *Honolulu Record*, 6 May 1954.

21. *Honolulu Record*, 13 May 1954.

22. *Honolulu Record*, 3 June 1954.

23. *Honolulu Record*, 5 August 1954.

24. Transcript of radio broadcast, 3 October 1954, file Japanese Radio Program, ILWU Headquarters, Honolulu.

25. Glenn Mitchell, Chairman, Republican Party County Committee, County of Hawaii, to Richard M. Nixon, 14 September 1954, LN Collection, ser. 320, folder Hawaii, Nixon Presidential Library and Museum, Yorba Linda, Calif.

26. *Honolulu Advertiser*, 25 June 1953.

27. *Honolulu Advertiser*, 14 May 1953.

28. *Honolulu Star-Bulletin*, 22 July 1953.

29. *Honolulu Star-Bulletin*, 19 January 1952.

30. *Honolulu Advertiser*, 13 January 1952.

31. *Honolulu Star-Bulletin*, 2 February 1952.

32. Lincoln Fairley, ILWU Research Director, ILWU, to Ann Berenson, 2 July 1946, box 37, ILWU Headquarters, San Francisco.

33. Minutes of Local 142 Executive, 30–31 July 1954, file Meetings, Local Executive Board, 1954, ILWU Headquarters, San Francisco.

34. *Honolulu Star-Bulletin*, 4 September 1951.

35. Yoshiko Hall, interview, 24 November 1975, notebook 12, Sanford Zalburg Papers, University of Hawaiʻi at Mānoa, Archives and Manuscripts (hereafter cited as Zalburg Papers).

36. *Honolulu Star-Bulletin*, 22 August 1952.

37. Robert McElrath, interview, 28 March 1975, notebook 25, Zalburg Papers.

38. Transcript of radio program (ILWU), 25 October 1955, University of Hawaiʻi at Mānoa, Special Collections.

39. *Honolulu Advertiser*, 5 December 1953.

40. *Honolulu Star-Bulletin*, 14 May 1952. See also *Honolulu Star-Bulletin*, 16 December 1953.

41. Press release from Matson Navigation, 13 March 1953, box 61, Joseph Farrington Papers, Hawaiʻi State Archives, Honolulu (hereafter cited as Farrington Papers).

42. *Honolulu Advertiser*, 4 August 1953.

43. Minutes of Local 142 Executive, 12–13 September 1953, file Meetings, Local Executive Board, 1953, ILWU Headquarters, Honolulu.

44. *Honolulu Advertiser*, 17 March 1953.

45. Minutes of Local 142 Executive, file Meetings, Local Executive Board, 1953, ILWU Headquarters, Honolulu.

46. Minutes, Local 142, 21–23 July 1953, file Meetings, of Local Executive Officers, 1953, ILWU Headquarters, Honolulu.

47. Minutes, Local 142 Executive, 28–30 May 1954, ILWU Headquarters, Honolulu.

48. Minutes, Meeting of Regional Staff, Local 142, 17 August 1955, file Local 142, Meetings of Local Officers and Regional Office Staff, 1955–1957, ILWU Headquarters, Honolulu.

49. Transcript of radio broadcast, 30 May 1958, file ILWU Japanese Radio Program, ILWU Headquarters, Honolulu.

50. Memorandum from Ernest Arena, Joseph Kealalio, Antonio Rania, to All Units and Divisions, 5 June 1952, file Meetings of Local Executive Officers and Steering Committee, ILWU Headquarters, Honolulu.

51. Minutes of Local 142 and Regional Staff, 9 December 1953, file Local 142, Meetings of Local Officers and Regional Office Staff, 1953–1954, ILWU Headquarters, Honolulu.

52. *Honolulu Advertiser*, 24 December 1952.

53. Louis Goldblatt to Harry Bridges, 14 December 1953, box 38, ILWU Headquarters, San Francisco

54. *Garden Island* (Kaua'i), 23 December 1953.

55. "Sugar Negotiations Reopening, HSPA Board Room," Honolulu, Friday, 9 October 1953, box 38, ILWU Headquarters, San Francisco.

56. "Confidential" Memorandum from Regional Office of ILWU to Sugar Negotiating Committee, 16 December 1954, Regional Office Circulars, 1951–1959, ILWU Headquarters, Honolulu.

57. "Confidential" Memorandum from Regional Director to Sugar Unit Chairmen, Full Time Officials, and Members of Sugar Negotiating Committee, 21 December 1953, Regional Office Circulars, 1951–1959, ILWU Headquarters, Honolulu.

58. Transcript of radio broadcast (ILWU), 3 February 1954, University of Hawai'i at Mānoa, Special Collections.

59. Transcript of radio Program (ILWU), 12 March 1954, University of Hawai'i at Mānoa, Special Collections.

60. Transcript of radio program (ILWU), 29 March 1954, University of Hawai'i at Mānoa, Special Collections.

61. *Honolulu Advertiser*, 21 October 1953.

62. *Honolulu Star-Bulletin*, 6 September 1952.

63. Transcript of radio broadcast, 12 October 1951, file ILWU Radio Program, October 1951, ILWU Headquarters, Honolulu.

64. Transcript of radio broadcast, 1 May 1952, file ILWU Radio Program, May 1952, ILWU Headquarters, Honolulu.

65. Minutes of ILWU Local Executive Officers, 20 December 1951, file Local 142, Meetings of Local Officers and Regional Office Staff, 1951, ILWU Headquarters, Honolulu.

66. Antonio Rania, Ernest Arena, et al., to Katsuro Kato, 28 February 1952, file Japanese Radio Program, ILWU Headquarters, Honolulu.

67. Unnamed correspondent to Bob McElrath, 12 July 1954, file National Office, Publicity, Radio Program, Crank and Fan Letters, ILWU Headquarters, Honolulu.

68. Unnamed correspondent to Bob McElrath, 22 May 1954, file National Office, Publicity, Radio Program, Crank and Fan Letters, ILWU Headquarters, Honolulu.

69. Robert McElrath to Myer Symonds, 8 March 1948, Regional Office Correspondence, Attorneys Bouslog and Symonds, 1947–1951, ILWU Headquarters, Honolulu.

70. Transcript of radio broadcast (ILWU), 10 June 1954, University of Hawai'i at Mānoa, Special Collections.

71. Transcript of radio broadcast, 31 August 1951, file ILWU Radio Program, August 1951, ILWU Headquarters, Honolulu.

72. Transcript of radio broadcast, 21 August 1951, file ILWU Radio Program, August 1951, ILWU Headquarters, Honolulu.

73. *Honolulu Record*, 4 March 1954.

74. *Honolulu Record*, 25 March 1954.

75. Transcript of radio broadcast, 16 May 1952, file ILWU Radio Program, May 1952, ILWU Headquarters, Honolulu.

76. *Honolulu Record*, 24 June 1954.

77. Transcript of radio broadcast, 1 October 1951, file ILWU Radio Program, October 1951, ILWU Headquarters, Honolulu.

78. Transcript of radio program, 30 November 1950, file ILWU Radio Program, November 1950, ILWU Headquarters, Honolulu.

79. Transcript of radio program, 8 January 1951, file ILWU Radio Program, January 1951, ILWU Headquarters, Honolulu.

80. Transcript of radio program (ILWU), 27 April 1954, University of Hawai'i at Mānoa, Special Collections.

81. Ray Jerome Baker to Warren Smith, 27 November 1954, box 33, Ray Jerome Baker Papers, Bishop Museum, Honolulu (hereafter cited as Baker Papers).

82. Ray Jerome Baker to Olga Eddy, 15 March 1952, box 33, Baker Papers.

83. Lincoln Fairley to Jack Hall, 15 July 1954, box 37, ILWU Headquarters, San Francisco.

84. Jack Hall's Labor Day Speech, 1947, unnamed file, ILWU Headquarters, Honolulu.

85. Transcript of radio broadcast (ILWU), 12 March 1954, University of Hawai'i at Mānoa, Special Collections.

86. Ray Jerome Baker to Warren Smith, 13 April 1954, box 33, Baker Papers.

87. Ray Jerome Baker to Warren Smith, 1 December 1954, box 33, Baker Papers.

88. Paul Crouch to Harlan Wood, 6 April 1954, box 41, Olin D. Johnston Papers, South Caroliniana Library, University of South Carolina, Columbia (hereafter cited as Johnston Papers).

89. Governor Oren Long to Senator Lyndon B. Johnson, 15 February 1952, Legislative Files, box 223, Lyndon B. Johnson Papers, Lyndon Baines Johnson Library, University of Texas at Austin (hereafter cited as LBJ Papers).

90. Arthur Compton to Senator Thomas Hennings, 10 January 1954, folder 2137, Thomas Hennings Papers, Western Historical Manuscripts Collection–Columbia, University of Missouri.

91. E. L. Sitton to Senator Lyndon B. Johnson, 27 February 1951, Legislative Files, box 223, LBJ Papers.

92. Proposal, July 1952, RG 1.1, ser. 214, box 1, Rockefeller Foundation Archives, Rockefeller Archives Center, Sleepy Hollow, N.Y.

93. *Honolulu Advertiser*, 14 April 1953, James Eastland Papers, University of Mississippi, Oxford (hereafter cited as Eastland Papers).

94. *Honolulu Star-Bulletin*, 1 May 1953, Eastland Papers.

95. Memorandum, "Filipino Communist Broadcast in Hawaii," n.d., Eastland Papers.

96. "Communist Press," n.d., Eastland Papers.

97. Memorandum, "Communist Daily Radio Broadcast in Hawaii," 24 April 1952, Eastland Papers.

98. Untitled memorandum, n.d., ca. 1953, Eastland Papers.

99. "Political Influence of Communist Party in Hawaii," n.d., James Eastland Papers.

100. Transcript of radio broadcast, 24 January 1954, file Japanese Radio Program, ILWU Headquarters, Honolulu.

101. Minutes of Oahu ILWU Council, 6 January 1946, file Oahu ILWU Council Minutes of Meetings, ILWU Headquarters, Honolulu.

102. Attorney Harlan Wood to Senator Olin Johnston, "personal by hand," 16 March 1954, box 41, Johnston Papers.

103. Statement by Senator James Eastland, 22 December 1953, Eastland Papers.

104. Clipping, *Baltimore Sun*, ca. 1953, box 146, J. B. Matthews Papers, Duke University, Durham, N.C.

105. Elwood Murray to Congressman Sam Rayburn, 20 April 1954, Sam Rayburn Papers, Center for American History, University of Texas at Austin (hereafter cited as Rayburn Papers).

106. Charles Francis to Senator Lyndon B. Johnson, 3 March 1952, Legislative Files, box 223, LBJ Papers.

107. Senator Willis Robertson to "Dear Clyde," 14 March 1953, box 148, Clyde Roark Hoey Papers, Duke University, Durham, N.C. (hereafter cited as Hoey Papers).

108. Senator Willis Robertson to Clyde Hoey, 13 March 1953, box 148, Hoey Papers.

109. *Honolulu Star-Bulletin*, 14 April 1953.

110. George Lehleitner to Mississippi State Legislature, 16 March 1954, file Statehood, John Sparkman Papers, University of Alabama, Tuscaloosa (hereafter cited as Sparkman Papers).

111. Alfred Yap to Senator Olin Johnston, 25 June 1953, box 41, Johnston Papers.

112. Alfred Yap to Sam Rayburn, 20 April 1954, Rayburn Papers.

113. Sam Rayburn to Alfred Yap, 30 April 1954, Rayburn Papers.

114. Senator Olin Johnston, Statement on Statehood, n.d., box 41, Johnston Papers.

115. *Congressional Record*, 23 April 1953, M-473, box 18, Farrington Papers.

116. Helen Jensen and Daisy Emsley to Senator George Smathers, 16 February 1954, box 41, Johnston Papers.

117. Helen Jensen and Daisy Emsley to Senator Clyde Hoey, 16 February 1954, box 148, Hoey Papers.

118. *Congressional Record*, 5 March 1953; *Chinese World* (San Francisco), 11 March 1953, 11-6, Governor Samuel Wilder King Papers, Hawaiʻi State Archives, Honolulu (hereafter cited as King Papers).

119. H. L. Hunt to Senator Eastland, 18 April 1953, Eastland Papers.

120. William N. Michels to Senator Sparkman, n.d., file Statehood, Sparkman Papers.

121. John T. Barker to Senator J. William Fulbright, 17 March 1954, BCN47 F11, J. William Fulbright Papers, University of Arkansas, Fayetteville.

122. Early Van Deventer to Senator Eastland, 5 March 1954, Eastland Papers.

123. James Stanley Frazer to Senator Sparkman, 1 March 1954, Sparkman Papers.

124. Leon L. Rice to Congressman Bryan Dorn, 25 February 1953, box 41, Bryan Dorn Papers, South Carolina Political Collections, University of South Carolina, Columbia (hereafter cited as Dorn Papers).

125. Tom O'Brien to Senator Johnston, 13 April 1954, box 41, Johnston Papers.

126. Senator Clyde Hoey to H. E. Stewart, 13 January 1954, box 148, Hoey Papers.

127. George Lehleitner to Senator Hoey, 18 July 1950, box 148, Hoey Papers.

128. Congressman Otto Passman to Samuel Wilder King, 13 April 1953, 116, King Papers.

129. Charles Campbell to Congressman Dorn, 15 March 1954, box 41, Dorn Papers.

130. *Washington Post*, 2 February 1952.

131. "Stenographic Transcript of Hearings before the Committee on Interior and Insular Affairs," US Senate, 8 January 1954, Eastland Papers.

132. Ibid.

133. Ibid.

134. *Honolulu Star-Bulletin*, 10 March 1954.

135. Jeff Kibre to Jack Hall, 8 January 1954, box 6, ILWU Headquarters, San Francisco.

136. *Honolulu Star-Bulletin*, 21 July 1949.

137. Governor Samuel Wilder King to Senator Hugh Butler, 4 March 1954, 11-6, King Papers.

138. "Report on the Statehood Mission to Washington, D.C., May 8–18, 1954," M-481, John Burns Papers, Hawai'i State Archives, Honolulu.

139. Executive Session Transcript, 26 February 1954, RG 46, box 28, Records of the US Senate, Internal Security Subcommittee of the Senate Judiciary Committee, NARA, Washington, D.C.

140. *For God and Freedom: The Voice of Christianform* 1, no. 1 (March 1954): 1, 11-6, King Papers.

141. *Honolulu Advertiser*, 17 March 1954.

142. *Honolulu Star-Bulletin*, 25 April 1953.

143. *Honolulu Advertiser*, 1 May 1955.

144. Testimony of Paul Crouch, Executive Session Transcript, 1 March 1954, RG 46, box 28, Records of the US Senate, Internal Security Subcommittee of the Senate Judiciary Committee.

145. Lincoln Fairley to William Glazier, 7 March 1947, box 38, ILWU Headquarters, San Francisco.

146. Jack Hall to Louis Goldblatt, 7 February 1946, box 6, ILWU Headquarters, San Francisco.

147. *Honolulu Star-Bulletin*, 22 June 1950.

148. Paul Steintorf to Ingram Stainback, 29 July 1946, RG 126, Office of the Territories, Classified Files, 1907–1951, box 658, NARA, College Park, Md.

149. Governor Ingram Stainback to Harold Ickes, 5 November 1945, RG 126, Office of the Territories, Classified Files, 1907–1951, box 657, NARA, College Park, Md.

150. Ricardo Labez to "All Locals and Units," 2 December 1946, box 37, ILWU Headquarters, San Francisco.

151. Ricardo Labez, Assistant Regional Director, to "All Island Strike Strategy Committee," 8 October 1948, box 37, ILWU Headquarters, San Francisco.

152. Minutes of Local 136, Oahu, Executive Board Meeting, 2 July 1946, Regional Office Correspondence, Miscellaneous, ILWU Headquarters, Honolulu.

153. William Glazier to Louis Goldblatt, 4 June 1947, box 37, ILWU Headquarters, San Francisco.

154. Local 137, ILWU, Honolulu, to President Harry S. Truman, 10 October 1945, file Local 136 Correspondence (Protest Letters, Etc.), ILWU Headquarters, Honolulu.

155. Frank Thompson et al. to C. A. Mackintosh, 10 October 1945, file Oahu CIO Council, ILWU Headquarters, Honolulu.

156. Jack Hall to William Glazier, 25 March 1948, Reading File, 1948, ILWU Headquarters, Honolulu.

157. *Information on the Territory of Hawaii for the Fiscal Year Ended June 30, 1953, Transmitted by the United States to the Secretary-General of the United Nations in Pursuant to Article 73 (3) of the Charter . . . Prepared by the Governor of Hawaii in Cooperation with the Department of the Interior. . .*, 11-30, King Papers.

158. Ricardo Labez to Pedro Magsalin, Manila, 25 June 1946, Regional Office Correspondence, Miscellaneous, 1944–1947, ILWU Headquarters, Honolulu.

159. Toyomasa Oshiro, Secretary, ILWU Memorial Association, to Louis Goldblatt, 20 May 1955, box 18l, ILWU Headquarters, San Francisco.

160. Louis Goldblatt to R. Vidimari, Secretary-Treasurer, Trade Unions International of Agricultural and Forestry Workers, Rome, n.d., box 37, ILWU Headquarters, San Francisco.

161. Louis Goldblatt to Vincente Lombardo Toledano, 17 February 1947, and Jesus Menendez to Louis Goldblatt, 11 August 1947, box 37, ILWU Headquarters, San Francisco.

162. Transcript of radio program (ILWU), 6 July 1954, University of Hawai'i at Mānoa, Special Collections.

163. Transcript of radio program (ILWU), 14 May 1954, University of Hawai'i at Mānoa, Special Collections.

164. William Glazier to G. G. Gelt, 20 October 1947, box 1, ILWU Headquarters, San Francisco.

165. Martha Ezralow to Louis Goldblatt, 23 August 1946, box 37, ILWU Headquarters, San Francisco.

166. Minutes of Havana meeting, 23 November 1947, box 37, ILWU Headquarters, San Francisco.

167. Louis Goldblatt to Congressman Vito Marcantonio, 6 August 1947, box 37, ILWU Headquarters, San Francisco.

168. Memorandum from William Glazier, 28 March 1951, box 37, ILWU Headquarters, Honolulu.

169. Minutes of Havana meeting, 25 November 1947, box 37, ILWU Headquarters, San Francisco. See also *Daily Worker*, 18 December 1947.

170. Minutes of International Sugar Conference, 12–17 April 1947, box 37, ILWU Headquarters, San Francisco.

171. William Glazier to Harry Bridges, 19 December 1946, box 37, ILWU Headquarters, San Francisco.

172. William Glazier to Harry Bridges, 24 October 1946, box 37, ILWU Headquarters, San Francisco.

173. Ferdinand Smith, Jamaica Federation of Trade Unions, to "Dear Brothers," 1 January 1959, Regional Office Correspondence, Trade Unions, Foreign, ILWU Headquarters, Honolulu.

174. Jack Hall to Louis Goldblatt, 24 January 1948, box 38, ILWU Headquarters, San Francisco.

175. Louis Goldblatt to Jesus Menendez, 2 May 1947, box 37, ILWU Headquarters, San Francisco.

176. Jack Hall to Congress of Labor Organizations, Manila, 28 May 1948, file ILWU Hawaii, History Files: 1948, Robeson Concert Tour Proceeds to Joven and Menendez Widows, ILWU Headquarters, Honolulu.

177. William Glazier to "National Officers," 10 December 1948, box 38, ILWU Headquarters, San Francisco.

178. Memorandum from William Glazier, 10 December 1948, Regional Office Correspondence, Inter-Office, Washington, 1945–1948, ILWU Headquarters, Honolulu.

179. Louis Goldblatt to Jacob Potofsky, 21 February 1948, box 37, ILWU Headquarters, San Francisco.

180. Louis Goldblatt to Felix D. Perez-Gil, Havana, 21 February 1948, box 37, ILWU Headquarters, San Francisco.

181. William Glazier to Louis Goldblatt, 21 October 1947, box 37, ILWU Headquarters, San Francisco.

182. Jack Kawano, Antonio Rania, Ernest Arena, et al., to Secretary of State George Marshall, 28 October 1948, file Local 150 Correspondence, ILWU Headquarters, Honolulu.

183. Harry Bridges to Editor, "Sydney Morning Herald," 9 January 1952, box 37, ILWU Headquarters, San Francisco.

184. Memorandum from US Embassy, Santiago, Chile, to Washington, D.C., 8 January 1953, RG 59, box 3279, Decimal File, 1950–1954, 720.0001/1-853, NARA, College Park, Md.

185. Alain Le Leap to President Dwight D. Eisenhower, 14 May 1954, file Union Defense Correspondence, 1953, ILWU Headquarters, Honolulu.

186. Letter from William Glazier, 15 December 1948, box 37, ILWU Headquarters, San Francisco.

187. Jack Hall to Francisco Aguirre, 19 November 1951, Regional Office, Reading File, 1951: July–December, ILWU Headquarters, Honolulu.

188. "Hernandez Defense Contribution Report," 16 April 1952, ILWU Hawaii, History Files, 1951, Protesting Persecution of Amada Hernandez and Other CLO Leaders, ILWU Headquarters, Honolulu.

189. Ricardo Labez, Jack Kawano, Antonio Rania, et al., to Modesto Farolano, Consul General of the Philippines, 2 March 1948, Reading File, 1948, ILWU Headquarters, Honolulu.

190. Resolution by ILWU Locals on "Labor Recruiters and Filipino Importation to California," 2–4 June 1950, ILWU Hawaii, History Files, 1950, Protesting Recruitment of Filipino and Labor to Work on California Farms, ILWU Headquarters, Honolulu.

Chapter 16. Radicals Advance—and Retreat

1. Ray Jerome Baker to Richard Liebes, 17 November 1955, box 34, Ray Jerome Baker Papers, Bishop Museum, Honolulu (hereafter cited as Baker Papers).

2. *Honolulu Star-Bulletin*, 1 December 1956.

3. *Honolulu Advertiser*, 1 December 1956.

4. Ray Jerome Baker to Betty Marion, 23 September 1957, box 4, Baker Papers.

5. Howard Hoddick, interview, 10 December 1974, notebook 23, Sanford Zalburg Papers, University of Hawai'i at Mānoa, Archives and Manuscripts (hereafter cited as Zalburg Papers).

6. *Honolulu Advertiser*, 6 December 1956.

7. *Honolulu Advertiser*, 4 December 1956.

8. *Honolulu Star-Bulletin*, 4 December 1956.

9. *Honolulu Advertiser*, 15 December 1956.

10. *Honolulu Star-Bulletin*, 30 November 1956.

11. *Hilo Tribune-Herald*, 3 March 1956.

12. *Hilo Tribune-Herald*, 13 November 1956.

13. *Honolulu Record*, 22 November 1956.

14. *Honolulu Record*, 25 October 1956.

15. *Honolulu Record*, 8 November 1956.

16. *Honolulu Advertiser*, 20 October 1956.

17. *Honolulu Record*, 8 November 1956.

18. *Honolulu Record*, 27 December 1956.

19. *Honolulu Record*, 15 November 1956.

20. *Honolulu Advertiser*, 11 June 1957.

21. *Honolulu Advertiser*, 10 June 1957.

22. Ray Jerome Baker to William Armstrong, 22 September 1956, box 10, Baker Papers.

23. Ray Jerome Baker to Henry Tibbets, 9 December 1956, box 10, Baker Papers.

24. *Honolulu Record*, 27 December 1956.

25. William Glazier to Jack Hall, 24 October 1956, box 6, ILWU Headquarters, San Francisco.

26. Memorandum to Files, 26 November 1956, ILWU Hawaii, History Files, 1956 Eastland Hearings, ILWU Publicity, ILWU Headquarters, Honolulu.

27. *Hilo Tribune-Herald*, 28 November 1956.

28. *Honolulu Advertiser*, 11 November 1956.

29. *Honolulu Advertiser*, 18 November 1956.

30. *Honolulu Advertiser*, 28 November 1956.

31. ILWU poster, ca. 1956, University of Hawai'i at Mānoa, Special Collections.

32. Minutes, "Expanded Oahu Division Executive Board," 12 December 1956, ILWU Hawaii, History Files, 1956 Eastland Hearings, ILWU Publicity, ILWU Headquarters, Honolulu.

33. Transcript of radio program (ILWU), 18 May 1954, University of Hawai'i at Mānoa, Special Collections.

34. Transcript of radio program (ILWU), 3 September 1954, University of Hawai'i at Mānoa, Special Collections.

35. Transcript of radio program (ILWU), 15 August 1955, University of Hawai'i at Mānoa, Special Collections.

36. *Honolulu Record*, 16 August 1956.

37. Transcript of radio program (ILWU), 23 March 1956, University of Hawai'i at Mānoa, Special Collections.

38. *Honolulu Record*, 1 September 1955.

39. *Honolulu Record*, 20 October 1955.

40. *Honolulu Record*, 16 February 1954.

41. *Honolulu Record*, 22 December 1955.

42. *Honolulu Star-Bulletin*, 27 November 1956.

43. *Honolulu Star-Bulletin*, 3 December 1956.

44. Frank Marshall Davis to Claude A. Barnett, 28 October 1956, part 2, reel 5, Claude Barnett Papers, Columbia University, New York (hereafter cited as Barnett Papers).

45. Frank Marshall Davis to Claude Barnett, 10 April 1950, part 2, reel 5, Barnett Papers.

46. *Honolulu Record*, 13 September 1956.

47. *Honolulu Record*, 20 September 1956.

48. *Honolulu Advertiser*, 28 November 1956.

49. *Honolulu Advertiser*, 10 June 1957. See also *Hilo Tribune-Herald*, 4 January 1957.

50. Myer Symonds, interview, 16 December 1974, notebook 19, Zalburg Papers.

51. *Honolulu Star-Bulletin*, 17 October 1956.

52. Jeff Kibre to Harry Bridges and Jack Hall, 4 December 1956, box 6, ILWU Headquarters, San Francisco.

53. *Honolulu Star-Bulletin*, 1 December 1956.

54. *New York Times*, 17 November 1956.

55. *Honolulu Advertiser*, 17 November 1956.

56. *Honolulu Advertiser*, 28 July 1955.

57. Report, 19 June 1956, US Senate Committee to Investigate the Administration of the Internal Security Act and Other Internal Security Laws, of the Committee on the Judiciary, New York City, Room 1530, 342 Madison Avenue, ILWU Hawaii,

History Files, 1956 Riesel-Jenner Attack on ILWU and Jack Hall Case, ILWU Headquarters, Honolulu.

58. *New York Daily Mirror,* 18 June 1956.

59. Lyle G. Phillips, "The Communist Grip in Hawaii," All-American Conference of National Organizations to Combat Communism, Hotel Roosevelt, Pittsburgh, 16 November 1957, University of Hawai'i at Mānoa, Special Collections.

60. Congressman Carroll Reece, "Communist Base in Hawaii" (analysis by Jan Jabrulka), 21 January 1957, University of Hawai'i at Mānoa, Special Collections.

61. Samuel Wilder King to Raymond Coll, 18 January 1956, 11-6, Governor Samuel Wilder King Papers, Hawai'i State Archives, Honolulu (hereafter cited as King Papers).

62. Hawaii Residents' Association, *Communism in Hawaii—A Summary of the 1955 Report of the Territorial Commission on Subversive Activities,* University of Hawai'i at Mānoa, Special Collections.

63. Allie Bates Jolley to Senator Olin Johnston, 1 April 1957, box 41, Olin D. Johnston Papers, South Caroliniana Library, University of South Carolina, Columbia.

64. *New York Herald Tribune,* 10 December 1956.

65. *Honolulu Star-Bulletin,* 9 September 1955. See also *Honolulu Record,* 19 January 1956.

66. *Honolulu Record,* 6 September 1956.

67. Testimony of William Stephenson, 16 October 1956, box 111, Herbert A. Philbrick Papers, Library of Congress, Washington, D.C.

68. Transcript of radio program (ILWU), 4 March 1955, University of Hawai'i at Mānoa, Special Collections.

69. Transcript of radio program (ILWU), 22 March 1955, University of Hawai'i at Mānoa, Special Collections.

70. Transcript of radio program (ILWU), 29 March 1955, University of Hawai'i at Mānoa, Special Collections.

71. Transcript of radio program (ILWU), 25 April 1955, University of Hawai'i at Mānoa, Special Collections.

72. *Honolulu Record,* 17 November 1955.

73. Raymond Dickson to Honorable Price Daniel, 5 May 1955, BCN46 F27, J. William Fulbright Papers, University of Arkansas, Fayetteville.

74. Drew L. Smith, *The Menace of Hawaiian Statehood* (New Orleans: Free Men Speak, 1957), box 146, J. B. Matthews Papers, Duke University, Durham, N.C.

75. *Hilo Tribune-Herald,* 4 January 1957.

76. Harold Lord Varney, "The Risk in Hawaiian Statehood," *Freeman* (3 May 1954), University of Hawai'i at Mānoa, Special Collections.

77. *Hilo Tribune-Herald,* 2 July 1953.

78. Report of the Hawaii Commission on Subversive Activities to the Governor of Hawaii re United Public Workers, 31 March 1954, University of Hawai'i at Mānoa, Special Collections.

79. Sherman Clemmons to Senator James O. Eastland, 28 January 1957, Subject Correspondence, 1958, Federal Government, Statehood, J. Strom Thurmond Papers, Clemson University, Clemson, S.C.

80. Transcript of radio program (ILWU), 13 January 1954, University of Hawai'i at Mānoa, Special Collections.

81. Transcript of radio program (ILWU), 19 January 1954, University of Hawai'i at Mānoa, Special Collections.

82. Transcript of radio program (ILWU), 15 September 1954, University of Hawai'i at Mānoa, Special Collections.

83. Transcript of radio program (ILWU), 12 July 1956, University of Hawai'i at Mānoa, Special Collections.

84. Ray Jerome Baker to Warren Smith, 15 February 1956, box 10, Baker Papers.

85. Transcript of radio program (ILWU), 23 March 1956, University of Hawai'i at Mānoa, Special Collections.

86. *Honolulu Star-Bulletin*, 11 July 1956.

87. Governor King to Ernest Gruening, 30 August 1955, 11-6, King Papers.

88. *Honolulu Advertiser*, 2 November 1955.

89. Transcript of radio program (ILWU), 14 January 1956, University of Hawai'i at Mānoa, Special Collections. See also *Hilo Tribune-Herald*, 15 February 1956.

90. Transcript of radio program (ILWU), 27 February 1956, University of Hawai'i at Mānoa, Special Collections.

91. *Honolulu Record*, 21 June 1956.

92. *Honolulu Record*, 15 December 1955.

93. Transcript of radio program (ILWU), 19 January 1954, University of Hawai'i at Mānoa, Special Collections.

94. *Honolulu Record*, 8 September 1955.

95. Ray Jerome Baker to Warren Smith, 11 March 1956, box 10, Baker Papers.

96. *Honolulu Advertiser*, 4 January 1957.

97. *Facts for 1958: A Sugar Year*, 1958, box 42, Norman Leonard Collection, Labor Archives and Research Center, San Francisco State University.

98. *Honolulu Record*, 12 April 1956.

99. Ray Jerome Baker to Warren Smith, 15 April 1956, box 10, Baker Papers.

100. Henry Walker Jr., interview, 22 August 1996, transcript, University of Hawai'i–West O'ahu, Center for Labor Education and Research.

101. *Honolulu Advertiser*, 25 February 1954.

102. Lorrin Thurston to Henry Kaiser, 14 July 1954, box 88, Henry Kaiser Papers, University of California, Berkeley (hereafter cited as Kaiser Papers).

103. Claude Jagger, Hawaii Economic Service, to Wallace Marsh, 26 October 1950, carton 62, Kaiser Papers.

104. Minutes of Central Labor Council, 3 August 1954, files of Hawaii's Old Central Labor Council, University of Hawai'i–West O'ahu, Center for Labor Education and Research (hereafter cited as files of Hawaii's Old Central Labor Council).

105. *Honolulu Star-Bulletin*, 25 October 1955.

106. Jack Hall to Louis Goldblatt, 6 September 1957, box 6, ILWU Headquarters, San Francisco.

107. Jack Hall to Louis Goldblatt, 23 October 1958, box 6, ILWU Headquarters, San Francisco. See also *Honolulu Star-Bulletin*, 23 October 1958.

108. *Honolulu Advertiser*, 13 October 1958.

109. *Honolulu Star-Bulletin*, 26 November 1958.

110. Jack Hall to Louis Goldblatt, 24 October 1958, box 6, ILWU Headquarters, San Francisco.

111. Ray Jerome Baker to Marshall McEuen, 14 March 1955, box 34, Baker Papers.

112. *Honolulu Star-Bulletin*, 24 September 1958. On the attempt to deport Rutledge, see *Honolulu Star-Bulletin*, 1 September 1953.

113. Jack Hall to Harry Bridges, 17 November 1958, box 6, ILWU Headquarters, San Francisco.

114. Frederick H. Otis, Secretary-Treasurer of Central Labor Council, to George Meany, 22 September 1954, files of Hawaii's Old Central Labor Council.

115. Minutes of Central Labor Council, 2 August 1955, files of Hawaii's Old Central Labor Council.

116. A. S. Reile, Business Representative, to Oscar Chapman, Department of Interior, 3 February 1951, files of Hawaii's Old Central Labor Council.

117. Jack Hall to J. R. Robertson, 30 September 1955, box 6, ILWU Headquarters, San Francisco.

118. Louis Goldblatt to Jack Hall, 25 October 1957, box 6, ILWU Headquarters, San Francisco.

119. Louis Goldblatt to Jack Hall, 2 August 1955, box 6, ILWU Headquarters, San Francisco.

120. Matsuki Arashiro, 26 January 1976, interview, notebook 17, Zalburg Papers.

121. Louis Goldblatt to Jack Hall, 13 September 1957, box 6, ILWU Headquarters, San Francisco.

122. James R. "Bob" Robertson, interview, 26 September 1974, notebook 26, Zalburg Papers.

123. Rachel Saiki, interview, 1 February 1976, notebook 31, Zalburg Papers.

124. Ibid.

125. Mitsuo Shimizu, interview, 24 January 1976, notebook 31, Zalburg Papers.

126. Comment by Sanford Zalburg, ca. 1975, notebook 12, Zalburg Papers.

127. Philip Maxwell, interview, 20 November 1973, notebook 24, Zalburg Papers.

128. Newton Miyagi, interview, 8 December 1975, notebook 24, Zalburg Papers.

129. Jack Hall to Louis Goldblatt, 24 January 1957, notebook 3, Zalburg Papers.

130. Wendell Carlsmith, interview, 21 February 1975, notebook 21, Zalburg Papers.

131. *Honolulu Beacon*, September 1964.

132. *ILWU Reporter*, 16 May 1956.

133. *Business Week*, 3 April 1956.

134. Ray Jerome Baker to Marshall McEuen, 14 March 1955, box 34, Baker Papers.

135. Ray Jerome Baker to Jane Bliss, 17 April 1955, box 34, Baker Papers.

136. Jeff Kibre to Jack Hall, 18 January 1957, Regional Office Correspondence, Inter-Office, Washington, 1956–1957, ILWU Headquarters, Honolulu. Farrington's spouse also served in the US Congress.

137. Jack Hall to Jeff Kibre, 14 November 1956, Regional Office Correspondence, Inter-Office, Washington, 1956–1957, ILWU Headquarters, Honolulu.

138. *Honolulu Advertiser*, 8 December 1956.

139. *San Francisco Sun-Reporter*, 25 February 1956.

140. *Hawaii Reporter*, June 1959, at ILWU Headquarters, Honolulu.

141. *Honolulu Advertiser*, 8 July 1956. See also Bob Krauss, *Johnny Wilson: First Hawaiian Democrat* (Honolulu: University of Hawai'i Press, 1994).

142. *Hilo Tribune-Herald*, 16 February 1956.

143. Remarks by Harry Bridges, September 1958, file Proceedings of Third Biennial Convention of ILWU Local 142, Honolulu, 25–28 September 1959, ILWU Headquarters, Honolulu.

144. Memorandum from Harold T. Swartz, Assistant Commissioner of Internal Revenue Service, 28 August 1959, and memorandum from US Senate, 10 December 1957, RG 46, box 135, Records of the US Senate, Internal Security Subcommittee of the Senate Judiciary Committee, National Archives and Records Administration, Washington, D.C.

145. *Honolulu Star-Bulletin*, 20 June 1957.

146. *Honolulu Star-Bulletin*, 19 October 1956.

147. *Maui News*, 19 March 1958.

148. *Honolulu Star-Bulletin*, 22 November 1956.

149. *Honolulu Star-Bulletin*, 21 September 1955.

150. *Hilo Tribune-Herald*, 21 September 1955.

151. *San Francisco Chronicle*, 3 May 1957.

152. *People's Daily World*, 10 October 1987.

153. Philip Eden, Research Department, ILWU, to Bernie Stern, Research Director, Mine, Mill and Smelter Workers Union, 10 May 1955, box 36, ILWU Headquarters, San Francisco.

154. Jack Hall's Labor Day Address, September 1955, notebook 10, Zalburg Papers.

155. Transcript of radio broadcast, 15 July 1954, University of Hawai'i at Mānoa, Special Collections.

156. Ray Jerome Baker to Warren Smith, 11 March 1956.

Chapter 17. Toward Statehood

1. *Honolulu Advertiser*, 21 January 1958. See also David Wellman, *The Union Makes Us Strong: Radical Unionism on the San Francisco Waterfront* (New York: Cambridge University Press, 1995).

2. Jeff Kibre, ILWU, Washington, D.C., to Louis Goldblatt, 11 March 1957, ILWU Hawaii, History Files, 1956, Eastland Hearings Correspondence, ILWU Headquarters, Honolulu.

3. *Honolulu Star-Bulletin*, 5 February 1957. See also H. Brett Melendy, *The Federal Government's Search for Communists in the Territory of Hawaii* (Lewiston, N.Y.: Mellen, 2002).

4. *Honolulu Star-Bulletin*, 23 July 1955.

5. *Honolulu Star-Bulletin*, 10 August 1954.

6. Jack Hall to Myer Symonds, 8 October 1953, file John E. Reinecke, ILWU Headquarters, Honolulu.

7. *Honolulu Advertiser*, 10 November 1954.

8. *Report of the Commission on Subversive Activities of the Legislature of the Territory of Hawaii* (28 February 1959), University of Hawai'i at Mānoa, Special Collections.

9. Transcript of radio broadcast, 18 February 1957, University of Hawai'i at Mānoa, Special Collections.

10. Hawaii Residents' Association, *Communism in Hawaii as Revealed in the Report of the Commission on Subversive Activities to the Legislature of the Territory of Hawaii* (1957), University of Hawai'i at Mānoa, Special Collections.

11. *Honolulu Advertiser*, 2 March 1958. See also *Honolulu Advertiser*, 24 October 1962.

12. *Honolulu Star-Bulletin*, 1 August 1960.

13. *Honolulu Advertiser*, 11 February 1958, Subject Series, box 15, Fred A. Seaton Papers, Dwight D. Eisenhower Presidential Library, Abilene, Kans. (hereafter Eisenhower Library).

14. Myer Symonds to Ben Margolis and Norman Leonard, 20 October 1958, box 5, folder 5, Smith Act Collection, Southern California Library for Social Studies and Research, Los Angeles.

15. *Honolulu Advertiser*, 3 May 1976.

16. Lyle G. Phillips, MD, "The Reds in Hawaii" (originally published in *American Mercury*, December 1956; reprinted by Hawaii Residents' Association, 1956), University of Hawai'i at Mānoa, Special Collections.

17. Transcript of radio broadcast, 16 February 1954, University of Hawai'i at Mānoa, Special Collections.

18. Frank Marshall Davis, *Livin' the Blues: Memoirs of a Black Journalist and Poet* (Madison: University of Wisconsin Press, 1992), 324–325.

19. Letterhead of Hawaii Foundation for American Freedoms, formerly Hawaii Residents' Association, Inc., 3 October 1962, box 157, Group Research Archives, Columbia University, New York.

20. *Honolulu Record*, 12 April 1956.

21. Louis Goldblatt to Jack Hall, 29 April 1958, notebook 3, Sanford Zalburg Papers, University of Hawai'i at Mānoa, Archives and Manuscripts (hereafter cited as Zalburg Papers).

22. Account of Sugar Negotiations, 16 January 1958, box 39, ILWU Headquarters, San Francisco.

23. Transcript of radio broadcast, 18 October 1955, University of Hawai'i at Mānoa, Special Collections.

24. Harriet Bouslog to Herbert Resner, 17 October 1947, box 42, Norman Leonard Collection, Labor Archives and Research Center, San Francisco State University.

25. David Jenkins, "The Union Movement, the California Labor School and San Francisco Politics, 1926–1988," Regional Oral History Office, Bancroft Library, University of California, Berkeley, 129.

26. Ricardo Labez, interview, 4 August 1974, notebook 30, Zalburg Papers.

27. *Honolulu Star-Bulletin*, 24 January 1958.

28. Ray Jerome Baker to Warren Smith, 15 April 1956, box 10, Ray Jerome Baker Papers, Bishop Museum, Honolulu (hereafter cited as Baker Papers).

29. *Honolulu Record*, 29 March 1956.

30. Yasuki Arakaki, interview, 23 April 1996, University of Hawai'i–West O'ahu, Center for Labor Education and Research.

31. *Honolulu Advertiser*, 18 March 1958.

32. *Honolulu Record*, 10 April 1958.

33. *Hilo Tribune-Herald*, 15 February 1958.

34. *Honolulu Star-Bulletin*, 17 April 1958.

35. Transcript of radio broadcast, 12 April 1956, University of Hawai'i at Mānoa, Special Collections.

36. *Maui News*, 22 December 1956. See also *Maui News*, "Workers at Pioneer Mill Company and Wailuku Sugar Company Receive One-Day Suspensions after Work Stoppage in Protest of Eastland Hearings," 5 December 1956; and *Hilo Tribune-Herald*, "1,700 Workers at Olaa Sugar Company Suspended for Walkout," 4 December 1956.

37. *Honolulu Advertiser*, 29 April 1958.

38. *New York Times*, 8 June 1958.

39. Ray Jerome Baker to Dr. and Mrs. Gay Morrow, 8 December 1958, box 10, Baker Papers.

40. Officers' Report, Part 1, circa 1959, file Proceedings Fourth Biennial Convention, ILWU Local 142, Honolulu, 23–26 September 1959, ILWU Headquarters, Honolulu.

41. Remarks by Jack Hall, 14 October 1960, notebook 3, Zalburg Papers.

42. Harry Bridges, interview, 1 June 1975, notebook 22-A, Zalburg Papers.

43. Philip Maxwell, interview, 20 November 1973, notebook 24, Zalburg Papers.

44. Minutes, ILWU Local 142, box 36, ILWU Headquarters, San Francisco.

45. Officers' Report, Part 1, Local 142, file Proceedings of Third Biennial Convention, ILWU Local 142, Honolulu, 25–28 September 1959, ILWU Headquarters, Honolulu.

46. *Honolulu Record*, 12 June 1958.

47. *Honolulu Record*, 5 June 1958.

48. *Honolulu Record*, 29 May 1958.

49. *Honolulu Star-Bulletin*, 3 July 1953.

50. *Honolulu Record*, 3 July 1958.

51. John Reinecke, interview, 9 March 1975, notebook 26, Zalburg Papers.

52. *Hawaii Reporter*, June 1959, at ILWU Headquarters, Honolulu.

53. *Hawaii Reporter*, 2 July 1959.

54. Transcript of radio broadcast, 3 February 1958, University of Hawai'i at Mānoa, Special Collections.

55. *Honolulu Advertiser*, 2 February 1952.

56. Transcript of radio broadcast, 18 March 1955, University of Hawai'i at Mānoa, Special Collections.

57. Minutes, Regional Staff, Local 142, 10 December 1956, file Local 142, Meetings of Local Officers and Regional Office Staff, 1955–1957, ILWU Headquarters, Honolulu.

58. Minutes of Local 142 Executive Board, 3–4 August 1956, file Local 142, Meetings of Executive Board, ILWU Headquarters, Honolulu.

59. Minutes of Meeting, 9 December 1953, file Local 142, Meetings of Local Officers and Regional Office Staff, ILWU Headquarters, Honolulu.

60. Transcript of IMUA radio broadcast, 19 August 1955, University of Hawaiʻi at Mānoa, Special Collections.

61. Transcript of IMUA radio broadcast, 29 August 1955, University of Hawaiʻi at Mānoa, Special Collections.

62. Transcript of radio broadcast, 18 January 1956, University of Hawaiʻi at Mānoa, Special Collections.

63. Press release, 9 March 1960, file Regional Office Press Releases, ILWU Headquarters, Honolulu.

64. Ray Jerome Baker to Dr. and Mrs. Richard Liebes, 21 December 1958, box 10, Baker Papers.

65. Transcript of radio broadcast, 10 February 1955, University of Hawaiʻi at Mānoa, Special Collections.

66. Letter from Ray Jerome Baker, 1 January 1953, box 33, Baker Papers.

67. Ray Jerome Baker to Warren, 10 December 1956, box 10, Baker Papers.

68. Ray Jerome Baker to Dr. and Mrs. Gay Morrow, 8 December 1958, box 10, Baker Papers.

69. Ray Jerome Baker to Richard Liebes, 30 September 1953, box 33, Baker Papers.

70. Ray Jerome Baker to Mildred Jensen, 7 April 1956, box 10, Baker Papers.

71. Christina Klein, *Cold War Orientalism: Asia in the Middlebrow Imagination, 1945–1961* (Berkeley: University of California Press, 2003), 245.

72. Lorrin Thurston to "My Dear Henry," 14 July 1954, box 88, Henry Kaiser Papers, University of California, Berkeley.

73. *Honolulu Record*, 25 July 1957. See also David Jenkins, "The Union Movement, the California Labor School and San Francisco Politics, 1926–1988," Regional Oral History Office, Bancroft Library, University of California, 1993, 129: Homosexuality "seemed to be accepted culturally and sexually among the Filipinos." The "amount of male copulation going on was enormous," though "given the slightest opportunity these same Filipino men would marry."

74. *Honolulu Record*, 11 July 1957.

75. *Honolulu Record*, 4 July 1957.

76. *Honolulu Record*, 20 March 1958.

77. *Honolulu Record*, 20 December 1956.

78. Press release, 1 August 1958, file Regional Office Press Releases, ILWU Headquarters, Honolulu.

79. Minutes, 23 October 1957, file Local 142, Meetings of Local Officers and Regional Office Staff, ILWU Headquarters, Honolulu.

80. Minutes, 3–4 August 1956, file Local 142, Meetings of Local Executive Board, ILWU Headquarters, Honolulu.

81. Minutes, 23 October 1957, file Local 142, Meetings of Local Officers and Regional Office Staff.

82. Memorandum, 23 June 1955, RG 59, box 2780, Central Decimal File, 1955–1959, 711.001/6-2355, National Archives and Records Administration (hereafter cited as NARA), College Park, Md.

83. Consul General, Genoa, to State Department, 12 March 1959, RG 59, box 96, 032, Bridges, Harry/31259, Central Decimal File, 1955–1959, NARA, College Park, Md.

84. US Embassy, Prague, to State Department, 25 March 1959, RG 59, box 96, 032, Bridges, Harry/32559, Central Decimal File, 1955–1959, NARA, College Park, Md.

85. Jeff Kibre to Jack Hall, 3 July 1959, Regional Office Correspondence, Inter-Office, Washington, 1956–1967, ILWU Headquarters, Honolulu.

86. Robert McElrath to Louis Goldblatt, 26 May 1958, Regional Office Correspondence, Inter-Office, San Francisco, ILWU Headquarters, Honolulu.

87. *Honolulu Record*, 22 November 1956: "One thing is certain: There was discontent which had been expressed for some time in the Hungarian press. Another thing is clear. The mass of workers took active part in the demonstrations which were routed by military action. Students and intellectuals who in many countries are drawn to theoretical Marxism took active part in the demonstrations. . . . [C]onditions of life for the people of Hungary were bad. . . . [S]omething is drastically wrong."

88. *Honolulu Record*, 20 December 1956: "Naturally I cannot condone what has transpired in Hungary," he said, while observing, "The Hungarians are fellow haoles. The Egyptians, being darker, are looked upon as 'different.' The native Kenyans are black, and white America has not learned to weep for the colored peoples of the world unless there is a political motivation. I wish this were not so."

89. Klein, *Cold War Orientalism*, 249.

90. Ray Jerome Baker to Warren Smith, 23 May 1956, box 10, Baker Papers.

91. Ray Jerome Baker to Katherine C. Feller, 20 February 1956, box 4, Baker Papers.

92. *Honolulu Record*, 30 May 1957.

93. *Honolulu Record*, 11 April 1957.

94. William S. White, oral history transcript, 21 June 1978, Lyndon Baines Johnson Library, University of Austin at Texas (hereafter LBJ Library).

95. George Reedy, oral history transcript, 21 May 1982, LBJ Library.

96. George Reedy, oral history transcript, 14 October 1983, LBJ Library.

97. George Reedy, oral history transcript, 23 May 1983, LBJ Library.

98. George Reedy, oral history transcript, 21 October 1983, LBJ Library.

99. Horace Busby, oral history transcript, 2 April 1989, LBJ Library.

100. Legislative Leadership Meeting, 4 March 1958, box 3, Whitman-Legislative Series, Eisenhower Library.

101. Thomas Kuchel, oral history transcript, 15 May 1980, LBJ Library.

102. Lillian Coltzer to Senator Lyndon B. Johnson, 16 March 1959, box 732, Senate, Subject Files, Lyndon B. Johnson Papers, LBJ Library (hereafter LBJ Papers).

103. Raymond Orr to Senator Lyndon B. Johnson, 19 March 1959, box 732, Senate, Subject Files, LBJ Papers.

104. Frank M. Gossett to Senator Lyndon B. Johnson, 9 March 1959, box 732, Senate, Subject Files, LBJ Papers.

105. Mr. and Mrs. Austin Burges to Senator Lyndon B. Johnson, 11 March 1959, box 732, Senate, Subject Files, LBJ Papers.

106. J. R. English to Senator J. William Fulbright, 18 February 1959, BCN99, F5, A76, J. William Fulbright Papers, University of Arkansas, Fayetteville.

107. Reverend Donald J. Ely to Senator J. Strom Thurmond, 2 July 1958, Subject Correspondence, 1958, Federal Government—Statehood, J. Strom Thurmond Papers, Clemson University, Clemson, S.C. (hereafter Thurmond Papers).

108. Stanley Morse, President of Grass Roots League of South Carolina, to "Dear Member," 18 March 1959, box 1, Erwin Allen Holt Papers, University of North Carolina at Chapel Hill.

109. William Rickard to Senator Thomas Hennings, 5 March 1959, folder 5100A, Thomas C. Hennings Jr. Papers, Western Historical Manuscripts Collection–Columbia, University of Missouri (hereafter Hennings Papers).

110. Hicklin A. Harrel to Speaker Sam Rayburn, 12 July 1958, box 3466, Sam Rayburn Papers, Center for American History, University of Texas at Austin.

111. Thomas Perry to Senator J. Strom Thurmond, 26 July 1958, Subject Correspondence, 1958, Federal Government—Statehood, Thurmond Papers.

112. George Mellen to Senator George Smathers, 26 March 1959, George A. Smathers Papers, Special and Area Studies Collections, George A. Smathers Libraries, University of Florida, Gainesville (hereafter Smathers Papers).

113. H. Brett Melendy, *Hawaii: America's Sugar Territory, 1898–1959* (Lewiston, N.Y.: Mellen, 1999), 271. See also Peter Hyun, *Man Sei! The Making of a Korean American* (Honolulu: University of Hawai'i Press, 1986); and Glynn Barratt, *The Russian View of Honolulu, 1809–1826* (Ottawa: Carleton University Press, 1988).

114. Ingram Stainback to Senator George Smathers, 30 January 1959, Smathers Papers.

115. Ingram Stainback to Senator Olin Johnston, 12 January 1959, box 71, Olin D. Johnston Papers, South Caroliniana Library, University of South Carolina, Columbia (hereafter cited as Johnston Papers).

116. Ingram Stainback to Senator Olin Johnston, 5 March 1959, box 71, Johnston Papers.

117. Senator Olin Johnston to Hattie S. Shirer, 19 March 1959, box 71, Johnston Papers.

118. Senator J. Strom Thurmond to Thomas Perry, 31 July 1958, Subject Correspondence, 1958, Federal Government—Statehood, Thurmond Papers.

119. Mrs. Emmitt Wieurscheske to Senator Lyndon B. Johnson, 28 February 1959, box 732, Senate, Subject Files, LBJ Papers.

120. F. S. Stephens, British Embassy, Washington, D.C., to Foreign Office, 4 December 1950, FO371/81743, National Archives (UK), London. Whitehall breathed a sigh of relief when a pared-down Hawai'i entered the Union. See "Confidential" Memorandum, 13 May 1953, FO371/103530, National Archives (UK), London: "I have been told by a Senator that there is pressure to include in the new state the island of Palmyra, despite the fact that it lies 1,100 miles from the main group. My informant understands that there was once a British claim to this island and asks whether this is still alive."

121. President Harry S. Truman to Vice-President Alben Barkley, 27 November 1950, FO371/81743, National Archives (UK), London.

122. Senate Committee on Interior and Insular Affairs, *Statehood for Hawaii*, 86th Cong., 2nd sess. (5 March 1959), report 80, folder 5100A, Hennings Papers.

123. Vice President Richard M. Nixon to Saigeo Soga, 19 August 1959, LN Collection, ser. 320, folder Hawaii, Nixon Presidential Library and Museum, Yorba Linda, Calif.

124. C. H. Kwock to President Eisenhower, 16 September 1959, Official File, Central File, OF 147-e, box 755, Eisenhower Library.

125. Comments by Sanford Zalburg, 9 April 1975, notebook 19, Zalburg Papers.

126. US Senate, *Tributes to the Honorable Hiram L. Fong of Hawaii in the United States Senate*, 94th Cong., 2nd sess. (22 September 1976), Hawai'i State Library, Honolulu.

127. Pat Duarte et al., *Visions of a Man: Tommy Trask and the ILWU* (Honolulu: Island Heritage, 1991), 10, 11.

128. Marc Levinson, *The Box: How the Shipping Container Made the World Smaller and the World Economy Bigger* (Princeton, N.J.: Princeton University Press, 2006), 65, 226, 274.

129. *New York Times*, 2 May 2008.

130. *Washington Post*, 30 April 2008.

131. Louis Goldblatt to Jack Hall, 24 June 1957, box 6, ILWU Headquarters, San Francisco.

132. Davis, *Livin' the Blues*, 317.

133. J. B. Matthews, *Communism and the NAACP*, Public Hearing in Tallahassee, Fla., 10 February 1958 (University of Virginia, Charlottesville).

134. Frank Marshall Davis to Claude A. Barnett, 6 August 1951, part 2, reel 5, Claude Barnett Papers, Columbia University, New York (hereafter cited as Barnett Papers).

135. Frank Marshall Davis to Claude A. Barnett, 12 March 1959, part 2, reel 5, Barnett Papers.

136. Howard Kimeldorf, *Reds or Rackets? The Making of Radical and Conservative Unions on the Waterfront* (Berkeley: University of California Press, 1988), 148.

137. American Committee on Africa to Maida Springer, 27 May 1960, RG-18-007, George Meany Memorial Archives, Silver Spring, Md.: "Here is the list of Kenya students which I promised you." On this list was "Barrack [*sic*] H. Obama."

138. Barack Obama, *Dreams from My Father: A Story of Race and Inheritance* (New York: Times Books, 1995). See also Davis, *Livin' the Blues*, 318: "Another student from Kenya split[,] leaving two pregnant blondes."

139. THP to Gloster Current, 27 September 1960, part 1, reel 2, #549, NAACP Papers, Duke University, Durham, N.C.

140. George Reedy, oral history transcript, 22 June 1984, LBJ Library.

141. Yoshiko Hall, interview (comments by Sanford Zalburg), 24 November 1975, notebook 12, Zalburg Papers. See also Bernard Stern, *Rutledge Unionism: Labor Relations in the Honolulu Hotel Industry, 1941–1967* (Honolulu: University of Hawai'i–West O'ahu, Center for Labor Education and Research), 1988.

142. Jack Hall to Louis Goldblatt, 19 September 1956, box 6, ILWU Headquarters, San Francisco.

143. *Honolulu Advertiser*, 1 July 1959.

144. *Honolulu Star-Bulletin*, 25 July 1959.

145. Comments by Sanford Zalburg, n.d., notebook 29, Zalburg Papers.

146. John A. Burns Oral History Project, 1975–1976, Hawai'i State Library, Honolulu.

147. *New York Times*, 18 November 1961.

148. *Honolulu Advertiser*, 20 June 1965.

149. *Honolulu Advertiser*, 14 January 1968.

150. *Voice of the ILWU*, January 1968.

151. Harriet Bouslog, interview, 11 March 1976, notebook 19, Zalburg Papers.

152. Transcript of Proceedings, 8 September 1948, Reinecke File, 318-2-1, Corr.: Commissioner, DPI Hearing Transcript, Hawai'i State Archives, Honolulu.

153. *Honolulu Advertiser*, 29 November 1984.

154. *ILWU Dispatcher*, 25 March 1995, ILWU Headquarters, San Francisco.

155. *Honolulu Advertiser*, 5 March 1993.

156. *Honolulu Star-Bulletin*, 1 June 1959.

157. *Honolulu Advertiser*, 26 January 1954.

158. *People's Daily World*, 7 January 1988.

159. Duarte, *Visions of a Man*, 15.

160. Sanford Zalburg, *A Spark Is Struck! Jack Hall and the ILWU in Hawaii* (Honolulu: University of Hawai'i Press, 1979), xvii.

161. Bill Bailey, interview, 27 June 1973, notebook 28, Zalburg Papers.

162. John Elias, interview, 30 April 1981 (conducted by Sid Rogers), Labor Archives and Research Center, San Francisco State University.

163. John Reinecke interview, 9 March 1975.

164. J. R. Robertson, interview, 26 September 1974, notebook 26, Zalburg Papers.

165. Comments by Sanford Zalburg, 28 March 1975, notebook 25, Zalburg Papers.

166. Ben Dillingham, interview, 30 January 1976, notebook 29, Zalburg Papers. See also H. Brett Melendy, *Walter Francis Dillingham, 1875–1963: Hawaiian Entrepreneur and Statesman* (Lewiston, N.Y.: Mellen, 1996).

167. *Honolulu Record*, 23 February 1956.

168. *Honolulu Record*, 18 April 1957.

169. *Honolulu Record*, 13 June 1957.

170. *Honolulu Record*, 4 April 1957.

171. Transcript of radio broadcast, 26 August 1954, University of Hawai'i at Mānoa, Special Collections.

172. Remarks by John Burns, September 1959, file Proceedings of Third Biennial Convention, ILWU Local 142, Honolulu, 25–28 September 1959, ILWU Headquarters, Honolulu.

Index

Page numbers in italics refer to photographs.

About the Author

Gerald Horne is Moores Professor of History and African-American Studies at the University of Houston. He has been an author or editor of thirty books, including *The White Pacific: U.S. Imperialism and Black Slavery in the South Seas after the Civil War.*

Production notes for Horne | *Fighting in Paradise*

Cover design by Julie Matsuo-Chun.

Text design by inari with display type in Trade Gothic Lt Std
and text type in Janson Text LT Std

Composition by inari

Printing and binding by Sheridan Books, Inc.

Printed on 50 lb. House Opaque, 606 ppi